MW01199059

PLLS
Papers of the Langford Latin Seminar
ISSN 1740-8652
Sixteenth Volume
2016

ARCA
Classical and Medieval Texts, Papers and Monographs

54

General Editors
Neil Adkin (University of North Carolina, Chapel Hill)
Francis Cairns (The Florida State University)
Robin Seager (University of Liverpool)
Frederick Williams (Trinity College Dublin)
Assistant Editor: Sandra Cairns

ISSN 0309–5541

PAPERS OF THE LANGFORD LATIN SEMINAR

Sixteenth Volume
2016

Greek and Roman Poetry
The Elder Pliny

Edited by
Francis Cairns and
Roy Gibson

FRANCIS CAIRNS

Published by Francis Cairns (Publications) Ltd
116 Shrewsbury Rd, Prenton, CH43 8SP, U.K.

www.francis-cairns.co.uk

First published 2016

Copyright © Francis Cairns (Publications) 2016

British Library Cataloguing in Publication

A catalogue record for this book is available from the British Library

ISBN 978-0-905205-59-5

The Greek fonts used in this work are available from
www.linguistsoftware.com
+1-425-775-1130

Printed and bound by CPI Group (UK) Ltd, Croydon, CR0 4YY

CONTENTS

Preface   vi

Greek and Roman Poetry

Nigel Nicholson (Reed College)
    Four Reasons not to have an Epinician   3

Alex Hardie (University of Edinburgh)
    Callimachus at the Mouseion (the Hymn to Delos)   39

Annemarie Ambühl (Johannes Gutenberg-Universität Mainz)
    Literary Love Triangles: Berenice at Alexandria
    and Rome   155

Alberto Canobbio (Università di Pavia)
    Lucilius and Horace: from criticism to identification   185

The Elder Pliny

Eugenia Lao
    Taxonomic Organization in Pliny's *Natural History*   209

Aude Doody (University College Dublin)
    The Authority of Greek Poetry in Pliny's *Natural
    History* 18.63-65   247

Trevor Murphy (University of California, Berkeley)
    Notes from Underground: the Curious Katabasis
    of Dionysodorus   269

Trevor S. Luke (The Florida State University)
    Pliny the Elder on Pythagoras   285

Sandra Citroni Marchetti (Università di Firenze)
    Cicero as Role-Model in the Self-Definition of Pliny
    the Elder   315

Preface

PLLS 16, the sixth volume of *Papers of the Langford Latin Seminar*, continues the series which began with five volumes of *Papers of the Liverpool Latin Seminar* (1976–1985), followed by five volumes of *Papers of the Leeds International Latin Seminar* (1988–1998).

PLLS 16 contains (in revised, usually enlarged, and annotated form) some of the papers presented at Langford Colloquia and Seminars of the Department of Classics of The Florida State University over the years 2012 to 2014, together with supplementary articles contributed at the request of the editors. Most of the papers in The Elder Pliny section originated in the Langford Seminar of November 2012, 'The Greek and Roman Culture of Pliny the Elder', directed by Professor Roy Gibson.

The editors have been greatly assisted in the task of assembling *PLLS* 16 by a number of anonymous referees, to whom they express their gratitude.

FRANCIS CAIRNS
The Florida State University &
Faculty of Classics, Cambridge

ROY GIBSON
University of Manchester

December 2015

Greek and Roman Poetry

Four Reasons not to have an Epinician[*]

Nigel Nicholson
Reed College

Among the memorials that celebrated athletic victories in the late archaic and early classical period, epinician is today, by virtue of the accidents of survival, the most visible. It is easy to assume it was also the dominant form of memorial in its day also, and certainly some of the greatest victors from this period, both equestrian and gymnastic, were celebrated in epinician: Astylus of Croton with seven Olympic crowns; Hippocleas of Thessaly, Ergoteles of Himera and Xenophon of Corinth with two each; the famous boxers Glaucus of Carystus, winner of nineteen Panhellenic crowns, and Diagoras of Rhodes, winner of the period and father of a family of over-achieving Olympians; and the dynastic hippotrophs Arcesilas of Cyrene, Theron of Acragas, and Hieron of Syracuse.[1]

More striking, however, are the many absences from this list. Victors not celebrated in epinician include some of the greatest athletes and some of the most prominent public figures: the triple Olympic victors who met in the boxing in 480, Euthymus of Epizephyrian Locri and Theogenes of Thasos; Leontiscus of Messene, twice successful in the pancration at Olympia, Philo of Corcyra whose two Olympic boxing victories exceeded those of his more famous father Glaucus of Carystus, and Timasitheus of Delphi, a great warrior and winner of two Olympic and three Pythian crowns; another triple Pythian victor with a distinguished war record, Phayllus of Croton, who fought at Salamis; the brothers Telemachus and Agias of Pharsalus, both Olympic victors with more than ten Panhellenic wins to their names; Gelon, tyrant of Gela, and soon to be tyrant of Syracuse, and Damaratus, king of Sparta,

[*] I want to express my gratitude here to Francis Cairns and the department at Florida State for the generous invitation to speak at the Langford Seminar in 2013 and their kind hospitality during my visit. While this article does not derive from the paper delivered there, I did have the chance to explore some of the work in Nicholson (2015) there, and part of this work is predicated on that.
[1] Astylus: Sim. 506; Hippocleas: Pi. *Py.* 10; Ergoteles Pi. *Ol.* 12; Xenophon: Pi. *Ol.* 13; Glaucus; Sim. 509; Diagoras: Pi. *Ol.* 7; Arcesilas: Pi. *Py.* 4–5; Theron: Pi. *Ol.* 2–3; Hieron: Pi. *Ol.* 1, Pi. *Py.* 1–3, Bacch. 3–5.

both victors in the Olympic chariot race; and the greatest Olympian of all, with victories at six consecutive festivals, Milo of Croton.[2]

Yet little thought is put to why so many victors, and so many great victors, did not appear in epinician. In some cases serendipity was surely to blame, a simple failure to connect with a poet, or a missed opportunity, but there were structural factors also, more basic facts about the form and its production, that made it unattractive to some victors, and it is these factors that this paper will explore.

Any discussion of victors who do not appear in epinicians must confront the limitations of our sources; absence of evidence for epinician does not automatically constitute evidence that epinician was absent. In many ways we are very lucky with epinician, however, certainly rather luckier than with other classical genres. Pindar is the only Greek lyric poet, and epinician the only lyric genre, to have come down to us through a manuscript tradition, and, while five or six odes have fallen away from the end of the book of Isthmian odes, some information is known about these losses, including some of the victors and cities celebrated, and we can conclude that few odes have been lost in transmission.[3] Bacchylides' epinicians, few enough to be collected into a single book by an Alexandrian editor, have been largely supplied by the sands of Oxyrhynchus, and, again there is little reason to think that we lack much of the outline that was known to the Alexandrians.[4] How the Alexandrians were able to collate the works of the lyric poets remains mysterious, but the number of obscure victors celebrated in the extant odes, and the inclusion of odes for victors who had won only at minor contests (Pindar's *Nemean* 9, two odes tacked on to Pindar's

---

[2] For these victors, see Moretti (1957) nos.115, 140, 157, 185, 190–2, 201, 271, and Moretti (1953) no.11. On Philo's relation to Glaucus, see Rausa (1994) 46–7 and Smith (2007) 99, *contra* Löhr (2000) 34–5. Other great victors not listed here include Anochos of Tarentum (Moretti (1957) no.130), a winner in the stade and the diaulos, Ischomachus and Tisicrates of Croton (nos.148 and 166), both twice victors in the sprint, and Crison of Himera (no.294), three times a sprint victor. As a very rough indication, about 14% of the Olympic victors listed by Moretti (1957) between and including the years 520 and 440 are known to have been celebrated in epinicians by Pindar, Bacchylides or Simonides.

[3] On Pindar's lost Isthmian odes, see d'Alessio (2012).

[4] For the argument that 14B belongs in the same book as the odes of the British Museum papyrus, see Fearn (2009) 23–5. While it seems reasonable to think that Pindar and Simonides might have been thought of by victors as obvious producers of epinician, to call Bacchylides an epinician poet might be to mischaracterize his output. Even among the fifteen identifiable odes of his book, many seem to be special or atypical commissions: five celebrate victors from his home island (1–2, 6–8), and three or four more celebrate victories for which a second ode by a different poet — in all cases Pindar — was also commissioned (3–5, 13). Fundamentally, Bacchylides was a lyric poet who, among his many lyric works, produced some epinicians when he was persuaded to do so.

Isthmian odes, and Bacchylides 13), as well as odes whose relation to athletic celebration is more distant (Pindar's *Nemean* 11 and Bacchylides 14B), strongly suggest that, through whatever means, the Alexandrian editors were able to make thorough collections and that absences are few.[5]

On the other hand, we are much less fortunate with Simonides and almost wholly ignorant of more local producers. Simonides composed as many as seven books of epinicians,[6] but only fragments survive, and in a heavy majority of cases we do not know who Simonides celebrated. About less famous and more local producers of epinician, we are even more in the dark. The ode known as Pindar's *Olympian* 5 is all that survives from contemporary production by other authors.[7]

Despite these challenges, arguments can be made, however. First, there is no reason to assume that an epinician ode produced by a local poet carried the same meaning as an ode produced by one of the famous producers of the form. Part of what was obtained with an ode from Pindar, Bacchylides or Simonides was membership in an interstate community of victors defined by the reach and fame of each of these lyric poets; the simple act of retaining such a poet carried a definite value, regardless of any difference in quality. The genre may have extended well beyond its most famous three practitioners, but it is justifiable to treat these in separation from any larger mass of production precisely because of their fame and international status. The question before this paper is thus, more properly, why victors avoided epinicians by the three famous epinician poets.

Second, for the most famous athletes, strong arguments can be made that they were not celebrated in epinician. Athletes such as Milo,

---

[5] Many of the victors celebrated in Pindar's Isthmian and Nemean odes are otherwise unknown: Melissus, Herodotus and Strepsiades of Thebes, Deinias and Aristocleidas of Aegina, and Aristagoras of Tenedos. The final two lost Isthmian odes seem not to have celebrated Isthmian wins, but local victories; see d'Alessio (2012) 48–57. Pi. *Ne.* 11 and, seemingly, Bacch. 14B (Fearn (2009) celebrate the installation of a past victor as a civic functionary; this may also be true of Pi. *Ne.* 3 (Pfeijffer (1999) 197–8, 218–27, cf. Currie (2005) 333–5). Although quotations of epinician probably relied on their collection in Alexandrian editions, it is also worth noting how few seemingly epinician quotations do not have a home; cf. d'Alessio (2012), Bacch. fr. 1. Hubbard (2004) suggests that physical copies of the odes were circulated soon after the performance, at least for Pindar and Bacchylides.

[6] Lowe (2007) 174–5. The larger confusion in how Simonides' works are classified in later authors suggests a greater diversity and fluidity than was evident in the works of Pindar and Bacchylides. Lowe (2007) 175–6 suggests that any reference to an athletic victory would have ensured that a poem was classified as an epinician.

[7] On the authorship of *Ol.* 5, see Barrett (2007) 46–53, *contra* Hamilton (1972) 342–9, and Mader (1990) 109–13. Earlier production is represented only by the few fragments collected under Ibycus' name. These indicate some patrons. See Rawles (2012).

Phayllus or Euthymus were so famous in antiquity, and so often referred to, that it is reasonable to suppose that the patronage of an epinician poet would at some point in our surviving sources be mentioned or implied, had there been an ode, as it was, for example, for Astylus, Glaucus, Hieron and Diagoras, four of the victors from the period most referenced by later authors.[8]

Third, and more important, sufficient numbers of epinician odes survive to reveal significant patterns in the usage of epinician, whether about how families commissioned epinicians, or what parts of the Greek world retained the poets. While being aware of the limitations of epinician as a source, we should also be aware of its richness: we have all or almost all of over fifty odes by Pindar and Bacchylides and significant fragments of several more that include information about the victors being celebrated; beyond this, we have evidence for nearly a full book's worth of the victors Simonides celebrated.[9] For Pindar and Bacchylides, the evidence is excellent, and overall five of twelve or thirteen books of epinicians by these poets provides an excellent sample size from which to draw certain sorts of conclusions.

Based on this sample, I will argue in this paper that four structural reasons made epinicians authored by Pindar, Bacchylides or Simonides unattractive or unavailable to many patrons: the limited geographic range of the poets themselves, local agonistic practices that did not include such celebrations, the particular politics of the form of epinician, and the basic expense to commission and perform (and reperform) an epinician.

---

[8] Astylus: Didymus, *De dubiis apud Platonem lectionibus*, Miller (1965) 403; Timaeus the Sophist, *Lexicon Platonicum*, Dübner (1839) 1000a.21–5; Photius, *Lexicon*, *s.v.* περιαγειρόμενοι; Suda, *s.v.* περιαγειρόμενοι. Glaucus: Quint. *Inst.* 11.2.14. Hieron: Aelian *VH* 4.15, 9.1, Suda s.v. Βασιλεὺς μέγας. Diagoras: Gorgon, *FGrH* 515 F18 (=schol. ad Pi. *Ol.* 7, Drachmann (1903) 195).

[9] Anaxilas of Messene (Sim. 515), Astylus of Syracuse (506), Glaucus of Carystus, Leocrates of Athens (510, with Molyneux (1992) 33–45), the Thessalians Scopas, Antiochus, Aleuas and the sons of Aeatius (510, 511, Theoc. 16.42–7, with Molyneux (1992) 118–30), Eualcides of Eretria (530), Crius of Aegina (507; see n.11 below), and certainly one, if not both of Eritimus and Ptoiodorus of Corinth (519A fr. 21, 519B fr. 13, with Barrett (2007) 98–117), plus various victors of unknown cities: Orillas (514, with Nicholson (2005) 223 n.13), Agatharchus (510, with Molyneux (1992) 44–5), and Athenaeus (519 fr. 120b). Simonides did not produce an epinician for Xenocrates of Acragas, however; see Podlecki (1979) 6–7, Molyneux (1992) 233–4, *contra* schol. ad Pi. *Is.* 2, inscr. a, and Hornblower (2004) 187.

I. Limited Geographic Range of the Poets

The first observation suggested by the extant epinicians is that, with the obvious exception of the Greeks of Sicily, the three great epinician poets for the most part actually served few patrons whose hometowns were more than a few days travel away, whether by boat or mule. Of the forty-eight odes known to have been collected under Pindar's name, seventeen are for victors from Sicily and southwestern Italy. Of the remaining thirty-one, twenty-five are for victors within 200 miles of Pindar's hometown of Thebes (and twenty-four within 100 miles): six for Boeotian victors, twelve for Aeginetan victors, and victors from Thessaly, Argos, Corinth, Athens, Opuntian Locri and Megara.[10] Of Bacchylides' fifteen known odes, three celebrate Sicilians, and eleven of the remaining twelve celebrate victors from Bacchylides' home island of Ceos or places within 200 miles of the island: Thessaly, Phlius, Aegina, and Athens. Such comprehensive data are not available for Simonides, but we do know that, as well as praising victors from Sicily, he composed epinicians for Athenians, Aeginetans and Euboeans, and was particularly identified in later periods with praise poetry for Thessalian patrons — a similarly restricted geographical range to that of his fellow Cean, Bacchylides.[11]

The very limited evidence provided by the poets' other productions supports the hypothesis that the poets worked mostly closer to home. While, as with the epinicians, we do see commissions for towns and patrons outside this range (Abdera, Macedon, Sparta, Tenedos, and perhaps Chios, as well as Sicily), the same towns and regions are again prominent: Corinth, Athens, Aegina, Ceos, Thessaly, Boeotia.[12]

The numbers thus suggest that the poets themselves acted as a brake on epinician production, discouraging victors from more distant cities

[10] Of the odes lost from the book of Isthmian odes, three are known to have been for an Aeginetan, a Megarian and a Rhodian. D'Alessio (2012) suggests that there was a second ode for an Aeginetan and then two odes for local victors in local victories in Athens and Corinth. C. Morgan (2007) 219–35 analyses the production of Pindaric epinicians by region relative to a different criteria, the kinds and numbers of victories celebrated in each ode.

[11] That the famous Crius fragment came from an ode celebrating the Aeginetan, rather than mocking a defeated opponent is surely clear from the commentary of the highly informed John Tzetzes (Holwerda (1960) 672, Molyneux (1992) 48, 60 n.80, *contra* Rawles (2013) 184 n.26); see also Poltera (2008) 306–7. For Simonides' patrons, see Molyneux (1992) and n.9 above.

[12] For a possible Pindaric commission from Chios, see Hornblower (2004) 145–56. On Simonides' patrons, see Molyneux (1992). It seems unlikely that Simonides did, in fact, execute a dedicatory epigram for Milo's Olympic statue (Molyneux (1992) 81–3), but, even if he did, an epigram did not require travel to Italy, as there was no choral performance to accompany the dedication, and the dedication was at Olympia.

from seeking odes. Certainly some distant victors were able to attract the poets — most obviously those from Sicily and southwestern Italy collected around Theron and Hieron, but also some from Cyrene, Tenedos, Metapontum and Rhodes — but the numbers suggest that these commissions required some additional justification or motivation on the part of the poets, above and beyond the reasons needed to accept a commission from a more local patron.

The attractions of Hieron's court in Sicily were clearly many — Phrynichus, Aeschylus and, probably, Xenophanes were lured there, as well as Simonides, Bacchylides and Pindar. These attractions surely included the grandeur of his entertaining, the generosity of his patronage, the glory to be won by the poets who visited, and the chance to mix with some of the great artists of the era.[13] Perhaps the same was true of the courts of the Emmenids in Acragas and the Battiads in Cyrene, but other commissions will require different explanations, whether curiosity, friendship, or multiple opportunities: Pindar's odes for the Rhodians Diagoras and Casmylus (perhaps completed on the same journey), his ode for the Cyrenean Telesicrates (completed well before his odes for Arcesilas), and Bacchylides' ode for Phaiscus of Metapontum's son, Alexidamus.[14]

While some more distant areas were able to attract the major epinician poets, a significant number of others were rarely celebrated or never celebrated; as Catherine Morgan reminds us, "citizens of very few states commissioned odes, let alone in any number."[15] Places devoid of epinician include: many of the cities in Italy; Crete; the northern Aegean; the eastern Aegean and the coast of Asia Minor; Cyprus; the Black Sea; and Massalia.[16] How many of these areas boasted significant populations of successful athletes is hard to judge. Some of these areas seem not to have competed in mainland athletics at all, even if they engaged with the Panhallenic sanctuaries in other ways

[13] On the literati who gathered at Hieron's court, see Luraghi (1994) 354–68, Bonanno (2010) 181–209, and K. Morgan (2015) 87–132.

[14] Diagoras' ode looks back on his whole career, and is thus difficult to date, but the Olympic victory, which was won in 464, provides a terminus post quem; cf. Currie (2011) 287 n.75. Golden (2004) 32 tentatively suggests 462 as a date for Casmylus' Isthmian victory, which probably postdates his Pythian win (d'Alessio (2012) 37), and certainly postdates Diagoras' Olympic victory in 464; the two odes might certainly have been performed as part of the same trip east. Pi. *Py.* 9 was certainly completed while Telesicrates was still actively competing; he won the Pythian sprint in 466, 8 years after his victory in the hoplite race (schol. ad Pi. *Py.* 9, inscr. a, b), but the later victory is not recorded in the ode. Arcesilas' chariot win came in 462, two years before his Olympic chariot win (Moretti (1957) no.268).

[15] C. Morgan (2007) 216.

[16] Cf. Hornblower (2004) 144–5 (eastern Aegean and Asia Minor), 156–9 (Cyprus, Thasos and Crete).

(Massalia, the Black Sea, Cyprus), but some areas certainly enjoyed success in athletic competition (Crete, Italy, the northern and eastern Aegean) and it is likely that the few victors that we know of were not the only ones who enjoyed success at Panhellenic venues, since our sources skew heavily towards Olympic victory only.[17] As this paper will show, a lack of epinician in areas with athletic successes to their names could be explained in other ways, but one significant reason for more distant patrons seems simply to have been the distances involved: a long journey was not insuperable, but it provided a significant hurdle for the poets.

The above survey assumes that most epinician odes were performed first in the victor's hometown, and that the poet who composed them was present for the performance. Christopher Eckerman has demonstrated that short odes were not a particular type of ode intended for performance at the place of victory, and, while it is possible, though, I think, unlikely, that some odes (say, for equestrian victors who could guarantee that they would be returning) were first performed at the following festival (and quite likely that they were reperformed on such occasions), the majority were surely intended for an initial performance in the victor's hometown.[18] There is some evidence that the poet did not always travel with the ode; internal evidence in two of Pindar's odes suggests that a chorus leader might have deputized, though it is quite possible that a chorus leader would have been needed when the poet was present anyway, and that, for whatever artistic reasons, these are the only two odes that make reference to this chorus leader.[19] Setting up a choral lyric performance was a complex process involving singing, dancing and musical accompaniment, and it is most likely that the poet was involved on the site, at least in the vast majority of occasions.[20] There were thus perhaps some options for victors who

[17] For victors from Thasos, Mytilene, Samos, and Miletus, see Hornblower (2004) 144, 157 and Moretti (1957) nos.201, 209, 225 and 226. For Cleomedes of Astypalaea, see Moretti (1957) no.174. For Crete and southern Italy, see below, especially nn.21, 32–3, 35, 47, and also Hornblower (2004) 157–9, 189. There is no evidence for a victor from a Black Sea colony specifically, but there is reason to think a Byzantine athlete won at Olympia (Loukopoulou and Laitar (2004) 917).

[18] Eckerman (2012), also (2011). For the compelling suggestion that the Panhellenic sanctuaries served as sites for reperformance of odes, see Hubbard (2004) 71–80, Currie (2004) 60, (2011) 301–8.

[19] Pi. Ol. 6.88, Is. 2.47. I have suggested elsewhere, for example, that one motivation for including the chorus leader is a desire to frame the work of the charioteer or driver (Nicholson (2005) 64–94).

[20] This in turn assumes that the premiere of an epinician was for the most part chorally performed, but this assumption is increasingly safe. Budelmann (2012) 173–90 has shown that the symposium (as opposed to a large feast or banquet) was not the primary site of performance, though it was envisaged as a possible site for performance), and

lived far away and could not tempt one of the great epinician poets to visit, but these can only have been rarely (if at all) exercised, and will not change the overall picture offered here.

II. Local Agonistic Practice

The patterns of production of the extant epinicians suggest that a second, and more pointed, reason for a lack of epinicians was that epinician was not among the standard ways that victors celebrated their victories in certain cities and towns, a factor that would have seriously undermined its utility as a vehicle for celebration. Athletics provided an arena in which prestige could be won within a home community, but within that community (or at least within a particular sector of the that community) local rules may have governed how that prestige was claimed. Some events may have been more prestigious than others, just as Aeginetans seem to have privileged the gymnastic events over the hippic, Spartans in the latter part of the fifth century to have privileged the hippic over the gymnastic, Cretans to have favored the long runs, or Crotoniates to have favored the sprints.[21] The value of different venues may have varied, with all panhellenic crowns bringing great prestige in some communities, but Nemean and Isthmian crowns carrying a more decidedly secondary status in others.[22] In some cases, as for example

---

scholars such as Currie (2004) 63–9, (2005), (2011), Ferarri (2012) and Krummen (2014) have collected evidence for the performance of particular epinicians within pre-existing religious festivals.

[21] Aegina: Hubbard (2001) 391–2. Even extremely wealthy patrons like Lampon, who commissioned multiple odes, did not engage in chariot racing; cf. Nicholson (2005) 169, 188–190. Sparta: Paus. 6.2.1, Golden (1998) 174, Hodkinson (1999) 160–5. Crete seems to have encouraged long-distance runners specifically; it also produced the victor in the long run in 448 (POxy II.222.26, Moretti (1957) no.296), and in the games of the Ten Thousand at Trapezus in 400 over sixty Cretans competed in the event (Xen. *Anab.* 4.8.27). See also Hornblower (2004) 158–9. Crotoniate runners were said to have finished in the top seven spots in one Olympic sprint, and its sprinting prowess gave rise to at least two proverbs, "The last of the Crotoniates is the first of the Greeks," and "All other towns prove vain against Croton"; see Strabo 6.1.12, schol. ad Theoc. 4.33, *fr.* adesp. 1270 Kock, Moretti (1957) 68–83, Giangiulio (1989) 102–6, Mann (2001) 164–7.

[22] Aeginetan odes seem to treat all Panhellenic victories as particularly special, with some propensity to offer grand totals of Panhellenic victories specifically (Pi. *Ol.* 8.62–6, 74–6, *Ne.* 6.57–9, Bacch. 12.36–41, although this latter may include non-Panhellenic wins; cf. also 13.196 which seems to focus on crown games, but refuses to provide the precise number; this is true even when an Olympic victory is being celebrated, as in Pi *Ol.* 8. By contrast, Nemean and Isthmian wins are treated more separately, and more like local wins, in many odes for victors from elsewhere: Pi. *Ol.* 7.80–7, 9.83–99, 13.28–46, 13.98–113, *Ne.* 10.21–36, 10.41–8, *Is.* 4.19–30, Bacch. 10.21–35. This distinction is different to that drawn by C. Morgan (2007) 221–35, who

the Argive Theaios' victories in the Argive Heraea, non-panhellenic victories may have carried unusual weight, or at least counted for more than an Isthmian or Nemean win.[23] Similarly, the forms in which the victory was celebrated were themselves sources of prestige, but they too were governed by local rules. Just as some communities — Aegina, Thebes, Ceos, Sicily in the time of Hieron, and Thessaly — competed in the commissioning of epinicians,[24] so for others epinician seems to have had no value within the local agonistic economy.

It has long been suggested that Spartans as a group avoided epinician.[25] Spartans certainly had plenty of victories to celebrate in the era of epinician, and were reliable patrons of statues and other monuments at Olympia.[26] But, although there is evidence that a Spartan was an early adopter of epinician, commissioning an ode, or at least a proto-ode, from Ibycus around the middle of the sixth century,[27] there is no evidence that any Spartan was celebrated by an epinician from Simonides, Pindar or Bacchylides.[28]

Distance may have played a role here, but there are reasons (beyond

---

separates odes where lesser victories are given attention from those where they are rarely mentioned. What is being flagged here is the way in which Nemean and Isthmian victories are included in odes where they are included.

[23] Pi. *Ne* 10. Similarly the Tlapolemeia, Diagoras' local festival, receives a more prominent billing than the Isthmian and Nemean games in Pi. *Ol*. 7.78–82, while the Aeginetan Delphinia and Heraea are given more lofty positions in Pi. *Py*. 8.61–80.

[24] C. Morgan (2007) 219 notes that epinician production peaks for Sicily, Aegina, central Greece and Ceos. Aegina boasts at least 12 of the extant epinicians, including Pi. *Is*. 9; in addition, Simonides wrote an epinician for Crius of Aegina (see n.11 above) and d'Alessio offers evidence of a second Aeginetan ode lost from the end of Pindar's book of Isthmian odes. Sicily and southwest Italy boasts 20 of the extant odes (with Syracuse and Aetna bagging 10 and Acragas 5), Thebes 5 odes for four victors, and Ceos 5 odes for three victors. In addition to one extant ode for a Thessalian from Pindar (Pi. *Py*. 10) and two from Bacchylides (14, 14B), Simonides wrote at least four epinicians for Thessalian patrons: Scopas, Aleuas, Antiochus and the sons of Aeatius (Sim. 510, 511, Theoc. 16.42–7, Molyneux (1992) 118–30). Hamilton (1974) 35–8 sees praise of the homeland as a particular structural feature of Pindar's odes for Aeginetans. Fearn (2010) 176–80 suggests that it was a particular feature of Aeginetan odes that they celebrated other family victors.

[25] Golden (1998) 81, Hodkinson (1999) 170–6, (2000) 317–12, C. Morgan (2007) 215–16, but cf. Hornblower (2004) 235–43. For a discussion of possible cultural factors behind this avoidance, see section III.

[26] Hodkinson (1999) 173–6, C. Morgan (2007) 215–16. Victors: Moretti (1957) nos.149, 157, 160, 195, 211, 216, 237, 305, 315. Dedications are recorded for nos.149, 160, 195, 305, 315. Note also that in 470s the Spartans erected a stele for Chionis, a great Spartan sprinter from the seventh century, and around the same time erected a statue for Eutelidas, a seventh-century youth pentathlete. See Moretti (1957) no.42, Hodkinson (1999) 165–7 and Christesen (2010).

[27] Golden (1998) 77, Hornblower (2004) 21, Rawles (2012) 6–10.

[28] As d'Alessio (2012) 52 notes, it would be very rash to assume that the reference to a Spartan in the fragmentary ode celebrating a victory in the Corinthian Hellotia refers to the victor.

specific arguments about what those factors were) to think that cultural
factors provide the dominant explanation for the lack of Spartan
interest in odes from the great epinician poets. The first reason is
simply the numbers: there were a lot of Spartan victors, and no Spartan
epinician from Pindar or Bacchylides, and no suggestion of one from
Simonides.[29] The second is that at least one of the poets, Bacchylides,
composed a different kind of commission for the Spartans, a dithyramb.[30] If Sparta was far away, at least one of the poets had an interest
in making that journey.[31] Third, Tarentum, Sparta's most successful
colony and the city most closely identified with Sparta, also seems, as a
rule, to have avoided epinician. Tarentum was a major participant in
Panhellenic and local athletic contests in the fifth century, and yet no
epinicians are known to have been composed for this active and
successful athletic community. The Oxyrhynchus victor list credits
Tarentines with Olympic victories in 476, 472 and 468, two in the
pentathlon, and another Tarentine pentathlete, the famous trainer Iccus,
presumably won his victory at Olympia in the 440s.[32] In addition,
excavations in the necropolis have revealed the extent to which the
Tarentine elite underpinned their privileged status through athletic victories at lesser venues in the fifth century (or at least the display of
prestigious objects linking the owner to athletics). Numerous prize Panathenaic vases have come from these graves, and one tomb, Tomb C,
even featured one Prize Panathenaic at each corner of the
sarcophagus.[33]

A second Italiote city also seems to have avoided epinician
deliberately: Croton. Croton boasted an even more impressive athletic
pedigree than Tarentum, at least until the Persian wars. In fact, during
the sixth century, Croton was the dominant athletic power at Olympia,
with particular success in the sprint, although that was not its only
source of success.[34] Milo won six wrestling crowns in a row at

---

[29] Cf. Hornblower (2004) 235–43, who agrees that the evidence for any Pindaric
epinician is weak, but argues that "there is no reason why Pindar *could* not have
written such a victory ode" (243).

[30] Bacch. 20. Hornblower (2004) 240–43 suggests that Pindar wrote a paean or
dithyramb for Sparta also.

[31] As Hodkinson (1999) 171 notes.

[32] Moretti (1957) nos.212, 230, 238, 307.

[33] Lo Porto (1967). Lo Porto records six fifth-century Prize Panathenaics found in the
excavations, and suggests that more were taken from the same necropolis before the
excavation started. It is unlikely that the occupant of Tomb C won all four of vases in
his tomb, *contra* Lo Porto (1967) 84; boxing and pentathlon is an unlikely combination. More likely, the four vases represent family successes. Neils (2001) 130
suggests, however, that the vases were purchased second-hand.

[34] Mann (2001) 164–7, with Moretti (1957) 68–83.

Olympia, and on his seventh visit, lost to another Crotoniate, Timasitheus, while the Phayllus who fought at Salamis won two Pythian crowns in the pentathlon as well as one in the sprint.[35] Yet there is only one Crotoniate who is known to have received an epinician — Astylus of Croton, the seven time Olympic victor. Astylus was not a regular Crotoniate, however; he relocated to Syracuse, presumably joining Gelon's synoecism in 485/4, after winning his first two crowns in 488, and, given that the remaining fragment of his ode hails Astylus as having won more local victories than any other athlete of his era, it makes most sense to conclude that he commissioned his epinician after moving to Syracuse, late in his career.[36] Given that Croton's successes date to the early period of epinician, our ignorance of most of Simonides' output must make this conclusion tentative, but it is surely safe to conclude that if Milo and Phayllus, at least, had received an epinician, some trace of those commissions would remain in later sources, as it does for Astylus'. That Astylus likely commissioned his epinician only after leaving Croton is particularly suggestive; it implies that, while epincian could be countenanced in Sicily, it was simply not the lingua franca of victory celebration in Croton.

There are reasons to believe that victors from Cretan cities too, as a whole, avoided epinician. As noted above, Crete was known for its long-distance runners, and one Olympic victor is recorded in 448; a second Olympic victor from the archaic period, Diognetus, cannot be dated, but Moretti puts his win in 488.[37] Perhaps most significant, however, is another departure, in this case Ergoteles of Cnossus, who joined Theron's reconstitution of Himera in 476/5.[38] Ergoteles was a double-Olympic champion, indeed a double period winner, and it seems likely that he was already excelling in the long run when he

[35] Milo and Timasitheus: Moretti (1957) nos.122, 145. Phayllus: Moretti (1953) no.11, Paus. 10.9.2.

[36] Sim. 506. Poltera (2008) 295–6, by contrast, considers the ode to belong to the early part of Astylus' career because of the focus on local victories, but cf., for example, Pi. Ol. 13.113. On Astylus' relocation to Syracuse, see Luraghi (1994) 288–304.

[37] Moretti (1957) nos.181 and 296. Moretti (1957) no.158 also suggests that the Titas celebrated on a vase found in Athens was from Crete and that the Icadion who won in 456 was also Cretan.

[38] Mann (2001) 245 n.81, Catenacci (2005) 33, Barrett (2007) 79–80, Hornblower (2004) 157–9. Hornblower (2004) 195–6 suggests that Ergoteles first resided briefly in Acragas; Acragas had Cretan connections, having been founded by Gela, itself a joint foundation of Crete and Rhodes. For Ergoteles' record, see Moretti (1957) no.224. Ergoteles commissioned his epinician (Pi. Ol. 12) before his second Olympic victory, but the statue he dedicated at Olympia (Paus. 6.4.11, SEG 11.1223a, Moretti (1957) no.224, Ebert (1972) no.20) records his full slate of victories. For the refoundation of Himera, see Diod. Sic. 11.48.3–49.4, with Luraghi (1994) 349–51, Bonanno (2010) 85–101.

relocated, and indeed that Theron invited him to relocate to Himera because of his promise in running. While there is no record of a Cretan epinician, Ergoteles, as Astylus before him, commissioned an epinician when he moved to Sicily. Sicily was by then an epicenter of epinician and epinician was an obvious way for a Sicilian to claim prestige.[39]

Distance may certainly have been a factor in the general absence of epinician from Crete and Croton, though it should be observed that both Astylus and Ergoteles had moved further away from the centers of epinician when they secured epinicians from Simonides and Pindar. Several cities closer to the poets' hometowns also make intriguing case studies, however: the towns of Arcadia, particularly Mantinea, and, perhaps, the towns of Achaea also.[40]

Mantinea was extraordinarily successful in the youth contests at Olympia in the late archaic and early classical periods — a more successful version of Aegina, with significantly more Olympic wins claimed by its young athletes, as well as at least one famous adult win.[41] Unlike Aeginetans, however, Mantineans seem to have disdained epinician; there is no trace of any Mantinean commission. Other Arcadians towns were less successful than Mantinea, but they certainly won victories, with Heraea claiming some fine successes.[42] As with Crete and Croton, there are no known epinicians from Arcadians still living in Arcadia, but a transplant did commission one, Hagesias of Stymphalus.[43] Again, this seems telling. The only Arcadian

---

[39] The date of Ergoteles' ode is contested. Barrett (2007) 78–97 and Hornblower (2004) 83–4 challenge the earlier consensus date of 470, dating the ode to 466, after the fall of the Deinomenids (when epinician largely ceased to be part of the Sicilian agonistic economy), but see also Catenacci (2005) and Nicholson (2015) for defenses of 470.

[40] C. Morgan (2007) 216 notes that the absence of epinicians from Arcadia and Achaea.

[41] Open victory: Dromeus of Mantinea, who won the pancration when Theogenes was a competitor (Moretti (1957) no.202). Youths: at least three, and perhaps five, Mantinean youths won victories at Olympia between 500 and 460: Epicradius (Paus. 6.10.9; dated by Moretti (1957) no.193 to 484), Protolaus (6.61; dated by Moretti (1957) no.256 to 464), and Cyniscus (6.4.11; dated by Moretti (1957) no.265 to 460), and perhaps Pytharchus (Paus. 6.7.1; dated by Moretti (1957) no.254 to 460) and Agametor (Paus. 6.9.9, dated by Moretti (1957) no.163 to 500). Moretti's dates for Agametor and Pytharchus are primarily based on the situation of their dedications. All but Pytharchus won the boys' boxing. See also Nicholson (2005) 127–8.

[42] Dromeus of Stymphalus won the long run twice (Moretti (1957) no.188), Tellon of Oresthasion won the boys boxing in 472 (no.231), and Heraea enjoyed a number of successes, largely through one family: Damaretus was the first, and second, winner of the hoplite race in 520 and 516 (Moretti (1957) no.132), his son was a double pentathlon winner (no.189), and his grandson a double winner in the wrestling (no.313). An (unrelated) victor in the boys' boxing is also known (no.205). Moretti (1957) no.314 dates a Dipaean's win to 440.

[43] Pi. Ol. 6. The ode could certainly have been performed in Stymphalus as well as Syracuse (Hubbard (2004), Calame (2012) 307–14); if so, it must have made for an unusual celebration in the Arcadian town.

we know to have commissioned an epinician did so once he no longer resided in Arcadia.

Peloponnesian Achaea too lacks epinician, but it also does not seem to have boasted the same population of victors. On the one hand, the story of Oebotas' curse implies that athletes from Achaean towns had no success at Olympia for nearly two hundred years until 460 (or at least not enough success to prevent the story from circulating).[44] On the other hand, the story also implies that successes followed after that date,[45] and, suprisingly, we do in fact know of some successes before that date, including at least one very flashy victory, a triple victory by the same athlete at the same games.[46] Moreover, the story also implies that success at Olympia might otherwise have been expected, that athletes from the (Peloponnesian) Achaean region were active participants in the games, and perhaps successful at lesser contests — otherwise Oebotas' curse had little point and the story would have had little purchase on the Achaean (or wider Greek) imagination. Certainly there are no known epinicians for Achaean athletes, and this raises an interesting possibility. Given that Achaean identity seems, as Jonathan Hall has argued, to have crystallized in southern Italy, and to have been exported from there to the northern Peloponnese, it was perhaps in imitation of the Achaean Italian cities or the cities that came to be understood as Achaean — primarily Croton, but also Sybaris, Caulonia, Metapontum and Poseidonia — that the Peloponnesian Achaeans avoided epinician.[47]

---

[44] On the story of Oebotas' curse, see Paus. 6.3.8, 7.17.6–7, 13–14, Bohringer (1979) 12–13, Kurke (1993) 152–3.

[45] Once the curse was lifted, according to the story, Sostratus of Pellene won an Olympic victory (Paus. 7.1.7.14, Moretti (1957) no.263); given that Oebotas was honored in 460, we can conclude that Sostratus was thought of as winning in 460 also. Sostratus may be a fictional character, however, perhaps confused with a real victor, Socrates (Paus. 6.8.1); a cult hero of the same name was honored outside Dyme, the dominant city in western Achaea which took over Oebotas together with his original hometown of Paleia (Paus. 7.17.8).

[46] In 512 Phanas of Pellene won the sprint, the diaulos and the hoplite race (Moretti (1957) no.142), and in 496 Pataecus of Dyme won the first kalpe race (Moretti (1957) no.171).

[47] Hall (2002) 58–65. Sybaris seems to have been successful at Olympia (Fischer-Hansen, Nielsen and Ampolo (2004) 296–7, and Moretti (1957) no.71 and (1987) 81–2), but, given that it was destroyed in 510, successful Sybarites had few opportunities to commission or avoid epinician; Poseidonia had at least one Olympic victor in the era of epinician, Parmenides, winner of the sprint and diaulos in 468 (Moretti (1957) no.235); Caulonia seems to have seen Olympic success only later (Moretti (1957) no.379); but, given that Croton was its mother-city, it was likely active in athletics before that; Metapontum also seems to have boasted no Olympic wins, although a Metapontine did win at Delphi (and compete at Olympia), and was celebrated in an epinician ode, Bacch. 10. In Nicholson (2015), I dated this ode to after 450. This ode seems to have been an anomaly, the only ode for a victor from the cities of southern

One final case worth considering is Macedonia. Pindar and Bacchylides both composed praise poetry for one of the Macedonian kings, Alexander, the son of Amyntas, but there is no trace of an epinician.[48] The Macedonians certainly competed in the games at the end of the fifth century (Archelaus seems to have won the four-horse chariot at both Olympia and Delphi), but it is less clear that they had successes to celebrate, or were even seeking to win prestige through these venues, earlier in the century. The victory of Alexander himself in the sprint reported by Herodotus is certainly a fabrication created as part of a larger effort on the part of the Macedonian kings to create a Hellenic profile for themselves (the fact that Alexander is said to have finished joint first is particularly suspicious), but Herodotus' retelling of the story does suggest that Macedonians were competing by Herodotus' time, and is perhaps evidence that Alexander had himself competed, even if he had not won.[49] It is hard to believe, however, that encomia, but not epinicians, would have been acceptable. While Felix Budelmann has shown that the two types of poetry were correlated with different performance venues, it is clear that many of the families that commissioned encomia from Pindar, Simonides and Bacchylides also commissioned epinicians.[50]

Whatever the situation with Macedon, there are good reasons to believe that at least in some other areas epinician was not a form of celebration that was part of the normal way that the prestige of victory was claimed from the victor's home community. Such norms would not have been absolute, and could have been ignored if the victor's family had particular reasons to seek an epinician, but these norms would have seriously undermined, or at least threatned, one of the main points of an epinician, to secure prestige within the home community. Nevertheless, such situations might explain those instances where a community is represented by a single extant epinician. Strong reasons are certainly needed to think that a single epinician is an anomaly when we lack so much of Simonides' output,[51] but one such anomalous epinician might

---

Italy identified as Achaean.

[48] Pi. Fr. 120–1, Bacch. Fr. 20B.

[49] Archelaus: Moretti (1957) no.349. On Hdt. 5.22, see Hall (2001) 167–72, (2002) 154–68 and Fearn (2007) 116–18.

[50] Pindar composed encomia and epinicians for the Emmenids (Fr. 118–19, 124a-b, *Ol.* 2–3, *Py.* 6, *Is.* 2), the Deinomenids (Fr. 124d-126, *Ol.* 1, *Py.* 1–3), Xenophon of Corinth (Fr. 122, *Ol.* 13), the family of Aristagoras of Tenedos (Fr. 123, *Ne.* 11), Bacchylides composed encomia and epinicians for the Deinomenids (Bacch. 3–5, 20C), and Simonides presumably composed encomia and epinicians for the Scopads (Sim. 542, with Molyneux (1992) 118–30).

[51] I am not convinced, for example, that epinician was a rarity in Corinth, as C. Morgan (2007) 228–31 argues. Morgan notes that Pi. *Ol.* 13 was not the first ode

be represented by Bacchylides' ode for Alexidamus of Metapontum. As noted above, epinician seems to have been a rarity in the Achaean cities of Italy and the Peloponnese; it was also a rarity in Italy as a whole.[52] A second strong possibility is Pindar's ode for the Argive Theaios.[53]

III. The Politics of Epinician Form

The reasons behind these large scale absences of epinicians by Pindar Bacchylides and Simonides could be various — established practice, conservatism, or taste, for example — but one kind of reason repays further investigation, and that is local politics. Stephen Hodkinson, for example, has argued that the absence of epinician from Sparta should be traced to a more centralized and complete control of choral performance that prevented individual victors or their families establishing a civic chorus to celebrate their victories or appropriating existing choruses for this purpose.[54] While attractive, this hypothesis must also confront serious objections. While Hodkinson offers evidence that honors to Olympic victors in Sparta were controlled in

---

commissioned by the Oligathidae, but it is worth adding that Barrett (2007) 98–117 argues that Simonides composed two odes for the family, and that d'Alessio (2012) 52 argues that one of the patrons celebrated in Pindar's lost Isthmian odes was also Corinthian, so that epinician was not simply a feature of one family's celebratory practice. Cities nearby certainly commissioned epinician, including Athens, Megara (d'Alessio (2012) 39–48) and Phlius, and epinicians must have been familiar from reperformance at the Isthmian festival. On the other hand, it is suggestive that epinician seems to have been absent from Corinth's colonies, with the exception of Syracuse, where epinician could certainly be understood as a genre promoted by imports, the Geloan Deinomenids, in imitation of foreign (Agrigentine or Euboean) practice. (The Euboean influence would have come from the emigration of Glaucus to Leontini and Camarina; see Nicholson (2015).) Corcyra, for example, enjoyed regular success at Olympia (Moretti (1957) no.118, 119, 155, 161, 168), and among these victors appears the intriguing example of Philo of Corcyra (no.161), a double winner in the open Olympic boxing, whose father, Glaucus of Carystus, commissioned an ode from Simonides (on the relationship, see Rausa (1994) 46–7, Smith (2007) 99, *contra* Löhr (2000) 34–5), but who himself does not seem to have been celebrated in epinician. No epinicians are recorded for Epidamnus, but the city seems to have been less successful than Corcyra. The one known victor is Cleosthenes of Epidamnus (Moretti (1957) no.141), who won the Olympic chariot race in 516, and seems to have been the first such victor to dedicate a full-size equestrian group (Smith (2007) 123–4).

[52] In Italy, the only parallel is the pair of odes for Hagesidamus of Epizephyrian Locri, Pi. *Ol.* 10–11. Anaxilas installed his son as ruler of Rhegion and was celebrated by Simonides as Anaxilas of Messene (see Sim. 515 and Heraclides Lembus, *Pol.* 25,a and Luraghi (1994) 215–16) and, as noted above, Astylus' ode was likely produced in Syracuse.

[53] See C. Morgan (2007) 227–35, 249–61.

[54] Hodkinson (1999) 170–3, (2000) 317–19; also Golden (1998) 81, C. Morgan (2007) 216–17.

certain ways, it is clear that Spartans were used to celebrating their athletic successes both at home and abroad, and that they used the dedications they made to promote their own families and factions. In the sanctuary of Athena Chalkioikos on the Spartan acropolis around 440 Damonon was allowed to erect (or not prevented from erecting) the famous stele that proclaimed his many minor victories at great length; it would have been a surprise if someone had objected, since, in commemorating his victories there, he was following established practice.[55] Perhaps most revealing, however, are the stelai commemorating the long-dead Chionis at Olympia and in Sparta; as Paul Christesen has demonstrated, these monuments were a specifically Agiad initiative, designed to regain some of the lost influence of that family.[56] To subscribe to Hodkinson's hypothesis about Sparta and epinician thus means believing that the state as a whole prevented the use of choral performance to promote individual interests, but was much less strict in its regulation of the use of public monuments for the same ends, and that, while the Spartan elite was unable or unwilling to rein in the self-promotion of families or factions in public monuments, it favored and was able to maintain a unified position regarding choral performance. Hodkinson may be right, however; there is so much we do not know about the workings of Spartan society.[57]

It is certainly much harder to provide convincing reasons for the large-scale absences than to provide convincing evidence for the absences themselves. A more promising place to expose the politics of epinician is through comparison with a different celebratory vehicle that turns out to have been in competition with epinician: orally transmitted narratives that cast the victor as a hero. I argue elsewhere that a genre of narratives that cast athletes as heroes — often, though not exclusively, as Heracles — operated in the late archaic and early classical period. One type of these narratives was relatively complex, the narrative of disrespect analyzed by Joseph Fontenrose,[58] according to which a great athlete is denied the honors due to him on his return from the games, but, when disaster falls upon the home community, those honors are paid. Others are more simple. One simply tells how the great athlete performs some exceptional, heroic feat outside of the games, such as winning a battle or killing a monster, while other basic

---

[55] Hodkinson (1999) 152–76, C. Morgan (2007) 216–17.

[56] Christesen (2010).

[57] Hornblower (2004) 235–9. Hornblower's argument that epinician did not require choral performance is, I believe, misconceived, however. While reperformance certainly did not require choral performance, the genre was fundamentally a choral one, and the initial or primary performance was surely choral. Cf. Budelmann (2012).

[58] Fontenrose (1968).

types ascribe divine birth, metamorphosis or the ability to be in two places at once to the victor. Abnormal size and exceptional physical strength, as well as a lack of control are also typical motifs, as well as a death in which the hero-athlete's body disappears.[59]

Drawing on the groundbreaking work of Bruno Currie,[60] I have argued that these narratives were not the result of some long, decentralized and relatively random process of exaggeration, but were intentionally generated by the victor (or, indeed, by the victor's family or hometown in cases where the victor is long dead) as a way to capitalize on the prestige of his victory, much like an epinician. Some victors used their statues to generate these narratives, as Theogenes, and, later, Polydamas of Scotussa,[61] or created unusual public monuments such as huge boulders that they claimed to have lifted.[62] Others provided spectacular public demonstrations of their strength, such as lifting up cattle or wrestling wild animals.[63] Others sought to shape their lives — and even their deaths — in imitation of Heracles, dressing up as Heracles in battle, as Milo, or pursuing adventures that followed in the great hero's footsteps, as Philippus of Croton, or even committing suicide through self-immolation, as Timanthes of Argos.[64] Perhaps the most effective method of generating a lasting narrative was for an athlete to insert himself into a pre-existing cult, as Currie argues that Euthymus of Epizephyrian Locri did. In this way the cult not only framed the athlete as a hero, but provided a regular venue for the retelling of the narrative.

That this kind of narrative stood in competition with epinician is suggested by the behavior of the victors themselves. Victors who sought to create narratives that cast them as heroes seem to have avoided epinician: Milo, who went into battle against the Sybarites carrying his Olympic crowns and dressed as Heracles; Euthymus, who inserted himself into the riverine cult of the Hero of Temesa on the Tyrrhenian side of Locri's territory; Theogenes of Thasos, whose statues cast him as a second Heracles; Cleomedes of Astypalaea, never a victor at Olympia, but heroized in his hometown, after, presumably,

[59] Nicholson (2015).

[60] Currie (2002); see also Currie (2005).

[61] For Theogenes' statues at Olympia and Delphi, see Ebert (1972) no.37.3–4, 8–9, *IvO* no.153, with Moretti (1957) 88, and Moretti (1953) no.21.3–4, 8–9. For the comparison to Heracles, see Currie (2005) 134 and n.84. Polydamas: Paus. 6.5.1–7.

[62] Cf. Bybon (Moretti (1953) 4–5), Eumastas of Thera (*IG* XII.3.449) and Euthymus (Ael. *VH* 8.18).

[63] Milo: Lucian, *Charon* 8, Athen. 10.412e-413a (= Phylarchus, *FGrH* 81 F3). Amesinas of Barce: Philostr., *Gym.* 43; Euseb. *Chron.* 243–4, text of Christesen (2007) 393.

[64] Milo: Diod. Sic. 12.9.5–6. Philippus: Hdt. 5.47, with Hdt. 5.43, Diod. Dic. 5.9, and Malkin (1994) 203–18; Timanthes: Paus. 6.8.4.

inserting himself into a local cult; and Timanthes of Argos who immolated himself when he could no longer string his bow.[65] We certainly do not possess a full knowledge of epinician, but the fame and frequent mentions of the first three of these victors provides a strong guarantee that they, at least, did not commission epinician.

The most striking evidence of the incompatibility of the two genres comes from Astylus of Croton. Astylus was a patron of epinician, commissioning an ode from Simonides, but he was also the subject of a failed heroizing narrative, presumably articulated in Croton, the city he left. This narrative told how, on his departure, his townsmen showed their disrespect for him by tearing down his statue and turning his house into a prison. Yet, in contrast to the typical disrespect narrative where imprisonment and the abuse of statues is followed by plague or famine, no retribution followed for the Crotoniates.[66]

Analysis of the two forms supports the conclusion that epinician was incompatible with such heroizing narratives. In three aspects in particular their visions are opposed. First, the world of epinician is a world of Greek cities and sanctuaries linked together in a dense network. Epinician links together not only the victor's hometown and the place of victory, but the poet's own town of Thebes, mother-cities and colonies, allies, and the various places where the victor has won other victories, including the more obscure contest locales such as Athens, Argos, Arcadia, Megara and Aegina. The two most important festival sites, Olympia and Delphi, are often evoked in concrete detail with numerous specific features mentioned: at Olympia, Pelops' tomb, the Altis, the hippodrome, the olive trees, the hill of Kronos, the altars and the river Alpheus, and, at Delphi, the sacred way, the temple of Apollo, the treasuries and dedications.[67]

The implication of this geographical vision is that the victor moves easily between Greek cities and sanctuaries, and exiles and transplants are consequently prominent among the patrons: Astylus moved from Croton to Syracuse, Ergoteles from Cnossus to Himera, Hagesias from Stymphalus to Syracuse, Glaucus from Carystus to Corcyra and then to Leontini and Camarina, Psaumis from somewhere, perhaps Aetna, to

---

[65] For Cleomedes, see Paus. 6.9.6–8. Only two victors who were subjects of heroizing narratives commissioned epinician, Diagoras of Rhodes and Glaucus of Carystus. This overlap likely points to the ways in which different interests sought to claim the prestige of these victors for themselves.

[66] Paus. 6.13.1. For the epinician, see Sim. 506. I should make clear here that for Currie (2005) epinician did not stand in opposition to these narratives, but rather represented one possible step in a bid for heroization.

[67] Olympia: Pi. *Ol.* 1.90–3, 3.17–24, 3.33–4, 6.64–70, 8.1–3, 8.9, 9.3, 9.7, 10.43–50, [Pi.] *Ol.* 5.5, 17–18. Delphi: Pi. *Py.* 4.3–4, Pi. *Py.* 7.10–12, *Ne.* 7.34–6, Bacch. 3.17–21.

Camarina, and, of course, Hieron and Chromius from Gela to Syracuse and Aetna.[68] The epinician victor seems to move above the polis, to work on a higher plane. Prominent among the victors are those promoting synoecisms or new foundations: Diagoras (and presumably Casmylus) of Rhodes, the Ceans Argeius, Lachon and probably Liparion, Theaios of Argos, Psaumis of Camarina, and Hieron and Chromius.[69]

By contrast, the heroizing narratives avoid this wide view. The site of the victory is mostly left in the background, and the action of the narrative takes place in the victor's home polis, creating a sense of a much more independent community and emphasizing the full territory of the polis, rather than focusing on the built-up center. More often than not, the action is in the countryside, in agricultural or wild spaces, or in the sea off the coast: the athlete-heroes perform agricultural tasks, or quasi-agricultural tasks, fixing ploughs, wrestling with cattle, chasing hares, swimming in the sea, or they die in wilderness areas, lost in rivers or caves or eaten by wolves.[70] When they do appear in the towns, they are often at odds with the spaces, sent into exile, imprisoned, or destroying a school.[71] In some ways it would have been better if the victor had not left the countryside. One humorous twist on the heroizing lore surrounding Milo tells how he was comprehensively bested in rock lifting and bull wrestling by Titormus, a self-deprecating Aetolian cowherd who never competed. In desperation, Milo exclaims, "Zeus, have you not begotten a second Heracles in this man?"[72]

A second difference of vision in the two forms relates to the economy they imagine or project. As Leslie Kurke has demonstrated, epinician sought to accommodate aristocrats to the reality of their cities, by providing a public language through which commodity exchange could be understood in accord with an aristocratic ideology of exchange and expenditure on their cities as an activity that advanced the

---

[68] For Glaucus, see Nicholson (2015); for Psaumis, Nicholson (2011).

[69] Diagoras: Hornblower (2004) 131–4, Cairns (2005) 70–2, 85–8 and Kowalzig (2007) 224–66. That Casmylus, like Diagoras was known as "of Rhodes" in *AP* 16.23, rather than of one of the cities on Rhodes, suggests that he advertised himself as such; cf. Hornblower (2004) 142. Argeius: Nicholson and Gutierrez (2012) 99–101, and for Lachon and Liparion, cf. Bacch. 6.5, 6.16, 8.14. Theaios of Argos: C. Morgan (2007) 249–57 and Kowalzig (2007) 170–8. Psaumis: [Pi.] *Ol.* 5.8 and Nicholson (2011). Hieron: Pi. *Py.* 1. Chromius: Pi. *Ne.* 9.1–3.

[70] Agricultural tasks: Philostr., *Gym.* 13 (Polymestor), Paus. 6.10.1–2 (Glaucus), and n.63 above. Sea: Philostr., *Gym.* 43 (Tisander), Paus. 6.11.6–9 (Theogenes). Deaths: Paus. 6.5.8–9, 6.6.10, 6.14.8, Gell. 15.6, Ael. *VH* 8.18.

[71] Imprisoned: Euthycles in Callimachus 186–7 (Massimilla) / 84–85a (Harder) and Oenomaus, *Detectio Praestigiatorum* apud Eusebius *Praep. Evang.* V.34.14–17 (= fr. 12.80–105 Mullach). Destroying a school: Paus. 6.9.6–8.

[72] Aelian *VH* 12.22, 14.47b.

stability and glory of their families.[73] Commodity exchange was a frequent subject in Pindar's epinicians; it must also have been frequent in Simonides' epinicians, given the later picture of the poet as venal and clashing with his patrons over money.[74] By contrast, the heroizing narratives typically avoid engaging with a world in which commodity exchange seemed to be encroaching on new territory: the exchanges that are central to these narratives are the exchange of honor — of crowns, of sacrifices — for great deeds done, whether that honor is paid or withheld. This difference is flagged by Herodotus in his only, and very brief, reference to Milo. At the end of his lengthy story on the Crotoniate doctor Democedes, who grew wealthy through his medical practice, Herodotus notes briefly, and mischievously, that when he had succeeded in escaping the Persian King, he married Milo's daughter, securing the match by paying out a large sum of money.[75]

A third difference of vision comes in the idea of victor the two forms promote. In the heroizing narratives, the victor is either explicitly or implicitly marked as a hero: born of a god, celebrated in cult, or framed by their hero-like deeds as existing on a different plane than ordinary mortals. By contrast, epinician represents a rejection of the vision of the athlete as a literal hero, a viable object of hero cult, and represents instead an assurance that the victor belongs within the community as a regular citizen, not outside of it or on its margins. Epinician's victor is defined primarily by his athletic feats, not by some extraordinary deed of strength done elsewhere. He is, therefore, special, but not unique, and the club that the epinician victor is enrolled in by virtue of his victory is an expansive one. While the victors celebrated in the heroizing narratives are adult gymnasts who have won at Olympia, or been robbed of a victory they should have won at Olympia, epinician celebrates not only the great gymnasts, but also equestrian victors, youth victors, victors at other Panhellenic venues, and indeed victors at local contests. Where the hero-athlete's great power can often turn against his home town, epinician's victors, the genre assures us, will settle back easily into their home city on their return.[76]

---

[73] Kurke (1991) 225–56.

[74] For this tradition, see Bell (1978).

[75] Hdt. 3.137. On Herodotus' treatment of exchange in the Polycrates section of the text more generally, see Kurke (1999) 101–29. Note also that one heroizing narrative, that of Euthycles of Locri, does engage with issues of commodity exchange, as his imprisonment turns on the misreading of a gift as a bribe. Partly because of this significant difference, I have argued in Nicholson (2015) that this narrative dates a few decades later, to the time of radical democracies in Syracuse and Croton. For the sources of Euthycles' story, see n.71 above.

[76] For the threat posed by the victor, see Fontenrose (1968) and Kurke (1993).

That these different visions were deployed in the service of competing political visions is shown by the case of two Olympic victors from Epizephyrian Locri, Hagesidamus, victor in the youth boxing in 476, and the great Euthymus, who won the open boxing in 484, 476 and 472, and only missed out on four straight crowns because of an epic defeat by another true great, Theogenes, in 480. At some point in the few years following 476, Hagesidamus was celebrated in a pair of odes by Pindar, one short and one long, *Olympians* 10 and 11, but, while Euthymus was celebrated in statues erected both at Olympia and in Locri, no trace of an epinician remains. Given Euthymus' celebrity and prominence in the anecdotal tradition, it is surely safe to conclude that this is because there was no epinician. Euthymus was also remembered instead in an orally transmitted heroizing narrative, likely generated during the 470s, that told how he drove away the "Hero of Temesa," a vampire-like revenant and abandoned member of Odysseus' crew that was said to have demanded the regular tribute of a maiden from Temesa, a small, indigenous community on the northern seaboard of Locri's territory. Euthymus did indeed become a cult hero, worshipped in a Locrian cult during and after his lifetime.[77]

Specific elements in the different celebratory vehicles make it clear that different political visions were being pursued through the celebrations of the two victors, as the two vehicles take opposed positions on Locri's relationship with Syracuse and its tyrant Hieron. Syracuse had had interests in Locrian territory since the time of Gelon, but immediately prior to the games of 476 it had protected Locri's western border from Anaxilas of Messene, with the result that in *Pythian* 2, using one of Locri's most resonant images as a synecdoche for the whole polis, Pindar was able to represent Locri as a maiden protected by Hieron.[78] Hagesidamus' epinician makes it clear the family supported Locri's affiliation with — and subordination to — Syracuse. The ode is part of a sequence of odes produced by Pindar to celebrate three Olympic victories in 476 that delineate the newly affirmed reach of Hieron of Syracuse: *Olympian* 1, for Hieron himself,

---

[77] For the sources on Euthymus, see Moretti (1957) no.191, Currie (2002), Nicholson (2013) 12–15 and (2015). For the statues, see Paus. 6.6.6, *IvO* no.144, and Pliny *NH* 7.152 = Callimachus 202 (Massimilla) / 99 (Harder). For the legend of the Hero, see Callimachus 201–2 (Massimilla) / 98–99b (Harder), Strabo 6.1.5, Pausanias 6.6.7–10, Aelian *VH* 8.18, Suda, s.v. Εὔθυμος. For its date, see Nicholson (2014) 12–15, (2015). Callimachus' version likely did proceed to the inauguration of the cult; cf. Pliny *NH* 7.152 = Callimachus *Aetia* 202 (Massimilla) / 99 (Harder).

[78] *Py.* 2.18–20. On Anaxilas' invasion or threatened invasion of Locri, see Luraghi (1994) 224, 349, Bonanno (2010) 75–84. Gelon built some sort of building in Locri: Athen. 12.542a (= Duris *FGrH* 76 F19), with Bonanno (2010) 73–4. For the maiden as a symbol of Locri, see Redfield (2003) 83–150, 241–91, 309–85.

Olympians 2 and 3 for Theron of Acragas, and *Olympians* 10 and 11 for Hagesidamus.[79] The odes for Hieron and Hagesidamus are specifically linked by the image of Ganymede that concludes *Olympian* 10. This was likely a Deinomenid image, since it seems that the famous terracotta of Zeus abducting Ganymede adorned the newly completed Syracusan treasury at Olympia.[80]

Euthymus' heroizing narrative of his defeat of the Hero of Temesa represents Locri in a very different light, as independent, powerful in its own right, protecting its own and focused on its neighbor to the east, Croton. Far from being protected by Syracuse, in this narrative Locri is the protector, with the part of the maiden played by Temesa, a small community in the north-eastern reaches of its territory, recently taken from Croton.[81] Syracuse is simply not a part of this vision.

These opposed positions on relations with Syracuse fit the two forms well. The epinician vision of the victor as part of a network of victors and of his city as part of a network of cities is deployed to buttress and justify Locri's linkages to Hieron and Syracuse, while epinician's focus on navigating a more complex, increasingly commodified economy also served to aid integration into the Syracusan empire with its expanding trade networks and dominant coinage standards.[82] By contrast, the isolated, extraordinary victor of the heroizing narrative, with its focus on the rural areas of its own territory rather than relations with other cities and its refusal to address the spread of coinage and commodity exchange, very much fits a refusal to accommodate to Syracuse's military and economic sphere. Locri is to find its identity and value in the organization of its own spaces, not in relations with other cities.

In Locri, then, it is clear that the choice of commemorative vehicle correlated with the fundamental politics of the vehicle: epinician was the best vehicle for Hagesidamus' family to promote their vision of

---

[79] Theron had challenged Hieron in the wake of Gelon's death (Luraghi (1994) 321–34, 346–7, Bonanno (2010) 39–69, 85–124), but the complex of odes signals his integration into Hieron's regime also. See Nicholson (2014) 18.

[80] *Ol.* 1.43–5, 10.99–105, with Neer (2012) 181–2. For the completion date of the treasury, see Luraghi (1994) 314–18.

[81] Nicholson (2014) 13–15, (2015).

[82] For Locri's relations with the Syracusan trade networks, see Giudice (1989) 47–61. The dominance of Syracusan standards was ensured by the huge issues of Syracusan coins after 480 as well as the expansion of Geloan issues (Holloway (1987) 14–15), the new issues of Leontini and Aetna on the same standard that began c.475, the closing or mothballing of area mints on other standards (Naxos, Selinus), and the shift of Rhegium and Messene to the same standard. On the coinage of the area, see Rutter (1997) 101–39. For the complex treatment of commodity and gift exchange in *Ol.* 10, see Kurke (1991) 225–39, Nicholson (2014) 19–20.

connection to Syracuse, while a heroizing narrative was an excellent vehicle for Euthymus' rejection of this connection. Euthymus had the opportunity to commission an epinician ode (Pindar clearly made himself available to some victors at the 476 games, and visited Euthymus' hometown), and lived in a town where epinician was at least not unthinkable, if indeed not, seemingly, a normal part of athletic celebration, yet he did not commission one. The analysis of the politics of epinician form offered here suggests that this was not the result of happenstance, but of conscious choice, that Euthymus actively avoided epinician because of a political orientation built in to the form.[83]

There are other intriguing situations where victors in the same community pursue these different forms — in Argos Timanthes sought to frame himself as a hero, while Theaios commissioned an epinician; in Aegina, while many athletes commissioned epinicians, Taurosthenes generated a hero narrative involving a spectral appearance on the island on the day of his victory — but the remains of the heroizing narratives are usually so exiguous that it is difficult to determine whether the political orientation of the athlete celebrated there is different from that of the epinician athletes.[84] One other promising possibility is, however, offered by Cleomedes of Astypalaea.

There is no epinician for an Astypalaean athlete, but the epinician commissioned by Diagoras of Rhodes offers a good sense of the possibilities for a victor from an Aegean island. While, as Francis Cairns argues, Diagoras and his family were surely opposed to the spread of Athenian power and the inclusion of their city, Ialysos, within the Delian league,[85] they did not promote the isolation of Ialysos. Instead, the ode promotes both the synoecism of the three cities of Rhodes, Ialysos, Kameiros and Lindos, and strong links to the larger Dorian world and their putative mother-city of Argos specifically.[86]

---

[83] For Currie (2002), Euthymus' choice seems to be due to Euthymus' personal desire to be heroized.

[84] Timanthes: Paus. 6.8.4. Theaios: Pi. *Ne.* 10. Taurosthenes: Paus. 6.9.3 and Currie (2005) 131. For Aeginetan epinician, see Burnett (2005), Kowalzig (2007) 181–223, Fearn (2010) 175–226, Morrison (2011). Taurosthenes is often overlooked in discussions of Aeginetan athletic culture, yet the fact that this narrative dates to the period after Athens' successful siege of the island in the mid 450s seems significant. Later Aeginetan epinicians, at least, are often pro-Athenian; cf. Figueira (1993) 205–13.

[85] Cairns (2005) 69–70.

[86] Synoecism: Hornblower (2004) 131–4, Cairns (2005) 70–72, 85–8 and Kowalzig (2007) 224–66. The ode tells how Tlepolemus, described as the founder of the island (30), was the king of Tiryns (78; also 29), and left the Argolid (33) to come to Rhodes. The Rhodians are also represented as "Argive" (19). A heroizing narrative certainly developed around Diagoras (schol. ad Pi. *Ol.* 7.inscr.a, c, with Currie (2005) 130–1), but it would be wrong to conclude that he and his faction were the ones promoting it. Not only did he frame himself as an epinician victor, but he also, in contrast to the

By contrast, the heroizing narrative of Cleomedes seems to sever or oppose links with Astypalaea's mother-city. The narrative told how Cleomedes was denied an Olympic crown because he killed an opponent during their boxing match. On returning to Astypalaea, in his grief he tore down a school, killed the children inside and hid in a chest a temple. When the chest was opened, he had disappeared, however, and the Delphic oracle commanded the Astypalaeans to honor him as a hero.[87] There is little here of the kind of specific details that illuminated the politics of Euthymus' narrative, but the identity of Cleomedes' luckless opponent is significant: Iccus of Epidauros. While Astypalaea's colonial heritage seems to have been contested, Epidauros was at the least one of the cities that was framed as Astypalaea's mother-city in this period.[88] The narrative thus seems designed to separate the island from its Dorian mother-city, without suggesting any competing linkage. Given this vision, the form is well chosen. While Diagoras' vision of a well-connected Rhodes fits epinician, the vision encoded in Cleomedes' narrative fits the inward-looking vision of the heroizing form.[89]

While epinician embodied a certain political orientation, statue dedications were more flexible. Both epinician patrons and victors who sought their own heroization commissioned statues in healthy numbers.[90] It is probably a mistake, however, to treat statue dedications as a single genre or as unified in their ideology. There were clear differences in design, iconography, and the kind of information offered

---

heroizing narratives, framed himself as a father, as the placement of his sons' Olympic statues makes clear (Paus. 6.7.1–3, Löhr (2000) 61–4, 183–4, Smith (2007) 99). These statues certainly encouraged narratives that framed Diagoras as a mortal patriarch whose existence was continued by his family: Cic. *Tusc.* 1.46.111, Plut. *Pel.* 34, Gell. 3.15.3

[87] Paus. 6.9.6–8.

[88] Reger (2004) 737.

[89] Cleomedes does not seem to have won at Olympia, since there is no mention of a statue in Paus. 6.9.6–8; the story seems to be occasioned by the statue of Philo of Corcyra, who presumably benefitted from Cleomedes' supposed disqualification to win in 492 as well as 488. To garner such a reputation, however, Cleomedes must have been a great victor, with victories at other panhellenic contests, so that epinician was a viable choice for him. The date of Cleomedes' narrative is harder to judge. A date some years after the loss, and during the Athenian occupation of the Aegean — and perhaps around the time of Diagoras' epinician — fits well. Such a date would not mean that Cleomedes was not involved in the generation of narrative. A spectacular death may well have been part of the generation of some such narratives, but a theatrical representation may also have sufficed.

[90] Thus, Euthymus (above n.77), Theogenes (Olympia: Ebert (1972) no.37.3–4, 8–9, *IvO* no.153, with Moretti (1957) no.201; Delphi: Moretti (1953) no.21.3–4, 8–9), Milo (Paus. 6.14.6), Timanthes (Paus. 6.8.4) and Taurosthenes (Paus. 6.9.3) all boasted statues at Olympia, as well as elsewhere. Cleomedes cannot have had a statue at Olympia, since he did not win an Olympic crown.

on the pedestal — with some statues emphasizing the moment of crowning or, more directly (like those of Theogenes or Polydamas of Scotussa) suggesting a comparison to some hero, and others (like those of Glaucus of Carystus, Telesicrates of Cyrene or Diagoras' son Acusilaus) emphasizing the competition or the event in which the athlete competed.[91] These differences would certainly repay a detailed study, but one hypothesis worth testing is that statues can in fact be categorized according to whether they represent the victor as a hero or as an athlete.

The formal opposition between epinician and the heroizing narrative and the specific examples of the narratives of Euthymus and Cleomedes combine to make a strong argument that epinician had a particular, in-built political meaning that did not suit the agendas of every victor. Epinician was a flexible vehicle, but it could not be turned to every purpose, and one reason why a patron might not have commissioned an epinician was that he did not want to be associated with its politics or that epinician was not a welcoming vehicle through which to promote his own political agenda.

IV. Expense

A number of patterns that emerge from the extant epinicians suggest that, in addition to access, local culture and politics, expense constituted one further significant obstacle to commissioning an epinician.

First, there are very few repeat commissions (that is, later commissions for later victories) once those patrons who enjoyed the full resources of the state are excluded from consideration. When tyrants, kings and their lieutenants are set to one side, and the short odes that come paired with a longer ode discounted, only two patrons seem to have commissioned multiple epinicians: Melissus of Thebes and Lampon of Aegina.[92]

Second, there are very few repeat commissions from patrons who

---

[91] Theogenes' dedicatory inscription emphasized that he won the boxing and the pancration at a single festival, a feat similar to the double victory attributed to Heracles at Olympia, where Theogenes also attempted it (cf. Currie (2005) 134 and n.84), while a relief on Polydamas's pedestal (Paus. 6.5.1–7) showed (or described) him, among other things, wrestling a lion. Glaucus' statue showed him in action (Paus. 6.10.3), while that of Telesicrates included a helmet (schol. ad *Py*. 9, inscr. b) and that of Acusilaus boxing thongs (schol. ad *Ol*. 7, inscr. c).

[92] Melissus: Pi. *Is*. 3, 4. Lampon: Pi. *Ne*. 5, *Is*. 5, 6, Bacch. 13. Note that the Oligathidae of Corinth commissioned more than one ode, but in each case different members of the family seem to have been involved. Cf. Barrett (2007) 98–117.

were not hippotrophs. Lampon is the only exception here, since Melissus was from a hippotrophic family, and all the tyrants, kings and their lieutenants celebrated by the epinician poets raced horses for their wins.[93]

Third, there are several examples of victors who do not commission a second ode when they win a more prestigious victory later, even when that victory is much more prestigious. Hippocleas of Thessaly, whose victory as a youth in the Pythian sprint is celebrated in Pindar's *Pythian* 10, went on to win two victories as an adult at Olympia, but no further ode was commissioned.[94] Telesicrates of Cyrene celebrated his Pythian victory in the hoplite race in 474 in an epinician, but not his victory in the sprint eight years later.[95] Timodemus of Acharnae commissioned *Nemean* 2 to celebrate a Nemean win, a win that is represented as the first step in building a great record, but no ode to celebrate his later Olympic win.[96] Similarly, as Eusebius' various datings of Bacchylides' activities suggest, at least one of the victors celebrated by Bacchylides for a lesser victory went on to win at Olympia without celebrating that feat,[97] while, less dramatically, Ergoteles of Himera, who celebrated the victories he had won to date, which included an Olympic and two Pythian wins, in the short *Olympian* 12, did not return for a second ode when he won a second Olympic victory in 464 and completed a double period.[98]

One might argue that these absences suggest that one ode was sufficient to commemorate an athlete's excellence. Recent scholarship has stressed that an ode could be regularly reused, and this is surely correct.[99] Whether reuse of an old ode was the optimal means of celebrating a new victory is another question, however, and a fourth pattern, that almost all the patrons who enjoy (or had enjoyed) the resources of the state commission new odes for new victories, suggests that a new ode was preferable. Hieron commissioned a total of seven odes from Pindar and Bacchylides, celebrating his Pythian victories in the horse race after 478, and then commissioning one or more odes whenever he had a more prestigious win: his Olympic horse race in

---

[93] Hieron: Pi. *Ol.* 1, *Py.* 1–3, Bacch. 3–5; Xenocrates and Theron: Pi. *Ol.* 2–3, *Py.* 6, *Is.* 2. Chromius: Pi. *Ne.* 1 and 9. Cf. also Psaumis: Pi. *Ol.* 4, [Pi.] *Ol.* 5.

[94] Moretti (1957) no.175. *Py.* 10 seems to have been commissioned by someone outside the immediate family, Thorax; cf. *Py.* 10.64–6, schol. ad *Py.* 10.99a, b.

[95] Schol. ad Pi. *Py.* 9, inscr. a, b.

[96] Moretti (1957) no.262.

[97] Schmidt (1999) 82–5.

[98] Moretti (1957) no.224.

[99] Currie (2004), Hubbard (2004) 75–80.

476, his Pythian chariot in 470 and his Olympic chariot in 468.[100] Xenocrates' family celebrates his Isthmian win with an ode, even though the prior and more prestigious Pythian win had already been celebrated by Pindar.[101] Hieron's lieutenant Chromius commissioned an ode to celebrate his Nemean win when he had already commissioned one to celebrate a win at the Adrasteia, while Psaumis of Camarina, who I have argued had also been one of Hieron's close associates, followed up a locally commissioned epinician that celebrated a mule-cart win with a Pindaric ode to celebrate his chariot success.[102] The only exception to this pattern is Arcesilas of Cyrene, who did not follow up the remarkable epinician production for his Pythian win of 462 when he won the Olympic chariot race in 460.[103] The wealthiest private patrons followed the practice of the tyrants and their followers: Lampon commissioned odes for the victories of both his children, with separate odes for Phylacidas' two victories.[104]

A fifth pattern is that a number of victors seem to have waited until the end of their athletic careers before they commissioned an ode. This suggests that those victors from most elite families who imagined an epinician celebration expected that they would only commission one ode. In this group belong Diagoras of Rhodes, Epharmostus of Opuntian Locri, Xenophon of Corinth, Theaios of Argos, Cleander of Aegina, the victor celebrated by Bacchylides' tenth ode, and perhaps also Herodotus of Thebes.[105] Two of the names in this list should surprise us: Xenophon came from a family with at least one ode in its past, as well as the wealth to dedicate perhaps a hundred women to a local temple ("a public service of a character and scale normally seen on the level of state religion," as Bruno Currie observes), while Diagoras, while not at the time part of the ruling family of Ialysos, came from the royal family that had ruled the city, and probably very

[100] 478: Pi. *Py*. 3. 476: Pi. *Ol*. 1, Bacch. 5. 470: Pi. *Py*. 1, Bacch. 4. 468: Pi. *Py*. 2, Bacch. 3. I follow Young (1983) in seeing *Py*. 2 as celebrating the Olympic chariot win.

[101] Pi. *Py*. 6 and *Is*. 2.

[102] Chromius: Pi. *Ne*. 1 and 9. Psaumis: Pi. *Ol*. 4, and [Pi.] *Ol*. 5, with Nicholson (2011).

[103] For his Olympic win, see Moretti (1957) no.268. In 462, Arcesilas commissioned Pi. *Py*. 5, while an exile seems to have commissioned the extraordinary *Py*. 4, by far the longest of the odes.

[104] Pi. *Ne*. 5, *Is*. 5, 6, Bacch. 13.

[105] Pi. *Ol*. 7, 9, 13; *Ne*. 10; *Is*. 1, 8; Bacch. 10. See Currie (2011) 271 n.9, 287 n.75 for Pi. *Ol*. 7 and *Ne*. 10; Pi. *Ol*. 12 seems a less good candidate, not only because Ergoteles clearly continued competing at a high level after the commissioning of the ode, but also because the commissioning of the ode seems to have been tied to Hieron's commissioning of Pi. *Py*. 1; see Nicholson (2015). Bacch. 14B, Pi. *Ne*. 3 and Pi. *Ne*. 11 belong in a different category, since, although they come at the end of an athlete's career, they all seem to have been occasioned by some sort of civic appointment; cf. Fearn (2009).

recently. Diagoras' family may, however, have had considerable amounts of their wealth confiscated when the Athenians incorporated the city, and the island as a whole, into the Delian league, but a generation later, Diagoras' son Dorieus was still able to finance a squadron of ships.[106]

A sixth indication that odes were especially costly is the number of odes that make one of their main goals the celebration of more than one victor, or of a whole line of family victories. Several odes figure more than one victor prominently, at the start of the ode, and some have for this reason been designated by scholiasts as celebrating two victors.[107] Less dramatically, many odes, while primarily honoring an individual victory, take care to name victors among the ascendants or other relatives of the victor.[108] One striking example is Pindar's *Pythian* 8. This ode celebrates the victory of Aristomenes of Aegina in the youth wrestling at Delphi, but it also carefully records the victories of two uncles on his mother's side, Clitomachus, who won at the Isthmus, and Theognetus who won at Olympia. That Theognetus was not celebrated in his own epinician is a surprise, given that he was celebrated in Aristomenes' ode and that epinician was certainly established on Aegina by the time of his victory, in 476. Theognetus was commemorated by a memorable statue dedicated at Olympia, but the family did not commission an ode. One plausible explanation is that, while a statue was within the means of the family of Aristomenes' mother, it was only the family of Aristomenes' father that could afford an epinician.[109]

The story with statues appears, in fact, to be very different. Several victors are said to have been celebrated by more than one statue, and it seems to have been normal practice to dedicate a statue both at one or even two of sites of victory and at a sanctuary in one's hometown.[110] Similarly, families with statues for two or more family members at

---

[106] Xenophon: Pi. Fr. 122 and Currie (2011) 292. For Diagoras, cf. Cairns (2005) 64–5, 69–70, 86–88, and Currie (2011) 283–7, with Paus. 6.7.4.

[107] Pi. *Ol* .8 (with schol. ad *Ol*. 8), *Py*. 10, *Ne*. 8 (with schol. ad *Ne*. 8. inscr); cf. also Pi. *Py*. 11 and Hamilton (1974) 104–10. Fearn (2010) 179 suggests that the Alexandrian editorial practice of determining a single honorand misrepresents such odes. For the ode as the possession of a house rather than an individual, see Kurke (1991) 32–54.

[108] Pi. *Ol* .2, 9, 13, *Py*. 8, 11, *Ne*. 4, 5, 6, 8, *Is*. 2, 6, 8. Cf. also *Ol*. 6 and *Is*. 4, and Fearn (2010) 176–80.

[109] Pi. *Py*. 8.35–7, Paus. 6.9.1. On Theognetus, see Moretti (1957) no.217.

[110] Euthymus and Astylus had statues at Olympia (Paus. 6.6.6, *IvO* no.144; Paus. 6.13.1), and orally transmitted stories recorded that they also had statues in sanctuaries at home (Pliny *NH* 7.152 = Callimachus 202 (Massimilla) / 99 (Harder); Paus. 6.13.1). Theogenes had statues in Olympia and Delphi (Ebert (1972) no.37.3–4, 8–9, *IvO* no.153, with Moretti (1953) no.21.3–4, 8–9), Phayllus in Delphi and Athens (Paus. 10.9.2, Moretti (1953) no.11, Raubitschek (1949) no.76), and cf. the stelai set up to commemorate Chionis of Sparta (Paus. 3.14.2–3 and 6.13.1–2, with Christesen (2010)).

Olympia alone are much more common than families with odes for two or more family members.[111] The assumption made in the notorious story told by one of the scholiasts to Pindar's *Nemean* 5 that an ode and a bronze statue would have cost the same is thus, in all likelihood, mistaken.[112]

If expense was indeed part of the explanation for this difference, what made an ode so much more expensive than a statue? One possibility is simply that the work of the great lyric poets was more highly valued than the work of the great sculptors, perhaps because there were so many more sculptors who were known beyond their home regions or perhaps because the lyric poem was simply more highly valued than the statue. But the second commission of Melissus of Thebes suggests a different answer. Melissus' two odes are unique in the Pindaric corpus, in that they share the same meter, something not true of any other pair of odes, whether for the same victor or not. Yet the two pieces were not originally composed together because *Isthmian* 4 celebrates only Melissus' victories in the pancration, with his Isthmian win to the fore, while the triad known as *Isthmian* 3 celebrates both this Isthmian pancration win, and a Nemean chariot win (*Is.* 3.9–13). How long a delay came between the two compositions is unknown; presumably, it could have been brief or extended, depending on when Melissus became head of his family and took over the responsibility for the family's equestrian endeavors.[113]

Spencer Barrett argues that the particular instantiations of the metrical scheme in the two pieces implies that the piece celebrating both the Nemean and Isthmian victories was not meant to be added to the first to form a single, unified ode, but to be performed as its own ode, and Richard Hamilton's structural analysis comes to the same conclusion.[114] Why, then, link the two odes in this way, when in the other instances where Pindar completes a second commission for the same victor, he invents a new metrical scheme? One reason lies perhaps in

---

[111] Examples include: the Diagorids, who boasted six statues at Olympia (Paus. 6.6.2, 6.7.1–7); Philo of Corcyra and Glaucus of Carystus (Paus. 6.9.9–10.3); Alcaenetus, Hellanicus and Theantus of Leprea (Paus. 6.7.8); Damaretus, Theopompus and Theopompus (jr.) of Heraea (Paus. 6.10.4–5); and Aristeus and Cheimon of Argos (Paus. 6.9.3). See further Löhr (2000) 6–152, and, for the relationship of Philo and Glaucus, Smith (2007) 99.

[112] Schol. ad. *Ne.* 5.1a.

[113] Golden (1998) 117–23 notes that equestrian victors are usually considerably older than gymnastic ones, but the gap was likely reduced at the lesser festivals. That Melissus' family had already been involved in chariot racing, though without success in the Panhellenic contests, is stated by Pi. *Is.* 4.25–9. On the metrical relationship between the two odes, see Barrett (2007) 162–7.

[114] Hamilton (1974) 111, Barrett (2007) 162–7.

the fact that different kinds of victories are involved. The shared meter certainly blurs the boundaries between the equestrian and gymnastic victories of Melissus, as if they are the same sorts of achievement, an idea that did not command universal assent.[115] A second reason may also have been at work, however. Richard Hamilton suggests that the shared metrical scheme might instead mean that the two odes "were sung by the same chorus."[116] One plausible reason to use the same chorus was, therefore, that it reduced the cost of choral performance, whether by obviating the need for the chorus to be trained in two different metrical and choreographical schemes or because a chorus trained in this scheme was already available. With the welcome exception of Bruno Currie, scholars rarely consider the cost of the performance itself, but training a chorus, as well as hiring and training one or more musicians, was a truly significant expense, as the Athenian liturgical system demonstrates; Peter Wilson observes that in the late fifth century the closest comparison in scale to the expenditure that an individual choregus might lay out on an impressive suite of tragedies was the annual tribute paid by the small city-states of the Athenian empire.[117] Just as the production of a set of tragedies would have been expensive, so too would have been the choral performance and the choral reperformance of an ode, but the fact that the same metrical, musical and choreographical scheme was being used surely cut down on the cost.

Whatever the reason for the precise shape of *Isthmian* 3, and whatever the reason for the expense of epinician odes, these patterns make it clear that there were obstacles other than access, local culture and politics to commissioning an epinician. There were a lot of patrons who enjoyed access to the poets, had the ability to fund one commission, and enjoyed a local culture congenial to epinician, but did not return for a second commission. Few families, we must conclude, even from the elite, could afford more than one ode. It follows that some cannot have been able to afford even one ode, and that the simple expense of an epinician production is one reason why victors were not celebrated in the form.

---

[115] Nicholson and Heintges (2010) 24–5. Opposition to such a vision was encoded in the heroizing narratives considered above, since no equestrian victor was the subject of such a narrative.

[116] Hamilton (1974) 111.

[117] Currie (2011); Wilson (2003) 87–95, with Lys. 19.42, 21.1–5.

Conclusion

Undoubtedly there were many random reasons for victors not being celebrated in an epinician from Pindar, Bacchylides or Simonides: absent connections, missed meetings, schedules that did not match up or political troubles at home. Personal taste surely played a part too; the vision one scholiast had of a patron preferring a bronze statue to an ode may be an absurd vision for a patron who actually commissioned an ode, but it is a plausible vision in general terms.[118] But such reasons can only be conjectured, and this paper has focused on those reasons to which we have some access, the structural reasons for not commissioning an epinician. The individual cases may not all be compelling — specific elements of a given patron's situation may offer a more plausible reason in some cases — but, as a whole, the corpus of epinician exhibits various telling patterns of patronage that mark out four impediments to commissioning an ode from the three great practitioners of the genre: the distance between the patron's hometown and those of the poets'; local agonistic culture; the politics of epinician form; and the expense of commissioning and performing an epinician.

There are certainly limits to the evidence offered here, but the corpus of surviving material and the patterns of patronage that it exhibits (including what we know of Simonides' patrons) are strong enough that it would be a surprise if Oxyrhynchus threw up a book of Simonides' odes that did not reinforce these conclusions. While it is important to recognize what we do not have, it is also important to recognize how much does remain, and that we can answer certain sorts of question with what remains. The basic questions asked here about patronage allow the scattered testimonies concerning Simonides to factor into the argument.

The main limitation of the evidence used here is that it is restricted to the three great epinician poets. I argued above that their odes should be separated out from epinicians produced by poets only known locally precisely because they were internationally renowned and active. It is worth noting in closing that some of the structural impediments noted here likely would not have applied, or have applied less to epinicians from local producers. Certainly distance would not have been an issue, by definition, and the expense was surely reduced, although the expenses of performance would have remained. Local agonistic culture

---

[118] Schol. ad Pi. *Ne.* 5.1a. Note also that at least some ancient commentators seem to have referred the apparent lack of an ode by Pindar for Hieron's Olympic chariot victory to Hieron's preference for Bacchylides' poetry; see schol. ad Pi. *Py.* 2.166d, and cf. Jebb (1905) 20–2, 200–3. On this apparent absence, see Young (1983) 42–8.

would surely have prevented some such commissions, but perhaps the most interesting question is whether the form would have carried the same political meanings. The evidence provided by the ode collected among Pindar's works and known as *Olympian* 5 is mixed.[119] On the one hand, the ode certainly fits the victor into a built up urban space (σταδίων θαλάμων... ὑψίγυιον ἄλσος, "a high-limbed grove of strong chambers," [*Ol.*] 5.13) and marks him as part of the interstate aristocracy, by creating a fully realized vision of Olympia, with its twelve altars, the hill of Cronus and the river Alpheus. On the other hand, the ode is also more interested than other odes in the wider territory of the victor's hometown, the rivers, lakes and irrigation canals of Camarina ([*Ol.*] 5.9–12). But one ode is truly an inadequate sample on which to base conclusions about such productions.

Bibliography

Athanassaki, L. and Bowie, E. (2011). (edd). *Archaic and Classical Choral Song: Performance, Politics and Dissemination.* Berlin

Barrett. W.S. (2007). *Greek Lyric, Tragedy, & Textual Criticism: Collected Papers.* Oxford

Bell, J. (1978). 'Κίμβιξ καὶ σοφός: Simonides and the Anecdotal Tradition' *QUCC* 28.29–86

Bohringer, F. (1979). 'Cultes d'athlètes en Grèce classique; propos politiques, discours mythique' *REA* 81.5–18

Bonanno, D. (2010). *Ierone il Dinomenide: Storia e Rappresentazione.* Kokalos Suppl. 21. Pisa

Budelmann, F. (2012). 'Epinician and the *Symposion.* A Comparison with the *Enkomia*' in Carey, Agocs and Rawles (2012) 173–90

Burnett, A. 2005. *Pindar's Songs for Young Athletes.* Oxford

Cairns, F. (2005). 'Pindar *Olympian* 7: Rhodes, Athens, and the Diagorids' *Eikasmos* 16.63–91

Calame, C. (2012). 'Metaphorical Travel and Ritual Performance in Epinician Poetry' in Carey, Agocs and Rawles (2012) 303–20

Carey, C., Agocs P. and Rawles R. (2012). (edd.) *Reading the Victory Ode.* Cambridge

Catenacci, C. (2005). 'La data dell' 'Olimpica' 12 di Pindaro' *QUCC* 81(3).33–9

Christesen, P. (2007). *Olympic Victor Lists and Ancient History.* Cambridge

— (2010). 'Kings Playing Politics: The Heroization of Chionis of Sparta' *Historia* 59.26–73

---

[119] On the authorship of Pi. [*Ol.*] 5, see n.7 above.

Currie, B. (2002). 'Euthymos of Locri: A Case Study in Heroization in the Classical Period' *JHS* 122.24–44

— (2004). 'Reperformance Scenarios for Pindar's Odes' in Mackie (2004) 49–69

— (2005). *Pindar and the Cult of Heroes*. Oxford

— (2011). 'Epinician Choregia: Funding a Pindaric Chorus' in Athanassaki and Bowie (2011) 269–310

D'Alessio, G. (2012). 'The Lost *Isthmian* Odes of Pindar' in Carey, Agocs and Rawles (2012) 28–57

Drachmann, A. (1903). (ed.) *Scholia Vetera in Pindari Carmina*. Vol 1. *Scholia in Olympionicas*. Leipzig

Dübner, F. (1839). (ed.) 'Lexicon Platonicum (e cod. Coislin. 345)' in J. Baiter, J. Orelli, and A. Wincklelmann (edd.) *Platonis opera quae feruntur omnia: accedunt integra varietas lectionis Stephanianae, Bekkerianae, Stallbaumianae, Scholia et nominum index*. Zurich. 971–1008

Ebert, J. (1972). *Griechische Epigramme auf Sieger an Gymnischen und Hippischen Agonen*. Abhandlungen der Sächsischen Akademie der Wissenschaften zu Leipzig, Philologisch-Historische Klasse, 63.2. Berlin

Eckerman, C. (2011). 'Pindar's *Pythian* 6: On the Place of Performance and an Interpretive Crux' *RhM* 153.1–8

— (2012). 'Was Epinician performed at Panhellenic Sanctuaries?' *GRBS* 52.338–60

Fearn, D. (2007). 'Narrating Ambiguity: Murder and Macedonian Allegiance' in E. Irwin and E. Greenwood (edd.) *Reading Herodotus: A Study of the Logoi in Book 5 of Herodotus' Histories*. Cambridge. 98–127

— (2009). 'Oligarchic Hestia: Bacchylides 14B and Pindar, *Nemean* 11' *JHS* 129.23–39

— (2010). 'Aeginetan Epinician Culture' in D. Fearn (ed.) *Aegina: Contexts for Choral Lyric Poetry: Myth, History, and Identity in the Fifth century BC*. Oxford. 175–226

Ferrari, F. (2012). 'Representations of Cult in Epinician Poetry' in Carey, Agocs and Rawles (2012) 158–72

Figueira, T. (1993). *Excursions in Epichoric History: Aeginetan Essays*. Lanham

Fischer-Hansen, T., Nielsen, T. and Ampolo, C. (2004). 'Italia and Kampania' in Hansen and Nielsen (2004) 249–320

Fontenrose, J. (1968). 'The Hero as Athlete' *CSCA* 1.73–104

Giangiulio, M. (1989). *Ricerche su Crotone arcaica*. Pisa

Giudice, F. (1989). *Vasi e frammenti "Beazley" da Locri Epizefiri e ruolo di questa città lungo le rotte verso l'Occidente. Catalogo a cura di S. Valastro e F. Caruso. Vol. 1*. Catania

Golden, M. (1998). *Sport and Society in Ancient Greece*. Cambridge

— (2004). *Sport in the Ancient World from A to Z*. London

Hall, J. (2001). 'Contested Ethnicities: Perceptions of Macedonia within

Evolving Definitions of Greek Identity' in I. Malkin (ed.) *Ancient Perception of Greek Ethnicity.* Cambridge, Mass. 159–86

— (2002). *Hellenicity: Between Ethnicity and Culture.* Chicago

Hamilton, R. (1972). 'Olympian Five. A Reconsideration' *AJPh* 93.324–329

— (1974). *Epinikion: General Form in the Odes of Pindar.* The Hague

Hansen, M. and Nielsen, T. (2004). (edd.) *An Inventory of Archaic and Classical Poleis. An Investigation conducted by The Copenhagen Polis Centre for the Danish National Research Foundation.* Oxford

Hodkinson, S. (1999). 'An Agonistic Culture? Athletic Competition in Archaic and Classical Spartan Society' in S. Hodkinson and A. Powell (edd.) *Sparta: New Perspectives.* London. 147–87

— (2000). *Property and Wealth in Classical Sparta.* London

Holloway, R. (1987). 'The Coinage Production of the Sicilian Greek Mints of the Sixth and Fifth Centuries B.C' in G. Depeyrot, T. Hackens and G. Moucharte (edd.) *Rythmes de la production monétaire, de l'antiquité à nos jours. Actes du colloque international organizé à Paris du 10 au 12 Janvier 1986.* Louvain-la-Neuve. 11–20

Holwerda, D. (1960). (ed.) *Scholia in Aristophanem. Pars IV: Jo. Tzetzae Commentarii in Aristophanem. Fasc. II: Commentarium in Nubes.* Gröningen

Hornblower, S. (2004). *Thucydides and Pindar: Historical Narrative and the World of Epinikian Poetry.* Oxford

Hornblower, S. and Morgan C. (2007). (edd.) *Pindar's Poetry, Patrons, and Festivals: From Archaic Greece to the Roman Empire.* Oxford

Hubbard, T. (2001). 'Pindar and Athens after the Persian Wars' in D. Papenfuss and V. Strocka (edd.) *Gab es das griechische Wunder? Griechenland zwischen dem Ende des 6. und der Mitte des 5. Jahrhunderts v. Chr.* Mainz. 387–400

— (2004). 'The Dissemination of Epinician Lyric: Pan-Hellenism, Reperformance, Written Texts' in Mackie (2004) 71–93

Jebb, R. (1905). (ed.) *Bacchylides. The Poems and Fragments.* Cambridge

Kowalzig, B. (2007). *Singing for the Gods: Performances of Myth and Ritual in Archaic and Classical Greece.* Oxford

Krummen, E. (2014). *Cult, Myth, and Occasion in Pindar's Victory Odes.* tr. J.G. Howie. Arca 52. Prenton

Kurke, L. (1991). *The Traffic in Praise: Pindar and the Poetics of Social Economy.* Ithaca

Kurke, L. (1993). 'The Economy of *Kudos*' in L. Kurke and C. Dougherty (edd.) *Cultural Poetics in Archaic Greece: Cult, Performance, Politics.* New York. 131–63

Kurke, L. (1999). *Coins, Bodies, Games, and Gold: The Politics of Meaning in Archaic Greece.* Princeton

Lo Porto, F. (1967). 'Tombe di atleti tarentini' in U. Zanotti-Bianco (ed.) *Atti e Memorie della Società Magna Grecia.* Roma. 31–98

Löhr, C. (2000). *Griechische Familienweihungen: Untersuchungen einer*

Repräsentationsform von ihren Anfängen bis zum Ende des 4. Jhs. V. Chr.
Internationale Archäologie Bd. 54. Rahden, Westphalia

Loukopoulou, L. and Laitar, A. (2004). 'Propontic Thrace' in Hansen and
Nielsen (2004) 912–23

Lowe, N. (2007). 'Epinikian Eidography' in Hornblower and Morgan (2007)
167–76

Luraghi, N. (1994). *Tirannidi arcaiche in Sicilia e Magna Grecia da Panezio di
Leontini alla caduta dei Dinomenidi.* Florence

Mackie C. (2004). (ed.) *Oral Performance and its Context.* Leiden

Mader, W. (1990). *Die Psaumis-Oden Pindars (0.4 und 0.5): ein Kommentar.*
Commentationes Aenipontanae 29. Innsbruck

Malkin, I. (1994). *Myth and Territory in the Spartan Mediterranean.*
Cambridge

Mann, C. (2001). *Athlet und Polis im archaischen und frühklassichen
Griechenland.* Hypomnemata: Untersuchungen zur Antike und zu ihren
Nachleben 138. Göttingen

Miller, E. (1965). (ed.) *Mélanges de littérature grecque contenant un grand
nombre de textes inédits.* Amsterdam

Molyneux, J. (1992). *Simonides: A Historical Study.* Wauconda, Ill

Morgan, C. (2007). 'Debating Patronage: The Cases of Argos and Corinth' in
Hornblower and Morgan (2007) 213–64

Morgan, K. (2015). *Pindar and the Construction of Syracusan Monarchy in the
Fifth Century B.C.* Oxford

Moretti, L. (1953). *Iscrizioni agonistiche greche.* Rome

— (1957). 'Olympionikai. I vincitori negli antichi agoni olimpici' *MAL* 8.55–
198

— (1987). 'Nuovo Supplemento al Catalogo degli Olympionikai' *MGR* 12.67–
91 (Studi pubblicati dell'Istituto italiano per la storia antica 39)

Morrison, A. (2011). 'Pindar and the Aeginetan patrai: Pindar's Intersecting
Audiences' in Athanassaki and Bowie (2011) 311–36

Neer, Richard. (2012). *Greek Art and Archaeology c.2500–c.150 BCE.* New
York

Neils, Jennifer. (2001). 'Panathenaics in the West' in M. Bentz, and N.
Eschbach (edd.) *Panathenaïka: Symposion zu den Panathenäischen
Preisamphoren, Rauischholzhausen 25.11.-29.11.1998.* Mainz. 125–30

Nicholson, N. (2005). *Aristocracy and Athletics in Archaic and Classical
Greece.* Cambridge

— (2011). 'Pindar's *Olympian* 4: Psaumis and Camarina after the
Deinomenids' *CPh* 106.93–114

— (2013). 'Cultural Studies, Oral Tradition, and the Promise of
Intertextuality' in Y. Baraz and C. van den Berg (edd.) *Intertextuality* (=
AJPh 134). 9–21

— (2015). *The Poetics of Victory in the Greek West: Epinician, Oral Tradition
and the Deinomenid Empire.* Oxford.

Nicholson, N. and Gutierrez, A. (2012). 'Doctors, Trainers and Athletes in Bacchylides Ode 1' *Nikephoros* 25.79–114

Nicholson, N. and Heintges, E. (2010). 'Aging, Athletics and Epinician' *Nikephoros* 23.105–38

Pfeijffer, I. (1999). *Three Aeginetan Odes of Pindar: A Commentary on Nemean V, Nemean III, and Pythian VIII.* Leiden

Podlecki, A. (1979). 'Simonides in Sicily' *PP* 34.5–16

Poltera, O. (2008). *Simonides lyricus: Testimonia und Fragmente. Einleitung, kritische Ausgabe, Übersetzung und Kommentar.* Basel

Raubitschek, A. (1949). *Dedications from the Athenian Acropolis: A Catalogue of the Inscriptions of the Sixth and Fifth centuries B.C.* Cambridge, Mass

Rausa, F. (1994). *L'imagine del vincitore: L'athleta nella statuaria greca dall' età arcaica all' ellenismo.* Rome

Rawles, R. (2012). 'Early Epinician: Ibycus and Simonides' in Carey, Agocs and Rawles (2012) 3–27

— (2013). 'Aristophanes' Simonides: Lyric Models for Praise and Blame' in E. Bakola, L. Prauscello and M. Telò (edd.) *Greek Comedy and the Discourse of Genres.* Cambridge. 175–201

Redfield, J. (2003). *The Locrian Maidens: Love and Death in Greek Italy.* Princeton

Reger, G. (2004). 'The Aegean' in Hansen and Nielsen (2004) 732–93

Rutter, N.K. (1997). *The Greek Coinages of Southern Italy and Sicily.* London

Schmidt, D. (1999). 'An Unusual Victory List from Keos: IG XII, 5, 608 and the Dating of Bakchylides' *JHS* 119.67–85

Smith, R. (2007). 'Pindar, Athletes and the Early Greek Statue Habit' in Hornblower and Morgan (2007) 183–239

Wilson, P. (2003). *The Athenian Institution of the Khoregia: The Chorus, the City and the Stage.* Cambridge

Young, D. (1983). 'Pindar *Pythians* 2 and 3: Inscriptional ποτέ and the 'Poetic Epistle'' *HSCPh.* 87.30–48

Callimachus at the Mouseion
(the *Hymn to Delos*)[*]

Alex Hardie
University of Edinburgh

Contents

Introduction		40
I. Κύνθιος before Callimachus		43
(a) Kynthos and its Cults	43	
(b) The Homeric Hymn to Apollo	45	
(c) Pindar's Twelfth Paean	49	
II. Apollo Kynthios, Zeus and the Ptolemaic Dynasty		56
(a) A Challenge to the Reader	56	
(b) Delos as Nurse	58	
(c) Zeus Kynthios	62	
III. Nymphs, Nurture and Song		66
IV. Gods, Elements and Reconciliation		74
(a) Hera and Leto	74	
(b) Poseidon	78	
(c) Zeus, and Pindar's First Hymn	83	
(d) Space, Elements and Song	87	
V. Apollo Kynthios and the Muses		98
(a) Proem, θυμός and Inspiration	98	
(b) 'My Goddesses'	107	
(c) Swans, Apollo, Muses and Deliades	109	
(d) Delos as 'Musical Space'	112	
(e) Philitas and Aratus	118	
VI. τὰ πρῶτα φέρεσθαι ἐκ Μουσέων		121
Appendix I. *HZeus* 1–3 as Programmatic Book-ἀρχή		131
Appendix II. Artemis		135
Appendix III. The 'Goats of Kynthos' (αἶγες Κυνθιάδες)		139
Bibliography		144

[*] I am grateful to Professor Frederick Williams for critical comment, encouragement, and bibliographical advice. The conclusions of this essay are of course advanced on my own responsibility.

INTRODUCTION

This paper takes its departure from an item of Apolline nomenclature. In the proem to the *Hymn to Delos* (*HDelos*), Callimachus introduces the god as 'Kynthios' (10), an adjective which, so far as can be determined, had been in general circulation only with reference to the Kynthos hill itself.[1] No explanation is offered for the epithet as an epiklesis of Apollo or for its association with the god as 'lord of songs' (Φοῖβον ἀοιδάων μεδέοντα, 5), whereas the familiar epiklesis 'Delios', proclaimed by Asteria/Delos towards the end of the hymn (268–9), receives an explicit derivation (ἀπ' ἐμεῖο/ Δήλιος Ἀπόλλων κεκλή-σεται).[2] The new title was to be highly influential for later poets writing in the Callimachean tradition; but since earlier usage of Kynthios and its bearing on the hymnist's purposes in *HDelos* have not been explored to any depth, its colouring and associations remain oddly opaque.[3] Among other consequences, the relationship between landscape and music, a central theme of *HDelos*, is obscured; attempts to understand Delos as a symbol of Callimachean literary values do not take account of the part played in its song-formation by the island's most prominent physical feature;[4] and the place of Kynthos in the relationship (cultic and literary) between Apollo and Artemis is not explored at all. As an innovation in divine nomenclature, then, Ἀπόλλων Κύνθιος invites closer inspection.

Apollo's musical domain was rarely the object of formal sacral observance or title. But rich traditions of choric worship and music-making at the god's cult centres had helped link his various geographical identities with his patronage of music;[5] and as a Cyrenaean with family connections to the civic cult of Apollo, Callimachus was well qualified to explore this interplay of cult, territory and music.[6] The epilogue to the *Hymn to Apollo* (*HApollo*), projecting Apollo Karneios

---

[1] Κύνθιος is a certain restoration (Lascaris) from the *recentiores* DdLM, and from a marginal correction of confused readings in the MSS. For a claimed Parian epigraphic reference to Artemis Kynthia, see p.45.

[2] For the "Delos-*aition*" and the "Delios-*aition*", Ukleja (2005) 212–15.

[3] Verg. *Ecl.* 6.3; *Georg.* 3.36, with Thomas's comment; Hor. *Odes* 1.21.2; Prop. 2.35.80. Clausen (1976), (1977).

[4] Bing (1988) 94–6; 119–24; Slings (2004); cf. Giuseppetti (2013) 19–20.

[5] Cult activity in honour of Apollo Μουσάγετης appears in the third century: cf. Fraser (1970) 120 n.6. For extended analyses of music and cult at the great centres, see Kowalzig (2007), indexed at 477–8.

[6] Cyrene: Acosta-Hughes–Stephens (2012) 3–10 give a good account of the family, political, and intellectual setting. C.'s family connections with the cult of Apollo at Cyrene (Petrovic [2011] 283–5) are relevant to his championship of the god's interests at Alexandria.

at Cyrene as champion of Callimachean literary values, and aligning the god with 'my king' (26–7: Ptolemy Philadephus), offers a well-known example.[7] In this article I argue that *HDelos* presents a complementary (and in all probability, contemporary) perspective on Apollo as a musical god and divine patron of singers for the Ptolemaic era.[8]

Callimachus' application of Κύνθιος to Apollo cannot be understood in isolation from the cult environment on Delos and the traditions of Delian poetry. My analysis of the hymn is accordingly prefaced by a review (§I) of Kynthos' presence in the pre-Callimachean record (the reader who wishes to proceed immediately to Callimachus will find full back-referencing in §§II–VI). The Kynthian prolegomena include Artemis' early presence on the hill, and accounts of the Homeric *Hymn to Apollo* (*HHApollo*) and Pindar's twelfth *Paean*, in which the Kynthian cult of Zeus plays a conspicuous part. The pre-Callimachean material is then (§II) brought to bear on Apollo Kynthios in *HDelos*, his relationship to the Delian landscape, and the significance of his paternal inheritance for the Ptolemaic dynasty.

Alongside Kynthian Apollo, *HDelos* addresses, or refers to, the Muses in no fewer than four places (5, 7, 82, and 252). It is the only hymn in the collection that mentions them at all, and indeed it offers the earliest set-piece Callimachean treatment of the goddesses and their association with Apollo. This is the main subject of §VI, and here again, the interface between poetry and cult comes into consideration. W.H. Mineur (1984) sought to associate *HDelos* with the shrine of the Muses (the Mouseion) within the royal complex at Alexandria.[9] His hypothesis of the hymn's occasion drew sceptical comments from reviewers;[10] but it was to Mineur's great credit that he focused directly

---

[7] Cameron ([1995] 407–9) plausibly argued for a date around 270 for *HApollo* (in my view, however, 'my king' (27) cannot be identified with Magas at Cyrene). See also next n.

[8] *HApollo* and *HDelos* as complementary texts: signalled by the 'Delian palm' and singing swan at *HApoll.* 4–5; and for evidence that Apollonius read them as such, see below, n.123. Dating: Bing (1988) 91–3 dates *HDelos* in the period 275–259; Gigante Lanzara (1990) 19 suggests 270–264; Giuseppetti (2013) 35 suggests "seconda metà degli anni '70". In my view, 273/2 is probable: with F.T. Griffiths (1977–78), I believe (primarily on the evidence of 'window' intertextual reference to C.'s Pindaric models: below, n.183) that Theocritus *Idyll* 17 was written after *HDelos*; *Idyll* 17 depicts Arsinoe as living, thus, the *terminus ante quem* for *HDelos* must fall well before the sister-queen's death (generally assigned to 270; 268 is possible).

[9] The fullest account of the foundation of the Mouseion from a historical perspective, its institutional character, relationship to the library and the court, and significance as a collegiate setting is Weber (1993), 74–101, superseding *RE* XVI.801–12 (Müller-Graupa). Pfeiffer (1968) 96–104 and Fraser (1972) 305–19 remain fundamental.

[10] Mineur (1984) 10–16; 118: the suggestion that *HDelos* was a birthday offering to Ptolemy Philadephus on the occasion of C.'s admission to the Mouseion is still periodically re-cycled, but was rightly rejected by Hopkinson (1985) 250 and A. Griffiths

on the relationship between the Muses of *HDelos* and the Muses of the institution to which the poet belonged, an issue that is mostly skirted around in scholarly comment, or treated only in the sketchiest terms.[11] For the modern reader, it is true, assessment of institutional allusions in this area is an uncertain business: when we read ἐκ Μουσέων at *HDelos* 5, for example, how are we to tell whether Callimachus is referring generally to the divine patronesses of song or specifically to the goddesses of the Alexandrian cult? That said, within the book of *Hymns*, *HDelos* presents a useful test case for Callimachus' deployment of the Muses in relation to their collegiate cult, and my own conclusion is that the hymn does indeed have a regal-institutional context at Alexandria: in §VI, I argue that it proceeds on a figurative song-journey to Delos from the Muses of the Mouseion, depicted as Panhellenic goddesses of Apolline song.

A feature of *HDelos* that must have impressed its first audience is an extensive divine and semi-divine apparatus, embracing territorial Nymphs that extend across the Greek-speaking world and naming (or referencing) all but two members of the Greek Dodekatheon. The central sections (§§III and IV) offer connected accounts of this extraordinary parade of divinities, their role in the story of Delos, and their theological characters (in anthropomorphic form, civic cult and philosophical *ratio physica*). These analyses will provide the basis for a fuller appreciation (§V) of the relationship between the Muses and Apollo as musical patrons of Callimachus as singer-kitharist, and of Delos as a focal point of Callimachus' hymnic programme.

HDelos is an exceptionally rich and rewarding poem, universal in range and fully representative of the resources (prose as well as poetry) being gathered together in the Alexandrian Library at the time of writing. It has been the subject of intensive analysis in recent decades, with two recent monographs, three commentaries, several substantial book-parts and many articles.[12] Yet much remains to be explored, at

---

(1988) 231. Giuseppetti allows for performance at the Mouseion, but his comments on occasion ([2013] 39–43) are inconclusive: "Per un carme come questo ... nessuno scenario è implausibile, a Delo come ad Alessandria."

[11] Bing (1988) 44; Weber (1993) 87–95; 351–3; Morrison (2011) 342–3 touches on the institutional relevance of the Mouseion to Callimachus' "learned Muses" as deployed in the *Aetia* (this paper would have benefited from closer engagement with relevant secondary literature). The Mouseion as a Callimachean 'context' is touched on by Acosta-Hughes–Stephens (2012) 12, but is not further developed.

[12] The bibliography on *HDelos* offered here is by no means comprehensive. I saw Gigante Lanzara (1990), Giuseppetti (2013) and Stephens (2015) at a late stage in drafting, so that their materials have not always been incorporated to the extent that might have been merited (specific debts, e.g. new or unfamiliar intertexts, are acknowledged, as are significant areas of overlap, or difference, in argumentation).

micro- and macro-level, and in what follows emphasis is placed on Callimachus' encouragement to his readers to analyse intertextual references, intratextual correspondences and etymological associations, and to draw appropriate inferences. (To reduce distraction, I have consigned much textual analysis to footnotes.) In addition, any attempt at fresh interpretation nowadays must also take into account the high levels of verbal and conceptual overlap between *HDelos* and the five other *Hymns*, in particular those to Zeus, Apollo and Artemis. The question whether the *Hymns* as we have them were conceived and written as a six-part unity inevitably arises, and in what follows, I reflect a growing sense among Callimachean scholars that the correspondences do indeed represent sustained authorial planning and organization.[13] In Appendix I, a further item of evidence is offered for the proposition that the *Hymns* were composed as a planned collection (Appendices II and III proceed on the same basis). Features that may point towards that conclusion will be noted as they occur in the main text, but the analysis of *HDelos* offered here is not materially dependent on the existence of unitary design.

I. ΚΥΝΘΙΟΣ BEFORE CALLIMACHUS

(a) Kynthos and its Cults

Rising to a little over 100 metres above the sacred city and its plain, the rocky summit ridge of Kynthos is Delos' most prominent physical feature.[14] On one account, promulgated by Antimachus, the hill-name was given a mythic genealogy (Kynthos, son of Oceanus), and was evidently applied to the island as a whole; and it is possible that Κύνθιος too was in some contexts drawn into a whole-island frame of reference.[15] Certainly, its absence of cultivation will have contributed

---

[13] For reflections on book-form, Haslam (1993) 115, Hunter and Fuhrer (2002), Acosta-Hughes–Stephens (2012) 133–7. Ukleja (2005) 21–107 offers a detailed case for a planned "sextet".

[14] For a physical and geological account, based on autopsy in 1901, see Cook (1914–40) I.918 n.3: "Kynthos, partly because of its dominating position, partly because of its proximity to the sea, looks more of a mountain than it really is …".

[15] Steph. Byz. 226.19–227.1 M., s.v. Δῆλος· ἐκαλεῖτο δὲ Κύνθος ἀπὸ Κύνθου τοῦ Ὠκεανοῦ, καὶ Ἀπόλλων Κύνθιος. Cf. also 393.15 M. (as emended: Antimachus fr. 12 M.; *Thebaid*), with Matthews (1996) 106–7, citing Plin. *Nat.* 4.66 *hanc* [sc. Delon] *Aristoteles ita appellatam tradit, quondam repente apparuerit enata, Aglaosthenes Cynthiam, alii Ortygiam, Asteriam, … Cynthum* [Matthews; *Cynethum*, codd.] … With *Cynthiam*, cf. perhaps Limenios *Paean* 11–12 (text at Furley–Bremer [2001] 92–4; later 2nd cent. BC) Κυνθίαν … νῆσον. I assume that the ancient ascription of *HHApollo* to 'Kynaithos' (Burkert [1979]), notwithstanding verbal proximity to 'Kynthios' (and to Pliny's *Cynethus*, as transmitted), is coincidental.

to the emphasis on 'rockiness' in literary accounts of the island, as also to the Delian paradox of physical barrenness combined with the island's cult celebrity and the rich sacrificial offerings it attracted.[16]

In the Hellenistic era and later, the summit of Kynthos was dominated by the joint cults of Zeus Kynthios and Athena Kynthia, located in the 'Kynthion'. Athena Kynthia appears in an archaic inscription from the Delion on Paros, evidently reflecting a parent-cult on Delos; and the recovery of geometric vases inscribed to Zeus on the site of the later Kynthion is also suggestive of an early summit-cult. Both cults can be assumed to have been active on Delos by the fifth century, but there appears to have been only one cult statue, presumably of Zeus, until around 150 BC.[17]

A sanctuary on the east side of Kynthos has been linked, on the basis of votary reliefs, with Euripides' reference to 'Artemis Lochia who has her dwelling by the Kynthian cliff'.[18] Artemis' principal Delian shrine, the Artemision (around 700 BC, with earlier structures), reveals that her presence long preceded Apollo whose first temple dates to around 540: she, or a near-eastern predecessor, evidently brought early associations with human fertility and childbirth to Delos (perhaps specifically to Kynthos, a pre-Greek name);[19] and he, the incoming *kouros*-god, developed a cult-legend that paired him with the long-established Artemis as siblings or indeed birth-twins.[20]

---

[16] Thus, 'rocky Delos' at *HHApoll.* 16, κραναῇ ἐνὶ Δήλῳ; 26, κραναῇ ἐνὶ νήσῳ; 72, κραναήπεδος. Cf. also Pind. *Pae.* 7b.47 Ma. (C2 Ru.) εὐαγέα πέτραν; fr. 33c.9 Ma. πέτραν. Kynthos as rock: *HHApoll.* 141; Aristoph. *Clouds* 597; Pind. *Pae.* 12.8 Ma. (G1 Ru.); cf. fr. 60b col. 2.14 Ma. (G4 Ru.). 'Delian paradox': Ukleja (2005) 76; Kowalzig (2007) 59–60; Giuseppetti (2013) 208–16. For Delian terrain, cf. Strabo 10.5.2 Ἡ μὲν οὖν Δῆλος ἐν πεδίῳ κειμένη ἔχει τὴν πόλιν καὶ τὸ ἱερὸν τοῦ Ἀπόλλωνος καὶ τὸ Λητῷον· ὑπέρκειται δὲ τῆς πόλεως ὄρος ψιλὸν ὁ Κύνθος καὶ τραχύ, ποταμὸς δὲ διαρρεῖ τὴν νῆσον Ἰνωπὸς οὐ μέγας.

[17] Hellenistic cults on the Kynthion: Bruneau (1970) 222–32. Cult statue(s): Hamilton (2000) 194, 219. See also the still-useful note at Cook (1914–40) I.918 n.3. Athena on Paros: *IG* XII.5.210; Kontoleon (1966) 207–8 (see below, n.23 for his restoration of Zeus Kynthios in *IG* XII.5.390). Dedications to Zeus: Plassart (1928) 57–8. A sanctuary to Zeus Hypsistos occupied the southern end of the summit: Bruneau (1970) 240–41.

[18] Eur. *IT* 1097–9 ποθοῦσ' Ἄρτεμιν λοχίαν,/ ἃ παρὰ Κύνθιον ὄχθον οἱ/κεῖ .... Bruneau (1970) 191–5, with Planche I, figs. 4 and 5; cf. Kowalzig (2007) 63, with n.25.

[19] Kowalzig (2007) 119–20, stressing Artemis' priority on Delos and Apolline exploitation of prior patterns of Artemis-cult. For her cult in Asia Minor, and association with near-eastern counterparts, see Farnell (1896–1909) II.472–82; and cf. Solomon (1994) 43–4, who sees Delos as originally "sacred to the goddess of fertility and childbirth". See also Bryce (1983) for a separate but illuminating account of Leto's arrival in Lycia (Xanthos), Artemis' priority (with Anatolian antecedents), the late intrusion of the Greek divine triad, and the local cultural and political context.

[20] *HHApoll.* 16–17 (cited below, p.46) claims separate births in different places, Delos and 'Ortygia'. The location of Artemis' 'Ortygia' was contested (Allen, Halliday, Sikes

Artemis is occasionally found in cult harness with the birth-goddess Eileithyia, in their conjoined names, but on Delos the two retained separate cult identities and precincts.[21] Eileithyia appears in literary accounts of Leto's parturition (as does Artemis herself, within the tradition that she was the elder by one day, and assisted in Apollo's delivery); and Leto's choice of the barren island to give birth, a recurring topic of Delian religious song, is evidently linked to this early association with birth cult.[22] That all this was further associated with Kynthos in cult as well as legend is suggested by the (putative) site of the shrine of Artemis Lochia. But 'Kynthian Artemis', [Ἀρτεμίδ]ος Κυνθί<η>ς, restored by Hiller von Gaertrigen in an archaic inscription from the Delion on Paros is far from secure, and in any case unparalleled as a cult epiklesis of Artemis.[23] As regards Apollo, there is no archeological evidence for worship on Kynthos, and Κύνθιος is not found as an Apolline cult epiklesis.[24] When Aristophanes speaks of the 'Kynthian rock' as Apollo's domain (*Clouds* 595–6), he is flattering the god on his intrusion into that space in the late-sixth century *HHApollo*, and on his subsequent reception of choric honours there (below, [b], [c]): he is not reflecting a distinct 'Kynthian' cult identity.[25]

(b) The Homeric Hymn to Apollo

The Delian section of *HHApollo* is the founding text for Leto's choice of Delos as Apollo's birthplace, for his nursing, acquisition of godhead and association with Kynthos. This is how the hymnist introduces the topography of the birth (16–18):

---

on line 16): see below, (b) for Callimachus' implicit 'correction'. Rutherford (2001) 368 suggests that Pindar's consistent representation of the pair as twins is otherwise a rarity; Kowalzig (2007) 61 observes apparent suggestions of twin birth in the postnatal iconography of Leto, in particular a black figure image of mother and twins (?) on a later 6th cent. amphora (*LIMC* VI.1.258, s.v. 'Leto', no. 10). Observe also the 4th cent. portrayal (Euphranor) of Leto *puerpera*, holding Apollo and Artemis (Plin. *Nat.* 34.77).

[21] Artemis Eileithyia: *LIMC* II.1.676, s.v. 'Artemis', nos. 721a, 722; III.1.686. Artemis Lochia is by far the more common cult identity.

[22] See the excellent account of Kowalzig (2007) 59–68.

[23] *IG* XII.5.390 and addendum (Paros); rejected by Kontoleon (1966) 207–8 (who restores Δι]ὸς Κυνθίο, as counterpart of Athena Kynthia, at *IG* XII.5.210), against Rubensohn (1962) 144, who implausibly hypothesises a separate paired cult of 'Kynthian' Apollo and Artemis on a Parian 'Kynthos'.

[24] Le Roy (1973) 286, with bibliography.

[25] Aristoph. *Clouds* 595–7 ἀμφί μοι αὖτε Φοῖβ' ἄναξ/ Δήλιε, Κυνθίαν ἔχων/ ὑψικέρατα πέτραν; the final phrase is Pindaric (cf. *Etym. Magn.* p. 504 K.). The cult epiklesis is, of course, Δήλιε; the ode continues with interwoven references to worship of Artemis at Ephesus (strikingly separated from her Delian sibling), Dionysus on Parnassus, Athena at Athens. For possible cult-political nuances, cf. Kowalzig (2007) 115.

τὴν μὲν ἐν Ὀρτυγίῃ, τὸν δὲ κραναῇ ἐνὶ Δήλῳ,
κεκλιμένη πρὸς μακρὸν ὄρος καὶ Κύνθιον ὄχθον,
ἀγχοτάτω φοίνικος ὑπ' Ἰνωποῖο ῥεέθροις.

[Leto bore ...] her [Artemis] on Ortygia and him [Apollo] on rocky
Delos, leaning against the long rise of the Kynthian hill, very close to
the palm, below the streams of Inopos.

Ten lines later (25–6), seeking Apollo's guidance, the hymnist asks
whether he should sing ... ὥς σε πρῶτον Λητὼ τέκε .../ κλινθεῖσα πρὸς
Κύνθου ὄρος κραναῇ ἐνὶ νήσῳ (... of how Leto bore you first, leant
against the hill of Kynthus, on the rocky island), with assonance of
posture (κλινθεῖσα) and hill (Κύνθου). Leto is later said to give birth in
a different posture, kneeling on a plain (118, λειμῶνι μαλακῷ; i.e.
below the hill).[26] The 'leaning' posture (κεκλιμένη [17]/κλινθεῖσα [26])
is accentuated in order that Leto's form may complement the territorial
sweep from hill to sea; and indeed the goddess-in-landscape is echoed
in 'beaches sloping (κεκλιμέναι [24]) to the sea', of the god's wider
territories. The Delian topography of Leto's parturition is thus aligned
with the vertical (mountain to beach) axis of the god's later domains;[27]
and this 'vertical' aspect is a recurring feature in treatments of Kynthos
in Pindar and Callimachus.[28]

Here is the full sequence of birth-events (*HHApollo* 117–39): Eileithyia arrives in Delos, and parturition begins; Leto plants her knees on
the meadow and clasps the palm tree; Earth smiles; moment of birth;
attendant goddesses raise the *ololyge*;[29] goddesses wash the infant 'in a
holy and pure manner', with sound-allusion to the paean-cry in the address ἤϊε (120, lord); they swaddle him; Leto does not nurse, but
Themis feeds with divine nectar/ambrosia; Apollo bursts out of his
bindings (presaging the unbounded extension of his worship, from tiny
Delos), assumes his godhead and divine attributes (bow, cithara and
prophecy) and takes to his feet. Delos then flowers with gold,

---

[26] Not, therefore, understood to be born 'on' Kynthos (see Le Roy [1973] 283–5, with
conclusions at 286, locating the event "dans la plaine, non loin de la basse vallée de
l'Inopos ... et probablement dans le hiéron"). Two direct attestations of Kynthian birth
can however be cited: *AP* 15.25.9 (late) has Apollo and Artemis as Κυνθογενὴς ...
φύτλη; the other (below, n.30) occurs in a Hellenistic work.

[27] The useful term 'vertical axis' is that of Philip Hardie (1986), 267–85. Sloping terrain:
Richardson (2010), 13–15. Le Roy (1973) 284–5 is troubled by issues of scale (Leto,
Kynthos and palm); but Richardson, ibid. 85, on 16–18 rightly pictures Leto as a
supernaturally large goddess; cf. Janko on *Il.* 13.17–20.

[28] For the vertical axis in Pindar, below p.51. It is also a prominent feature in the
Apolline architecture of Hor. *Odes* 3.4: A. Hardie (2008) 101–2; (2010) 244.

[29] *HHApoll.* 119–22: θεαὶ δ' ὀλόλυξαν ἅπασαι./ ἔνθα σὲ ἤϊε Φοῖβε θεαὶ λόον ὕδατι καλῷ/
ἁγνῶς καὶ καθαρῶς, σπάρξαν δ' ἐν φάρεϊ λευκῷ/ λεπτῷ νηγατέῳ· περὶ δὲ χρύσεον
στρόφον ἧκαν. Paean-cry and *ololyge* are distinct, notwithstanding word-play on the
paean-cry in ἤϊε (cf. *Etym. Magn.* p. 469.50–51 K.); cf. Rutherford (2001) 19–20; 48.

transformed for the supreme moment of Apolline birth from rock to divinely fertile terrain (child-birth and care is readily associated with fecundity of landscape, but as a recurring topic in Delian birth-poetry, this miraculous correlation of floral/arboreal and maternal fertility reflects the unique verdant impact of the divinity on the barren island).[30]

The hymnist then turns to Apollo's pattern of movements, on Kynthos and around the wider world (140–42):

> αὐτὸς δ' ἀργυρότοξε ἄναξ ἑκατηβόλ' Ἄπολλον,
> ἄλλοτε μέν τ' ἐπὶ Κύνθου ἐβήσαο παιπαλόεντος,
> ἄλλοτε δ' ἂν νήσους τε καὶ ἀνέρας ἠλάσκαζες.

> And you, far shooting lord Apollo, you of the silver bow, at one time made your way upon rocky Kynthos, and at another time you frequented islands and their peoples.

From Kynthos, the mobile god extended his terrestrial domains; and that outward movement has its inward counterpart in festival worshippers converging from the wider world (146–50). Kynthos emerges as the literary focus for patterns of 'outward' cult expansion and 'inward' convergence of worshippers. Yet Artemis' pre-Apolline presence on Delos (and Kynthos) arouses suspicion that the Homeric hymnist is minimising Artemis' Delian identity in order to promote an Apolline agenda; and that the latter extends to a presence on Kynthos intended to offset (?the birth-cult of) Artemis. Kynthos, in other words, may have become a contentious area in a sibling-relationship prone to (hymnic) rivalry. Callimachus, who displays marked sensitivity to the siblings' Delian relationship, seems to have shared the sense that Apollo's cult has been embellished at the expense of Artemis. At *HApollo* 59–61, he 'corrects' *HHApollo*'s report (16–17) of Artemis' separate birth on 'Ortygia': narrating Apollo's construction of the Delian horn altar, the *keraton*, he identifies 'Ortygia' as Delos itself (59), names Artemis (60), and makes her contribute the product of her assiduous hunting of

---

[30] *HHApoll.* 135/9 χρυσῷ δ' ἄρα Δῆλος ἅπασα/ ἤνθησ' ὡς ὅτε τε ῥίον οὔρεος ἄνθεσιν ὕλης. It is as a variant of this Delian miracle-fertility topic that Euripides' chorus of exiles speaks (*IT* 1097–1102) of Artemis *Lochia* dwelling by the 'Kynthian hill, the palm with tender foliage, the sprouting laurel and the sacred shoot of the grey olive …' (all three were understood to retain their leaves: Emped. 30 A 70 D–K; 571 Bo.). Cf. also Eur. *Hec.* 458–61; *Ion* 919–22; *PLitGoodspeed* 2 col. vi Powell (fr b col. I Meliadò) 19–20]ν ἠύκομος τέκε Λητώ/]κορυφαῖς λασιώτιδος ὕλης (observe correspondence of Leto's hair [ἠύκομος] and the hill-foliage: a further assimilation of landscape and goddess: for the rhetorical figure, cf. Eustathius on *Il.* 14.326); Hor. *Odes* 3.4.65–6 … *natalemque silvam/ Delius … Apollo*; *HDelos* 262 χρύσειον δ' ἐκόμησε γενέθλιον ἔρνος ἐλαίης.

'Kynthian goats' (61, Κυνθιάδων).[31] At *HArtemis* 7, the child-goddess asks Zeus to grant πολυωνομίη 'in order that Phoebus should not contend (ἐρίζῃ) with me'; and indeed Apollo has been 'many-named' in *HApollo* (70, πάντη δὲ τοι οὔνομα πουλύ). In *HDelos*, Apollo is granted the epiklesis Κύνθιος; yet in *HApollo* itself, Artemis retains hunting rights on the hill and does so to support her brother (Appendices II, III).

With *HHApollo* in view, Vergil was to depict the god on the heights of Kynthos, on his springtime return from Lycia to 'set up the choruses anew', while worshipping nations combine around his altars.[32] In this vignette, inward movement to Kynthos replaces its outward counterpart in *HHApollo*, and fifth century theoric *choroi* enter the scene. From his acquired vantage point upon Kynthos, the Delian Apollo receives incoming Delian paeans, and surveys the musical-festive setting of paean-performance at his sanctuary below.

The Homeric hymnist illustrates in his own *persona* the pattern of outward and inward movement, and the juxtaposition of 'local' (Delos) and world-wide: the (sc. Panhellenic) *HHApollo* will carry praise of the Deliades to foreign cities (175); and the Deliades are to reciprocate by securing the hymnist's preeminent fame with future visitors to their island.[33] The Deliades' representation of foreign speech (162–4) exemplifies hospitable acceptance;[34] and "holistic representation of their

---

[31] Cf. also Furley–Bremer (2001) 106. With C.'s choice of the horn altar for this central 'correction' (as I see it) of *HHApollo*, compare the performance-location attested by the *Certamen* (presumably known to C. from Alcidamas' *Mouseion*): 'Homer' sailed to Delos for the Ionian *panegyris* and recited the hymn 'having taken up his stance at the horn altar' (316, σταθεὶς ἐπὶ τὸν κεράτινον βωμόν). The testimony (*Cert.* 320–21) that the Delians 'inscribed the hymn on a white panel and dedicated it in the temple of Artemis' bears on the dating of the hymn, on her contemporary status on Delos and on the fact that Apollo's temple was arguably too recent to house a 'Homeric' composition (see West [1999] 382). Burkert (1979) 61–2 observed of the hymn that "Artemis is hardly mentioned and definitely has to stand back ...". If the dedication is historical, perhaps a Delian effort to placate the goddess whose erstwhile dominance *HHApollo* itself was helping bring to an end. Separately, the reference to Delos, the palm and the 'altar of Apollo' at *Od.* 6.162–3 (with non-Delian Artemis, and Leto, at 102/106 and 151) presents a problem of dating in relation to the formation of the *Odyssey*: might the lines be an 'Apolline' addition (of an otherwise unknown visit to Delos), with the aim of back-dating the horn altar to the time of 'Homer'? West (2014) 35–43 dates the *Odyssey* to the last third of the seventh century, but comments (ibid. 87) that the poet might well have seen "the palm tree by Apollo's altar on Delos".

[32] *Aen.* 4.143–8; Vergil departs from his model for the Aeneas/Apollo comparison, Apollonius' Jason/Apollo counterpart at *Arg.* 1.307–9, in ignoring the latter's Apolline temple (ie cult) setting, and separating god (on Kynthos) from worshippers around the *altaria*; possibly an acknowledgement of the literary status of his model in *HHApollo*.

[33] For the "panhellenization" of the Deliades' reputation (and comparison to the Helikoniades), Nagy (2009) 25; but the Deliades remained a local chorus, as did their antecedent landscape nymphs.

[34] Deliades and *theoria*: Rutherford (2013) 238–9. 'Acceptance': 48; 64; cf. *HDelos* 69, 154, 223. For standard hospitality at Delos, cf. Verg. *Aen.* 3.79 *accipit*; 83 *hospitio*,

audience" (Peponi) becomes a musical analogue for the wider world.[35] The quasi-hymnic treatment of the Deliades marks them as the 'universal' ritual voice of their island, and perhaps also as a terrestrial analogue of the chorus of singing Muses.[36]

(c) Pindar's Twelfth Paean

Pindar twice refers to Kynthos. One reference survives only in an isolated scrap of papyrus (fr.60b col. 2.14 Ma. [G4 Ru.]): Κυνθίῳ πα[, where πα[ρὰ κρημνῷ and πα[γῷ have been proposed as supplements. In the preceding line, σκοπαι χοραγ[may connect with the hill as vantage-point (see below). There is no obvious reference to divine birth. References to an 'army' or 'host' (col 1.8,]ώων στρατῷ; perhaps ἡρ]ώων 'of heroes', i.e. Greeks) and possibly an 'oracle' (col. 1.12, χρηστ]ήριον) suggest, as a possible context, the attempt of King Anius, in obedience to an oracle, to delay the Trojan expedition at Delos with an offer of nine years' sustenance on Kynthos (Lyc. *Alex.* 569–83; and cf. especially 574, Κυνθίαν ... σκοπήν).[37] 'Choric leadership' is clear in χοραγ[, but the identities of the 'leader' and the 'chorus' are lost: possibly Artemis, but more probably Apollo as archetypal *choregos* (if so, standing apart from the human chorus, on Kynthos [σκοπαι], as in Vergil's choric scenario: above, p.48).[38] The scraps could again point to Kynthos as a focal point for Delian choruses.

Pindar's principal surviving reference to Kynthos, in the twelfth *Paean* (fr. 52m Ma.; G1 Ru.), is of altogether greater significance. The

---

with Horsfall. For Deliades as facilitators of Delian *theoriai*, Richardson (2010) 91. With imitation of foreign speech, cf. *Etym. Magn.* p. 612.14–17 K., s.v. ξενίζειν· τὸ ξενικῇ χρῆσθαι τῇ φωνῇ καὶ μὴ ἐπιχωρίῳ· ... σημαίνει καὶ ... τὸ ὑποδεχέσθαι ξένον.

[35] For a valuable analysis, scc Peponi (2009), esp. 64–8.

[36] Quasi-hymnic: thus, the envoi (166), coupled with that to Apollo and Artemis: Nagy (2009) 23; Richardson's note at 165–6. Peponi (2009) 65–7 suggests that the Deliades as "archetypal" chorus, representing "*all* peoples' voices", may be an adaptation of the archetypal divine chorus of Muses; Nagy (2009) 19–26 argues independently that the Deliades are "local Muses" of Delos; Giuseppetti (2013) suggests "riflesso terreno del coro delle Muse", comparing Hes. *Theog.* 25 with *HHApoll.* 157. The choric Muses as the divine paradigm for choruses of young girls and boys was of course embedded in early Greek lyric practice: Calame (1997) 30–31; 49–53; 74–5; 90; 222–3; Lonsdale (1993) 33; 115; 194–5; A. Hardie (1996) 224 (on the choric Delphides assimilated to local Muses). It was elaborated in the identification of the choric voice with the Muses and in the concept of choric performance as the epiphany of the Muse herself: A. Hardie (2013) 19–26.

[37] Anius had a hero-cult on Delos dating from the 6th century: Hamilton (2000) 187. Lycophron alludes to *HHApoll.* 142 ἠλάσκαζες (Apollo in the wider world after Kynthos) at 575 ἠλάσκουσιν (Greeks on Kynthos, beside Inopos); see Appendix III.

[38] For the *choregos*, see the full discussion in Calame (1997) 43–73 (Apollo, 49–53).

intelligible portion of the papyrus fragment reads, with selected restorations, as follows:[39]

[ ]με[......]ων ἰο[-
πλό]κοισιν ἐννέ[α Μοί]σαις.
μ]άλα δ᾽ Ἀρτέμιδ[ος Λα]τώϊον Ἀσ[τερία
λέ]χος ἀμφέπο[ισ᾽ ἄν]θεα τοιά[σ-
δ᾽]ὑμνήσιος δρέπῃ· θαμὰ δ᾽ ἔρ[χεται   5
Να]ξόθεν λιπαροτρόφων θυσί[α(ι)
μή]λων Χαρίτεσσι μίγδαν
Κύ]νθιον παρὰ κρημνόν, ἔνθα [
κελαινεφέ᾽ ἀργιβρένταν λέγο[ντι
Ζῆνα καθεζόμενον   10
κορυφαῖσιν ὕπερθε φυλάξαι π[ρ]ονοί[ᾳ,
ἀνίκ᾽ ἀγανόφρων
Κοίου θυγάτηρ λύετο τερπνᾶς
ὠδῖνος· ἔλαμψαν δ᾽ ἀελίου δέμας ὅπω[ς
ἀγλαὸν ἐς φάος ἰόντες δίδυμοι   15
παῖδες, πολὺν ῥόθ[ο]ν ἴεσαν ἀπὸ στομ[άτων
Ἐ]λείθυιά τε καὶ Λά[χ]εσις· τελε[ί]αι δ᾽ ὀλ[ολυγαί
κα]τελάμβανον.[...]
ἐπ]εφθέγξαντο δ᾽ ἐγχώριαι
ἀγ]λαὸς ἃς ἀν᾽ ἔρκε[.]...[20
... χ]αρὰν τότ᾽ ἄρ᾽ ἀκταίνοντο

... with the nine violet-[tressed?] Muses. And especially [?] you, attending the Letoian [?] birth-bed [of?] Artemis, As[teria?], pluck the flowers of such hymning. And often comes from Naxos [...], in the company of the Charites, [for?] the sacrifice of sleekly-reared sheep, to the Kynthian cliff, where [...] it is related that Zeus, he of the dark clouds and bright thunder, taking his seat above the heights, mounted guard with providence, when the mild-mannered daughter of Coeus was released from her sweet birth-pang. When the twins shone like the sun, proceeding towards the bright light, Eleithyia and Lachesis emitted many a sound-wave from their mouths. And [fulfilling *ololygai* ?] seized ... [the whole island?]; and auto-chthonous [nymphs?] uttered the refrain ... glorious ... defence [?] ... So then, joy they radiated [?].

Identification of the fragment as a paean (and the title tentatively attached to it by Snell–Maehler, 'For the Naxians, to Delos') is an in-ference from the book-contents of *POxy* 1792, and from the internal reference to Naxian *theoria* proceeding to Delos, accompanied by song. In addition, D'Alessio has plausibly suggested on the basis of the pro-

---

[39] The text given here is based on Rutherford (2001) 364–5 (with selected restorations by Grenfell and Hunt, Lobel, Deubner and Snell as recorded in Rutherford's apparatus, and in the Teubner edition [1989] of Maehler). I am indebted to Rutherford's trans-lation and commentary (ibid., 365–72); see also Furley–Bremer (2001) 109–12; Kowalzig (2007) 60–67.

cessional element that the ode may have been identified in antiquity as a *prosodion*.[40]

The destination of these processional Naxian *theoriai* as a regular event (θαμά), 'by the Kynthian crag' (8, Κύ]νθιον παρὰ κρημνόν) is of immediate interest. It introduces Zeus' oversight of the twin births from a vantage point above the summit, a reference that Plassart (followed by Le Roy, Rutherford and Kowalzig) connected with the cult of Zeus Kynthios.[41] It reads like a cult aetiology (thus, λέγο[ντι, 9), ostensibly fixed in local lore as an explanation for Zeus' presence above Kynthos.[42] Rutherford's further suggestion that Athena too was named seems less likely, since the foundational exercise of *pronoia* is ascribed to Zeus, acting as supreme benevolent protector.[43] Zeus takes his seat ὕπερθε (above) Kynthos, and brings a new dimension to the 'vertical axis', since Zeus will have descended from *ouranos* to this vantage point. It is relevant both for Zeus' protective purposes and for the sequel in *HDelos* (pp.63f., 91) that the Homeric antecedents for καθεζόμενον κορυφαῖσιν (9–10) describe Zeus sitting alone on Ida, having descended from heaven to keep protective watch over the Trojans (Ἴδης ἐν κορυφῇσι καθέζετο .../ οὐρανόθεν καταβάς, *Il.* 11.183–4; cf. 8.45–6, 51–2). His Pindaric guardianship (φυλάξαι), directed to the safe delivery of two younger members of his new Olympian order, may also suggest that Apollo's own paeanic role as 'guard' is inherited from his father's action in guarding his own birth:[44] Apollo, we are reminded, is the true son of Zeus.[45]

[40] D'Alessio (1997) 28. For Naxian and other theoric choruses at Delos, Kowalzig (2007), 56–128 ("Dancing on Delos"), esp. 101; Rutherford (2013) 240. For Naxos and Apollo Delios, Kowalzig (2007) 74; and for a survey of views on the 'Oikos of the Naxians' as possible first temple of Apollo on Delos, Jockey (1996) 169–73.

[41] Plassart (1928) 64; Le Roy (1973) 283 ("Ce passage ... ne fait que confirmer les données de l'archéologie: le Cynthe est la montagne de Zeus, non celle d'Apollon"); Rutherford (1988) 65–75, esp. 71–2; Rutherford (2001) 366–7; Kowalzig (2007) 72–3. Furley–Bremer (2001) offer no specific comment. Cf. Soph. *Trach.* 1191 (Zeus' cult site on Oeta) τὸν Οἴτης Ζηνὸς ὕψιστον πάγον; ibid. 436–7 for lightning associated with summit-cult (and cf. P's. ἀργιβρένταν).

[42] For λέγοντι in cult/temple aetiology, cf. Pind. *Nem.* 7.84, introducing Aeacus, 'ruler of cities', through Zeus' intercourse with Aegina, to explain why it is appropriate to praise Zeus, 'king of gods', in δάπεδον ... τόδε (this holy precinct) i.e. the Aeginetan Aeaceum (so Bury [1890] 123; 141; contra, Carey [1981] 172, who under-weights interplay with 34 ἐν Πυθίοισι ... δαπέδοις). Cf. also Aesch. *Eum.* 4 (of an unorthodox account of the succession at Delphi) ὡς λόγος τις, with Sommerstein's note.

[43] Rutherford (2001) 367, documenting Athena Pronoia's association with the Leto-myth. Athena appears in Delian paeans for the Athenians (*PMG* 519 frr. 35.3; 55.7), but Naxos' relationship with Delos was troubled in the mid 5th century: Kowalzig (2007) 101 notes the probably troubled political context; the Naxian revolt dates probably to the early 460's: Hornblower (1991) 221–2; Milton (1979).

[44] A. Hardie (1998) 259–60 (on Hor. *Odes* 4.6.27), citing Theogn. 781–2, Philodamus *Paean in Dionysum* 12 (recurring refrain); add Limenios *Paean* 31; Stat. *Silv.* 1.4.16.

Other relevant background (Zeus' passion for Asteria, and the common parentage of Asteria and Leto) is omitted, at least in this fragment.[46] The text of what precedes and follows the Zeus Kynthios-*aition*, though defective in places, does however yield musical content, typical of Delian paeans, bearing on the present paean-performance and on the origins of Apolline song. The cries of Eileithyia and Lachesis are probably to be identified with the τελε[ί]αι δ' ὀλ[ολυγαί (fulfilling *ol[olygai*) plausibly restored at 17, with reference to the delivery of a ritually correct utterance completing a sacral action.[47] They seem also to allude to the paean-cry (etymologised in ἴεσαν; compare the goddesses' *ololyge* and implicit paean-cry at *HHApollo* 119–20 [above, p.46]).[48] These cries 'took hold' of something, presumably 'the whole island' *vel sim.*, thereby producing a musical-territorial effect that prompts the responsive utterance of the native Nymph-chorus (ἐπ]εφθέγξαντο δ' ἐγχώριαι).[49] The autochthonous and terrestrial Nymph-

---

Cf. also ἔρκε[at Pind. *Pae.* 6.22 (D6 Ru.), with Call. *HDelos* 24 (Apollo as ἕρκος of Delos). Cf. esp. Apollo's defence of Troy at *Pae.* 6.90–95 (D6 Ru.), reflecting Zeus' inclinations (against Athena's resistance), but ultimately thwarted by Zeus' unwillingness to overturn fate.

[45] For Artemis' assertion of her lineage by adopting a role associated with Zeus, cf. Bing and Uhrmeister (1994) 25 on *HArtemis*. Cf. also Eur. *Her.* 687–700 (paeanic celebration of Heracles' εὐγενία as Διὸς παῖς, compared to Deliades' temple-paeans for Apollo as Λατοῦς εὔπαιδα γόνον); and for the shouted recognition of a true son of Zeus, see below, n.101. Limenios' 'Athenian' aetiology of the paean (*Paean* 11–18, as restored) depicts the newborn Apollo 'leaving the Kynthian island' (11, λιπὼν Κυνθίαν νᾶσον) for Athens, where he is greeted by instrumental song echoing on a 'hilly eminence of Tritonis', and rejoices as he 'receives in his mind and recognises the will of Zeus' (16–17, νόῳ δεξάμενος ἀμβρόταν/ Δι[ὸς ἐπέγνω φρέ]ν'); hence, says Limenios, the epiklesis 'Paieon' bestowed by the entire citizen body. If the printed text is accurate (see Furley–Bremer [2001] 97 for disputed reading of Δι[), Apollo infers that Zeus intends him to be 'Healer' (i.e., a helper god, benign to mortals); and given that Limenios' highly allusive paean (below, n.85) has transferred the birth-song scenario from Delos to Athena's hill, it is tempting to connect Apollo's reception of the first, 'Athenian', paean, and his inference about Zeus, with Κυνθίαν.

[46] For the familial relationship between Asteria and Leto, Pind. Pae. 7b.44 (C2 Ru.) (Asteria also as Κοίου θυγάτηρ; cf. *Pae.* 12.13); Rutherford (1988) 68 n. 17; Depew (1998) 168–9.

[47] This formulation is taken from Rutherford (2001) 48, commenting on Aesch. *Sept.* 267–9 (combined paean cry and *ololyge*) and citing Hesychius τ 414, s.v. τελεσίερον παιᾶνα. For *ololyge* marking the end of a sacral action, Karanika (2009) 71–3.

[48] Rutherford (2001) 368 notes the paeanic reference in ῥόθ[ο]ν, documented at 170 n.9. Add the etymologising reference to the paean-cry ἰή/ἰή; ἰέ, in ἴεσαν (cf. Rutherford, ibid., 25 with n.7); and observe etymologising πολύν (of Apollo). Cf. esp. Simon. *PMG* 519 fr. 35b.9–10 ἱέμενοι ἐνοπὰν .../[ ] εὔφαμον ἀπὸ φρενὸς ὁμορρόθο[υ. Paean-cry is conventionally associated with males and *ololyge* with females, but the gender-distinction is not rigidly observed in literary/aetiological contexts: Rutherford, ibid. 19–20; 48.

[49] For this combination of light and sound, Pindar may have in mind the epiphany of Apollo to the Krisaeans at *HHApoll.* 440–47: radiating flashes and looking like a star, the god lights the sacred fire, the gleam of which 'occupied all Krisa'; Krisaean

singers, are thereby aligned through song with the attendant goddesses, and supply the choric Deliades with their own *aition* in the shouts that greeted Apollo's birth (below).[50]

There is more to be said on the "birth-shout" (Kowalzig) as *aition* for song-ritual at Delos. The 'twin children proceeding to the light' (15–16, ἐς φάος ἰόντες δίδυμοι/ παῖδες) echo the processional movement (5, ἔρ[χεται) of the Naxian paeanic/prosodic chorus, such that the latter is the musical re-enactment of the birth(s).[51] The musical references in the fragmentary lines 1–5 include a figure said to 'attend Leto's birth-bed' and 'pluck the flowers of hymning such as this'. 'Asteria' from ασ[(3, Lobel) would project the virgin island-nymph either as hymnist or as present-day subject of hymning ('Delos' is of course already a *persona loquens* in *HHApollo*).[52] Rutherford's 'hymning such as this' (τοιά[σ-/δ']ὑμνήσιος) suggests a mythical song presented as predecessor of the present one:[53] it is then re-enacted in the Naxian choric *theoriai*, that is, in paeans/prosodia 'for Delos', εἰς Δῆλον. Figurative 'flowers' (ἄν]θεα) of hymning echo the 'violet' hair-colouring or violet-flower crown (Snell's ἰο-/πλό]κοισιν) of the

---

women respond with *ololyge*; Karanika (2009) 68–9; 74–5.

[50] ἐγχώριαι may signify choric groups native to a particular region (cf. Calame [1997] 31–2) but it cannot here refer to local women (as Kowalzig [2007] 64–7), if only because pre-Apolline Delos was uninhabited (thus *HHApoll.* 78 ... χήτει λαῶν); so, rightly, Furley–Bremer (2001) 112; Rutherford (2001) 365 is undecided. The *choros* of Deliades is a component of the *chōra*; cf. *Pae.* 6.139 (D6 Ru.), where νύμφη Aegina is the ἐπιχώριον νῶτον of Mt Hellanios. Callimachus' reworking (also of *HHApoll.* 119) at *HDelos* 255–8 brings out the nymph-Deliades' instant acquisition of Eileithyia's *melos*: ὁ [sc. Apollo] δ' ἔκθορεν, αἱ δ' .../ νύμφαι Δηλιάδες, ποταμοῦ γένος ἀρχαίοιο,/ εἶπαν Ἐλειθυίης ἱερὸν μέλος, αὐτίκα δ' αἰθήρ/ ... ἀντήχησε ... ὀλολυγήν; noted by Bing (1988) 109 (n.35); cf. also Fantuzzi–Hunter (2004) 367.

[51] ἰόντες reflects the regular use of verbs of motion in a figurative sense in processional hymns; cf. *Pae.* 7b.12; Aristoph. *Birds* 851 8, with Dunbar. Cf. also the 'processional' (epiphanic) birth in Leto's appeal at *HDelos* 214 ἤπιος ἕξιθι κόλπου, with McKay (1962b) 182–3. For paeanic ritual re-enactment, see Kowalzig (2007) 67–8. Furley–Bremer ([2001] 111) suggest that it is Apollo who 'frequently comes from Naxos' with the Charites; but the only clear parallel for the joint progression of god and chorus seems to be lines 4–8 of the Athenian paean for the *Pythais* of 138 or 128 BC (Furley–Bremer [2001] 85–92, with commentary; Rutherford [2013] 183–4), re-enacting the myth that Apollo came from Delos to Delphi by way of Athens (cf. Aesch. *Eum.* 9–11). No such connection appears to exist for Naxos.

[52] Personified Delos: Giuseppetti (2013) 86. Delos is also personified in an Attic vase-painting of c. 440–30: *LIMC* III.1.368–9 (Bruneau); Gallet de Santerre (1976). Asteria in Pindar: *Pae.* 7b.43–9 Ma. (C2 Ru.); cf. fr. 33c.5–6; Bing (1988) 97–110; Rutherford (2001) 250–51; 370–71. For attendance at the birth, cf. the dual role, birth and teaching, ascribed to the nymphs of Kynthos by Claudian *Gig.* 120–24.

[53] For this nuance, see Dunbar on Aristoph. *Birds* 769–72, citing Stesich. 212.1–2 *PMGF*, 173 Finglass; Pind. *Isth.* 4.27, Aristoph. *Peace* 796–7, Bacchyl. 20.3; cf. also D'Alessio (2013) 124, on Bacchyl. 20.3.

Muses;[54] but the figure also reflects miraculous flowering in the Apolline birth-tradition;[55] and song/Muses combined with 'Delian' flowering is juxtaposed with birth and parturition with reference (sadly, uncertain in sense) to Artemis (Ἀρτέμιδ[ος Λα]τώϊον .../ λέ]χος). The suggestion within this cluster of motifs is that Artemis is in some way associated with the 'music' that originated with the birth.[56] Such associations are considered further in Appendix II.

The 'nine Muses' (ἐννέ[α Μοί]σαις) signal allegiance to the Hesiodic chorus, and they parallel Pindar's invocation of the Helikonides to validate departure from 'Homer' in another Delian paean, (7b.15–20 [C2 Ru.]).[57] Here, they are juxtaposed with the Charites, who are themselves given a processional role, 'mixed up with' (μίγδαν, 7) the Naxian sacrificial offerings.[58] The figure suggests

[54] For ἰόπλοκος and allied epithets, of Muses, cf. Pind. *Pyth.* 1.1; *Isth.* 7.23; Bacchyl. 3.71; *PMG* 1001. For the possibility that ἰόπλοκος refers to a flower-crown, and not hair-colour, Irwin (1996) 390–92. Compare Pindar on the birth of Apollo's son Iamos in *Ol.* 6: ἰόπλοκος of mother Euadne (30) echoed in ἴα ('violets') radiating around the infant's body (55); and the concluding prayer (105) ἐμῶν δ' ὕμνων ἄεξ' εὐτερπὲς ἄνθος (cause the pleasure-giving flower of my hymns to grow), links Pindar's figurative 'flower-hymn' with fertile growth, with birth, and with the Muses (εὐτερπές in strophic correspondence with the nurturing μελίφθογγοι δ' ἐπιτρέψοντι Μοῖσαι [21], hence allusion to Muse Euterpe [Hutchinson]). The two birth-accounts have been connected by Schmitz (1970) 28; Salvador (1997) 46 n.34.

[55] *HHApoll.* 135; 139; Irwin (1996) 387–9, citing Verg. *Ecl.* 4.23. At *HDelos* 193, cf. Apollo's comparison of the pre-birth floating Asteria to asphodel, ἀνθέρικος, perhaps with reference to Delos' latent capacity for divine flowering (for Apolline/Delian associations, cf. Plut. *Sept. Sap. Conv.* 14, cited by Bing [1988] 121).

[56] Furley–Bremer (2001) 110 restore vocative Ἄρτεμι, suggesting that Artemis herself "'gathers flowers of hymn-making' in welcome for Apollo ...". I think this is unlikely to give the appropriate sense; but were it on the right lines, Artemis' integration into Apolline music would be still more marked.

[57] Assessment in this area involves the authenticity of the only reference to the canonical number in the Homeric epics, at *Od.* 24.60–62, where 'all nine Muses, responding with beautiful voice' sing a dirge over Achilles' pyre. In my view, this alludes to the *Theogony*: the rhetorical point is that the entire Muse-chorus sings in the aspect of their choric identity that Hesiod had represented in the etymology of Calliope (ὀπὶ καλῇ) (A. Hardie [2009] 15–16); Pindar evidently interpreted the passage thus in designating the dirge-singing Muses in the same scenario as *Helikoniai* (*Isth.* 8.57–62; A. Hardie [2013] 31 for Pindar's awareness also of Ibycus' deployment of the Helikonian Muses in an earlier departure from Homer). For the Helikonides in *Pae.* 7b (C2 Ru.), see Rutherford (2001) 249–50.

[58] For Charites and Muses, see Harder (2012) II.120–21, on Call. *Aetia* fr.3–7b Ha. With μίγδαν in mixed voice/instrumental performance, cf. Aristoph. *Birds* 771 συμμιγῆ βοήν; Limenios *Paean* 13–14 μελίπνοον δὲ Λίβυς αὐδὰν χέω[ν λωτὸς ἀνέμελ]πεν ἁ-/ δεῖαν ὄπα μειγνύμενος αἰόλ[οις κιθάρι]ο[ς/ μέλεσιν ...; Hor. *Odes* 4.15.30 *Lydis remixto carmine tibiis*, with Thomas. For 'mixing' and harmony in Pindar, see Steiner (1986) 53. For mortals Χαρίτεσσι μίγδαν cf. also Schol. Flor. 16–17 on Call. *Aetia* fr. 2 Ha. σ(υμ)μείξας ταῖς Μού[σαις (sc. Callimachus). The phrase is perhaps re-worked at *Aen.* 4.145 (Lycian Apollo returns to Delos, above p.48; and cf. Simon. *PMG* 519 fr. 55.1) *instauratque choros, mixtique altaria circum/ Cretes ....*

an 'aural' epiphany of the Charites, as harmonious instrumental accompaniment to the processional paean/*prosodion* (we may also recall the instrumental, possibly processional, Charites on the right hand of the statue of the Delian Apollo).[59]

Finally, Lobel's restoration of line 21 and his illustrations for ἀκταίνοντο offer an attractive combination of 'raising' (with a nuance of quivering, or perhaps darting/radiating) and 'joy'.[60] First syllable ἀκτ- would connect with ἀελίου δέμας, evoking ἀκτῖνες (the 'rays' of the sun) so that the light-sound combination would be sustained in a joyful terrestrial reflection of the gods' birth, sent up to the sky from Delos.[61] As will be seen in more detail later, Pindar is drawing on a cluster of miraculous effects (flowering, stilled elements, echoing land-scape) that greeted the first Apolline (birth) epiphany, and all sub-sequent epiphanies. In χ]αράν, we should have the 'joy' etymologically associated with χόρος and χῶρα as territorial dancing-ground, thus elegantly reflecting ἐγχώριαι and also recalling the Naxian choric Χάριτες.[62] Incoming choruses (with their Charites-in-performance) will thus reflect the joyous sound first created at the twin birth by a native landscape chorus identified with its *chōra*.

In honouring the Delian triad, choric *theoriai* from Naxos come to Kynthos, the domain of Zeus Kynthios. All that follows from that action, the births, the miraculous sun-on-earth effects, the interplay of light and sound in the island-Nymphs' response to the goddesses' paean-cries, Asteria(?) as recipient(?) of 'hymning' exemplified in the present paeanic worship of the Naxians, is the product of Zeus' *pronoia* exercised on the vertical axis from 'above' Kynthos. Thus, Kynthos is

---

[59] Good discussion of Delian Charites at Furley–Bremer (2001) 111. Processional Charites: cf. *Pae.* 5.6 (D5 Ru.) (Athenians for Delos) σὺν Χαρίτ[εσσι μολόντα. In Eumelus' *Prosodion to Delos* (696 *PMG*) the (singular) Muse embodies the processing chorus. For Charites and statue of Apollo, Pfeiffer (1952); Bruneau (1970) 56–60. The tradition (ps.-Plutarch *de Musica* 1136a–b) that their instruments (lyre, pipes and syrinx) accompanied the Hyperborean offerings to Delos again suggests sacral-processional significance.

[60] Lobel compared Hesych. υ 563, s.v. ὑποακταίνοντο, glossed as ἔτρεμον, and surmised a variant of ὑπερικταίνοντο (*Od.* 23.3, the old lady's toes twinkling [sc. with joy, διὰ τὴν χαράν: *Etym. Magn.* p. 779.13 K., s.v. ὑπερικταίνοντο]). See also *LSJ* under all three verb-forms.

[61] For association of paean-cry with Apollo as sun 'sending out' rays, *Etym. Magn.* p. 469.50–53 K., s.v. ἰηιε For miraculous light-effects accompanying divine epiphany, see Seaford's note on Eur. *Bacch.* 1082–3.

[62] Cf. again (n.54) the birth of Iamos in *Ol.* 6, where the child is 'bathed in rays' (ἀκτῖσι) from violets at the find-spot. One etymology (Macr. *Sat.* 1.17.7 derived 'Apollo' ἀπὸ τοῦ ἀποπάλλειν τὰς ἀκτῖνας. For the etymologies of χόρος, χῶρα, χαρά/χαίρω (also χεῖρ), Plat. *Laws* 654a; *Etym. Magn.* p. 813.47–9 K., s.v. χόρος; Calame (1997) 19–20 (n.3); Lonsdale (1993) 115.

re-positioned as the local (Delian) domain of Zeus, as well as the Apolline focal point for incoming choruses.

II. APOLLO KYNTHIOS, ZEUS AND THE PTOLEMAIC DYNASTY

(a) A Challenge to the Reader

After Apollo's birth, Delos addresses the 'great one' (266), namely Gaia/Ge, whose identity is defined and expanded (267) as the 'continents and islands': these are the future world-wide domains of Apollo to whom the sacred island now presents the new god. She utters a twin prediction (268–70): 'from me will Apollo be called "Delian" and no other land will be as dear to any other god … as I to Apollo'. Discharging the action attributed to her in the opening lines of the hymn, Delos is indeed 'first to praise [Apollo] as a god' (6); and contrary to what Hera has said about illegitimacy (240–43), Delos' magniloquent speech proclaims the god's acceptance as nursling, and seals his legitimisation.[63] Although the first public enunciation of the name 'Apollo', the accent is on Δήλιος, and it recalls the kind of name (epiklesis) aetiology that we find in Limenios' 'Athenian' account of Apollo Paieon.[64]

Delos' actions as nurse, including her ringing proclamation of Apollo Delios, take us back to the proem and recall the introduction there of Apollo Κύνθιος (10). Kynthos itself has not however been named in the intervening narrative, a striking omission discreetly

---

[63] Hera's speech 240–48 suggests the illegitimacy of Zeus' children by other unions; cf. Giuseppetti (2012) 470. Delos' action in picking up the child-god (264) signifies her assumption of responsibility for rearing him *vice* his mother; cf. esp. *HHDem.* 286 (there is an analogous 'acceptance' action, nurse from father, documented by Hunter on the parallel scene at Theocr. *Id.* 17.58–9). The action is perhaps also analogous to the Roman father's 'lifting' (*tollere*) his child to signify acceptance and legitimacy. For involvement of a nurse in naming a child, cf. *Od.* 21.403–4, where Eurykleia appeals to Penelope's father (visiting) for help in naming the new-born Odysseus. Cf. also Soph. *Ajax* 545–82 for Ajax's command to a servant to 'raise' Eurysakes to his father (545), leading to reflection on inherited qualities as a legitimate son (547) and on actions consistent with his given name (574–6). For the theme of illegitimate offspring elsewhere in *HDelos*, see Giuseppetti (2013) 113–14.

[64] With κεκλήσεται (269), cf. Limenios *Paean* 17–18 ἀνθ' ὧν ἐκείνας ἀπ' ἀρ-/ χᾶς [sc. an Athenian birth-paean] Παιῆονα κικλήσκ[ομεν. Cf. also Aesch. *Eum.* 7–8 ('Phoebus' taken as additional name in gratitude for grandmother Phoebe's 'birthday gift' of Delphi). For Zeus naming a son (Dionysus, to Thebes) and simultaneously acting as first performer of the dithyramb, after the child's purification in Dirke, Eur. *Bacch.* 526–9, with Battezzato (2013) 95. For post-natal purification and naming, see Ginouvès (1962) 235–8 (the purifying bath); Parker (1983) 50–52 (*amphidromia*, purification by encircling the hearth with the child).

underlined in the statement that Leto 'leaned' (ἐκλίθη) against the palm tree (209–10) and not (as so prominently in *HHApollo*: p.46) against Kynthos.[65] Then in Delos' post-natal prophecy, the designation of half-brother Hermes' birthplace as πάγος ... Κυλλήνιος (272, Cyllenian crag) transfers a personal epithet (as in Ἑρμῆς Κυλλήνιος) to his mountain, a device that echoes the transfer of *Kynthios* in the reverse direction, from hill to god.[66]

As observed at the outset (p.40), *Delios* from Delos is a perfectly obvious epiklesis, while the parallel, and innovative, Κύνθιος is not at all obvious.[67] It is not to be assumed that Callimachus is simply alluding to the association of god and hill trailed in the Homeric *Hymn to Apollo*. Nor is it likely that he has used *Kynthios* as a loose synonym for *Delios* (above, p.43).[68] Rather, he has thrown out a challenge to his readership; and the puzzle gains in interest from the explicit *aition* of *Delios*, and also from the contrast between the world-wide reverberation of *Delios* and the local focus of *Kynthios*.[69] It will be argued here that in constructing these polarities, Callimachus deploys a distinctive mode of internal cross reference, whereby our reading of the 'musical topography' of Delos, and hence the rationale for Apollo as *Kynthios*, must be built up by a process of inference from topographical

---

[65] For analysis of Leto's upright birth-posture in *HDelos* in terms of contemporary advances in obstetrics, Most (1981) 191–6. This 'modern' medical knowledge, derived from Herophilus, is a component of the advanced learning that the hymnist brings from the Alexandrian Mouseion to Delos (below, §§III, V).

[66] Κυλλήνιος of Hermes: *Od.* 24.1, *HHHerm.* 304, etc. The only near-contemporary parallel for application to the mountain is *A.Pl.* 188.1 Εἰνοσίφυλλον ὄρος Κυλλήνιον αἰπὺ λελογχὼς by Theocritus' friend Nicias (thereafter, only Nonn. *Dionys.* 13.277): evidently not an imitation of *HDelos*; perhaps from Philitas' *Hermes*. On musical aspects of the parallel between Hermes/Kyllene and Apollo/Kynthos, see below p.111: they are foreshadowed in ἀοιδάων μεδέοντα (5, of Apollo); cf. *HHHerm.* 2, Κυλλήνης μεδέοντα (the first extant use of the participle other than for Zeus, and other than in the vocative: Mineur [1984] 55). For epigraphic application to Apollo, Kontoleon (1966) 203. This note supplements Michalopoulos (2012) 382–3, on C.'s use of μεδέων of Ptolemy at *HZeus* 86 and Apollo at *HDelos* 5 to effect "la liaison entre Apollon, Zeus et Ptolémée ..."; I do not agree with Michalopoulos (2007) 70–72 that *HDelos* 5 itself imitates the Homeric μεδέων of Zeus .

[67] Delos/*Delios*: Depew (1998) 179–82; Fantuzzi–Hunter (2004) 366–9.

[68] Bruneau (1970) 169 is wrong, in this instance, to claim "Kynthios est ... un synonyme poétique de Délios".

[69] Contrast also the way *HHApollo* supplies regular *aitia* for cult titles: 372–4 (Pythios), 385–7 (Telphousios), 493–6 (Delphinios); cf. Ambühl (2005) 326–7; Henrichs (1993) 128–33. The contrast between the obvious and the concealed rationale exemplifies what Bing (1988) 141 well describes as "a larger pattern – one of play between that which is δῆλον and ἄδηλον"; cf. Fantuzzi–Hunter (2004) 366–9, with useful comment on explicit and implicit aetiologies in *HDelos*.

analogues catalogued elsewhere in the hymn, and signposted for the reader by verbal and thematic echoes.[70]

(b) Delos as Nurse

Callimachus gives full anthropomorphic force to the old metaphor of island as 'nurse' (2). He combines it with the related motif of landscape nymphs as nurses of divine or semi divine beings, and clarifies κουρο-τρόφος (which may be wet or dry nurse) in τιθήνη (10).[71] That Leto herself does not nurse Apollo is no surprise, since she does not do so in *HHApollo* (Themis feeds the newborn with nectar and ambrosia), and contemporary representations of nursing mothers are in any case strikingly rare.[72] Whether the island's role as (wet-) nurse is entirely Callimachus' invention is uncertain. He will however have been aware of Hesiod's genealogy (*Theog.* 404–10) whereby 'Asteria' and Leto were sisters, a sibling relationship which, though it is not stressed in *HDelos*, is certainly present (below, p.72); and aunt-nurses are of course paralleled elsewhere (the classic example in myth being Ino and Dionysus).[73]

Prooemial references to Delos' post-birth actions as 'nurse', washing and swaddling (6), are paired with further nursing actions after the birth-narrative: she lifts Apollo and places him on her lap; and he 'sucked the sweet breast' (ὁ δὲ γλυκὺν ἔσπασε μαζόν, 274). The 'sweet breast' belongs, of course, to Delos acting as 'wet nurse', as fore-shadowed in the proem;[74] and the collocation there of τιθήνη and Κύνθιος (10) invites the reader to consider Kynthos itself as the 'breast'

---

[70] Schmiel (1987) offered an introduction to the structural and thematic significance of verbal repetitions in *HDelos*. Critical appreciation of this aspect was placed on a new footing by Ukleja (2005).

[71] τροφός/κουροτρόφος of places: e.g. Ithaca, *Od.* 9.27; Soph. *OT* 1089–91; *OC* 760; Eur. *Bacch.* 105. Landscape nymphs as nurses of gods/heroes: *HHAphr.* 256–80, with Richardson; Strabo 14.1.20 (Ephesian 'Ortygia' as midwife and nurse to Artemis); Price (1978) General Index, s.v. 'Nymphs'. For C.'s departure from *HHApollo*, see Depew (1998) 162 with n.22; Most (1981) 189; 190 n.7; Ukleja (2005) 207 n.714. For further detail on the anthropomorphic representation of Asteria, Nishimura-Jensen (2000) 290–92; and for a good treatment of the physical and personified island at 11–27, see Giuseppetti (2013) 208–16.

[72] Bonfante (1997) 174, 184. I am grateful to Professor Elizabeth Gebhard for discussion of this topic and for bibliographical assistance.

[73] For Asteria and Leto, see below, nn.130, 167 (and cf. Giuseppetti [2013] 120, noting their joint presence on the Pergamene Gigantomachia frieze). Ino: Price (1978) 141; Pache (2004) 135–80. Ino is later drawn into association with the role of aunt-nurses in the Roman cult of Mater Matuta: Ov. *Fast.* 6.485–8, 559–62; Plut. *Quaest. Rom.* 17, 267e. For aunt-nurses, cf. also Pers. *Sat.* 2.32–40.

[74] This is notwithstanding her virginal status: for breast-feeding by virgin goddesses, cf. Newbold (2000) 14 (Nonnus' *Dionysiaca*). Artemis was honoured as Kourotrophos in a Laconian festival of nurses (the *Tithenidia*: Price [1978] 139–40).

at which he was nursed. Were that to be the case, the attribution of Κύνθιος as an additional epiklesis to the Delian god would represent the hymnist's personal reward to Delos for her services as Apollo's wet nurse.[75]

μαζός as 'hill' (Scots 'pap') offers some encouragement for a connection with Kynthos, and indeed Pliny (*Nat.* 4.66) preserves the name Dimastus (two-breast) for the hills of neighbouring Mykonos.[76] Yet at this point it cannot be over-emphasised that the idea of a barren piece of rock acting the role of nurturing breast represents an extraordinary paradox, in that child-care is so closely associated with fertility of landscape. For this reason, the golden transformation of Delos (§I [a], [b]) takes on added significance, and analogues (within *HDelos* and beyond) with 'wet' rocks/mountains as breasts or nurses are especially important. The role of the Inopos is central to this story, as is the Callimachean claim that the stream was fed from the flooding (and fertilising) Nile.[77] The centrality of the wet-nursing relationship to Callimachus' design is deftly unscored in Asteria/Delos' initiative in calling out to 'Leto', i.e. by name (203–4): in Iris' subsequent report to Hera, ὀνομαστί (224) 'unintentionally' puns on μαστός.

Pindar had already visualised the island-nymph in female form, Ἀστερίας δέμας (*Pae.* 5.42 [D5 Ru.], the body of Asteria).[78] In *HDelos*, the landscape/anatomical reference of μαζός is supported by μαστός of the island of Samos (48–50, concluding a summary of Asteria's wanderings):

---

[75] For interplay of reciprocity and naming, cf. Bing (1988) 110–11.

[76] For hill and breast, see Mineur's note, including possible allusion to contemporary anatomical theory. For mountain as figurative 'wet-nurse', cf. Pind. *Pyth.* 1.20 χιόνος ... τιθήνα. Cf. also Braswell's note on Pind. *Pyth.* 4.8; and on topographical analogues for body parts, Adams (1981) 253–5. The analogy is widespread, and may (like the Paps of Anu in Ireland) carry associations with maternal divinities.

[77] Nile: Bruneau (1970) 17; (1990) 554. See Bing (1988) 136–7; 141 for Nile/Inopos, the background in subterranean river-lore, and the cross-reference to Inopos flooding at the birth. The notion of Nilotic underground channels and fertilisation of islands certainly pre-dates C.: Giuseppetti (2013) 14 well compares Eur. *Bacch.* 406–8 (Cyprus), with Dodds's commentary. The connection with Delos is of Ptolemaic origin (cf. Bonneau [1964] 174–6, 280, 282) and may well be a Callimachean innovation: see below, p.72; also Appendix III, p.143f. on Lyc. *Alex.* 576.

[78] McKay (1962) 18–19, citing *Pyth.* 4.8. *Paean* 6 (Delphi) supplies an aetiological parallel, the personification of Aegina, 'shining star of Zeus Hellanios' (125–6) as virgin daughter of the river god Asopus (134–5) and as physical embodiment of Zeus' own seat, Mt Hellanios itself (139): this is the location of the love-making that produced Aiakos and established Aegina's fame and power; A. Hardie (1996) 228; Rutherford (2001) 325–6. Cf. also *HHAphr.* 256–8, where Aeneas is nursed by 'the deep-breasted mountain-Nymphs' (sc. of Ida).

ἢ νήσοιο διάβροχον ὕδατι μαστόν
Παρθενίης (οὔπω γὰρ ἔην Σάμος), ἧχί σε νύμφαι
γείτονες Ἀγκαίου Μυκαλησσίδες ἐξείνισσαν.

[sc. you swam towards] ... the breast of the Virgin Island, irrigated
by water (it was not yet Samos), where the nymphs of Mykalessos,
neighbours of Ankaios [sc. king of Samos], entertained you as a
guest.

διάβροχον ὕδατι echoes *Bacchae* 1051, of Kithairon: ἢν δ' ἄγκος ἀμφί-
κρημνον, ὕδασι διάβροχον (there was a valley [observe ἄγκος/Ἀγκαίου]
irrigated by waters);[79] in *HDelos*, allied to μαστόν, this suggests a
figurative 'wet breast'; and the associated mountain-Nymphs of
Mykalessos (on the Mykale promontory) who 'entertained' Asteria
further imply liquid sustenance provided for a guest.[80] That Callimachus intended the 'Samos-breast' to supply an analogue for the
'Delos-breast' is implicit in further parallels: Parthenie/Samos' change
of name (cf. 39–40 [Delos], οὔπω ... οὐδέπω with 49 [Samos], οὔπω);
Parthenie/Samos and Asteria/Delos as 'virgins'; and Asteria/Delos' hospitable acceptance of Leto and Apollo (39; 51–4).[81] The reader is thus
encouraged to read across 'μαστός irrigated by water' from Samos to
Delos, and to understand the latter's μαζός as a Delian landscape feature (Kynthos).[82] Furthermore, if διάβροχον ὕδατι (irrigated by water)

[79] Cf. also ἄβροχος (*HZeus* 18: Rhea's requirement for water to wash newborn Zeus),
with Stephens (2003) 98–9 on the associations with Nilotic inundation. For comparison of irrigated mountain to woman, cf. Eur. *Androm.* 116 (with Stevens): the
weeping Andromache's self-comparison to an irrigated rock (Mt Ida and its streams).
For the same figure of Niobe at Call. *HApoll.* 22–4, see below, n.84.

[80] Kuiper (1896) 122–3. διάβροχον ὕδατι μαστόν is paralleled in two epigrams on Apelles' painting of Aphrodite Anadyomene. In *Anth. Plan.* 178 (Antipater of Sidon)
Apelles represents 'Kypris rising from the sea, her mother'; then, 'grasping her hair,
soaked with water (διάβροχον ὕδατι χαίταν), in her hand, she squeezes the foam from
the wet locks'. In Archias' imitation (*Anth. Plan.* 179), Apelles 'saw Kypris naked, as
she was being born from the sea, her wet-nurse (τιθηνῆτορος), and represented her
thus, still squeezing with sturdy hands her hair soaked with the foam of the water'
(διάβροχον ὕδατος ἀφρῷ). If the *HDelos* parallel (διάβροχον ὕδατι in same *sedes*) is in
play, Antipater may have substituted χαίταν for μαστόν in order to recall and contrast
the conventional action of a baby reaching for its mother's breast. Archias' 'wet nurse'
vice Antipater's 'mother' would be consistent with such a reading. If correct, it would
underscore the Callimachean analogue between Samos as island/hill μαστός and
Kynthos as Apollo's Delian μαζός. The resemblance between 'Apelles' and 'Apollo'
might or might not be fortuitous.

[81] The Samos/Delos 'welcome' parallel is confirmed obliquely by ἐπεμίσγετο (39, Leto-
Delos), recalling *Od.* 6.205 and 241, ἐπιμίσγεται (in Nausicaa's welcome to Odysseus
to Scheria/Corcyra) (Kuiper [1896] 122), in combination with C.'s Κέρκυρα φιλο-
ξεινωτάτη (156), with reference to the same *Odyssey* episode (D'Alessio ad loc.; cf.
Od. 6.121, φιλόξεινοι), and echoing ἐξείνισσαν (50); the cross-reference is further
marked by Iris on Mimas at 157, mainland mountain opposite Chios (48, Χίον: see
next n.).

[82] Stephens (2015) 189 observes "μαστός portends Asteria's role as future nurse of

is read across to the stream water of Kynthos, then the Nilotic Inopos (again, by implication) supplies the god with sustenance.[83] Apollo's rejection, jointly, of Thebe and Kithairon as his 'dear nurse' (φίλη τροφός, 97), offers another parallel for mountain as component of territorial 'nurse' (underscored by allusion to Kithairon in διάβροχον ὕδατι at line 48).[84] The epithet γλυκύν in context conveys the divine sweetness of Apollo's sustenance, akin to the sweetness of the honey fed to the infant Zeus (*HZeus* 48) and of the nectar/ambrosia that was the distinctive diet of gods; but Callimachus' readers, I would suggest, are invited to infer that 'Kynthian' Apollo's equivalent sustenance derived from the Nile, and from Egypt.

On this reading, 'Apollo Kynthios' reflects Delos as wet nurse, and Kynthos the 'sweet breast' (γλυκὺν ... μαζόν) at which he was nursed.[85] In *HHApollo*, the divine sustenance fed to the infant by Themis (124–5) prompted his instant progression to godhead, including

---

Apollo". For further references within the hymn-book, cf. *HZeus* 48 (Appendix III). Cf. also *HDem*. 95, μαστός metonym for (weeping) 'wet-nurse'; in combination with Μίμαντι χίων (91, snow-melt on Mimas opposite Chios: last n.) this is directly related to *HDelos* 48, Χίον ... μαστόν. For stream/breast figure, cf. Stat. *Silv*. 4.5.33–4 (Septimius as immigrant to Rome) *quis fonte Iuturnae relictis/ uberibus neget esse pastum?* For city/water/mountain nurture of Apollo, cf. *Culex* 13–15 *sive educat illum/ Arna Chimaereo Xanthi perfusa liquore/ seu decus Asteriae* ....

[83] The implicit analogy between hill-streams and breast-milk is paralleled in Pausanias' account of Mt Leibethrion in the Helikon range (9.34.4): no doubt reflecting a literary source (Euphorion?) he speaks of images of Nymphs and Muses, and then of two spring-sources similar in shape to female breasts and sending up 'water like milk'. For river water in Apollo's nurture, see last n. and below pp.69–70, 71f.

[84] Gigante Lanzara (1990) 99 rightly sees rejection of Thebes as negative counterpart to selection of Delos, and compares Soph. *OT* 1091 (Kithairon as 'nurse' of Oedipus); Giuseppetti (2013) 135. The Niobe-sequel appears at *HApoll*. 22–4, where she is a weeping rock (δακρυόεις ... πέτρος, 22), the blasphemer κακογλώσσοιο γυναικός, *HDelos* 96) now silently mouthing (a travesty of a statue) (μάρμαρον ἀντὶ γυναικὸς ὀιζυρὸν τι χανούσης, 24): an evil counter-example of a 'wet' rock (and silent misery in contrast to Delos' magniloquent joy). The parallel is reinforced (a) by ἐστήρικται (*HApoll*. 23), cf. ἐνεστήρικται at *HDelos* 13 (below, n.307), and (b) Apollo's dissociation from Thebes εὐαγέων δὲ καὶ εὐαγέεσσι μελοίμην (*HDelos* 98) with punning reference to Pindar's εὐάγεα πέτραν ('conspicuous rock'; *Pae*. 7b.47 [C2 Ru.]).

[85] I have not found any replay of Kynthos as breast. There is a speculative but not impossible pun at Limenios *Paean* 11–12 (a section in which Delos, Libya and Athens are allusively cross-referenced): having left Κυνθίαν νᾶσον, Apollo hears the first (Athenian) paean γαλ[όφῳ πρῶνι] Τριτωνίδος (see above, n.45). Otherwise, *decus Asteriae* (*Culex* 13–15, cited above, n.82) which, in context, may represent a sound-sense echo of the Pindaric Ἀστερίας δέμας (*Pae*. 5.42 [D5 Ru.]), in the same lineage as Vergil's *tellus* = 'Dēlos' at *Aen*. 3.73 (Barchiesi [1994] 439 n.4). Claudian (*Gig*. 120–24) has nymphs on Kynthos as teachers and birth-attendants (*exclamant placidae Cynthi de vertice Nymphae,/ Nymphae, quae rudibus Phoebum docuere sagittis/ errantes agitare feras, primumque gementi/ Latonae struxere torum, cum lumina coeli/ parturiens geminis ornaret fetibus orbem*), followed by Delos herself speaking as Apollo's nurse (126–7) *si te gratissima fudit/ in nostros Latona sinus* ....

his function as prophet of the will of Zeus (132); and together with the authenticating attendance of goddesses at the birth, it certified the legitimacy of the new god, and his claim to his divine inheritance from Zeus.[86] In *HDelos*, by contrast, Apollo is already acting as prophetic divinity from the womb, anticipating his Delphic role (90), guiding his mother to his birthplace (88–98; 162–95), and revealing the will of the *Moirai* (165).[87] So what bearing might the Kynthian 'breast' and its sustenance have on Apollo's entry upon his divine inheritance, and his legitimisation? To address that question, we need to take account of Zeus' presence on the summit of Kynthos.

(c) Zeus Kynthios

In §I, Kynthos emerged as a focal point for visiting theoric choruses to Delos, associated with their 'reception' by Apollo. In §VI, these local associations will be brought to bear on the god's reception of Callimachus and his hymn on Delos. But in the twelfth *Paean*, Pindar had plainly presented Kynthos as the domain of Zeus, and the cult of Zeus Kynthios had thereby acquired 'literary' status around the middle of the fifth century. By the later 270's, moreover, construction of the Kynthion, begun after Delos gained independence from Athens (314 BC), was approaching completion, and the sanctuary had become a major focal point for Delian worship of Zeus Kynthios (principally) and Athena Kynthia.[88] At the time of writing, then, 'Kynthios' as a sacral epiklesis indubitably belonged to Zeus; and it is difficult to suppose that Callimachus was unaware of this or that he applied the epithet to Apollo without thought for the father's principal local cult.[89] The application (in enjambement) of the epiklesis to Apollo (Ἀπόλλων/ Κύνθιος, 9–10), will surely have sprung a major surprise on its first audience.

That Zeus was indeed in the poet's mind at this juncture is suggested by a 'wet-nurse' parallel between *HZeus* and *HDelos*: the goat-μαζόν of Amalthea that fed Zeus is in my view (Appendix III) echoed in the hill-

---

[86] Legitimisation: so Most (1981) 190 n.7, noting the parallel with Zeus' action, with Leto, in welcoming Apollo to his court at Olympus with nectar. See above, n.63 for Hera's views on illegitimacy.

[87] Cf. Ambühl (2005) 324.

[88] Bruneau (1970) 225; Hamilton (2000) 194.

[89] This was not simply a local cult: the dedicants at the Kynthion were "international and male" (Hamilton [2000] 194). Pfeiffer (1952) 29 observes that "Callimachus had the most intimate knowledge of the sacred island". Whether he visited Delos is quite uncertain: Pfeiffer (ibid. 26) tentatively accepted Callimachus' claim not to have been a sea-goer (cf. *Aetia* fr. 178.27–30 Pf.). See now Harder (2012) II.984.

μαζόν of Asteria/Delos.[90] Further internal evidence for Zeus' bearing on Apollo Kynthios will be offered below. Here, the suggestion that Callimachus has applied a Zeus-epiklesis to Apollo may be compared with the latter's activities as builder of cities and layer of foundations at *HApollo* 55–64: Albert Henrichs observed that the child-god here moves into spheres associated with Zeus Πολιεύς and Poseidon Θεμελιοῦχος, albeit without deployment of those titles.[91] Explicit play on cult epithets between Apollo and Zeus had however appeared in tragedy, at *Rhesus* 355: the Trojan chorus greets Rhesus on his unexpected arrival as 'for me, Zeus Φαναῖος'; in their delight, they apply an Apolline epiklesis to Zeus in order to cap their earlier prayer (224–32) for an epiphany of Apollo; and for the choristers personally, Rhesus now represents something better, an 'epiphany' of Zeus himself.[92]

Pindar's twelfth *Paean* presents itself as the most obvious extant antecedent for Callimachus' *Kynthios*, and the reader is prepared for Pindarising material from the outset: in the first line, θυμέ, τίνα echoes *Nemeans* 3.26 (below, p.100f.), and τὴν ἱερήν .../ Δῆλον echoes τὰν δ' ἱεράν/ [...] Κῶν in Pindar's first *Hymn*.[93] Further debts to the first *Hymn* have been documented, as also to Pindar's Delian paeans: 5 (D5 Ru.), 7b (C2 Ru.) and 12 (G1 Ru.);[94] and among identified points of

---

[90] Cf. Ukleja (2005) 247 n.836. On most conventional dating, *HZeus* is earlier than *HDelos*: Fraser (1972) I.652, II.915, n.284, with bibliography; Cameron (1995) 261); Hunter (2003) 3–5 (preference). See below, Appendix I, for the hypothesis of unitary composition.

[91] Henrichs (1993) 129 (but θεμείλια already at *HHApoll.* 254, 294). These are instances of a wider phenomenon: see the comments of Hunter and Fuhrer (2002) 160, on Athena's 'usurpation' of an 'Artemis' role: "The inherited pantheon was a dynamic system of overlapping relations, narratives and spheres of influence."

[92] Liapis (2007) esp. 382–6 identifies the Apolline epiklesis, but adds unpersuasive suggestions of 'mystery' allusion. The chorus deploys the epiklesis in a private capacity (thus, μοι, 355) in order to suggest that for them personally, Rhesus' arrival is (like) that rarest of events, an 'epiphany' of Zeus (Φαναῖος etymologised from epiphany: Plut. *De E apud Delph.* 385c). The following invitation to Phrygia to speak of Zeus as *Eleutherios* ('Liberator'), marks the choric cross-over from personal reaction to public role.

[93] D'Alessio (2005) 128–31, re-editing Pind. fr. 33a.2–3 Ma.; cf. Giuseppetti (2012) 473–8, rightly stressing (478) the role of the Pindaric Heracles' expedition against the Koan Meropes in effecting the "ordinamento dell'universo il cui primo movente è Zeus". D'Alessio (ibid. 133; and [2009] 135) well observes the parallel with *HDelos* 1 (marked also in the later reference to Kos as Χαλκιόπης ἱερὸν μυχὸν ἡρωίνης, 161); McKay (1962) 142–3 noted (but over-emphasised) the centrality of the island-nurse parallel between the two, and C.'s correction of Kos' inclusion in the catalogue of refusals at *HHApoll.* 42 (*HDelos* 47–8).

[94] For the modified Pindarising agenda announced in the first line, see Cahen (1930) 155, and Giangrande (1988). On Pindaric influence, see Wilamowitz (1924) 63, 65; Bing (1988) 91–110; Depew (1998); Ukleja (2005) 129–41, and 'Stellen' s.v. 'Pindaros: *Paiane*; *Fragmente*'; and Giuseppetti (2013) 86–97 (particular emphasis on the first *Hymn*). For other possible paeanic antecedents, see Rutherford (1990) 182–3. I am not

contact with the twelfth is the Callimachean Ares' malign mountain-top 'guard' (ἐφύλασσε, 64), now understood to recall and reverse the Pindaric Zeus' benign guardianship from above Kynthos.[95]

Pindaric provenance, along with reference to Zeus, is indicated at two points in the *Aetia* where Apollo is addressed as Κύνθιε (Kynthian). The first, from *Acontius and Kydippe* (*Aet.* fr. 67.5–6 Ha.) refers to a sacrificial procession concluding an Apolline festival: ἦ γάρ, ἄναξ, ὁ μὲν ἦλθεν Ἰουλίδος ἡ δ᾽ ἀπὸ Νάξου,/ Κύνθιε, τὴν Δήλῳ σὴν ἐπὶ βουφονίην (For, lord, he came from Ioulis, she from Naxos,/ Kynthian, to the sacrifice of oxen at Delos, for you).[96] The reader knows, of course, that the 'Kynthian' is Apollo; yet the divine identity is briefly open to question (with *anax* alone, it could be Zeus Kynthios), and momentary ambiguity is confirmed in what follows: Δήλῳ and σὴν placed between τὴν and βουφονίην (literally, your Bouphonia, the one at Delos) implies contrast with another *bouphonia*, in another city and to another god, patently with reference to the well-known Attic festival for Zeus on the Acropolis.[97] On this basis, we might infer that Κύνθιε echoes Apollo Kynthios at *HDelos* 10; that Kydippe's provenance 'from Naxos' (ἦλθεν ... ἀπὸ Νάξου) echoes the Naxian *theoria* in the Pindaric model for *HDelos* (ἔρ[χεται Να]ξόθεν, *Pae.* 12.6 [G1 Ru.]);[98] and that the allusion to the Attic Bouphonia for Zeus echoes the *HDelos* interplay between that god and Apollo.

The second echo of Apollo Kynthios occurs in the speaker's dialogue with Apollo's Delian statue (*Aet.* fr. 114 Ha.).[99] The latter confirms that it/he is 'Delian', 'golden', and belted (2–5), and is then questioned thus (6–7): τεῦ δ᾽ ἕνεκα σκαιῇ μὲν ἔ]χεις χερὶ Κύνθιε τ[όξον,/ τὰς δ᾽ ἐπὶ δεξιτερῇ] σὰς ἰδανὰς Χάριτας; ([For what reason] do you hold the bow, Kynthian, in the [left] hand, and your lovely Charites [in the right]?). As at *Aetia* fr. 67.6 Ha., we have a vocative address Κύνθιε in the sixth line; as in *HDelos*, *Kynthios* is paired with *Delios*;

---

persuaded by the parallels between *HDelos* and Pindar *Pythians* 4 suggested by Meillier (1995) 137–9, 147–8.

[95] The inversion is noted by Most (1981) 190, Bing (1988) 108–109 (n.35), and Ambühl (2005) 316 n.408.

[96] Bruneau (1970) 65–6 (citing Callimachus); 76. For the choric/processional context, see Harder (2012) II.554–5; 572–3.

[97] Harder (2012) II.555 notes the Attic Bouphonia, but does not connect with Kynthios. On the Attic festival, Burkert (1983) 136–42. The apparently commonplace comparison of the pair to 'stars of their islands' (νησάων ἀστέρες, 8) sustains allusion to *HDelos*: Asteria/Delos as island-star (38; cf. Pind. fr. 33b.6 Ma.); and the anomalous form νησάων, deployed only at *HDelos* 66 and, of Delos, 275 (Harder).

[98] There is a sound-echo of Pindar's Να]ξόθεν in C.'s ἄναξ, ὁ μὲν, arguably fixed by C.'s internal play between ἄναξ and (the 'translation' of Ναξόθεν) ἀπὸ Νάξου.

[99] The line numbering given here assumes (a) the separation of fr. 114.1–3 Pf. (= fr. 113f Ha.) and (b) the loss of one line from the start of the papyrus remains.

and as in the Pindaric paean/prosodion, the Charites embody the god's instrumental music (*Pae.* 12.7 [G1 Ru.], Χαρίτεσσι μίγδαν).[100]

The 'Kynthian' echoes in the *Aetia* help confirm the integration into *HDelos* of Pindar's reference to the Delian cult of Zeus. This cultic interplay between father and son carries dynastic implications for the Ptolemies. In prophesying 'another god' (165, Ptolemy Philadelphus) at the hymn-centre, Apollo predicts 'he will know the ways of his father' (170), and thereby aligns his own birth with that of Philadelphus, and with the latter's legacy from Ptolemy I Soter. The father/son dimension is enriched by *Kynthios*: nurtured by the hill that is sacred to Zeus, Apollo will be the latter's true (Delian) son.[101] The dynastic resonances go further. As 'highest offspring of the Saviours' (Σαωτήρων ὕπατον γένος, 166), Philadelphus is son of a 'Saviour' king (Ptolemy I Soter), a title certainly intended to recall Zeus Soter.[102] Apollo himself is seldom addressed as Soter (rather, he is the guardian god: above, p.51); and tellingly, his intervention against the Gauls at Delphi, immediately advertised as preserving the *soteria* of the *Hellenes*, was the occasion for sacrifices to Apollo as Pythios, but to Zeus as Soter. Callimachus' dynastic point lies in Apollo and Philadelphus as sons of Zeus Soter and Ptolemy I Soter.

The connection between prooemial Κύνθιος and the central comparisons of gods and kings is set up by the verb αἰνεῖν (praise):[103] Delos 'first praised' (ἤνεσε πρώτη, 6) Apollo 'as god'; the hymnist hopes for Apollo Kynthios' praise (αἰνήσῃ, 10); Apollo predicts Philadelphus'

---

[100] For the Apolline Charites at Delos, above, nn.58, 59; Bruneau (1970) 43–4.

[101] For the general scenario, cf. esp. Aesch. *Suppl.* 583–9 (Zeus' protection of Io from Hera in his sacred grove by the Nile; Epaphus as true son of Zeus): ἔνθεν πᾶσα βοᾷ χθών [sc. Egypt]/ 'φυσιζόου γένος τόδε Ζηνός ἐστιν ἀληθῶς·/ τίς γὰρ ἂν κατέπαυσεν Ἥ-/ ρας νόσους ἐπιβούλους;'/ Διὸς τόδ' ἔργον· καὶ τόδ' ἂν γένος λέγων/ ἐξ Ἐπάφου κυρήσαις. For Io as model for Leto, see Ambühl [2005] 316 n.407; 353–4. For C.'s double father/son analogue, cf. Opp. *Cyn.* 1–9 (Antoninus/Severus :: Apollo/Zeus). With ἤθεα, cf. Nonn. *Dionys.* 46.15–18 (Pentheus rejects Dionysus' nursing by Rheia and suggests he was nursed by, and got his character from, Semele): εἴρεο καὶ Κορύβαντας, ὅπῃ ποτὲ κοῦρος ἀθύρων/ μαζὸν Ἀμαλθείης [cf. *HZeus* 48–9] κουρο-τρόφον [cf. *HDelos* 2] αἰγὸς ἀμέλγων/ Ζεὺς δέμας ἠέξησε, καὶ οὐ γλάγος ἔσπασε [cf. *HDelos* 274] Ῥείης./ ἤθεα σῆς δολίης ἀπεμάξαο καὶ σὺ τεκούσης. For moral influence imbibed in breast-feeding: Gell. *NA* 12.1.20 *in moribus inolescendis magnam fere partem ingenium altricis et natura lactis tenet* ...; and cf. Coleman on Stat. *Silv.* 4.5.35–6.

[102] So Gigante Lanzara (1990) 124. The main evidence for Zeus Soter at Alexandria in the period 290–70 is his statue on the lighthouse at Pharos, recorded by Posidippus (AB 115.1, 10); Fraser (1972) 18–20. For Zeus Soter, see *RE* Xa.362–3; Suppl. XV.1055–7. Zeus Soter on Delos: Bruneau (1970) 233–5. Muccioli (2013) 81–94, on Ptolemy I Soter, refers (85) for an association with Zeus Soter to Koenen (1983) 154 n.35 (recording numismatic evidence for the king wearing the aegis of Zeus). For a probable Soteria festival at Alexandria in the 270s (*OGIS* 36) see Foertmeyer (1988) 100 n.33.

[103] On the import of these verbal repetitions, see Bing (1988) 119–21.

future praise (αἰνήσεις, 189). The rationale for Κύνθιος lies in the Pindaric relationship between son and father, Apollo and Zeus Kynthios;
its enunciation in *HDelos* sets up an analogue for the father/son
dynamics of the Ptolemaic dynasty;[104] and *HDelos* itself enacts the
predicted praise of Apollo's oracular predictions.

III. NYMPHS, NURTURE AND SONG

HDelos covers an extraordinary geographical range: the far north, the
Greek mainland, the Aegean and Mediterranean islands, the Ionian
coast, the Ethiopian source of the Nile. The geography and topography
of the Greek-speaking world are prominent features of early
Alexandrian poetry, certainly reflecting the imperial (maritime and
territorial) interests of the Ptolemaic dynasty, but no doubt contributing
to the appeal of these works for a Panhellenic readership as well as for
their domestic audiences.[105] In addition to what has been termed the
"geopoetic" representation of places in poetry, however, *HDelos* has
much to say about the integration of territory and music. This feature
was touched on at the outset with reference to Delos as a symbol for
Callimachus' poetry, and again in analysis of the twelfth *Paean*
(§I[c]).[106] How, then, does Callimachus' association of physical landscape with song and dance relate to his hymnic purposes, in particular
to his praise of Delos' nurture of Apollo as *kourotrophos*?

As the catalogues of islands, cities, regions, rivers and mountains
unfold, a pattern is laid down of locations identified as Nymphs, with
interwoven cross-references, integral to the fabric of the hymn, among
Nymph-groups.[107] Plural 'Nymphs' appears six times (49, 83, 84, 85,
109, 256), all with reference to landscape or to natural features (trees);
the singular 'nymph' appears three times, of Melia (79), of Hera as wife
of Zeus (215), and of the unnamed 'Delian nymph' (or 'bride') at 323.

---

[104] Theocr. *Id.* 17.58–76 has often been compared: Philadelphus's birth on Cos;
personification of island as (wet-) nurse; P. as true son of his father; Cos' address to P.,
including Apollo's love for Delos/P's love for Cos; the postnatal triple call of Zeus'
eagle. See Hunter (2003) 142–53; and for a good statement of Theocritus' debt to C.,
Ambühl (2005) 347 (see also below, n.183).

[105] Asper (2011), with reference to *Aetia* and *Iambi*. See especially Bing (2005) on the
Milan Posidippus. For the Panhellenic appeal of the *Hymns*, Hunter and Fuhrer (2002)
144–5, 146–57.

[106] Bing (1988) 125 speaks of the "blending of physical and musical within the circling
motif". The background is explored in A. Hardie (2006) 53–7.

[107] See Larson (2001) 8–11 ("Nymphs in the Landscape"); I have capitalised 'Nymphs'
throughout.

There is much in this kaleidoscopic, anthropomorphised, review of Greek topography that Pindar would have recognised. What is new is the associated parade of overt learning (vouchsafed often in parentheses, ostensibly for the benefit of readers), the hymnist's thirst for accurate knowledge, and his disposition to question the veracity of his sources. Just after the first quarter of the hymn (81.5/327), he pauses to initiate a scholarly exchange, ostensibly improvised, with the Muses (82–5):[108]

> ἐμαὶ θεαὶ εἴπατε Μοῦσαι,
> ἦ ῥ' ἐτεὸν ἐγένοντο τότε δρύες ἡνίκα νύμφαι;
> 'νύμφαι μὲν χαίρουσιν, ὅτε δρύας ὄμβρος ἀέξει,
> νύμφαι δ' αὖ κλαίουσιν, ὅτε δρυσὶ μηκέτι φύλλα.'

> My goddesses, tell me, Muses,
> did trees of a truth come to exist at just the same time as Nymphs?
> 'Nymphs do rejoice when water makes trees grow;
> Nymphs yet weep when trees no longer have their leaves.'

ἐτεόν is a Homeric term, applied to the detached, somewhat sceptical, tone in which Hellenistic poets sometimes query the testimony of their predecessors.[109] The aorist ἐγένοντο (83) signals a 'theogonic' framework, and Melia's 'co-eval tree' at line 81 (ἥλικος ... δρυός) directs us to *Theogony* 187, where Gaia gives birth to 'Nymphs whom they call Meliai' and where primordial status is implied for both nymphs and (ash) trees.[110] The question also picks up Aphrodite's account of mountain-dwelling Nymphs as intermediate beings, neither mortal nor immortal, in *HHAphrodite* (259–72), and the statement (264–8) that 'at the same time as they [sc. the nymphs] are coming into existence, pines ... or oaks grow up ... on high mountains ... and they are called precincts of the immortals.' Invited to verify received wisdom as to the nature, origin and status of tree-Nymphs (Hamadryads), the Muses offer a gnomic reference to the nurturing power of rain water. This brings Presocratic (Empedocles) zoogony/botany into play:[111] trees as the first things to grow from earth; the nurturing power of water/wetness; and the general loss of leaves as a consequence of water-deficit in the heat

---

[108] For the dynamics of this question and answer exchange, see p.108f.

[109] Cf. Arat. *Phaen.* 30, with Kidd's note, suggesting reference to Epimenides; Nic. *Ther.* 10 (Hesiod).

[110] Hes. *Theog.* 187. The scholiast's comment Μελίας δὲ διὰ τὸ ἅμα τοῖς δένδρεσι γίνεσθαι shows that the line featured in discussion of the nymph/tree question. Mineur (1984) 118–19 gets the right general sense. For the theogonic reference of ἐγένοντο, cf. Hes. *Theog.* 46, 106, 108, 116, 123, etc.

[111] Sources in Diels–Kranz *Fragmente der Vorsokratiker* I.296–7, 31 A 70 (= frr. 571–77 Bo.), esp. Aetius 5.26.4 (fr. 571 Bo.) καὶ τὰ μὲν [δένδρα] ἐλλιπὲς ἔχοντα τὸ ὑγρὸν ἐξικμαζομένου αὐτοῦ τῷ θέρει φυλλοροεῖν. Cf. also fr. a(i) 9 M-P; 25–39 In.

of summer. Moreover, the alternating joy and sadness of the Nymphs looks like an anthropomorphic representation of Presocratic (Empedocles and Anaxagoras) teaching on plants' capacity for pleasure and pain, preserved in the pseudo-Aristotelian *de Plantis* (where leaf-fall is cited in argument).[112] Callimachus' subtle mix of scientific physiology (here, the elements earth and water) and traditional anthropomorphism is further sustained in ὄμβρος ἀέξει, patently with reference to the Homeric Διὸς ὄμβρος ἀέξει (*Od.* 9.111, 358), and perhaps also to associated scholarship on Homer's representations of mountain, tree and water Nymphs as 'daughters of Zeus'.[113]

The Muses too are of course daughters of Zeus (Hes. *Theog.* 25, etc., κοῦραι Διός), and their response to the hymnist offers a verbal hint of their ancient kinship with Nymphs: the striking symmetry in sound and *sedes* of χαίρουσιν and κλαίουσιν (84–5) is paralleled (albeit with word-change) only in Hesiod's address to the Helikoniades (*Theogony* 104–5, where χαίρετε and κλείετε open successive lines).[114] Following as it does upon Callimachus' description of Nymph-*choreia* on Helikon, this distinctive parallel is unlikely to be fortuitous: indeed, it may well carry further reference to the contemporary deployment of Hamadryads as Muse-surrogates (familiar to us from Vergil and Propertius, where they are presumably modelled on Hellenistic antecedents).[115]

---

[112] This work is an expansion by Nicolaus of Damascus of a lost Aristotelian treatise, and it survives in an Arabic version, itself translated into Latin in the 13ᵗʰ century. Emped. 30 A 70 and 59 A 117 (fr. 577 Bo.); *Anaxagoras autem et Abrucalis* [i.e. Empedocles] *desiderio eas* [sc. *plantas*] *moveri dicunt, sentire quoque et tristari delectarique asserunt; quorum Anaxagoras animalia esse has, laetarique et tristari dixit, fluxum* [Meyer, D–K; *flexum* Latin MS] *foliorum argumentum assumens.* Bollack (1969) III.511–12; Inwood (2001) 186–7.

[113] Schol. *Od.* 4.477 … οἱ ποταμοὶ ἐκ Διὸς πληροῦνται, ὥς που ἔφη [sc. Homer] 'καί σφιν Διὸς ὄμβρος ἀέξει'. οἵῳ λόγῳ καὶ τὰς νύμφας Διὸς θυγατέρας λέγει, 'νύμφαι κρηναῖαι, κοῦραι Διός'. ἔτι 'νύμφαι ὀρεστιάδες, κοῦραι Διός', ἐπειδὴ καὶ τὰ ἐν τοῖς ὄρεσι φυτὰ τῷ τοῦ Διὸς ὕδατι τρέφεται. This last passage (*Il.* 6.419–20) attracted scientific analysis of the Nymphs as natural 'powers': Eustathius explains the genealogy of tree-nymphs (including Hamadryads) in elemental terms as the wetness and heat that accompany the Nymphs from *aer* and *aither*. For ὄμβρος as the element water in Empedocles, Wright (1981) 23.

[114] For the sound-play (here of course implicit in the intertext), cf. Bion *Ep. Adon.* 91, 94; and for the etymological nexus linking 'weeping' and 'praising', *Etym. Magn.* pp. 516.52–8 K., s.v. κλαίω.

[115] Kennedy (1982) 377–82, arguing for a model in Cornelius Gallus: the key text is *Ecl.* 10.52–4 on the growth of Gallus's *amores* with the growth of the trees on which they are inscribed (*crescent* ... *crescetis*), allied to the Hamadryads (62). For Hamadryads and Muses with Apollo on Helikon, cf. Himerius' parable (*Or.* 66 Col.) of Apollo's anger with the Dryads and Hamadryads for their incongruous attempt to join the Muses' chorus dancing to his lyre, and pass themselves off as 'goddesses' and Muses, together with Helikon's indignant intervention. Reinsch-Werner (1976) 189–90 rightly observes interplay between the Helikonian Nymphs and the Hesiodic Muses.

More fundamentally, the reader is left to ponder how the primordial
zoogony might bear on the origins and nature of the Muses, and on the
era in which they came into existence.[116] That Muse-puzzle aside, the
programmatic exchange is highly informative for Callimachus' innovative approach to the Nymphs: he combines scientific physiology with
traditional anthropomorphism and mythic genealogy, in a synthesis perhaps best paralleled in contemporary poetry in Aratus' *Phaenomena*.[117]
But such syntheses were nothing new in high poetry: they have a major
Pindaric antecedent in the first *Hymn*, where traditional genealogy is
evidently blended with Milesian cosmological ideas.[118]

The nurturing (kourotrophic) role of rivers, glimpsed earlier of
Inopos in relation to Kynthos as 'breast' (visible also in Leto's exchange with Peneius), is central to what follows.[119] Callimachus' treatment is best approached through Hesiod who, at *Theogony* 337–45, had
represented Oceanus and Tethys as the parents of Rivers (with a
catalogue of names headed by the Nile); Tethys then (346–8) 'gave
birth to the sacred family of Kourai [West's reading] who with lord
Apollo and Rivers nurture men from boyhood' (τίκτε δὲ Κουράων
ἱερὸν γένος, αἳ κατὰ γαῖαν/ ἄνδρας κουρίζουσι σὺν Ἀπόλλωνι ἄνακτι/
καὶ ποταμοῖς). Callimachus first refers to this seminal text at line 17,
where, uniquely as extant, the two names, Ὠκεανόν and Τηθύν, each
occupy the same *sedes* as their counterparts at *Theog.* 368; at line 45,
καναχηδὰ ῥέοντος is a well-known echo of *Theog.* 367 ποταμοὶ καναχηδὰ ῥέοντες; and at line 324, κουρίζοντι ... Ἀπόλλωνι varies *Theog.*
347 κουρίζουσι ... Ἀπόλλωνι (again, identical *sedes*). The Hesiodic
passage thus frames the kourotrophic content of *HDelos*, underscores

---

[116] On the conventional parentage (Mnemosyne and Zeus), and on the Hesiodic order of
Zeus' wives (*Theog.* 915–17), the Muses were born before Apollo and Artemis; the
order was fluid, but that the Muses pre-existed Apollo may reasonably be assumed for
HDelos. The view that an 'elder' Muse-group, daughters of Ouranos and Ge (i.e. the
Titans' generation), preceded the 'younger' (sc. Hesiodic) Muses is attributed to
Musaeus 2 B 15 D–K (Schol. Apoll. Rhod. 3.1) and Mimnermus (fr. 13 W. (Paus.
9.29.4]); the former were invoked by Alcman (5 fr. 2 col. ii.28–9 *PMGF*; 81 Cal.; cf.
Diod. 4.7.1). The matter attracted scholarly attention at the Mouseion and Aristarchus
is recorded as accepting that 'the Muse was the daughter of Ouranos' (Schol. Pind.
Nem. 3.16b [iii.43.19 Dr.]); *AP* 9.26.9–10 (Antipater of Thessalonica) plays on the
Ouranos/Ge genealogy.

[117] Cf. Gee (2013) 22–33.

[118] A. Hardie (2000) 24–5, with bibliography cited there for elements of continuity
between Hesiod and Milesian cosmologists.

[119] Kourotrophic rivers, and the association of fertility and nurture: Borthwick (1963),
esp. 231; also Price (1978) 124; 195. For the kourotrophic Nile, central to Delos'
nursing role, see below, Appendix III. Apollonian hair-cult is also relevant: Schol.
Theog. 347 σὺν Ἀπόλλωνι ἄνακτι· καὶ γὰρ Ἀπόλλωνι καὶ ποταμοῖς οἱ νέοι ἀπέκειρον
τὰς κόμας διὰ τὸ αὐξήσεως καὶ ἀνατροφῆς αἰτίους εἶναι. On *HHApollo*, *HDelos* and
the aetiology of kourotrophic ritual at Delos, Graf (1993) 102–8.

the nurturing role of rivers, and supplies a telling association of flowing water with sound (καναχηδά), hence potentially with song as well.[120]

The 'sacred song of Eileithyia' is uttered at the moment of birth by 'Delian Nymphs, offspring of an ancient river' (256, Νύμφαι Δηλιάδες, ποταμοῦ γένος ἀρχαίοιο). Who are these riverine Nymph-singers? The scholiast claims the 'ancient river' is Inopos, which was certainly a 'river' but was not (in context) 'ancient'. The circumlocution points in the first instance to the kourotrophic Nile, transmitting its fertilising flood (n.77) through Inopos at the moment of birth (206–8), as 'grandfather' of the Deliades; yet beyond the Nile may lie its (Hesiodic) father Oceanus, the very first river and thus ἀρχαῖος in the sense of ἐξ ἀρχῆς (ἀρχέγονος Ὠκεανός, in Nonnus' phrase [40.550–51]).[121] But like the 'Thessalian' Nymph-daughters of the Peneius, who are introduced in parallel phrasing (109) Νύμφαι Θεσσαλίδες, ποταμοῦ γένος and who evidently represent 'all Thessaly' (cf. πᾶσα ... Θεσσαλίη, 139–40), the Delian Nymphs represent all Delos, earth as well as river-water.[122] An Apollonian identification of river-nymphs and territory at *Arg.* 2.686– 713 (the 'sacred island' of Thynias) offers confirmation: the 'Korykian Nymphs' (Parnassian landscape around the cave), 'daughters of

---

[120] καναχηδά of (pipe) music already at Pind. *Nem.* 8.15. Directly relevant is Williams' account ([1978] 87–9) of Oceanus as source of all rivers, and as literary figure (with particular reference to Homer as source of inspiration to successor-poets). The correlation of stream water and song is of course ancient, and widespread: cf. e.g. A. Hardie (1996) 225–26, 233–34; (2010a) 47–51.

[121] Inopos, as a spring fed by the subterranean waters of a 'parent' source is a (virgin) 'daughter': see Harder (2012) II.110, on *Aetia* fr. 2b,2 Ha. For ἀρχαῖος in this sense, cf. Pind. fr. 30.5 Ma. (Themis) ἀρχαίαν ἄλοχον Διός. Nonnus' ἀρχέγονος, if accented ἀρχεγόνος may carry the active sense of first begetter: see *LSJ* s.v. For a possible Alcaeic antecedent of Nile/Inopos at Delphi (Kephisus/Kastalia) see below, Appendix II, with n.358.

[122] Moero's near-contemporary assimilation of Hamadryads to water-nymphs (*AP* 6.189.1) Νύμφαι Ἀμαδρυάδες, ποταμοῦ κόραι, is clearly related to *HDelos* 109 and 256, and to the Muse-exchange, and underscores creative interplay of Hellenistic Nymphs: the 4-word line openings Νύμφαι ... ποταμοῦ only in C. and Moero, Νύμφαι ... γένος only in C. and *AP* 9.329.1 (Leonidas, imitating Moero, Νύμφαι ἐφυδριάδες, Δώρου γένος). Moero's 'Hamadryads' have been amended (Meineke; cf. Gow–Page *HE* II.415 [2679]); but for Hamadryades and water, cf. Nonn. *Dionys.* 22.101–3 (Hamadryad on her debt to Dionysus as son of Zeus): ... ὅττι ῥεέθρων/ ὑγροτόκους ὠδῖνας, ὅττι δρύας αἰὲν ἀέξει/ ὀμβρηρῇ ῥαθάμιγγι ... ὑέτιος Ζεύς; and for a possible etymological connection, cf. *Etym. Magn.* p. 256.3–5 K., s.v. δενδρυάζειν: παρὰ τὸ δρύας, δρύαζειν καὶ δενδρυάζειν. σημαίνει καὶ τὸ καθ' ὕδατος δύεσθαι καὶ κρύπτειν ἑαυτόν. Relevant Latin texts include Cat. 61.22–5 *ramulis/ quos Hamadryades deae/ ludicrum sibi roscido nutriunt umore* (paired with Helikonian *nympha ... Aganippe* [29–30]); Prop. 1.20.32–7; *Culex* 95 *fontis Hamadryadum* (text corrupt), with Kennedy (1982) 377–82. Postgate (1896) is still relevant, but dismissive of problem-passages; better, Fedeli on Prop. 1.20.12. See also Myers (1994) 230–33 for the possible influence of C.'s Hamadryads on their Augustan counterparts.

Pleistos', are first singers of the Delphian paean-shout (711):[123] Πολλὰ δὲ Κωρύκιαι νύμφαι, Πλείστοιο θύγατρες,/ θαρσύνεσκον ἔπεσσιν, Ἰήιε κεκληγυῖαι. Here again, riverine landscape Nymphs are instrumental in creating song; yet their Apolline song underlines the apparent anomaly of the Delian Nymphs' 'song of Eileithyia', a non-Apolline performance which calls for clarification (see below, Appendix II).

Callimachus deploys the Deliades first as singing landscape Nymphs, and then (296) as their contemporary choric counterparts, and thereby embraces the kourotrophic cycle of nurture and education, both for the musical *kouros*-god and for generations of *kouroi* and *kourai* on Delos.[124] The *aition* for Apollo's own kourotrophic role lies in his nurture by Delos (and Leto; see below), and in the choric content of his education;[125] and while Apollo's role as chorus-leader is not celebrated, it is implicit in the kithara-playing Theseus leading the chorus of Athenian *paides* (312–13).[126]

As the god grows, and nursing merges into early education, the νύμφαι Δηλιάδες have a singular counterpart in the 'Delian Nymph' (323, Δηλιὰς ... νύμφη) said to have 'invented' the ritual encirclement of altar and olive trunk as a 'game' for the toddler god.[127] Who is this educator? Not, surely, 'a Delian Nymph' (i.e. some anonymous member of the troupe) in such a critical role: rather, we should think (in the first instance) of the island-Nymph Delos herself, in nurse-play with her charge.[128] This entails reading the 'invention' clause as an explanatory (narrative) addendum to the description of the play-ritual in the hymnist's address to Asteria, connected by ἅ (323) as demonstrative (=

---

[123] The entire passage deserves separate treatment, as evidence for Apollonius' complementary reading of *HDelos* and *HApollo*. Of immediate interest for *HDelos*: (a) the paean-shout (*HApollo*) uttered first by Delphian (*HApollo*) landscape nymphs (*HDelos*); (b) the paean-shout as 'healer' (?), cf. 701 and below on *HDelos* 214); (c) 'window' reference to Pindar's first *Hymn* (fr. 33d.3 Ma., Leto Κοιογενής) in Κοιογένεια (710); (d) Apollo's unshorn hair ἀδήλητοι (709); (e) the *aition* set within Orpheus' song marking the new cult of Apollo of the Dawn (686–7).

[124] For the choric character of kourotrophy and education in the Hyperborean context, see Lonsdale (1994) 36–7; cf. Calame (1997) 105–9.

[125] Calame (1997) 109, with bibliography: "There is ... a close link between the nurturing character of Apollo and that of the island ...".

[126] For the role of the choregos (including Theseus on Delos), see Calame (1997) 43–73.

[127] Delian education of Apollo: the proem to the *Culex* invokes Apollo and appends the following list of cult sites (13–17): *sive educat illum/ Arna Chimaereo Xanthi perfusa liquore,/ seu decus Asteriae, seu qua Parnasia rupes/ hinc atque hinc patula praepandit cornua fronte,/ Castaliaeque sonans liquido pede labitur unda*. Apollo is *kouros* god, subject to nurture (*educat*) in three possible sites, 'Asteria', plus Lycia and Delphi, where the latter two are characterised in terms of mountain-riverine landscape.

[128] Variation between singular nymph and plural nymph-collective is paralleled in e.g. the nymph(s) of Nysa: Larson (2001) 93–4. In *HDelos*, Melia (νύμφη 80) is singular representative of the *Meliai*.

τά). Equally possible (and no more awkward) is a reference within the address to Asteria, to Leto as 'Delian bride' (sc. of Zeus), where ἅ carries its customary relative force.[129] νύμφα Διὸς (215, of Hera) lends support to this alternative reading, as does Leto's appearance in the envoi (326). Either reading, Delos or Leto, seems valid, and I would suggest that both are present, that the syntactical ambiguity is deliberate, and that it highlights a progressive assimilation of the two sisters, Nymph and goddess, within *HDelos*.[130] The functions and identities of mother and nurse converge in this concluding reference to kourotrophic care.

These components (rivers, physiological science, nurture, birthsong, and assimilation of goddess to 'Delos') may be seen in relation to one another in the events following Leto's landing. She settles beside the Inopos (206, ἕζετο δ᾽ Ἰνωποῖο παρὰ ῥόον), at which point the hymnist discloses, outside the narrative of events and in the manner of a geographer, that 'Gaia sends up the Inopos in deepest flood at the time when the Nile descends in full flow from the Ethiopian crag' (κρημνοῖο ... Αἰθιοπῆος). Leto's exhaustion is manifested in 'damp [literally 'southern rainy'] sweat', a physical reaction that sets up an analogue between her body and cascading river-water (together with an implicit scientific explanation for the Nile flood as the product of rain from the south winds).[131] The goddess is thus assimilated to the (extended) Delian-Ethiopian landscape, just as the reclining Leto of *HHApollo* complements the sloping landscape of Kynthos (above, p.46).

---

[129] The only other possible deployments of demonstrative ἅ (unhomeric) as a sentence opening in Callimachus (*HZeus* 69 and *HDelos* 284, as printed) could both be read as relative pronouns within a single sentence; both, as it happens, are also connected with Zeus.

[130] Assimilation to Delos: πότνια (123, Leto; 312, Delos). Both respect Hera's allocated domain: 73–4 (Leto does not go to Argos) οὐ γὰρ ἐκείνας/ ἀτραπιτοὺς ἐπάτησεν, ἐπεὶ λάχεν Ἴναχον Ἥρη; and 247–8 (Hera acknowledges Asteria's respect for her marriage bed) ἐμεῖο/ δέμνιον οὐκ ἐπάτησε. Both identify with Leto's capacity for pity (*Etym. Magn.* p. 564.18–19 K., s.v. Λητώ): 151–2 (Leto to Peneius) τῆσδε ἀντ᾽ ἐλεημοσύνης, cf. Stephens (2015) 203; and the lacuna at 201 may have contained a reference to Asteria's pity for Leto's grievous condition. Both display/respect χάρις: Leto at 152 χάριτος δέ τοι ἔσσετ᾽ ἀμοιβή; Asteria as charged/acknowledged by Hera (246) κακῶς ἐχαρίσσατο Λητοῖ. In addition, Plato etymologises Leto's name from 'the willing one' (*Crat.* 406a κατὰ τὸ ἐθελήμονα εἶναι), cf. ἐθέλει (4), ἐθέλουσαν (195) of Asteria/ Delos. See below, n.167.

[131] On νότιος δὲ διὰ χροὸς ἔρεεν ἰδρώς (211), Stephens (2015) 214 comments "'damp', because southerly winds were thought to bring rain." C. reflects the debated issue of the origin of the Nile flood: Herodotus had rejected snow-melt (2.22), without understanding the role of seasonal rains (cf. e.g. Strabo 2.3.3). On Leto's weakness, see Stephens, ibid. and Gigante Lanzara (1990) 139, on ἀλυσθενέουσα (212).

Leto does not, however, summon Eileithyia (contrast line 132), probably because that goddess remains under Hera's control, as in *HHApollo*, and Iris, who there duped Hera to fetch her, is realigned with Hera.[132] Instead, in a weakly-voiced prayer (212, εἶπε δ᾽ ἀλυσθμαί-νουσα), she appeals to Apollo himself for his (epiphany in) birth (212–15). The appeal (211), in particular ἤπιος, reflects Leto's own gentle personality, and it prefigures Apollo as the healer-god (Ἰήιος, Παι-άν);[133] yet it appears to offer no connection with the paean-cry, and indeed the repeated κοῦρε (212, 214) arguably distances the utterance from the παῖ-address characteristic of paean-aetiology.[134] A separate association with song may nevertheless be in play: two names in this passage, Ἰνωποῖο and Αἰθιοπῆος, were derived from the distinct senses of ὄψ ('voice' and 'face' respectively), and so the presence of etymo-logising is worth considering:[135] 'Inopos', etymologised from 'strength of voice', offers an immediate contrast with Leto's weakness of utterance (above), and at longer range, a link forward to the 'far-reaching' (255, ἐπὶ μακρόν) utterance of the riverine Deliades singing the *melos* of Eileithyia (255–7); and this reading would yield a further correspondence between the flooding Inopos (at 263) and Asteria/Delos' magniloquent speech (juxtaposed, at 266–73). All of which would reinforce a 'familial' association between Deliades and the Inopos-Nile; on this reading of the sequence of events, moreover, the Deliades' singing of the Eileithyia-song will represent a blending of old and new song, and will participate in the ultimate song-led reconciliation (below, Appendix II).

Callimachus' association of nurture and song did not of course originate with him. The Muses had their place in Hellenistic nymph-

---

[132] This is signalled at *HDelos* 215 (hymnist to Hera) νύμφα Διὸς βαρύθυμε, σὺ δ᾽ οὐκ ἄρ᾽ ἔμελλες ἄπυστος/ δὴν ἔμεναι (followed by Iris' intelligence) recalling *HHApoll.* 97 μούνη δ᾽ οὐκ ἐπέπυστο μογοστόκος Εἰλείθυια (kept on Olympus by Hera until tipped off by Iris). Cf. also (with Stephens) *HDelos* 222 (Leto) ἔνδοθι νήσου with *HHApoll.* 92 (all goddesses present on Delos except Hera and Eileithyia) θεαὶ δ᾽ ἔσαν ἔνδοθι πᾶσαι: aside from Asteria/Delos, Leto is alone in *HDelos*. For Iris' alignment with Hera, see below, p.92–3 with n.208.

[133] Paean to Apollo as healer: *HHApoll.* 516–19; cf. Apoll. Rhod. *Arg.* 2.701, 712; Ruther-ford (2001) 24–5. ἤπιος: of Leto, Hes. *Theog.* 406–7 (daughter of Titans Phoebe and Coeus) Λητὼ … μείλιχον αἰεί/ ἤπιον ἀνθρώποισι καὶ ἀθανάτοισι θεοῖσιν (her sister Asteria at 409). ἤπιος of Asclepius: Herod. *Mime* 4.18; Makedonikos *Paean to Apollo and Asclepius* 20; and esp. *Etym. Magn.* p. 434.15–18 K., s.v. ἤπιος.

[134] Williams (1975) 82, 85, on *HApoll.* 97–104; Rutherford (2001) 24–7.

[135] Etymology of 'Inopos': *Etym. Magn.* p. 471.30–32 K., s.v. Ἰνωπός· ὄνομα ποταμοῦ· ἀπὸ τοῦ ἲς ἰνός, καὶ τοῦ ὄψ ὀπός. ὃ σημαίνει τὴν φωνήν. This presumably reflects a lost literary text in which Inopos and 'voice' were explicitly juxtaposed. For etymology of 'Aethiops', see Stephanie West's note on *Odyssey* 1.22. For ὄψ (voice) in the paean, Limenios *Paean* 14 (of the *aulos*). Cf., perhaps, the fragmentary Pind. *Pae.* 3.93–4 (D3 Ru.)]ν σθένος ἱεράν/ χαλκ]έοπ᾽ αὐλῶν ὀμφὰν

nurture; and their ancient kinship with Nymphs, alluded to in the Callimachus' Muse-exchange (above) extended to care of the young, so that Muses are found alongside Nymphs as nurses and teachers of gods (Dionysus) as well as of favoured musicians.[136] The Muses' interest in nurture and education is variously documented in vase-painting, Platonic texts on education, and classroom Muse-cult.[137] Philoxenus the dithyrambist evidently spoke of the Muses as his *syntrophoi* (co-nurses) and/or *tithenai* (wet-nurses), and later reflections of that manifesto-text suggest a close association of the Muses as nurses of poets with the Muses in public and private cult.[138]

IV. GODS, ELEMENTS AND RECONCILIATION

(a) Hera and Leto

On the face of things, *HDelos* presents a pretty unequal contest. Hera, queen of Olympus, gripped by apparently irreconcilable anger, seeks through subordinate agents of terror to create terrestrial chaos in pursuit of what she sees as her personal interests. Leto, by contrast, is the mildest and most compassionate of goddesses (n.133), careful to respect Hera's cult domains (73–4), magnanimous even in disappointment (150–52), and deeply affectionate towards her unborn child (212–14). Certainly, she is conscious of carrying 'Zeus' children' (111); and Apollo himself compensates forcefully for her lack of aggression (below, n.146). But Callimachus' Leto is quite different from the character who cannily negotiates with Delos in *HHApollo*: alone, and ignorant of what 'the Fates' have in store, she is footsore (117), weighed down at the extremity of her pregnancy, and bewildered (116–17; 213). How, then, are we to 'read' Hera's persecution?

The proximate cause of Hera's anger is her awareness (57–8) that Leto alone will bear a son dearer to Zeus than Ares. She had good grounds for concern, in the light of Zeus' blistering attack on the

---

[136] Kourotrophic rivers and Muse-cult: Borthwick (1963) 230–31. Nymph-nurses of Dionysus: Larson (2001) 85–7; 181–2; 92–5. Muse-nurses identified as Nymphs: Eustathius on *Od.* 5.205. For a general account of Nymphs and Muses, see Otto (1956) 9–20, 23–31.

[137] Men. Rhet. *RG* III.413.25–6 Sp. (Euripides as nursling of the Muses).

[138] Queyrel (1988). See also A. Hardie (1997) 30–31 and Cairns (2000): these articles were written independently, but came to similar conclusions as regards Machon's and Hermesianax' reflections of an original text of Philoxenus. Cairns' view that the Muses as *syntrophai* are 'co-nurses' and not 'co-nurslings' is clearly right (as is his suggestion that Philoxenus' text was a programmatic antecedent for Callimachus). I also argued for the association of the texts with the cult of the Muses.

wounded Ares at *Iliad* 5.889–95 as the 'most hateful' (ἔχθιστος) of all gods, one who (says Zeus) takes his character and love of strife from his mother. Zeus directs Paieon to heal the wound, but intimates that if he were not his son, Ares would be consigned to the company of the Titans below Tartarus, so ἀίδηλος is he: 'destructive', of course, but with play on 'unseen' (sc. in Hades/Ἀίδης), and, as will emerge, of special interest for (formerly ἄδηλος) Delos.[139] Leto owes her unique place (μούνη, 57) in this theogonic scheme to her distinctively mild and compassionate character (above, and n. 133), traits that Zeus evidently wished to be passed on to his son (and daughter); and indeed Apollo is praised in *HApollo* (103–4) as 'a helper from the moment your mother gave birth to you'. The providential Zeus is breeding a new god, a benign terrestrial presence, as a component of a reformed Olympian authority.[140] Hera correctly foresees the displacement of her uniformly divisive son in the new dispensation, and seeks to prevent it by halting the birth: a hopeless venture in the nature of things, but also because (the Iliadic) Ares is himself such a childish, blustering and generally unsatisfactory character:[141] significantly for the reader's estimation of this god and his prospects of success, Ares' cacophony and its fearful impact at *HDelos* 140 takes its verb (reading homophonic ἔβραχεν ἦχος) from the fearful roar of the wounded and ineffectual Ares of *Iliad* 5 (859). It is also significant that ἦχος has its sequel in ἄραβος σάκεος (147, rattling of the shield), with Homeric reference both to the clanging of armour and to the symptoms of fear (chattering of teeth): Ares' 'echo' intimidates, but does no more.[142]

The ancient reader knows, however, that the Zeus/Hera marriage itself is indissoluble, notwithstanding patterns of turbulence, and that Hera's anger, whether directed at her husband personally or at the broader fulfilment of his will, must ultimately give way to some form of reconciliation: in the long term, Hera has a positive role to play in the workings of fate.[143] Within this narrative pattern, a recurrent feature is Hera's personal insecurity and concern for status, a character trait exquisitely exploited in Iris' address, reporting unwelcome developments

---

[139] The barb is guaranteed by the recall (900–1) of Paieon's earlier (401–2) treatment of the wounded Hades himself. For formerly ἄδηλος Delos, *HDelos* 53; and observe also the absence of 'Hades', conjoined to that of Ares' horses (277) οὐδ' Ἀίδης ... οὐδ' ἵπποι Ἄρηος.

[140] Cf. Arat. *Phaen.* 5 (the Stoic Zeus) ὁ δ' ἤπιος ἀνθρώποισι/ δεξιὰ σημαίνει, where Kidd cites Hes. *Theog.* 407 (above, n.133). Cf. also *HDelos* 214 (Leto to Apollo, with both immediate and longer term significance) ἤπιος ἔξιθι κόλπου.

[141] See Kirk's notes on *Il.* 5.872–87, 906, and esp. 890–1 ("Ares, whenever he is most fully personified in *Il.*, represents the worst and least heroic side of warfare.").

[142] *Il.* 4.504, 10.375, cited by Mineur (1984) 155, ad loc.

[143] Feeney (1984); Cairns (1989) 203.

on Delos (*HDel.* 218–27): in slavish near-hysteria, she seeks to appease and reassure Hera by projecting her Olympian powers on a level dangerously close to those of Zeus (whom she denigrates without naming, alongside Asteria).[144] And in instituting a vicarious reign of terror on earth, Hera has indeed sought to usurp the authority of the supreme god.[145] Yet she fails to act on the appeal for direct terrestrial action that accompanies her agent's (accurate, but not quite complete) intelligence report, precisely because she cannot act: Asteria has rejected her threats (203) and called her bluff.[146] Contrary to Iris' hymnic urgings (226, δύνασαι γάρ), she has no further recourse. An 'unintentional' pun (χέρα/Hera) by Iris in οὐ χέρα δείδιμεν ἄλλην/ θηλυτέρην (220, we fear no other feminine hand) highlights the paradox: 'Hera' inspires fear like no other goddess; but her 'hand', *qua* symbol of strength and compulsion, is emphatically 'feminine' (with undertones of 'gentleness': *LSJ* s.v. θῆλυς II.1), implicitly incapable of enforcement.[147]

Hera responds in what at first looks like a masterpiece of insecurity and rationalisation, charged with resurgent anger. Initially avoiding direct address or reference to Leto, she speaks to all Zeus' sexual partners (and by implication, those who lie in the future) as Ζηνὸς ὀνείδεα (240, shameful objects of Zeus), illegitimate liaisons which are yet acknowledged as 'marriages' (240, γαμέοισθε): affecting disdain, and indeed satisfaction with the outcome, she wishes that all such ὀνείδεα might wed and give birth 'thus' (240, οὕτω νῦν) in obscurity; and for good measure she 'quotes', from *HHApollo* (77–8), Delos' expressed

---

[144] Stephens (2015) 215–17 offers a good account, observing (215) that γνησίη (220, legitimate) "goes to the heart of the matter – Hera's fear for her own status". Iris duly acknowledges that Hera is supreme among 'goddesses'; but σὰ δὲ πάντα (219) recalls standard hymnic praise of Zeus.

[145] The concluding appeal (226–7), that Hera should defend her agents on earth (οἵ σεῖο πέδον πατέουσιν ἐφετμῇ), will be familiar to a modern readership: a brutal (but ultimately doomed) regime inflicted at the behest of an authoritarian ruler who remains remote from the realities. In context, πέδον πατέουσιν implies trespass on earth (cf. 74, 248), as well as the tramp of the soldier's boot (cf. Aesch. *Ag.* 1357).

[146] Both Apollo and Hera/Ares/Iris 'threaten': the difference is that Apollo's threats will, we know, be carried through to fulfilment, whereas Hera's will not. Bing (thesis as cited at Ukleja [2005] 60 n.277) observes etymologising play between ἀπειλήσας (87) and Apollo. The threat motif goes back at least to theft of Apollo's cattle: *HHHermes* 374; Alc. fr 308 V. (*POxy* 2734 fr. 1.15–16 Ἀπόλλω[ν/] αὐτῷ ἀπειλήσας; Schol. ABD *Il.* 15.256 ἀπειλοῦντος … Ἀπόλλωνος; Hor. *Odes* 1.10.10–11 *puerum minaci/ voce dum terret*). Cairns (1983a/2012) 30–32/207–9. Cf. also Call. *Aet.* fr. 18.6 Ha., …Ἰήιε, πολλὰ δ' ἀπείλει where Harder cites *Il.* 23.862–5 and 872 for 'vows' to Apollo). Apollo's capacity to counter the threats of others as future 'guardian' of Delos, underpins Asteria's robust rejection (οὐ … ἐφύλαξα) of '*your* [sc. Hera's] 'threats' (ἀπειλάς, 203; cf. ἠπείλησεν, 125; ἀπειλητῆρες, 69): this item is omitted from Iris' report!

[147] For the 'feminine' implications, cf. Nonn. *Dionys.* 8.55–6 (Envy, disguised as Ares, provokes Hera) ἦ ῥα καὶ αὐτῆς/ εἰς Σεμέλης ὑμέναιον ἐθηλύνθη χόλος Ἥρης;)

fear that in accepting Leto she risks rejection by Apollo, to become the haunt of 'black seals'.[148] Hera thus far rationalises her failure to prevent Apollo's birth in terms of the pre-Apolline obscurity of Asteria/Delos. Choking back resurgent anger, Hera then sidesteps Iris' vituperation, recalls that Asteria had not trespassed on her personal domain (her marriage-bed), and appears grudgingly to find within that memory the reassurance she needs to bow to the inevitable. Again in doing so, she 'quotes' from poetry, in this case Homer's account of Hera's own sexual deception of Zeus on Ida and specifically Hypnos' recollection, as she attempts to co-opt him into the plot, of Zeus' fury at his part in an earlier deception (*Il.* 14.256–61): Zeus would have 'thrown me from the *aither* into the sea'; Zeus was restrained from throwing Hypnos out of heaven only by reluctance to cause offence to Night, with whom Hypnos had taken sanctuary (261, μὴ Νυκτὶ θοῇ ἀποθύμια ἔρδοι).[149] Zeus' checking of his own anger on that occasion, and his reasons for doing so, parallel Hera's on the present occasion; and like δέμνιον (248) of her marriage bed, the 'quotation' underlines her recollection of their enduring relationship. Her speech thus concludes on a dignified note, acknowledging Leto by name, and bestowing on Asteria a mark of regal respect (247, ἀλλά μιν ἔκπαγλον τι σεβίζομαι) that will lead ultimately to Delos' graduation to the rank of goddess.

One way of 'reading' the saga, then, is as a study in divine psychology in the tradition of the acutely-observed interplay of personalities in the *Iliad*. Conspicuously absent, however, is the personality of Zeus. To be sure, we are regularly reminded that he is somewhere off-stage, for he is named eight times (38, 58, 111, 215, 240, 248, 259, 272);[150] and yet the disclosure that he 'had taken away [Hera's] anger' (259, ἐπεὶ χόλον ἐξέλετο Ζεύς) comes as a complete surprise. The reader is left wondering how the reconciliation has been effected, how Zeus' action relates to Hera's final speech, and indeed what concealed implications it might carry for the musical sequence that follows, and for the cycle

---

[148] *HHApoll.* 77 φῶκαι … μέλαιναι in residence; *HDelos* 242–3 φῶκαι/ εἰναλίαι giving birth. ὄνειδος was etymologised (*Etym. Magn.* 626.15–17 K., s.v.) as 'disgraceful sight', accentuating the proper 'invisibility' of such marriage and birth in the obscurity of (pre-Apolline) Asteria/Delos.

[149] The parallel with the Homeric *hapax* is well observed by Stephens (2015) 219. For Hera's momentarily resurgent anger, see also her note on possible aposiopesis at line 246; and for surging anger within a speech, compare the ominous dynamics of the Ovidian Juno's claim to be the eponymous goddess of month June at *Fasti* 6.21–64 (esp. 35–51).

[150] Hera is named seven times, and the seventh namings of Zeus and Hera (259) associate them in reconciliation, seven lines after seven circuits of Delos by Apollo's singing swans (251–2, ἑβδομάκις).

of anger, chaos and reconciliation as a whole. For this part of the hymnic design, one obvious line of approach lies through Apollo's relationship with the providential Zeus already observed in its 'Kynthian' context. It would be wrong, however, to focus on the agency of Zeus to the exclusion of all others, for in addition to Zeus, Hera and Apollo, we encounter no fewer than seven senior Olympians in *HDelos*: in total, nine members of the standard list of Twelve Gods (Dodekatheon) are named;[151] a tenth, Hestia, is referenced in a concluding assimilation of the immobile Delos at the centre of the Kyklades to the goddess who alone remains, unmoving, at the centre of the gods' house (325);[152] and only Athena and Demeter (subjects of the fifth and sixth *Hymns*), are absent. A Delian Dodekatheon was constructed towards the end of the fourth century, and while its composition remains quite uncertain, it is unlikely to have coincided with the standard list.[153] In parading the gods, however, Callimachus accentuates the 'universal' and Pan-hellenic, embracing a cult-pantheon which was common to many cities, and which for that reason was taken by Alexander to conquered territory: the poet may well have had in view a Ptolemaic cult-foundation in the Tychaion, close to the Mouseion.[154] As will be seen in the case of Poseidon, each god has a distinctive part to play in the Delian scheme of things.

(b) Poseidon

Poseidon's personality, like that of Zeus, is largely absent from *HDelos*, and perhaps for that reason critics have neglected his role. In a work that combines a pronounced anthropomorphic dimension with scientific doctrine and cult aetiology, however, it is worth asking whether the absences of 'personality' may themselves point to the presence of impersonal forces alongside (or in accommodation with) the mythic apparatus and the gods' civic cult centres. This would be consistent with the treatment of Nymphs in *HDelos*, as analysed in the previous

[151] For the standard list of Twelve Gods, see C. Long (1987) 140–41, 317–19.

[152] For the Hestia-comparison, Faulkner (2010), 59–61, and (observing fixity) Giuseppetti (2013) 107, 222. For Hestia and the Dodekatheon, see Plat. *Phaedr.* 247a, with Yunis (2011) 140 (Zeus leads eleven contingents of gods) μένει γὰρ Ἑστία ἐν θεῶν οἴκῳ μόνη. τῶν δὲ ἄλλων ὅσοι ἐν τῷ δώδεκα ἀριθμῷ τεταγμένοι θεοὶ ἄρχοντες κατὰ τάξιν ἣν ἕκαστος ἐτάχθη.

[153] For the cult, and attempts to reconstruct its membership, see Bruneau (1970) 438–41; C. Long (1987) 182, 198–201. Leto, though not an Olympian, was presumably a member of the Delian Dodekatheon.

[154] For the Dodekatheon as an 'integrative feature' of Greek civic religion (notwithstanding regional variations), see Rutherford (2010) 46, a feature which will have had special resonance for early Ptolemaic Alexandria. For a good discussion of the evidence for Alexander, and Alexandria, see C. Long (1987) 212–16.

section. The interplay of all three components (the so-called *theologia tripertita*) may be observed in Callimachus' delineation of Poseidon's assistance to Zeus in securing the intersection of Delos and Leto.[155]

Poseidon appears three times in *HDelos*. He is named twice (101, 271), in each case (Helikē and Corinth) in connection with a prominent cult site. His first appearance, however, is as the unnamed μέγας θεός (30) in Callimachus' suggestion as to the hymnic praises that Delos might wish to hear (30–32):

> ἢ ὡς τὰ πρώτιστα μέγας θεὸς οὔρεα θείνων
> ἄορι τριγλώχινι τό οἱ Τελχῖνες ἔτευξαν
> νήσους εἰναλίας εἰργάζετο ...;

> Is it how, as the very first thing, the great god, striking the mountains
> with the three-barbed weapon which the Telchines fashioned for him,
> made of them islands in the sea ... ?

The hymnist opens with a primordial (thus, πρώτιστα) *nesogonia*, the creation of islands by the 'great god', levering mountains into the sea with his trident.[156] The vignette is strongly anthropomorphic but conveys negative implications as an exercise in force and compulsion (ἀνάγκη).[157] It is nonetheless welcome to Delos, we infer, because it sets up a hymnic foil for her distinctive celestial origins and for her entirely voluntary acquisition of fixed-island status. Our first impression of the anthropomorphosed, primordial Poseidon is at best ambiguous, and that is why we are left to infer his identity from the anonymised μέγας θεός (hence also the variant wording for his emblematic τρίαινα). The Delian sequel, in which Asteria 'offers ground for Apollo's birth' (51, γενέθλιον οὖδας) and plants the 'roots of her

---

[155] For Poseidon on Delos, Bruneau (1970) 257–67; he takes the view (258) that Poseidon is given no role in the Callimachean fixture. For Poseidon's collaboration with Zeus in stabilising Delos and facilitating Leto's parturition, cf. Hyg. *Fab.* 140 (an otherwise unknown version); Lucian *Dial. Mar.* 9 τὴν νῆσον τὴν πλανωμένην, ὦ Πόσειδον ... ταύτην, φησὶν ὁ Ζεύς, στῆσον ἤδη καὶ ἀνάφηνον καὶ ποίησον ἤδη δῆλον ἐν τῷ Αἰγαίῳ μέσῳ βεβαίως μένειν στηρίξας πάνυ ἀσφαλῶς· cf. Ael. Aristid. *Or.* 3 (Poseidon) καὶ ἔστι γε οὓς καὶ ἀνέφηνεν ἐκ τῆς θαλάττης, ὡς τόν τε Ἀπόλλω καὶ τὴν Ἄρτεμιν. καὶ τούτων μὲν ὁ Ζεὺς εἰκότως ἂν χάριν αὐτῷ εἰδείη, ὅτι οὔτε τὴν Λητὼ περιεῖδεν ἐλαυνομένην πάντα τὸν χρόνον ὑπὲρ ὧν ἐτύγχανεν, οὔτε τὴν γένναν αὐτοῦ μικροῦ γε ἐξαμεληθεῖσαν. Contrast Nonn. *Dionys.* 33.336–40, where the aroused Poseidon pursues Asteria around the ocean until Apollo roots her immoveably. For Terentius Varro's *theologia tripertita* and its Hellenistic antecedents, see Lieberg (1982). Hor. *Odes* 3.4 again supplies a comparator: A. Hardie (2010) 195–7.

[156] Cf. Hes. *Theog.* 116; Aristoph. *Birds* 695. *Nesogonia* is Bing's term, (1988) 112. For primordial Telchines, see Mineur (1984) 79.

[157] There is an implicit critique in the contrasting σὲ δ' οὐκ ἔθλιψεν ἀνάγκη (35, of Asteria), which is echoed (along with μέγας θεός of Poseidon) in Ἀναγκαίη μεγάλη θεός (122). For related material on Zeus, force and compulsion in the 'tragic' background, see also Giuseppetti (2013) 110–21 (on *Prometheus Vinctus* and *HDelos*).

feet in the waves of the Aegean sea' (54; ῥίζας), recalls how Poseidon 'rooted' the mountains he rolled into the sea (35; ἐρρίζωσε), but it accentuates Asteria's retained capacity (notwithstanding her involuntary sea- and wind-borne movements in the meantime) to exercise free will at the crucial juncture, a character trait of great symbolic significance for the transition to the 'Apolline' era.[158] And now, in a present-day sequel, the γενέθλιον οὖδας stabilised by the 'feet' of Asteria/Delos provides 'safe ground' (306, ἀσφαλὲς οὖδας) for the dancing 'foot' (ποδί) of the chorus-girls (i.e. the modern Deliades [296]).[159] Both epithets connect with Poseidon: Genethlios was a widespread cult epiklesis, and ἀσφαλές echoes the Delian worship of Poseidon Asphaleios (appropriate for the 'immovable' island traditionally immune from earthquakes).[160] Furthermore, the island's (rooted) 'foundations' (260, θεμείλια) relates to the Delian cult of Poseidon *Themeliouchos* and in combination, to the Callimachean Apollo (*HApoll.* 57, 58, 64; p.63 with n.91).[161]

Three allusions to Poseidonian cult titles thus suggest positive alignment with Apollo's birth, and indeed with Delos as a safe platform for choric music. A famous (sc. 'future') cult-site of Poseidon supplies a further connection. Asteria, addressed (with her future Kykladean 'chorus' in view) as 'music-loving' (φιλόμολπε), makes her final journey from Euboea 'destined to see the Kyklades, laid out in the round' (198, Κυκλάδας ὀψομένη περιηγέας). She is followed, as it were in procession, by 'Geraistian seaweed' (199, τοι μετόπισθε Γεραίστιον εἴπετο φῦκος), evidently the uprooted product of the seabed, thrown up

---

[158] Delos' 'willing' acceptance of Leto (195, ἐθέλουσαν) is in polar opposition to past ἀνάγκη; for its Apolline force, cf. Aeschylus' treatment of the peaceful passage of the Delphic oracle from Themis to Phoebe (*Eum.* 5) θελούσης [sc. Themis], οὐδὲ πρὸς βίαν τινός, with Somerstein's note.

[159] There is some quiet humour in the capacity of the ground to withstand the beating it receives from the choric feet (306, ποδὶ πλήσσουσι); cf. 321–2 βωμόν ... ῥησσόμενον. With Delos as safe dancing ground, contrast Melia's experience of Helikonian *choros*, ὑποδινηθεῖσα 'whirled away from beneath' (79–82).

[160] Cf. esp. Lucian *Dial Mar.* 9 (cited n.155) στηρίξας πάνυ ἀσφαλῶς. For the cult and festival, Bruneau (1970) 260–64; Robertson (1984) 6; cf. Johannson (2001) 87–9. Poseidon and Apollo are also associated at Delphi: Aesch. *Eum.* 27 (connected with river Pleistos); Aristonoos *Paean* 34 (Furley–Bremer [2001] 45–52); Paus. 10.24.4.

[161] Poseidon Themeliouchos on Delos: *ID* 290.116; Bruneau (1970) 265. The concept of 'roots' is widespread in Greek cosmogony: see Schibli (1990) 70–71. For roots, foundations and Poseidon Asphaleios, cf. Opp. *Hal.* 5.679–80 (concluding prayer) γαίης δ' ἀστυφέλικτα Ποσειδάων ἐρύοιτο/ Ἀσφάλιος ῥιζοῦχα θεμείλια νέρθε φυλάσσων. Cf. also Hes. *Theog.* 816 (foundations/roots of Ocean), with West's note; Call. fr. 623 Pf. (ῥιζοῦχε Ποσειδῶν), with Pfeiffer's note; *RE* II.1726 (Jessen); V A.1625 (Kruse). Poseidon could also destroy: for the rampaging god wrecking foundations and uprooting trees, cf. Nonn. *Dionys.* 21.90–106.

by storm off Euboean Geraistos and attaching itself to Asteria:[162] this is an emblem of Poseidon (sc. the future Geraistios) that represents that god's control of the seas (and of sea-storms) and also foreshadows the island's auto-rooting, soon to follow.[163] What then are we to make of this highly symbolic final journey? We recall that Apollo's final injunction to Leto, 'bear me thither' (195, sc. to the unnamed floating 'island'), had intimated that the destination is a moving target, carried by sea and tide as well as the winds (193–4); and yet their early intersection is not a matter of happenstance, since the future participle ὀψομένη (198) signifies Asteria's predestined arrival among the Kyklades and not any conscious 'intention' on Asteria's part. We are to infer the assistance of Poseidon, operating through a combination of sea-currents and wind in the one domain where Ares and Iris (thus Hera) are impotent; and this inference is supported by comparison/ contrast with a sea-storm raised by the malign Poseidon in the *Odyssey* (5.286–331, esp. 286–90; also 339–40, 366–7, 375–9), an episode evoked earlier in Apollo's comparison of Asteria to an asphodel (193).[164] Asteria's sighting of Leto and courageous initiative in addressing her (and defying Leto) is itself modelled on the sea goddess Ino-Leukothea's sighting of, and pity for, the struggling Odysseus, and her courageous initiative in thwarting Poseidon and instructing Odysseus on how to save himself (*Od.* 5.333–50). We can now appreciate Apollo's juxtaposition of θάλασσα and ἐθέλουσαν (end-lines at 194–5): the 'sea' (that is, Poseidon; cf. 33) has brought Asteria to the Kyklades and to intersection with Leto; and her 'willing' character has prompted her bold initiative in hailing Leto.[165]

We are presented with an implicit contrast between the old Poseidon and his discreet Delian role, *qua* 'sea', in effecting the fated intersection: this contrast in time-zones, between the primordial and that of the Delian narrative, is brought out by repetition of τὸ παλαιόν (37, just after the *nesogonia*) in οὔ τι παλαιόν (198, of the final 'Geraistian' journey to the Kyklades); and the contrast between old and new is underscored by contrast with the malign Poseidon of the *Odyssey*.[166]

---

[162] Seaweed as product of storms: *Il.* 9.7 (*hapax*).

[163] Cf. esp. Posidipp. AB 20.5–6 (addressing Poseidon in the context of a vast boulder cast up on the shore at Alexandria (AB 19, 20), and surely echoing *HDelos*: νῦν δέ, Γεραίστι᾽ ἄναξ, νήσων μέτα τὴν Πτολεμαίου/ γαῖαν ἀκινήτην ἴσχε καὶ αἰγιαλούς.

[164] Bing (1988) 120–21 (but Apollo alone does not "select his conduit into the world"). Further details of this intricate intertext in Gigante Lanzara (1990) 134.

[165] Leukothea's 'pity' for Odysseus supports Mineur's suggestion ([1985] 184) that Asteria is motivated by pity as well as by 'willingness' (both character traits are shared with her sister: see above, n.130).

[166] Cf. Burkert (1985) 139 (Poseidon in the Homeric poems): "never winged with youth but always decidedly a member of the older generation."

πρώτιστα takes us to a different, distant, era, one characterised by
'compulsion', and it is to this same 'old' era that Asteria's 'flight' from
'marriage to Zeus' belongs (*HDelos* 38): φεύγουσα points to attempted
rape, and its unfavourable reflection on Zeus, already present in Pindar,
is strongly implied in the echoing 'flight' of the Greek regions, landmarks and rivers in the face of Hera's threats.[167] In the Callimachean
terms set out in *HZeus*, this 'old' era might best be located after Zeus'
overthrow of the Titans (Πηλαγόνων ἐλατῆρα) and before his incul-
cation of justice into what remained of the 'descendants of Ouranos'
(δικασπόλον Οὐρανίδῃσι).[168] All this lays down a kind of base-position
for what will emerge as a pattern of divine moral progression, reflected
most immediately in Poseidon's 'Delian' conduct , and more distantly
in the mature controlling role of the supreme god.[169]

    In addition to the positive Poseidonian role suggested here, the old
Poseidon functions as a reference point for the primordial character of
Ares' Delian actions. The latter seeks, in effect, to return to the past and
to usurp Poseidon's ancient powers to re-shape the land- and sea-scape.
Thus, the incipient threat to obliterate Peneius (Poseidon's creation:
Hdt. 7.179.4) with the ripped-up Mt Pangaion (133–5) picks up
Poseidon's formation of islands from levered-out mountains (30–35);
and the reaction of the landscape, 'all Thessaly dances in fear' (139–
40), recalls the figurative language of earthquake, reinforced by
reference to the Iliadic Poseidon shaking mountains.[170] Spreading

---

[167] Pindar: I incline to Rutherford's view ([2001] 250–51 that at line 42, the chorus-
narrator clothes the myth of attempted rape and its aftermath in disbelief; but there are
real difficulties in reading the key question τί πείσομα[ι; (42; 'what shall I [sc. 'Pindar'] believe'?; or 'what shall I [sc. Asteria] suffer?'); for a contrary view, see Furley–
Bremer (2001) 105. C.'s Asteria (38) φεύγουσα Διὸς γάμον (first naming of Zeus) is
echoed in the flight of lands, etc., at 70 (bis), 71, 72, 75, 103, 105 (treated contemp-
tuously by Apollo [95, to Thebe] φεῦγε πρόσω); cf. 310. Pindar's οὐκ ἐθέλο[ισα]/
Κοίου θυγάτηρ (the daughter of Coeus being unwilling [sc. to submit to Zeus]) is
especially telling both for Asteria's character and for 'early' Zeus: contrast C.'s
ἐθέλουσαν (195, of Asteria's willingness to accept Leto). Pindar's 'daughter of Coeus'
elsewhere designates Leto (Rutherford [2001] 250 n.23), and here he implicitly
contrasts Asteria with Leto, 'the willing one' (Plat. *Crat.* 406a), while appearing to
align (indeed almost to merge) the two sisters in other respects (hence ambiguity of
grammar/reference in τᾶς [50]); for the assimilation of the two, see above, n.130.

[168] This goes some way to explaining the dichotomy in *HZeus* between on the one hand
Zeus' acquisition of powers (65–6), not by lot but by 'deeds of your hands, your force
and might which you have set beside your throne' (ἔργα δὲ χειρῶν,/ σέ τε βίη τό τε
κάρτος, ὃ καὶ πέλας εἷσαο δίφρου) and on the other his concern for mankind and
justice and his establishment of an orderly division of responsibilities; see below, (c)
on Pindar's first *Hymn*.

[169] A striking parallel for Zeus' moral progression appears in Horace's account of Jupiter's
terror at the onslaught of the Giants: *Odes* 3.4.49; A. Hardie (2010) 224–5.

[170] Ares/Peneius and Poseidon: observed by Bing (1988) 112 n.37. Dancing and earthquake: Eur. *Erechth.* fr. 370.48–9 (Poseidonian earth-shaking at Athens) ὀρχεῖται δὲ

cacophony, shaking/'dancing' landscape and quivering fear across the Greek lands converge in the monstrous, counter-musical, epiphany of the war god: it is of course the antithesis of Apolline cult, which will extend from Delos and win acceptance and choric response from all Greek-speaking cities.[171] But it is ultimately pointless, since unlike Poseidon, Ares is unable to carry through his intentions: he is 'on the point of' sending Pangaion down upon Peneius (134, μέλλεν); but he does not actually do so, resorting instead to the equivalent of sabre-rattling. This fall-back works up to a point, because like any noise made by Ares (cf. *Il.* 5.862–3) it spreads fear; but in the end, the Callimachean Ares matches his counterpart in *Iliad* 5 as a god of bluff and bluster.

Poseidon, as a main source of discord in the *Odyssey*, also illuminates the conduct of the Callimachean Hera: he can obstruct Odysseus' return, but he cannot prevent it, and in due course, as predicted by Zeus at the outset, 'Poseidon will surrender his anger' (*Od.* 1.77–8, Ποσειδάων δὲ μεθήσει/ ὃν χόλον). A reconciliation of sorts is indeed effected between the god and his mortal adversary, as it is between Hera and Zeus in *HDelos*.[172] Vergil evidently observed this Callimachean version of Poseidon's progression, for the Neptune of the *Aeneid* is allied with the will of Jupiter, favourable to Aeneas and opposed to the chaotic machinations of Juno; and so he had good reason, it seems, to allude to *HDelos* in headlining the benign role of Neptune and the sea-goddesses in the Delos-episode of *Aeneid* 3 (73–4): *sacra mari colitur medio gratissima tellus/ Nereidum matri et Neptuno Aegaeo* (A sacred land is hallowed in the middle of the sea, very dear to the mother of the Nereids and to Aegean Neptune; trans. Horsfall).[173]

π[ό]λεος πέδον σάλωι·/ [ ].ἐμβάλλει Ποσειδῶν πόλει. Cf. esp. Poseidon's earthquake at Nonn. *Dionys.* 21.90–104 (land dancing [ὠρχήσατο] 102). And with *HDelos* 137–8 ἔτρεμε δ' Ὄσσης/ οὔρεα καὶ πεδίον, cf. *Il.* 13.18–19 (unique combination) τρέμε δ' οὔρεα μακρὰ καὶ ὕλη/ ποσσὶν ὑπ' ἀθανάτοισι Ποσειδάωνος ἰόντος ....

[171] Epiphany: for the sound of Ares' arms in auditory epiphany of the war-god, cf. esp. Ov. *Fast.* 5.549–52 (Mars Ultor).

[172] For Poseidon/Odysseus as a model for reconciliation after discord, see Cairns (1989) 189–90.

[173] Observe the sense of calm conveyed by this spondaic line. For the Delos-episode and *HDelos*, see Barchiesi (1994) and Horsfall (2006) 91–5. Vergil has his own reasons for deploying Neptune: not only the god's broad sympathies (*Neptunia Troia*, *Aen.* 3.3), but his resistance to the chaotic usurpation of his powers by Aeolus, at Hera's behest (*Aen.* 1.65–80; 124–56), a conceptual parallel for Ares in *HDelos*; cf. also Cairns (1989) 95 n.38.

(c) Zeus, and Pindar's First Hymn

A larger story, the moral progression of a divine regime, and of its
leader, now emerges from within the Delos narrative. Asteria, who
once resisted Zeus' rough wooing, now resists Hera's efforts to turn the
clock back, and in consequence is the (celestial) exception to Poseidon's primordial creation of islands by compulsion. Amelioration of
primordial governance is symbolised by Zeus' marriage to Leto (herself
of Titan descent), whose humane personality — shared with her 'kourotrophic' sister — will be passed on to her offspring, 'a son dearer to
Zeus than Ares.' We recall Pindar's Kynthian Zeus, the supreme god
who took providential guard over Delos to ensure the safe deliverance
of the helper god; and in *HDelos*, the son is saluted in his turn as
Kynthian Apollo.

Zeus has given a lead through the creation of an extended family
and a new generation of gods. To appreciate *HDelos* more fully as an
account, or at least a reflection, of Zeus' progress to mature divine governance, we may turn to another universal poem, Pindar's first *Hymn*.
Addressed in all probability to Apollo at the Theban Ismenion, it contained a theogonic narrative of the marriages of Zeus sung by the
Muses (under the direction of Apollo Mousagetes) at the wedding of
Cadmus and Harmonia.[174] The fixing of Delos acts as a terrestrial
microcosm for universal stability and reconciliation after the
Titanomachy, under the direction of the victorious 'saviour Zeus' (fr.
30.5 Ma., σωτῆρος ... Δίος).

The relevance of such poetry for Callimachus' *Hymns* has been
documented in an analysis of *HZeus* by Susan Stephens:[175] she shows
that the treatment of Zeus' birth is situated "within the context of the
earlier theogonic discourses of Hesiod, Epimenides, and Orphic and
rationalist traditions", and that Callimachus' account in *HZeus* of Zeus'
accession to power involves a similar engagement with the theogonic
tradition. The interest of the first *Hymn* for Delos lies in part in its

---

[174] Stephens (2015) 160, citing D'Alessio (2009). That the first *Hymn* was addressed to
Apollo and was performed at the Ismenion had been argued at some length by me (A.
Hardie [2000] 35–7, developing a footnote of Jane Harrison): D'Alessio (2009) 140–
42 advanced this as "the easiest hypothesis", citing only the Harrison footnote (which
does not specify the Ismenion; but D'Alessio separately (141 n.34) cited my article in
order to reject the suggestion that the hymn might have been a "*tripodephorikon* for
the Ismenion sanctuary". On that point, I would accept the difficulty of including such
a work among the *Hymns*; yet the prominence of Apolline tripods at the Ismenion (cf.
Pind. *Pyth*. 11.4–5), and their putative association with the Theban leadership of the
Boeotian Confederacy, remains of interest for the hymn's political setting.

[175] Stephens (2003) 77–114, esp. 79–91 (quotation from 91). She appends (114–21) a
brief account of *HDelos*, with a focus different that under discussion here.

treatment of the Delos myth within a theogonic narrative which incorporates and revises earlier cosmology.[176] In *HDelos*, the pre-Apolline relationship between *ouranos* and earth remains precarious, and vulnerable to the chaos engendered by Hera and her allies. Like Pindar, Callimachus presents his materials within a hymn-performance (located of course in present time), and he places the principal actions within a mythic context. Pindar uses his mythic context, the Theban wedding of Cadmus and Harmonia, to create a narrative of prior theogonic events (successive marriages of Zeus; his reconciliation with the Titans [fr. 35 Ma.]). Callimachus too reaches further back (Poseidon; Zeus/Asteria; nymphs and zoogony; and the pre-history of, for example, Samos), but he does so in his own *persona* as hymnist. By contrast, within the mythic context of the Delian narrative, he discloses what lay in the (then) future, through the unborn Apollo's prophecies; and he thereby reaches forward both to Apollo's legendary actions (the oracle at Delphi, the slaughter of Niobe), and to a contemporary historical *telos* in the reign of Philadelphus over 'willing' subjects (167), which, with the defeat of the latter-day 'Titans' (the Gauls), comes full circle to the founding myth of Zeus' divine regime.[177] Both poets also present materials outside their respective mythic contexts (Pindar's direct address to Delos [fr. 33c Ma.] as a hymnic adjunct to the narrative of the fixture [fr. 33d Ma.] may be an example). In each case, the hymnist moves backwards and forwards in time-zones, deploying universal (hence timeless) theological and cosmological statements alongside traditional anthropomorphic myth.

Although we have only a single fragment from Pindar's reconciliation narrative, Zeus' release of the Titans from their bonds (fr. 35 Ma.), its content can be inferred in outline from the miraculous fixture of Delos upon 'adamantine pillars' arising from earth-grown, tree-like foundations on the sea-bed (fr. 33d Ma.): the tree-pillars are surmounted by the island-stone to create a four-pillar cosmos-in-miniature, modelled on the architecture of a Greek temple.[178] The very antitheses of the earth-born γηγενεῖς, these pillars combine the Delian motifs of miraculous growth and fixture and represent the constructive use to which the powers of compulsion and confinement (sc. of the Titans, in

---

[176] A. Hardie (2000) 19 n.4 (bibliography); 23–6.

[177] The first *Hymn*, as a universal history, places Thebes within a cosmic conceptual frame, and suggests that civic ideals mirror the principles on which the cosmos itself is founded; A. Hardie (2000) with further references.

[178] Four-pillar cosmic model: A. Hardie (2000) 28–9; add Hes. *Theog.* 778–9 (Styx' mansion set on silver pillars reaching to *ouranos*); Schibli (1990) 69–77 on Pherekydes' 'cosmic tree'. Delos as 'temple': A. Hardie, ibid., citing G. Kirkwood; see also Furley–Bremer (2001) 139.

adamantine chains and on pillars) have now been put; and the entire island edifice, itself a 'star on earth' (fr. 33c.6 Ma., κυανέας χθονὸς ἄστρον), stands as a symbol of the reconciliation of Ge and Ouranos under Zeus' new order.[179] There is a strong case, on this basis, for conjecturing a narrative sequence leading from Zeus' victory in the Titanomachia and the confinement of the Titans to a reconciliation process in which Zeus married the Titan Coeus' daughter Leto and released the Titans, and thence to Leto's arrival on Delos, and its fixture as microcosm. Whether, and in what way, Hera's displeasure was registered is not known: hymnic reticence might have constrained explicit treatment; alternatively, her marriage to Zeus may post-date the union with Leto.[180]

At all events, Zeus' reconciliation with the Titans has a Theban sequel in the wedding of Harmonia (daughter of Ares and Aphrodite) and Cadmus (now reconciled with Ares). And the fixture of Delos has a musical sequel in the 'godbuilt sound' and 'straight music' of Apollo and the Muses (fr. 35c Ma., θεόδματον κέλαδον; fr. 32 Ma., μουσικὰν ὀρθάν) on that occasion. The Muses, fathered by Zeus for this express purpose, now celebrate his cosmic creation for a mortal (Theban) audience in their first terrestrial performance. Pindar's audience will have connected their θεόδματον κέλαδον with his hymnic address to Delos (fr. 33c.1 Ma.) χαῖρ', ὦ θεοδμάτα (hail, o godbuilt one), hence with the metaphorical assimilation of the four-pillared microcosm-island to a temple (fr. 33d.7–8 Ma.). Thus, a quasi-hymnic address to Delos exploits the island's fixture to set up an analogue between hymnic song and temple as honours to gods; and herein may lie one influence upon the Callimachean idea that hymnic poetry is a necessary component in the fully-realised creation of divinity, as *HDelos* itself helps to complete Delos' graduation to divine status.[181] The Pindaric antecedent for Callimachus' 'metapoetical' Delos, based upon an architectural 'island as temple' metaphor, sets up a further analogue between the universal poem and the cosmos itself (as also between the poet and Zeus as divine artificer).[182] But Pindar also ascribes the first terrestrial perform-

---

[179] For detailed argumentation, see A. Hardie (2000) 29.

[180] Pindar (like Hesiod *Theog.* 918–23) could have presented the marriage with Hera as the culminating *gamos* in the series, after Leto: thus Snell (1982) 77–8; there are unresolved difficulties as to the point at which Pindar's Zeus fathered the Muses.

[181] For an insightful reading of Pindar's creation of the Muses in order to hymn Zeus' creation, in relation to Callimachus' representation of Artemis' growth and progression in *HArtemis*, see Bing and Uhrmeister (1994) 28, citing Snell (from the German edition: in the 1982 translation, p. 78). For Hellenistic interest in comparison of hymns with other divine honours, cf. Theocr. *Id.* 22.223 γεράων δὲ θεοῖς κάλλιστον ἀοιδαί, with Sens (1997) 223.

[182] Poem and cosmos, poet and Zeus: A. Hardie (2000) 38, with works cited there. On

ance of the Muses to Thebes, and it may be that in echoing Pindar's opening survey of Theban figures (fr. 29 Ma.), associating Melia with Helikon, and then rejecting Thebe and Kithairon as his nurse, Callimachus was countering the Theban/Aonian focus of performed *mousike* in the first *Hymn*.[183]

(d) Space, Elements and Song

The recurring figure of the circle in *HDelos* has long been understood as a spatial and territorial analogue for choric song (thus, for example, the encircling Kyklades are explicitly compared to a chorus [300–301]). Less fully commented is the recurring juxtaposition of circle and straight line (another feature that *HDelos* has in common with Pindar's first *Hymn*):[184] among many examples, Hesperus looking down upon Delos 'surrounded by sound' (302–3) combines a vertical axis with encircling noise, as a sequel to the circular positioning of the 'choric' Kyklades (300–1); the singing swans that encircle Delos are followed by the fixture of the vertical lyre strings (253–4), then by the vertical rise of the Deliades' *melos* and its re-echo downwards by *aither* (249–58); and Ares offers a 'counter-musical' example, beating [sc. straight] spear against 'round' shield (136–7, 140, 147), and sending out an echo that travels laterally in a line from North East to South West.

A more elaborate combination, again negative, of circle and vertical axis appears in Apollo's prophesy of the Gauls' invasion of Greece, where the vast encirclement of Delphi (ἀμφιπεριστείνωνται, 179) is juxtaposed with the (vertical) rise of smoke from Gallic incendiarism. Furthermore, the Gauls are compared to the (circular) Milky Way, 'equal in number to stars when they flock most thickly in the air' (175–6):[185] as 'late born Titans', they are thus likened to a monstrous

---

'metapoetical' Delos, see below, §V(d).

[183] A. Hardie (2000) 20. Taken together at 77, Melia and Ismenos recall their juxtaposition in the first line (fr. 29.1 Ma.) and thus the marriage of Melia and Apollo, founding myth of the oracular Ismenion; this features elsewhere in Pindar (*Paeans* 7 [D7 Ru.] and 9 [A1 Ru.]; *Pyth*. 11), including as performance venue: see now the discussion in Kowalzig (2007) 371–82 (overlooking A. Hardie [2000]). The relationship between Thebe in *HDelos* and the first *Hymn* is I think put beyond doubt by Theocritus at *Id.* 17.67, Δῆλον κυανάμπυκα (in a passage otherwise closely related to *HDelos*): it echoes Thebe's appearance in the first *Hymn's* third line, κυανάμπυκα Θήβαν, and thereby acknowledges C.'s *comparatio* of Thebe and Delos; and indeed this comparison was itself foreshadowed by Pindar's own correlation of Thebe κυανάμπυκα and Delos as κυανέας χθονὸς ἄστρον (fr. 33c.6 Ma.); both Pindaric passages are noted also by Hunter (2003) 148, but without the conclusions drawn here.

[184] A. Hardie (2000) 25, 27–8.

[185] The Milky Way as τὸ γάλα (Aristot. *Meteor.* 345b31–346b10; Arat. *Phaen.* 476, with Kidd), with play on Γαλάται (etymology attested at Isid. *Orig.* 9.2.104, 14.4.25; and cf. esp. the *lactea colla* of the Gauls at Verg. *Aen.* 8.660); C. alludes in πλεῖστα κατ'

counter-chorus, and as 'white stars' on earth, they represent a sacrilegious antithesis to the terrestrial 'star' Asteria and to its encircling island chorus.[186] As the embodiment of barbarian 'Ares', the Gauls also represent the antithesis of the widely-claimed epiphany of Apollo that put them to flight.[187]

Within these richly allusive descriptions of Ares and the Gauls, a larger concept is in play, namely the potentially chaotic disturbance of the universe and its elemental equilibrium by the uncontrolled action of wind. Hermann Schibli sensed allusion, in the 'seven-chambered cave of the North Wind' (65, ἑπτάμυχον βορέαο ... σπέος) as stable for Ares' horses, to the sixth-century *Heptamuchos* (or *Theokrasia*, or *Theogonia*) of Pherekydes of Syros:[188] this early prose work, by a 'mixed theologian' (Aristot. *Meteor.* 1091b8; that is, one who 'does not account for everything mythically') combined divine genealogy, physical elements and cosmogony; and it placed the 'daughters of Boreas' as guardian storm-goddesses (doubtless embodying winds) in Tartarus.[189]

ἠέρα to the Aristotelian view of the Milky Way as location of πυκνότατα καὶ πλεῖστα καὶ μέγιστα τῶν ἄστρων (*Meteor.* 346a10, cf. 28) operating by combustion at the outermost *aer* (*Meteor.* 345b.30–32; 346a9, etc.). As circle: *Meteor.* 345b.25 τὸν τοῦ γάλακτος κύκλον; Arat. *Phaen.* 476–8, etc. In astronomical theory, these stars are nourished (cf. βουκολέονται?) by 'airlike', 'smokey' exhalations (ἀναθυμίασις) from earth (*Meteor.* 341b.8–10; Cic. *Nat.* 2.83 ... *exspirationibus et aer alitur et aether et omnia supera*, with Pease; Sen. *NQ* 6.16.2): contrast, therefore, with elemental (air/ fire) overtones, the Nilotic sequel, where the rebel mercenaries 'expire', ἀποπνεύσαντας (186) in 'fire' (186, ἐν πυρί).

[186] 'Titans' as counter-chorus is paralleled, significantly, in Hor. *Odes* 3.4: A. Hardie (2010) 258–9, 268–9. The Gauls as 'choric counterpart' to Asteria/Delos/Kyklades is suggested by intertextual reference (Gigante Lanzara [1990] 129) to Achilles' Myrmidons compared to wolves, their bellies glutted with prey (*Il.* 16.163 περιστένεται δέ τε γαστήρ), thus with intertextual word-play with 'star'. It is fixed by a complex intratext between ἀμφιπεριστείνωνται, stars, the quasi-sacrificial smoke at Delphi (179), the interplay of sight and hearing (179–81) and the address to Asteria at 300–3: Ἀστερίη θυόεσσα, σὲ μὲν περί τ' ἀμφί τε νῆσοι/ κύκλον ἐποιήσαντο καὶ ὡς χόρον ἀμφεβάλοντο·/ οὔτε σιωπηλὴν .../ Ἕσπερος, ἀλλ'αἰεί σε καταβλέπει ἀμφιβόητον. For a large, white, choric body as 'terrestrial stars', cf. Apul. *Met.* 11.10 (initiates in the procession of Isis): ... *linteae vestis candore puro luminosi .... hi capillum derasi funditus verticem praenitentes, magnae religionis terrena sidera ....*

[187] Epiphany: Champion (1995) 215–17. Cf. esp. Justin. 24.8.6 (eye-witness accounts of Apollo's epiphany) *nec oculis tantum haec se perspexisse, audisse etiam stridorem arcus ac strepitum armorum* and compare (a) *HDelos* 125, the epiphany of Ares on Haemus (Peneius to Leto) ἀπαύγασαι (followed by the clashing of arms) and (b) 180–85, the Gauls' as 'barbarian Ares' at Delphi οὐκέτι μοῦνον ἀκουῇ/ ἀλλ' ἤδη παρὰ νηὸν ἀπαυγάζοιντο φάλαγγας (followed by the list of armaments heard and seen at the temple). Consistent with these Apolline/Ares antitheses is Gigante Lanzara (1990) 131, reading the Gaul's κακὴν ὁδόν (184) as reversal of the Delphian ἱερὴ ὁδός leading to the sanctuary.

[188] Schibli (1990) 40 nn.77, 79; Stephens (2015) 190–91. Syros is in the Kyklades, not far from Delos.

[189] Schibli (1990) 40, 45.

Here we may glimpse an antecedent of later theories whereby cataclysmic phenomena such as earthquakes and volcanoes are caused by subterranean winds.[190] In *HDelos*, wind plays an intermittently disruptive role (see below), and in stabling Ares' horses in the cave of Boreas, Callimachus aligns the god with destructive winds.[191] At the same time he draws in the association of winds with Titans and Giants (itself based on the 'Titanic' genealogy of the winds in the *Theogony* [378–80]), hence also with Titanomachy: thus, the shield-clashing sequel to Ares' stabling of horses evokes the Hesiodic Titanomachy, and its cataclysmic impact upon earth and heaven (136, ἐσμαράγησεν; cf. *Theog.* 679, γῆ δὲ μέγ' ἐσμαράγησεν, same *sedes*);[192] and the landscape, including 'windswept' Pindus (138, δυσαεῖς), shakes (sc. as in an earthquake: above, n.170). There follows a comparison with Briareos, pinioned and shifting under Aetna, again with earthquake-effects (142, σείονται μυχὰ πάντα); and the vignette of the volcano πυρὶ τυφομένοιο (smouldering with fire) alludes to another challenger for cosmic power Typhaon/Typhos (also pinioned under Aetna, at Pind. *Pyth.* 1.15–16), and by extension to that monster's Hesiodic (and etymological) identification with winds.[193]

In these multiple allusions to wind, cataclysm and Titano/Typhonomachy, Callimachus comes strikingly close to the symbolic deployment of the winds in the *Aeneid*, where Philip Hardie has shown good reason

---

[190] For this, its physiological interpretation, and association with Titanomachy, see the now-classic account of P. Hardie (1986) 90–97. There is no incompatability between Pherekydes' storm goddesses as 'guardians' and the destructive power of winds: the power to guard can be the obverse of the power to destroy; and we may compare the varied conditions in myth of the 'Hundred-handers', sometimes imprisoned in Tartarus (see below, on Briareos), sometimes guardians of the Titans.

[191] For the claimed destructive power of 'Boreas' himself against city-walls, cf. *HDel.* 25–6. For Ares' horses assimilated to storm-winds, cf. (a) for the commonplace comparison, *Il.* 10.437 (Rhesus' horses) θείειν δ' ἀνέμοισιν ὁμοῖοι; and esp. Apoll. Rhod. *Arg.* 1158 Ποσειδάωνος ἀελλόποδες ... ἵπποι; (b) Leto's accusation (112–13) that the river Peneius in flight is 'competing with the winds', though he is 'not in a horse race'; (c) as parallel for C.'s 'stabling' (ηὐλίζοντο), applied figuratively to the winds, Quint. Smyrn. 14.482 (Aeolus' cave of winds) ἔνθ' ἄνεμοι ... δυσηχέες ηὐλίζοντο, surely echoing a Hellenistic original (also relevant is δυσηχέες, the malign echo of the entrapped winds, associated with war and death in Homer and to be compared with the Callimachean 'echo' ([ἠ̃χος], 140) of Ares' weapons); see below, n.209.

[192] Reinsch-Werner (1976) 177–9.

[193] See esp. Reinsch-Werner (1976) 180–82, also connecting C.'s portrayal of Hephaestus with that in Hesiod's Typhonomachy at *Theog.* 862–7 (again, in a simile); the allusion is fixed by *HDel.* 141 πυρὶ τυφομένοιο/ *Theog.* 867 πυρὸς αἰθομένοιο. For Typhaon/ Typhoeus and winds, see P. Hardie (1986) 94–5, citing *Theog.* 869–80 ἐκ δὲ Τυφωέος ἔστ' ἀνέμων μένος ὑγρὸν ἀέντων (but with the exception of Notos, Boreas and Zephyros), with an extended description of their destructive powers on sea and land. For Hesiodic Typhoeus as antecedent of Pherekydes' cosmic challenger Ophioneus, see Schibli (1990) 93–6.

to think that Vergil was influenced by allegorising interpretation of
Hesiodic theomachy in meteorological terms, as "seasonally recurring
struggles between cold and warm exhalations in the course of which all
parts of the world suffer disturbance"; and again, "[t]he Hesiodic
battles are interpreted [sc. in Byzantine commentaries] as descriptions
of the storms which accompany the seasonal opposition of the elements
…".[194] If Hardie is right in suggesting that this kind of physiological
allegoresis derives ultimately from the older Stoa, then it may well
have been in gestation at around the time that Callimachus was
writing.[195] The rhetorical term ἀλληγορία itself is not attested before
the first century BC, but defensive readings of certain 'scandalous' passages of Homer as representing a physical or moral subtext goes back
at least to Theagenes of Rhegium (and perhaps to Pherekydes before
him), and will have developed gradually, no doubt embracing advances
in Presocratic philosophy (including the elemental theories of Empedocles).[196] Of direct interest for *HDelos* is evidence of a Peripatetic
reading of Delos in Pindar's first *Hymn*: Theophrastus adduced Pindar's address to the island as 'daughter of Pontus' (fr. 33c.3 Ma.) in
support of his view that islands emerge from the subsiding sea (a
component of his theory of the diminution and coalescence of elements
[στοιχεῖα]).[197] Theophrastus used αἰνιττόμενος (hinting cryptically) of
what he took to be Pindar's own allusion to his own theory, a term that
later acquired a wide field of allusive reference, up to and including
full-fledged allegory.[198] The value of this text lies in the interest of
Delos as a subject of poetry for the leader of the Peripatetics, a school
which had close personal contacts with the early Mouseion;[199] and
indeed Theophrastus' (Pindaric) αἰνιττόμενος may offer a clue to the

---

[194] P. Hardie (1986) 95–6.

[195] P. Hardie (1986) 95. For a careful, if sceptical, analysis of early Stoic activity in this
area, underlining the importance of allusive etymologising, see A. Long (1992), esp.
57–64.

[196] Feeney (1991) 8–11; for Pherekydes, see Schibli (1990) 99 n.54.

[197] Theophr. *Phys. Opin.* fr. 12 θυγατέρα γὰρ Πόντου τὴν Δῆλον εἴρηκε τὸ λεχθὲν
αἰνιττόμενος. There follows a complex analysis of diminution of sea and of Ge, then
of lessening air into the 'one entity of fire'. For Pindar's four-element cosmos in the
first *Hymn*, cf. Philo *de Plant. Noe.* 127 (Zeus asks whether he has omitted anything in
his creation) … εἴ τι ποθεῖ μὴ γενόμενον τῶν ὅσα κατὰ γῆς καὶ καθ᾽ὕδατος ἢ ὅσα κατὰ
τὴν μετάρσιον ἀέρος ἢ τὴν ἐσχάτην τοῦ παντὸς φύσιν οὐρανοῦ γέγονεν. Philo does
not cite Pindar: for the (probably indirect) relationship to the first hymn, see A. Hardie
(2000) 33–4 (and for other elemental features, ibid. 27 with n.69).

[198] See Nünlist (2009) 225–7 (excluding instances from allegoresis).

[199] Brink (1946) 11–12; this is not to exaggerate institutional Peripatetic influence on the
Mouseion: cf., with varying degrees of scepticism, Brink (1946) 26; Pfeiffer (1968)
95–7; Lynch (1972) 121–3; and (for a more positive view) Fraser (1972) 314–16.
Ptolemy I Soter invited Theophrastus to Alexandria (Diog. Laert. 5.37) and succeeded
in attracting Demetrius of Phaleron.

appeal of Delos as metapoetical symbol: not just 'small' and 'pure', that is, but a medium for the recovery of the ἄδηλον through the δῆλον, and thus for the allusive character of Callimachean hymnic poetry.[200] With Theophrastus' elemental reading in view, therefore, I would now offer an outline account of 'elemental' references and symbolism in *HDelos*, beginning with Ares and Hera.

Ares' mountain-top, 'guarding' (ἐφύλασσε, 64), reverses the Pindaric Zeus' benign guardianship from above Kynthos (above, p.51), and at the same time picks up the Iliadic Zeus' positioning on Ida, between heaven and earth.[201] To that subversion of Zeus' distinctive mountain-top location may be added a cosmic/elemental dimension within the same passage: Hera takes up her observation post 'within the *aither*' (αἰθέρος εἴσω, 59), an elemental positioning potentially at odds with her traditional identification as the lower 'air' (ἀήρ).[202] In her anger, Hera has infringed the aetherial/fiery domain of Zeus, and *physica ratio* would seem to be in play, alongside traditional anthropomorphism: the cause of Hera's particular anger with Leto lies in the coming birth of a son 'more dear [to Zeus] than Ares' (58), where juxtaposed φιλαίτερον Ἄρεος sets up wordplay with αἰθέρος (59) and also, by anagrammatic suggestion, between Ἄρεος and implied ἀέρος.[203] In physiological terms, Apollo will be 'more dear than Ares' because the the war-god's realm, like that of his mother, lies in the

---

[200] Cf. Bing (1988) 141; above, n.69.

[201] Zeus and mountain-tops: Cook (1914–40) I.124–48. With Ares ἥμενος ὑψηλῆς κορυφῆς (63), cf. *Il*. 14.157 (Zeus) ἐπ' ἀκροτάτης κορυφῆς ... ἥμενον, a variant on the formula at *Il*. 8.51 and 11.183 echoed by Pindar. Ares stables his horses (ἵππω) in the cave of the (destructive) North Wind (64–5) while Zeus 'shed thick air' (κατὰ δ' ἠέρα πουλὺν ἔχευεν, 50) over his horses (ἵππω, 41). Zeus 'between heaven and earth': *Il*. 8.46 (his horses take him to Ida) μεσσηγὺς γαίης τε καὶ οὐρανοῦ ἀστερόεντος (this is the realm of ἀήρ: cf. ἠέρα above, as 'stable').

[202] Hera and *aer*: Plat. *Crat*. 404c (cited next note). *RE* VIII.398 (Eitrem); Baxter (1992) 'Index of Greek Words' s.v. Ἥρα; Feeney (1991) 9 (citing *Il*. 21.6–7); 88 n.109 (citing Apoll. Rhod. 3.210–11, 4.578, 646–8); 132, 329. Zeus and *aither*: Cook (1914–40) I.25–33; Schibli (1990) 43–4; cf. Feeney (1991) 149–51, 329; and see below, nn.205, 210. αἰθέρος εἴσω (59) is not readily paralleled; the closest extant conjunction of the words is *Il*. 16.364–5 (Zeus sends a storm) ὡς δ' ὅτ' ἀπ' Οὐλύμπου νέφος ἔρχεται οὐρανὸν εἴσω/ αἰθέρος ἐκ δίης, where the Homeric scholia, and in particular Eustathius' comments indicate ancient puzzlement over the topography of cloud and storm, with attempts to equate οὐρανὸν εἴσω with *aer*, and αἰθέρος ἐκ δίης with Zeus' higher domain. For Aristarchus' view that in Homer ἀήρ means the 'lower air', see Williams (1978) 20, on *HApollo* 5.

[203] Nonnus picks up the φιλαίτερον/αἰθέρος play at *Dionys*. 10.307–8 (αἰθέρι/φιλαίτερον: Dionysus prefers life as Maionian Satyr to *aither*/Olympus, and relinquishes the appurtenances of Zeus' power to other sons). For Ares and air, see next n. With the implicit Ares/*aer* anagram (as I see it), cf. the Socratean etymology at *Crat*. 404c ... ἴσως δὲ μετεωρολογῶν ὁ νομοθέτης τὸν ἀέρα Ἥραν ὠνόμασεν ἐπικρυπτόμενος, θεὶς τὴν ἀρχὴν ἐπὶ τελευτήν.

turbulent lower air, whereas Apollo (the future sun-god) will be a god of the bright sky, elementally aligned with aetherial 'Zeus'.[204] The presence of elemental symbolism is further signalled in Hera's concluding declaration of regard for Asteria/Delos (247–8): ἐμεῖο/ δέμνιον οὐκ ἐπάτησε, Διὸς δ' ἀνθείλετο πόντον (she did not leave her imprint on my bed; but chose the sea instead of Zeus), where the implicit equivalence of Zeus and 'sky' is clear enough.[205] Elemental and scientific allusion may be further illustrated from the fate of the Gallic rebels (185–6) αἱ δ᾽ ἐπὶ Νείλῳ/ ἐν πυρὶ τοὺς φορέοντας ἀποπνεύσαντος ἰδοῦσαι (... and some [shields] seeing their bearers expiring in fire by the Nile ...): Callimachus is here making play around Herodotus' explanation for the absence of exhalation of air from the Nile (2.26, τῆς αὔρης δὲ πέρι, ὅτι οὐκ ἀποπνέει), namely ambient heat.[206]

The element *aer*, benign in fine weather, is subject to periodic turbulence (wind, rain, cloud and storm) and thus to disruptive forces which, if not held in check by the providence of Zeus, will threaten the cohesion of the cosmos. Within the elemental identification of *aer* with Hera, such meteorological irruptions may be represented in poetry as the goddess's inner mental turmoil and anger:[207] in *HDelos*, Hera's intrusion on *aither* is the corollary of her intense anger, urged on by Iris

---

[204] Ares and *aer*: cf. (a) *Il.* 5.355–6 Ares sitting aside from battle, his spear and horses leant against air/cloud (ἠέρι δ' ἔγχος ἐκέκλιτο καὶ ταχέ᾽ ἵππω); (b) *Il.* 5.889–95, Zeus' fury with Ares, the renegade son who takes his character and love of strife from his mother, together with Homer's preceding Ἄρης/ἀήρ simile (864–5, cited below, n.209); and (c) *HDelos* 173 and 176, the Gauls as Κελτὸν ... Ἄρηα compared to the (Milky Way) stars κατ᾽ ἠέρα (above, n.185). Add Apoll. Rhod. *Arg.* 1033–4 (Ἀρήιον ὄρνιν speeding δι᾽ ἠέρος); and for Ares and cloud, Nonn. *Dionys.* 10.301. Ἄρης and ἀήρ both have ἀείρω (lift) among their etymologies: *Etym. Magn.* pp. 23.8, 140.20 K., s.vv.; *HDelos* 133–4 has Ἄρης, ἀείρας at successive line-ends (cf. Moschus *Eur.* 144). There is elemental significance in Hera's watch (σκοπιὴν ἔχεν, 59) matched by Ares (σκοπιὴν ἔχει, 126, recalling *Od.* 8.285, where Ares watches Hephaestus and Aphrodite): the Hera-watch recalls *Od.* 8.302 (σκοπιὴν ἔχεν in the same *sedes*: the sun keeps watch for Hephaestus on Ares and Aphrodite), and thereby underlines her presumptuous intrusion into the fiery domain. For striking Vergilian illumination of *HDelos* 58–9, cf. Verg. *Aen.* 12.790–92 ... *Martis anheli* [i.e. Mars as metonymic battle (cf. *HDelos* 173), combined with 'gasping', sc. for air]./ *Iunonem interea rex omnipotentis Olympi* [the shining mountain/sky: Maltby (1991) s.v.]/ *adloquitur fulva pugnas de nube tuentem* (cf. *HDelos* 59, σκοπιὴν ἔχεν; Servius ad loc.: *de aere, de elemento suo*); and cf. also the post-reconciliation sequel at 842 *interea excedit caelo nubemque relinquit* (thereby, resuming her elemental location as *aer* while clearing the sky of the *fulva nubes*).

[205] For 'Zeus' as 'sky' in Aratus' *Phaenomena*, see Kidd (1997) 162 (citing lines 224, 253, 259, 756).

[206] Hdt. 2.26 ... κάρτα ἀπὸ θερμέων χωρέων οὐκ οἰκός ἐστι οὐδὲν ἀποπνέειν, αὔρη δὲ ἀπὸ ψυχροῦ τινος φιλέει πνέειν. This relates back to Herodotus' theory of winds, heat and rain in relation to the Nile (25–6). 'Exhalations' may also be relevant to C.'s comparison of Gauls to Milky Way stars: above, n.185.

[207] P. Hardie (1986) 229; Feeney (1991) 150.

(here a 'lower-air' meteorological phenomenon, beholden in slave-like subservience to Hera alone);[208] and the chaotic power of wind, like the malign interplay of noise and echo (hence of air as the medium of sound), is a recurring theme, deftly associated with Ares.[209] The scientific explanation for such phenomena focused on "the perpetual alternation of antagonism and rapprochement between the elements of *aer* and *aether* ...".[210] these phenomena had their anthropomorphic counterpart in the recurrent quarrels and reconciliations of Zeus and Hera; and indeed the overlay of *aither* upon *aer* lent itself, in sexual terms, to figurative *coniunctio*.[211]

Hera does not feature in what survives of any known Delian paean; and again, while Pindar appears to have adopted a four-element cosmos in the first *Hymn*, and certainly narrated the reconciliation of Zeus and Titans, there is no sign of Hera in what remains. We cannot, therefore, account for the reconciliation simply and solely by reference to Zeus' role in the Pindaric models:[212] on the contrary, there must be a worked-through Callimachean rationale for this central development, however dependent for full recovery and interpretation it may be upon (marked) intertextual allusion. The reading that follows offers an outline approach, starting with the hymnic reticence of the key line (259), οὐδ' Ἥρη νεμέσησεν, ἐπεὶ χόλον ἐξέλετο Ζεύς (and Hera found no fault, since Zeus had taken away her anger). Reticence is evident also in the delicately oblique allusion to Zeus' relationship with Leto (39), following Asteria's flight: οὔπω τοι χρυσέη ἐπεμίσγετο Λητώ (not yet did

---

[208] Iris: cf. the Homeric (also *HHApoll.* 107, Iris fetches Eileithyia from Olympus) ποδήνεμος ὠκέα Ἶρις. *Etym. Magn.* p. 475.39 K., s.v.: σημαίνει καὶ τὴν νεφελώδη ζώνην. *LIMC* V.1.742; 747–8. In *HDelos*, her 'airy' character and subservience is exquisitely conveyed in her breathless fear (217, ἀσθμαίνουσα) before Hera; see above, n.204 (Vergil's *anheli Martis*) and n.185 (expiring Gauls); below, n.261 (breathless Melia).

[209] Ares as agent of 'wind': see above, n.191. Signalled at 138–9 δυσαεῖς ἐσχατίαι Πίνδοιο, with which (and with cross-reference to Ares' post at *HDelos* 63), cf. *HArt.* 114–15 (Artemis's chariot), Αἵμῳ ἐπὶ Θρήικι, τόθεν βορέαο κατάιξ/ ἔρχεται ... δυσάεα κρυμὸν ἄγουσα. Fundamental is Homer's extended 'air-wind' simile of the wounded Ares (*Il.* 5.864–5) οἵη δ' ἐκ νεφέων ἐρεβεννὴ φαίνεται ἀήρ/ καύματος ἐξ ἀνέμοιο δυσαέος ὀρνυμένοιο .... Malign 'echo': *HDelos* 140 τοῖος ἀπ' ἀσπίδος ἔβραμεν [ἔβραχεν] ἦχος (from *Il.* 5.859). For the scientific association of noise and air, see Aristot. *De Aud.* 800a1–17. 'Echo' and air: Emped. 31 A 86.29–30 D–K; Aristot. *De Anima* 419b25–7; *De Aud.* 802a17–19, etc. *Etym. Magn.* p. 440.30 K., s.v. ἦχος· ...ἡ εἰς ἀέρα χεομένη φωνή.

[210] Quotation from Feeney (1991) 150; he cites Plutarch ap. Euseb. *Prae. Ev.* 85c–86d for the Plataean Daedala festival (enacting the rupture and reconciliation of Hera and Zeus) as a ritual representation of the "tussle between *aer* and *aether*".

[211] Cf. Cic. *ND* 2.66, with Pease ad loc.; Serv. *Aen.* 1.47; Corn. *Epidr.* 3; A. Hardie (2010) 236–7, with n.58.

[212] Contrast, e.g., Giuseppetti (2013) 121. The conundrum (another Callimachean challenge to the reader) is not resolved by Mori (2012).

golden Leto have dealings with you), where 'you' is Asteria, but in context, ἐπεμίσγετο acquires secondary sexual colouring from the neighbouring Διὸς γάμον (38). At one level, then, Callimachus may be offering a 'coy' allusion to Hera's positive memories of sexual re-lations between herself and Zeus, an inference supported by Hera's reference to her marriage-bed (247–8, cited above), and by her 'quotation' of a scene from her own sexual deception of Zeus on Mt Ida, in *Iliad* 14.[213] This Homeric event is referenced at several places in *HDelos*. Thus, οὐδ' Ἥρη νεμέσησεν (259) echoes οὐ νεμεσητόν (16), where 'no blame attaches to' praise of Delos' choric leadership of pro-cessions to Oceanus and Tethys, a reminder of Hera's deceitful claim to Zeus that she plans to visit Oceanus and Tethys to effect a reconcili-ation and restore their sexual relationship, which has been interrupted by χόλος.[214] On that occasion, Hera's response when Zeus presses her to have sex there and then, is that visibility to the other gods will be a source of disgrace for her (336, νεμεσσητὸν δέ κεν εἴη): Zeus works around the objection by drawing a cloud over matters.

The *Iliad* 14 encounter between Zeus and Hera is again referenced when Delos, on her way 'to see' (198, ὀψομένη) the Kyklades, spots Leto and comes to a halt (200): ὡς δ' ἴδες, [ὡς] ἔστης (and as you saw, so you stood); similarly, Zeus on Ida spots Hera, is overwhelmed by *eros*, and stands before her (294–7): ὡς δ' ἴδεν, ὡς μιν ἔρως ... φρένας ἀμφεκάλυψεν ... στῆ δ' αὐτῆς προπάροιθεν ... ἔκ τ' ὀνόμαζεν· Ἥρη ... (and as he saw, so did love cloud his wits ...; and he stood before her ... and addressed her by name: 'Hera ...').[215] The text of *HDelos* is defective at this point, but that it relates to *Iliad* 14 seems clear enough: the point seems to lie in the unobtrusive intimation (unremarked by commentators) that Delos finally comes to a standstill (ἔστης) on spotting Leto; and thus, that her final stabilisation, and the emotions that accompanied it, are correlated intertextually with Zeus' enduring love for Hera.

---

[213] For reticence on the Hera/Zeus sexual relationship, cf. Call. *Aet.* fr. 75.4–5 Ha., with Harder (2012) II.584–5. χόλον ἐξέλετο Ζεύς (259) reverses Homeric φρένας ἐξέλετο Ζεύς, itself twice used of mental derangement, but in the context of reconciliation scenes (*Il.* 6.234, 19.137); the former involves Glaucus' exchange of gold armour for Diomedes' bronze (near-proverbial: Plat. *Symp.* 219a, χρύσεα χαλκείων), and is thus germane to C.'s context, following the re-echo of the birth-song from αἰθήρ/ χάλκεος (257–8) and preceding the 'golding' of Delos, χρύσεα (260, and successive lines).

[214] *Il.* 14.304–6 (Hera to Zeus) τοὺς [Oceanus and Tethys] εἶμ' ὀψομένη, καί σφ' ἄκριτα νείκεα λύσω·/ ἤδη γὰρ ... ἀλλήλων ἀπέχονται/ εὐνῆς καὶ φιλότητος, ἐπεὶ χόλος ἔμπεσε θυμῷ.

[215] The same text is imitated at Theocr. *Id.* 2.82 (on which see Gow's note). With C.'s ὀψομένη (198, Asteria's last journey), cf. *Il.* 14.205, 301, 304, all in the same *sedes*, of Hera's claimed intention to 'see' Oceanus and Tethys.

Within the narrative sequence of *HDelos*, however, it is difficult to infer that Zeus has literally resumed sexual relations with Hera, or that his action in removing her anger can be understood simply in personal terms, as the corollary of such a resumption. Rather, we are prompted through Hera's positive memory of love-making with Zeus to recall their mythic intercourse, to reflect on its elemental symbolism, and to read it into Callimachus' narrative merger of the mythic and anthropomorphic with the physical and scientific. Whether the physiological interpretation of the Zeus/Hera scene on Ida as the union of *aither* and *aer* had achieved currency by this time is not quite certain; yet given the literary evidence associating both Hera and Ares with elemental air and wind, it is tempting to read οὐδ' Ἥρη νεμέσησεν (259) in meteorological terms as a reference to (no) 'wind', unobtrusively cued by recall of οὐ νεμεσητόν (16) and its verbal play with ἠνεμόεσσα (11, of Delos), and paralleled elsewhere in Apolline epiphany by topical 'calmness of weather', 'absence of wind' (νηνεμία).²¹⁶ To substantiate this line of approach, we may turn to the sequence of events following Hera's concession speech, and within it to the elemental dimension of song accompanying and following the birth of Apollo.

Hera's concession reflects awareness of her inability, through her appointed aerial agents (Ares, Iris), to control the seas (that is, the independent maritime authority of Poseidon, now evidently aligned with the providence of Zeus for Asteria's final sea-journey to her intersection with Leto). After the concession, we read (249) ἡ μὲν ἔφη. κύκνοι δὲ .../ ... Πακτωλὸν ἐκυκλώσαντο λιπόντες/... περὶ Δῆλον ... (She spoke; and the swans ... leaving Pactolus circled around Delos ...), where μέν ... δέ associates the swans' action with Hera's speech, implying that it is a responsive sequel to what she has said.²¹⁷ Hera's elemental conclusion, Διὸς δ' ἀνθείλετο πόντον (see above) is articulated as the divine personification of air: she is speaking, in other words, in audible epiphany through the medium of *aer*, and it is this, I

---

²¹⁶ Calm/absence of wind: see below, nn.223, 224. νέμω is common to the two etymologies: *Etym. Magn.* pp. 103.40, 600.29–30 K., s.vv. ἄνεμος, Νέμεσις. Cf., perhaps, *Anth. App.* 6 (*Oracula*) 58 ἰσόν τοι Δῆλόν τε Καλαύρειάν τε νέμεσθαι/ Πυθώ τ' ἠγαθέην καὶ Ταίναρον ἠνεμόεσσαν. At Quint. Smyrn. 14.421–2, Athena's anger as the Greeks near windy Euboea foreshadows the winds that will be sent to wreck the fleet: νεμέσησεν Ἀθήνη/Εὐβοίης ... ἠνεμοέσσης. Separately, Iris' reference to Zeus as τὸν αἴτιον ... ὀργῆς (the one responsible for your anger) may echo early physiological accounts of the mythic Zeus as (sc. the physical force) αἴτιος for life: cf. e.g. Cornutus ap. *Etym. Magn.* p. 408.52–5 K., s.v. Ζεύς; Schol. *Il.* 1.399–406.

²¹⁷ ἡ μὲν ἔφη ... δὲ is unhomeric, but is exactly paralleled at *HAth* 82, where Night's blinding of Tiresias, though separate from Athena's speech of condemnation, is its consequence.

suggest, that prompts the swans' response.[218] Callimachus offers a complementary perspective on the swan's song in *HApollo*, where the bird 'sings beautifully in the air', presaging the god's epiphany (5, ὁ δὲ κύκνος ἐν ἠέρι καλὸν ἀείδει): in *HDelos*, that epiphanic phenomenon is given an *aition* embracing the singing swans' aerial 'midwifery' role (documented below, p.109) in effecting the birth of the god, and thus in facilitating his first epiphany.[219]

Swan-songs traditionally resonate with the landscape around or below.[220] That is not quite the case in *HDelos*: rather, Apollo is born, and the Delian landscape Nymphs respond to the god's birth-epiphany with the 'far-sounding' (255, ἐπὶ μακρόν) 'sacred *melos* of Eileithyia', which rises vertically, to the 'bronze *aither*' (257–8), which in turn 'sings [echoes] back the piercing *ololyge* in response'.[221] This sequence re-works topical descriptions of the impact of divine epiphanies, imminent or in progress: miraculous light and sound effects that link earth and heaven;[222] and the calming, and silencing of the natural world (land, sea, air/wind, beasts).[223] Of special interest is Aristophanes'

---

[218] For 'voice' epiphany from celestial regions, cf. Eur. *Bacch.* 1078–9 (Dionysus) ἐκ δ' αἰθέρος φωνή τις ... ἀνεβόησεν. With Iris' stillness and alertness (ears pricked up) awaiting Hera's voiced command (230–32) cf. the maenads' awaiting Dionysus' epiphanic command at *Bacchae* 1086–7. Hera as 'air' could serve benign musical purposes (wind instruments): cf. esp. *App. Anth.* 6.124.6; A. Hardie (2007) 553. Birds and *aer* (hardly requires illustration): *Il.* 3.7; Aristoph. *Birds* 550–51; Aristot. *De Incess. Anim.* 714a9; Apoll. Rhod. *Arg.* 2.933, 1034; Moschus *Eur.* 144; Verg. *Georg.* 1.375; Williams (1978) 20 on *HApoll.* 6. The combination of swans and air (clouds) is more prominent in Latin authors: Verg. *Aen.* 7.698–705, with Horsfall; 12.253–4; Hor. *Odes* 4.2.25; Plin. *Nat.* 10.32; A. Hardie (2010a) 42–4.

[219] The *aition* explains why the swans later became the servants/singers of Apollo; consequently Wilamowitz's emendation μέλλοντες (for MS μέλποντες) 'future singers', has much to commend it: it offers verbal play on 'song' (i.e. μέλος; cf. 257), and is not incompatible with the swans' singing 'midwifery' role, which is not performed *qua* present servants of Apollo. For reviews of other suggested solutions, Mineur (1984) 207–8; Ukleja (2005) 258 n.863; Stephens (2015) 220 (adopting the neat, but unconvincing θεοῦ μέλλοντος: the speaking Apollo of *HDelos* is fully aware of his own godhead). θεράποντες might be considered (cf. Plat. *Phaed.* 85a; Aelian *NA* 2.32, 6.19; and for ἱεροὺς Ἀπόλλωνος, Dionys. *De Avibus* 2.20), with possible word play on πόντον and λίποντες; but this crucially lacks the essential, aetological, futurity of the swans' service of Apollo.

[220] Thus *Il.* 2.459–63; Apoll. Rhod. *Arg.* 4.1300–2; Verg. *Aen.* 7.698–705.

[221] 'Length' is associated with the swan's neck, as extended in flight (Schol. Aesch. *Prom.* 793). Cf. *HApoll.*5 (swan sings in the air, i.e. in flight) and 7 (the god is not far away [μακράν]). Otherwise, I have found parallels for the transfer of length from swan-neck to song-projection and landscape only in Latin poetry: cf. esp. Verg. *Aen.* 7.700–2 *longa canoros/ dant per colla modos, sonat amnis et longe/ pulsa palus*; A. Hardie (2010a) 41 n.82.

[222] See above p.55, for light/sound in Pindar's twelfth *Paean*. Cf. esp. Eur. *Bacch.* 1082–3 (column of fire between heaven and earth), with Dodds's note ad loc. Cook (1914–40) II.114–17 offers extensive parallels.

[223] Mesom. *Hymn* 2.1–4 (to Apollo/Sun) εὐφαμείτω πᾶς αἰθήρ,/ γῆ καὶ πόντος καὶ πνοιαί,/

description of the swans' hymn to Apollo in *Birds*, which certainly re-
works a major lyric antecedent:[224] the swans' combined song and wing-
beat penetrates (and clears) cloud and the clear sky quenches the [sc.
stormy] sea; the song amazes the gods and prompts a responsive (Zeus-
like) thundering from Olympus and a *melos* from Charites and Muses.
At the centre of this combined epiphany and swan-song is the 'clear/
windless sky' (νήνεμος αἴθρη; cf. *Thesm.* 43 ἐχέτω δὲ πνοὰς νήνεμος
αἰθήρ).[225] In *HDelos*, this is the αἰθὴρ χάλκεος, the bright, clear, sky
which the Deliades' *melos* of Eileithyia has reached, and from which
the 'piercing cry' (258, διαπρυσίην ὀλολυγήν) is echoed in response;[226]
and this is the positive sequel to Hera's disruptive intrusion αἰθέρος
εἴσω (59). It is against this Aristophanic/lyric background, combining
epiphany, song and the calming effect of the νήνεμος αἰθήρ on the

---

οὔρεα, τέμπεα σιγάτω,/ ἦχοι φθόγγοι τ' ὀρνίθων. Aristoph. *Birds* 769–84 (cited next.
n.); *Thesm.* 43–5 (pastiche: Agathon's servant) ἐχέτω δὲ πνοὰς νήνεμος αἰθήρ,/ κῦμα
δὲ πόντου μὴ κελαδείτω/ γλαυκόν. 46–8 πτηνῶν τε γένη κατακοιμάσθω,/ θηρῶν τ'
ἀγρίων πόδες ὑλοδρόμων/ μὴ λυέσθων. Eur. *Bacch.* 1084–5 (following Dionysus'
voice from *aither*, and a column of fire between *ouranos* and *gaia*) σίγησε δ' αἰθήρ,
σῖγα δ' ὕλιμος νάπη/ φύλλ' εἶχε, θηρῶν δ' οὐκ ἂν ἤκουσας βοήν. Limenios *Paean* 7–9
(Furley–Bremer [2001] 93) (birth of Apollo) πᾶ[ς δὲ γ]άθησε πόλος οὐράνιος
[ἀννέφελος ἀγλαός·/ νηνέμους δ' ἔσχεν αἰθήρ ἀε[λλῶν ταχυπετ]εῖς [ὀρ]όμους, λῆξε δὲ
βα-/ρύβρομον Νη[ρέως ζαμενὲς ο]ἶδμ' ἠδὲ μέγας Ὠκεανός .... Anon. hymn to Apollo
(ap. Euseb. *Praep. Evang.* III.14.4f., cited by Furley–Bremer [2001] 95) 5–6 (during
Leto's parturition) ἵστατο μὲν γᾶ, ἵστατο δ' ἀήρ,/ πάγνυτο νᾶσος, πάγνυτο κῦμα. Cf.
also Pind. *Pae.* 3.13–17 (D3 Ru.), with the valuable commentary of Rutherford (2001)
277–9.

[224] *Birds* 769–72: τοιάδε κύκνοι/ .../ συμμιγῆ βοὴν ὁμοῦ πτε-/ ροῖσι κρέκοντες ἴαχον
Ἀπόλλω/ ... 776–83 διὰ τ' αἰθέριον νέφος ἦλθε βοά·/ πτῆξε δὲ φῦλά τε ποικίλα
θηρῶν,/ κύματά τ' ἔσβεσε νήνεμος αἴθρη·/ .../ πᾶς δ' ἐπεκτύπησ' Ὄλυμπος·/ εἷλε δὲ
θάμβος ἄνακτας· Ὀλυμπιά-/ δες δὲ μέλος Χάριτες/ Μοῦσαί τ' ἐπωλόλαξαν. (Just so
did swans ... beating wings in unison, raise a harmonious whoop for Apollo ...; their
whooping pierced the cloud of heaven; the manifold tribes of beasts were cowed, and
the cloudless clear air quenched the waves ... All Olympus reverberated, amazement
seized its lords, and the Olympian Graces and Muses replied in cheerful song ...;
trans. Henderson [Loeb]). Henderson suggests reminiscence of Apollo's swan-drawn
chariot-ride to and from the Hyperboreans in Alcaeus' paean to Delphian Apollo (fr.
307 V.); but cf. also the Sapphic and Pindaric paeans described by Himerius *Or*. 46.6
(discussed by Rutherford [2001] 278 in relation to *Paean* 3 [D3 Ru.]). See below,
p.110f. for C.'s reflection of the swan's self-accompaniment by wingbeat, and the
analogy to the lyre.

[225] Cf. Apoll. Rhod. *Arg.* 1.1154–5 (αἰθὴρ νήνεμος calms the sea, prompting benign *eris*
among the oarsmen).

[226] In the only extant parallel for the phrase, Nonnus evidently detected a Callimachean
reference to the former hostility of *aither*, perhaps with χάλκεος Ἄρης (*Il.* 5.859) in
view (*Dionys.* 20.363): Nereus consoles Dionysus on defeat by Lycurgus, with the
claim that he had also faced Ἥρη καὶ μενέχαρμος Ἄρης καὶ χάλκεος αἰθήρ. Nonnus
was surely right, for C.'s aetherial 'echo' recalls the cacophonous echo of spear on
shield at line 140. Nereus adds (in a phrase that goes to the heart of the mythical/
physical interface) πολλάκι σὸς γενέτης πρόμος αἰθέρος εἴκαθεν Ἥρη (often has your
father, lord of the *aither*, yielded to Hera).

world below, that Zeus' 'elemental' role in removing Hera's anger can best be understood.[227]

Callimachus' correlation of song-sound and elements (earth-water Nymphs, air and *aither*) further suggests familiarity with Empedocles' physiological conception of his own didactic *epos*, a point that will not be pursued here save to note that Empedoclean 'elemental' poetics were embraced and developed by Roman poets, and that among these treatments is at least one (Ovidian) evocation of the Callimachean swans circling Delos.[228]

V. APOLLO KYNTHIOS AND THE MUSES

The main aim of this section is to illuminate the relationship between Apollo and the Muses as presented in *HDelos*, together with the musical relationships between Delos and the Muses, and between Apollo and Delos. All three are announced in the proem, and it is to this that we turn first.

(a) Proem, θυμός and Inspiration

> Τὴν ἱερήν, ὦ θυμέ, τίνα χρόνον – ἢ πότ'; – ἀείσεις
> Δῆλον Ἀπόλλωνος κουροτρόφον; ἦ μὲν ἅπασαι
> Κυκλάδες, αἳ νήσων ἱερώταται εἰν ἁλὶ κεῖνται,
> εὔυμνοι· Δῆλος δ' ἐθέλει τὰ πρῶτα φέρεσθαι
> ἐκ Μουσέων, ὅτι Φοῖβον ἀοιδάων μεδέοντα   5
> λοῦσέ τε καὶ σπείρωσε καὶ ὡς θεὸν ᾔνεσε πρώτη.
> ὡς Μοῦσαι τὸν ἀοιδὸν ὃ μὴ Πίμπλειαν ἀείσῃ
> ἔχθουσιν, τὼς Φοῖβος ὅτις Δήλοιο λάθηται.
> Δήλῳ νῦν οἴμης ἀποδάσσομαι, ὡς ἂν Ἀπόλλων
> Κύνθιος αἰνήσῃ με φίλης ἀλέγοντα τιθήνης.[229]   10

---

[227] For a vivid illustration of where cosmic and elemental conceptions of song-epiphany was to lead by the second century AD, cf. the anonymous *Hymn to Pan* inscribed at Epidaurus (*IG* IV² 1.130; Furley–Bremer (2001) 192–8): the pipe music of the god as cosmic dancer evokes the response of all earth and sea and its echo reaches 'star-faced Olympus', 'sprinkling the assembly of gods with immortal Muse'.

[228] Empedocles' physiological conception of his *epos*: A. Hardie (2013a), esp. 227–32. Elements and poetry at Rome: A. Hardie (2002) 203–5 (the *Georgics* and elemental harmony in the poet); (2008) 99–102 (Hor. *Odes* 3.4 and elemental Muses/Camenae); (2010a) 47–51 (Ovid *Metamorphoses* 14, and the elemental character of the fictitious Canens; esp. p. 49 for the Callimachean swans).

[229] Text: the transmitted reading of line 1 may be explicable in part by the emotional state of the singer (hence ἢ ποτ' in parenthesis here). The combination τίνα χρόνον and ἢ πότ' is supported by Ukleja's identification ([2005] 84) of a Demosthenic parallel (*Ol.* 3.16): τίνα γὰρ χρόνον ἢ τίνα καιρόν, ὦ ἄνδρες Ἀθηναῖοι, τοῦ παρόντος βελτίω ζητεῖτε; ἢ ποθ' ἃ δεῖ πράξετ', εἰ μὴ νῦν; the implication, at all events, is that a hymn is

Of her that is sacred, O my heart, for what period of time – or when?
  – will you sing,
of Delos, Apollo's child-nurse? Certain it is, all
the Kyklades, most sacred of islands that repose in the sea,
are fine for hymning. But Delos aspires to take first things
from the Muses, for that Phoebus lord of songs
she cleansed and swaddled, and was the first to acknowledge as a
  god.
As the Muses, for the singer who sings not of Pimpleia,
feel abhorrence, so Phoebus does for him who forgets Delos.
To Delos now shall I vouchsafe her share of the path of song, that
  Apollo
Kynthios should acknowledge me as one who takes thought for his
  dear wet-nurse.

In a well-known study of the epilogue to *HApollo*, Elroy Bundy analysed this opening (and the sequel at 28–9) in terms of traditional
(rhapsodic and lyric) formulae of hymnic subject selection and apology
directed towards winning the favour of the god/dess and avoiding his/
her displeasure.[230] Bundy's conclusion, that the singer is concerned
about the consequences of hymning Delos and not Apollo, has receded
from view in recent scholarship, but it remains a valuable insight into
the apologetic issues in play. Apollo's capacity for displeasure with the
chorus that fails to honour him, or otherwise falls short of his hymnic
expectations, is a familiar topic which is explored at length in
HApollo.[231] Bundy did not however take full account of the address to
the θυμός, with the result that the dynamics of the first-person decision
to proceed 'now' (νῦν, 9) to a Delos-song, and the role of the Muses in
that process, are still to be explained.

It is the θυμός, addressed as a distinct component of the singer's
persona, which 'will sing' (ἀείσεις, 1). The θυμός as something distinct
from the self, and as interlocutor for the 'I' figure, is present in Homer
and is applied to song-composition by Pindar (*Nem.* 3.26–8; cited below).[232] Its function as organ of prophecy and poetry had arisen from

---

long overdue.

[230] Bundy (1972), esp. 66, 74–5.

[231] For possible fear of Apolline anger at Pind. *Pae.* 7b.7 [C2 Ru.], see Rutherford (2004)
246. The fear of the Apolline child-chorus is a major component of Hor. *Odes* 4.6: A.
Hardie (1998) 281–4.

[232] Cf. Onians (1951) 13; 66–7; Dodds (1951) 16; 25–6 (nn.98, 99); Sullivan (1981) 152–
3; 154–5. *Phren* exhibits similar characteristics: cf. esp. Terp. fr. 2 G. ἀειδέτω φρήν.
See Sullivan (1989) 151–2 (on φρήν in Pindar) for "independent activity on the part of
the *phren* within the person and the possibility of opposition between the individual
and this psychic entity". Again, the *phren* may be associated with singing: at *Ol* 7.8,
the *phren* is "the source of Pindar's song"; it is "receptive to the influence of the
Muses, and it produces the intricate beauty of an epinician ode." Interplay between
θυμός and Muses is present already in Ibycus S151 *PMGF*, where the Muses' inter-

the belief that an altered mind state prompting abnormal behaviour is the product of divine action upon it; and it is by virtue of an inspirational god's action on the θυμός that a seer or singer becomes ἔνθεος, hence the medium for utterance of the god's words. In addressing his θυμός, an I-figure may or may not engage with it at a conscious level, *qua* mediating organ between god and 'self'.[233]

It follows that where a statement about a singer's θυμός (*animus*) is accompanied by a reference to Muse(s), possible influence of the goddess(es) should be taken into consideration.[234] This can be documented for Callimachus: in dialogue with a Muse at *Aetia* fr. 31c Ha., it is 'my heart' (ἐμὸς θυμός) that puts a follow-up question;[235] then, the variant reading 'came upon [my] heart' (θυμὸν ἐπήιεν) recorded in a commentary on a lost Muse-address in the *Aetia* suggests Muse-inspiration; and again at *Iamb.* 13.15, a reference to θυμός turns up in an explicitly 'inspirational' context.[236] In *HDelos* too, the prooemial references to the Muses (5, 7) suggest that the singer's θυμός may be subject to their inspirational influence, and thus that the proem may, at least in part, represent the Muses' 'response' mediated through the θυμός. Such a reading is consistent with the closest Pindaric parallel, at *Nemeans* 3.26–8 (with explicit distinction between θυμός and I-figure):[237] θυμέ,

---

vention cuts across the poet's determination (ἐπιθύμιον) to hymn Polycrates alone, and arises (by implication) from their prior inspirational action on the poet's θυμός. This reading supplements A. Hardie (2013).

[233] Cerc. fr. 7.6–10 P., addresses the θυμός as 'fisherman and hunter of the Pierides'. For a literary-critical view of ὦ θυμέ as (analogous to) address to the Muse, cf. Eustathius on *Il.* 1.1, citing Aristoph. *Knights* 1194. For ὦ θυμέ as a component of critical terminology, and the assumption that simple imperatival self-command in Pindar is directed to the Muse, cf. e.g. Schol. *Ol.* 1.18, 7.92, 9.110. In epic and lyric poetry where there is no reference to θυμός or Muses, self-generated answers to ostensibly rhetorical requests for information might also be understood to come from the Muses: Schol. Apoll. Rhod. 2.1090–1094a; Harder (1988) 3; cf. Bundy (1972) 79 n.95.

[234] Giuseppetti (2013) 50 rightly sees θυμός as "la sede per eccellenza dell' ispirazione poetica". Cf. Hor. *Odes* 3.4.20 *non sine dis animosus infans* with ps.-Acro ad loc. *tamquam si numen sibi inesse velit intellegi*; on the same passage, Porphyrio comments ... *divinitatis cuiusdam, quam in se esse intellegere vult*; A. Hardie (2008) 95–6.

[235] In reported dialogue at *Aet.* fr. 178.21 Ha., C. bids Theogenes 'tell me, in response to my questions, all that my θυμός longs to hear from you': the θυμός is stimulated by an exchange that carries the speaker along in a state akin to inspiration (or 'emotional inspiration', A. Hardie [1998] 245–7, with reference to Plato's *Phaedrus*). The poet's angry address to his θυμός at *Aet.* fr. 75.4–5 Ha., restraining sacrilegious disclosure should not be taken as a counter-example; among possible influences yet to be fully explored are Empedocles' Muse-dialogues at frr. 9 In. (2W.) and 14.1–3 In. (5.1–3 W.).

[236] *Iamb.* 13.15: Acosta-Hughes (2002) 80. *Aetia* fr. 2g Ha., to be located between the fragmentary end of the *Aetia* Prologue and the start of the Helikonian Dream: Harder (1993); Harder (2012) 112–13; 116–17 offers Muse-intervention last in her survey of suggested interpretations, supplying χόρος or ἑσμός (sc. of the Muses) as subject, and comparing *Batr.* 1.

[237] Giangrande (1988) 270 cites *Nem.* 3.26 and *Ol.* 2.89 as the only extant examples of

τίνα πρὸς ἀλλοδαπάν/ ἄκραν ἐμὸν παραμείβεαι;/ Αἰακῷ σε φαμὶ γένει
τε Μοῖσαν φέρειν. (My heart, to what alien headland are you turning
aside my ship's course? To Aiakos and his race I bid you bear the
Muse. trans. Race [Loeb].) The speaker is critical of digression by the
θυμός, fearing that the 'poem-journey' will pass by (παραμείβεαι) the
chosen subject; yet the command to carry 'the Muse' (i.e. the ode as inspired utterance) to Aeacus (in Aegina) is still addressed to the medium
through which the Muse is communicating with the poet.[238]

As an opening enunciation of subject, however, Callimachus' θυμός-
address is unique, and it will surely have taken its first audience by surprise. The clarity and immediacy of subject in his other hymn-openings
is replaced by uncertainty. Urgent and emotional questions imply anxiety that the θυμός (like Pindar's) may 'pass by' Delos and neglect the
island as song-subject altogether.[239] We are not told what has prompted
this uncertainty, but it is worth considering the θυμός-address in its
hymn-book location: it follows hymns to Apollo and Artemis which
refer only briefly and obliquely to the island, and not by name;[240] and
whereas *HHApollo* has Delos at the heart of its 'Delian' section, the
focal points of Callimachus' *HApollo* are Delphi and Cyrene. Delos, on
this reading of the hymn-book, has been lurking ἄδηλος in the background, but has indeed been neglected.[241]

The singer takes his θυμός to task in a *prooimion*, the part of the
performance that 'precedes the οἴμη', that is, the 'song' (or 'song-
journey') announced at line 9.[242] The term derives from the rhapsodic/

---

[238] juxtaposed θυμέ and τίνα: the former offers much the closer context (Muse-reference,
song-journey, 'passing by', late poem); in the latter, a pause in sense between the two
words is marked in some editions by a full stop.

[238] This address is the sequel to the kletic hymn to the Muse that opens the ode (Pfeijffer
[1999] 199–200; 241–2; 243–68); it implies that she is intervening to disrupt the
hymnist's original purposes, just as the Muses disrupt Ibycus' intentions in S151
PMGF (above, n.232).

[239] The implication of 'passing by' is picked up in Leto's arrival (see below, p.120f. on
lines 204–5, compared to Aratus *SH* 109), in Iris' report to Hera (224) Ἀστερίη δ'
ὀνομαστὶ παρερχομένην ἐκάλεσσεν, and at the end (316–17) τίς δέ σε ναύτης/ ...
παρήλυθε ...;. Emotion: ὦ θυμέ has been assessed as informal/familiar (Giangrande
[1968] 58–9; [1988]); but ὦ in vocative address may express intense emotion (id.
[1968] 55; Williams [1973] 60), as at Eur. *Med.* 1057–8, parodied at Aristoph. *Acharn.*
450, 480.

[240] Thus, *HApoll.* 5 (the 'Delian palm'), 59 ('Ortygia': identified, but observe avoidance
of 'Delos') and 61 ('Kynthiades' [goats]). *HArt.* offers 'Egyptian Inopos' (171). *HZeus*
opens with allusion to a Pindar-poem for Leto and Artemis, possibly performed on
Delos (Appendix I); if so, the island has been lurking unseen from the outset.

[241] Giuseppetti (2013) 50 suggests that the poet's address "mostra il suo stupor per il fatto
che l'isola abbia dovuto attendere tanto a lungo per ricevere un 'inno' in suo onore."

[242] For etymologies of *prooimion* from *oimos* (road) or *oime* (song), Aristot. *Rhet.* 3.14.1,
1414b21; Quint. *Inst.* 4.1.1–3. See Sansone (2007) 257–8; Power (2010) 187–8. For
the etymology, its application to Homeric Hymns, and the later integration of

citharoedic tradition of performing a separate hymnic *prooimion* before
the main recitation (Callimachus will have been aware that *HHApollo*
is termed a *prooimion* by Thucydides).[243] Unlike the hymn-*prooimia* in
the Homeric collection, however, this θυμός-address is integrated into
the larger performance of *HDelos* as a 'conventional' rhetorical preamble. Yet its distinct, quasi-hymnic, function as an appeal to the organ
of singer-inspiration is still evident, and it can best be understood as a
substitute for an appeal to the Muse(s):[244] significantly, θυμέ at the
opening of this 'fourth hymn' occupies the same first-line metrical
sedes as Μοῦσα in the fourth Homeric hymn (to Hermes; the first such
Muse-appeal in the collection). There is however no explicit indication
that the hymnist is consciously seeking to access the Muse(s) through
his θυμός, or that they are engaged. Indeed the proem might be read at
face value along apologetic lines, as the singer's advocacy of a Delos-
song, and as a *captatio benevolentiae* aimed at Apollo. Readers are left
to ponder whether the singer is inspired, or whether this *prooimion*
simply articulates such thoughts as have occurred to him independently.[245]

That the Muses are indeed engaged is discreetly signalled in what
follows. Thus, the case for singing about Delos is advanced on the basis
of privileged access (ordinarily unknowable to the mortal singer) to
Delos' own aspirations, as also to the grounds on which she entertains
them; ἐθέλει … ὅτι … πρώτη signals a higher source of information (a
nuance later confirmed in Apollo's privileged awareness of Asteria/
Delos' 'willingness' to receive Leto [195] κείνην γὰρ ἐλεύσεαι εἰς ἐθέλουσαν). These aspirations entail a revisionist account of Apollo's
nursing, with Delos now acting in full anthropomorphic mode, as
distinct from the traditional 'island as nurse' metaphor in κουροτρόφον

---

rhapsodic *prooimia* into the larger performance, see Aloni (1980), esp. 30–32; 33–4;
38. For Homeric Hymns as rhapsodic 'preludes', Richardson (2010) 1–2.

[243] The 'prize' reference in τὰ πρῶτα φέρεσθαι (4) reflects the agonistic context of many
hymnic *prooimia*: cf. Aloni (1980) 31; Power (2010) 190–93; Richardson (2010) 1–2
on *HHApollo*.

[244] Here, and in the musical rituals attested at the end of the hymn, C. may be commenting
on technical aspects of choral song and *kitharoedia*, including the function of the
prooimion and its relationship to the *hymnos*. Power (2010) 201–3 offers relevant
comments on prooemial developments in early choral lyric, and on the relationship of
kitharist to chorus. Praise of host cities by visting/competing singers may have been a
component of kitharoedic *prooemia*: Power (2010) 192–3.

[245] Cf. Sansone's (2007) analysis of Socratic etymologising in *Phaedrus* 266d around
prooimion as a rhetorical term for "the first thing that comes into the mind of the
speaker", as distinct from Muse-inspired speech. The dialogue offered an influential
treatment of 'inspiration', including dramatic uncertainty as to whether Socrates
speaks under its influence, and if so, in what ways: A. Hardie (1998a) 245–6 traces the
influence of the *Phaedrus* on Juvenal 3.

alone: she 'washed and swaddled' Apollo, actions which in *HHApollo* (120–22) were performed by attendant goddesses.[246] But to revise the founding 'Homeric' account was no small matter, as Pindar had emphasised in calling on the Helikonian Muses to validate his version of Asteria's escape from Zeus (*Pae.* 7b.11–20 [C2 Ru.]). In *HDelos*, as a further sophistication, Delos herself is cited as authority for her own actions as nurse, within her (stated) wish 'to win first things from the Muses' (4–5, ἐκ Μουσέων): we may infer that the island-nymph's aspirations are articulated with the authority of the Muses, an inference confirmed by *Paean* 7b (C2 Ru.), where the participle οὐκ ἐθέλοισα is applied to Asteria/Delos (43; refusal of marriage to Zeus) within the Muse-inspired narrative. Thus, the Callimachean pairing of ἐθέλει (4) and ἐθέλουσαν (195) sets up a significant relationship with οὐκ ἐθέλοισα in a major Pindaric treatment of Asteria/Zeus; and Muse-inspired articulation of her wishes sets up common interests between Delos and the Muses at the outset.[247] The intertexts also take over from *HHApollo* and Pindar a pronounced element in the character of Asteria/Delos, independence of judgment.[248]

Two further intertexts substantiate this emerging Muse-engagement. The first, referenced by ἐκ Μουσέων (5), is Hesiod's juxtaposition of Muses and Apollo as divine forebears of 'singers and kitharists' in the proem to the *Theogony* (94–5):[249] ἐκ γάρ τοι Μουσέων καὶ ἑκηβόλου Ἀπόλλωνος/ ἄνδρες ἀοιδοὶ ἔασιν ἐπὶ χθόνα καὶ κιθαρισταί (for it is from the Muses and far-shooting Apollo that there are mortal singers and kitharists on earth). Here, the direct intertextual relationship is cued by genitive form Μουσέων (each unique in its poem; otherwise Μουσάων); and its immediate point lies in the obligations placed upon professional singers by Apollo and the Muses as their patron deities (7–8). Callimachus' singer/Muse relationship is however given an oddly negative projection in the reversal (ἔχθουσιν) of Hesiod's φίλωνται (see below and n.250). The second textual allusion, cued by οἴμης ([way of] song), is to the divine inspiration of Homeric bards: 'singers', says Odysseus (*Od.* 8.480–81), 'have their share of honour because the

---

[246] Bing (1988) 110 observes that κουροτρόφον "as yet conceals the coming play on personification", but does not explore the dramatic implications.

[247] ἐθέλει/ἐθέλουσαν also echo/vary the *HHApollo* treatment of the island's unwillingness to accept Apollo on the grounds of his fearsome pre-natal reputation: thus 46, εἴ τίς οἱ γαιέων υἱεῖ θέλοι οἰκία θέσθαι and 51 (Leto to Delos) ἐθέλοις. The exact nuance of ἐθέλει at 4 is however closer to e.g. Pind. *Nem.* 7.90, of the *laudandus*' reasonable expectation of future prosperity.

[248] On this quality, Giuseppetti (2013) 16.

[249] The intertext is observed by Reinsch-Werner (1976) 323–5. Μουσάων: *Theog.* 1, 36, 93, 100; *HDelos* 252. Μουσέων reappears at *Aet.* fr. 2.2 Ha. (Harder [2012] 102).

Muse teaches them songs and loves the tribe of singers'(οἴμας Μοῦσ' ἐδίδαξε, φίλησε δὲ φῦλον ἀοιδῶν); and addressing Demodokos he adds (487–8) 'I praise you beyond all: either the Muse taught you ... or Apollo' (ἔξοχα ... <u>αἰνίζομ</u>' ἀπάντων·/ ἢ σέ γε Μοῦσ' ἐδίδαξε, ... ἢ σέ γ' Ἀπόλλων); and again Phemios, pleading with Odysseus, claims (22.347–8) that 'the god has implanted all manner of song in my *phrenes*'. Through these textual references Callimachus (as the I-figure hymnist) looks directly towards the patronage and inspiration of singers as a professional group by Apollo and the Muses, and to the praise, honour and protection that accrue to them in consequence.

The reader may conclude that the singer of *HDelos* is embarking on this οἴμη with the active encouragement of the inspiring Muses, and in their company. The gnomic analogue Muse:Pimpleia::Apollo:Delos offered at lines 7–8 reflects, not without mischievous humour, the Muses' own perspective and their interest in singer-commemoration of their birthplace, under its newly-fashionable name, ostensibly projected as a rationale for Apollo's positive expectation of a Delos-song.[250] The first entry of the I-figure, in the undertaking Δήλῳ νῦν οἴμης ἀποδάσσομαι (9), thus represents the singer in his ἔνθεος state, and it is in that condition (Muses and mortal speaking conjointly) that he sets his sights upon 'praise' from Apollo Kynthios at the destination of his song-journey, Delos.

Yet it is unclear whether the singer is aware (at the conscious level and for dramatic purposes) that the Muses are thus engaged. Nor is it clear whether he has consciously (again, in his dramatic *persona*) referred to the antecedent texts summarised above, or whether they, together with the rest of the proem, are products of unheralded divine inspiration. This deep uncertainty, and the option of reading the proem at two different levels, is part of Callimachus' design: he is drawing, as I see it, on a distinct treatment of Muse-inspiration in Greek choral lyric, dramatic interplay where the Muses' engagement is not immediately evident to the mortal singer, or where he may be diffident as to their favour. An early example of a singer who is ἔνθεος without realising it appears in Ibycus' encomium for Polykrates (S151 *PMGF*).[251] Again, in Plato's *Phaedrus* (235c), Socrates' immersion in poetry read

---

[250] Hence the reversal (ἔχθουσιν, 8) of Hesiod's φίλωνται in the same *sedes* at *Theog.* 97: Muse-alienation is normally expressed as at *Aetia* fr. 1.2 Ha., Μούσης οὐκ ἐγένοντο φίλοι (Telchines), where 'not friends' may be litotes for 'enemies' (cf. Theocr. 1.141). For Muses' love and revulsion cf. *Iamb* 13.50–51, 58–9: Acosta-Hughes (2002) 98–9. The Muses' 'hatred' at *AP* 9.251.1 (Euenus) is mock-serious, thus helpful in recognising the paradox at *HDelos* 7–8. Liban. *Or.* 23.27 and *Epp.* 469.4 refer to enmity towards the Muses (i.e. literary culture).

[251] A. Hardie (2013) 19–30.

and heard is treated as a form of inspiration, operating at sub-conscious level to stimulate fluency in dramatic dialogue.[252]

Further uncertainty surrounds the status of Delos as hymnic subject. Is 'sacred Delos' an island (Nymph) or a goddess? Alone of the addressees in the *Hymns*, she is not addressed, or spoken of, as 'god(dess)', a further reason, perhaps, for the anxiety conveyed in the opening lines. As a matter of fact, itinerant Hellenistic poets were developing new ways of praising the cities and islands that they visited, together with their resident gods, and *HDelos* can be read as a sophisticated exemplar for this distinctive pattern of professional *epideixis*.[253] Contemporary poets were also exploring the relative status, human and divine, of subjects and of singers, and on one view, presented by Theocritus at *Idyll* 16.3, 'the Muses are goddesses: goddesses sing of gods'.[254] In other words, as 'goddesses', the Muses do not hymn beings of a lower order. In *HDelos*, Callimachus too is experimenting with the boundaries of the 'hymn', the relative status of singer and subject, and the engagement or otherwise of the Muses.

Delos' own hymnic expectations are implicit in her claim to post-natal actions which in *HHApollo* (120–22) are performed by goddesses, and are underlined by her further claim to have 'first acknowledged Apollo *as a god*' (6, ὡς θεόν). She now lays claim (ἐθέλει) to hymnic reciprocity 'from the Muses', such that the Delos-song will represent long-delayed recompense, at the level of divine (hymnic) honours, for her founding actions as Nymph-nurse.[255] The inspiring Muses themselves mediate Delos' expectations (sc. of divine honours), and they go on (see below) to finesse the issue of Apollo's possible displeasure at the transfer of hymnic focus from himself (sc. as addressee of paeans inscribed εἰς Δῆλον) to his nurse as newly divine honorand of a ὕμνος

---

[252] For the concept, and reflections in Longinus (*de Subl.* 13.2) and Lucian (*Menippus* 1), see A. Hardie (1998a) 247–8 (the *Phaedrus*, Umbricius' unconscious inspiration, and recalled reading, in Juvenal 3).

[253] See Guarducci (1929); also A. Hardie (1983) 15–21; and add Cameron (1995) 47–8.

[254] Hunter (2003) 94–6; 104, on shifting rhetorical categories of praise (in this case, island as goddess). With one exception (*HArt.* 2), C. eschews the word *hymnos* and its verb. Praise of countries, including islands, was already a standard element in the travel-genres and elsewhere: cf. Men. Rhet. 345.17–19.

[255] For the figurative role of the hymnist in 'creating' a divinity, see the suggestions of Bing and Uhrmeister (1994) 28 on *HArtemis*. The recompense/reciprocity motif, observed in general terms by commentators (Bing [1988] 110–11; Ruffy [2004] 49), is brought into sharp focus by Aphrodite's arrival at Cyprus (itself an analogue for Leto's arrival on Asteria/Delos): ἣν ἐπενήξατο Κύπρις/ ἐξ ὕδατος τὰ πρῶτα, σαοῖ δέ μιν ἀντ' ἐπιβάθρων: with significant echoes for Delos of (a) τὰ πρῶτα (4) of D's expectation of return from the Muses; and (b) ὕδατος ἄχνην (14), with interplay with Aphrodite's emergence from sea 'foam'.

εἰς Δῆλον.[256] In acting thus through the singing I-figure, the Muses themselves seek to honour Delos as a new goddess, and it is in this context that the song-journey becomes an act of sharing (Δήλῳ νῦν οἴμης ἀποδάσσομαι): Delos is to assume divine status by virtue of the hymnic recognition represented by *HDelos* itself; and by the same token, as a new goddess, she is to receive a newly-created share of sung honours, within the existing, finite, hymnic honours to which Muses and singer are committed.[257] One response, then, to the opening question τίνα χρόνον; (for what period?) is that by virtue of her inclusion within the (Callimachean) hymnic canon, Delos will 'always', or 'from now on, indefinitely' be the subject of song.

The creation of a new 'share' within a finite song-resource must entail concessions by gods whose own existing 'share' will be to that extent diminished. Herein may lie a part-rationale for the honour done to other members of the Dodekatheon, in particular Zeus and Poseidon (§IV[b], [c]). But of course it is Apollo as principal honorand of paeans εἰς Δῆλον, who stands to lose (part of his) 'hymn-share' from the creation of a new ὕμνος εἰς Δῆλον. Callimachus' solution to the delicate negotiation between god and island is far-reaching: first, the singer draws the Muses into the musical scenario; second, and (as the reader knows) speaking under inspiration, he sets as his main objective a favourable reception at Delos from 'Kynthian Apollo', the god at the location from which he traditionally observes incoming Delian paeans (pp.47f., 55f.); third, he elevates Apollo in that musical role to (quasi)-cult status with the new epiklesis Κύνθιος, enunciated here for the first time, but arguably advancing his early claim, as presented in *HHApollo*, to a place on Kynthos alongside Artemis (above, p.47f); fourth, the potential risk of requiring Apollo to share hymnic honours with Delos is offset by a (quasi-)cult title extended to him from his own father, Zeus; and fifth, the *aition* of the new epiklesis, Kynthos as the breast at which Apollo suckled, and through which he imbibed the waters of the Nile, is there to reassure the god as to the fitness of hymnic praises now, at last, under way for Delos from Egypt itself. In *HZeus*, the distribution of divine domains in *HZeus* had included the

---

[256] Cf. Bundy (1972) 66, 74–5.

[257] Theocritus (*Id.* 17.48–50) interprets the verb thus in describing Aphrodite's intervention to deify Berenike 'before she embarked on [Charon's] ship', and 'allocated her share of divine honours' (ἀπεδάσσαο τιμᾶς). For the simplex form of the primordial division of divine property and honours, Hes. *Theog.* 112 δάσσαντο. For a new god's new share, and the requirement on others to concede space, cf. Verg. *Georg.* 1.33–5 (Octavian) ... *qua locus .../ panditur — ipse tibi iam bracchia contrahit ardens/ Scorpius et caeli iusta plus parte reliquit.* There are good comments on *HDelos* as the island-goddess's 'just share', and as offerings of the Muses by Giuseppetti (2013) 51.

allocation to Apollo of 'those who well know the ways of the lyre' (77, Φοίβου δὲ λύρης εὖ εἰδότας οἴμους): in *HDelos*, that exclusively musical focus is reprised in Φοῖβον ἀοιδάων μεδέοντα and οἴμης ἀποδάσσομαι, deployed to ensure that the Delian god receives the hymn *qua* patron god of song.[258]

These tightly organised praises come to Delos with the authority of the hymnist's Muses, and on the basis of a community of interest between them and the island they are honouring. The nature of the relationships between Muses and Delian nymph(s), and between Muses and Apollo is the subject of the next two part-sections.

(b) 'My Goddesses'

The next explicit reference to Muses occurs at the point where the singer breaks off his narrative of the fleeing Boeotian landscape, following Melia's concern for her co-eval tree on Helikon, and digresses into the learned enquiry at lines 82–5 (above, p.67f.):

> ἐμαὶ θεαὶ εἴπατε Μοῦσαι,
> ἦ ῥ' ἐτεὸν ἐγένοντο τότε δρύες ἡνίκα Νύμφαι;
> 'Νύμφαι μὲν χαίρουσιν, ὅτε δρύας ὄμβρος ἀέξει,
> Νύμφαι δ' αὖ κλαίουσιν, ὅτε δρυσὶ μηκέτι φύλλα.'

> My goddesses, tell me, Muses,
> truly, do there come into being trees at just the same time as
>   Nymphs?
> 'Nymphs do rejoice when water makes trees grow;
> Nymphs yet weep when trees no longer have their leaves.'

Reworking epic Muse-invocation, the singer puts a question to which the Muses are invited to respond (εἴπατε).[259] Lines 84–5 are in my view to be understood as the Muses' response, presented verbatim and modelled on the (equally cryptic) address by the Muses to Hesiod at *Theo-*

---

[258] Reprised: the correspondence of οἴμους (*HZeus*) and οἴμης (*HDelos*) is clear enough; εὖ εἰδότας (*HZeus* 77) alludes to the etymology of ἀοιδός (cf. *HZeus* 59, 70) from 'knowing very well', hence the echo in Φοῖβον ἀοιδάων: A. Hardie (2000a). ἀποδάσσομαι has no verbal counterpart, but is broadly relevant to the allocation/selection of different divine domains described at *HZeus* 57–79. ἐκ δὲ Διὸς βασιλῆες (*HZeus* 78, following the Apollo reference) cites Hes. *Theog.* 96, in the same passage as that referenced in the proem to *HDelos*.

[259] εἴπατε: cf. Hes. *Theog.* 114–15; *Il.* 2.484–5. Muse(s) as 'goddess(es)' is epic in origin, but appears in other genres by the later fifth century: *Il.* 1.1, 2.485; Hes. *Theog.* 24; *Scutum* 205–6; *HHApoll.* 518–19; Aristoph. *Peace* 816–17; Apoll. Rhod. 2.511–16, 4.1–2; Theocr. *Id.* 10.25, 16.3, 22.116, *Ep.* 10.1 Gow (*AP* 6.338); Verg. *Ecl.* 10.70, *Aen.* 7.41 (*diva*), 7.641 *pandite nunc Helicona deae* ...; 645 *divae*; Val. Flacc. 6.41; Stat. *Silv.* 1.2.4; *Ciris* 93, 98; Him. *Or.* 62.56; cf. 66.15–16 Col.; Liban. *Or.* 11.188. Reinsch-Werner (1976) 187–93 offers an excellent analysis of oracular context, intertexts and re-working of epic Muse-invocation.

gony 26–8; but whereas the Hesiodic address is narrated as the Muses' own initiative, this couplet is presented as a Muse-response without signposting, other than εἴπατε.[260]

The exchange takes forward the exploration of the Muse-singer relationship begun in the proem. There, intervention was unsolicited, and the singer speaks in his own *persona*; here, the Muses respond and make a brief epiphany, albeit through the voice of the hymnist, as *personae loquentes*. In so doing, they confirm his favoured status, a professional successor to Hesiod as recipient of the Muses' wisdom. The response itself, couched in cryptic language and symmetrical form, is akin to an oracle and in that sense it looks forward to Apollo's 'oracular' intervention with Thebes and underlines the Muses' kinship to Apolline interests.[261] But this is no oracle: rather, the Muses comment on a learned ζήτημα of a kind associated with the Alexandrian library and with membership of the Mouseion.[262] This in no way implies that Callimachus is turning his back on traditional notions of 'inspiration'; rather, he supplements them with these Muses' distinctive capacity to address contemporary issues of scholarship, taking account of scientific advances, by virtue of their omniscience as 'goddesses' (θεαί).

ἐμαὶ θεαί denotes the particular goddesses who protect the interests of singers, and to whom our singer owes professional allegiance.[263] It reflects the singer's professional, occupational descent from, and allegiance to, 'the Muses' as is represented by the Hesiodic passage (*Theog.* 94–7) referenced in the proem. The appended Μοῦσαι clarifies the identity of these θεαί (ἐμαί does not particularise within Muses as a sub-group of goddesses). On the contrary, the singer regards all Muses, whatever their geographical location or cult identity, as the same Panhellenic goddesses who had been born in Pimpleia but who nonetheless

---

[260] On the Muses' response, Wilamowitz (1924) II.67; Mineur (1984) 117–18; Morrison (2011) 343–4. Bing (1988) 42 and D'Alessio (2007) 142 both suggest intentional uncertainty. The conventions of exchanges with Muses might have featured more prominently in discussion of the issue: see Harder (1988), and for lyric background to unsignposted, unsolicited, Muse intervention, A. Hardie (2013) 19–26.

[261] Ambühl (2005) 343–4, notes the oracular parallel with Apollo's prophecy. C. sets this up in Melia's fearful response to the auditory epiphany of Ares, and the latter distorts the impact of Apolline epiphany on Sybil/prophetess: cf. *Anth. App.* 6.145.4 (oracular) ἄσθματα δινήεντα. For whirling δῖναι, cf. Plut. *Mor.* 404e; and for 'panting', cf. Verg. *Aen.* 6.48 *pectus anhelum*, with Horsfall's comment; Luc. 5.191 *anhelo ... meatu*. The cult reference is to the Melia-Apollo marriage and Teneros as seer at the Theban Ismenion.

[262] Plato (*Crat.* 406a) etymologises 'Muse' from μῶσθαι in the sense ζήτησις ('enquiry'): this is directly relevant to the way the singer first addresses (and characterises) them in *HDelos*.

[263] Cf. Pind. *Nem.* 3.1, where the Muse, addressed as 'our mother', is the lineal parent of the *genos* of singers. Ov. *Met.* 10.149, *mea Musa*, signifies 'my [Roman] Muse'.

retain local interests and cult-identities. Hesiod had assimilated the local Helikoniades to the Panhellenic Olympian Muses in his first encounter (*Theog.* 24–5), and there too they were designated first (24) as θεαί and then (25) as Μοῦσαι.

(c) Swans, Apollo, Muses and Deliades

Immediately after Hera's declaration of respect for Asteria (244–8), and as an 'aerial' reflection of what she has said (see above, §IV [d]), swans encircle Delos, where Leto is finally in the process of parturition (249–55):[264]

> κύκνοι δὲ θεοῦ μέλλοντες ἀοιδοί
> Μῃόνιον Πακτωλὸν ἐκυκλώσαντο λιπόντες   250
> ἑβδομάκις περὶ Δῆλον, ἐπήεισαν δὲ λοχείῃ
> Μουσάων ὄρνιθες, ἀοιδότατοι πετεηνῶν
> (ἔνθεν ὁ παῖς τοσσάσδε λύρῃ ἐνεδήσατο χορδάς
> ὕστερον, ὁσσάκι κύκνοι ἐπ' ὠδίνεσσιν ἄεισαν)·
> ὄγδοον οὐκέτ' ἄεισαν ...   255

> and swans, the god's singers-to-be,
> leaving Maeonian Pactolus, circled
> seven times around Delos, and accompanied the parturition in song,
> birds of the Muses, most songful of winged creatures
> — for that reason did the boy attach as many strings to the lyre,
> later, as the swans sang over the birth-travails;
> an eighth time they did not sing ...

Eileithyia is absent (above, p.73 and n.132), and the swans act as substitute 'midwives', facilitating Apollo's birth through song.[265] Their singing (ἐπήεισαν δὲ λοχείῃ and ἐπ' ὠδίνεσσιν ἄεισαν) brings into play the sound association of ὠδή/ἀοιδή (song) and ὠδίς (birth pang): this epodic wordplay is reminiscent of Plato's association of song and midwifery, and the etymology (ὠδή from Leto's ὠδίς) was already present in a Euripidean ode for the Delian Artemis Λοχεία.[266]

---

[264] Text: for the emendation μέλλοντες (Wilamowitz) see above, n.219.

[265] McKay (1962) 168–9, citing Meineke, observes (but does not develop) the swans' epodic role. Eileithyia/midwife: contrast *HHApoll.* 115–16, with Haslam (1993) 118–19; also *HDelos* 132 (Peneius to Leto) κάλει μόνον Εἰλήθυιαν, an action omitted in the event; cf. Mineur [1984] 206. Her absence is reflected in later variants (a) that there was no midwife (Eustath. on *Od.* 6.160 μαῖα γὰρ φασιν οὐκ ἦν), (b) that the palm acted as substitute (Nonn. *Dionys.* 27.273 μαιώσατο φοῖνιξ), and (c) that (firstborn) Artemis took the role.

[266] *IT* 1097–1105 (with several points of correspondence with the swan-passage: Kuiper [1896] 173). The chorus speaks of Delos, ποθοῦσ᾽ Ἄρτεμιν λοχίαν,/ ἃ παρὰ Κύνθιον ὄχθον οἰ-/ κεῖ .../ .../ ..., Λατοῦς ὠδῖνα φίλαν,/ λίμναν θ᾽ εἰλίσσουσαν ὕδωρ/ κύκλιον, ἔνθα κύκνος μελῳ-/ δὸς Μούσας θεραπεύει. C.'s verb/noun combination echoes Plato's figurative account of midwives' epodic song facilitating birth (*Theaet.* 149d.) καὶ μὴν καὶ διδοῦσαί γε αἱ μαῖαι φαρμάκια καὶ ἐπάδουσαι δύνανται ἐγείρειν τε τὰς

Swans are etymologically associated with circularity;[267] and they circle Delos as (in Hekataios of Abdera's account) clouds of musical swans circled the Hyperborean temple of Apollo, accompanying the 'all-harmonious *melos*' of singers and citharists.[268] Harmony is again implicit in the Callimachean swans' 'seven times, but not an eighth', linked to the stringing of the lyre.[269] The main lines of musical symbolism are clear enough: the swans are aerial prototypes for professional singers and kitharists in service to the Muses and to Apollo as a kithara-playing Musagetes.[270] There are overlaps with citharoedic *prooimia*:[271] joint allegiance to Apollo and the Muses, the invention of the seven string lyre, and the analogy between the swans' wings and lyre-playing as instrumental accompaniment to singing.[272] But Callimachus also has

---

ὠδῖνας καὶ μαλθακωτέρας ἂν βούλωνται ποιεῖν (cf. Philostr. *Vit. Apoll.* 1.5). For ὠδίς and ὠδή, cf. Him. *Or.* 12.38 Col., and esp. *Or.* 41.4 Col. Δῆλον μὲν δὴ τὴν νῆσον λαχοῦσαν τὰς θείας ὠδῖνας Ἀπόλλωνος ἅπασαι λύραι ᾠδὴν καὶ μέλος πεποίηντα ....

[267] *Etym Magn.* p. 544.5 K., s.v. κύκνος; *Etym. Gud.* p. 334.17–22, s.v. κολοιός (from the circle formed by the swan's throat), 353.5–12, s.v. κύκνος. The circling swans connect by antithesis with the Gauls, likened to the Milky Way as they encircle Delphi (above, p.87f.); the connection might have been set up by visual witnesses among the processing (theoric!) Delphian boys departing from Tempe in preparation for the Septerion festival (proposed by Pfeiffer, *app. crit.* 177b for the lacuna after 176, modified by Bing [1988] 129–31; cf. Ukleja [2005] 241–44, accepting the modified [departure] scenario; was Hekataios perhaps a source? See next n.).

[268] Hekataios 264 *FGrH* 12, ap. Ael. *NA* 11.1: ... καταπέτεται κύκνων ἄμαχα τῷ πλήθει νέφη, καὶ περιελθόντες τὸν νεὼν καὶ οἱονεὶ καθήραντες αὐτὸν τῇ πτήσει ... ὅταν οὖν οἵ τε ᾠδοὶ τῇ σφετέρᾳ μούσῃ τῷ θεῷ προσάδωσι καὶ μέντοι καὶ οἱ κιθαρισταὶ συγκρέκωσι τῷ χορῷ παναρμόνιον μέλος, ἐνταῦθά τοι καὶ οἱ κύκνοι συναναμέλπουσιν ὁμορροθοῦντες ... Mineur (1984) 208; Giuseppetti (2013) 224. C. composed *HDelos* in the generation after Hekataios (a protégé of Ptolemy I Soter at Alexandria) produced his monograph on the Hyperboreans, to which C.'s account of the Hyperboreans may be indebted: *RE* VII. 2750–69, esp. 2755–57 (Jakoby); Fraser (1972) I.496–7; II.717 n. 7; Mineur (1984), 'General Index', s.v. 'Hecataeus of Abdera'.

[269] The intertextual reference (Mineur [1984] 211) is to *Il.* 5.436–9 (Apollo tacitly protects Aeneas against Diomedes three times, but overtly upbraids the latter on his fourth charge); Ovid *Met.* 13.610–11 looks through *HDelos* 251–5 to this passage, in depicting Memnon's birds circling harmoniously three times, then splitting into warring factions; A. Hardie (2010a) 49–50 (n.112).

[270] For Callimachus and the analogue of swan and singer, again in relation to Muses and Apollo, see Harder (2012) II.86–7, on Call. *Aet.* 1.39–40 Ha. The role of the kithara-playing chorus-leader is explicit in Theseus as first Athenian *theoros* (312–16).

[271] See Beecroft (2008) 228–9, on Terp. fr. 1 G. (swan's wings); 232–4, on Terp. fr. 4 G. (seven-string lyre); 237–8, on Terp. fr. 8 G. (libations to Apollo and the Muses). Sacral setting and Muse cult is especially prominent in the Terpandrian tradition: Schol. *Il.* 22.391; Power (2010) 391.

[272] Wing-beat and lyre: *Hom. Hym.* 21 (Apollo) Φοῖβε σὲ μὲν καὶ κύκνος ὑπὸ πτερύγων λίγ'/ ἀείδει ὄχθη ἐπιθρῴσκων ποταμὸν πάρα .../ Πηνειόν· σὲ δ' ἀοιδὸς ἔχων φόρμιγγα λίγειαν/ ἡδυεπὴς ... αἰὲν ἀείδει. Cf. Alc. fr. S2 *PMGF* (= Terp. fr. 1 G.); Aristoph. *Birds* 771–2 (with Dunbar); Anacreontea fr. 60.5; Ov. *Met.* 13.607–8 *volucris/ insonuit pennis*; Philostr. *Vit. Apoll.* 1.5; and esp. Philostr. Jun. *Imag.* 1.9.4; 1.11.3. For Hellenistic interest (Aristarchus) in κύκνος ὑπὸ πτερύγων as the 'beginning' of a work (*prooimion*?) by Terpander, Power (2010) 188 (noting the relevance of Minoan-

a lyric intermediary in view, in the shape of whichever poem is re-
worked in Aristophanes' Apolline swan-song at *Birds* 769–84 (where
again the motif of singing swans' self-accompaniment by wing-beat
appears).

Six words representing 'singing', 'singers' and 'song' in the swan-
passage pick up a similar concentration (four) in the proem, including
Apollo as 'lord of songs' (Φοῖβον ἀοιδάων μεδέοντα, 5). There, as we
saw (n.66), μεδέοντα overlaps with Hermes and derives from his Homeric hymn (2) Κυλλήνης μεδέοντα, the first item in a pattern of interplay (gods and hill-epithets) between Apollo/*Kynthios* and Hermes/
Kyllenios. Callimachus' 'correction' of Hermes' invention of the seven-
string lyre, as recorded in the Homeric *Hymn to Hermes* (51), extends
this half-brother interplay to embrace the substance of Apollo's musical
role, his command of the lyre, and so to integrate it with his identity as
Kynthios.[273]

The Deliades' response, indebted to Pindar's Delian ἐγχώριαι (*Pae.*
12.16–19 [G1 Ru.]), is characterised as the 'sacred *melos* of Eileithyia',
evidently the *aition* of a later hymn (see below, p.124 on Olen) but also
as, in some sense, the indigenous landscape counterpart of the visiting
swans' epodic midwifery. Aerial and landscape song combined to create what might be termed a Delian 'musical space' comparable to the
Hyperboreans' temple and of course prefiguring the unceasing song and
dance of the present-day Deliades and male chorus (302–6). Asteria/
Delos has already been addressed as φιλόμολπος (197) as she proceeds
to the (choric) Kyklades (above, p.80), a lyric epithet associated with
Apollo and the Muses, and her intrinsic identification with song and
dance is now instantiated through the landscape Deliades.[274] The idea
of 'musical space' can be refined by an allusion, through the swans, to
another Euripidean evocation of song: Μουσάων ὄρνιθες, ἀοιδότατοι
πετεηνῶν (252) takes us to *Helen* 1107–10, where the nightingale is
'most songful melodious bird' (ἀοιδοτάταν/ ὄρνιθα μελῳδόν) and
perches in 'μουσεῖα', trees filled with bird-song.[275] μουσεῖον is a

_____

Mycenaean swan-neck *kitharai*). The issue is relevant to the relationship between
prooimion and *nomos*, hence to Olen's *nomos* (*HDelos* 304–5; below p.124).

[273] *HHHerm.* 51 ἑπτὰ δὲ συμφώνους ὀίων ἐτανύσσατο χορδάς; cf. *HDelos* 253 ἔνθεν ὁ
παῖς τοσσάσδε λύρῃ ἐνεδήσατο χορδάς. For C., *HHHermes* and *HHApollo* on seven-
string lyre-aetiology, McKay (1962) 166–7; Mineur (1984) 210. Cf. also Power (2010)
474 for promulgation of the Hermes version (it was to feature again in Eratosthenes'
Hermes).

[274] Stesich. 193.10 *PMGF* (90 Finglass) with Finglass's commentary; cf. Corinna 692 fr.
2.5 *PMG* (choric activity following a Muse-invocation?); at Alc. S1 *PMGF*, it is
unclear if the address is to a Muse or Apollo: see Davies ad loc.; applied to Aegina at
Pind. *Nem.* 7.9. (cf. 'streams of the Muses' at 12).

[275] This important intertext is guaranteed by Theocr. *Id.* 12.7 ἀοιδοτάτη πετεηνῶν, which

Euripidean favourite for musical places sacred to the Muses:[276] it embraces inspirational landscape, and performed song as the auditory epiphany of the Muse(s) such that the Muse(s) may at one and the same time inspire a song, and be identified with its divine sound-in-performance;[277] and its Hellenistic currency as a sacral-musical figure is guaranteed by its development by Plato, with reference to the topography of the *Phaedrus*, the cicadas singing overhead in the service of the Muses, and the Muse- (and Nymph-) inspired *logoi* of philosophical discourse.[278] Euripides' μουσεῖα is echoed in Callimachus' Μουσάων; and following the response of the Delian Nymphs, we are encouraged to view the island as (in Plato's phrase: n.278) τὸ Νυμφῶν ... μουσεῖον, the *mouseion* of the Nymphs. At the root of this musical conception lies the kinship of Panhellenic Muses and local Nymphs (as validated by the Muses themselves: above, p.67f.), here exemplified in the Deliades (old and present-day) as indigenous and terrestrial 'equivalents' of the chorus of Muses (above, p.49). It required, however, the intersection of the Muses' swans and the landscape Deliades to create this musical space; and in that intersection, we may observe the creation of prototypes for the present-day visiting singer-kitharist in the service of Apollo and the Muses and for the local choric Deliades.

(d) Delos as 'Musical Space'

Peter Bing has argued that Callimachus saw Delos (and the hymn) as "a potential vehicle for a programmatic statement", and that the island is a "metaphor for [Callimachus'] poetic principles", that is, for the virtues

---

imitates C.'s phrasing but re-applies it to Euripides' nightingale.

[276] The bird-*mouseion* is a Euripidean innovation: cf. Eur. *Alcmene* fr. 89 K. χελιδόνων μουσεῖον, replicated (of the twittering of bad poets) at Aristoph. *Frogs* 93 χελιδόνων μουσεῖα. Relevant, therefore, that C.'s Μουσάων ὄρνιθες is replicated by Theocritus (*Id.* 7.47) in Μοισᾶν ὄρνιχες of those who 'crow against Homer'; like *Frogs* 93, this represents bad poets in the sacral service of the Muses, and may well allude to the Mouseion. Timon's reference (fr. 60 W.) to members of the Mouseion squabbling Μουσάων ἐν ταλάρῳ (in the bird-cage of the Muses) sustains the figure, and parallels the institutional sense of 'Muses' in this context. For further play on the Euripidean theme (re-applied to Sophocles), cf. Philostr. *Imag.* 395 K. ὁ δὲ τῶν ἀηδόνων χορὸς καὶ τῶν ἄλλων ὀρνέων μουσεῖα σαφῶς ἡμῖν τὰ τοῦ μελιχροτάτου Σοφοκλέους ἐπὶ γλῶτταν ἄγει. Cf. also Parnassus as *mouseion* at Eur. fr. 665c.19 M. (Melanippe the Wise): M's mother, a νύμφη θεσπιῳδός (Nymph singer of prophecies) is swept away from her μουσεῖον on the Κωρύκιον ὄρος.

[277] A. Hardie (2002) (2008) 71–9 (on Hor. *Odes* 3.4); (2013) 216–20 (on Empedocles). 'Hearing' is a key motif in the literary experience of auditory epiphany: thus (*HDelos* 29) τί τοι θυμῆρες ἀκοῦσαι; cf. Call. fr. 227.1 Pf. (auditory epiphany of Apollo) ἔνεστ' Ἀπόλλων τῷ χορῷ· τῆς λύρης ἀκούω. Hor. *Odes* 3.4.5–6 *auditis?... audire ... videor*.

[278] *Phaedr.* 278b–c καταβάντε ἐς τὸ Νυμφῶν νᾶμά τε καὶ μουσεῖον, ἠκούσαμεν λόγων. See Yunis (2011) 175–7 (cicadas), 240 (*mouseion* and Muse-guidance).

of smallness, refinement and purity. Bing's account was supplemented by Simon Slings' reading of *HDelos* as a "partial allegory" of island for poetry.[279] To this might be added Delos' attraction as a vehicle for the recovery of the ἄδηλον through the δῆλον, with reference to the allusive character of Callimachean hymnic poetry (above, p.90f.). But this line of criticism has received little by way of positive development, perhaps because both treatments isolate a relatively small proportion of the text for metapoetical analysis; and the limited amount of explicitly programmatic material in *HDelos* (of the kind presented at the conclusion of *HApollo*) may have discouraged further exploration. But it can be assumed that Callimachus' readers will have been critically receptive to implicit programme statements, whereby the subject of the poem, or significant elements within it, may symbolise the poem itself.[280] And certainly, it is hard to suppose that in composing a work that has so much to say about song, the young Callimachus neglected the opportunity for self-reflexive content, conveying some conception of his own work as a hymnist. But the reader is confronted by the issue of what might be termed complementarity within the hymn-book: are we to read what Callimachus says about song in *HDelos* alongside comparable materials in the other hymns, as part of a coherent approach to hymnic poetry, or as separate and unrelated items? I suggested earlier above, p.106, with n.257) that the action of 'sharing the way of song' (9, οἴμης ἀποδάσσομαι) in the proem to *HDelos* echoes the allocation of divine provinces in *HZeus*, and Apollo's patronage of 'those who well know the ways of the lyre' (77, Φοίβου δὲ λύρης εὖ εἰδότας οἴμους); but are we take that echo, together with the Apolline *aition* of the seven-string lyre at *HDelos* 253, as a significant pointer to the hymnist's own musical *persona*, a latter-day singer-kitharist (or chorus-leader)?[281] Again, Bundy observed parallelism between *HApollo* 106 (οὐκ ἄγαμαι τὸν ἀοιδὸν ὃς οὐδ ὅσα πόντος ἀείδει) and *HDelos* 8–9 (ὡς Μοῦσαι τὸν ἀοιδὸν ὃ μὴ Πίμπλειαν ἀείσῃ/ ἔχθουσιν), and took the view that the proem to *HDelos* is counterpart to the 'apologetic' epilogue to *HApollo*.[282] But do *HApollo* and *HDelos* present literary programmes that are in any meaningful sense complementary?

---

[279] Slings (2004). The issue is touched on but not further developed by Giuseppetti (2013) 19.
[280] Thus, Theocritus' first *Idyll*, where an agonistic cup, with its contents, is a programmatic symbol of the idyll: see Cairns (1983).
[281] On possible self-reflection by the Callimachean hymnist, see below, p.123f.
[282] Bundy (1972) 45–6; 74–5.

To pursue these issues, and to relate them to the presence of the Muses in *HDelos*, I turn now to the the the second proem, addressed to Delos, as the hymnist figuratively arrives at the island (28–30):[283]

> εἰ δὲ λίην πολέες σε περιτροχόωσιν ἀοιδαί,
> ποίῃ ἐνιπλέξω σε; τί τοι θυμῆρες ἀκοῦσαι;
> ἢ ὡς τὰ πρώτιστα μέγας θεός ...

> But given that exceeding many songs are in circulation around you, with what kind shall I weave you in? What will it befit your heart to hear? How, in the very first place, the great god ...

The singer is in *aporia* as he juxtaposes 'many [sc. Apolline] songs' encircling Delos with his own song;[284] but instead of asking Delos 'How shall I hymn you?' (as the Homeric hymnist had asked Apollo [20] πῶς ... σ' ὑμνήσω;), he asks 'With what *kind* of song (ποίῃ) shall I weave you in?' ποίῃ signals continuing uncertainty as to the island's status as honorand (above, p.105).[285] *Aporia* is articulated in the terminology of poetic craftsmanship: how to 'weave' Delos into song;[286] and what content will best 'fit' Delos' heart (θυμῆρες)? This is the *persona* of the poet-artificer, the ποιητής (with learned allusion to its etymology from ποιότης) integrated with the hymnic uncertainty of ποίῃ, and ostensibly lacking the Muses' guidance.[287] The appearance is misleading however for (notwithstanding the diffidence implicit in the

---

[283] For the hymnist's notional visit to Delos, see below p.121f.

[284] λίην πολέες ... ἀοιδαί alludes etymologically (Ἀ[intensive]-πόλλων) to Apolline song. For a priamel-format distinction between 'many' and hymnist, cf. *HApoll.* 69–71 (on Apolline nomenclature). Prop. 3.1.15 *multi, Roma, tuas laudes annalibus addent*, also in an Apolline context, makes much the same etymological-programmatic point as *HDel.* 28–9. Civic choruses: cf. 279 πᾶσαι δὲ χορούς ἀνάγουσι πόληες, with probable play between πόληες (cities) and πολέες (many) (28), marked by lexical choice πολέες over πολλαί (see Mineur [1984] 76, for the scholiast's puzzlement; and for *polis* and *polloi*, *Etym. Magn.* p. 680.8 K., s.v. πόλις). For the Hellenistic paean-titles, Fantuzzi and Hunter (2004) 371.

[285] ἐνιπλέξω σε suggests weaving a crown of praise (Nisbet–Hubbard on *Odes* 1.26.7), picking up the epinician figure of Delos' 'first prize' (4) vis-à-vis the (encircling) Kyklades (for the crown of song/victor's crown analogue in Pindar, cf. Steiner [1986] 54); the figure is anticipated by 'songs that run around' (περιτροχόωσιν ἀοιδαί) which in turn effect transition from the preceding passage on city walls (for *stephanos* as circle 'running around', and for association with walls, *Etym. Magn.* p. 455.52–4 K., s.v. θριγκῷ).

[286] With ἐνιπλέξω of weaving together different poetic materials, cf. Call. fr. 203.17 Pf. (*Iamb.* 13), ἐμπέπλεκται (discussed below). For Callimachean weaving of old elements into a new song, cf. also Stephens (2002–2003) 14; 21–22; and for the Pindaric background, Steiner (1986) 54–5.

[287] The etymology is not directly attested in a Greek source, but is guaranteed by Suetonius (*de poetis* 2) ap. Isid. *Orig.* 8.7.2 *poetae inde sint dicti ... quia forma quadam efficitur quae* ποιητής *dicitur, poema vocitatum est eiusque fictores poetae* (cf. esp. Prop. 2.34.79–80, of Vergil: *tale facis carmen docta testudine quale/ Cynthius* [!] *impositis temperat articulis*).

question format) ἢ ὡς τὰ πρώτιστα signals that divine inspiration may well be active: it refers to Hesiod's narrative, where the Muses open 'their' account of primordial beginnings (there, as here, unknowable to the poet) with the birth of Chaos (*Theog.* 116, πρώτιστα). And yet, the very fact that the hymnist's question was directed to Delos herself might lead us to suppose that any inspired response has come from her;[288] and this apparent inspirational overlap of Delos and Muses is reinforced by the echo of the poet's θυμός (1) through which he accesses the Muses, in θυμῆρες (29, of Delos' own θυμός). Taken together, these features should encourage the reader to explore further the nature of the relationship between island and Muses.

I suggested earlier (above, p.111f.) that this relationship might be understood in terms of analogy: the island as '*mouseion* of the (Delian) Nymphs', a musical space first created by the intersection of visiting and local singers, the Muses' swans and the landscape Deliades. In the second proem, the visiting hymnist wants to know how his song is to address a location already encircled by Apolline songs. Speaking as craftsman-poet, he alludes to an earlier visitor to Delos, the Homeric hymnist: 'Homer', we need to recall, had praised the Deliades' imitation of the voices of visiting Ionians as 'fitting' them so well (*HHApollo* 164, οὕτω σφιν καλὴ συνάρηρεν ἀοιδή), 'that each might say he was speaking himself': the local chorus, in other words, brought the sound of foreign tongues and places to Delos. The Callimachean visitor aspires to do something different: in 'weaving' Delos into his song, he wants the musical landscape embodied by the Delian Nymph/ goddess to be 'heard' (ἀκοῦσαι) and thereby to 'fit' her own θυμός.[289] In terms of poetic craftsmanship, this means recalling earlier Delian songs and 'weaving' them together into a new song; but at another level, the craftsman is blended with inspired poet, bringing a woven hymn-artefact from the Muses (cf. 5, ἐκ Μουσέων) to an inspirational place. Here we first glimpse the profound reciprocal engagement of

---

[288] *HHApoll.* 25 ἢ ὥς σε πρῶτον Λητὼ τέκε … is rightly cited, but the parallel underlines the difference between πρῶτον and τὰ πρώτιστα (the latter also at *HHApoll.* 407, but in a quite different context). Hesiod: the view expressed in a scholium ad loc: 'at this point the Muses' account starts' will have originated in Hellenistic criticism. For πρώτιστα of the Muses' own utterances, Hes. *Theog.* 24; Pind. *Nem.* 5.25; and cf. also Call. *Aet.* 1.21 Ha. (Apollo's intervention), with Harder's note ([2012] 56–7). For the Muses informing on 'first things', cf. e.g. *Il.* 11.218–19; 14.508–9; 16.112–13; Bacchyl. 15.47; Call. *Aet.* 7.c.6–7 Ha.; Verg. *Aen.* 7.40; Stat. *Theb.* 1.4. For the addressee acting as substitute Muse and 'participat[ing]' in the genesis of her own hymn', see Bing and Uhrmeister (1994) 32, on *HArt.* 183–8.

[289] For the reference to 'fitting' (ἀραρίσκω), hence 'pleasing' (ἀρέσκον) in -ῆρες, cf. Hesych. θ 879, s.v. θυμῆρες· ἀρέσκον ψυχῇ *Etym. Magn.* p. 458 K., s.v. θυμάρης.

Callimachus' inspired and crafted hymn with the musical space (the figurative *mouseion*) that is Delos the island.

Fortunately for our understanding of this complex passage, Callimachus was to return to the travel and inspiration issues raised in *HDelos*, in the programmatic/polemical thirteenth *Iamb*. In terms evidently designed to recall *HDelos*, Callimachus rehearses criticism of his own failure, *qua* iambic poet, physically to visit Ephesus; and he responds to allegations that he is divorced both from the physical location of his claimed literary model (Hipponax) and from the divine inspiration of the Muses.[290] The criticism includes these assertions (13–18):

> ... Ἔφεσον, ὅθεν περ οἱ τὰ μέτρα μέλλοντες
> τὰ χωλὰ τίκτειν μὴ ἀμαθῶς ἐναυόνται·
> ἀλλ' εἴ τι θυμὸν ἢ 'πὶ γαστέρα πνευσ.[
> εἴτ' οὖν ἐπ ... ἀρχαῖον εἴτ' ἀπαι.[
> τοῦτ' ἐμπ[έ]πλεκται καὶ λαλευσ[
> Ἰαστὶ καὶ Δωριστὶ καὶ τὸ σύμμικτον.

> ... Ephesus, whence those preparing to produce the limping measures [sc. choliambs] are not unlearnedly inspired. But if something inspires [sc. C.'s] heart or belly, whether old or [untutored?] this is woven in, and babbling ... in Ionic and Doric and in the mixed up way ....

The points in common between iamb and hymn are as follows: inspiration from place visited, and from engaging/mixing with its (Ionian) people; mingling of inspiration and poetic workmanship; alignment of inspiring Muses with literary model; and interweaving the source of inspiration itself into the poem. Callimachus' rejoinder includes the claim (58–9) that the Muses 'have flown by [sc. his detractors], being afraid lest they hear badly of themselves' (παρέπτησαν/ καὐται τρομεῦσαι μὴ κακῶς ἀκούσωσι·), a reprise of the 'passing by' motif in *HDelos*, together with a deft reversal of the notion of song as auditory Muse-epiphany.

Before proceeding further with the Muses' relationship to Delos and the Deliades, we may consider possible symbolism of the Delian horn altar, the focal point (312, 321) of the rituals of choric encirclement described at the end of *HDelos*. Callimachus describes the construction of the altar by the four-year-old Apollo at *HApollo* 57–64: introduced as an analogue for the god's 'weaving' (57) of city-foundations, it is 'woven' (61), with 'walls', from the horns of 'Kynthian' goats. This 'weaving' action has been interpreted by some scholars as a metaphor

---

[290] On *Iamb* 13, see Acosta-Hughes [2002] 60–103, esp. 74–81, 99–103. The poem as a whole is of great interest for the travel and inspiration concepts in *HDelos*.

for the composition of poetry;[291] and it is for consideration whether Callimachus intends the reader to cross-refer the altar (as Apolline arte-fact) to the 'woven' hymn (as Callimachean song-artefact). There is some encouragement for reading the two passages as complementary texts in the immediately preceding praise, in *HDelos*, of Apollo as divine protector, without requirement for defensive walls (23–7): the point lies in Delos' 'sacred' status (cf. the opening τὴν ἱερήν …) and immunity from invasion;[292] thus, association with the Delian altar (itself an analogue for Apolline city-foundation) as focal point for that status, readily comes to mind, and is reinforced by the (sc. choric) songs that 'run around' (28, περιτροχόωσιν) Delos, songs that will have been performed at or near the altar.[293]

'Running around' (28) has a sequel at the altar in the invention of the sailors' encirclement ritual as *paignia* and source of laughter for the young Apollo (316–24). The analogue, unobserved to the best of my knowledge, is between sailors running around the altar while being beaten and a spinning top wheeled around by whip-strokes (321, ὑπὸ πληγῇσιν).[294] It recalls Pittacus' advice to a consultant to observe boys 'spinning their swift hoops with blows' (Callimachus *Ep.* 1.9–10 Pf. [*AP* 7.89], οἱ δ' ἄρ' ὑπὸ πληγῇσι θοὰς βέμβικας ἔχοντες/ ἔστρεφον … παῖδες).[295] This short poem (a Callimachean *paignion*?) has been inter-preted by Enrico Livrea as a literary manifesto, and in my view is later in date than *HDelos*, perhaps written as an epigrammatic guide to the ending of our hymn.[296] In any case, the point of the hymnic analogue

---

[291] Wimmel (1960) 66–9; Acosta-Hughes (2002) 136–7. Contra: Williams (1978) 57. The reading is supported by the poetic associations of *Kynthiades*, to be considered in Appendix III.

[292] For the implications of 'sacred' status, including impunity from invasion, Tarn (1924). With Apollo as ἕρκος (24), substitute for walls, cf. *Il.* 1.283–4 (Achilles) and Theocr. *Id.* 22.220: see Sens (1997) 221.

[293] The analogue of altar and island is confirmed in the concluding address to Delos as unmoving 'hearth'/Hestia of the Kyklades (325, ἱστίη ὦ νήσων εὐέστιε), as the Scholiast observed: ἑστία ἐστὶ μέντοι κυρίως ὁ βωμὸς ὁ ἐν μέσῳ τῷ δόμῳ ἑστώς· ἐπειδὴ οὖν ἡ Δῆλος ἐν μέσῳ τῶν Κυκλάδων ἔστηκε, δοκεῖ ὥσπερ ἑστία τις καὶ βωμὸς εἶναι.

[294] 'Running around': cf. Hesych. δ 817, s.v. Δηλιακὸς βωμός· τὸ περιτρέχειν κύκλῳ τὸν ἐν Δήλῳ βωμὸν καὶ τύπτεσθαι. ἤρξατο τούτου Θησεύς, χαριστήριον τῆς ἀπὸ τοῦ λαβυρίνθου φυγῆς.

[295] Suda β 236, s.v. βέμβηξ cites *Ep.* 1.9–10, and later notes ὡς τροχὸς ὃς μάστιγι δακόμενος στρέφεται; perhaps 'biting' links the two parts of the *paignion* in *HDelos*.

[296] Livrea (1995). Relative dating: see below Appendix III on Call. *Ep.* 62 Pf. and *HApollo*. Livrea (1995) 480 notes parallels with the Prologue to the *Aetia*. Separately, the Delian olive tree is the subject of two references in the *Iambi* (4.84, 13.62): see Acosta-Hughes (2002) 100–102 for the interrelationship of the three texts and meta-poetical significance, on the working assumption of *HDelos'* priority: add that at *Iamb.* 13.61–2 (meagre scrapings of 'finger-tips' compared to morsels from the Delian olive, signifying the exclusion of Callimachus' critics from this source of literary inspiration)

lies with Apollo as the boy wielding the whip that spins the sailor-circle/'top' around the great horn-altar which he has just woven (sc. as a four year old [cf. 324, κουρίζοντι], *HApollo* 58–64). It encourages readers, as they near the end of the hymn, to think carefully about the element of *paignion* within it; and, we may infer, the singer hopes that, like the encirclement ritual of the visiting sailors, his hymn will evoke the god's benign 'laughter' (the reverse of his chilling 'threats'), and will achieve the opening objective of praise by Callimachus' own 'invention', Apollo Kynthios.[297]

A striking feature of Callimachus' hymn-fabric is the way in which its many component elements are brought together by a tissue of interlinking analogues and (in the case of Ares, and the Gauls as latter-day Titans) polar opposites. The hymn itself participates in these patterns: as woven artefact, it is analogous to the *keraton*, itself the sacral 'hearth' of the island and focal point of choric performance; and as inspired song, its performance represents the audible epiphany of the Callimachean Muses in the musical space of Delos. Pindar's first *Hymn* offers a comparable physical-musical analogue between a (Theban) performance by Apollo and the Muses and the fixture of Delos, modelled on the architecture of a Greek temple (above, pp.85, 86).[298] This reflects the place of *mousike* within a well-ordered universal governance, where his own hymn-performance is integrated with the cosmos it describes; and the Muses, as led by Apollo, are the divine intermediaries who enable contemporary poets to give terrestrial effect to musical order and harmony within the sacred performance-space. How far the figurative comparisons of poem and temple were taken by the Greek poets of the Hellenistic era is not certain, but with the help of a closely related Roman perspective from Vergil's *Georgics*, the final section of this article (§VI) will consider whether *HDelos* itself might be read as a figurative *mouseion*.

(e) Philitas and Aratus

What emerges from the foregoing, unsurprisingly, is a strong 'sacral' dimension to Callimachus' orientation as poet-singer: like Theocritus in

---

δακτύλοις plays on ὀδακτάσαι (*HDelos* 322), and on the sailors' loss of the use of their hands (323, χεῖρας ἀποστρέψαντας).

[297] *HDelos* and *paignion*: cf. Bing (1988) 142. For divine laughter as a topic of epilogue/ envoi, see Bundy (1972) 50–51. For Apollo's laughter at a pleasing ritual, cf. Pind. *Pyth.* 10.36 (Hyperboreans). For Apollo as 'threatening' god see above, n.146; and for his smiles/laughter replacing anger, *HHHermes* 420–21 (on hearing Hermes' lyre); Hor. *Odes* 1.10.12 *risit Apollo*.

[298] For poem as 'treasure-house of song', cf. Pind. *Pyth.* 6.7–18; Timoth. *Persae* (791 *PMG*) 232–3.

Dioscuri (*Idyll* 22), Callimachus will sing 'such things as the Muse wishes, and in whatever manner is pleasing to her';[299] but as is so often the case, it is the precise character and delineation of the poet's Muses that matters for programmatic purposes. Theocritus' allegiance to the Muses in *Dioscuri*, he discreetly intimates, is conditioned by membership of the Mouseion;[300] and in the final section, it will be argued that Callimachus' allegiance also lies with the Muses of that sacral institution. This is not to suggest uniformity of outlook among the Alexandrian *philologoi* (the evidence points in quite the opposite direction); but just as Callimachus aligns his Muses with scientific interests as a reflection of the encyclopaedic pursuits of the Mouseion, so he may have sought to align them with the literary values of his older contemporary, and founder-member of the Mouseion, Philitas.[301] Thus, the epilogue to *HApollo* is generally understood to allude to Philitas' *Demeter*, and in the proem to *HDelos* (2), ἦ μέν in address to θυμός is otherwise found only in the *Hermes* (fr. 4.1 Sp., Odysseus' soliloquy). That context has general relevance for Callimachus' interplay between Apollo and Hermes in relation to their hills/epithets (above, p.57) and to their dealings over the lyre (above, p.111). Moreover, the self-address of the Philitan Odysseus is interwoven in the *HDelos* proem with echoes of the Homeric Odysseus' introduction of himself to the Phaeacians, in a programmatic juxtaposition of epic and refinement in the preamble to a hymn that narrates Asteria's wandering.[302] Again, following the first-line re-working of a reference to Kos in Pindar's first *Hymn* (above, p.63), a linguistic allusion to Philitas, the Koan mentor of Ptolemy Philadelphus (and founder-member of the Mouseion), brings a sharply contemporary focus to *HDelos* as hymnic praise of the island-nurse.

[299] *Id.* 22.116–17 εἶπέ, θεά, σὺ γὰρ οἶσθα· ἐγὼ δ᾽ ἑτέρων ὑποφήτης/ φθέγξομαι ὅσσ᾽ ἐθέλεις σὺ καὶ ὅππως τοι φίλον αὐτῇ, and see Sens (1997) 156–7 ad loc. for the Homeric antecedents of 117.

[300] *Id.* 22.221–3 ὕμιν αὖ καὶ ἐγὼ λιγεῶν μειλίγματα Μουσῶν,/ οἵ᾽ αὐταὶ παρέχουσι καὶ ὡς ἐμος οἶκος ὑπάρχει,/ τοῖα φέρω. Juxtaposed with the Muses' contribution, ἐμος οἶκος (my storehouse) alludes to the οἶκος μέγας of the Mouseion where the *philologoi* shared their common table (Strabo 17.1.8, cited below, n.339). The mix of Muses' and poet's contributions is not as innovative as sometimes supposed: cf. e.g. Pind. *Nem.* 3.1–9.

[301] *HApollo*/Philitas: Williams (1978) 93–4; Spanoudakis (2002) 288–93. Similarly, Theocritus first Idyll, an implicit, non-polemical, programme, makes honorific allusions to distinguished (near-) contemporaries, including Philitas. See Cairns (1983) 98; 105–6.

[302] The first figurative use of κουροτρόφος is at *Od.* 9.27, in Odysseus' speech. Cf also ἦ μέν at 29; superlative plus εἰν ἁλὶ κεῖνται at 25; superiority of Ithaca to surrounding islands at 22–3. The parallel between Odysseus and Delos is brought out explicitly in comparison of Asteria to an asphodel blown around at sea, modelled on *Od.* 5.327–32 (Odysseus' raft like thistle at sea): Bing (1988) 121.

Aratus, by contrast, was not a member of the Mouseion, and at
HDelos' time of writing he was at the court of Antigonas Gonatas at
Pella. Notwithstanding Callimachus' admiration for his work (e.g. *Ep.*
27 Pf., *AP* 9.507), it is unclear whether they ever met (or indeed
whether any attempt was made to attract him to Alexandria).[303] At all
events, he is referenced in Delos' address to Leto (204), echoing these
lines from the κατὰ λεπτόν collection (*SH* 109):[304]

> ὦ Λητοῖ σὺ μὲν ἤ με σιδηρείη Φολεγάνδρῳ
> δειλὴν ἤ Γυάρῳ παρελεύσεαι αὐτιχ᾽ ὁμοίην.

> O Leto, you will presently pass by me as like either to rough (iron-
> clad) Pholegandros, poor one that I am, or to Gyaros.

Delos' implication that she is in fact qualitatively different from other
members of the Kyklades group is of course fully developed in *HDelos.*
The Aratean appeal to Leto is verbally echoed in Apollo's direction to
Leto to head for Delos: thus, κείνην γὰρ ἐλεύσεαι εἰς ἐθέλουσαν
(*HDelos* 195) deftly varies Aratus' δειλὴν ... παρελεύσεαι (*SH* 109.2);
and Delos' 'willingness' (195, ἐθέλουσαν) to receive Leto is evidenced
by the anxiety of her Aratean counterpart that she will be 'passed
by'.[305] We know that Callimachus' Leto, under guidance from Apollo,
will not 'pass by' Delos, and that the hymnist's θυμός will not do so,

---

[303] Brink (1946) 13–14; Kidd (1997) 3–5. The *Phaenomena* was also praised in a poem
by a Ptolemy (but probably Philopator): Fraser (1972) 780.

[304] Wilamowitz (1924) 63 observed the relevance of the two lines for Leto's arrival at
Delos: "Wichtig kann ein Gedicht des Aratos gewesen sein ...". Possibly from a hymn
to Apollo: *RE* Suppl. X.28–9 (Ludwig); Lloyd-Jones and Parsons on *SH* 109. Text: that
Strabo read δειλῇ with Γυάρῳ seems likely, since the text is cited to illustrate Gyaros'
poverty; but (unless we read ἤ δειλῇ [Meineke]), it produces a highly suspect hiatus.
σιδηρείη may contrast with Delos' divine golden flowering after Apollo's birth
(*HHApoll.* 135, etc.); the Pholegandros/Gyaros link lies in the belief that mice on the
latter consumed its iron deposits (Aristotle ap. Ael. *NA* 5.14). For 'Delos' as με ...
δειλήν (printed by Maass [1892] 228–9 and Wilamowitz) cf. esp. *AP* 9.408.3
(Antipater of Thessalonica): Delos complains 'alas, for me in my misery (ἐμὲ δειλήν,
exclamatory accusative) by how many ships of the Greeks am I now passed by'. On
Antipater and *HDelos*, see Ypsilanti (2010), but without reference to the Aratean
window intertexts. Aratus' source for the rare με ... δειλήν may have been *Od.* 20.115
ἐμοὶ δειλῇ (self disparagement by mill-worker), in which case cf. also δειλαί ...
ἀλετρίδες at *HDelos* 241–2 of Hera's wish for secret/concealed births for Zeus'
children.

[305] The urgency and emphasis of Delos' appeal (204) πέρα, πέρα εἰς ἐμέ, Λητοῖ (cross,
cross to me, Leto) plays on the Aratean anxiety, with reference to περάω = 'pass
through', 'go beyond'. The motif is beautifully picked up in Iris' attack on Asteria's
eagerness at 224 (to Hera): Ἀστερίη δ᾽ ὀνομαστὶ παρερχομένην ἐκάλεσσεν. The
Aratus background helps read the issue of Delos' motivation, rightly highlighted by
Haslam (1982) 120 commenting on line 195. There is also good comment on the
'willing'/'unwilling' motif, linked to Asteria/Delos' personal independence of mind, in
Giuseppetti (2013) 106–7.

either. The motif is nicely rounded off in the pious behaviour of sailors, none of whom 'pass by' — παρήλυθε — the island without visiting (316–20). That Callimachus is re-working Aratus (and not vice versa) is I think most likely and may be signalled in ἀρητόν (205, just after Leto's arrival).[306] If this is intentional, then Aratus' own name-reference at *Phaenomena* 2 might be compared: in hymning Asteria/Delos, Callimachus may have been signalling awareness of Aratus' engagement on a poem about 'stars'.[307] The programmatic significance lies in the well-known Aratean virtue of *leptotes*, and in the existence of a Delian model in a collection entitled κατὰ λεπτόν.[308]

VI. ΤΑ ΠΡΩΤΑ ΦΕΡΕΣΘΑΙ ΕΚ ΜΟΥΣΕΩΝ

The visiting sailors' ritual has been read as an analogue for the poet and his 'journey', at the point where he ends the hymn and takes his leave of Delos.[309] This attractive proposal is supported by a further echo of *HDelos* at the end of the thirteenth *Iamb*:[310] there, in his rejoinder to the critics who have attacked his failure to visit Ephesus, Callimachus claims that they will themselves be no more inspired or competent than if they were to (sc. visit Delos and) pare morsels from the Delian olive trunk. The polemical point depends, of course, on recognition of the motif of the imaginary visit in *HDelos*. The hymnist's notional visit is consistent with other features, in particular the figure of song as journey, introduced in the proem (οἴμης, 9) to connect the hymn with the figures of travel and arrival in choral lyric.[311] The link passage that

---

[306] The possibility of nameplay at *HDelos* 205, allied (a) to the verbal ambiguity of ἀρητόν, 'longed for', 'accursed', 'unspeakable' (see Mineur [1984] 185–6) with (b) allusion to ἀραῖη, 'longed-for' in ἀραιή (191) is perhaps supported by Verg. *Georg.* 3.4–6: *quis .../ ... inlaudati nescit Busiridis aras?* [bi-lingual play on 'curses'; cf. ἀρητόν]/ *cui non dictus* [cf. *Phaen. 2* ἄρρητον, with Bing (1990)] *... Latonia Delos.*

[307] In this context, with πόντῳ ἐνεστήρικται (13, the wandering Delos, 'set/fixed in the sea'), cf. (a) Homeric unicum at *Il.* 21.168 (Achilles and Asteropaeus), γαίῃ ἐνεστή-ρικτο, with wordplay Asteropaeus/ ἐνεστήρικτο; (b) Aratus' use of the verb for fixed stars (ἐστήρικται, *Phaen.* 230, 234, 351, 500; all concluding spondaic lines). C. too uses the simplex of another rock/woman, Niobe, at *HApoll.* 23 λίθος ἐστήρικται (concluding spondaic line).

[308] On the Aratean title, and λεπτός, Maass (1892) (sceptical); Reitzenstein (1931) 25–40; Cameron (1995) 321–28, esp. 324, 326. On λεπτός and weaving: Stephens (2002–3), 14–15.

[309] Hunter (2011) 249–50 observes "a parallelism ... between the passing sailors and the poet on his own journey", and suggests that the episode functions as a hymnic closure-device, "as the poet is about to take his leave of the island".

[310] For this important reminiscence, see Acosta-Hughes (2002) 99–103.

[311] For journey-figures at the beginning and end of poems, cf. Bing (2005) 122 n.9. For the figure, and its grounding in the travels of the itinerant singer, Steiner (1986) 76–86,

follows (11–27) presents topics of the rhetorical *epibaterion* (arrival speech/poem): it suggests that the speaker approaches from the sea, observes the island's physical setting and directly addresses her on arrival as 'dear Delos' (27).[312] Other suggestive features include Delos' choric visit to Oceanus and Tethys (17–21), Aphrodite's payment of a figurative 'boarding', or 'landing' fee on arrival at Cyprus (22, ἀντ' ἐπιβάθρων), and the intimation in ἀκοῦσαι (29) that Delos herself will actually 'hear' the hymn.[313] The hymnist is thus acting the part of a singing worshipper: he is visiting the island; but, as οἴμης ἀποδάσσομαι makes clear, the journey and the song are one and the same: there is no visit to Delos, and we are meant to understand that it is an inspired fiction (we may compare the explicit failure physically to visit Ephesus in the thirteenth Iamb).

No occasion is announced, however, and we are not told for what purposes the hymnist makes this imaginary singing visit. In a figurative sense, Delos herself commissions the hymn 'from the Muses' (4–5): Δῆλος δ' ἐθέλει τὰ πρῶτα φέρεσθαι/ ἐκ Μουσέων (Delos aspires to take first things/ from the Muses). A god could indeed instruct the composition of a hymn;[314] but Delos' claim to hymnic honours cannot be taken literally as a requirement placed on Callimachus by the Delians.[315] Rather, it alludes to civic commission as one of several contexts for the composition and performance of song. There is a further allusion to prize-competition (in this case among the Kyklades for primacy in the Muses' priorities). And at yet a third level, Callimachus offers a variant on the motif of song as sacral offering, that is, as figurative 'first fruits' and in that sense parallel to the various theoric offerings described at the end of the hymn: for the metaphor, compare the opening of Germanicus' *Aratea* (3–4; to Tiberius): *te veneror, tibi sacra fero doctique laboris/ primitias* (it's you I worship, to you that I bear

esp. 77–9. For epic poem as 'voyage', Hunter (1993) 84 (Apollonius); and for an analogue between the chariot that carries Artemis to Olympus and C.'s hymn, see Bing and Uhrmeister (1994) 26–7.

[312] Mineur (1984) 59–60, citing Cairns (1972) 212–13 for topics of the rhetorical *epibaterion*; Hopkinson's sceptical tone ([1985] 250) is misplaced. For C.'s exquisite suggestion of arrival by sea, see Appendix III. The disparagement of Delos as 'fitter for sheerwaters than racecourse for horses' (ἐπίδρομος ... ἵπποις [12]), reverses the topic of spectacular public sites such as ἵππων δρόμους in arrival encomia; cf. Men. Rhet. *RG* III.386.25 Sp.

[313] Choric visit: thus Stephens (2015) 183, rightly observing that the procession "prefigures the *theoriai* to Delos at the end of the poem."

[314] Thus, Macedonikos' inscribed paean to Apollo and Asklepios (Furley–Bremer [2001] 228–33 [7.5]) was composed τοῦ θεοῦ προστάξαντος.

[315] Meillier (1979) 188 supposes (without citing 4–5) that *HDelos* was indeed composed "à la demande des Déliens eux-mêmes et pour une fête locale."

sacral offerings, and the first fruits of my learned labour).[316] All three contexts are figuratively in play, but it is song as 'offering' that is of most immediate interest, in that it suggests that the parallelism between the hymn and Delian ritual is not confined to the visiting sailors: rather, it brings the full range of choric *theoria*, as described in lines 274–315, into consideration of the hymn's occasional setting and of the hymnist's dramatic *persona*.[317] Such a 'theoric' context would certainly be consistent with third-century patterns of regal *theoria* from Alexandria to Delos.[318] Within *HDelos*, the hymnist as *theoros* would also be consistent with various 'processional' references, themselves a reflection of theoric journeys to, and processions on, Delos.[319] Moreover as a theoric hymn that reflects upon its own journey, *HDelos* might might well have Pindar's twelfth paean among its generic antecedents, if it is correct to identify that work as a *prosodion* (a processional poem).[320]

HDelos has much to say about song-performance, its origins, its instrumentation and its divine patrons. A focal point, closely interlinked with the proem and with the concluding musical rituals, is the swan-passage (above, §5[c]); and it is for consideration whether the conjunction of visiting swans and the indigenous chorus of Deliades, the joint patronage of Apollo and Muses, and the associated *aition* of the seven-string lyre, represents self-reflection on the part of the singer, and if so to what degree. Is this a purely objective account of Apolline-Delian music, or is it in some sense prototypical for the role of Callimachus' I-figure himself? This large issue bears on Callimachus'

---

[316] Cf. Mineur (1984) 14, comparing 283–4 οἱ μέν τοι καλάμην τε καὶ ἱερὰ δράγματα πρῶτοι/ ἀσταχύων φορέουσιν, and 298–9. Cf. Fernandez-Galiano (1976–80) 187 ("primicias"). With Germanicus' *primitias*, cf. Gell. *NA Praef.* 13 *primitias quasdam et quasi libamenta ingenuarum artium dedimus*; *TLL* X.2.1253.37–45. Cf. also Theocr. *Id.* 22.221–3 (hymn to Dioscuri) ὑμῖν αὖ καὶ ἐγὼ λιγεῶν μειλίγματα Μουσῶν ... φέρω: the inspired hymn (cf. 116–17) is borne to the Dioscuri as sacral offering both 'from the Muses', and 'consisting of the Muses' (i.e performed hymn as 'Muse'): Sens (1997) 221–2.

[317] Theoric offerings: Rutherford (2013) 110–25, esp. 114–16, on *aparchai*. For 'bringing a song', ibid. 239–43 (including Olen).

[318] Alexandrian/Lagid *theoria* to Delos: Bruneau (1970 511 – 33; Rutherford (2013) 287–8. The Ptolemaic Nesiarch based on Delos sponsored choric performances by the Deliades: Rigsby (1980).

[319] Theoric processions: Rutherford (2013) 206–8. Processions in *HDelos*: 17–22 (Delos leads the island-procession to Oceanos and Tethys); 75–8 (processional flight of Boeotian landscape features); 197–9 (Asteria's processional journey to 'see' the Kyklades, followed by Poseidonian seaweed from Geraistos); 283–95 (journey of the Hyperborean offerings). Given the fundamental importance of *theoria* as 'viewing' (Rutherford [2013] 142–8), add perhaps, Hesperus as observer of Delian song (καταβλέπει, 304). Cf. also Verg. *Ecl.* 6.86 *processit Vesper*; and for Hesperus' concluding role in the Alexandrian procession of Philadelphus, Athen. 197d; Foertmayer (1988).

[320] D'Alessio (1997) 28.

hymnic *persona* and definitive treatment lies beyond the scope of this article. But the parallel I have suggested with the Homeric hymnist (above, p.115) may encourage the reader to consider the relationship between the visiting singer and the choric Deliades (might they perform his hymn?); and we are, I think, bound to ask whether Theseus' (Apolline) role as kithara-playing chorus-leader at the Delian altar, again theoric in character (*HDelos* 312–15), is in any sense an antecedent for the Callimachean hymnist. More obviously relevant to Callimachus' hymn-offering is the '*nomos* of the Lycian old man' brought to Delos by Olen (304–6) and performed by female and male choirs:[321] this hymn, a text of which was available to Pausanias, is cryptically delineated but would appear, for Callimachean purposes, to have represented the first hymnic replication of the 'sacred *melos* of Eileithyia' uttered by the landscape-nymph Deliades (256–7);[322] and in that sense it might also be read as an antecedent of *HDelos*. There, for the present, the issue must be left, with the interim conclusion that Callimachus appears to present himself as a theoric singer-kitharist modelled not just on the Homeric hymnist, but perhaps also on the composers of choric *prooimia* as well. Certainly, *HDelos* deserves to be brought into consideration of the issue of 'choric' performance, real or imagined, of the *Hymns*.

It might be argued from the foregoing (as also from the figurative conventions of travel and arrival in Greek lyric poetry) that *HDelos* was, in reality, intended for performance on the island. As already noted, however, it is overwhelmingly likely that Callimachus meant the hymnist's travel to be read as inspired fiction, whereby he is transported in imagination to the island. The hymn cannot have been composed as an integral component of any Delian sacral occasion: it touches at many points on Delian tradition, culture, and worship; but, as the introduction of Apollo Kynthios indicates (and the concluding *paignion* confirms), the poem as a whole is an invention that could

---

[321] Olen is described as θεοπρόπος (305), properly an 'oracle delegate': Rutherford (2013) 98–9.

[322] Pausanias (8.21.3) is aware of several hymns attributed to Lycian Olen 'for the Delians', but specifies only that to Eileithyia. At 9.27.2, he adds that the hymn to Eileithyia identified her (not Aphrodite) as 'mother of Eros'. Of especial interest in that context is C.'s rare epithet ἀμφιβόητον (resounding all around) of Delos in the preceding line (303): it recalls C.'s own revision of Antagoras' hymn to Eros at *HZeus* 2, where he replaces ἀμφιβόητον (celebrated everywhere) of Eros' lineage with ἀμφήριστον (disputed); see Stephens (2003) 79–80. That C. emphatically associates the performance of Olen's hymn with the crowning of Aphrodite's image (δὴ τότε καί..., 307) cannot be coincidental: it is a placatory gesture to offset her anticipated displeasure at exclusion from Olen's song, and by extension at C.'s reference to that song.

have had no formal place in Delian sacral observance.[323] The suggestion that it was written for a federal celebration of the Delian *Ptolemaieia* by the Nesiotic League might be thought to carry more weight: *HDelos* reflects Delos' role in the central administration of the League;[324] it refers to a 'gathering of islands' (modelled on the Ionian festival in *HHApollo*), and it alludes to an earlier thalassocracy (Minos).[325] Indeed, the hymn's positioning of the League as the successor to earlier political communities would bear further investigation. Yet the island references (as well as the central tribute to Kos) go well beyond the membership of the League, and it is difficult to see how a Hymn to Delos, universal in scope and asserting the island's precedence over all other islands, could have been accommodated within a Nesiotic festival.[326] On the other hand, there is nothing here that would have been inappropriate in an Alexandrian celebration of Ptolemaic maritime power, and there is much, including the prominence of Poseidon, that would have been familiar to a cosmopolitan audience at Alexandria.[327] Of course, for all we know, the hymn might have been heard later on Delos, perhaps in an epideictic ἀκρόασις of the kind recorded in civic decrees honouring visiting poets; but that is a quite different proposition from the composition of a hymn 'for' a celebration of federal *Ptolemaieia*.

The Egyptian setting of *HDelos* is implicit in the first reference to the Nile (185, the deaths of the Gallic mercenaries); and as the Nile flows underground from Egypt to Delian Inopos, so our hymn is to be read as emanating from Alexandria.[328] Embracing almost all areas of

---

[323] For an analysis of fiction, poetic authority and the divine in *HZeus*, see Stephens (2003) 79–91; 113–14. The *Phaedrus* (again) supplies the cardinal text, the influence of which can be traced as late as Juvenal 3: A. Hardie (1998a).

[324] Stephens (2015) 162; Weber (1993) 303–4; on the Nesiotic *koinon*, dynastic festivals and Delian *theoria* as a component of the political context, Giuseppetti (2013) 26–9, 31–3.

[325] Thus, in the sequel to πρῶτα φέρεσθαι we read (16–18): ἀλλά οἱ οὐ νεμεσητὸν ἐνὶ πρώτῃσι λέγεσθαι,/ ὁππότ' ἐς Ὠκεανόν τε καὶ ἐς Τιτηνίδα Τηθύν/ νῆσοι ἀολλίζονται, ἀεὶ δ' ἔξαρχος ὁδεύει. The congregation of islands recalls the agonistic Ionian festival on Delos (*HHApollo* 146–52), but with playful allusion (ἀολλίζονται) to an alternative etymology of Αἰολεῖς, *vice* the 'Homeric' Ἰάονες ἠγερέθονται (147): διὰ τὸ ἐκ πολλῶν ἐθνῶν συνηθροῖσθαι· ἀπὸ τοῦ αἰολίζω (*Etym. Magn.* p. 37.25–6 K., s.v.). But these are the 'large' islands, which were not, of course members of the Nesiotic League.

[326] The membership of the Nesiotic League is not recorded, but appears to have been centred on, if not confined to, the Kyklades: Merker (1970) 158; cf. Reger (1994) 39–40.

[327] The Milan Papyrus of Posidippus has added to understanding of the literary projection of Ptolemaic geopolitical interests: see Bing (2005); and cf. esp. AB 20.5–6 (to Poseidon).

[328] Possible Egyptian influences on *HDelos* have not been taken into consideration here. I have difficulty in seeing how some pharaonic allusions detected by commentators could have been accessible to a wider Greek readership unless they had been explicitly

ancient Greek learning, it is manifestly the intellectual product of the
Library. In addition, the four references to the Muses considered in the
previous section point to it being the joint work of inspired singer and
Muses, and invite consideration of institutional reference to the royal
Mouseion. The Muses' presence, like that of other Greek divinities, was
most readily experienced within their own sacred space.[329] The fundamental importance of the inspirational setting had been registered in
two influential texts: the first, Hesiod's encounter with the Muses on
their sacred mountain (*Theogony* 22–34) was to provide Callimachus
with the Helikonian setting of the *Aetia*, on a site by this time graced
with a famous Mouseion; and the second, Socrates' inspirational experience in Plato's *Phaedrus*, at the 'Nymphs' stream and *mouseion*'
(278b, τὸ Νυμφῶν νᾶμά τε καὶ μουσεῖον), reflected the establishment
of the Academy itself as a Mouseion, and was among Theocritus' sources for the quasi-sacral staging of the first *Idyll* (libation to the Muses;
143–5). Similarly, I would suggest, the allusive process whereby Callimachus experiences the Muses' inspiration, and encouragement to proceed to a Delos-hymn, may best be understood as unfolding within
their sacred domain.

Callimachus alludes intertextually at the outset to the sacral-
collegiate aspect of his work, and other texts from the archaic era and
later depict in sacral terms the relationship between singer-kitharists as
an occupational group and the Muses as their professional patrons.[330]
The extent to which this material can be taken literally, as reflections of
sacral observance by professional singers, cannot now be known (in at
least some instances, sacral terms may be used with purely metapoetical force, to signify the act of composition). Yet the cumulative
evidence of some form of cult *realia* associated from an early period
with the professional status of the singer is not to be set aside as figurative adornment or pious fiction. By the Hellenistic era, certainly, Mouseia of different kinds (civic, private, schoolrooms, joint shrines with
other divinities and heroised poets) were being established across the
Greek-speaking world.[331] With the advent of precincts, altars, priest-
hoods, sacrifices, statuary, and cult-regulation, the educated public's

---

treated in Greek writings that are the subject of intertextual reference by C., hence part
of the Greek 'reception' of Egypt. One example, the regal dimension to the Egyptian
goat-cult of Mendes, is considered in Appendix III. But in general, I share Weber's
reservations ([1993] 376–88).

[329] For the general point, see Rutherford (2013) 13.

[330] A. Hardie (2005a) 14–20; Power (2010) 331–6; 385–93.

[331] There is no comprehensive treatment of Mouseia: *RE* XVI.797–821 (Müller–Graupa)
provides an introduction. Boyancé (1972) remains essential for the philosophical Mouseia,
with Lynch (1972) 108–27; Fraser (1972) 312–16; cf. A. Hardie (1997) 21–3; 30–31.

direct experience of the Muses was changing. Their very name, when governed by a preposition (thus, ἐν Μούσαις; παρὰ ταῖς Μούσαις), could refer to their shrine; and a small but growing body of evidence reveals that poets in the early Hellenistic era were prepared to reflect these institutional realities in their work.[332]

A character in the first *Mime* of Herodas, extolling the delights of Egypt (1.26–36), places 'Mouseion' (Μουσῆον, 31) at the exact centre of her list, preceded by 'the precinct of the *Theoi Adelphoi*, the king …'. The dynastic context had been integral to the remarkable Library and Mouseion programme from the outset, as the Ptolemies set out to establish Alexandria as a Greek intellectual centre. They were not, of course, the first Macedonian monarchs to appropriate the cult of the Muses: Archelaos had set the pattern at the end of the fifth century, giving the Muses a spectacular new setting in their original homeland, and promoting Aegae as a centre of Greek culture.[333] Pimpleia itself owes its Hellenistic currency to these Macedonian initiatives, and to the challenge they presented to Helikon (Thespiae later responded with the invention of an original, autochthonous Muse-cult of its own). The Macedonian claim to the Muses is recalled in 'Pimpleia' (*HDelos* 7), but it is treated with transparent humour ('the Muses hate the singer who sings not of Pimpleia'), possibly in an effort to distance presentation of the Muses from the polemical challenges of earlier times. Be that as it may, the birthplace analogue between Pimpleia and Delos carries with it, as a corollary, an 'outward extension' analogue between the Muses

---

[332] See Derow and Forrest (1982) on a Chian inscription (late 3rd/early 2nd cent.) honouring (probably) Hermocles, known from Delphi as a hymnist of Apollo; he has established and paid for a shrine to the Muses (and probably Rome), wishing (31–2) [τὰς τῶν] Μουσῶν τιμὰς συναύξειν ταῖς πολίταις (31–2) and acknowledging (34) τὴν περιγεγονυῖαν τῆι πόλει δόξ[αν ἀπὸ τῶν ποιητῶν]. Posidippus (AB 118.1; *SH* 705) addresses Μοῦσαι πολιήτιδες, clearly the Muses of a civic Mouseion, and presumably at Pella; the same poem refers to Pimpleia and addresses Apollo as 'Kynthios' (8–9). Posidipp. AB 63.9–10 (with Scodel's restoration of 10) records a statue of Philitas set up in a Mouseion (Cos or Alexandria: A. Hardie [2003]): ἐκ Πτολε]μαίου δ' ὧδε θεοῦ θ' ἅμα καὶ βασιλῆος/ ἄγκειμ]αι Μουσέων εἵνεκα Κῷος ἀνήρ. At Herodas *Mime* 8.71–2, τὰ μέλεα πολλοὶ κάρτα …/ τιλεῦσιν ἐν Μούσηισιν, the critical action of τιλεῦσιν (ripping apart the poems) will take place ἐν Μούσηισιν (in the shrine of the Muses); cf. Athenaeus 629a for an epigram on a dancer teaching ἐν Μώσαις (in the precinct of the Muses [sc. of Helicon/Thespiae]). See n.300 above for an allusion to the Mouseion at Theocr. *Id.* 22.222.

[333] For these actions, and the response of Thespiae with the invention of the Aloades' autochthonous cult of three Muses, see A. Hardie (2006) 59–61. Pimpleia was in the *chora* of Dion, site of a major Macedonian festival in honour of Zeus and the Muses; and it acquired an association with Orpheus as Muse-son and as warrior-initiator: *RE* XX.1387–89 (J. Schmidt). In this context, Giuseppetti (2013) 52–3 observes the juxtaposition of Pimpleia and address to Apollo Kynthios at Posidipp. AB 118.8–9 (*SH* 705).

and Apollo, so that the wider efficacy of the Muses is presented as, in effect, a function of the world-wide acceptance of Apolline music. The Muses' cult extension to Helikon and by implication to the Alexandrian Mouseion, are jointly referenced in the Helikonian context of the learned enquiry addressed (82–5) to 'my goddesses'.

Callimachus does not juxtapose the Muses with Ptolemy. But the king is directly identified with praise of Apollo in *HDelos* (188–90):[334]

> ἐσσόμενε Πτολεμαῖε, τά τοι μαντήια φαίνω.
> αἰνήσεις μέγα δή τι τὸν εἰσέτι γαστέρι μάντιν
> ὕστερον ἤματα πάντα.

> Ptolemy who are to be, these are the prophecies I reveal for you. Greatly will you praise the prophet yet in the womb, in after time for all your days.

The action of μαντήια φαίνω is represented by the recording of the Apollo's prophecy in *HDelos* itself (162–95), and of course the same passage simultaneously represents Ptolemy's reciprocal praise of the μάντις. Ptolemaic praise is thus articulated by the hymnist, who thereby makes good the prophecy, and whose own hymn is thus revealed to have been predicted by Apollo. The alignment of king and hymnist is reinforced by the echo (p.65f.) of the proem in αἰνήσεις. Thus, as *HDelos* unfolds, it ceases to be a purely personal initiative by the singer: it takes on dynastic significance, in which the workings of fate (165, ἐκ Μοιρέων of Philadelphus and Kos) are aligned with the obligations now placed by Delos upon the Muses (ἐκ Μουσέων, 5); and it is the regal centrepiece which points decisively to the royal foundation of the Mouseion at Alexandria as the scene of this hymn. The dramatic location of *HDelos*, as I see it, is not at the Delian altar but in the Mouseion itself: this is where the hymnist receives his inspiration; and when he addresses 'my goddesses' and asks the Muses to 'speak' (82), we may (with Mineur) picture a gesture towards the shrine's cult statuary. Again, we might suppose Apollo's direct address to Ptolemy, the majestic ἐσσόμενε Πτολεμαῖε (188), to be uttered in the presence of the king, who would thus participate in the performance-scenario. Horace's fourth Roman Ode, addressed to the Muses in their shrine in the presence of the princeps, offers a close Augustan analogue.[335]

---

[334] Text: the reading, as between MSS φαίνω and POxy 2225 [Φοίβ]ου, is uncertain: the former conveys the sense of an Apolline oracular epiphany to the future king, and αἰνήσεις … μάντιν then conveys a clear sound-sense reciprocity for μαντήια φαίνω; see further Giuseppetti (2013) 124 n.8 (citing *Od.* 11.96 καὶ τοι νημερτέα εἴπω), 137. For the case for 'Phoebus', see Stephens (2015) 211.

[335] A. Hardie (2008) 107; (2010) 298–304.

Apollo is not addressed directly in *HDelos* other than as god-in-embryo by Leto (212–14), and this may be a reflection of his status as a distant god, who will receive the hymn at Delos as, in formal terms, a subsidiary *laudandus*. Ptolemy Philadelphus showed little political interest in the cult of Apollo, and Callimachus' motives for fostering a distinctive interest in Apollo, while according relatively little overt attention to Dionysus (contrast Theocritus *Id*. 17.112–16), lie beyond the scope of this paper; but on the basis of the analysis of Apollo and the Muses in §V, I believe that Mineur was right to connect his presence in *HDelos*, and his prediction of Ptolemy's future praise, with the latter's patronage of the Mouseion.[336] We know nothing about Apollo's presence in the Mouseion, but it is inherently likely that his traditional role as leader of the Muses was depicted there, in painting or statuary. The thirteenth *Iamb*, a poem (as we have seen) of special interest for understanding *HDelos* (fr. 203.1 Pf.), begins Μοῦσαι καλαὶ κἄπολλων, οἷς ἔγω σπένδω (Fair Muses and Apollo, to whom I make libation); and while sacral language of this sort can of course have a metapoetical dimension (the poem itself as an offering, or libation), it is illustrative of an element in early Greek lyric poetry, the joint worship of Apollo and the Muses, that cannot be dismissed as wholly figurative in origin or character.[337] The association was strong enough at Alexandria to be celebrated in a Ptolemaic festival for Apollo and the Muses (attested by Vitruvius [7 *Praef.*] and to be assigned to the reign of Philopator, towards the end of the third century).[338]

The Mouseion gathered its scholarly personnel from various parts of the Greek world, and operated on a collegiate basis, as a κοινόν. Its members shared its resources, financial and otherwise, and Strabo speaks of *philologoi* 'participating in the Mouseion'.[339] This shared institutional culture bears on the language of sharing adopted at the outset

---

[336] Mineur (1984) 179; cf. Stephens (2015) 211.

[337] Thus, the anonymous line preserved at Dionys. Hal. *Comp.* 17 σοι Φοῖβε Μοῦσαί τε σύμβωμοι; and another fragment (sometimes attributed to Terpander) at *Anal. Gramm.* 6.6 K. σπονδεῖος δ' ἐκλήθη ἀπὸ τοῦ ῥυθμοῦ τοῦ ἐν ταῖς σπονδαῖς ἐπαυλομένου τε καὶ ἐπαδομένου οἷον 'σπένδωμεν ταῖς Μνάμας παισὶν Μούσαις/ καὶ τῷ Μωσάρχῳ Λατοῦς υἱεῖ'. Cf. Plut. *Mor.* 743c (before a private discussion about the Muses) ... σπονδὰς ἐποιησάμεθα ταῖς Μούσαις, καὶ τῷ Μουσηγέτῃ παιανίσαντες ..., where there can be no question of metaliterary reading. For hymn-singing in accompaniment to libation, cf. also the adscript to an Erythrean paian (Furley–Bremer [2001] 162 [6.1.1]) ὑμνεῖτ(ε) ἐπὶ σπονδαῖς Ἀπόλλωνος κυανοπλοκάμου/ παῖδα Σέλευκον; Plut. *Tit. Flam.* 16.6.

[338] Fraser (1970) 119–121. For paucity of interest in Apollo at Alexandria, Fraser (1972) I.196.

[339] Strabo 17.1.8 τῶν δὲ βασιλείων μέρος ἐστι καὶ τὸ Μουσεῖον, ἔχον περίπατον καὶ ἐξέδραν καὶ οἶκον μέγαν ἐν ᾧ τὸ συσσίτιον τῶν μετεχόντων τοῦ Μουσείου φιλολόγων ἀνδρῶν. ἔστι δὲ ἐν τῇ συνόδῳ ταύτῃ καὶ χρήματα κοινὰ καὶ ἱερεὺς ὁ ἐπὶ τῷ Μουσείῳ, τεταγμένος ... ὑπὸ τῶν βασιλέων ....

by the hymnist (9): Δήλῳ νῦν οἴμης ἀποδάσσομαι. Might the hymn itself be read as a figurative *mouseion*? It travels in imagination to Delos as the embodiment of the goddess Muses and as their offering to Delos; it represents the gathered intellectual resources of shrine and Library; and its celebration of Delos is elaborated not only through textual evocation of classical authors, but also with reference to contemporary and near-contemporary authors who were laying the foundations of that remarkable institution.

There was a precedent of sorts in Alcidamas' 'Mouseion', a prose work on poets and poetry. But the most revealing extant testimony as to the reception of *HDelos* as an embodiment of the Muses comes from Rome.[340] In the proem to the third *Georgic*, following ostensible rejection of Delos as a commonplace (!) poem-subject (6), Vergil depicts a future epic as a poem-temple constructed of marble (12). The temple will house Muse-statues brought from Greece (11: Vergil's *templum* is modelled jointly on the Roman shrine of the Muses in the Aedes Herculis Musarum and on the temple of Palatine Apollo, under construction). At the centre of this poem-temple will be 'Caesar' (16). In the inspired role of poet-priest Vergil is transported to the location in imagination, and leads cattle in procession to sacrificial slaughter (21–3). He surveys the future scene: on the (metapoetical) curtain that rises on the dramatic productions, *Britanni* will be 'inwoven' (25, *intexti*); and temple doors will be engraved with scenes from Greek and Roman warfare, culminating in the Nile 'inundating' (with war) and 'columns rising with ships' bronze' (that is, civil-war rostra-trophies). Paired with this extended ekphrastic figure, at the end of the second *Georgic*, is Vergil's self-portrayal as the Muses' neophyte priest bearing their *sacra*: there, he seeks the Muses' acceptance in order to access scientific understanding of the workings of the celestial cosmos; but, diffident (as I-figure) as to the outcome of his prayer, Vergil goes on to project the sister-Nymphs as terrestrial counterparts to the Muses, and thus as an alternative source of wisdom on the various landscape domains they represent; and the representation of terrestrial Nymphs in contemporary *choreia* is illuminated through Spartan parthenaic *choreia*, Mt. Taygeta itself 'traversed by maidens' (487–8).

Despite his ostensible rejection of Delos (*Georg.* 3.6), Vergil's twinned inspirational centrepiece is cited here at length by way of conclusion, because it could scarcely be bettered as a summation in essence of *HDelos* itself. A single window reference will underline the close textual engagement: Vergil's 'rising columns', *surgentes* ...

---

[340] On all that follows, see A. Hardie (2002) 187–90, 193–4, 194–200.

columnas (29), looks through *HDelos* to the rising κίονες of Pindar's first *Hymn* (fr. 33d.6–9 Ma.), while the trophy ships' *rostra* relate to Callimachus' Gallic shield-trophies (*HDelos* 185–7). Other influences, not least the scientific perspective of Empedocles, are engaged; but that Vergil should so clearly place *HDelos* at the heart of his programmatic exploration of the celestial and terrestrial, as also of the mythical and contemporary, is remarkable. A further interpretive gain lies in the theoric and processional context of Vergil's inspired transposition from poem-composer to priest-leader of a sacrificial procession (3.21–3): here, I would suggest, is a Roman sequel to our Callimachean singer-hymnist positioned in imagination as choric procession-leader at the Delian altar.

That the *manes Callimachi* would have appreciated Vergil's signal (yet ostensibly negated, thus ἄδηλον), homage to Δῆλος and to *HDelos* may be assumed. Perhaps Apollo Kynthios himself — evoked within the temple statuary as *Troiae Cynthius auctor* alongside Trojan *nomina* sprung from Jupiter — might have been moved to recognition, approval and praise.

APPENDIX I. *HZEUS* 1–3 AS PROGRAMMATIC BOOK-APXH

There is neglected programmatic evidence for unitary design in Callimachus' book of *Hymns*, in the opening lines of the first hymn. It has long been recognised that the poet had Pindar in view in writing *HZeus* 1–3:

> Ζηνὸς ἔοι τί κεν ἄλλο παρὰ σπονδῇσιν ἀείδειν
> λώιον ἢ θεὸν αὐτόν ...
> Πηλαγόνων ἐλατῆρα

> What better to hymn at libations of Zeus than the god himself ... driver of the Giants

Compare Pind. fr. 89a Ma.

> τί κάλλιον ἀρχομένοισιν ἢ καταπαυομένοισιν
> ἢ βαθυζωνόν τε Λατώ
> καὶ θοᾶν ἵππων ἔλατειραν ἀεῖσαι;

> What is finer, in beginning or coming to an end, than to sing both of deep-breasted Leto and the driver of swift horses?[341]

---

[341] Ziegler (1913) 352–3; Merry (1914) 48–9; cf. Fuhrer (1988) 60 n.19. The parallel is noted, but not further developed, by McLennan (1977) 26 and D'Alessio (2007) 64 n.1.

As was recognised, apparently independently, by Ziegler (1913) and Merry (1914), Callimachus here reworks θοᾶν ... ἔλατειραν ἀεῖσαι (of Artemis) in ἀείδειν ... θεὸν ... ἐλατῆρα. Less obvious, and hitherto un-remarked, is the variation of τί κάλλιον in the near-anagram τί κεν ἄλλο, followed by λώιον in the sense of κάλλιον.[342] Alongside this intertextual reading is a suggestive parallel in Euripides (1087 *TrGF*; context unknown): εὐφημία γὰρ παρὰ σπονδαῖσι κάλλιστον (good speech is the fairest thing to accompany libations), a line that would seem to resonate with Xenophanes' sympotic injunctions concerning hymnic *euphemia*, prayer and libation (fr. 1.13–15 W.) and his famous prohibition of accounts of 'the battles of Titans and Giants' and other such 'fictions of predecessors' (ibid. 21–2). Such exclusions Calli-machus himself, of course, proceeds to ignore (Πηλαγόνων ἐλατῆρα).[343]

The Pindaric lines are known from an ancient commentary on an Aristophanic parody, where they cited as 'the opening of a *prosodion* [processional poem] by Pindar' (Schol. *Knights* 1264; ἀρχὴ προσοδίου Πινδάρου). That Apollo too featured in this processional ode, jointly honoured with Leto and Artemis, would be consistent with what is known of Pindar's odes for performance on Delos, and may be implicit in an echo of Theognis (below); but his original presence cannot be assumed.[344] At all events, Callimachus' opening intertext springs a

---

[342] The mix is observed and again re-worked by Theocritus in the *Encomium to Ptolemy*: *Id.* 17.116–17 (poets praise Ptolemy) τί δὲ κάλλιον ἀνδρί κεν εἴη [cf. ἔοι τί κεν]/ ὀλβίῳ ἢ κλέος ἐσθλόν ... ἀρέσθαι; see below, n.346 for likely correspondence with Theognis in proem; and cf. 7 Πτολεμεῖον ἐπιστάμενος καλὰ εἰπεῖν/ ὑμνήσαιμ'.

[343] C. immediately plunges into literary dispute (ἀμφήριστον, 5) and falsehood (ἐψεύ-σαντο, 7), both contrary to the spirit of the Xenophanean symposium, but both none-theless constituting the fifth foot of 'spondaic' lines: surely with ironic reference to the association of the metrical foot with the solemnity of 'spondaic' flute music accom-panying libations (Dionys. Hal. *Dem.* 22; Pollux 4.79; *Anal. Gramm.* 6.6 K.; cf. Plut. *Mor.* 35a). Underlying the wit is a neglected feature in the relative dating of the *Phaenomena* and the *Hymns*, i.e. the incidence of spondaic lines, and specifically the parallelism of *HZeus* 53 (the Kouretes protect the infant Zeus), ending καὶ μή σεο κουρίζοντος, with *Phaen.* 32 (the same scenario), ending ὁ μιν τότε κουρίζοντα; and of *HZeus* 7, ending ἐψεύσαντο, with *Phaen.* 35 Δικταῖοι Κούρητες ὅτε Κρόνον ἐψεύ-δοντο. Aratus is describing the Katasterism of figures involved in Zeus' protection. Were the two poets sharing their work as it progressed, or is one echoing the other? See below, Appendix III, on the Katasterism of Capella/Mazos.

[344] Aristophanes' chorus goes on to address (Pythian) Apollo (1270), and later (1298–99) concludes with a parodic appeal (to a named contemporary) ἴθ' ὦ ἄνα ... ἔξελθε (go, oh lord, go out ...), phrases in which Wilamowitz (1919) 54–7 detected further Pindaric parody; he concluded that Aristophanes had in view a single ode for Delphi. Yet the components of the parody need not come from the same ode, and Leto/Artemis in a 5th cent. *prosodion* points rather to Delos; for joint Delian celebration with Apollo, cf. Kowalzig (2007) 61–2. Cf also (briefly) D'Alessio (1997) 29. The particle combi-nation τε ... καί is listed by Slater (1969) 257 (s.v. καί B1) among those where "τε is

surprise, in that it does not concern Zeus, his immediate hymnic subject, but brings into play the subject of his third hymn (Artemis) and a protagonist (Leto) of the fourth, to Delos.

The background presence of Apollo might nonetheless be suggested by a close antecedent to Pindar's twin participles ἀρχομένοισιν ἢ καταπαυομένοισιν, the first invocation in the Theognidean corpus, addressed to Apollo:

> ὦ ἄνα, Λητοῦς υἱέ, Διὸς τέκος, οὔποτε σεῖο
>   λήσομαι ἀρχόμενος οὐδ᾽ ἀποπαυόμενος,
> ἀλλ᾽ αἰεὶ πρῶτόν τε καὶ ὕστατον ἔν τε μέσοισιν
>   ἀείσω·

> Oh lord, son of Leto, offspring of Zeus, never shall I omit you in opening, nor in leaving off, but always first, last and at the centre shall I sing of you, ...[345]

Strikingly, Theognis then devotes three couplets (5–10) to Apollo's birth on Delos (relevant for the location of Pindar's *prosodion*); and his second invocation (11–15) is to Artemis. The Theognidean ὦ ἄνα is post-Homeric and is regularly applied to Apollo (rarely to others), whereas in Homer vocative ἄνα (without ὦ) is addressed to Zeus alone.[346] Callimachus combines the two, addressing Zeus as ὦ ἄνα (8, cf. 33), which in turn links forward to ὦ ἄνα in address to Apollo at *HApollo* 79. With the loss of most of the Pindaric *prosodion*, it is unclear whether ὦ ἄνα in *HZeus* reflects that text (cf. Aristoph. *Knights* 1298, above, n.344); yet there is perhaps enough in what we have to suspect implicit programmatic linkage between the proem to *HZeus* and the second, third and fourth hymns in the collection.

The case for programmatic linkage within the Hymn-book is strengthened by a visible forward connection to the fifth hymn, set up by Zeus as Πηλαγόνων ἐλατῆρα (driver of the Giants): recalling the Pindaric Artemis as ἵππων ἔλατειραν, the phrase foreshadows Athena as

---

superfluous"; that is, as I understand it, without emphasis on first or second component: in general, contrast Denniston (1954) 515.

[345] For the influence of this passage, cf. esp. Arat. *Phaen.* 14 (Ζευς) τῷ μιν ἀεὶ πρῶτόν τε καὶ ὕστατον ἱλάσκονται; Apoll. Rhod. 2.213–14 (cited next n.). Theocritus seems to have had Theognis' opening in view at *Id.* 17.3–4 (among men [ἀνδρῶν bis], Ptolemy praised first, last, and at centre); for this, and the relationship between *Id.* 17 and *HZeus*, cf. Hunter (2003) 97–8.

[346] ὦ ἄνα to Apollo: *HHApoll.* 179, 526; Theogn. 1; Pind. *Pyth.* 9.44; Bacchyl. fr. 4.58 M. cf. Aristoph. *Knights* 1298 (parody: see n.344). Of special interest is Apoll. Rhod. 2.213–14 (Phineus the Apolline prophet): ὦ ἄνα, Λητοῦς/ υἱέ recalls the Theognidean proem, in a passage that also re-works the opening proem of the epic (1.3–4: see Hunter [1993] 91), where of course the poet is inspired by Apollo (1.1) ἀρχόμενος σέο, Φοίβε. Other figures: Pind. *Pyth.* 12.3 (Persephone); *APApp.* 80.1 (Proteus); cf. [Eur.] *Rhesus* 827 (Hector). Ζεῦ ἄνα: *Il.* 3.351, 16.233; *Od.* 17. 354.

driver of horses, and provides the mythological analogue for the wagon and horses bringing her image from the sanctuary:[347] (61–2) ἐλαύνοι/ ἵππως (she drove her horses); (141–2) χαῖρε καὶ ἐξελάοισα, καὶ ἐς πάλιν αὖτις ἐλάσσαις/ ἵππως (Hail both as you drive out, and as you drive the horses back in), a closure that echoes both lines 61–2 (above) and the figurative opening, where Athena is said not to wash herself πρὶν κόνιν ἱππειᾶν ἐξελάσαι λαγόνων (before driving dust from the horse-flanks). This latter action, though habitual, is exemplified in Athena's horse-cleansing on return (8) τῶν ἀδίκων … ἀπὸ γαγενέων (from the lawless earthborn): her 'horse-driving' (and cleansing) is thus associated with the Gigantomachy, hence with Zeus both as Πηλαγόνων ἐλατῆρα and as 'dispenser of justice to the gods' δικασπόλον Οὐρανίδῃσι (*HZeus* 3).[348]

This leaves the sixth hymn (Demeter) for consideration. It stands in a particularly close relationship to the fifth;[349] but whereas Athena's procession is depicted at the moment of its inception, Demeter's ritual is coming to an end, as evening falls and her ceremonial basket processes back to the sanctuary (1, τῶ καλάθω κατιόντος); the two final components of the book thus exemplify hymning the gods at the outset and the conclusion of the respective ceremonies. Demeter's κάλαθος-scenario is reflected in the incidence of words beginning in καλ-, and in particular (with etymological reference) καλός.[350] The highest concentration occurs in lines 15–28, where the hymnist summarises, then rejects, three episodes distressing to Demeter; threefold 'thrice' (13–15, τρίς, τοσσάκι, τρίς) is then balanced by threefold κάλλιον, introducing preferable subject areas (19, 20 [juxtaposed with καλάμαν], 22). This appears to be the only truly programmatic application of κάλλιον extant, other than Pindar fr. 89a Ma. Callimachus however applies it to the selection of narrative episode (κάλλιον ὡς …) and not to the choice of the goddess as hymnic addressee: in this respect, the re-working may be compared with the opening of *HArtemis* where ἄρχμενοι ὡς (4) introduces the hymnist's selection of the opening narrative episode; and again, we may suspect that Callimachus has re-deployed Pindar's ἀρχο-

---

[347] Cf. Bulloch (1985) 3–4, 11, 115–16; Stephens (2015) 233–4.

[348] The long-range wordplay λαγόνων/Πηλαγόνων appears to confirm the latter as the correct reading at *HZeus* 3; but κόνιν … ἐξελάσαι (6) creates an analogue between driving off the Giants (pollutant earth-/mud-born adversaries) and cleansing/purifying the horses of the earth-dust.

[349] See Hopkinson (1984) 13–17 for points of correspondence and contrast.

[350] The καλ- root in the following lines: 1, 3, 15, 18, 19 (bis), 22, 25, 28, 41, 120; cf. also 75, 97 (with *Od.* 8.549–50). Etymologies: *Etym. Magn.* p. 485.23 K., s.v. κάλαθος· κυρίως εἰς ὃν τὰ κάλλη ἀποτίθεται; ibid. 27, s.v. κάλαμος· παρὰ τὸ καλῶς ἀμᾶσθαι.

μένοις from the selection of hymnic honorand to the treatment of the subject's story (that is, from the 'what?'/'whom?' to the 'how?').

APPENDIX II. ARTEMIS

Artemis is generally thought to be absent from *HDelos*; and the reader is left wondering whether Callimachus has separate births in view (as at *HHApoll.* 15–16: Apollo on Delos, Artemis on 'Ortygia'). I suggested earlier (p.47f.) that in *HApollo* Callimachus corrects *HHApollo* on this score, and depicts the goddess hunting on Kynthos in order to offset her near-exclusion from that work. The evidence for her presence in *HDelos* and its resonances in *HApollo* and *HArtemis* is therefore worth reviewing.

Leto's awareness that she is carrying twins is apparently explicit in her appeal that 'the children [τέκνα] of Zeus be born' in the river Peneius.[351] The final line (326) χαίροι δ' Ἀπόλλων τε καὶ ἣν ἐλοχεύσατο Λητώ (farewell Apollo too, and her to whom Leto gave birth) is an unambiguous envoi to the Delian triad, embracing both births.[352] And while Artemis is not mentioned by name in the lines dealing with Apollo's birth, she does appear in the Iris/Hera episode (215–48) that bridges the onset of parturition and the actual birth, where Iris is compared to the hunting goddess's hound (228–31). Again, the name of one of the three Hyperborean maidens at line 292, Oupis, is a cult name of Artemis (cited at *HArt.* 204, 240).

The naming of Artemis at a key juncture in the parturition, albeit as huntress, might encourage the reader to ponder her Delian function as birth-goddess (as celebrated by Euripides, *IT* 1097–1105: above, pp.44, 109 n.266). As Λοχεία, she overlapped with Eileithyia, but had a separate cult and shrine on Kynthos.[353] In *HDelos*, Eileithyia is recalled in the Deliades' 'sacred *melos*' (257), but she is not summoned by Leto, despite Peneius' earlier injunction (132) κάλει μόνον Εἰλήθυιαν (just

---

[351] *HDelos* 111 τὰ Ζηνὸς ἐν ὕδατι τέκνα τεκέσθαι. Cf. *HHApoll.* 14 (of Artemis and Apollo) ἐπεὶ τέκες ἀγλαὰ τέκνα. Mineur (1984) 137 understands 111 as a reference to the twins; cf. Stephens (2015) 199: "the plural seems to indicate that Artemis has not yet been born." See also Stephens' summary of variant traditions, ibid. 102.

[352] For a good defence of this position against efforts to amend, see Gigante Lanzara (1990) 177–8.

[353] *IT* 1097–1105 ποθοῦσ' Ἄρτεμιν λοχίαν,/ ἃ παρὰ Κύνθιον ὄχθον οἰ-/ κεῖ .../ .../ ..., Λατοῦς ὠδῖνα φίλαν,/ λίμναν θ' εἰλίσσουσαν ὕδωρ/ κύκλιον, ἔνθα κύκνος μελῳ-/ δὸς Μούσας θεραπεύει (... longing for Artemis of childbirth, who dwells beside the Kynthian hill ..., dear offspring of Leto, and the lake rolling around its circular water, where the melodious swan serves the Muses). Kuiper (1896) 173 is right to suggest that C. had this chorus in view.

call Eileithyia). Rather, within the hymn-book as we have it, τειρομένη (211, of Leto's birth-pains) echoes not only τειρομένην ὠδῖσι (61, [sc. Leto] suffering distress from her labour pains), but also *HArtemis* 21–2, ὑπ' ὠδίνεσσι γυναῖκες/ τειρόμεναι (women suffering distress from labour pains), at the point where Artemis undertakes to be a goddess of childbirth, responding to appeals for help from women in travail. (τειρομεν- is the first word of the line on all three occasions.) Again in *HDelos*, Artemis Λοχεία is glimpsed in the swans' 'midwife' song (251) ἐπήεισαν δὲ λοχείῃ, an allusion reinforced in the last-line reference to her own birth (326), καὶ ἣν ἐλοχεύσατο Λητώ.[354] And there is a further allusion to Artemis in the διαπρυσίην ὀλολυγήν (258, penetrating *ololyge*) echoed back by *aither*: this phrase derives from the Homeric *Hymn to Aphrodite*, where Artemis' interests as virgin goddess of hunting and dancing include φόρμιγγές τε χοροί τε διαπρύσιοί τε ὀλολυγαί (19, lyres and choruses and penetrating *ololygai*).

What are we to make of these glimpses of Apollo's sister? Starting with the cluster of apparent references to Artemis as Delian birth goddess that associate her also with music and fertility, we may recall comparable clusters in the the Euripidean *IT* chorus, and perhaps also in Pindar's twelfth *Paean* (above, p.55).[355] Artemis' credentials as a musical goddess, already prominent in *HArtemis*, thus come under consideration.[356] Of special interest is the opening of Callimachus' catalogue of Nymph-dances at *HArtemis* 170–71: ἡνίκα δ' αἱ νύμφαι σε χορῷ ἔνι κυκλώσονται/ ἀγχόθι πηγάων Αἰγυπτίου Ἰνωποῖο … (when the Nymphs circle you in dance, near the streams of Egyptian Inopos …). The oblique reference to Delos, wrapped up in a designation of its river as Αἰγυπτίου Ἰνωποῖο, must have challenged any reader who had not first seen its explicit counterpart at *HDelos* 206–8: there, the hymnist speaks directly to the reader, explains the subterranean link from Nile to Inopos, and thereby elucidates the Delian choric scenario in *HArtemis*. The Nymphs who dance around Artemis by the Inopos cannot, of course, be other than the νύμφαι Δηλιάδες, ποταμοῦ γένος ἀρχαίοιο, the riverine descendants of Nile and Oceanus. For a further pointer towards this inference, we may compare *HDelos* 306 (of the girls singing Olen's hymn) ποδὶ πλήσσουσι χορίτιδες ἀσφαλὲς οὖδας (the choric dancers beat the safe ground with their foot), where the rare

---

[354] Cf. Stephens (2015) 221: "the potential allusions to Artemis *Lochia* may substitute" (sc. for Eileithyia).

[355] The text is unfortunately unclear at what may well be a relevant juncture (3) ἐννέ[α Μοί]σαις/ μ]άλα δ' Ἀρτέμιδ[ος Λα]τώϊον Ἀσ[τερία/ λέ]χος ἀμφέπο[ισ' ἄν]θεα τοιά[σ-/ δ'] ὑμνήσιος δρέπῃ·

[356] Bing and Uhrmeister (1994) 30–32.

formation χορίτιδες recalls Artemis' selection of χορίτιδας Ὠκεανίνας (choric Ocean-Nymphs) as her companions at *HArtemis* 13. This additional point of contact between *HDelos* and *HArtemis*, connecting the present-day girl-choruses of Delos (the modern Deliades) with Artemis' Nymph-companions, offers a further link to Oceanus, the source of all rivers and the riverine 'ancestor' of the terrestrial Nymph-Deliades (above p.69f.).[357]

It follows that in singing (*HDelos* 257) the 'sacred *melos* of Eileithyia', the Deliades are reflecting Artemis' own role as goddess of childbirth, and arguably the pre-birth of Artemis herself. Several consequences would flow from such a reading of her disguised presence at the birth. In the first place, we should have a narrative rationale for Callimachus' rapid sequence ὁ δ' ἔκθορεν, αἱ δ' ἐπὶ μακρόν/ .../ εἶπαν ..., and for the striking simultaneity of ὁ δ' and αἱ δ': Apollo has leapt forth in response to the swans; and as his twin Artemis nears birth, the Deliades themselves will perform the swans' epodic role, thereby assuming the function of Eileithyia in relation to the birth of their future choric leader; and this is why *aither* responds with an 'Artemisian' *ololyge*. Another consequence flows from the Callimachean invention, as I see it, of the Nile–Inopos connection. This was based in part on pre-existing testimony of such island–Nilotic connections, but in all probability it re-works Alcaeus' delineation of the Delphian Kastalia in (perhaps the greatest loss to early Apolline song) the *Paean* to Apollo:[358] there, according to a summary account in Himerius, Kastalia is an offshoot of the Kephisos in flood, and it flows in silver in response to Apollo's first, swan-borne, epiphany at Delphi. Thus, the purely Apolline epiphanic response of Delphian waters would in *HDelos* be combined with the landscape-riverine response to the very first (birth) epiphany of Artemis. In short, *HDelos* balances the visiting swans' obstetric and (later) singing service to Apollo by the

---

[357] Cf. *Il.* 21.195–7 with Richardson's comments; Hes. *Theog.* 337–70; Pind. fr. 326 Ma.; Williams (1978) 88–9, on *HApoll.* 105. For choric dance in the Delian *Artemisia*, see Bruneau (1970) 198–9. *HArt.* 13 is echoed at Nonn. *Dionys.* 16.125–32, where χορίτιδες are paired with Χάριτες of Orchomenos, in service of Aphrodite (cf. also *Dionys.* 24.261, 31.20, 34.37, 41.225); Diosc. fr. 25.4–5 ἀμφὶς ἐκυκλώσαντο χορίτιδες ἐννέα Μοῦσαι/ καὶ Χαρίτων χόρος .../ ὡς νέον ἄλλον ἴδον Διονύσιον. Nonnus' consistent attachment to the Charites of Orchomenos suggests that Callimachus is echoing an earlier (Philitan?) etymologising association of χορίτιδες with Χάριτες (hence also with Aphrodite, thereby supplying a further onward link to the wreathing of Aphrodite at 307–8).

[358] Alcaeus fr. 307 V (c) (Himerius *Or.* 48.11 Col.) ῥεῖ καὶ ἀργυροῖς ἡ Κασταλία κατὰ ποίησιν νάμασι, καὶ Κηφισσὸς μέγας αἴρεται πορφύρων τοῖς κύμασι, τὸν Ἐνιπέα τοῦ Ὁμήρου μιμούμενος. βιάζεται μὲν γὰρ Ἀλκαῖος ὁμοίως Ὁμήρῳ ποιῆσαι καὶ ὕδωρ θεῶν ἐπιδημίαν αἰσθέσθαι δυνάμενον. For the Kephisos/ Kastalia link, Paus. 10.8.10.

indigenous Deliades' obstetric and (later) choric service to Artemis. Finally, it should be observed that Eileithyia is in no way discredited in *HDelos*: rather, she is juxtaposed with Artemis as birth-goddess, helps through divine embodiment within her sung *melos* to effect Artemis' birth, and so serves as *aition* for the easy birth narrated by the goddess herself at *HArt*. 25. Here then is a further cosmic reconciliation of old and new divinities, to be associated for all time with the indigenous Nymphs of Delos.

HDelos thus supplies the hymn-reader with an explanation for Artemis' acceptance of the role of birth-goddess at *HArt*. 20–25, as also for the part played in this role-allocation by the *Moirai* at the very moment of her own birth (for their juxtaposition with Eileithyia, cf. Pind. *Pae.* 12.17 [G1 Ru.]). Her birth, in contrast to Apollo's, was trouble-free: 25, ἀμογητί. But that Leto calls on Apollo to effect his own birth (*HDelos* 214) suggests that the bewildered goddess was utterly focused on her son, and as yet ignorant of Artemis' role (about to be realised) as a βοηθόον who would respond to appeals from women in travail (*HArt.* 21–5).

With such a reading of Artemis in *HDelos*, if it is on the right lines, the inference is clear that *HArtemis* and *HDelos* were composed for sequential reading within the hymn-book. It might be added that Artemis' striking progression to civic responsibilities, which was observed by Bing and Uhrmeister, but which they were at a loss to explain from within *HArtemis* itself, finds its internal hymn-book *aition* in her hunting co-operation with Apollo's childhood construction of the Delian *keraton* at *HApollo* 60–61, itself an analogue for the god's foundation of cities (see below, Appendix III).[359] But why should Callimachus have chosen to disguise Artemis' place in *HDelos* in this way? Perhaps her rivalry with Apollo, explicitly admitted at *HArtemis* 7; perhaps the hymnist's defensive objective not to incur collateral divine damage in promoting Delos to the divine ranks as he responds to the Muses' prompt; and perhaps also the hymnist's acknowledgement of Artemis' own Muse-like patronage of song and dance in her own honour, and thus his difficulty in ever 'forgetting' Artemis (*HArt.* 1–2).[360]

Alongside the implicit *HApollo* correction of her historic Delian displacement in *HHApollo* (above, p.47f.), Artemis' association with choric song finds implicit aetiological explanation in *HDelos*; and her

---

[359] Bing and Uhrmeister (1994) 25.

[360] Bing and Uhrmeister (1994) 28: "it is *she* who makes possible his song" (sc. about herself!).

old association with Kynthos finds discreet recognition in her hunting
and birth roles in *HApollo* and *HDelos*.

APPENDIX III. THE 'GOATS OF KYNTHOS'
(ΑΙΓΕΣ ΚΥΝΘΙΑΔΕΣ)

At *HApollo* 60–61, Artemis the huntress supplies the materials for
Apollo's construction of the Delian horn altar (*keraton*) from αἰγῶν/
Κυνθιάδων (Kynthian goats). The adjective, a new formation, invites
comparison with Κύνθιος at *HDelos* 9–10 (also in enjambement).[361]
The 'goats of Kynthos' appear again in a Callimachean epigram recording the (fictitious) dedication of a bow to Artemis (*Ep.* 62 Pf.; *AP*
6.121): there, Κυνθιάδες addressed in line 1 are revealed to be αἶγες
only in line 4 (the ostensible point is to offer reassurance that the bow
which has 'emptied' the mountain of the Κυνθιάδες is now dedicated to
Artemis and no longer in active service); and the reader is led initially
to think that landscape nymphs embodying the Kynthos Hill are
addressed.[362] The epigram, evidently the later text, may suggest the
possibility of an allusion to Nymphs in αἰγῶν/ Κυνθιάδων as well; and
that such an allusion is indeed present is supported by parallelism with
the preceding αἶγες ... ἐπιμηλάδες (*HApoll.* 50–51) where the adjective
is cognate with ἐπιμηλίδες (protectresses of flocks), an attested Nymph-
title, and additionally implies the fertility of goats under Apollo's
care.[363] Such an intrinsic relationship between the hill and the goats
conceived, born and nurtured upon it might best be understood by
reference to their respective κέρατα ('horns' and 'crests'):[364] it is from
these κέρατα that Apollo has woven the *keraton*; and the altar thus
represents the hill itself, but in miniature and as a civilising artefact.
The respective roles, of Apollo as founder of cities and Artemis as

---

[361] For the formation, see Williams (1978) 52; cf. Lanzara (1990) 84.

[362] D'Alessio (2007) 268 (on *Ep.* 62) "non di ninfe compagne di Artemide si tratta, ma di
capre." On the coinage and its suggestion of nymphs in *HApollo*, see Williams (1978)
52; also McKay (1968) 174.

[363] For full discussion of these terms, see Williams (1978) 51–3. For attestation of *epi-
melides*, see Larson (2001) 292 n.64, 297 n.17.

[364] *LSJ* s.v. κεράς I.1 and V.6; Frisk (1973) I.826–7. Key items of evidence are (a)
Aristoph. *Clouds* 596–7 (to Apollo) ... Δήλιε, Κυνθίαν ἔχων ὑψικέρατα πέτραν'; (b)
Etym. Magn. p. 504 K. s.v. κεραβάτης: ὁ τὰ ἀκρωτήρια τῶν ὀρέων, τουτέστι τὰς
κορυφὰς, βαίνων, οἱονεὶ ὀρειβάτης. κέρατα γὰρ καλοῦσι πάντα τὰ ἄκρα, ὥς φησι
Πίνδαρος· ὑψικέρατα πέτραν [fr. 325 Ma.] ἀντὶ τοῦ ὑψηλὰ ἀκρωτηρία; and cf. further,
(c) ὑψίκερων and cognate terms of 'high-horned' animals (*Od.* 10.158; Bacchyl. *Dith.*
2.22; cf. Soph. *Trach.* 507–8), and also of goat-god Pan at Nonn. *Dionys.* 16.187.
'Keraton' itself is the modern name of a hill on Crete, near Dikte.

huntress in the wild, thus complement one another.[365] And Artemis'
personal association with the Nymphs around Inopos (that is, on
Kynthos) as argued above (Appendix II) adds a further territorial
dimension to this careful balance between the siblings.

Goats do not appear explicitly in *HDelos*, but there is an intertextual
allusion to the animals at *HDelos* 12, two lines after 'Apollo Kynthios',
within the hymnist's comment as, in imagination, he approaches the
island from the sea (12):[366] αἰθυίης καὶ μᾶλλον ἐπίδρομος ἠέπερ ἵπποις
(rather more course for the seagull than for horses, trans. Stephens).
This is a reference to Telemachus' description of Ithaca in *Odyssey* 4
(following up Callimachus' proem-reference to the island as nurse):
'lovely for goat-grazing rather more than horse grazing' (606, αἰγίβοτος
καὶ μᾶλλον ἐπήρατος ἱπποβότοιο).[367] The Callimachean reader who
spots the reference will recognise that αἰγίβοτος has been displaced by
the diving sheerwater, because the notionally arriving hymnist is
recording his first glimpse of Delos from the sea; but the underlying
allusion to goats is retained. This represents the essential character of
Delos as barren lump of rock, the most prominent component of which
is rocky Kynthos itself. The *keraton*, constructed from the horns of the
only animal that could thrive and achieve fertility on the unfertile
ground of the hillside, is the focal point for visiting worshippers,
sacrificial offerings and choric performances, and thus a symbol of the
Delian juxtaposition of indigenous poverty and imported wealth
(above, p.44).

The interplay of goats and nymphs in *HApollo* has an explicit
counterpart in *HZeus*, where Amaltheia suckles the infant Zeus (48–9
σὺ δ᾽ ἐθήσαο πίονα μαζόν/ αἰγὸς Ἀμαλθείης): 'Amaltheia' is unexpectedly identified as goat-nurse and not as the Nymph of that name,
and the surprise is heightened by μαζόν, revealed to be the goat's teat.
In the background lies a Cretan tradition of katasterism: thus, Aratus on

---

[365] For the mix of wildness and civilisation in *HArtemis*, cf. Bing and Uhrmeister (1994)
21, 24–5, 28.

[366] Gigante Lanzara (1990) 72 well describes the poem "spalancando dinanzi agli occhi
l'immagine delle sconfinate vastità marine intorno all' *isola lontana*, un limbo di terra
aperto ai venti, percorso dai volidei gabbiani ..." (my italics): this rightly suggests a
deictic sense 'yonder' (as well as an internal back-reference) to κείνη (11), as the ship-
borne visitor notionally descries the distant island. Observe also the sailing speaker's
observation (15) of ἁλίπλοοι inhabitants; and cf. Arat. *Phaen.* 296–8 (offshore sailors
compared to sheerwaters looking towards the beach) ἴκελοι ... αἰθυίῃσι/ πολλάκις ἐκ
νηῶν πέλαγος περιπαπταίνοντες/ ἥμεθ᾽, ἐπ᾽ αἰγιαλοὺς τετραμμένοι. The sheerwater,
like Asteria, dives into the sea: *Od.* 5.353. For sea-dominated 'first view', cf.
Giuseppetti (2013) 208. For the divine 'prequel' to κείνη (11) of the speaker's arrival,
cf. 195 κείνην (Apollo); 213 αὔτη (Leto).

[367] Well observed by Gigante Lanzara (1990) 73; see Giuseppetti (2013) 213–16 for
Ithaca as a parallel example of a poor/sterile island; Stephens (2015) 182.

the star Capella in the constellation Auriga (*Phaen*. 163):[368] ... Αἴξ ἱερή, τὴν μέν τε λόγος Διὶ μαζὸν ἐπισχεῖν (... the sacred Goat, whom indeed legend holds to have tendered her breast to Zeus).[369] Now, the goat-nurture of Zeus links forward to Apollo and to Asteria/Delos in various ways. μαζόν (48–9) itself is paralleled at *HDelos* 274 (ὁ δὲ γλυκὺν ἔσπασε μαζόν), and for what it may be worth it corresponds in poem-location (lines 48–9) with the Samian μάστον/ Παρθενίης. Then, Zeus' secondary feed on honey (49, ἐπὶ δὲ γλυκὺ κηρίον ἔβρως) echoes the 'Homeric' Apollo's early feeding at *HHApollo* 127 (κατέβρως); and the honeycomb makes its first appearance as Πανακρίδος ἔργα μελίσσης (the product of Panakridan bee), so that another nymph (Melissa, sister of Amaltheia) is represented as a creature which, like the goats of Kynthos, is adjectivally identified with the sparse sustenance of the mountain on which it/she operates.[370] There is no mention of Amaltheia's cornucopia (κέρας); but perhaps γλυκὺ κηρίον constitutes a 'Melissan' counterpart (and sound-reference?).

Within these clusters of topography, nymphs, and infant gods, the αἶγες of *HApollo* act as an indirect link between Kynthos (with the nurture of Apollo) and Cretan Ida (with the goat-nurture of Zeus). The associated childhoods create linkages within the mountain nomenclature attached to each god (this is after all Callimachus' point of departure for the treatment both of Zeus [*HZeus* 4, Δικταῖον ἀείσομεν ἠὲ Λυκαῖον], and of Delian Apollo [*HDelos* 10, Κύνθιος]). The theme of katasterism, prominent in the early 'Cretan' passages of Aratus' *Phaenomena*, may also be relevant to Asteria, the star that fell from heaven to earth as rock/nymph, in that Capella evidently acquired the additional name 'Mazos';[371] but the date of that development is uncertain, and since further investigation would involve the dating of the *Phaenomena* relative to the *Hymns* as well as later treatments, it cannot be pursued for present purposes.

The prominence of goats in *HZeus* and *HApollo* may have a further resonance, in the name Αἴγυπτος both as river (Nile) and country.[372]

---

[368] Cretan tradition: the various accounts are well presented by Gantz (1996) I.41–2; cf. *LIMC* I.582–4 (all representations are late). For the influence of Epimenides' *Cretica* cf. 3 B 21–24 D–K: observe the presence in the tradition of Aigikeros (goat-horned) and Aigipan (goat-Pan).

[369] Crinagoras: *AP* 9.224.5–6 (goat speaks with reference to Augustus): ἥξω δ' αὐτίκα που καὶ ἐς ἀστέρας· ᾧ γὰρ ἔπεσχον/ μαζὸν ἐμόν, μείων οὐδ' ὅσον Αἰγιόχου. The allusion to Aratus is clear; but I am unsure what, if anything, to make of Crinagoras' use of two verbs, ἐκένωσεν (1) and εἰργάσατο (4) which appear in identical form in Call. *Ep.* 62.3 and 4 Pf. (εἰργάσατο in the same *sedes*).

[370] Melissa: McLennan (1977) 83; *RE* XV.526–7 (Van der Kolf).

[371] Hübner (1991).

[372] For *Aigyptos* (masculine) as river-name, *Od.* 4.477, etc. Schol. Lyc. *Alex.* 116.

Herodotus (2.46) and others record the special place of the goat (local name *mendes*) in religious life on the Delta: the goat-god Mendes had a major cult at the city of the same name, and was identified with Greek Pan. The rationale for this cult, certainly as understood by Greek writers, lay in the interplay of the fertilising and nurturing power of the river and the sexual proclivities of the goat.[373] Aelian (*NA* 3.33) credits the Nile with the phenomenon of multiple births among Egyptian goats: λέγεται ὁ Νεῖλος αἴτιος εἶναι εὐτεκνότατον παρέχων ὕδωρ (the Nile is said to be the cause, supplying water most conducive to conception). Strabo (15.22) says much the same about Egyptian women; and he cites Aristotle (fr. 284 R.) for the view that the Nile is πολύγονον ... καὶ τρόφιμον (highly productive and nurturing). The 'fertility' association of goat and river gave rise to at least one recorded etymology of (river) Αἴγυπτος, from αἰγίποτος (drunk by goats), and perhaps also for a variant διὰ τὸ αἶγας πίονας ἔχειν (through having fat goats).[374] The interest of these matters for Greek audiences, and the rich interplay of concepts and lexical choices to which they gave rise, may be seen in Pindar's reference to the scandalous coupling of goats and women at Mendes (fr. 201 Ma.): Αἰγυπτίαν Μένδητα, πὰρ κρημνὸν θαλάσσας/ ἔσχατον Νείλου κέρας, αἰγιβάται/ ὅθι τράγοι γυναιξὶ μίσγονται (... Egyptian Mendes, furthermost branch of the Nile by sea-cliff, where goat-mounting billy-goats couple with women). This tightly organised passage alludes to the conversion of land to 'sea' by the Nile's flooding, and also to what was evidently a spectacular, if occasional, aspect of Mendes fertility-cult.[375] It is all tied together in witty wordplay: goats

---

[373] What follows is indebted to Borthwick (1963). R. Griffith (1997) offers a related collection of evidence on Egypt and goats.

[374] *Etym. Magn.* p. 29 K., s.v. Αἴγυπτος. ἢ αἰγίποτος παρὰ τὸν τράγον, ὃν Αἰγύπτιοι σέβουσιν, ἐξαιρέτως δὲ τοὺς Μενδησίους. ἢ διὰ τὸ αἶγας πίονας ἔχειν. Cf. *Etym. Gen.* α 169; *Etym. Gud.* α 37. Cf. Lyc. *Alex.* 847–51: Menelaus, in search of Helen, comes to Egypt, described as θερειπότους γύας (lands that drink water in summer) and the Nile, described as 'stream of Asbystes'. He will sleep with δυσόδμοις θηρσί (evil-smelling beasts), with immediate reference to Proteus' seals (*Od.* 4.404–7; 441–6), but with secondary allusion (oracular double meaning) to the rank smell of goats (for a further analogue between Proteus' seals and goats, cf. [Theocr.] *Id.* 8.49–52, with Schol.); Menelaus will tolerate this for the sake of the Αἴγυας κυνὸς τῆς θηλύπαιδος (the Aigyan [sc. Laconian] bitch, bearer only of female children, i.e. Helen), where Αἴγυας (850) picks up γύας (847) and alludes to Αἴγυπτος, thus again to goats; θηλύπαιδος alludes to the Nile's efficacy for conception of male children (Schol. Aesch. *Suppl.* 858; Borthwick [1963] 232). θερειπότους may play on θηρσί, hence Αἴγυπτος/αἰγίποτος: see below for an internal parallel with Inopos at *Alex.* 573–6.

[375] For 'sea' created by Nile flood, cf. Hdt. 2.97.1 (where towns are compared to Aegean islands); Strab. 17.1.4. Pindar's reference to the cliff and the sea cannot have been fully understood by Aelius Aristides (*Or.* 48.112, observing that the area is an extensive plain). Mendes-cult: Hdt. 2.46 (scandalised); cf. Thompson (1955) 201 n.34, with reference to Mendes as 'Living *ba*, chief of young women'.

coupling γυναιξί; river-κέρας and goats (and perhaps κρημνόν); Αἰγυπτίαν and αἰγιβάται. The wider interest for *HDelos* lies in the combined fertilising and kourotrophic powers of the Nile feeding through to barren Delos/Kynthos, and in the goat as an 'Egyptian' extension and symbol of Nilotic fertility and nurture. A specific and contemporary focus is also visible in two items concerning the family of Ptolemy Philadelphus: the king is reported to have sent consignments of Nile water to his daughter Berenike on her marriage to Antiochus II, perhaps in the expectation that this would aid conception of a male child;[376] and again, Philadelphus' sister-wife was closely identified with Mendes after her death (and perhaps before), appearing in (Hellenising) iconography with a ram's horn woven into her hair.[377]

We may now turn to Lycophron's Kynthos. The *Alexandra* prophecy includes an oracle vouchsafed to Anius, Delian Apollo's king-priest, to the effect that the Greek army might pause for nine years on the island, and that 'blameless sustenance' would there be available to all: ... Κυνθίαν ὅσοι σκοπὴν/ μίμνοντες ἠλάσκουσιν Ἰνωποῦ πέλας,/ Αἰγύπτιον Τρίτωνος ἕλκοντες ποτόν (such as stay and frequent the Kynthian hill beside Inopos, drawing the Egyptian drink of Triton, *Alex.* 574–6). The reference is of course to the subterranean sourcing of Inopos from the Nile (here, 'Triton'). Αἰγύπτιον ... ποτόν (Egyptian ... drink) looks like an etymologising allusion to Αἴγυπτος from αἰγίποτος (twinned with θερειπότους at line 847: above, n.374). There is a further Egyptian reference in τροφὴν ἀμεμφῆ (blameless sustenance), evidently with name-play on 'Memphis':[378] 'blameless', because Anius' daughters, instructed by the god Dionysus, can produce sufficient corn, wine and oil for the sojourning host; but in the context, perhaps 'blameless' also because the Greeks will not breach the Egyptian taboo on sacrificing (and eating) goats (Hdt. 2.46), and will not take Kynthian goats that have drunk the Nilotic waters of Inopos. Lycophron is clearly drawing allusively on earlier authorities (the scholia refer to Hipponax); and among his sources for the Anius episode, it was suggested earlier (p.49), may be a Pindaric ode for Delos, featuring Kynthos.

I make the working assumption that Lycophron's juxtaposition of Ἰνωποῦ and Αἰγύπτιον reflects its only extant parallel, at *HArtemis* 171 (choric nymphs encircling the goddess ἀγχόθι πηγάων Αἰγυπτίου Ἰνω-ποῖο: above, Appendix II, arguing for Callimachus' invention of the

---

[376] Polyb. fr. 73 ap. Athen. 45c; Borthwick (1963) 231–2 (see above, n.374).
[377] Thompson (1955), an important and neglected article.
[378] Cf. Eur. *Hel.* 462–3 (old woman) τί δὴ τὸ Νείλου μεμπτόν ἐστί σοι γάνος;/ (Menelaus) οὐ τοῦτ' ἐμέμφθην; *Orac. Sib.* 11.236 (explicit); *Etym. Magn.* p. 579 s.v. μέμφομαι (explicit).

river-link).[379] Nonetheless, a demonstrable connection between Calli-machus' αἶγες Κυνθιάδες and Αἴγυπτος seems beyond reach. πίονα μαζόν/ αἰγὸς (*HZeus* 48–9) offers some encouragement, in view of the variant derivation of Αἴγυπτος from τὸ αἶγας πίονας ἔχειν (above, n.374), but here the absence of any geographical reference to Egypt means that the allusion is not assured.

We are however left with a reasonably solid series of connections. Zeus' nurturing goat 'Amaltheia' is cross-referenced to the two hill-'breasts' of *HDelos*, including of course Kynthos itself; goats and Nymphs are in part assimilated, and goats are drawn into Callimachus' exploration of the kourotrophic powers of water; and the linkage of Nile to Inopos creates a further, Egyptian, dimension to this nexus of fertility and culture, transferred with the Nile-waters to Delos. That the goats participate in this Nilotic/Egyptian connection, as they appear to do in Lycophron's (arguably interpretative) version, remains an inference.

Bibliography

Acosta-Hughes, B. (2002). *Polyeideia: The Iambi of Callimachus and the Archaic Iambic Tradition.* Berkeley, etc.

Acosta-Hughes, B. and Stephens, S.A. (edd.) (2012). *Callimachus in Context. From Plato to the Augustan Poets.* Cambridge and New York

Acosta-Hughes, B., Lehnus, L., and Stephens, S. (edd.) (2011). *Brill's Companion to Callimachus.* Leiden and Boston

Adams, J.N. (1981). 'Cunus, Clunes and their Synonyms in Latin' *Glotta* 59.239–64

Aloni, A. (1980). '*Prooimia, Hymnoi*, Elio Aristide e i cugini bastardi' *QUCC* 4.23–40

Ambühl, A. (2005). *Kinder und junge Helden. Innovative Aspecte des Umgangs mit der literarischen Tradition bei Kallimachos.* Hellenistica Groningana 9. Leuven, etc.

Asper, M. (2011). 'Dimensions of Power: Callimachean Geopoetics and the Ptolemaic Empire' in Acosta-Hughes, Lehnus and Stephens (edd.) 155–77

Athanassaki, L., Martin, R. and Miller, J.F. (edd.) (2009). *Apolline Politics and Poetics.* Athens

Austin, C. and Bastianini, G. (edd.) (2002). *Posidippi Pellaei quae supersunt omnia.* Milan

Barchiesi, A. (1994). 'Immovable Delos: *Aeneid* 3.78–93 and the Hymns of Callimachus' *CQ* 44.438–43

---

[379] See now Hornblower (2015) 27–30, esp. n.83.

Battezzato, L. (2013). 'Dithyramb and Greek Tragedy' in B. Kowalzig and P. Wilson (edd.) *Dithyramb in Context*. Oxford. 93–110

Baxter, T.M.S. (1991). *The Cratylus: Plato's Critique of Naming*. Leiden, etc.

Beecroft, A.J. (2008). 'Nine Fragments in Search of an Author: Poetic Lines Attributed to Terpander' *CJ* 105.223–41

Bethe, E. (1937). 'Das archaische Delos und sein Letoon' *Hermes* 72.190–201

Bing, P. (1988). *The Well-Read Muse: Present and Past in Callimachus and the Hellenistic Poets*. Göttingen

— (1988a). 'A Note on the New "Musenanruf" in Callimachus' Aetia' *ZPE* 74.273–75

— (1990). 'A Pun on Aratus' Name in Verse 2 of the *Phainomena*?' *HSCP* 93.281–5

— (2005). 'The Politics and Poetics of Geography in the Milan Posidippus, Section One: On Stones (AB 1–20)' in Gutzwiller (ed.) 119–40

Bing, P. and Uhrmeister, V. (1994). 'The Unity of Callimachus' Hymn to Artemis' *JHS* 114.19–34

Bollack, J. (1969). *Empédocle*, III. *Les origines*. Paris

Bonfante, L. (1997). 'Nursing Mothers in Classical Art' in A.O. Koloski-Ostrow and C.L. Lyons (edd.) *Naked Truths: Women, Sexuality and Gender in Classical Art and Archeology*. London and New York. 174–96

Bonneau, D. (1964). *La crue du Nil divinité Égyptienne: à travers mille ans d'histoire (332 av. – 641 ap. J.-C.)*. Paris

Borthwick, E.K. (1963). 'The Oxyrhynchus Musical Monody and Some Ancient Fertility Superstitions' *AJP* 84.225–43 [repr. in *Greek Music, Drama, Sport, and Fauna. The Collected Classical Papers of E.K. Borthwick*, ed. C. Maciver. Prenton, 2015. 29–42]

Boyancé, P. (1972). *Le culte des Muses chez les philosophes grecs*. 2ⁿᵈ edn. Paris

Brink, K.O. (1946). 'Callimachus and Aristotle: An Inquiry into Callimachus' ΠΡΟΣ ΠΡΑΞΙΦΑΝΗΝ' *CQ* 40.11–26

Bruneau, P. (1970). *Recherches sur les cultes de Délos à l'époque hellénistique et à l'époque impériale*. Paris

— (1990). 'Deliaca (VIII)' *BCH* 114.553–91

Bryce, T.R. (1983). 'The Arrival of the Goddess Leto in Lycia' *Historia* 32.1–13

Bulloch, A.W. (1985). *Callimachus: The Fifth Hymn*. Cambridge Classical Texts and Commentaries 26. Cambridge

Burkert, W. (1979). 'Kynaithos, Polycrates and the Homeric Hymn to Apollo' in G.W. Bowersock, W. Burkert, and M.J.C. Putnam (edd.) *Arktouros: Hellenic Studies Presented to Bernard M.W. Knox*. Berlin. 53–62

— (1983). *Homo Necans: the Anthropology of Ancient Greek Sacrificial Ritual and Myth* (trans. P. Bing). Berkeley and Los Angeles

— (1985). *Greek Religion* (trans. J. Raffan). Oxford Blackwell

Bury, J.B. (1890). *The Nemean Odes of Pindar*. London

Cahen, E. (1930). *Les Hymnes de Callimaque. Commentaire explicatif et critique*. Paris

Cahen, E. (1961). *Callimaque*. 5th edn. Paris

Cairns, F. (1972). *Generic Composition in Greek and Roman Poetry*. Edinburgh

— (1979). *Tibullus: A Hellenistic Poet at Rome*. Cambridge

— (1983). 'Theocritus' First Idyll: The Literary Programme' *WS* n.s. 17.89–113

— (1983a). 'Alcaeus' Hymn to Hermes, *POxy.* 2734 Fr. 1 and Horace *Odes* 1.10' *QUCC* 42.29–35

— (1989). *Virgil's Augustan Epic*. Cambridge

— (2000). 'A Testimonium to a New Fragment of Philoxenus of Cythera?' *ZPE* 130.9–11

— (2006). *Sextus Propertius: The Augustan Elegist*. Cambridge

— (2012). *Roman Lyric. Collected Papers on Catullus and Horace*. Berlin and Boston

Calame, C. (1997). *Choruses of Young Women in Ancient Greece: Their Morphology, Religious Role, and Social Functions* (trans. D. Collins and J. Orion). Lanham, etc.

Cameron, A. (1995). *Callimachus and his Critics*. Princeton

Carey, C. (1981). *A Commentary on Five Odes of Pindar: Pythian 2, Pythian 9, Nemean 1, Nemean 7, Isthmian 8*. Salem N.H.

Champion, E. (1995). 'The Soteria at Delphi: Aetolian Propaganda in the Epigraphical Record' *AJP* 116.213–20

Clausen, W. (1976). 'Cynthius' *AJP* 97.245–7

— (1977). 'Cynthius: An Addendum' *AJP* 98.362

Cook, A.B. (1914–40). *Zeus. A Study in Ancient Religion*. Vols. I–III. Cambridge

Cusset, C., Le Meur-Weissman, N., Levin, F. (edd.) (2012). *Mythe et pouvoir à l'époque hellénistique*. Hellenistica Groningana 18. Leuven, etc.

D'Alessio, G.B. (1997). 'Pindar's "Prosodia" and the Classification of Pindaric Papyrus Fragments' *ZPE* 118.23–60

— (2005). 'Il primo Inno di Pindaro' in S. Grandolini (ed.) *Lirica e teatro in Grecia. Il testo e la sua ricezione*. Naples. 113–49

— (2007). *Callimaco. Inni, Epigrammi, Ecale: Introduzione, traduzione e note*. 4th edn. Vol. I. Milan

— (2009). 'Re-Constructing Pindar's First Hymn: The Theban "Theogony" and the Birth of Apollo' in Athanassaki, Martin and Miller (edd.) 129–47

Denniston, J.D. (1954). *The Greek Particles*. 2nd edn. Oxford

Depew, M. (1998). 'Delian Hymns and Callimachean Allusion' *HSCP* 98.155–182

Derow, P.S. and Forrest, W.G. (1982). 'An Inscription from Chios' *ABSA* 77.79–82

Dodds, E.R. (1951). *The Greeks and the Irrational*. Berkeley and Los Angeles

Eichgrün, E. (1961). *Kallimachos und Apollonios Rhodios.* Diss Berlin

Erskine, A. (1995). 'Culture and Power in Ptolemaic Egypt: The Museum and Library of Alexandria' *G&R* 42.38–48

Faulkner, A. (2010). 'Callimachus and his Allusive Virgins: Delos, Hestia, and the "*Homeric Hymn to Aphrodite*"' *HSCP* 105.53–63

Fantuzzi, M. and Hunter, R. (2004). *Tradition and Innovation in Hellenistic Poetry.* Cambridge

Farnell, L.R. (1896–1909). *Cults of the Greek States.* Vols I–V. Oxford

Feeney, D.C. (1984). 'The Reconciliations of Juno' *CQ* 34.179–94

— (1991). *The Gods in Epic: Poets and Critics of the Classical Tradition.* Oxford

Fernandez-Galiano, E. (1976–80). *Lexico de los Hymnos de Calímaco.* 4 Vols. Madrid

Foertmeyer, V. (1988). 'The Dating of the Pompe of Ptolemy Philadelphus' *Historia* 37.90–104

Fraser, P.M. (1970). 'Aristophanes of Byzantion and Zoilus Homeromastix in Vitruvius. A note on Vitruvius VII, Praef. §§4–9' *Eranos* 68.115–22

— (1972). *Ptolemaic Alexandria.* Oxford

Frisk, H., (1973). *Griechisches etymologisches Wörterbuch*, 2nd edn. Heidelberg

Fuhrer, T. (1988). 'A Pindaric Feature in Callimachus' *AJP* 109.53–68

Funaioli, M.P. (1993). 'I Fiumi e gli Eroi. Osservazioni sulla technica compositiva e sulla datazione dell' *Inno a Delo* de Callimaco (e dell' *Idillio* XVII di Teocrito)' *Philologus* 137.206–15

Furley, W.D. and Bremer, J.M. (2001). *Greek Hymns.* Volume II: *Greek Texts and Commentary.* Tübingen

Gallet de Santerre, H. (1958). *Délos primitive et archaïque.* Paris

— (1976). 'Athènes, Délos et Delphes d'après une peinture de vase à figures rouges du Ve siècle avant J.-C.' *BCH* 100.291–8

Gee, E. (2013). *Aratus and the Astronomical Tradition.* Oxford

Giangrande, G. (1968). 'On the Use of the Vocative in Alexandrian Epic' *CQ* 18.52–9

— (1988). 'Callimaque et Pindare: Un détail stylistique et littéraire' *AC* 57.269–70

Gigante Lanzara, V. (1990). *Callimaco: Inno a Delo.* Biblioteca di Studi Antichi 65. Pisa

Ginouvès, R. (1962). *Balaneutikè. Recherches sur le bain dans l'antiquité grecque.* Paris

Giuseppetti, M. (2012). 'Mito e storia nell' *Inno a Delo* di Callimacho' in Cusset, Le Meur-Weissman and Levin (edd.) 469–94

— (2013). *L'isola esile. Studi sull' Inno a Delo di Callimaco.* Seminari Romani di Cultura Greca, Quaderni 16. Rome

Graf, F. (1993). *Greek Mythology: An Introduction* (trans. T. Marier). Baltimore and London

Griffith, F.T. (1977–78), 'The Date of Callimachus' *Hymn to Delos*' *Maia* 29–30.95–100

Griffith, R.D. (1997). 'Criteria for Evaluating Hypothetical Egyptian Loan-Words in Greek: The Case of Αἴγυπτος' *ICS* 22.1–6

Griffiths, A. (1988). Review of Mineur (1984), *JHS* 108.230–34

Guarducci, M. (1929). *Poeti vaganti e conferenzieri dell'età ellenistica: ricerche di epigrafia greca nel campo della letteratura e del costume.* Memorie della R. Accademia nazionale dei Lincei. Rome

Gutzwiller, K. (ed.) (2005). *The New Posidippus. A Hellenistic Poetry Book.* Oxford

Hamilton, R. (2000). *Treasure Map: A Guide to the Delian Inventories.* Ann Arbor

Harder, A. (1988). 'Callimachus and the Muses: Some Aspects of Narrative Technique in *Aetia* 1–2' *Prometheus* 14.1–14

— (2012). *Callimachus.* Aetia. Oxford

Harder, M. A., Regtuit, R.F., Wakker, G.C. (edd.) (1993). *Callimachus.* Hellenistica Groningana I. Groningen

Hardie, A. (1983). *Statius and the Silvae: Poet, Patrons and Epideixis in the Graeco-Roman World.* Liverpool

— (1996). 'Pindar, Castalia and the Muses of Delphi (the Sixth Paean)' *PLLS* 9.219–57

— (1997). 'Philitas and the Plane Tree' *ZPE* 119.21–36

— (1998). 'Horace, the Paean, and Roman *Choreia* (*Odes* 4.6)' *PLLS* 10.251–93

— (1998a). 'Juvenal, the *Phaedrus*, and the Truth about Rome' *CQ* 48.234–51

— (2000). 'Pindar's 'Theban' Cosmogony (the First Hymn)' *BICS* 44.19–40

— (2000a). 'The Ancient "Etymology" of ἀοιδός' *Philologus* 144.163–75

— (2003). 'The Statue(s) of Philitas (P.Mil. Vogl. VIII 309 Col. X.16–25 and Hermesianax fr. 7.75–78 P.)' *ZPE* 143.27–36

— (2005). 'The Ancient Etymology of *Carmen*' *PLLS* 12.71–94

— (2005a). 'Sappho, the Muses, and Life after Death' *ZPE* 154.13–32

— (2006). 'The Aloades on Helicon: Music, Territory and Cosmic Order' *A&A* 52.42–71

— (2008). 'An Augustan Hymn to the Muses (Horace *Odes* 3.4). Part I' *PLLS* 13.55–118

— (2010). 'An Augustan Hymn to the Muses (Horace *Odes* 3.4). Part II' *PLLS* 14.191–317

— (2010a). '"Canens' (Ovid *Metamorphoses* 14.320–434)' *SIFC* 8.11–67

— (2012). '*Hypsipyle*, Dionysus Melpomenos and the Muse in Tragedy' *PLLS* 15.143–89

— (2013). 'Ibycus and the Muses of Helicon' *MD* 70.9–36

— (2013a). 'Empedocles and the Muse of the *Agathos Logos*' *AJP* 134.209–46

Hardie, P. (1986). *Virgil's Aeneid: Cosmos and Imperium.* Oxford

Haslam, M.W. (1993). 'Callimachus' Hymns' in Harder, Regtuit and Wakker (edd.) 111–25

Headlam, W. (1922). *Herodas. The Mimes and Fragments.* Cambridge

Henrichs, A. (1993). 'Gods in Action: the Poetics of Divine Performance in the *Hymns* of Callimachus' in Harder, Regtuit and Wakker (edd.) 127–47

Hopkinson, N. (1984). *Callimachus: Hymn to Demeter. Edited with an Introduction and Commentary.* Cambridge

— (1985). Review of Mineur (1984), *CR* 35.249–52

Hornblower, S. (1991). *A Commentary on Thucydides. Vol.1, Books I-III.* Oxford

— (2015). *Lycophron: Alexandra.* Oxford

Horsfall, N. (2006). *Virgil, Aeneid 3. A Commentary.* Leiden and Boston

Hübner, W. (1991). 'Capella = Μαζός?' *Hermes* 119.356–66

Hunter, R. (1993). *The Argonautica of Apollonius. Literary Studies.* Cambridge

— (2003). *Theocritus: Encomium of Ptolemy Philadelphus.* Berkeley, Los Angeles and London

— (2006). *The Shadow of Callimachus.* Cambridge

— (2011). 'The Gods of Callimachus' in Acosta-Hughes, Lehnus and Stephens (edd.) 245–63

Hunter, R. and Fuhrer, T. (2002). 'Imaginary Gods? Poetic Theology in the *Hymns* of Callimachus' in *Callimaque.* Fondation Hardt Entretiens XLVII. Geneva. 143–87

Inwood, B. (2001). *The Poem of Empedocles.* 2nd edn. Toronto, etc.

Irwin, M.E. (1996). 'Evadne, Iamos and Violets in Pindar's *Sixth Olympian*' *Hermes* 124.385–95

Jockey, P. (1996). 'Le Sanctuaire de Délos à l'époque archaïque' *Topoi* 6.159–97

Johannson, M. (2001). 'The Inscription from Troizen: A Decree of Themistocles?' *ZPE* 137.69–92

Karanika, A. (2009). 'The *Ololygê* in the *Homeric Hymn to Apollo*: from Poetics to Politics' in Athanassaki, Martin and Miller (edd.) 67–78

Kennedy, D. (1982). 'Gallus and the Culex' *CQ* 32.371–89

Kidd, D. (1997). *Aratus: Phaenomena.* Cambridge

Koenen, L. (1983). 'Die Adaptation ägyptischer Königsideologie am Ptolemäerhof' in E. van t'Dack et al. (edd.) *Egypt and the Hellenistic World.* Leuven. 143–90

Kontoleon, N.M. (1966). Review of Rubensohn (1962), *Gnomon* 38.202–11

Kowalzig, B. (2007). *Singing for the Gods. Performances of Myth and Ritual in Archaic and Classical Greece.* Oxford

Kuiper, K. (1896) *Studia Callimachea I: de Hymnorum I–IV Dictione Epica.* Leiden

Larson, J. (2001). *Greek Nymphs: Myth, Cult, Lore.* Oxford

Le Roy, C. (1973). 'La naissance d'Apollon et les palmiers déliens' *BCH*

Suppl. 1.263–86

Liapis, V.J. (2007). 'Zeus, Rhesus, and the Mysteries' *CQ* 57.381–411

Lieberg., G. (1982). 'Die Theologia Tripertita als Formprinzip antiker Denkens' *RhM* 125.25–53

Livrea, E. (1995). 'From Pittacus to Byzantium: The History of a Callimachean Epigram' *CQ* 45.474–80

Long, A.A. (1987). 'Stoic Readings of Homer' in R. Lamberton and J.J. Keaney (edd.) *Homer's Ancient Readers: The Hermeneutics of Greek Epic's Earliest Exegetes*. Princeton, N.J. 41–66

Long, C.R. (1987). *The Twelve Gods of Greece and Rome*. Leiden, etc.

Lonsdale, S.H. (1993). *Dance and Ritual Play in Greek Religion*. Baltimore and London

— (1994). '"Homeric Hymn to Apollo": Prototype and Paradigm of Choral Performance' *Arion* 33.25–40

Lynch, J.P. (1972). *Aristotle's School: A Study of a Greek Educational Institution*. Berkeley, etc.

Maass, E. (1892). *Aratea*. Berlin

Marinatos, Sp. (1936). 'Le temple géométrique de Dréros' *BCH* 60.214–85

Matthews, V.J. (1996). *Antimachus of Colophon. Text and Commentary*. Leiden, etc.

McKay, K.J. (1962). *The Poet at Play: Kallimachos, the Bath of Pallas*. Leiden

— (1962a). *Erysichthon: a Callimachean Comedy*. Leiden

— (1968). 'A Hellenistic Medley' *Mnemosyne* 21.171–5

McLennan, G.R. (1977). *Callimachus: Hymn to Zeus*. Testi e Commenti/Texts and Commentaries 2: Istituto di Filologia Classica Urbino/Birkbeck College, London. Rome

Meillier, C. (1979). *Callimaque et son temps. Recherches sur la carrière et la condition d'un écrivain à l'époque des premiers Lagides*. Lille

— (1995). 'L'éloge royal dans l'*Hymne à Délos* de Callimaque. Homère, Pindare, Callimaque: une dialectique de l'épique et du lyrique' in L. Dubois (ed.) *Poésie et lyrique antiques*. Villeneuve d'Ascq. 129–48

Merker, I.L. (1970). 'The Ptolemaic Officials and the League of the Islanders' *Historia* 19.141–60

Merry, M.T. (1914).'Callimachus' Debt to Pindar and Others' *Hermathena* 18.46–72

Michalopoulos, I.D. (2007). 'Intertextualité et allusion historique dans le préambule de *l'Hymne à Délos* de Callimaque' *BAGB* 2007.69–74

— (2012). 'Le Dieu, Le Souverain et le Poète: Callimaque et la Philosophie Politique' in Cusset, Le Meur-Weissman and Levin (edd.) 373–95

Milton, M.P. (1979). 'The Date of Thucydides' Synchronism of the Siege of Naxos with Themistokles' Flight' *Historia* 28.257–75

Mineur, W.H. (1984). *Callimachus. Hymn to Delos*. Leiden

Mori, A. (2012). 'Reconciliation and Ceaseless Wrath: Paradoxical Hera in Apollonius and Callimachus' in Cusset, Le Meur-Weissman and Levin (edd.) 319–36

Morrison, A. (2011). 'Callimachus' Muses' in Acosta-Hughes, Lehnus and Stephens (edd.) 329–48

Most, G.W. (1981). 'Callimachus and Herophilus' *Hermes* 109.188–96

Muccioli, F. (2013). *Gli epiteti ufficiali dei re ellenistici.* Stuttgart

Myers, K.S. (1994) '*Ultimus Ardor*: Pomona and Vertumnus in Ovid's *Met.* 14.623–771' *CJ* 89.225–50

Nagy, G. (2009). 'Perfecting the Hymn in the Homeric *Hymn to Apollo*' in Athanassaki, Martin and Miller (edd.) 17–44

Newbold, R.F. (2000). 'Breasts and Milk in Nonnus' *Dionysiaca*' *CW* 94.11–23

Nishimura-Jensen, J. (2000). 'Unstable Geographies. The Moving Landscape in Apollonius' *Argonautica* and Callimachus' *Hymn to Delos*' *TAPA* 130.287–317

Nock, A.D. (1930). 'Sunnaos Theos' *HSCP* 41.1–62

Nünlist, R. (2009). *The Ancient Critic at Work: Terms and Concepts of Literary Criticism in Greek Scholia.* Cambridge

Onians, R.B. (1951). *The Origins of European Thought about the Body, the Mind, the Soul, the World, Time, and Fate.* Cambridge

Otto, W.F. (1956). *Die Musen und der göttliche Ursprung des Singen und Sagens.* Darmstadt

Pache, C.O. (2004). *Baby and Child Heroes in Greece.* Urbana and Chicago

Parker, R. (1983). *Miasma. Pollution and Purification in Early Greek Religion.* Oxford

Peponi, A.-E. (2009). '*Choreia* and Aesthetics in the Homeric *Hymn to Apollo*: The Performance of the Delian Maidens (Lines 156–64)' *CA* 28.39–70

Petrovic, I. (2011). 'Callimachus and Contemporary Religion: The *Hymn to Apollo*' in Acosta-Hughes, Lehnus and Stephens (edd.) 264–85

Pfeiffer, R. (1952). 'The Image of the Delian Apollo and Apolline Ethics' *Journal of the Warburg and Courtauld Institutes* 15.20–32

Pfeijffer, I.L. (1999). *Three Aeginetan Odes of Pindar: A Commentary on Nemean V, Nemean III, & Nemean VIII.* Leiden, etc.

Plassart, A. (1928). *Les sanctuaires et les cultes de Mont Cynthe.* Paris

Postgate, J.P. (1896). 'On the Alleged Confusion of Nymph-Names, with Especial Reference to Propertius, I 21 and II 32. 40' *AJP* 17.30–44

Power, T. (2010). *The Culture of Kitharôidia.* Washington

Price, T.H. (1978). *Kourotrophos. Cults and Representations of the Greek Nursing Deities.* Leiden

Queyrel, A. (1988). 'Les Muses à l'école' *AK* 31.90–102

Reger, G. (1994). 'The Political History of the Kyklades 260–200 B.C.' *Historia* 43.32–69

Reinsch-Werner, H. (1976). *Callimachus Hesiodicus. Die Rezeption der hesiodischen Dichtung durch Kallimachos von Kyrene.* Berlin

Reitzenstein, E. (1931). 'Zur Stiltheorie des Kallimachos' in Ed. Fraenkel and others, *Festschrift Richard Reitzenstein.* Leipzig and Berlin. 23–69

Richardson, N. (2010). *Three Homeric Hymns: To Apollo, Hermes, and Aphrodite.* Cambridge

Rigsby, K.T. (1980). 'Bacchon the Nesiarch on Delos' *AJP* 101.194–6

Robertson, N. (1984). 'Poseidon's Festival at the Winter Solstice' *CQ* 34.1–16

Rubenson, O. (1962). *Das Delion von Paros.* Wiesbaden

Ruffy, M.V. (2004). *La fabrique du divin: Les Hymnes de Callimaque à la lumière des Hymnes homériques et des Hymnes épigraphiques.* Liège

Rutherford, I. (1988). 'Pindar on the Birth of Apollo' *CQ* 38.65–75

— (1990). '*Paeans* by Simonides' *HSCP* 93.169–209

— (2001). *Pindar's Paeans. A Reading of the Fragments with a Survey of the Genre.* Oxford

— (2010). 'Canonizing the Pantheon: The Dodekatheon in Greek Religion and its Origins' in J.N. Bremmer and A. Erskine (edd.) *The Gods of Ancient Greece: Identities and Transformations.* Edinburgh. 43–54

— (2013). *State Pilgrims and Sacred Observers in Ancient Greece. A Study of Theōriā and Theōroi.* Cambridge

Salvador, J.A. (1997). 'Iamos and ἴα in Pindar (*O* 6, 53–57)' *QUCC* 56.37–59

Sansone, D. (2007). 'An Ingenious Etymology in Plato, "Phaedrus" 266D7–9' *CQ* 57.253–8

Schibli, H.S. (1990). *Pherekydes of Syros.* Oxford

Schmiel, R. (1987). 'Callimachus' *Hymn to Delos*: Structure and Theme' *Mnemosyne* 40.45–55

Schmitz, H. (1970). *Hypsos und Bios. Stilistische Untersuchungen zum Altrealismus in der archaischen griechischen Chorlyric.* Berne

Seier, K. (1993). *Die Peneios-Episode des Kallimacheicheischen Deloshymons und Apollonios von Rhodos. Zur Datierung des dritten Buchs der Argonautika,* in Harder, Regtuit and Wakker (edd.) 177–95

Sens, A. (1997). *Theocritus: Dioscuri (Idyll 22).* Göttingen

Slater, W.J. (1969). *Lexicon to Pindar.* Berlin

Snell, B. (1982). *The Discovery of the Mind in Greek Philosophy and Literature,* trans. T.G. Rosenmeyer. New York

Solomon, J. (1994). 'Apollo and the Lyre' in J. Solomon (ed.) *Apollo: Origins and Influences.* Tucson and London. 37–46

Spanoudakis, K. (2002). *Philitas of Kos.* Leiden, etc.

Steiner, D. (1986). *The Crown of Song: Metaphor in Pindar.* London

Stephens, S.A. (2002–2003). 'Linus' Song' *Hermathena* 173–174.13–28

— (2003). *Seeing Double: Intercultural Poetics in Ptolemaic Alexandria.* Berkeley, etc.

— (2015). *Callimachus: The Hymns. Edited with Introduction, Translation and Commentary.* Oxford and New York

Sullivan, S.D. (1981). 'The Function of *thumos* in Hesiod and the Greek Lyric Poets' *Glotta* 59.147–55

— (1989). 'A Study of *phrenes* in Pindar and Bacchylides' *Glotta* 67.148–89

Tarn, W.W. (1924). 'The Political Standing of Delos' *JHS* 44.141–57

Thompson, D.B. (1955). 'A Portrait of Arsinoe Philadelphos' *AJA* 59.199–206

Too, Y.L. (1991). ''Ηρα Παρθενία and Poetic Self-Reference in Pindar 'Olympian' 6.87–90' *Hermes* 119.257–64

Ukleja, K. (2005). *Der Delos-Hymnus des Kallimachos innerhalb seines Hymnensextetts.* Münster

Vallois, R. (1924). 'Topographie délienne. I: L'Artémision, le Monument des Hyperboréennes, l'Olivier sacré, et le Kératôn' *BCH* 48.411–45

Vestrheim, G. (2000). 'Meaning and Structure in Callimachus' Hymns to Artemis and Delos' *Symb. Osl.* 75.62–79

Weber, G. (1993). *Dichtung und höfische Gesellschaft.* Stuttgart

West, M.L. (1999). 'The Invention of Homer' *CQ* 49.364–82

— (2014). *The Making of the Odyssey.* Oxford

White, H. (2001). 'Notes on Callimachus' Hymn to Delos' *Myrtia* 16.315–18

Wilamowitz-Moellendorff, U. von (1919). 'Lesefrüchte' *Hermes* 54.46–74

— (1924). *Hellenistische Dichtung in der Zeit des Kallimachos.* Berlin

Williams, F. (1973) 'ὦ in Theocritus' *Eranos* 71.52–67

— (1978). *Callimachus: Hymn to Apollo. A Commentary.* Oxford

— (1993). 'Callimachus and the Supranormal' in Harder, Wakker and Regtuit (edd.) 217–25.

Wilson, P. (2009). 'Thamyris the Thracian: the archetypal wandering poet?' in R. Hunter and I. Rutherford (edd.) *Wandering Poets in Ancient Greek Culture: Travel, Locality and Pan-Hellenism.* Cambridge. 46–79

Wimmel, W. (1960). *Kallimachos im Rom. Die Nachfolge seines apologetischen Dichtens in der Augusteerzeit.* Wiesbaden

Wright, M.R. (1981). *Empedocles: the Extant Fragments.* Yale

Ypsilanti, M. (2010). 'Deserted Delos: A Motif of the 'Anthology' and its Poetic and Historical Background' *GRBS* 50.63–85

Yunis, H. (2011). *Plato: Phaedrus.* Cambridge

Ziegler, C. (1913). 'Zum Zeushymnos des Kallimachos' *RhM* 68.336–54

Literary Love Triangles
Berenice at Alexandria and Rome[1]

Annemarie Ambühl

Johannes Gutenberg-Universität Mainz

1. Introduction

A cluster of love triangles appears in a group of Greek and Roman texts centered on Berenice II (best known from Callimachus' *Lock of Berenice* and its Latin version by Catullus) and her later analogues. These texts feature (at least) three pairs of royal lovers, whose fates span almost the whole epoch of Hellenism, including its aftermath in the early imperial period; discussion of them will move from Alexandria to Rome and back to the Near East, with a brief final excursion into the history of modern reception. The first 'love-affair' involves the Ptolemaic rulers Ptolemy III Euergetes and his wife Berenice II (mid third century BCE), the second her distant relative Cleopatra, the last Ptolemaic queen, and Julius Caesar (their affair is possibly reflected in the story of Dido and Aeneas in Vergil's *Aeneid*), and the third the Flavian emperor Titus and the Jewish queen Julia Berenice, a namesake of the Egyptian Berenice from the Hellenised Herodian dynasty. All these relationships contain a love triangle of some sort, either literally — there is a rival in love, or metaphorically — the couple's happiness is threatened, usually by the male partner's obligations to the state.[2]

---

[1] My paper's title was originally suggested by the theme ('Unusual Angles') of the Fall 2013 Langford Seminar at Florida State University, where an earlier version of it was presented. I thank the Seminar Director Ruurd Nauta, my co-speakers and the audience for stimulating discussion, the anonymous referees for their helpful comments, and Francis and Sandra Cairns for editorial assistance with the final version (it goes without saying that any remaining flaws are my own).

[2] While the love triangle already constitutes a fertile motif in classical myth and literature, some scholars have explored its metaliterary significance; so, for example, Nagle (1988) draws an analogy between erotic triangles involving mythical characters and the narrative triangle involving Ovid, the literary tradition and his readers in the *Metamorphoses*. Here I likewise apply the term in a wider sense to intertextual and intercultural relationships.

The starting point for comparison and analysis of the literary representations of these three couples is the well-known motif of the 'unwilling farewell'.[3] This motif is already found in early Greek epic, lyric and drama, most commonly in the form of a separation of two lovers by fatal circumstances. In most cases the husband leaves his wife to go to war, as Hector takes leave of Andromache in the *Iliad* or as Protesilaus parts from Laodamia in tragedy.[4] The crucial role of this motif in the plot of Callimachus' *Lock of Berenice* has long been noted, as has its influence on Latin poetry (see below §§2 and 3). Since the motif and its linguistic markers — often forms derived from ἄκων or *inuitus* — are so widely diffused in Greek and Latin love poetry, I focus, in order to validate intertextual links within the corpus of texts studied, on combinations of formal and contextual signals (e.g. verbal allusions reinforced by anaphora or polyptoton) occurring in love stories with an Egyptian, Libyan or Near Eastern setting and/or which are associated with the name Berenice.

I also move beyond poetry and trace the motif in historiography and biography, noting possible cross-generic connections between poetry and seemingly factual narratives; in some cases the allegedly historical facts look to have been shaped after fictional patterns and not vice versa. I argue, for example, in §§4 and 5 that literary motifs associated with the Hellenistic Berenice have been transferred to historiographical texts dealing with the other Berenice. While the associative identification of the two Berenices has been recognised in studies dealing with the history of their reception (see below §6), it has only rarely been noticed that the beginnings of this process can be traced back to the ancient texts.[5]

On yet another level, I address the relationship between the different historical and cultural contexts and literatures of Alexandria and Rome by concentrating on the interconnections between literary patterns and

---

[3] For this term see Acosta-Hughes (2008). More generally on expressions of unwilling-ness and regret and appeals to necessity or compulsion as topoi of the syntaktikon (the farewell speech of a departing traveller) and the propemptikon see Cairns (2007) 38–57.

[4] The tragic love story of Protesilaus and Laodamia, which apart from a brief mention in Homer's Catalogue of Ships (*Il.* 2.695–702) is mainly based on a lost play by Euri-pides, and which features the unwilling departure theme twice (Protesilaus' departure for the Trojan War and his departure after his brief return as a ghost), was analysed by Pelliccia (2010–2011), who studied the ramifications of the 'Protesilaus and Laodamia theme' in a wide range of Greek and Latin texts (on the *Coma Berenices* see esp. 149–52, 187–93).

[5] For the *communis opinio* see Sprondel–Schröder (2013) 176: "Die histor[ischen] Hin-tergründe und lit[erarischen] Figurationen der beiden Gestalten wurden in der nach-ant[iken] Rezeption häufig miteinander vermischt, wobei manchmal einzelne weitere Aspekte anderer Namensträgerinnen hinzutraten."

their political and ideological background; a key focal point will be the representation of female rulers at Alexandria and Rome. This approach accords with recent trends in scholarship on Hellenistic literature, where, in addition to emphasis on formal aesthetics, the political agenda has been emphatically reintroduced.[6] However, it was precisely the eminently political character of much Alexandrian poetry that generated the seeds of conflict when it was adapted in Roman literature. Although Alexandrian poetry was an admired model for Romans, the Ptolemaic empire was seen as an oriental-style monarchy — a political and ideological 'other' to Rome. But, as the Roman republic mutated into the principate, the distinction was blurred: generals and statesmen such as Pompey, Caesar, M. Antonius and Octavian-Augustus experimented with various forms of Hellenistic ruler-representation, and Rome became 'Alexandrianised'. This development was reflected in contemporary literature, where political and ideological tensions were explored within the reception and transformation of Hellenistic poetry. The literary fates of the two Berenices can thus be seen as one of the strands spanning the gulf between Alexandria and Rome.

2. Origins
Berenice II, Ptolemy III Euergetes, and the Lock

The self-representation of the Ptolemaic dynasty has been studied intensively in recent years, mainly with respect to Ptolemy II Philadelphus and his sister-wife Arsinoe II.[7] The Philadelphoi played a crucial role in shaping Ptolemaic ideology; the ingredients of this ideology were taken over and further developed by their successors up to the last and most famous Ptolemaic queen, Cleopatra VII. The Ptolemies were one of the few ancient dynasties in which, probably following Egyptian as well as Macedonian precedent, female members played a visible public role, although the extent of their actual political power is still contested.[8] Central elements of the official image shaped by the Philadelphoi, such as the cult of the divinised rulers and the

---

[6] See e.g. Weber (1993), Stephens (2003), Fantuzzi–Hunter (2004), Hunter (2006), Acosta-Hughes–Stephens (2012), and Harder–Regtuit–Wakker (2014). For political readings of Catullus see Du Quesnay–Woodman (2012).

[7] On Ptolemy II Philadelphus see McKechnie–Guillaume (2008), on the couple Müller (2009), and on Arsinoe II Carney (2013).

[8] The roles and representations of the Ptolemaic queens have been much discussed: e.g. Macurdy (1932) 102–223; Pomeroy (1984) 3–40; Hazzard (2000) esp. 82–159; Carney (2011); Prioux (2011); Caneva (2014). For the historical background of the Ptolemaic empire see Hölbl (2001).

concept of sibling-marriage, return under Ptolemy III Euergetes and Berenice II.[9] This third Ptolemaic royal couple is also well known from documentary papyri, inscriptions and portraits, but for present purposes I focus on a poetic text which mirrors and at the same time humorously subverts such official images: Callimachus' *Lock of Berenice*, the crowning elegy of his four-volume *Aetia*.[10] It is a prime example of the complex interactions between the ideology of Ptolemaic rule, the court patronage of arts and sciences, and the creative imagination of a highly innovative Alexandrian poet.

In 245 BCE, Berenice II dedicated at the temple of Arsinoe-Aphrodite Zephyritis a lock of her hair, which she had vowed for her husband's safe return from the Syrian War; it mysteriously disappeared from the temple. The court astronomer Conon then discovered a new constellation in the night sky, which he named after Berenice's lock, and Callimachus immortalised the pseudo-historical *aition* of the lock's catasterism in his elegy.[11] This seemingly playful text focuses on central topics of the Ptolemaic agenda such as the creation of a public image for Berenice II in emulation of her predecessor Arsinoe II and (a debated issue) the Greek-Egyptian dual perspective of the dynasty.[12] The offering of a lock of hair and its catasterism can be associated with Greek hero cults as well as with Egyptian cosmology, and it thus opens up a wide frame of reference which served to legitimise Ptolemaic rule over Egypt.[13] The *Lock of Berenice* thus projects the imperial ideology

---

[9] Clayman (2014), perceptively (if in some cases speculatively), discusses her reflections in Hellenistic literature; cf. also Clayman (2011); (2014a); van Oppen de Ruiter (2015).

[10] Pfeiffer's monumental edition of Callimachus (1949) — 112–23 on the *Coma Berenices* (fr. 110 Pf.) — was followed by the commented editions of the *Aetia* by Massimilla (2010) — see esp. 148–61, 464–509 (on fr. 213 M.), and Harder (2012) — see I.289–304, II.793–854 (on frr. 110–110f H.). Marinone (1997) is a comparative edition of Callimachus and Catullus. The texts of Callimachus and Catullus are quoted here after Harder (2012 = H.), as are the translations (sometimes slightly adapted).

[11] The offering of the lock seems also to have been commemorated in Berenice's official iconography; cf. Carrez-Maratray (2008) and Clayman (2014) 101–2. Pantos (1987) esp. 350–1 tentatively interpreted as an illustration of her vow a seal apparently portraying her with short hair at the back of her head.

[12] On the *Lock of Berenice* as a complex reflection of Ptolemaic royal ideology mediating between Greek/Macedonian and Egyptian cultural and religious concepts and highlighting the public role of the female members of the dynasty, see the seminal article by Gutzwiller (1992). Cf. also Koenen (1993) 89–113; Selden (1998) 326–54; Carrez-Maratray (2008); Hauben (2011); Llewellyn-Jones–Winder (2011); Clayman (2011), (2014) 97–104, 127–8, and (2014a) 94–6. Visscher (forthcoming) proposes a political reading of the poem in the context of the Third Syrian War. For the historical background see Hölbl (2001) 46–51, 105.

[13] On the Greek background of the lock-offering see Nachtergael (1980) and Gutzwiller (1992) 369–73; on Egyptian associations with Isis-Hathor see Selden (1998) 337–51, Jackson (2001), who associates the Lock of Berenice with the Lock of Isis, i.e. Red

of the Ptolemies onto a cosmic canvas.

However, as has recently been argued, the new queen's position was not as secure as it seems in retrospect: Berenice brought with her a scandalous reputation from her youth at Cyrene.[14] She had been entangled in a love triangle there with her fiancé Demetrius the Fair and her mother Apame, who had called off Berenice's earlier engagement to Euergetes only to become herself involved with her new son-in-law. Berenice had allegedly taken an active role in a plot to kill her unfaithful lover in the bedroom, a brave deed which reaffirmed her alliance with Euergetes, and to which the *Coma Berenices* alludes with that implication.[15] In the turbulent times around the outbreak of the Third Syrian War she also had to compete for Euergetes' attentions with his full sister Berenice Syra, widow of king Antiochus II and thus also a potential bride for Euergetes (another potential love triangle). Seen from this perspective Callimachus' poem, far from being a poetic fantasy, was instrumental in refashioning Berenice's image as the courageous and passionate sister-wife of Ptolemy Euergetes, although in their case the sibling relationship was feigned for dynastic reasons since they were actually cousins.[16]

Regrettably the *Lock of Berenice*, along with the majority of Callimachus' works, has not survived, and is known only partially through papyrus finds; but Catullus' Latin version (Poem 66) survives. Although Catullus' creative energy should not be underestimated (see below §3), Poem 66 is a fairly reliable guide to the overall plot, if not

---

Coral, Llewellyn-Jones–Winder (2011), and Clayman (2014) 100–1.

[14] See Llewellyn-Jones–Winder (2011) 247–54; Clayman (2014) 14–41, 97–104, 125–7, 179–80, and, more speculatively, 78–97, 105–20.

[15] Cat. 66.25–8 (*at <te> ego certe/ cognoram a parua uirgine magnanimam./ anne bonum oblita es facinus, quo regium adepta es/ coniugium, quod non fortior ausit alis?*) seems to be reflected in Call. fr. 110.26 H. (μεγάθυμον ?), as restored by Pfeiffer (1975) 104, and possibly in some scholia (fr. 110f H.); cf. Harder (2012) II.809–11, 854. The full story is told in Justin 26.3.2–8 (after Pompeius Trogus), whereas Hygin. *Astr.* 2.24.2 (= 110b H.) explains the epithet as referring to another brave deed of the young Berenice, her assistance to her father in a battle (cf. frr. 387–8 Pf.; but see Chiesa (2009), who also connects these fragments with the murder of Demetrius the Fair and interprets them as an elegiac wedding poem for Berenice); on the history of scholarship on these passages see Benedetto (2008).

[16] Cat. 66.21–2 (*et tu non orbum luxti deserta cubile,/ sed fratris cari flebile discidium*); cf. Call. fr. 110.45 H. See Gutzwiller (1992) and Clayman (2014) 127–8, who interprets this "earliest ... evidence for the officially sanctioned myth that Berenice II and Ptolemy III were siblings" as "the creative merger of the two Berenices in the imagination of a great poet ..., both a graceful response to the death of Berenice Syra, and the first step in an extended campaign to fashion Berenice II as a new Arsinoe II." On the ambiguous reflections of brother-sister marriage in Hellenistic poetry see Krevans (2012).

for the reconstruction of the lost parts of the Greek text.[17] In it the personified lock tells its own story, and from its heavenly position complains about its fate: even its recently acquired honours as a star cannot compensate for the loss of its mistress, from whose head it was cut off against its will. In both the Greek and Latin versions the talking lock oscillates between male and female roles, even though in Greek its grammatical gender is predominantly male (βόστρυχος: Callimachus fr. 110.8 H.; πλόκαμος: 47, 62) and in Latin female (*coma*: Catullus 66.51, 93; cf. *caesaries*: 8; but *crines*: 47).[18] In Callimachus it is the queen's male lover and brother of his sister locks who miss him dearly (fr. 110.51 H.: ἄρτι [ν]εότμητόν με κόμαι ποθέεσκον ἀδε[λφεαί]. But allusive links with Sappho's epithalamia suggest a female persona, with the lock as a young bride forced against her will to leave her beloved mistress to get married; this female perspective is reinforced by a verbal parallel with Apollonius' Medea, who cuts off a lock for her mother when leaving home (*Argonautica*. 4.27–31), and on a later occasion swears that she did not join Jason and the Argonauts of her own free will (4.1019–24).[19] Through such subtle intertextual links Berenice's lock is cast in the role of the third party excluded from the marital bliss of the royal couple, for which it was sacrificed.

The plot of the *Lock of Berenice* is thus constructed around two scenes of unwilling departure, viewed from the emotional perspective of the wife and the lock respectively. Berenice was deprived of her

[17] On the notorious problems of reconstructing Callimachus' text from Catullus' idiosyncratic Latin version, see the editions cited in n.10 and the methodically cautious overview by Bing (2009), especially *re* Pfeiffer's reconstruction (1975 [originally 1932]). Warden (2006) and De Wilde (2008) concentrate on Catullus' technique and motives as a translator and poet. Despite the tendency to ascribe the highly emotional tone to Catullus (see also n.33), Callimachus' elegy has been defined as "a celebration of royal conjugal love [in] the form of a lyric lament of separation and longing" (Acosta-Hughes (2008) 2 = (2010) 63). In what follows, when only Catullus is quoted, it means that the (hypothetical) Greek equivalent lines have been lost.

[18] While Callimachus' lock is defined as a maiden by Gutzwiller (1992) 373–85 and as a male by Koenen (1993) 94–5, Vox (2000) emphasizes the gender ambiguity; cf. also Barchiesi (2001) 145, 189–90 nn.8 and 9; Fantuzzi–Hunter (2004) 87; Acosta-Hughes (2008) 5 and (2010) 67–8; Höschele (2009) 149–51. Hutchinson (2008) 54–5 with n.19 calls the lock "a miniaturization of Berenice" that mirrors her experiences from various angles.

[19] Sappho fr. 94.5 L–P: Ψάπφ', ἦ μάν σ' ἀέκοισ' ἀπυλιμπάνω; Apollon. *Arg.* 4.1021–2: μὴ μὲν ἐγὼν ἐθέλουσα σὺν ἀνδράσιν ἀλλοδαποῖσιν/ κεῖθεν ἀφωρμήθην. See Vox (2000); Acosta-Hughes (2008); (2010) 47–9, 62–78; Pelliccia (2010–2011) 150, 157–8; Hall (2011) 617–20. The *Odyssey* includes other poetic models: Calypso must release Odysseus whom she wants to retain; there however the emphasis is on Odysseus staying with her against his will (5.155: παρ' οὐκ ἐθέλων ἐθελούσῃ — contrast the polyptoton '*inuitus inuitam*' at Sueton. *Tit.* 7.2, see §4 and n.49; cf. *Od.* 5.177: οὐδ' ἂν ἐγώ γ' ἀέκητι σέθεν σχεδίης ἐπιβαίην, and 10.489 (Circe): μηκέτι νῦν ἀέκοντες ἐμῷ ἐνὶ μίμνετε οἴκῳ).

husband immediately after the wedding night (Catullus 66.11–14: *nouo ... hymenaeo*; 15: *nouis nuptis*; 20: *nouo uiro*; cf. Callimachus fr. 110.13/14 H.); this caused her to be tormented by love-sickness (66.19–25, 29–30), as lovers are unwilling to be separated from the body of their beloved (66.31–2: *an quod amantes/ non longe a caro corpore abesse uolunt?*). But then, after the temporary separation of the loving spouses is ended by their happy reunion, the lock has to leave its mistress for good as a thank-offering for the king's victorious return from the war. The lock proclaims that it was forced to do so against its will and (ironically) swears an oath by the very head to which it formerly belonged. In Catullus the crucial distich reads: *inuita, o regina, tuo de uertice cessi,/ inuita: adiuro teque tuumque caput* (66.39–40: Against my will, queen, did I part from your head,/ against my will: I swear it by you and your head). In the Greek original only the pentameter containing the oath has been preserved (fr. 110.40 H.): σήν τε κάρην ὤμοσα σόν τε βίον (I swear by your head and by your life). It would be tempting to try to reconstruct the Greek hexameter from the Latin version, had not papyrus finds demonstrated the futility of most such attempts; but we may at least presume that Callimachus used a form of ἄκων or οὐκ ἐθέλων.[20] As we shall see, the motif of unwilling farewell runs as a common thread through later re-workings of the Berenice theme.

3. Distant relatives
Cleopatra and Caesar between Egypt and Rome
(*alias* Dido and Aeneas between Carthage and Italy)

In Callimachus' poem, the motif of the irreversible separation of lovers is playfully transferred from Berenice to the lock *qua* tragicomic victim. For two later couples the parallel process had a more serious, indeed a fatal, outcome. Almost two hundred years after Ptolemy and Berenice, another pair of lovers occupied the stage at Alexandria, Julius Caesar, fresh from his victory at Pharsalus, and Cleopatra, the last Ptolemaic queen. As has long been recognised, the image of Cleopatra in Augustan literature was shaped mainly by Octavian, whose propaganda attacked the 'un-Roman' involvement with her of M.

---

[20] In his detailed study of this motif and its variants in Greek and Latin poetry Pelliccia (2010–2011) 208–13 discusses the various possibilities for supplementing the text of the *Lock of Berenice*. Cf. also Clausen (1970) 91; Pfeiffer (1975) 105–6; Harder (2012) 2.811. In the intertexts from Sappho (ἀέκοισ') and Apollonius (μὴ ... ἐθέλουσα) quoted in n.19 both phrases figure.

Antonius, while pushing her affair with his adoptive father Caesar into the background.[21] Moreover, since the relevant parts of Livy's history have been lost (cf. the *periochae* for books 112 and 113), we are left with Lucan's fictional re-working of this episode, short comments by Suetonius and the Greek imperial versions by Plutarch, Appian and Cassius Dio.

Caesar's *Bellum Civile* 3.107 and posthumous *Bellum Alexandrinum* (33) offer exclusively political motives for his dealings with Cleopatra, followed by a brief statement of his departure for Syria — no trace, then, of an unwilling departure or of the emotionality surrounding that of Ptolemy III. Yet later historians' and biographers' versions elaborate on Caesar's love affair at Alexandria. Plutarch reports a view that the Alexandrian war was unnecessary and "a shameful and hazardous escapade, inspired by his passion for Cleopatra" (*Caesar* 48.5: ἔρωτι Κλεοπάτρας ἄδοξον αὐτῷ καὶ κινδυνώδη γενέσθαι), but he gives only a brief mention of Caesar's leaving her for Syria while she was pregnant with his son Caesarion (49.10: καταλιπὼν δὲ τὴν Κλεοπάτραν ... ὥρμησεν ἐπὶ Συρίας).[22] Suetonius' narrative of events (*Diuus Iulius* 35), more or less follows the historical record, while Caesar's love affairs are treated under a separate heading (52); there is a hint of a conflict between Caesar's erotic and military interests during his trip with Cleopatra up the Nile, for "he would have gone through Egypt with her in her state-barge almost to Aethiopia, had not his soldiers refused to follow him" (52.1: *eadem naue thalamego paene Aethiopia tenus Aegyptum penetrauit, nisi exercitus sequi recusasset*).[23]

The sequence of events comprising Caesar's brief love affair at Alexandria, his hasty departure for Syria and his swift victory at Zela against Pharnaces of Pontus (*Bellum Alexandrinum* 77.1),[24] reads surprisingly like the plot of the *Lock of Berenice*. There Ptolemy immediately after his wedding-night departs for the Third Syrian War (66.11– 14: *qua rex tempestate nouo auctus hymenaeo/ uastatum finis iuerat*

---

[21] Becher (1966) presents a chronologically and thematically arranged collection of the Greek and Latin literary sources for Cleopatra. For the ideological bias of the texts and especially Augustan poetry see Wyke (2002) and Syed (2005) 177–93; cf. also Gall (2006). Turner (2010) compares Lucan's account to the other extant sources. Roller (2010) has published a biography of Cleopatra VII in the same series as Carney (2013) on Arsinoe II and Clayman (2014) on Berenice II.

[22] Tr. Pelling (2011).

[23] Tr. Rolfe (1914). On the trip see also Appian *B.C.* 2.90. Lucan's Caesar by contrast is motivated by scientific curiosity and a wish to explore the sources of the Nile; he says that he would even give up the civil war for this (*B.C.* 10.188–93). On this episode and its chronological problems see Lord (1938); Turner (2010) 200–1; Roller (2010) 65–7.

[24] The locus of Caesar's aphorism '*ueni, uidi, uici*' (Suet. *Iul.* 37.2; cf. Plut. *Caes.* 50; Dio 42.48.1).

Assyrios,/ dulcia nocturnae portans uestigia rixae,/ quam de uirgineis gesserat exuuiis;[25] after a brief campaign during which he conquers the whole of Asia, he returns victoriously to his Berenice (66.35–6: *is haud in tempore longo/ captam Asiam Aegypti finibus addiderat*).[26]

Are these parallels a mere coincidence or are we dealing with a conscious literary reminiscence? The basic historical facts are not in doubt, and the efficiency and speed of Caesar's campaign are in line with his usual strategy of self-representation. But later writers, especially the imperial Greek historians, were arguably inspired by Hellenistic literature to enrich the historical narrative with a romantic touch.[27] Indeed, in Dio's version (42.45.1) there is a possible echo of the unwilling farewell passage from the *Lock of Berenice*:[28]

> She [Cleopatra] would have detained him [Caesar] even longer in Egypt or else would have set out with him at once for Rome, had not Pharnaces not only drawn Caesar away from Egypt, very much against his will (πάνυ ἄκοντα τὸν Καίσαρα), but also hindered him from hurrying to Italy. (tr. Cary [1916])

Just as Euergetes left for the Syrian War, so it was the war against Pharnaces that forced the unwilling Caesar to leave Cleopatra behind, with the crucial difference that Caesar did not return to Egypt.[29] Their reunion was postponed until Cleopatra's notorious stay at Rome — a diplomatic visit or a lovers' reunion? Cassius Dio refers to negative reactions at Rome (43.27.3):[30]

> But he incurred the greatest censure from all because of his passion for Cleopatra — not now the passion he had displayed in Egypt (for that was matter of hearsay), but that which was displayed in Rome itself. For she had come to the city with her husband and settled in

---

[25] In contrast to this dramatized plot, the actual wedding may have taken place somewhat earlier, and in any case Berenice had been betrothed to Euergetes for several years before; cf. Clayman (2014) 35–9.

[26] Visscher (forthcoming) traces the rhetoric of empire back to Callimachus' Ptolemaic context.

[27] See the general remarks on the later authors' "romanticizing view of Cleopatra and Caesar" in Turner (2010) 208–9. Interestingly, the idea that the '*docta puella*' Cleopatra might herself have stylized her relationship with Caesar after the model of Callimachus' (and Caesar after Catullus') *Lock of Berenice* has been proposed by Pelliccia (2010–2011) 206–8.

[28] See Pelliccia (2010–2011) 207 n.159, who cautiously warns that this might be a coincidence, given Dio's predilection for the term. In the parallel passages on Titus and Julia Berenice the term does not occur, which however might be due to Xiphilinus' paraphrase (see below §4).

[29] Only as an afterthought does Dio add that the departure from Egypt was also in Caesar's own political and military interests (42.47.1: οὔτε εὐπρεπῆ οὔτε λυσιτελῆ οἱ τὴν ἐν τῇ Αἰγύπτῳ διατριβὴν ἐνόμισεν εἶναι).

[30] He had used a similar strategy of indirect criticism earlier when describing Caesar's stay in Egypt (42.44).

Caesar's own house, so that he too derived an ill repute on account of
both of them. He was not at all concerned, however, about this, but
actually enrolled them among the friends and allies of the Roman
people. (tr. Cary [1916])

The scandal of Cleopatra's visit to Rome, which had repercussions too
in the contemporary correspondence of Cicero,[31] draws attention to
another triangle, the one involving Caesar, his wife Calpurnia and his
mistress Cleopatra (and on her side also her brother-husband Ptolemy
XIV); it also draws attention to the conflicting forms of government of
Rome and Egypt. Hosting Hellenistic royalty at Rome was standard
procedure, but scholars still debate the extent to which Caesar during
his brief dictatorship consciously experimented with various forms of
Hellenistic ruler representation. It may well have been one outcome of
his involvement with Cleopatra; the resulting tensions may have helped
to bring about his ultimate murder.[32]

Catullus' choice of Callimachus' *Lock of Berenice* as the model for
his Poem 66 may have been motivated primarily by his professed
adherence to the Alexandrian style and the congenial presence in the
Callimachean text of leitmotifs of his own oeuvre — grief for his dead
brother, his painful separation from his beloved Lesbia, and more
generally the love triangle that was to become so prominent in Latin
love elegy.[33] But there was plausibly influence from the contemporary
political background, as the internal strife for power within the
Ptolemaic dynasty drew Roman imperial interests towards Egypt on the
eve of the civil wars that would bring an end to independent Ptolemaic
rule. Such a political reading of poem 66 has recently been advocated
by Ian Du Quesnay with reference to the Egyptian connections of the
orator Hortensius — the dedicatee of Catullus 66 according to its

---

[31] Cicero's negative remarks on the arrogance exhibited by the queen during her sojourn
at Caesar's gardens across the Tiber might have been partly motivated by a personal
grudge against her (*Att.* 15.15.2: *reginam odi. ... superbiam autem ipsius reginae, cum
esset trans Tiberim in hortis, commemorare sine magno dolore non possum*). Cf.
Gruen (2003) 270, who in his critical review of the sources concludes that for political
reasons Cleopatra did not come to Rome for one extended stay but for two short visits,
the first one in 46 BCE and the second one immediately preceding Caesar's murder in
44 BCE; cf. Roller (2010) 71–4. For other views see Harders (2010) 64–6.

[32] On the issue see most recently Stevenson (2015) 139–80, who argues that Caesar did
not actively seek kingship.

[33] On love, separation, and death as leitmotifs in Catullus 66 and the group of longer
poems see especially Clausen (1970), Warden (2006), De Wilde (2008), and Höschele
(2009); for further literature see also Ambühl (2014). On Callimachus' *Coma
Berenices* and other elegies from the *Aetia* as models for Roman love elegy, mediated
through Catullus, see Puelma (1995), Videau (1997), and Binder–Hamm (1998). On
the love triangle and jealousy as constituents of Roman love elegy see recently Caston
(2012).

companion piece (Poem 65) — and his participation in the efforts to restore Ptolemy XII to his throne in the early fifties BCE.[34] A later date is also possible since the relative chronology of Catullus' poems as well as the year of his death are notoriously uncertain.[35] So the notion that Catullus' *Coma Berenices* reflects Caesar's erotic involvement with Cleopatra in Egypt in 48/47 BCE cannot absolutely be excluded, although if Catullus dedicated it to the orator Q. Hortensius Hortalus, who died in 50 BCE, that scenario would not work.[36]

Even if it cannot be proved that Caesar and Cleopatra were associated with their Ptolemaic predecessors during Caesar's lifetime, there is a strong argument that the association was made in the Augustan age, and that Catullus 66 was retrospectively associated with Caesar and his divinisation. At Catullus' first mention of the new constellation, the phrase '*e Bereniceo uertice caesariem*' (66.8) could with hindsight have been read as evoking Caesar's name as well as the comet, the 'hairy star' that announced his apotheosis in the fashion of Hellenistic ruler-cult.[37] Such a political re-reading of Catullus' *Coma Berenices* is suggested not only by Ovid's *Metamorphoses*, which ends with Caesar's catasterism, just as Callimachus' *Aetia* ends with that of the lock, but by an earlier hint in the *Aeneid*.[38] In one of the most controversial instances of intertextuality in Latin poetry, Vergil makes Aeneas, at his meeting with Dido in the underworld, quote almost literally the lock's

[34] Du Quesnay (2012) 153–62. For another possible political background of Catullus' translation see Konstan (2007) 82–4, who associates Ptolemy and Berenice with Pompey's eastern campaigns and his marriage to Caesar's daughter Julia. Cf. also Tatum (1997) 488–94; Warden (2006) 129–30; Acosta-Hughes–Stephens (2012) 229–33.

[35] The *communis opinio* has Catullus die by the end of the 50s BCE, but certain scholars date some of his poems to the early 40s (e.g. Newman (1990) 180–1, 407). In Ambühl (forthcoming) I read Catullus 64 in the political context of the civil war of 48 BCE, again in connection with a reworking of a Callimachean poem (*Hymn to Delos*).

[36] For the chronological uncertainties see Du Quesnay (2012) 160, who rejects the alternative identification with Hortensius' son, who died at Philippi in 42 BCE (ibid. 156; cf. Tatum (1997) 489). In any case, although Caesar was a friend of the family (Suet. *Iul.* 73), Catullus seems to have been critical of Caesar's transgressions; would he have sympathised with Cleopatra as the abandoned beloved?

[37] Cf. Nadeau (1982), Skulsky (1985) 452–3, Wills (1998) 288–9, Höschele (2009) 126–7 n.22, and especially Pelliccia (2010–2011) 207–8: "if Caesar toyed with the conceit of himself as Ptolemy going off to war from his latter-day Berenice, he certainly did not see himself as the lock as well. ... History had ... arranged to combine two of the lovers depicted in Catullus' poem, Ptolemy departing for Syria and the *coma* for the heavens, in the single extraordinary figure of Caesar." Catullus himself might have connected *caesaries* with *caedere* and thus with the cutting of Berenice's lock (for the ancient etymologies see Maltby (1991) 93–4 s.v. *Caesar* and *caesaries* and, more speculatively, Ahl (1985) 74–91 for wordplays with Caesar, hair, and slaughter).

[38] On the *Coma Berenices* and the *Metamorphoses* see Harder (2003) 302–306; Acosta-Hughes–Stephens (2012) 266–9; Myers (2012) 244–9; Gladhill (2012).

protestation of its unwilling departure from the queen's head in
Catullus (66.39: *inuita, o regina, tuo de uertice cessi*) and likewise
confirm it with an oath, strikingly sworn "by the stars" (*Aeneid* 6.458–
60: *per sidera iuro,/ per superos et siqua fides tellure sub ima est,/
inuitus, regina, tuo de litore cessi* (I swear by the stars, by the powers
above, by whatever is sacred in the Underworld, it was not of my own
will, Queen, I left your land, tr. Day Lewis [1986]).

Whereas earlier interpreters often limited themselves to asking
whether the quotation should be read as serious or ironic, Jeffrey Wills
has convincingly placed it within a complex of allusions to the *Coma
Berenices* spread over the *Aeneid* and expressing the leitmotifs of the
unwilling farewell, the oath, and the cutting of locks of hair.[39] Like the
Lock of Berenice, the *Aeneid* presents two separate scenes of farewell:
at Carthage Aeneas is seemingly unmoved by Dido's pleas and defends
his divinely sanctioned mission with a variant of the motif of unwilling
farewell (*Aeneid* 4.361: *Italiam non sponte sequor* – it is not of my own
free will that I am setting course for Italy).[40] Conversely, at their final
meeting in the underworld, Dido refuses to listen to his apologies and
turns away from him (6.469–76).

A further shared leitmotif is the love triangle. The *Lock of Berenice*
involves primarily Berenice, her husband and the cut-off lock. In the
Aeneid, Dido's relationship with Aeneas provokes the jealousy of
Iarbas and the other Nomad chiefs, while in the underworld Dido finds
comfort in the arms of her deceased husband Sychaeus, whose memory
she had betrayed for Aeneas. More importantly, the love triangle also
manifests itself in a more abstract form: Aeneas must sacrifice his love
for Dido for his love for the future Rome.[41] The fateful choice between
private affections and political realities also points to an extratextual
referent, since Dido as a foreign Libyan queen recalls not only the
Ptolemaic queen Berenice, but also her descendant Cleopatra and that

---

[39] Wills (1998), with bibliography. Subsequent treatments include Feldherr (1999) 107–
11; Barchiesi (2001) 143–6 (an English translation of his 1997 Italian article); Hardie
(2006) 34–40 and (2012) 229–38; Acosta-Hughes (2008), (2010) 75–8, and Acosta-
Hughes–Stephens (2012) 229–33, 238–9; Pelliccia (2010–2011) 149–52, 198–208;
Hall (2011) 616–20; Nauta (2011) 64–9. For more political readings see n.42 below.

[40] Cf. Aeneas' words only a few lines earlier (4.340–1: *me si fata meis paterentur ducere
uitam/ auspiciis et sponte mea componere curas* ...): even if the fates had let him
decide, he still would not have chosen Dido, but would have stayed in Troy. In Book 4
there is a doublet of the scene of Book 6, as Dido swears in front of her sister Anna
that she unwillingly performs the magical rites she intends to perform, which result in
her suicide (4.492–3: *testor, cara, deos et te, germana, tuumque/ dulce caput, magicas
inuitam accingier artis*).

[41] Skulsky (1985) 449–50, referring to *Aen.* 4.347 (*hic amor, haec patria est*) and to the
well-known palindrome *Roma/Amor*, notes that Aeneas' choice is not between love
and duty but between two irreconcilable loves.

queen's problematic relationship with Julius Caesar (and subsequently with M. Antonius).[42] The ambivalent reflections of Berenice and Cleopatra in the *Aeneid* thus confirm that, at Rome during the transition from the republic to the principate, the *Lock of Berenice* was read not merely as a purely literary exercise in Alexandrian poetics, but that its political undertones could be adapted to contemporary Roman politics.

4. The other Berenice
Julia Berenice and Titus between Jerusalem and Rome

The third and last couple were likewise torn between Rome and the East. Their story also revolves around an 'impossible' love-affair between a Roman ruler and an oriental queen who happens to be a namesake of the mistress of the lock: the Jewish queen Julia Berenice (hence a Roman citizen), mistress of Titus, the conqueror of Jerusalem and future Roman emperor, who left her when succeeding to the throne upon his father Vespasian's death in 79 CE.[43] Again, there is the problem of missing contemporary sources.[44] While the *Acts of the Apostles* and Josephus both mention Berenice's joint rulership with her brother Herodes Agrippa II, the Jewish historian silently passes over her relationship with Titus.[45] Apart from a short note on the youthful Titus'

---

[42] While Virgil's Dido has often been associated with the historical Cleopatra VII and her relationship with M. Antonius and with the fictional Cleopatras in Augustan literature (e.g. Cairns (1989) 57; Bertman (2000); Galinsky (2003); Syed (2005) 184–93; Reed (2007) 84–95), the triangle — Dido (and Aeneas); Berenice (and Ptolemy/the Lock); her descendant Cleopatra (and Caesar) — has mainly been acknowledged in political readings of the Callimachean allusion in *Aeneid* 6.640: besides the studies mentioned in n.39 above (i.e. Wills (1998) 288, Hardie (2006) and (2012) 234–5, Pelliccia (2010–2011) 150, 206–8, and Nauta (2011) 67–70), see also Nadeau (1982) 102–3, Skulsky (1985), Johnston (1987), and Clayman (2014) 184–6.

[43] More or less imaginative biographies of Julia Berenice have been written by Émile Mireaux (1951), Ruth Jordan (1974), Eugène Quinche (1978), and Sabino Perea Yébenes (2001). No less fanciful is Ronald Syme's (1991) fake 'reconstruction' of Tacitus' account of Titus and Berenice.

[44] The extant sources have been reviewed critically by Macurdy (1935; cf. 1937 84–91), Jones (1984) 59–63, 77–117, Wesch-Klein (2005), Vasta (2007), and Anagnostou-Laoutides–Charles (2015). On Quintilian's singular testimony that he pleaded on Berenice's behalf before an imperial *consilium* of which she herself was a member (*Inst.* 4.1.19), see Young-Widmaier (2002). On the historical background of the Herodian dynasty and its relations with Rome, mainly during the Jewish War, see Wilker (2007); specifically on Titus and Berenice cf. also Wilker's study (2008) of the political and personal relations between the Roman emperors and their client-kings.

[45] Considering Josephus' close ties with Agrippa II and Berenice as well as with the Flavian dynasty, he would have made a very interesting witness. On the politically coloured accounts of Berenice's role in the Jewish War in Josephus' different works see Krieger (1997) and Goodman (2012); on his stay at Rome, roughly contemporary

passion for queen Berenice at Tacitus *Histories* 2.2.1 and an even shorter note on her beauty and her financial generosity towards Vespasian at 2.81.2 — the Books dealing with Titus are not extant — their unhappy love story is mentioned only in passing by a few later writers such as (again) Suetonius and Cassius Dio.[46] The literary career of Julia Berenice was to reach its climax much later in early modern times (see below §6), when the reception of both Berenices eventually converges, but in my view the first stages of this association and cross-identification lie already in antiquity; this has been barely recognised so far because the texts belong to different epochs and genres.

The Ptolemaic and the Jewish Berenice are connected through a remarkable web of literary echoes that has its origins in the *Lock of Berenice* and its transfer from Alexandria to Rome.[47] The key-word *inuitus* which signals the quotation from Catullus' *Coma* in the *Aeneid* reappears in Suetonius in the context of the other Berenice's unfortunate relationship with Titus. Upon his accession to the throne, Titus is said to have given up his debauched way of life and to have assumed a wholly new character (7.1–2:); among other bad habits he gave up "his notorious passion for queen Berenice, to whom it was even said that he promised marriage. ... Berenice he sent from Rome at once, against her will and against his own" (... *propterque insignem reginae Berenices amorem, cui etiam nuptias pollicitus ferebatur; ... Berenicen statim ab urbe dimisit* *inuitus inuitam*).[48] The primary point of reference is obviously Aeneas' final farewell from Dido, but a Roman audience would probably also have linked the quotation with its origins in Catullus' and Callimachus' *Lock of Berenice*,[49] aided by the shared

---

with Berenice's, see den Hollander (2014) 263–279. On Berenice in Josephus and in the New Testament cf. also Ebel (2009).

[46] Tac. *Hist.* 2.2.1: *fuerunt qui accensum desiderio Berenices reginae uertisse iter crederent; neque abhorrebat a Berenice iuuenilis animus, sed gerendis rebus nullum ex eo impedimentum. laetam uoluptatibus adulescentiam egit, suo quam patris imperio moderatior*; 2.81.2: *nec minore animo regina Berenice partes iuuabat, florens aetate formaque et seni quoque Vespasiano magnificentia munerum grata.* On the first passage see also n.54 below.

[47] Most scholars have focused either on Vergil's intertextual relationship with Catullus (and indirectly with Callimachus) or on Suetonius' possible allusion to Vergil, without linking all three (or four) authors. The connections between the two Berenices have been rarely noticed, and then mostly in passing (see n.49 below); but cf. now Macrae (2015) esp. 416.

[48] Tr. Rolfe (1914). In the *Epitome de Caesaribus* ascribed to Aurelius Victor Berenice is idiosyncratically called Titus' wife (10.4: *Berenicis uxoris suae*); this is contradicted by the subsequent statement (based on Suetonius' version) that she was hoping for marriage when Titus sent her away at his accession (10.7: *Denique ut subiit pondus regium, Berenicen nuptias suas sperantem regredi domum et eneruatorum greges abire praecepit*).

[49] Cf. Wills (1998) 302 n.45: "The unusual wordplay at Suet. *Tit.* 7.2 ... suggests the

motif of the unwilling farewell.[50]

Titus and Berenice reappear a century or so later in Cassius Dio (who also featured Caesar and Cleopatra), although his Book 66 is preserved only in a Byzantine epitome by Xiphilinus, so that Dio's literary strategies and psychological motivations in this dramatic episode cannot be recovered fully. But the paraphrase reveals a telling difference between Suetonius and Dio. Suetonius focused wholly on Titus, and only with *inuitam* allowed us a glimpse of Berenice's feelings, but Dio seems to have told the story at least partly from her perspective (66.15.3–4):

> Berenice was at the very height of her power (Βερενίκη δὲ ἰσχυρῶς τε ἤνθει) and consequently came to Rome along with her brother Agrippa. The latter was given the rank of praetor, while she dwelt in the palace, cohabiting with Titus. She expected to marry him and was already behaving in every respect as if she were his wife; but when he perceived that the Romans were displeased with the situation, he sent her away (προσεδόκα δὲ γαμηθήσεσθαι αὐτῷ, καὶ πάντα ἤδη ὡς καὶ γυνὴ αὐτοῦ οὖσα ἐποίει, ὥστ' ἐκεῖνον δυσχεραίνοντας τοὺς Ῥωμαίους ἐπὶ τούτοις αἰσθόμενον ἀποπέμψασθαι αὐτήν).
>
> (tr. Cary [1925])

Moreover, again in contrast to Suetonius, Cassius Dio seems to have

---

enduring association of *inuitus* with namesakes of Berenice"; Pelliccia (2010–2011) 207 n.159: "The language Suetonius uses to report Titus' dismissal of his lover Berenice suggests that the theme may have become formulaically associated with the name (*Tit.* 7) …". Syme (1991) 652 reuses Suetonius' phrase in his invented Tacitean fragment (ch. 22): *posse Caesarem inflecti ut mittat vel inuitus inuitam* (see n.43 above). Macrae (2015) 416 likewise emphasizes the intentional and marked character of the "window allusion", holding that the polyptoton *inuitus inuitam* reflects the anaphora *inuita … inuita* from Cat. 66.39–40 and its divided repetition by Vergil (cf. also Wills (1998) 298); he also draws conclusions about the literary qualities of Suetonius' biographies. The polyptoton might also have tragic associations connected with the rupture of familial or marital relations: in [Aesch.] *PV* 670–1, Io relates that her father Inachus had to ban her from his house against his and her will because of Zeus' desire for her (ἐξήλασέν με κἀπέκλησε δωμάτων/ ἄκουσαν ἄκων), and at Eur. *Hippol.* 319 Phaedra hints that her stepson is unwittingly destroying her because of her uncontrollable passion for him (φίλος μ' ἀπόλλυσ' οὐχ ἑκοῦσαν οὐχ ἑκών). Again, at Aesch. *Suppl.* 227–8 Danaus complains about the impious man who wants to force his daughters to marry against their and their father's will (πῶς δ' ἂν γαμῶν ἄκουσαν ἄκοντος πάρα/ ἁγνὸς γένοιτ' ἄν;), while in *Rhet. ad Heren.* lines perhaps derived from Ennius' *Cresphontes* (fr. 53 Jocelyn; cf. Harder (1985) 5–7 for the problems of connecting them with Euripides' play) are quoted to illustrate a rhetorical dilemma — a daughter accuses her father of making her divorce her husband against their will (2.24.38: *sin est probus,/ cur talem inuitam inuitum cogis linquere?*).

[50] Valerius Flaccus' *Argonautica* might have constituted another poetic paradigm for Flavian and later audiences, but tantalizingly breaks off at the point where Jason is about to deliver an '*inuitus*'-speech in response to Medea's complaints about his supposed betrayal (8.467: *mene aliquid meruisse putas, me talia uelle?*): cf. Apollon. *Arg.* 4.395–409.

described two separate scenes of farewell: Berenice, after the first separation, that apparently occurred while Vespasian was still alive, returned to Rome but failed to move Titus, who in the meantime had become emperor and given up his former way of life (66.18.1):

> Titus after becoming ruler committed no act of murder or of amatory passion, but showed himself upright, though plotted against, and self-controlled, though Berenice came to Rome again (ὁ δὲ δὴ Τίτος οὐδὲν οὔτε φονικὸν οὔτε ἐρωτικὸν μοναρχήσας ἔπραξεν, ἀλλὰ χρηστὸς καίπερ ἐπιβουλευθεὶς καὶ σώφρων καίτοι καὶ τῆς Βερενίκης ἐς Ῥώμην αὖθις ἐλθούσης ἐγένετο). (tr. Cary [1925])

This doubling has puzzled modern historians who try to reconstruct the exact historical circumstances of Berenice's visits to Rome.[51] But Dio may have been aiming at dramatic effect rather than historical accuracy:[52] the doubling of the farewell scene is a standard ingredient of the texts so far examined. Dio may also have seen his descriptions of Berenice's two visits to Rome as companion pieces to his earlier chapters on Caesar and Cleopatra, where he alluded more overtly to the motif of unwilling farewell (42.45.1);[53] and Dio's failure to mention Titus' unwillingness to dismiss Berenice could be an enhancement of his imperial virtue.[54]

Through such subtle literary means, the Jewish Berenice is linked with the last Ptolemaic queen and indirectly also to Berenice II.[55] Julia

---

[51] On the number and timing of Berenice's visits see Braund (1984) and Keaveney–Madden (2003); the latter accept Suetonius' version of a single dismissal, whereas Wilker (2008) 180 n.80 prefers Dio's more detailed account. For the analogous scholarly controversy about Cleopatra's stay(s) at Rome see Gruen (2003) 269–70 and n.31 above.

[52] On Dio's affinities with the style of 'tragic history' see Hose (1994) 437–40. Macrae (2015) 417 however interprets Suetonius' reduction of the plot as a literary conceit.

[53] In Suetonius, too, Berenice's dismissal from Rome (*Tit.* 7.2: *Berenicen statim ab urbe dimisit inuitus inuitam*) is linked by a verbal echo to Cleopatra's, which, however, is presented in more diplomatic terms (*Iul.* 52): *..., quam denique accitam in urbem non nisi maximis honoribus praemiisque auctam remisit ...* (Finally he called her to Rome and did not let her leave until he had ladened her with high honours and rich gifts, tr. Rolfe [1914]).

[54] Braund (1984) 121 n.5 notes that Dio omits to describe Berenice's second dismissal after mentioning her return to Rome, unless this is due to the state of transmission (see n.28 above). Tacitus, too, in defending Titus from the accusation of having neglected his duties because of his passion for Berenice (*Hist.* 2.2.1, quoted in n.46 above) seems to respond to the epic and historiographical topos of the 'decadent general' associated with Homer's Odysseus, Apollonius' Jason, and Vergil's Aeneas, but also specifically with Caesar and M. Antonius in their relations with Cleopatra; cf. Sannicandro (2014).

[55] Although Wilker (2008) 180 notes that Mommsen's dictum about Berenice as a "Kleopatra im Kleinen" (Mommsen (1885) 540) is not drawn explicitly from the ancient sources, it is hinted at by them; on similarities with Plutarch's description of M. Antonius and Cleopatra see also Vasta (2007) 45f. and especially Anagnostou-Laoutides–Charles (2015).

Berenice's biography has several points of contact with that of Berenice II, despite the divergent nature of the extant sources.[56] Both were female members of Hellenistic dynasties bearing the official title of queen, and Julia Berenice's name testifies to the Hellenising tendencies of the Herodian dynasty; she also spent part of her life at Alexandria.[57] Both queens had a history of troubled marital relationships before their involvement with the most powerful men of their times, and Julia Berenice was rumored to have had an incestuous relationship with her brother Agrippa, which links her even more closely to her Ptolemaic prototype.[58] Berenice was accompanied to Rome by her brother (Cassius Dio 66.15.3), as Cleopatra had been by her brother-husband (43.27.3), so that malicious gossip could interpret their residence in the houses of their respective Roman lovers as a *ménage à trois*. In this light, it is highly intriguing that, according to Josephus (*Bellum Judaicum* 2.313–4) the Jewish Berenice had also publicly fulfilled a religious vow to shave her hair (ξυρήσεσθαι τὰς κόμας).[59] These co-incidences could have facilitated the association of the two Berenices in the ancient sources, an association perhaps instigated by Julia Berenice,

---

[56] Macurdy (1935) 253 = (1937) 91 sees in Julia Berenice "an aftermath of the glory and power which had belonged to Hellenistic queens before the Roman era". More speculatively, Anagnostou-Laoutides–Charles (2015) 31–5 associate Julia Berenice (and her vow, see below) with Isis by referring to the assimilation of Cleopatra to Isis in Augustan literature, but (apart from a passing reference on p.34, where she is erroneously called the wife of Ptolemy II Philadelphus) they do not link her with Berenice II, for whom an association with Isis is much better attested than for Julia Berenice; see Clayman (2014) 100–1 and n.13 above.

[57] Julia Berenice bears the official title of queen in an honorific inscription from Athens (*IG* III 556 = *CIG* 361: βασίλισσαν) and on a Latin euergetic inscription from Beirut (*AE* 1928, 82: *r]egina*); cf. Macurdy (1935) 246–8. For a new reconstruction of the latter inscription see Haensch (2006), who refutes the first reading by Cagnat (1928) on the grounds that the placing of Berenice's name and title before that of her brother would go against epigraphic conventions.

[58] On the scandalous circumstances surrounding the first marriage (or betrothal) of Berenice II see above §2. Julia Berenice had been married (or betrothed) first to M. Julius Alexander from a prominent Jewish family at Alexandria, then to her uncle Herod of Chalcis, and third to king Polemo II of Cilicia, a marriage which she herself dissolved after a short time. The rumours about her incest with her brother are mentioned only by Josephus — in a hostile context (*Antiquitates* 20.145–6: φήμης ἐπισχούσης, ὅτι τἀδελφῷ συνείη … ἐλέγξειν ᾤετο ψευδεῖς τὰς διαβολάς), and by Juvenal in connection with Berenice's famous diamond ring (in the misogynistic *Sat.* 6 (156–60, esp. 156–8: *deinde adamas notissimus et Beronices/ in digito factus pretiosior; hunc dedit olim/ barbarus incestae gestare Agrippa sorori*). They are usually rejected by modern scholars (e.g. Anagnostou-Laoutides–Charles (2015) 24–5), but they can be read as distorted reflections of the tradition of "Hellenistic philadelphic marriage" (Macurdy (1935) 249–51 and (1937) 86–9; cf. Krieger (1997) 11).

[59] Cf. Goodman (2012) 188 on Berenice taking the nazirite vow at the beginning of the Jewish revolt in 66 CE: "What could be a better demonstration of her commitment to Judaism and the Temple than the shaven head of the queen?"

who presented herself as a joint ruler with her brother in the tradition of her Ptolemaic namesake. If Berenice II had been immortalised, not by her fellow Cyrenean Callimachus but by Hellenistic historians who loved scandalous stories, and if Julia Berenice's love story had been told from her point of view by a congenial poet, the images of the two Berenices might have been reversed.[60]

5. Triangulations
The *Lock of Berenice* between Alexandria and Rome

The literary images of the three couples under discussion follow a declining ideological path. In Alexandrian poetry Berenice is celebrated as the new Ptolemaic queen, but from a Roman perspective eastern queens are seen as a potential danger to the Roman empire and are represented in an increasingly negative way, from Dido's ambivalent role in the *Aeneid* to the Egyptian seductress Cleopatra to the oriental-Jewish queen Julia Berenice.[61] My aim here, however, is not to recover the historical truth behind the ideologically biased (and moreover fragmentary) ancient evidence, but to detect literary patterns that may have shaped the perceptions of authors and readers alike.

From a wider perspective the three examples raise the issue of the function and transformation of such patterns in different genres and cultural contexts. Comparing and contrasting the official representation of the Ptolemaic queens with the evolving public role models for

---

[60] Clayman (2014) 179 states boldly: "Callimachus' 'Lock' is a window on the moment when Berenice transformed herself from murderess to Madonna." Cf. ibid. 5–6 on the sensationalist style of the Hellenistic historiographers, who focused on Berenice's youthful involvement in the murder of Demetrius the Fair (see above §2) and on the violent circumstances of her death in a court intrigue that may have been led by her own son (ibid. 172–3, 182–4). In contrast, nothing more is heard of Julia Berenice's fate after her separation from Titus.

[61] Macurdy's studies (1935 and 1937) exhibit an early feminist approach that uncovers the misogynistic stereotypes in the ancient texts; cf. Wesch-Klein (2005) 168–72 on the persistence of such prejudices in 19th-century historians. While most studies of Julia Berenice adduce political reasons for Titus' failure to marry her, either in the context of the opposition to his succession (Crook (1951); Rogers (1980); Jones (1984) 77–117; Levick (1999) 184–95; Vasta (2007)) or in that of the Roman populace's anti-Oriental and especially anti-Jewish feelings (Braund (1984); Castritius (2002) 167–9; Wesch-Klein (2005) 171; in general cf. Isaac (2004) esp. 440–91), some modern scholars still speculate about the personal reasons behind the affair and the possible attractions that a fifty-one year old Jewish widow (in 79 CE) could have had for Titus, eleven years her junior (e.g. Bengtson (1979) 54–5, 157–8; Murison (1999) 171; cf. also Quinche (1978) 145–6); Anagnostou-Laoutides–Charles (2015) 23 place the fertility issue in a dynastic context.

imperial women in the period of transition from the late republic to the early principate reveals a fundamental paradox. The female members of the Julio-Claudian and Flavian dynasties were promoted through the media of coins and statues in the tradition of Hellenistic queens, but they did not exert direct political influence,[62] whereas female descendants of the Hellenistic dynasties such as Cleopatra and Julia Berenice, who in their own kingdoms acted as powerful and up to a point independent queens, were excluded from official iconography at Rome — with the exception of Cleopatra, for whom Julius Caesar apparently set up a statue in the temple of Venus Genetrix on his forum.[63] Titus perhaps saw himself — or was posthumously construed — as a second 'Augustan' Aeneas who chose duty over love as part of the Flavians' attempt to distance themselves from the Julio-Claudians' involvement with 'bad' women (from Cleopatra to Nero's mother Agrippina and his mistresses) and to associate themselves with the principate's founder Augustus.[64] Consequently, Julia Berenice has left no tangible traces in Rome.[65] Instead Titus' daughter Julia was por-

---

[62] Current discussions have related the 'power' of imperial women to a Roman discourse on gender and politics in which the literary images of female members of the dynasty reflect the positive or negative evaluations of the respective emperors; see Wyke (2002) 215–21 and the contributions in Kunst–Riemer (2000) (esp. Riemer on the role of the emperors' wives and mistresses in Suetonius), in Temporini (2002) (esp. Castritius on the women of the Flavians), and in Kolb (2010) (esp. Harders on the Hellenistic *basilissa* as anti-model for the Roman *Augustae*, and Gregori–Rosso on the official image of Julia Titi). On the iconography of imperial women from the Julio-Claudian to the Severan dynasty see Alexandridis (2004); specifically on the programmatic coinage issued for Flavian women under Titus and Domitian (though none for Titus' earlier wives Arrecina Tertulla and Marcia Furnilla) cf. Alexandridis (2010).

[63] Appian *B.C.* 2.102; cf. Cassius Dio 51.22.1–3. For discussions about the significance of the statue (Caesar's homage to his mistress and mother of his son, token of Octavian's Egyptian triumph, or even an imperial fiction) and its possible reflections in Roman art see Wyke (2002) 206–7, 241; Gruen (2003) 259; Kleiner (2005) 135–56; Andreae et al. (2006); Harders (2010) 67–8; Roller (2010) 72, 174–5. M. Antonius went a step further by issuing official Roman denarii with double portraits of himself and Cleopatra in the tradition of Hellenistic royal couples; cf. Wyke (2002) 217–18; Kleiner (2005) 144–7; Roller (2010) 179–83.

[64] Suetonius mentions Titus' love for Berenice in close connection with the people's (unfounded) expectations that he would turn out to be a second Nero (*Tit.* 7.1: *denique propalam alium Neronem et opinabantur et praedicabant*). Cassius Dio (66.18.4–5) compares Titus with Augustus, again shortly after mentioning his dismissal of Berenice. On Titus as Aeneas cf. Wesch-Klein (2005) 164 and Vasta (2007) 87; Anagnostou-Laoutides–Charles (2015) acknowledge the association, but downplay the seriousness of Titus' relationship with Berenice.

[65] The modern identification of a bronze bust found at the Villa dei Papiri in Herculaneum as 'Berenice' is without foundation. Interestingly, Maltiel-Gerstenfeld (1980) interprets some coins bearing the portrait of a veiled woman with the inscription 'ΣΕΒΑΣΤΗ' and an anchor as belonging to a series prematurely issued by Agrippa II at Caesarea in 78–9 CE in anticipation of his sister Berenice's voyage to Rome for her wedding with the emperor — which did not take place; cf. Ebel (2009) 144–5.

trayed in a series of official portraits, during the reigns of both Titus and Domitian, and was divinised after her death, while Domitian's prematurely deceased son by his wife Domitia was deified too, and was represented on coins as a child on a globe surrounded by stars.[66] So it seems that the key ideological motifs associated with the Hellenistic queen Berenice II, catasterism and divinization, were transferred from Julia Berenice to the doomed third generation of the Flavian dynasty.[67] Interestingly, yet another leitmotif associated with both Berenice II and Julia Berenice reappears in connection with Julia Titi, although distorted by a hostile literary tradition, namely her alleged incestuous relationship with her uncle Domitian.[68]

We are thus thrown back on the literary texts, but we can at least try to compensate for this by taking into account their generic conventions and ideological biases. Regardless of their historical accuracy, the dramatic potential inherent in the texts about the two Berenices can be interpreted in terms of literary antitheses. In the *Lock of Berenice*, the conflict between love and war and the lock's futile protestations against its fate play out metapoetically the tensions between the innovative style of Callimachean elegy and traditional martial panegyric. In contrast, the biographers' and historiographers' versions of Cleopatra's and Julia Berenice's love affairs with Roman generals and statesmen are more serious in intent, but are also heavily biased in their anti-oriental stereotypes. But the central motifs associated with the first Berenice resonate through all of the later adaptations. Callimachus' poem on the wedding of Ptolemy and Berenice gradually mutates into a species of anti-epithalamium, as it is transposed into a problematic

[66] The dual Flavian strategy when dealing with the Julio-Claudian heritage is also visible in their iconography, which adopts some features of the Julio-Claudian women while innovating in other respects; cf. the bibliography cited in n.62 above, esp. Alexandridis (2010) and Gregori–Rosso (2010). Julia's deification is reflected in Martial's epigrams 6.3 and 6.13 (within a cycle on Domitian's restoration of Augustus' marital laws) as well as in 9.1. On the coins showing Domitia and her deified son see Castritius (2002) 179–80.

[67] These motifs also refer to the origins of the Julio-Claudian dynasty, insofar as the intra- and intertextual complex around hair, flames and comets in Vergil's *Aeneid* not only links Aeneas and his son Iulus with Julius Caesar, but also explicitly with Augustus (8.678–81); cf. nn.37 and 39 above. Generally on the role of catasterism in Hellenistic and Roman ruler representation see Bechtold (2011).

[68] Juvenal (*Sat.* 2.29–33), Pliny the Younger (*Epist.* 4.11.6), and Suetonius (*Dom.* 22) report that Julia died because of an abortion after having become pregnant by her uncle Domitian. These rumours might reflect plans to unite Domitian with his niece in a dynastic marriage on the model of Claudius' marriage to Agrippina, but they create a scandalous love triangle with Domitian's (ex-)wife Domitia (cf. Suet. *Dom.* 17.3 and 22; Cassius Dio 67.3.1–2). For a critical review of the sources as the remains of a 'smear campaign' against the last Flavian emperor by his successors see Vinson (1989), Jones (1992) 33–40, and Castritius (2002) 174–82.

wedding with a tragic outcome (Dido and Aeneas), a 'wedding' that (from a Roman perspective) never should have taken place (Caesar and Cleopatra) and finally, with Titus and Berenice, a promised wedding that never took place. It is this elegiac conflict between love and politics that forms the missing link between the Berenice figures in the Alexandrian and the imperial texts.[69]

6. Epilogue
The modern reception of the two Berenices

A few select examples from the *Nachleben* of the Berenices deserve mention.[70] In early modern literature the Jewish Berenice, whose unhappy love was not (as far as we know) treated by any ancient poet, was much more prominent than her Ptolemaic namesake. The leitmotif of the love triangle is psychologically explored and dramatically exploited, so that she becomes a tragic figure who is portrayed more sympathetically than in the Greek and Roman tradition, although Orientalist stereotypes still inform her characterisation as an Eastern queen.[71]

Already in French novels from the first half of the 17th century, among them Madeleine de Scudéry's *Lettres de Bérénice à Titus* (in *Les Femmes Illustres, ou les Harangues héroïques* of 1642), and Jean Regnauld de Segrais' unfinished four-volume novel *Bérénice* of 1648–9, the love of Titus and Berenice had aroused interest. Eventually, it assumed its classical form in Jean Racine's tragedy *Bérénice*, first performed in Paris in November 1670.[72] In its preface Racine printed

---

[69] In this I disagree with Le Leyzour (1992) 12 and Sprondel–Schröder (2013) 179, who claim that the multiple historical Berenices do not share an 'archetypical' nucleus, and that their conflation into a single mythical figure only starts with Racine. On the elegiac traits of Vergil's Dido see e.g. Feldherr (1999). Anagnostou-Laoutides–Charles (2015) place Julia Berenice in the Roman poetic tradition of the elegiac *domina* without drawing a connection to Catullus' and Callimachus' elegiac Berenice (see also n.56 above).

[70] Besides the overview in Sprondel–Schröder (2013), see the exhibition catalogue on the Berenices by Le Leyzour (1992) and the study of the Berenice myth in French literature by Goorah-Martin (1996), who all note the tendency to fuse the various Berenices. Mireaux (1951) 196–223, Akerman (1978), and Ebel (2009) 186–94 concentrate on the reception of Julia Berenice, but curiously, the motto taken from a poem by Paul Verlaine on Mireaux's title page turns around hair: "Est-elle brune, blonde, ou rousse? Je l'ignore." For the legacy of Titus and Berenice see also Zissos (2016).

[71] On Orientalism in French classical drama see Longino (2002) esp. 147–78.

[72] On *Bérénice* in the context of Racine's Roman tragedies see Ronzeaud et al. (1996) and Schröder (2009). In the same month, Racine's rival dramatist Pierre Corneille also

an anonymous Latin sentence which is a patchwork from Suetonius'
Life of Titus 7: *Titus Reginam Berenicen, cui etiam nuptias pollicitus
ferebatur, statim ab Urbe dimisit inuitus inuitam*. Then he compared
this famous historical passion to the tragic separation of Aeneas from
Dido in Vergil, without explicitly acknowledging the intertextual
ancestry of his Suetonian sentence in Catullus' translation of Callimachus' *Lock of Berenice* through the intermediacy of *Aeneid* 6.[73]
Typically Racine dramatises his plot further by introducing a semi-
historical third protagonist, King Antiochus of Commagene, who is
also in love with Berenice. This results in a love triangle similar to that
involving the first Berenice, where the lock is the excluded third party.
But in contrast to the *Lock of Berenice*, where at least the royal couple
lives happily ever after, in Racine's play all three protagonists finally
renounce fulfillment of their love.

The association between the two Berenices reached its peak when
the leitmotifs of the severed lock and its catasterism were explicitly
transposed to the Jewish Berenice: Albéric Magnard's opera *Bérénice*
(*Tragédie en musique*, 1909; première Paris 1911), which was clearly
inspired by Racine's play, transformed the newly-wed Alexandrian
Berenice's cutting of a lock as a love-token into a gesture of mourning
by the Jewish queen, newly abandoned by Titus. While sailing from
Rome back to Judaea she throws a lock of hair into the sea as a bitter
offering for Venus.[74] Finally, in the second part of Lion Feucht-
wanger's Josephus trilogy, written during his French exile in the
thirties (*Die Söhne*, 1935), Titus plans to surprise his beloved Berenice,
who has shorn her hair to complete a vow for the Jewish God, with the
news that the astronomer Conon has just discovered a new constellation

---

staged a play called *Tite et Bérénice*.

[73] Racine (*Œuvres completes, I: Théâtre – Poésie.* Édition présentée, établie et annotée
par G. Forestier, Paris 1999, p.450), who himself gives a rather free translation: "Titus,
qui aimait passionnément Bérénice, et qui même, à ce qu'on croyait, lui avait promis
de l'épouser, la renvoya de Rome, malgré lui, et malgré elle, dès les premiers jours de
son Empire." A connection to the *Coma Berenices* is suggested by Videau (1997) 38:
"... la reine élégiaque de Racine ressemble plus à la boucle de Catulle et Callimaque
qu'à leur princesse." On the intertextual chain extending from Callimachus and
Catullus via Vergil and Suetonius to Racine see now also Macrae (2015). While
Mueller (1974) esp. 208 cautions that Dido's role as a model for Bérénice does not
manifest itself at the level of plot construction, Sellstrom (1993) shows that Vergil's
Aeneid, along with Ariosto's *Orlando Furioso*, actually plays an important role as an
intertext of Racine's drama. More speculatively, as in the case of Dido and Cleopatra,
Racine's plot may allude to a historical figure, King Louis XIV's first love Marie
Mancini, whom he had to give up for dynastic reasons; cf. Quinche (1978) 153–62 and
Schröder (2009) 392.

[74] Magnard himself acknowledges the transfer of the motif from the Egyptian Berenice
in his preface; cf. Akerman (1978) 200; Le Leyzour (1992) 54–7; Goorah-Martin
(1996) 73.

and called it after her lock.[75] Here the circle is finally complete and the two historically independent Berenices are braided into a single fictional figure.

List of Works Cited

Acosta-Hughes, B. (2008). 'Unwilling farewell and complex allusion (Sappho, Callimachus and *Aeneid* 6.458)' *PLLS* 13.1–11

— (2010). *Arion's Lyre: Archaic Lyric into Hellenistic Poetry*. Princeton

Acosta-Hughes, B. and Stephens, S.A. (2012). *Callimachus in Context: From Plato to the Augustan Poets*. Cambridge

Ahl, F. (2985). *Metaformations: Soundplay and Wordplay in Ovid and Other Classical Poets*. Ithaca/London

Akerman, S. (1978). *Le mythe de Bérénice*. Paris

Alexandridis, A. (2004). *Die Frauen des römischen Kaiserhauses: Eine Untersuchung ihrer bildlichen Darstellung von Livia bis Iulia Domna*. Mainz

— (2010). 'The other side of the coin: The women of the Flavian imperial family' in N. Kramer and C. Reitz (edd.) *Tradition und Erneuerung. Mediale Strategien in der Zeit der Flavier*. Beiträge zur Altertumskunde 285. Berlin/New York. 191–237

Ambühl, A. (2014). '(Re)constructing myth: Elliptical narrative in Hellenistic and Latin poetry' in R. Hunter, A. Rengakos, and E. Sistakou (edd.) *Hellenistic Studies at a Crossroads: Exploring Texts, Contexts and Metatexts*. Trends in Classics Supplementary Volume 25. Berlin/Boston. 113–32

— (forthcoming). 'Thessaly as an intertextual landscape of civil war in Latin poetry' in J. McInerney and I. Sluiter (edd.) *Landscapes of Value: Natural Environment and Cultural Imagination in Classical Antiquity*. Leiden

Anagnostou-Laoutides, E. and Charles, M.B. (2015). 'Titus and Berenice: The elegiac aura of an historical affair' *Arethusa* 48.17–46

Andreae, B. et al. (2006). (edd.) *Kleopatra und die Caesaren. Katalog zur Ausstellung des Bucerius Kunst Forums, Hamburg, 28. Oktober 2006 bis 4. Februar 2007*. München

Barchiesi, A. (2001). 'Some points on a map of shipwrecks' in id. *Speaking Volumes: Narrative and Intertext in Ovid and Other Latin Poets*. London. 141–54

Becher, I. (1966). *Das Bild der Kleopatra in der griechischen und lateinischen Literatur*. Deutsche Akademie der Wissenschaften zu Berlin, Schriften der Sektion für Altertumswissenschaft 51. Berlin

---

[75] Already in Henri Balzac's novel *Histoire de la grandeur et de la décadence de César Birotteau* (1838), the protagonist, an inventor of hair oil, claims that Commagene (*Comagène*) derives from the Latin *coma* and was therefore chosen as the name of his kingdom by Antiochus, in Racine's tragedy the lover of queen Berenice, in honour of her famous hair.

Bechtold, C. (2011). *Gott und Gestirn als Präsenzformen des toten Kaisers: Apotheose und Katasterismos in der politischen Kommunikation der römischen Kaiserzeit und ihre Anknüpfungspunkte im Hellenismus.* Göttingen

Benedetto, G. (2008). '*Bonum facinus*: Catull. 66.25–28 tra Igino e Giustino' in P.F. Moretti, C. Torre, and G. Zanetto (edd.) *Debita dona: Studi in onore di Isabella Gualandri.* Napoli. 33–70

Bengtson, H. (1979). *Die Flavier: Vespasian, Titus, Domitian. Geschichte eines römischen Kaiserhauses.* München

Bertman, S. (2000). 'Cleopatra and Antony as models for Dido and Aeneas' *EMC* 44 n.s. 19.395–8

Binder, G. and Hamm, U. (1998). 'Die "Locke der Berenike" und der Ursprung der römischen Liebeselegie' in A.E. Radke (ed.) *Candide iudex: Beiträge zur augusteischen Dichtung. Festschrift für Walter Wimmel zum 75. Geburtstag.* Stuttgart. 15–34

Bing, P. (2009). 'Reconstructing Berenike's Lock' in id. *The Scroll and the Marble: Studies in Reading and Reception in Hellenistic Poetry.* Ann Arbor. 65–82

Braund, D. (1984). 'Berenice in Rome' *Historia* 33.120–3

Cagnat, R. (1928). 'Une inscription relative à la reine Bérénice' *Le Musée Belge* 32.157–60

Cairns, F. (1989). *Virgil's Augustan Epic.* Cambridge

— (2007). *Generic Composition in Greek and Roman Poetry. Corrected and with New Material.* Ann Arbor

Caneva, S.G. (2014). 'Courtly love, stars and power: The queen in third-century royal couples, through poetry and epigraphic texts' in Harder–Regtuit–Wakker (2014) 25–57

Carney, E.D. (2011). 'Being royal and female in the early Hellenistic period' in A. Erskine and L. Llewellyn-Jones (edd.) *Creating a Hellenistic World.* Swansea. 195–220

— (2013). *Arsinoë of Egypt and Macedon: A Royal Life.* Women in Antiquity. Oxford

Cary, E. (1916). (ed. and trans.) *Dio's Roman History, Vol. IV: Books 41–45.* Loeb Classical Library 66. Cambridge, MA

— (1925). trans. *Dio's Roman History, Vol. VIII: Books 61–70.* Loeb Classical Library 176. Cambridge, MA

Carrez-Maratray, J.-Y. (2008). 'À propos de la boucle de Bérénice: La publicité des reines lagides' in F. Bertholet, A. Bielman Sánchez, and R. Frei-Stolba (edd.) *Egypte, Grèce, Rome: Les différents visages des femmes antiques.* Travaux et colloques du séminaire d'épigraphie grecque et latine de l'IASA 2002 – 2006. Bern. 93–116

Caston, R.R. (2012). *The Elegiac Passion: Jealousy in Roman Love Elegy.* Oxford

Castritius, H. (2002). 'Die flavische Familie: Frauen neben Vespasian, Titus und Domitian' in Temporini (2002) 164–86

Chiesa, I. (2009). 'L'elegia 'In Magam et Berenicen' di Callimaco: 'In

Berenices nuptias'?' *Acme* 62.227–34

Clausen, W. (1970). 'Catullus and Callimachus' *HSCPh* 74.85–94

Clayman, D.L. (2011). 'Berenice and her lock' *TAPhA* 141.229–46

— (2014). *Berenice II and the Golden Age of Ptolemaic Egypt.* Women in Antiquity. Oxford

— (2014a). 'Historical contexts for two *aitia* from book III: "Acontius & Cydippe" (frr. 67–75 Pf.) and "Phrygius & Pieria" (frr. 80–83 Pf.)' in Harder–Regtuit–Wakker (2014) 85–102

Crook, J.A. (1951). 'Titus and Berenice' *AJPh* 72.162–75

Day Lewis, C. (1986). (trans.) *Virgil: The Aeneid.* Oxford World's Classics. Oxford

den Hollander, W. (2014). *Josephus, the Emperors and the City of Rome: From Hostage to Historian.* Ancient Judaism and Early Christianity 86. Leiden

De Wilde, M. (2008). 'Catullus' *Coma Berenices*: An investigation of a true interpreter's poetic licence and its reception by Apuleius' in C. Deroux (ed.) *Studies in Latin Literature and Roman History* 14. Collection Latomus 315. Bruxelles. 144–76

Du Quesnay, I. (2012). 'Three problems in Catullus 66' in Du Quesnay–Woodman (2012) 153–83

Du Quesnay, I. and Woodman, T. (2012). (edd.) *Catullus: Poems, Books, Readers.* Cambridge

Ebel, E. (2009). *Lydia und Berenike: Zwei selbständige Frauen bei Lukas.* Biblische Gestalten 20. Leipzig

Fantuzzi, M. and Hunter, R. (2004). *Tradition and Innovation in Hellenistic Poetry.* Cambridge

Feldherr, A. (1999). 'Putting Dido on the map: Genre and geography in Vergil's underworld' *Arethusa* 32.85–122

Galinsky, K. (2003). 'Horace's Cleopatra and Virgil's Dido' in A.F. Basson and W.J. Dominik (edd.) *Literature, Art, History: Studies on Classical Antiquity and Tradition. In Honour of W.J. Henderson.* Frankfurt am Main. 17–23

Gall, D. (2006). 'Geliebte Caesars, Verderben Marc Antons, Feindin Roms: Kleopatra in der Literatur der Antike' in Andreae (2006) 142–50

Gladhill, B. (2012). 'Gods, Caesars and fate in *Aeneid* 1 and *Metamorphoses* 15' *Dictynna* 9

Goodman, M. (2012). 'Titus, Berenice and Agrippa: The last days of the temple in Jerusalem' in B. Isaac and Y. Shahar (edd.) *Judaea-Palaestina, Babylon and Rome: Jews in Antiquity.* Texts and Studies in Ancient Judaism 147. Tübingen. 181–90

Goorah-Martin, A. (1996). *A la recherche de l'origine du mythe de Bérénice.* Mémoire de maîtrise soumis à la Faculté des études supérieures et de la recherche en vue de l'obtention du diplôme de Maîtrise ès Lettres Université McGill. Montréal

Gregori, G.L. and Rosso, E. (2010). 'Giulia Augusta, figlia di Tito, nipote di Domiziano' in Kolb (2010) 193–210

Gruen, E. (2003). 'Cleopatra in Rome: Facts and fantasies' in D. Braund and C.

Gill (edd.) *Myth, History and Culture in Republican Rome. Studies in Honour of T.P. Wiseman*. Exeter. 257–74

Gutzwiller, K. (1992). 'Callimachus' *Lock of Berenice*: Fantasy, romance, and propaganda' *AJPh* 113.359–85

Haensch, R. (2006). 'Die deplazierte Königin: Zur Inschrift AE 1928, 82 aus Berytus' *Chiron* 36.141–9

Hall, A.E.W. (2011). '"And Cytherea smiled": Sappho, Hellenistic poetry, and Virgil's allusive mechanics' *AJPh* 132.615–31

Harder, A. (1985). *Euripides' Kresphontes and Archelaos. Introduction, Text and Commentary*. Leiden

— (2003). 'The invention of past, present and future in Callimachus' *Aetia*' *Hermes* 131.290–306

— (2012). (ed.) *Callimachus: Aetia. Vol. 1: Introduction, Text, and Translation. Vol. 2: Commentary*. Oxford

Harder, M.A., Regtuit, R.F. and Wakker, G.C. (2014). (edd.) *Hellenistic Poetry in Context*. Hellenistica Groningana 20. Leuven

Harders, A.-C. (2010). 'Hellenistische Königinnen in Rom' in Kolb (2010) 55–74

Hardie, P. (2006). 'Virgil's Ptolemaic relations' *JRS* 96.25–41

— (2012). 'Virgil's Catullan plots' in Du Quesnay–Woodman (2012) 212–38

Hauben, H. (2011). 'Ptolémée III et Bérénice II, divinités cosmiques' in P.P. Iossif (ed.) *More than Men, Less than Gods: Studies on Royal Cult and Imperial Worship. Proceedings of the International Colloquium organized by the Belgian School at Athens (November 1 - 2, 2007)*. Studia Hellenistica 51. Leuven. 357–88

Hazzard, R.A. (2000). *Imagination of a Monarchy: Studies in Ptolemaic Propaganda*. Toronto

Hölbl, G. (2001). *The History of the Ptolemaic Empire*. Translated by T. Saavedra. London

Höschele, R. (2009). 'Catullus' Callimachean *hair*-itage and the erotics of translation' *RFIC* 137.118–52

Hose, M. (1994). *Erneuerung der Vergangenheit: Die Historiker im Imperium Romanum von Florus bis Cassius Dio*. Beiträge zur Altertumskunde 45. Stuttgart/Leipzig

Hunter, R. (2006). *The Shadow of Callimachus: Studies in the Reception of Hellenistic Poetry at Rome*. Cambridge

Hutchinson, G.O. (2008). *Talking Books: Readings in Hellenistic and Roman Books of Poetry*. Oxford

Isaac, B. (2004). *The Invention of Racism in Classical Antiquity*. Princeton

Jackson, S. (2001). 'Callimachus: *Coma Berenices*: Origins' *Mnemosyne* 54.1–9

Jocelyn, H.D. (1969). (ed.) *The Tragedies of Ennius. The Fragments Edited with an Introduction and Commentary*. Cambridge

Johnston, P.A. (1987). 'Dido, Berenice, and Arsinoe: *Aeneid* 6.460' *AJPh* 108.649–54

Jones, B.W. (1984). *The Emperor Titus*. London

— (1992). *The Emperor Domitian*. London

Jordan, R. (1974). *Berenice*. London

Keaveney, A. and Madden, J. (2003). 'Berenice at Rome' *MH* 60.39–43

Kleiner, D.E.E. (2005). *Cleopatra and Rome*. Cambridge, MA/London

Koenen, L. (1993). 'The Ptolemaic king as a religious figure' in A.S. Bulloch et al. (edd.) *Images and Ideologies: Self-Definition in the Hellenistic World*. Berkeley. 25–115

Kolb, A. (2010). (ed.) *Augustae: Machtbewusste Frauen am römischen Kaiserhof? Akten der Tagung in Zürich 18.-20.9.2008*. Herrschafts-strukturen und Herrschaftspraxis 2. Berlin

Konstan, D. (2007). 'The contemporary political context' in M.B. Skinner (ed.) *A Companion to Catullus*. Blackwell Companions to the Ancient World. Malden, MA. 72–91

Krevans, N. (2012). 'Virgins and brides in the land of brotherly love' in C. Cusset, N. Le Meur-Weissman, and F. Levin (edd.) *Mythe et pouvoir à l'époque hellénistique*. Hellenistica Groningana 18. Leuven. 303–18

Krieger, K.-S. (1997). 'Berenike, die Schwester König Agrippas II., bei Flavius Josephus' *JSJ* 28.1–11

Kunst, C. and Riemer U. (2000). (edd.) *Grenzen der Macht: Zur Rolle der römischen Kaiserfrauen*. Potsdamer altertumswissenschaftliche Beiträge 3. Stuttgart

Le Leyzour, P. (1992). (ed.) *Les Bérénices: Textes et figures. Musée National des Granges de Port-Royal, 14 mars - 15 juin 1992*. Paris

Levick, B. (1999). *Vespasian*. London

Llewellyn-Jones, L. and Winder, S. (2011). 'A key to Berenike's Lock? The Hathoric model of queenship in early Ptolemaic Egypt' in A. Erskine and L. Llewellyn-Jones (edd.) *Creating a Hellenistic World*. Swansea. 247–69

Longino, M. (2002). *Orientalism in French Classical Drama*. Cambridge Studies in French 69. Cambridge

Lord, L.E. (1938). 'The date of Julius Caesar's departure from Alexandria' *JRS* 28.19–40

Macrae, D.E. (2015). '*Invitus invitam*: A window allusion in Suetonius' *Titus*' *CQ* 65.415–8

Macurdy, G.H. (1932). *Hellenistic Queens: A Study of Woman-Power in Macedonia, Seleucid Syria, and Ptolemaic Egypt*. Baltimore

— (1935). 'Julia Berenice' *AJPh* 56.246–53

— (1937). *Vassal-Queens and Some Contemporary Women in the Roman Empire*. The Johns Hopkins University Studies in Archaeology 22. Baltimore

Maltby, R. (1991). *A Lexicon of Ancient Latin Etymologies*. ARCA 25. Leeds

Maltiel-Gerstenfeld, J. (1980). 'A portrait coin of Berenice sister of Agrippa II?' *Israel Numismatic Journal* 4.25–6

Marinone, N. (1997). (ed.) *Berenice da Callimaco a Catullo. Testo critico, traduzione e commento*. Nuova edizione ristrutturata, ampliata e aggiornata. Bologna

Massimilla, G. (2010). (ed.) *Callimaco, Aitia: Libro terzo e quarto*.

Introduzione, testo critico, traduzione e commento. Pisa

McKechnie, P. and Guillaume, P. (2008). (edd.) *Philadelphus II and his World*. Mnemosyne Supplements 300. Leiden

Mireaux, É. (1951). *La reine Bérénice*. Paris

Mommsen, T. (1885). *Römische Geschichte. 5: Die Provinzen von Caesar bis Diocletian*. Berlin

Mueller, M. (1974). 'The truest daughter of Dido: Racine's *Bérénice*' *CRCL* 1.201–17

Müller, S. (2009). *Das hellenistische Königspaar in der medialen Repräsentation: Ptolemaios II. und Arsinoe II.* Beiträge zur Altertumskunde 263. Berlin/New York

Murison, C.L. (1999). *Rebellion and Reconstruction: Galba to Domitian. An Historical Commentary on Cassius Dio's Roman History Books 64–67 (A.D. 68–96)*. American Philological Association Monograph Series 37. Atlanta

Myers, K.S. (2012). 'Catullan contexts in Ovid's *Metamorphoses*' in Du Quesnay–Woodman (2012) 239–54

Nachtergael, G. (1980). 'Bérénice II, Arsinoé III et l'offrande de la boucle' *CE* 55.240–53

Nadeau, Y. (1982). 'Caesaries Berenices (*or*, the hair of the god)' *Latomus* 41.101–3

Nagle, B.R. (1988). 'A trio of love-triangles in Ovid's *Metamorphoses*' *Arethusa* 21.75–98

Nauta, R. (2011). 'Dido en Aeneas in de onderwereld' *Lampas* 44.53–71

Newman, J.K. (1990). *Roman Catullus and the Modification of the Alexandrian Sensibility*. Hildesheim

Pantos, P.A. (1987). 'Bérénice II Déméter' *BCH* 111.343–52

Pelliccia, H. (2010–2011). 'Unlocking *Aeneid* 6.460: Plautus' *Amphitryon*, Euripides' *Protesilaus* and the referent of Callimachus' *Coma*' *CJ* 106.149–219

Pelling, C. (2011). *Plutarch: Caesar, Translated with an Introduction and Commentary*. Oxford

Perea Yébenes, S. (2001). *Berenice, reina y concubina. El legado de la historia* 35. Madrid

Pfeiffer, R. (1949). (ed.) *Callimachus. Vol. I: Fragmenta*. Oxford

— (1975). 'ΒΕΡΕΝΙΚΗΣ ΠΛΟΚΑΜΟΣ' in A.D. Skiadas (ed.) *Kallimachos*. Wege der Forschung 296. Darmstadt. 100–52 (originally published in 1932)

Pomeroy, S.B. (1984). *Women in Hellenistic Egypt: From Alexander to Cleopatra*. NewYork

Prioux, É. (2011). 'Callimachus' queens' in B. Acosta-Hughes, L. Lehnus, and S. Stephens (edd.) *Brill's Companion to Callimachus*. Leiden. 201–24

Puelma, M. (1995). 'Die Aitien des Kallimachos als Vorbild der römischen Amores-Elegie' in id. *Labor et Lima: Kleine Schriften und Nachträge* (ed. by I. Fasel). Basel. 360–414 (originally published in 1982)

Quinche, E. (1978). *Bérénice: L'histoire et l'élégie*. Paris

Reed, J.D. (2007). *Virgil's Gaze: Nation and Poetry in the Aeneid*. Princeton

Riemer, U. (2000). 'Was ziemt einer kaiserlichen Ehefrau? Die Kaiserfrauen in den Viten Suetons' in Kunst and Riemer (2000) 135–55

Rolfe, J.C. (1914). (ed. and trans.) *Suetonius, Lives of the Caesars*, 2 vols. Loeb Classical Library 31, 38. Cambridge, MA

Rogers, P.M. (1980). 'Titus, Berenice and Mucianus' *Historia* 29.86–95

Roller, D.W. (2010). *Cleopatra: A Biography*. Women in Antiquity. Oxford

Ronzeaud, P. et al. (1996). (edd.) *Les tragédies romaines de Racine, Britannicus, Bérénice, Mithridate: Actes de la Journée d'étude du 18 novembre 1995 à Marseille, sous la direction de P. Ronzeaud, et de la Journée Racine en Sorbonne du 13 janvier 1996, sous la direction de P. Dandrey et A. Viala*. Littératures classiques 26. Paris

Sannicandro, L. (2014). 'Der 'dekadente' Feldherr: Caesar in Ägypten (Luc. 10)' *Mnemosyne* 67.50–64

Schröder, V. (2009). 'Re-writing history for the early modern stage: Racine's Roman tragedies' in A. Feldherr (ed.) *The Cambridge Companion to the Roman Historians*. Cambridge. 380–93

Selden, D.L. (1998). 'Alibis' *ClAnt* 17.290–412

Sellstrom, A.D. (1993). 'Intertextual configuration in *Bérénice*' in C. Gaudiani (ed., en collaboration avec J. Van Baelen) *Création et Recréation: Un Dialogue entre Littérature et Histoire. Mélanges offerts à Marie-Odile Sweetser*. Tübingen. 255–63

Skulsky, S. (1985). '"*Inuitus, regina...*": Aeneas and the love of Rome' *AJPh* 106.447–55

Sprondel, J. and Schröder, B. (2013). 'Berenike' in P. von Möllendorff, A. Simonis, and L. Simonis (edd.) *Historische Gestalten der Antike: Rezeption in Literatur, Kunst und Musik*. Der Neue Pauly Supplemente 8. Stuttgart/ Weimar. 175–86

Stephens, S.A. (2003). *Seeing Double: Intercultural Poetics in Ptolemaic Alexandria*. Berkeley

Stevenson, T. (2015). *Julius Caesar and the Transformation of the Roman Republic*. London

Syed, Y. (2005). *Vergil's Aeneid and the Roman Self: Subject and Nation in Literary Discourse*. Ann Arbor

Syme, R. (1991). 'Titus et Berenice: A Tacitean fragment' in id. *Roman Papers VII* (ed. by A.R. Birley). Oxford. 647–62

Tatum, W.J. (1997). 'Friendship, politics, and literature in Catullus: Poems 1, 65 and 66, 116' *CQ* 47.482–500 (reprinted in J.H. Gaisser (ed.) *Catullus*. Oxford Readings in Classical Studies. Oxford 2007. 369–98)

Temporini, H. Gräfin Vitzthum, (2002). (ed.) *Die Kaiserinnen Roms: von Livia bis Theodora*. München

Turner, A.J. (2010). 'Lucan's Cleopatra' in id., J.H.K.O. Chong-Gossard, and F.J. Vervaet (edd.) *Private and Public Lies: The Discourse of Despotism and Deceit in the Graeco-Roman World*. Impact of Empire 11. Leiden. 195–209

van Oppen de Ruiter, B.F. (2015). *Berenice II Euergetis: Essays in Early*

Hellenistic Queenship. Queenship and Power. New York

Vasta, M.S. (2007). *Titus and the Queen: Julia Berenice and the Opposition to Titus' Succession*. Illinois Wesleyan University Honors Projects Paper 1. Bloomington, IL (http://digitalcommons.iwu.edu/grs_honproj/1)

Videau, A. (1997). 'Catulle élégiaque: La "Boucle de Berénice"' *REL* 75.38–63

Vinson, M.P. (1989). 'Domitia Longina, Julia Titi, and the literary tradition' *Historia* 38.431–50

Visscher, M. (forthcoming). 'Imperial Asia: Past and present in Callimachus' *Lock of Berenice*' in M.A. Harder, R.F. Regtuit, and G.C. Wakker (edd.) *Past and Present in Hellenistic Poetry*. Hellenistica Groningana. Leuven

Vox, O. (2000). 'Sul genere grammaticale della Chioma di Berenice' *MD* 44.175–81

Warden, J. (2006). 'Catullus in the grove of Callimachus' in C. Deroux (ed.) *Studies in Latin Literature and Roman History* 13. Collection Latomus 301. Bruxelles. 97–154

Weber, G. (1993). *Dichtung und höfische Gesellschaft: Die Rezeption von Zeitgeschichte am Hof der ersten drei Ptolemäer*. Hermes Einzelschriften 62. Stuttgart

Wesch-Klein, G. (2005). 'Titus und Berenike: Lächerliche Leidenschaft oder weltgeschichtliches Liebesverhältnis?' in W. Spickermann et al. (edd.) *Rom, Germanien und das Reich. Festschrift zu Ehren von Rainer Wiegels anlässlich seines 65. Geburtstages*. Pharos 18. Sankt Katharinen. 163–73

Wilker, J. (2007). *Für Rom und Jerusalem: Die herodianische Dynastie im 1. Jahrhundert n. Chr.* Studien zur Alten Geschichte 5. Frankfurt am Main

— (2008). '*Principes et reges*. Das persönliche Nahverhältnis zwischen Princeps und Klientelherrschern und seine Auswirkungen im frühen Prinzipat' in A. Coşkun (ed.) *Freundschaft und Gefolgschaft in den auswärtigen Beziehungen der Römer (2. Jahrhundert v.Chr. – 1. Jahrhundert n. Chr.)*. Inklusion/Exklusion. Studien zu Fremdheit und Armut von der Antike bis zur Gegenwart 9. Frankfurt am Main. 165–88

Wills, J. (1998). 'Divided allusion: Virgil and the *Coma Berenices*' *HSCPh* 98.277–305

Wyke, M. (2002). '*Meretrix regina*: Augustan Cleopatras' in ead. *The Roman Mistress: Ancient and Modern Representations*. Oxford. 195–243

Young-Widmaier, M.R. (2002). 'Quintilian's legal representation of Julia Berenice' *Historia* 51.124–9

Zissos, A. (2016). 'The Flavian Legacy' in id. (ed.), *A Companion to the Flavian Age of Imperial Rome*. Chichester. 487–514

Lucilius and Horace: from Criticism to Identification

Alberto Canobbio
Università di Pavia

The brief *Life of Horace* that has come to us under the name of Porphyrio identifies Lucilius as Horace's model for the *Satires* (*vita Hor.* 2.5–7 H.): *[Horatius scripsit] sermonum duos <libros>, Lucilium secutus antiquissimum scriptorem.* Of course Porphyrio had grounds for doing so: Lucilius was the most important reference point for Horace, who talks about him in three of his own satires, the so-called literary satires (1.4; 1.10; 2.1).[1] But this is an unsatisfactory way of looking at the relationship between the two satirists: Horace did not simply 'follow Lucilius', but instead his view of Lucilius was developing over the period in which he composed the *Satires*, and the development can be perceived in the three poems in which he discussed Lucilius and his writings. Therefore a correct assessment of Horace's interactions with Lucilius requires us to track the changes in Horace's attitude and to read each of these three texts closely as a stage in Horace's on-going literary relationship with Lucilius. This involves recognizing that what Horace says about Lucilius in the three satires cannot be harmonized into a single judgement, but must rather be understood as three separate assessments and reassessments, each of which also has its own internal dynamics.[2]

---

* Paper given at the Langford Latin Seminar "Unusual angles" (Florida State University, Tallahassee, 8 November 2013). I thank Prof. Francis Cairns for his kind invitation and revision of my text, Sandra Cairns for her help with my English, and Prof. Ruurd R. Nauta and Prof. Kenneth J. Reckford for their helpful comments during the discussion. Horace is quoted from the text of Klingner (1959). A first, enlarged, Italian version of this paper is forthcoming as 'L'immagine di Lucilio nelle satire letterarie oraziane' in the journal *Athenaeum*.

[1] For commentary on Horace's satires see Fedeli (1994); Gowers (2012), book I; Freudenburg (in progress for Cambridge Greek and Latin Classics), book II; De Vecchi (2013); on the three literary satires see also Fraenkel (1957) 124–35; 145–53; Brink (1963) 156–77; LaFleur (1981).

[2] On Lucilius and Horace see Fiske (1920); Rudd (1966) 86–131; Scodel (1987); D'Anna (1995); Labate (1996) 426–34; Cucchiarelli (2001) esp. 15–20; 33–43; 50–52; 56; 58–63; 82 "la spinta all'identità con il predecessore (*alter Lucilius*) diviene

I. *Horatius alius Lucilius* (*Satire* 1.4)

In the three preceding satires, the so-called diatribe poems, Horace had indulged in personal criticism of other people. This could have led his contemporaries to see him as a second Lucilius. To evade this identification Horace begins *Sat.* 1.4 by claiming that his satire belongs to a tradition which does not have its roots in Lucilius (1–5):

> Eupolis atque Cratinus Aristophanesque poetae
> atque alii, quorum comoedia prisca virorum est,
> siquis erat dignus describi, quod malus ac fur,
> quod moechus foret aut sicarius aut alioqui
> famosus, multa cum libertate notabant.

In Rome personal vices were stigmatized by the censor's *nota*; according to Horace, Old Comedy performed the same function of social control in Athens by freely describing the bad behaviour of bad people (*siquis erat dignus describi ... multa cum libertate notabant*). Horace limits the Attic *onomasti komodein* to the sphere of *mores*;[3] he passes over the considerable political element in Old Comedy because it was despised by the Roman élite.[4]

Horace continues (6–8) by saying that Lucilius was simply a follower of the Old Comedy and changed only the metre (from dramatic metres to the hexameter):[5]

---

pretesto di ironia, molla alla diversità: *alius Lucilius*"; 86 "nella paradossalità di questo rapporto (Orazio *non* è Lucilio, ma pure si trova a 'ripetere' Lucilio: *alius*, e non *alter*) c'è il motore dell'importanza, così vistosa, assunta nei *Sermones* dalla figura di Lucilio"; 111ff. and *passim*; Schlegel (2010). Further developments of this much debated issue can be found in Labate (2012) on Lucilius' and Horace's victims, and in general works on Horatian satire, e.g. Freudenburg (2001) 15–124; Muecke (2007); Courtney (2013).

[3] Cf. Quint. 10.1.65 *antiqua comoedia ... insectandis vitiis praecipua*.

[4] In Cic. *Rep.* 4.11–12 Scipio Aemilianus recognizes that Old Comedy attacked revolutionary demagogues; but he also points out that bad citizens should be stigmatized (*notari*) by the censors, not by poets, and remembers that Old Comedy also attacked meritorious citizens such as Pericles. Moreover the Ciceronian Scipio reports that in Rome severe sanctions were applied against defamatory writings since the time of the Twelve Tables, and maintains that public men should be judged only by the magistrates and the laws, not criticised by poets. The Ciceronian text might be aiming at blaming the practice, not uncommon in his times, of attacking prominent politicians in defamatory poems (cf. e.g. Tac. *Ann.* 4.34.5 *carmina Bibaculi et Catulli referta contumeliis Caesarum leguntur*). It is interesting that this criticism is put in the mouth of Scipio Aemilianus, a friend of Lucilius: Lucilius indeed was rightly regarded as the founder of this practice (cf. below n.8). Cicero's Scipio is of course very different from the Scipio mentioned in Hor. *Sat.* 2.1.65–68 (see below §III), where both Scipio and Laelius appear not to be offended by the verses which their common friend Lucilius wrote against corrupt politicians like Metellus and Lupus.

[5] Lucilius began to write in the same iambic and trochaic metres used by Latin comic poets (and similar to the metres used in Greek comedy); the change of metre to which

> hinc omnis pendet Lucilius, hosce secutus,
> mutatis tantum pedibus numerisque, facetus,
> emunctae naris, durus conponere versus.

Horace could have found the evidence for this connection in Lucilius, if we interpret the fragment *archeotera ... unde haec sunt omnia* (1111 M.) as Fiske suggests,[6] or in Varro, according to Jahn and Leo;[7] but it may be also Horace's own conjecture. Indeed Horace's claim has some basis in the analogous contents of satire and comedy: *animus, res* and *lexis* of the two genres are similar; Old Comedy's *parrhesia* could be compared to Lucilius' *libertas*.[8] Historically speaking, however, it is very unlikely that Lucilius derived his satire from Attic comedy.[9] Even the change of metre which Horace mentions rules this out: metre was such a strong identifier of genre in antiquity[10] that by the very act of writing in a different metre from the poets of Old Comedy Lucilius, at least in his second collection, would have seen himself as engaging in a quite different activity. Horace's version of the origin of satire as expressed in *Sat.* 1.4 is therefore at most a half-truth belonging to a very conscious strategy of self-depiction.

In these lines Horace is only apparently respectful of Lucilius: his initial compliments — *facetus* (7), *emunctae naris* (8) — mutate quickly into harsh criticism. The spondaic word *durus* (8) introduces the greatest fault of Lucilius, who was *durus conponere versus* (9–11):

> nam fuit hoc vitiosus: in hora saepe ducentos,
> ut magnum, versus dictabat stans pede in uno;
> cum flueret lutulentus, erat quod tollere velles.

The weakness of Lucilius, who wrote thirty books of satires, i.e. several thousand lines, consists in unrestrained prolixity and disdain for *limae labor et mora* (Hor. *Ars* 291). Horace fixes his criticism of Lucilius on the reader's mind with two effective images. The first depicts Lucilius in a quite unsuitable position for writing poetry: the satirist is standing

---

Horace refers happened after the composition of the oldest books and therefore does not coincide with the absolute beginning of Lucilian satire.

[6] Cf. Fiske (1920) 281; Marx in his edition (75) conjectures that Lucilius «videtur scripsisse *nosce archaeotera illa unde haec omnia nata*».

[7] Cf. Cucchiarelli (2001) 33 n. 63.

[8] In Cic. *fam.* 12.16.3 Gaius Trebonius, author of *versiculi* against Antonius, justifies the violence of his attacks (*liberius invehimur*) by quoting Lucilius' *libertas* as a precedent.

[9] Rudd (1966) 89 considers this statement a simplification and exaggeration, cf. also LaFleur (1981) 1795 n. 9; Cucchiarelli (2001) 21.

[10] Cf. Labate (1996) 426 "è davvero significativo che, in questo caso [*Sat.* 1.4], Orazio giunga quasi a rovesciare i principi di classificazione che privilegiavano il metro come portatore di identità letteraria (una specie di dissociazione tra i *numeri* e gli *animi*, sottolineata dal contrasto *omnis/tantum*)".

on one foot[11] composing in a single hour two hundred lines. This hyperbolic number recalls Hortensius' five hundred thousand lines which Catullus contrasts with Cinna's *Zmyrna*, an epyllion which is a model of scrupulous poetic revision and Callimachean *doctrina*.[12] The second image is that of the muddy river: it is plainly Callimachean, and it is derived directly from the *Hymn to Apollo* (108–9). By deploying these two images, and especially the second, Horace indicates that he is practising literary polemic of a Callimachean type. The fact that Lucilius is as overflowing and muddy as Callimachus' Assyrian river makes him not Horace's model but the reverse of Horace, who here presents himself as a follower of the Callimachean poetics introduced into Rome by *poetae novi* such as Catullus and Cinna.

In *Sat.* 1.4 Horace is constructing his own poetic identity by stressing the differences between himself and Lucilius, whose attacks on his most distinguished contemporaries made him an unsuitable precedent. So Horace moves himself out of the shadow of Lucilius by parading as his model an older and more prestigious genre: Old Comedy; then he distances himself further from Lucilius by putting more stress on Lucilius' eventual abandonment of theatrical metres than his employment of the hexameter;[13] finally he evades being identified with Lucilius by contrasting Lucilius' prolixity with his own Callimachean brevity and polish.

Horace's attempts to make his reader look back to Old Comedy, rather than to Lucilius, as the direct model of his own satires continue at lines 23–5. Horace admits that he fears the reactions of the people criticised in his satires; he labels these people as *culpari dignos* so as to recall the phrase *dignus describi* of line 3, which denoted someone mocked by the Old Comedy poets. Old Comedy is also mentioned a little further on (39–48), when Horace raises the question whether his own satires, *sermoni propiora* (42), should be considered real poetry or not. In fact comedy also sits on the boundary between poetry and non-poetry by its use of everyday language: because it is in metre it is not prose, but otherwise it is ordinary speech (47–8): *nisi quod pede certo/ differt sermoni, sermo merus*.

The name of Lucilius reappears in *Sat.* 1.4 precisely in connection with the kind of speech involved in satire. At lines 56–7 Horace

---

[11] The phrase *stans pede in uno*, probably proverbial, indicates an action performed with great ease and little effort, cf. Fedeli (1994) 389; according to Cucchiarelli (2001) the word *pes* might have a metrical value (46 n.105) and the whole phrase a convivial origin (58 n.4).

[12] Cf. Catull. 95.1–4 and Bellandi (2007) 141–63, esp. 142 n.331 (comparison with Hor. *Sat.* 1.4.9–10), 144 n.336 (Hortensius as poet), 147 (opposition Cinna/Hortensius).

[13] This is to cover up the fact that Horace himself also uses the hexameter in his satires.

equates his *sermo* to that of Lucilius: *ego quae nunc,/ olim quae scripsit Lucilius*. This is an attempt to admit some commonality of material with Lucilius, but without making Lucilius his model. Indeed the chiasmus *ego… nunc/ olim … Lucilius* merely gives the chronological order without implying a hierarchy; moreover the strong antithesis between *nunc* and *olim*, adjacent in the text but on separate lines, implies detachment rather than continuity. Horace aims to present himself not as a second Lucilius but as a different Lucilius, different, that is, from the historical one. In fact Horace, like his predecessor, attacks bad people, but his targets are little-known *personae*,[14] and from the stylistic viewpoint he, unlike Lucilius, closely follows Callimachean aesthetics.

Horace's wish to distinguish himself from Lucilius is based on his fundamental view of what motivates satire. Horace does not think that satirical mockery originates from a malicious and venomous inclination to *maledicere*, even though someone accuses him of doing just this (78–9): *laedere gaudes/ … et hoc studio pravus facis*. Horatian satire is instead the poetic version of the teachings of Horace's *pater optimus*, who preserved the moral health of his son by training him to take a critical view of vicious persons and to find fault with them, but to do so with a smile (103–6):

> liberius si
> dixero quid, si forte iocosius, hoc mihi iuris
> cum venia dabis: insuevit pater optimus hoc me,
> ut fugerem exemplis vitiorum quaeque notando.

The teaching methods of Horace's father had already been employed by Demea, the father-character in Terence's *Adelphoe*, who says about his son's upbringing (414–16):

> nil praetermitto; consuefacio; denique
> inspicere, tamquam in speculum, in vitas omnium
> iubeo atque ex aliis sumere exemplum sibi.

Some scholars have been led by this passage to assimilate Horace's father to the character of *pater* in Roman comedy.[15] But Horace's *pater optimus* is very different from the comic father.[16] Horace's reference to

---

[14] The lower social importance of the satirical targets is due to the change of the socio-political context in which Horace operates: since the Augustan poet lacks the *libertas* of Lucilius, he attacks, with an essentially moral purpose, only minor people representing common human types. On the differences between the Lucilian *onomasti komodein* and Horatian aggressiveness cf. Labate (2012) esp. 270; 276; 282; 287–8; 292–3; also Labate (1996) 430–31.

[15] Cf. Freudenburg (1993) 34–9.

[16] Cf. Citroni Marchetti (2004) 18–25 esp. 18–20 "le parole del padre di Orazio non sono

the *Adelphoe* was intended only to evoke the connection between satire and comedy which Horace had asserted so forcefully at the beginning of *Sat.* 1.4; in fact the words *liberius* (103) and *notando* (106) openly recall *multa cum libertate notabant* (5). Horace uses this echo to connect his earlier claim that Old Comedy was his model in satire with his new, contrasting, claim that the true model for his satire came from his father.[17]

The introduction of Horace's father impacts on the relationship with Lucilian satire that *Sat.* 1.4 is determined to deny, and also reduces his dependence on Greek Old Comedy by suggesting the (pre-Quintilianic) idea that satire is a Roman, or even a domestic, invention, rooted in the pragmatism of the *mos maiorum*. Horace's earliest moral education by his father took place in the formative years that preceded his introduction to philosophical study on the Greek model; and Horace prioritises his father as a philosophic instructor when he makes him say that the *sapiens* (i.e. the Greek philosopher) will instruct Horace in the theory of good and evil, but that he himself can hand down the *mos maiorum* to his son and in this way preserve his innocence and reputation until he grows up and can fend for himself (115–20):

> sapiens, vitatu quidque petitu
> sit melius, causas reddet tibi; mi satis est, si
> traditum ab antiquis morem servare tuamque,
> dum custodis eges, vitam famamque tueri
> incolumen possum; simul ac duraverit aetas
> membra animumque tuum, nabis sine cortice.

By placing such stress on his father's moral training along traditional Roman lines, Horace presents his satire not as something destructive like that of Lucilius, but as something educative and morally uplifting.

II. *Lucilius prior Horatius* (*Satire* 1.10a)

Horace starts his second literary satire by commenting on what he had said in *Sat.* 1.4 and defending the position he had adopted in it (1–6):[18]

---

la stessa cosa che le parole di Demea: non lo sono pur essendo anche le stesse parole ed essendo ben riconoscibili come tali ... Padre e figlio sono dalla medesima parte mentre osservano gli altri e il loro modo di porsi, di cui il padre è responsabile, è scherzoso ... Siamo cioè all'opposto dei padri di commedia"; 28–30; 33–4

[17] Cf. Schlegel (2000) esp. 95; 101; 105–6; Citroni Marchetti (2004) 19–20.

[18] In some manuscripts this passage is preceded by eight lines, unknown to ancient commentators and most likely spurious, cf. Fedeli (1994) 509–10; Gowers (2012), 309–11. Even though the authenticity of these lines is still maintained by D'Anna (2005) 208–12 = (2012) 366–70, the aim of *Sat.* 1.10 is certainly not to show how

> Nempe incomposito dixi pede currere versus
> Lucili. Quis tam Lucili fautor inepte est,
> ut non hoc fateatur? At idem, quod sale multo
> urbem defricuit, charta laudatur eadem.
> Nec tamen hoc tribuens dederim quoque cetera; nam sic
> et Laberi mimos ut pulchra poemata mirer.

The poem starts with a confirmation: yes, Horace admits, I did criticize Lucilius, but I praised him too — up to a point. At line 1 Horace repeats his judgement on Lucilius: *durus conponere versus* (*Sat.* 1.4.8); however, unlike *Sat.* 1.4, Horace's *ego* is revealed immediately and abruptly (*dixi*), almost in a Lucilian way. But the most important difference between the two satires is that in 1.10 the initial sequence of praise and blame of Lucilius is inverted: the words of praise now follow those of disapproval and therefore are placed in a more memorable and rhetorically stronger position.[19] Although Horace starts *Sat.* 1.10 by censuring Lucilius for the roughness of his metrics, he then goes on to praise him for rubbing the city down with a lot of salt (3–4). This medical metaphor underlines not only the harshness of Lucilius' satire, but also its healing quality, since salt was rubbed on the skin to heal wounds.[20] The poetry of Lucilius, then, is being characterized as a kind of social therapy from which the whole *civitas* benefited: and such healing satire which condemns vice for a beneficial purpose is not unlike Horatian satire, inspired as it was by the moral teachings of Horace's *pater optimus*. In contrast to *Sat.* 1.4, where Horace offered a few words laudatory of Lucilius only to move sharply away from him, in 1.10 Horace moves closer to Lucilius, but to a Lucilius whose image he has altered: Lucilius is now described as Horace's pioneering predecessor in the correct kind of satire, but — and Horace emphasizes this yet again in line 6 where he compares Lucilius to Laberius — Lucilius did not achieve a high degree of poetic refinement. In other words the Augustan poet aims to present himself as the one who was able to convey the essence of what made Lucilius important (*sale multo/ urbem defricuit*) in a style suitable to the modern aesthetic.

In *Sat.* 1.10, then, Horace is more interested in differentiating himself from Lucilius in terms of stylistic elegance. But he now extends his

---

mendosus Lucilius is, as stated in the alleged first line, but rather to redeem the *inventor* of the satirical genre by inserting him in a wider discourse concerning the evolution of Latin literature, and not only that. In fact, as Scodel (1987) observes, Horace in *Sat.* 1.10 defines his satire not only in respect to Lucilius but also in respect to Callimachean poetics, a theme which leads him to in-depth discussion of *imitatio* and originality (cf. below n.32).

[19] Cf. D'Anna (2005) 97–8 = (2012) 355–6.

[20] Cf. Fedeli (1994) 511; further interpretations of this metaphor in Gowers (2012) 312.

discussion of poetic faults to include other poets, starting with Laberius. The image of Lucilius benefits from this widening of focus, because Lucilius is no longer the only target of Horace's criticism. This is shown in 7–19, where Horace combines the Callimachean ideals of brevity and variety (9–11) with exemplary use of the *ridiculum* (14) which he found in Greek Old Comedy (16). At the beginning and end of this section Horace mentions two *exempla cavenda* which draw attention away from Lucilius. In lines 7–8 Horace describes the mimes of Laberius as able only *risu diducere rictum auditoris* (to get a laugh out of the audience); this phrase compares the laughter of the audience to the physiological reaction of a brainless animal — *rictus* means literally the gaping mouth of an animal.[21] The animal imagery returns at the end of this section, where Horace mentions the singer Hermogenes, who is ironically called *pulcher* (17–18), and *simius iste*, that is to say Demetrius, a despicable imitator of the 'New Poets' Calvus and Catullus (18–19).[22] Neither of these two performers has any interest in Old Comedy, whose poets, according to Horace, are the ones to imitate (16–17).

Lucilius reappears at line 20, where one of his supporters claims: *at magnum fecit, quod verbis graeca latinis/ miscuit*. In his reply Horace does not censure Lucilius' tendency to mix Latin with Greek; this was a common practice in the philhellenic environment of the second century BC in circles such as that of the Scipios, before linguistic purism became predominant in Latin culture in the times of Cicero and Caesar. Instead Horace criticizes those people who, like Lucilius' admirer, still approve of mixing Latin and Greek a century after Lucilius, calling them culturally retarded (21 *seri studiorum*). Horace then gives another example to be avoided, the otherwise unknown Pitholeon of Rhodes,[23] and again he does this without involving Lucilius.

Horace's more positive approach to Lucilius in *Sat.* 1.10 now glances at a further element of contact between the two, since Horace claims that he also composed in Greek (31–3):

---

[21] Cf. Fedeli (1994) 512; Gowers (2012) 313.

[22] Hermogenes, already mentioned in *Sat.* 1.3.129, is paired with Demetrius again in *Sat.* 1.10.79–80 and 90.

[23] Cf. Hor. *Sat.* 1.10.21–3 *o seri studiorum, quine putetis / difficile et mirum, Rhodio quod Pitholeonti / contigit?* Bentley supposed that Horace would have ironically Graecized the already unusual *cognomen* of M. Otacilius Pitholaus, a freedman who emigrated from Rhodes, author of *maledicentissima carmina* against Caesar evidently characterized by the mix between Greek and Latin, cf. Fedeli (1994) 515; Gowers (2012) 319.

> atque ego cum graecos facerem, natus mare citra,
> versiculos, vetuit me tali voce Quirinus
> post mediam noctem visus, cum somnia vera.

We do not know whether Horace really wrote in Greek; in these lines he is plainly recreating the famous scene from the prologue to the *Aitia* in which the young Callimachus is instructed by Apollo to write refined poetry. In *Sat.* 1.10 Quirinus, the deified Romulus, takes the place of the Greek god of poetry and instructs Horace to write in Latin[24].

However, Callimachean poetics were not accepted by everyone in Rome; among the non-Callimachean poets there is the *turgidus Alpinus*, traditionally identified with Furius Bibaculus,[25] who wrote a mythological poem (perhaps an *Aethiopis*) and a historical poem on the Transalpine deeds of Caesar (36–7):

> turgidus Alpinus iugulat dum Memnona dumque
> diffingit Rheni luteum caput, haec ego ludo.

The metaphor of the muddy river, which in *Sat.* 1.4 referred to Lucilius (11 *cum flueret lutulentus*), is now directed against Furius, who *diffingit*[26] *Rheni luteum caput*. By treating Furius in this way Horace yet again masks his criticism of Lucilius by attacking another poet who rejects the Callimachean ideals and from whom he wishes to distinguish himself (37 *haec ego ludo*). Horace is again a Callimachean immediately afterwards, when he says that he cares neither for poetic competitions nor for applause in theatres: rather he values the greatest poets of his time, Fundanius, Pollio, Varius, and Virgil, who refined the genres of comedy, tragedy, epic, and bucolic (40–45) and who induced Horace to seek his literary space in satire, which appears as the only genre that has still development potential (46–9):

> hoc erat, experto frustra Varrone Atacino
> atque quibusdam aliis, melius quod scribere possem,
> inventore minor; neque ego illi detrahere ausim
> haerentem capiti cum multa laude coronam.

The differences between this self-presentation and that of *Sat.* 1.4 are notable. Horace's decision to devote himself to satire is presented in 1.10 as an unavoidable choice rather than as the result of the teachings

---

[24] Quirinus' admonition expressed by a comparison, likely proverbial (34–5 *in silvam non ligna feras insanius ac si/ magnas Graecorum malis inplere catervas*), is supported by literary, rather than nationalistic, reasons: Latin poetry is preferable to Greek poetry simply because it is a field less crowded and therefore more promising.

[25] Cf. Fedeli (1994) 518; Gowers (2012) 323.

[26] The manuscripts have *diffingit* (disfigures), but Fedeli (1994) 518–19 and Gowers (2012) 323–4 prefer Müller's conjecture *diffindit* (splits), which gives a very bloody *color* to the context (cf. 36 *iugulat ... Memnona*).

of his *pater optimus*, who now disappears from Horace's poetry along
with the educational aim of satire which he represented. Satire is now
for Horace not a genre derived from another (Old Comedy): it is an
independent literary form with an *inventor* (Lucilius)[27] and its own
tradition, but it has not yet reached its full maturity. Lucilius, who
Horace wanted to be distinguished from in *Sat.* 1.4, now becomes his
major reference point. Horace's satire is secondary to that of Lucilius
not only chronologically (as in 1.4.56–7 *ego quae nunc,/ olim quae
scripsit Lucilius*, see above), and Horace himself admits to being *inventore minor*: certainly he will not deprive Lucilius of his poetic wreath.

Now that Horace has modified his stance towards Lucilius, he can
return to his admission at the beginning of *Sat.* 1.10 that he had in his
first literary satire he had attacked Lucilius (50–52):

> at dixi fluere lutulentum, saepe ferentem
> plura quidem tollenda relinquendis. age quaeso,
> tu nihil in magno doctus reprehendis Homero?

Horace repeats that he had called Lucilius 'muddy' and attacks him
even more strongly than in *Sat.* 1.4 by saying that more of Lucilius'
lines should be thrown away than retained. However, Horace is now
directing his remarks not against Lucilius, but against a fictional
speaker, called ironically *doctus*, whom he asks whether in his opinion
the great Homer was faultless (52). Lucilius is now — for the first time
— a positive model for Horace, who affirms that Lucilius was right to
criticize, with a smile and without claiming superiority, great authors
like Accius and Ennius (53–5):

> nil comis tragici mutat Lucilius Acci?
> non ridet versus Enni gravitate minores,
> cum de se loquitur non ut maiore reprensis?

This is exactly Horace's own modus operandi, who has just described
himself as *inventore minor* (48) and who claims the right to criticize
Lucilius in 56–63:

> quid vetat et nosmet Lucili scripta legentis
> quaerere, num illius, num rerum dura negarit
> versiculos natura magis factos et euntis
> mollius ac siquis pedibus quid claudere senis,
> hoc tantum contentus, amet scripsisse ducentos
> ante cibum versus, totidem cenatus, Etrusci
> quale fuit Cassi rapido ferventius amni
> ingenium

[27] The identification of the *inventor* (48) of satirical genre with Lucilius (and not Ennius,
the first to write *saturae*) is argued by D'Anna (1979) 525–37 = (2012) 59–71.

In these lines Horace once more deflects criticism from Lucilius by attacking another literary target: Cassius Etruscus,[28] a tireless versifier who doubles the number of lines attributed in *Sat.* 1.4.9 to Lucilius (*scripsisse ducentos/ ante cibum versus, totidem cenatus*, 60–61) and at is characterized at 62–3 (*rapido ferventius amni/ ingenium*) with the defamatory metaphor of a muddy river already applied at 1.4.11 to the *lutulentus* archaic poet. The redemption of Lucilius is completed in the lines that follow (64–7):

> fuerit Lucilius, inquam,
> comis et urbanus, fuerit limatior idem
> quam rudis et Graecis intacti carminis auctor
> quamque poetarum seniorum turba

Horace calls Lucilius *comis, urbanus*,[29] and, even more significantly, *limatior*, a term which ascribes to the inventor of satire *labor limae*, the poetic quality that distinguishes him from the *turba* of archaic poets and one which is hard to find in a poet who is initiating a new genre not derived from Greek literature.[30] The attitude expressed here by Horace is quite different from that of *Sat.* 1.4. Not only is Lucilius, who lived before the major introduction of Callimacheanism to Rome, credited with the Callimachean quality of *labor limae*, but also with originality, because his poetry had no Greek predecessor. Horace now denies the connection between satire and Old Comedy asserted in *Sat.* 1.4, and at the same time abandons his criticisms of Lucilius. Lucilian satire is now put into the wider context of the history of Latin literature which, after the pioneering phase[31] and the bad poetry of Laberius (6–8) and *turgidus Alpinus* (36–7), has reached its golden age under Augustus — although some people still disdain the refinement of the new generation of poets (40–45) and either slavishly imitate the out-dated New Poets (18–19) or nostalgically support old-fashioned bilingualism (20–24).[32]

This evolutionary vision of Latin literature, hinted at 46–7 in Horace's choice of poetic genre (*hoc erat ... melius quod scribere possem*), gives him a new perspective on Lucilius, allowing him to minimise the differences between himself and Lucilius constructed as

---

[28] Cf. Fedeli (1994) 523–4; Gowers (2012) 331 "unknown".

[29] Cf. Cic. *de orat.* 2.25 *C. Lucilius homo doctus et perurbanus.*

[30] The *auctor* of line 66 has been identified either with Ennius, the first to write satires, or with Lucilius; however in this passage Horace is probably referring to any kind of *rudis* (i.e. unpractised by Greeks) poetry, cf. Fedeli (1994) 524. D'Anna (2005) 102–107 = (2012) 360–64 still maintains the identification with Ennius.

[31] Not only Lucilius, but even the poets criticized by him, i.e. Ennius and Accius (53–4), are representative of the pioneering phase.

[32] See Scodel (1987), esp. 206, 213, for a useful statement of Horace's stance between excessive admiration of Lucilius and superficial Callimacheanism.

an ennobling model. Horace, self-admittedly *inventore minor* but living
in a more advanced literary age, now identifies himself with Lucilius,
who has supplanted the authors of Old Comedy taken as models at the
beginning of *Sat.* 1.4. Those authors are still deemed worthy of imitation (*sunt imitandi*, 1.10.17), but they are pushed aside when Horace
concentrates on the history of Latin literature in a way that also
relegates his *pater optimus* to the background.

At line 68 Horace identifies with Lucilius by means of a fictional
time-shift: if Lucilius could somehow become a contemporary (i.e. an
Augustan) poet, he would be a 'Horace' (i.e. an adherent of *labor
limae*). This new Lucilius would redirect the aggressiveness of his
pugnacious *ingenium* into formal refinement, a concept encapsulated in
the amusing image of Lucilius scratching his head and biting his nails
while composing poetry (69–71):

> detereret sibi multa, recideret omne quod ultra
> perfectum traheretur, et in versu faciendo
> saepe caput scaberet vivos et roderet unguis.

The slovenly poet who dictated two hundred lines an hour standing on
one foot has now become a meticulous literary artist. But of course it is
Horace himself hiding behind the mask of the Augustan Lucilius.

III. *Horatius alter Lucilius* (*Satire* 2.1)

The process of identification between Horace and Lucilius which
started in *Sat.* 1.10 is completed in the first satire of the second book, a
sort of 'proem in the middle',[33] which was presumably the last poem to
be written;[34] this satire therefore represents both a continuation of the
critical discourse about Lucilius begun in the first book, and Horace's
final thoughts on the genre of satire (1–4):

> Sunt quibus in satura[35] videar nimis acer et ultra
> legem tendere opus; sine nervis altera quidquid
> conposui pars esse putat similisque meorum
> mille die versus deduci posse.

Horace says that some regard his satire as too aggressive (*nimis acer*),

---

[33] Mazzoli (1995) 7; (2009) 476.
[34] Cf. Fedeli (1994) 531–2
[35] The precise definition *in satura* is to avoid confusion with the *iambi*, published along
with the *liber alter* of the *sermones*. This is the first time that Horace used the eidetic
marker *satura*; the second (and last) mention of *satura* will occur in *Sat.* 2.6.17 *quid
prius inlustrem saturis musaque pedestri?*

whereas others consider it flabby (*sine nervis*). Clearly these judgements cannot both be correct, so each weakens the other; and the accusation of flabbiness becomes even more absurd with the taunt that a thousand lines like those of Horace could be written in a day. But the true purpose of these paradoxical statements is to make us think of Lucilius and of Horace's earlier criticism of him. Over-aggressiveness and lack of stylistic refinement are indeed the most evident faults of Lucilius, and now Horace, according to his critics, is competing with his predecessor in prolixity also: the expression *mille die versus* recalls the two hundred lines dictated in one hour by Lucilius standing on one foot. By asserting that his satire is accused of sharing Lucilius' faults, Horace is linking it with that of Lucilius, who has definitively become his *auctor* in *Satire* 2.1: in fact at line 34 Horace will say *sequor hunc*. This is a real declaration of dependence, representing the culmination of the gradual overlap between Horace and the 'Lucilius' (the Horatian, not the historical, Lucilius) who is to be described in the first part of this satire.

The *enjambement* in lines 1–2 stresses the phrase *ultra/ legem tendere opus*. This phrase has several implications. It refers to Horace's supposed violation of the rules about defamatory poetry,[36] but more generally it refers also to the law of poetic genre, which Horace in *Ars* 135 calls *operis lex*. The two elements, literary and legal, evoked by this phrase are fundamental themes of this satire[37] and they are particularly relevant because Horace begins his defence of his poetic choices by an imaginary conversation with the famous jurist Trebatius Testa.[38] In this conversation Horace represents himself as someone approaching a jurist in search of a legal ruling, i.e. a *responsum* (4–5):[39] *Trebati,/ quid faciam? praescribe*. When Trebatius replies, he advises Horace *quiescas* (5). Horace admits that this might be the best solution, but says he cannot sleep (7 *nequeo dormire*). This is an amusing

---

[36] The law against *mala carmina*, dating back to the Twelve Tables (see n.4 above), is mentioned in *Sat.* 2.1.79ff.; Horace creates a defusing *Witz* of epigrammatic flavour by pointing out that, if Octavian is the holder of the *iudicium* (both legal and literary), his poems will be considered *bona*, not *mala*, obviously from an artistic viewpoint, cf. Fedeli (1994) 550–53.

[37] Cf. Muecke (1995); Tatum (1998).

[38] C. Trebatius Testa was born at least twenty years before Horace (in *Sat.* 2.1 they are *pater optime*, 12, and *puer*, 60) at Velia, Lucania, coming therefore from the same region as Horace (cf. *Sat.* 2.1.34). Trebatius cultivated a warm friendship with Cicero, evidenced both by their correspondence (*Fam.* 7.6–22 are addressed to Trebatius, and he is mentioned in *Fam.* 4.1; 7.5; 11.27 and 28; 14.17) and by the dedication of the *Topica*; cf. Fraenkel (1957) 145–7; Fedeli (1994) 529–30; Muecke (1995) 207–10.

[39] Freudenburg (1990), esp. 192–3, 196–7 and 202–3, thinks that this legal framework conceals Horace's true, humorous, intention, which the words *acer, tendere, opus, sine nervis* (1–2), all capable of sexual innuendo, would already have suggested.

allusion to the so-called *agrypnia*, the insomnia during which
Hellenistic poets composed their refined and learned verses.[40] In other
words, Horace cannot stop writing poetry. Horace's response also
glances at the well-known declaration of Lucilius *ex praecordiis/ ecfero versum* (590–91 M.), which establishes a link between the body of
the poet and the writing of satire.[41] As a remedy for Horace's insomnia,
Trebatius first suggests a long swim and a lot of wine;[42] then he tells
Horace to take up a different poetic genre, namely an epic in praise of
Octavian's military achievements (10–13):

> TREB. aut si tantus amor scribendi te rapit, aude
> Caesaris invicti res dicere, multa laborum
> praemia laturus. HOR. cupidum, pater optime, vires
> deficiunt.

Horace in his reply calls Trebatius *pater optime*. This respectful mode
of address of course refers back to Horace's discussion of his own real
father in *Sat.* 1.4. Trebatius therefore has now assumed the role of a
guide to Horace and, paternally, he urges Horace to take a different
approach, more pragmatic and utilitarian, to poetry, and write martial
epic; but Horace lacks the strength (*vires*). Martial epic and the
proposal that Horace should write it constitute another allusion to
Lucilius, to whom in book 26 (from which the fragment *ex praecordiis
ecfero versum* also comes) a similar request was directed (620–21 M.):

> hunc laborem sumas laudem qui tibi ac fructum ferat.
> Percrepa pugnam Popili, facta Corneli cane.

The similarity between this fragment and Hor. *Sat.* 2.1.10–11 (quoted
above) has already been pointed out:[43] the two texts have in common
the presence of exhortative forms (*sumas, percrepa, cane* in Lucilius;
aude in Horace), the word *labor*, which here indicates the act of poetic
composition, and the benefits connected with eulogistic poetry.

   Trebatius goes on to mention Lucilius explicitly as a model (16–18):
*attamen et iustum poteras et scribere fortem,/ Scipiadam ut sapiens
Lucilius*. Here Trebatius is encouraging Horace to follow Lucilius in
writing encomiastic rather than psogistic poetry;[44] Lucilian aggressive-

---

[40] Cf. Callim. *Epigr.* 27 Pf.; Cinna fr. 11 Bl.; Lucr. 1.140–45; Labate (1992) 60 n.20;
    Fedeli (1994) 533.
[41] On this theme cf. Barchiesi–Cucchiarelli (2005).
[42] 2.1.7–9 *ter uncti/ transnanto Tiberim, somno quibus est opus alto,/ inriguumque mero
    sub noctem corpus habento*; these lines humorously flaunt expressions typical of
    juridical Latin.
[43] Cf. e.g. Fiske (1920) 375; Fraenkel (1957) 150; Rudd (1966) 107–8; Fedeli (1994)
    531; Mazzoli (1995) 8.
[44] Cf. Muecke (1995) 212 "Trebatius relies on a distinction between poetry of praise and

ness is ignored both here and at lines 27–9, where Horace situates his passion for writing poetry among human inclinations in general and presents *apertis verbis* Lucilius as his literary model:

> quot capitum vivunt, totidem studiorum
> milia: me pedibus delectat claudere verba
> Lucili ritu.

Lucilius is now portrayed as a serene old man who confides his secrets to his books and uses poetry as a way of presenting his entire personality to the reader, "non solo gli avvenimenti, ma anche l'intimità dei pensieri", as Labate states,[45], rightly highlighting how Horace's words suggest that satire not only functions as a diary, but also offers a model for living (30–34):

> ille velut fidis arcana sodalibus olim
> credebat libris neque, si male cesserat, usquam
> decurrens alio neque, si bene; quo fit ut omnis
> votiva pateat veluti descripta tabella
> vita senis. Sequor hunc, Lucanus an Apulus anceps.

This picture of Lucilius is quite different from Juvenal's *Lucilius ardens*,[46] and indeed from the muddy poet of *Sat.* 1.4. Horace is trying here to set aside the stylistic differences between himself and Lucilius and to ennoble his own image by identifying with Lucilius the autobiographer.[47] In this way Horace stresses an aspect of Lucilius' works ignored in his previous literary satires but of great relevance to his poetry.[48] Paolo Fedeli,[49] on this new image of Lucilius, talks of a religious atmosphere in which the ritual of writing poetry is conducted, where the books that contain and perpetuate all the life of the old man (*omnis vitae senis*)[50] turn into faithful companions (*fidi sodales*).

In the following lines Horace deems it necessary to speak once more about the aggressiveness of his satire (the other 'Lucilian' side of

---

poetry of vituperation that Aristotle puts right at the beginning of the development of literature" (cf. Aristot. *Poet.* 1448b.24–7).

[45] Labate (1996) 427.

[46] Juv. 1.165–167 *ense velut stricto quotiens Lucilius ardens/ infremuit, rubet auditor cui frigida mens est/ criminibus, tacita sudant praecordia culpa.*

[47] Harrison (1987) reads this passage, and the whole of *Sat.* 2.1, as irony, but his interpretation is not convincing.

[48] Despite the ambiguity due to the presence of the satirical *persona* beside the authorial *ego*; on this issue cf. Citroni (1993) 280–282; Freudenburg (1993) 3–10; Cucchiarelli (2001) 9–13; Gowers (2003) 56–58; Muecke (2007) 106–109; Freudenburg (2010).

[49] Fedeli (1994) 539.

[50] As Freudenburg (2010) 274 suggests, the adjective *omnis* linked to *vita senis* might evoke the memory of Lucilius who *omnis pendet* (*Sat.* 1.4.6) from Greek Comedy: in *Sat.* 2.1 indeed a new 'all-encompassing' image of Lucilius as autobiographer accompanies that of Lucilius as the poet of *onomasti komodein*.

Horatian poetry so carefully hidden in this passage of *Sat.* 2.1). As in
Sat. 1.4 — but this time without evoking the *pater optimus* — Horace
recalls his background,[51] claiming, almost facetiously, an influence on
his poetry exercised by the places of his childhood. Horace, *Lucanus an
Apulus anceps* (34), was born in the border colony of Venusia, which
was founded to prevent the bellicose peoples of South Italy from in-
vading Roman territory (35–9): for this reason an innately combative
attitude is not unexpected in a true *Venusinus*, one who however exploits his aggressiveness only for defence (39–41): *hic stilus haud petet
ultro/ quamquam animantem et me veluti custodiet ensis/ vagina tectus.*

In lines 57–60 Horace declares that poetry is his personal life-choice
and that, whatever the future brings, he will continue to write. This rash
assertion appears to the more experienced Trebatius to be the utterance
of a young man still ignorant of the rules of human relationships,
especially where behaviour towards powerful people is concerned (60–
62): *o puer, ut sis/ vitalis metuo et maiorum nequis amicus/ frigore te
feriat.* Horace answers him by recalling the example of Lucilius, but
this time the aggressive Lucilius (62–5):

> Lucilius ausus
> primus in hunc operis conponere carmina morem
> detrahere et pellem, nitidus qua quisque per ora
> cederet, introrsum turpis.

Lucilius here is a bold pioneer whose aggressiveness is now completely
justified and accepted by Horace. Despite its violence (e.g. *detrahere
pellem*), Lucilian satire performs the social function of laying bare
those who deceive the Roman *civitas* by concealing their vices under a
skin-deep morality.[52] Horace then (65–8) tackles the delicate question
of the relationship with political power: honest men like Laelius and
Scipio Aemilianus were never offended by their friend Lucilius, nor did
they feel regret because Lucilius attacked other members of the

---

[51] Cf. Mazzoli (1995) 9, who draws attention to the significant conjunction in the same
line (34 *sequor hunc, Lucanus an Apulus anceps*) of two distinct *origines*: the literary
origin of Horace's satire and the birthplace of the poet. This combination is probably
meant to emphasize the Italic connotations of satire, a feature already suggested by the
non-Roman origin of Lucilius and Horace and recognizable also in the audience of the
Lucilian text (10–11) and in some Horatian characters (11–14).

[52] Horace will repeat this concept in *Epist.* 1.16.40–45 *vir bonus est quis?/ "qui consulta
patrum, qui leges iuraque servat,/ quo multae magnaeque secantur iudice lites,/ quo
res sponsore et quo causae teste tenentur"./ sed videt hunc omnis domus et vicinia
tota/ introrsum turpem, speciosum pelle decora* (cf. *Sat.* 2.1.64–5); on these lines and
their relationship with *Sat.* 2.1 cf. Mazzoli (1995) 21–2; on Lucilius poet 'engagé' cf.
Labate (1996) 430, who rightly observes that this interpretation of Lucilian poetry
creates a more direct link with the interpretation of *comoedia prisca* in 'censorial' key
at the beginning of *Sat.* 1.4.

nobilitas like Metellus and Lupus.

The last two lines of this section (69–70) reassert Lucilius' status as a model in *Sat.* 2.1. They allude to two fragments that Giancarlo Mazzoli has suggested were part of the first book of Lucilius' satires, and concerned the trial of Lupus.[53] The first depicts the endemic moral corruption of the Romans: the citizens spend all day in the Forum deceiving one another with *blanditia* and *simulatio* (the typical behaviour of a person who is *nitidus* outside but *turpis* inside); the persistent traps laid for one another by the Romans turn fellow-citizens into enemies (*hostes*), in a social environment where everyone is seeking to disadvantage everyone else (1228–34 M.):

> nunc vero a mani ad noctem, festo atque profesto
> totus item pariterque die populusque patresque
> iactare indu foro se omnes, decedere nusquam,
> uni se atque eidem studio omnes dedere et arti,
> verba dare ut caute possint, pugnare dolose,
> blanditia certare, bonum simulare virum se,
> insidias facere ut si hostes sint omnibus omnes.

Horace's line 69 *primores populi arripuit populumque tributim* seems to recall Lucilius' attacks on both the people and the senatorial class for their degenerate behaviour (*totus item pariterque ... populusque patresque*), whereas the following line (70), in which Lucilius is called *uni aequos virtuti atque eius amicis*, clearly alludes to the well-known Lucilian fragment which contains a definition of *virtus* (1326–38 M.). At 1334–6 M. Lucilius says that virtue consists also in:

> hostem esse atque inimicum hominum morumque malorum,
> contra defensorem hominum morumque bonorum,
> hos magni facere, his bene velle, his vivere amicum

The acts of criticising bad people (*mali*) and supporting good people (*boni*), whose friendship must be sought at all times, are two sides of the same coin and they are both essential elements in Lucilius' idea of social morality. Lucilius' satire, including his aggressiveness and his personal attacks, is therefore a natural fulfilment, even if negative, of his moral responsibility within the social and political environment of Rome. The positive side of Lucilius' satire is represented by the auto-

---

[53] See Mazzoli (2009) esp. 485 on the hypothetical collocation in book 1 of the two Lucilian fragments, 1228–34 M. and 1334–6 M., quoted in the text (for the attribution to book 1 of the first see also Degl'Innocenti Pierini (1990) esp. 253–5). If this hypothesis is correct, Hor. *Sat.* 2.1 has intertextual links to both opening books of Lucilius' satires: book 26, the first chronologically, which includes 590–91 (*ex praecordiis*) and 620–21 (*hunc laborem sumas*) both quoted above (for further evidence, concerning book 30, also see Fiske (1920) 370–78); and book 1, cf. Mazzoli (2009) 477–8.

biographical features of his poetry, which Horace had already idealized when referring to the old poet's books as *fidi sodales* (29–34), and which are now referenced again in lines 71–7.

In these lines Horace describes a scene from the everyday life of the Scipionic era. He praises the moral qualities of Lucilius' friends (72 *virtus Scipiadae et mitis sapientia Laeli*) by recalling their affable and intimate relationships (73–4 *nugari cum illo et discinti ludere, donec/ decoqueretur holus, soliti*). The mention of the three famous friends of the past evokes another group of friends, the so-called circle of Maecenas — who is probably to be identified with the wise Laelius. Scipio Aemilianus could be the alter ego of the young Octavian, another famous man who was adopted, and who was distinguished for his military *virtus*.[54] Horace of course finds his natural counterpart in Lucilius,[55] who is presented as his superior in financial status (*census*) and talent (*ingenium*);[56] nothing is said however about *ars*, which is usually contrasted with *ingenium* in literary contexts.[57] The reader may well be meant to conclude that Horace is superior in *ars* to an archaic poet such as Lucilius. With this important omission Horace completes the construction of his own and Lucilius' literary identities, whose evolution has been developed in the three satires examined in this paper.

Conclusions

In *Sat.* 2.1 Horace constructs himself as a second Lucilius, but this is the end of a long and complex process during which Horace shrewdly selects the characteristics of his *auctor* so as to create a literary model

---

[54] Octavian is mentioned, always as *Caesar*, in two other important passages of *Sat.* 2.1: first at 19, with reference to a celebration of his deeds by Horace himself; second at 84, in the humorous conclusion of the poem, where Horace assumes that the *princeps* values his *carmina* positively; cf. above n.36.

[55] Cf. Labate (1996) 438 "Lucilio che gioca libero e rilassato con Lelio e Scipione, aspettando che siano cotti i legumi, simboleggia per Orazio un modello di rapporto gratificante, stimolante, ma capace di non interferire con le scelte di vita e di non snaturarne i valori."

[56] Hor. *Sat.* 2.1.74–77 *quidquid sum ego, quamvis/ infra Lucilium censum ingeniumque, tamen me/ cum magnis vixisse invita fatebitur usque/ invidia.*

[57] Cf. e.g. Cic. *Q.fr.* 2.10(9).2 *Lucreti poemata, ut scribis, ita sunt, multis luminibus ingeni, multae tamen artis*; Ov. *Am.* 1.15.13–14 *Battiades semper toto cantabitur orbe:/ quamvis ingenio non valet, arte valet*; Ov. *Tr.* 2.424 *Ennius ingenio maximus, arte rudis.* In the *Ars poetica* Horace claims that a real poet must have both these qualities (408–12): *natura fieret laudabile carmen an arte,/ quaesitum est; ego nec studium sine divite vena/ nec rude quid possit video ingenium; alterius sic/ altera poscit opem res et coniurat amice.*

in his image and likeness.[58] In *Sat.* 1.4 Lucilius was a muddy predecessor. In *Sat.* 1.10 he became the inventor of the satirical genre and Horace's pioneering model. Finally in *Sat.* 2.1 Horace is in every quality, except *ars*, the new Lucilius; but the question of *ars* is no longer taken into consideration. Lucilius' aggressiveness is allusively associated with *virtus*, and it is no longer *maledicere* but moral reprimand. It has moved away from the precepts of Horace's father, but is not inconsistent with them in its methodology and aims: bad people are criticized in order to protect good people. Above all it is the autobiographical elements in Lucilius' poetry, which are mentioned only in *Sat.* 2.1, that allow Horace to present himself in his last literary satire as the new and second Lucilius. But the converse is equally true. The Lucilius of *Sat.* 2.1, who portrays intimate details of his own life, is very similar to a second Horace. Indeed, this ultimate Lucilius almost anticipates the more mature Horace who, once he has finished composing satires, will turn in his second collection of *sermones* to the more friendly form of the *Epistles*.[59]

Bibliography

Barchiesi, A. and Cucchiarelli, A. (2005). 'Satire and the Poet: the Body as Self-Referential Symbol' in K. Freudenburg (ed.) *The Cambridge Companion to Roman Satire*. Cambridge. 207–23, repr. in Italian, revised, in Freudenburg, Cucchiarelli and Barchiesi (2007) 151–66

Bellandi, F. (2007). *Lepos e pathos. Studi su Catullo*. Bologna

Brink, C.O. (1963). *Horace on Poetry. Prolegomena to the Literary Epistles*. Cambridge

Citroni, M. (1993). 'L'autobiografia nella satira e nell'epigramma latino' in G.

---

[58] According to Cucchiarelli (2001) 38–40 and 111–12, in *Sat.* 2.1 the two sides of Lucilian poetry, aggressive and autobiographical, "convivono ormai integrati: e proprio a questo Lucilio bifronte Orazio si allinea" (39); "la corrispondenza tra Lucilio e il suo successore è ora vistosa, dopo tante riserve e diversificazioni. Ha tutta l'evidenza di un punto d'approdo" (112). On the Horatian Lucilius Cucchiarelli also observes that in ancient culture the *inventor* of a tradition is often an 'invention', not without distortions and anachronisms, of those who recognize themselves in that tradition (112): "così, Orazio ha lavorato, con un gioco di luci ed ombre, a disegnare il 'suo' Lucilio."

[59] Cf. Fedeli (1994) 531: "il mutato atteggiamento nei confronti di Lucilio dipende probabilmente dal fatto che la satira introduttiva del II libro in realtà è un carme con funzioni retrospettive, che prevede già gli ulteriori sviluppi della poesia oraziana"; 532 "il poeta si sente ormai maturo per una poesia di tipo autobiografico, in cui gli attacchi saranno la logica conseguenza dell'essere stato attaccato. Sembra proprio che qui Orazio stia già pensando a ciò che saranno le *Epistole*: un *sermo*, cioè, come le satire, ma senza essere satire."

Arrighetti and F. Montanari (edd.) *La componente autobiografica nella poesia greca e latina fra realtà e artificio letterario*. Atti del Convegno, Pisa, 16–17 maggio 1991. Pisa. 275–92

Citroni Marchetti, S. (2004). 'I precetti paterni e le lezioni dei filosofi: Demea, il padre di Orazio ed altri padri e figli' *MD* 53.9–63

Courtney, E. (2013). 'The Two Books of Satires' in H.-Ch. Günther (ed.) *Brill's Companion to Horace*. Leiden-Boston. 63–168

Cucchiarelli, A. (2001). *La satira e il poeta. Orazio tra Epodi e Sermones*. Pisa

D'Anna, G. (1979). 'Due note oraziane di lettura' in *Studi di poesia latina in onore di Antonio Traglia*. vol. II. Roma. 525–52, repr. in D'Anna (2012) 59–86

— (1995). 'La polemica antiluciliana di Orazio' in M.L. Coletti and P. Domenicucci (edd.) *Musis amicus*. Atti Convegno Internazionale di Studi su Q. Orazio Flacco (Chieti, 4–6 maggio 1993). Chieti. 211–24, repr. in D'Anna (2012) 313–26

— (2005). 'La decima satira di Orazio' *Paideia* 60.95–112, repr. in D'Anna (2012) 353–70

— (2012). *Studi oraziani*. A cura di A. Taliercio. Roma

Davis, G. (2010). (ed.) *A Companion to Horace*. Malden-Oxford

De Vecchi, L. (2013). (ed.) *Orazio, Satire*. Introduzione, traduzione e commento. Roma

Degl'Innocenti Pierini, R. (1990). 'Le battaglie del foro (per l'esegesi e la collocazione dei vv. 1228 ss. M. di Lucilio)' *Maia* 52.249–55

Fedeli, P. (1994). (ed.) *Q. Orazio Flacco, Le opere II, tomo secondo, Le satire*. Commento. Roma

Fiske, G.C. (1920). *Lucilius and Horace. A Study in the Classical Theory of Imitation*. Madison

Fraenkel, E. (1957). *Horace*. Oxford

Freudenburg, K. (1990). 'Horace's Satiric Program and the Language of Contemporary Theory in Satires 2.1' *AJPh* 111.187–203

— (1993). *The Walking Muse. Horace on the Theory of Satire*. Princeton

— (2001). *Satires of Rome. Threatening Poses from Lucilius to Juvenal*. Cambridge

— (2009). (ed.) *Oxford Readings in Classical Studies. Horace: Satires and Epistles*. Oxford

— (2010). '*Horatius Anceps*: Persona and Self-Revelation in Satire and Song' in Davis (2010) 271–90

Freudenburg, K., Cucchiarelli, A., and Barchiesi, A. (2007). (edd.) *Musa pedestre. Storia e interpretazione della satira in Roma antica*. Roma

Gowers, E. (2003). 'Fragments of Autobiography in Horace Satires 1' *CA* 22.55–91

— (2012). (ed.) *Horace, Satires Book I*. Cambridge

Harrison, G. (1987). 'The Confessions of Lucilius (Horace *Sat*. 2.1.30–34): A Defense of Autobiographical Satire?' *CA* 6.38–52

Klingner, F. (1959). (ed.) *Q. Horati Flacci opera*. 3rd edn. Leipzig

Labate, M. (1992). 'Le necessità del poeta satirico: fisiopatologia di una scelta letteraria' in I. Mazzini (ed.) *Civiltà materiale e letteratura nel mondo antico*. Macerata. 55–66

— (1996). 'Il sermo oraziano e i generi letterari' in H. Krasser and E.A. Schmidt (edd.) *Zeitgenosse Horaz. Der Dichter und seine Leser seit zwei Jahrtausenden*. Tübingen. 424–41, repr. in English in Freudenburg (2009) 102–21

— (2012). 'La satira e i suoi bersagli: dallo spazio della *civitas* allo spazio della corte' in M. Citroni (ed.) *Letteratura e civitas. Transizioni dalla Repubblica all'Impero. In ricordo di E. Narducci*. Pisa. 269–93

LaFleur, R.A. (1981). 'Horace and *Onomasti Komodein*: The Law of Satire' *ANRW* II 31.3.1790–1826

Mazzoli, G. (1995). 'Italicità oraziana' in A. Setaioli (ed.) *Orazio: umanità, politica, cultura*. Atti del Convegno, Gubbio, 20–22 ottobre 1992. Perugia. 7–22

— (2009). 'Fra diritto e poesia. I primi due libri delle Satire di Lucilio' in B. Santalucia (ed.) *La repressione criminale nella Roma repubblicana fra norma e persuasione*. Collegio di Diritto Romano 2007 Cedant. Pavia. 475–92

Muecke, F. (1995). 'Law, Rhetoric, and Genre in Horace, Satires 2. 1' in S.J. Harrison (ed.) *Homage to Horace. A Bimillenary Celebration*. Oxford. 203–18

— (2007). 'The *Satires*' in S. Harrison (ed.) *The Cambridge Companion to Horace*. Cambridge. 105–20

Rudd, N. (1966). *The Satires of Horace*. Cambridge

Schlegel, C. (2000). 'Horace and his Fathers: Satires 1.4 and 1.6' *AJPh* 121.93–119, repr. in C. Schlegel (2006) (ed) *Satire and the Threat of Speech. Horace's Satires, Book 1*. Wisconsin. 38–58

— (2010). 'Horace and the Satirist's Mask: Shadowboxing with Lucilius' in Davis (2010) 253–70

Scodel, R. (1987). 'Horace, Lucilius, and Callimachean polemic' *HSPh* 91.199–215, repr. in Freudenburg (2009) 212–30

Tatum, W.J. (1998). '*Ultra legem*: Law and Literature in Horace, *Satires* II 1' *Mnemosyne* 51.688–99, repr. in Freudenburg (2009) 231–42

The Elder Pliny

Taxonomic Organization in Pliny's *Natural History*

Eugenia Lao

The *Natural History* belongs to a group of texts whose compilatory manner of construction, knowledge-bearing status, and informative function make study of its organization a task of critical importance. These works, produced during the imperial era, have recently received the moniker 'knowledge-ordering texts', a term that aptly focuses attention on their essential and distinctive quality: a relationship to knowledge defined by an effort to collect and organize it.[1] Because it is upon the selection and arrangement of received knowledge that authors of such texts concentrate their energies and exercise their creativity, a critical approach oriented toward examining that very element of choice and juxtaposition would be more historically sensitive than criticism aimed at evaluating originality of content.[2] Organization is the point of works like the *Natural History*, and thus should provide the frame for discussing the character of their intellectual contribution.

The collection of essays first brought together to approach these works as knowledge-ordering texts represents an interesting new body of scholarship that has variously illuminated the relations between textual organization and cultural practice.[3] Separately from this scholarship, largely preceding it and developing over a longer period of time, is the research that has been done on organization in the *Natural History* itself, which bears a brief summary. Since the modern resurgence of interest in the elder Pliny in the latter part of the twentieth century,[4]

---

[1] The idea of isolating such a group of texts for special study, and of using the compilation and organization of knowledge as a primary criterion, is first established in König and Whitmarsh (2007). The phrase 'knowledge-ordering' (and 'knowledge-ordering texts') is used throughout the introduction, 3–39. For a similar view emphasizing only the idea of collection cf. Morgan (2011) 49–54.

[2] On the opportunities for innovation in the "arts of editing" and organization and their intellectual seriousness in antiquity, and on the misapplication of modern (Romantic) intellectual values to these texts, cf. König and Whitmarsh (2007) 9, 28–30.

[3] See esp. the essays in Part II of König and Whitmarsh (2007) 43–174.

[4] Visible especially through international conferences held in Italy, England, and France in the late 1970s and 80s: cf. Carey (2003) 11.

nearly ten pieces have accreted on the subject, numerically modest by
absolute standards but comprising a respectable proportion of Plinian
scholarship.[5] These studies are characterized by their brevity — none
exceeds the length of an article or a book chapter — and by their disparateness. Their short length probably has to do with the fact that
study of organization is not usually conducted as an end in itself, but
rather to serve another interpretive aim (this is especially true of the
more recent pieces, which are embedded within monographs). As for
their disparateness, a key influencing factor is that the arc of growth in
Plinian research since the beginning of its modern resurgence has been
rather long. It was not until very recently that we can discern the scholarship beginning to congeal around some common themes and problems.[6] It is perhaps to be expected that a subfield within a field that has
itself had trouble sustaining a coherent discourse will reflect the fragmentary nature of its context. Our current state of knowledge on Plinian
organization, then, is best summed up as one characterized more by
breadth than depth.

Despite the variety of observations and conclusions on offer, we do
find a recurring interest in using analysis of organization to elucidate
Plinian thought. This is in general a welcome enterprise, as it is a
natural telos in the study of any knowledge-bearing work to understand
its intellectual character. However, the view has been advanced that it
is not possible to derive from the text a coherent picture of the author as
an individual thinker. Trevor Murphy, citing the very compilatory features that scholars of knowledge-ordering texts emphasize, as well as
external evidence of Pliny's reliance on amanuenses and the presence
of numerous factual inconsistencies, expresses skepticism on the
matter. If a coherent thought or mentality is to be found in the work,
Murphy prefers to locate it not in the person of the author himself but
in the culture in which Pliny was implicated.[7]

It is notable that Murphy is reacting to a particular way of approaching the study of Plinian thought, and that is one that conceives of

---

[5] Della Corte (1982); Locher (1986); Conte (1994); Naas (2002) 171–234; Carey (2003)
    17–40; Murphy (2004) 29–48; Doody (2010) 25–30; Henderson (2011); Laehn (2013)
    6–31. My count deliberately leaves out discussions of organization and structure that
    are either too succinct or incidentally presented to be considered a dedicated study of
    the topic, as well as local analyses of sections or individual books, but the rest of this
    article will cite some of these other studies at various points.
[6] Notably, the work's relationship to Roman imperialism: cf. esp. Carey (2003) and
    Murphy (2004); Naas (2002) incorporates themes of Flavianism and imperialism in
    her far-reaching work. Doody (2010) 59–91 places imperialist readings within the long
    history of the politicization of encyclopedias. Reception is another emerging field: cf.
    e.g. Borst (1994); Doody (2010); Maraglino (2012); and McHam (2013).
[7] Murphy (2004) 8–11.

and seeks to explicate thought as a coherent body of ideas and beliefs.[8] This is an important question that would benefit from evolution in further discussion and debate, but which this article will leave aside. Let me, instead, make note of an alternative approach to thought that has arisen in classical studies and other humanistic disciplines, the cognitive approach, which has focused (among other things) on understanding the workings of mind as it is engaged in the production and reception of creative media.[9] A reorientation along these lines offers a profitable way to proceed on the valuable endeavor of relating the *Natural History*'s organization to thought. Because, as noted earlier, it was the arrangement (and selection) of material in such works that bore weight with the ancient reading and writing community, it makes sense for modern scholarship to decentralize idea-based approaches to understanding the *Natural History*'s contemporary significance as an intellectual product.[10] This is not to say that we should exclude the utility of idea-based discussions of Plinian thought (*pace* Murphy), but rather that we take better account of the ancient readership's manner of valorizing the text than we have thus far.

Further, if organization was where Pliny concentrated much of his intellectual effort, then it pays to try to unpack that process. Apart from the practical question of whether he relied on notecards, slaves, or his memory to sort information, at a basic cognitive level the task of organization involved Pliny in apprehending categories, identifying discontinuities among them, analyzing their relationships, configuring them in a logical structure, and so on. These mental operations are actions which I view as rooted in and shaped by the particulars of an individual's physical environment, society, and culture.

---

[8] Murphy (2004) 8 cites the major studies by Beagon (1992) and Citroni Marchetti (1991). Laehn (2013) has subsequently sought to explicate Pliny's political philosophical thought with the goal of "restoring his reputation as one of the greatest thinkers of his time" (5), but makes no mention of Murphy's arguments.

[9] In classical scholarship, cf. e.g. Small (1997); Bakker (1997); Minchin (2001) (whose introduction 1–31 cites extensively the work done outside of classics, much of it from the scientific perspective); Bonifazi, Drummen and de Kreij (forthcoming).

[10] Cf. the prefatory trope found in numerous compilatory and miscellanistic works commenting on the exercise of judicious selection (*memoratu digna* or equivalent) and order of material in their work (often in the form of a disingenuous claim that the material has not been consciously arranged): *inter alios* Sen. *Con.* 1.praef.4; V. Max. 1.praef.1; Plin. *NH* praef.17; Plin. *Ep.* 1.1; Gel. *AN* praef.1–17; Ath. *Deip.* 1b; also Ael. *NA* epilogue. The elder Pliny's (in)famous remark, reported by his nephew in *Ep.* 3.5.10, that "no book was so bad that one could not profit from some part of it" (*nullum esse librum tam malum ut non aliqua parte prodesset*), in the context of an account of his working methods of excerption, suggests a programmatic boast on the art of selection. It is interesting that one of Pliny's earliest readers, Aulus Gellius, chooses to take issue with Pliny's authorial choices: *AN* 10.12.17.

This brings me to my last point. Approaching thought as a culturally-shaped cognitive process brings Plinian criticism in closer dialogue with the growing field of scholarship on knowledge-ordering texts, whose emphasis on the interrelations of text and cultural practice gives a more enriched view of the ancient author as agent. Scholarly production is not seen as occurring within a hermetically sealed world of mind but rather is treated as part of embodied experience. The assumption of the author's embeddedness within a shared culture also means that recognition of the author's independence is tempered by a perspective that sees him as similar to others in his society. Thus conversations about what is Plinian may be less constrained by the need to identify uniqueness, by turning attention to those characteristics expressed in the text that are representative.

Taking the approach and methodology I have outlined above, this article will build on current scholarship on the *Natural History*'s organization in two ways. The main part of the article will show how a predominant mode of analysis has produced descriptions of the text that reveal a recurrent inattention to a conceptually significant issue: a kind of hierarchical organization that is not only an artificial structuring tool but also a reflexive feature of human cognition. Representational errors in one descriptive model exemplify the issues particularly well. After presenting my own analysis of the text in a manner that incorporates and emphasizes the overlooked structure, I will then use that analysis as a springboard for exploring some ways in which we might approach Plinian organizational thinking.

I hope it will become apparent from my discussion that I regard the task of analyzing the *Natural History*'s organization, to a degree that better complements the work's vast complexity, as one that requires much more space than the compass of a single article. In view of this I present my analysis and interpretations — some of which will be speculative in nature — as preliminary to future studies. In addition, this article is intended to compensate for the absence of a consistent dialogue among studies of the *Natural History*'s organization, which as I mentioned earlier may have produced a certain lack of cohesion. I will therefore preface my analysis with a detailed survey and discussion of the scholarship, so that the reader will have a context for my work. This survey will make up Part I; my contribution will follow it in Part II.

Part I: Critical Divergences

When one speaks of a work's organization the sense that typically springs first to mind is the way in which material in a text is arranged. This is the sense, for example, used in knowledge-ordering scholarship. For a work like the *Natural History*, which presents itself as continuous and thematically unified in a way that the miscellanistic *Attic Nights* or *Sympotic Questions* do not, speaking of organization in this sense amounts to speaking of the work's structure. The scholarship on organization in Pliny is so divergent, however, that even this definition is not something we can take for granted. Further, even after we isolate those scholars who interest themselves primarily in the work's structure or arrangement of material, we find among them differing methods of analysis. While from one perspective the differing approaches have left us still at the surface of practical knowledge about the *Natural History*'s organization, from another they have laid foundations for a number of theoretical and methodological issues that would benefit from synthesis. With this goal in mind, let us look at the differences.

The Semantics of Organization

The ambiguity of the word 'organization' in the Plinian critical lexicon arises from the fact that the work, in claiming the totality of nature as its theme, covers an epistemological domain coextensive with ancient natural philosophy. The intellectual weight of Pliny's chosen subject matter makes it both possible and desirable for scholars to extend their study of organization so that it includes explication of logical structures found in the text, from which may be derived a description of some rational system of thought. It is also possible for studies of organization in Pliny not to be at all concerned with discussing structures of thought — for the study of organization to be a straightforward, elementary exercise in describing the text's surface appearance. But for those who have wished to penetrate to thought, explication has assumed one of two forms: scholars have either used the arrangement of material in the text to reconstruct the character of its dominant rational system, or they have, without regard for the explicit arrangement of material, but focusing instead on implicit meanings carried by concepts deemed significant, discussed the epistemological frame that organizes the general thinking expressed in the text. The one approach results in a structural analysis of the text that is seen as *reflecting* the structure of (ancient) thought. The other produces no analysis of textual structure, because its focus is on discussing the cognitive structures underlying the work's expository content.

The three scholars responsible for giving us these two alternative approaches are Gian Biagio Conte, Francesco Della Corte, and Trevor Murphy.[11] Della Corte and Murphy are the ones who concern themselves with the text's structure; although Conte does address the arrangement of material at the end of his now-classic piece, he does so only in a curtailed section that does not form the main part of his discussion.[12]

Despite commonality of approach, Della Corte and Murphy take their analyses in profoundly divergent directions. For Della Corte the work's large-scale structure reflects the organizing influence of Greek natural philosophy, of which Pliny combines different strands. The first book of cosmology, largely founded on the pre-Socratic theory of elements that views the universe as composed of fire, air, earth, and water, sets up in Della Corte's view the expectation that Pliny would follow through by dividing the rest of his text into four parts. But instead the Aristotelian *scala naturae* underlies the tripartite division of most of the remaining text, which proceeds in sequence through the animal, vegetable, and mineral kingdoms.[13] Della Corte, however, is very much aware of departures from the philosophical principle, and indeed spends much of his article discussing the exceptions. Important to note in this connection is the block formed by Books 20–32, represented as a free-standing group in the diagram that accompanies his article, which interrupts the linearity of Pliny's exposition.[14] Otherwise most of the exceptions to the philosophical rule are observed in small-scale sequences formed by individual items.[15]

For Murphy, the text's structure reveals something even more essential than the influence of Greek philosophical thought. Analogical thinking, a basic reasoning structure of the human mind, is in his view the key to understanding the *Natural History*'s organization. A style of thinking that depends on the simultaneous perception of similarity and dissimilarity, analogical thinking enables the formation of categories and the act of classification, which constructs rules of inclusion or exclusion based on perceiving and comparing attributes. Murphy holds that the *Natural History* can be understood as continually establishing categories and then destabilizing them, in response to the competing claims of two kinds of analogical thinking: antithesis, which fore-

---

[11] For full citations see n.5.
[12] Conte (1994) 100–4 (with about 33 pages of text preceding this part).
[13] Della Corte (1982) 21, 25; cf. Beagon (2005) 20–1.
[14] Della Corte (1982) 25–6. His diagram is reproduced on p.229 below as Figure 1.
[15] Cf. esp. Della Corte (1982), 27–8, 32–4, 39.

grounds dissimilarity, and metaphor, which foregrounds similarity.[16] In practical terms Murphy seems to suggest that antithesis is an organizational principle that operates more strongly when one views the text in larger blocks: we can divide the work, he argues, into the oppositions of heaven/earth, treated in Books 2 and 3–6 respectively, and animate/inanimate: humans and animals, treated in Books 7–11, represent the animate, while plants and minerals, treated in 12–19 and 33–7 respectively, represent the inanimate; Books 20–32, on medicines derived first from plants, then animals, also juxtapose inanimate with animate.[17] But when one descends to the level of individual items, the disruptive effects of the "playful metaphor", which "posits correspondences between different categories", exert a more noticeable influence, and can explain what might appear to be a random or illogical sequencing of topics.[18]

One interesting point of similarity between Della Corte and Murphy is that both perceive an organizational tension between larger and smaller scales, where a logical principle followed at the larger scale is abandoned, if not overturned, at the smaller.[19] This tension or inconsistency is one of the features that promotes an impression of the text as random or unpredictable. Whether or not the text is as random as it has appeared is a matter I will take up at the end of the article; for now, let us simply continue to pursue the distinction between these two scholars and Conte. Conte, from a certain perspective, bridges Della Corte and Murphy's work in that he touches on how both ancient philosophy and analogical thinking function as organizing principles in the *Natural History*. His main object, however, is not to illustrate how these modes of thought can be traced through the text's arrangement of material, but to explain how they underlie and inform Pliny's manner of framing nature.[20] For this explanation Conte focuses on the pervasiveness of anthropocentric thought, an analogical mode of thinking that uses man as the paradigm against which external reality is figured, and which has been traditionally cited as a major difference between ancient and modern conceptualizations of nature.[21] Insofar as the piece deals with

---

[16] Murphy (2004) 29–32, 36–48.
[17] Murphy (2004) 29–30, 41–2.
[18] Murphy (2004) 45.
[19] Della Corte (1982) 25–6: "Benché nelle strutture portanti della «Storia naturale» si riconosca un disegno illuminato, un *instructus ordo* (XXIX 59), quando poi si scende ad esaminare più da vicino il contenuto dei singoli libri, ci si avvede che un certo disordine ... confonde la linearità dell'esposizione". Cf. Murphy (2004) 44: "In fact, failure to proceed according to set principles is a general characteristic of the *Natural History*".
[20] Conte (1994) 76–100.
[21] For concrete examples of analogical thinking cf. esp. 78–9, 92–4; on the distinction

organization in the *Natural History*, it does so primarily through attention to its organization of the world.[22]

Conte's discussion of the philosophical sources behind Pliny's representation of nature has now received a fuller treatment by Beagon,[23] but his unusual manner of approaching the subject as a matter of cognitive organization is worth dwelling on for a moment. Because in his brief and dense survey of ancient natural philosophical thought Conte finds occasion, every now and then, to use modern science as a contrasting point of reference, one of the piece's main rhetorical effects (if subsidiary point) is to underscore the disjunction between ancient and modern conceptualizations of nature.[24] This disjunction, I submit, is instructive to keep in mind when undertaking the sibling tasks of explaining the text's structure and elucidating the thought behind it. When analyzing structure, it is necessary to identify the key concepts that the text arranges in a sequence, and convenient to translate those concepts into the modern scholar's native language. Since, however, the two languages give expression to non-equivalent modes of thought (particularly two so far separated from each other as ancient and modern), sometimes the act of translating apparently equivalent concepts in fact effects transformations in their implicit framing that can affect our perception of their logical relationship to other concepts, and thereby impact our analysis of structure. In other words, it is important that we be aware of framing disjunctions as an issue that imposes on the act of translation itself, particularly when translation accompanies the process of describing an alien system of thought.

Consider, for example, Murphy's argument that a sequence of antitheses organizes the work's largest categories, so that the oppositions of heaven and earth are first dealt with, followed by the animate humans and animals vs. the inanimate plants and minerals. The idea of heaven and earth as opposites is perhaps influenced by a folk directional perspective (down vs. up) that is easy enough for us to countenance, as is the idea that animal life possesses a special quality of

---

between ancient and modern science cf. 82–3, 97.

[22] The distinction between organization construed as textual arrangement and organization seen as a perspectival frame is one that Conte himself makes, just before he concludes his piece with an abbreviated discussion of the work's structure (100): "In short, at least two organizational lines coordinated with one another run through the text of the *Naturalis historia:* one articulates it (implicitly) according to 'mental' connections like the teleology mentioned above or a certain symbolic anthropocentric thought, while the other (explicitly) fashions the external order of the material treated".

[23] Beagon (1992).

[24] Cf. in addition to the pages cited in n.22, comments on 90, 95, 97, 98.

vitality and mobility not shared by its two biological counterparts.[25] But are these the attributes that Pliny emphasizes?

Pliny's conceptualization of the heavens and earth is based on the philosophical model of the two-sphere universe, where external reality is viewed as an enclosed space in which the terrestrial sphere is suspended at the center of the celestial sphere.[26] Following the tradition of cosmographic and geographic texts, it is the peculiar method of the *Natural History*'s first five books (Books 2–6) to describe visually where celestial bodies and geographical landmarks are physically located in relation to each other. A spatial logic governs all these books, so that in Book 2 the exposition proceeds, step-by-step, from the fixed stars, stamped on the firmament and located at the farthest point from earth (7), to the region of space occupied by the planets (32–101), to the sublunary region (102–53), until finally it reaches the earth itself (154–248). The maritime perspective of the *periplus* then structures the subsequent description of earth in Books 3–6.[27] In view of the graphical orientation of these books and the concentric imagery underlying Pliny's discussion of heavens and earth, the dominant impression left by Pliny's presentation of these concepts is not a relationship of antithesis, but rather one defined (among other things) by morphological likeness, a difference in magnitude, and a nested configuration.

As for whether or not the quality of animation distinguishes humans and animals from plants and minerals, the proems to Books 7 and 12 provide some clarification. At the beginning of Book 7, Pliny announces his intention to treat a large category of entities, which he calls *animantia*, defined by the attribute of vitality (7.1): "the nature of living beings that dwell in this same [universe] is worthy of no less contemplation than practically any other part, even if here too the human mind is incapable of pursuing the subject in its entirety" (*animantium in eodem natura nullius prope partis contemplatione minore, etsi ne hic quidem omnia exsequi humanus animus queat*).[28] Subsequently Pliny introduces the immediate subject of Book 7, human beings, and then proceeds to compare them unfavorably to *animalia* as well as *animantia*, alternating between the two categories. For the most part Pliny's usage suggests that *animantia* is synonymous with

---

[25] Cf. *OED* online s.v. animate, adj. and n.: "A. *adj.* 1. Endowed with life, living, alive; (esp. in later use) alive and having the power of movement, like an animal".

[26] Cf. the ps-Arist. περὶ κόσμου; Della Corte (1982) 21.

[27] Murphy (2004) 135, with further bibliography.

[28] All translations of Pliny are my own; quotations are drawn from Mayhoff's 1892–1909 Teubner edition.

animalia: for example, he writes that humans alone of *animantia* are given to grief (*uni animantium luctus est datus*, 7.5), or that unlike other *animantia* humans cannot live peaceably with their own kind (*denique cetera animantia in suo genere probe degunt*, 7.5).

In one significant instance, however, Pliny uses *animantia* in a way that indicates that he does not regard the category as confined to animals. Excoriating humans for being the only one of all *animantia* to lack their own protective covering, Pliny enumerates a long list of animal attributes — shells, hides, spines, fur, bristles, hair, down, feathers, scales, fleeces — but concludes by adducing the protective covering of trees (7.2): "even tree-trunks [nature] has safeguarded from frost and heat with bark, sometimes a double layer" (*truncos etiam arboresque cortice, interdum gemino, a frigoribus et calore tutata est*).[29] From this remark it appears that for Pliny, *animantia* is a category that includes plants.

The proem to Book 12 provides further support for this view. Having completed his discussion of animals in the preceding five books, Pliny again turns to announce a new subject:

> animalium omnium quae nosci potuere naturae generatim membratimque ita se habent. restat ut neque ipsa anima carentia — quandoquidem nihil sine ea vivit —, terra edita, et inde eruta, dicantur ac nullum sileatur rerum naturae opus.

> All animals' natures possible to know, considered kind by kind and limb by limb, are as I describe. This is what remains: to discuss the very items that also do not lack the soul (seeing that nothing lives without it), the products of earth, and then after that the things dug up from it, and for no work of nature to be passed over in silence.
>
> *NH* 12.1.1

Although Pliny's circumlocutions are striking, it is clear that he is here announcing a partition that extends over the rest of the whole work: he will first treat of plants, what he calls "the products of earth" (*terra edita*), and then of minerals, "the things dug up from it" (*terra eruta*). With some rhetorical effort Pliny makes a point of characterizing plants as an entity distinguished by the possession of *anima* — of accommodating them within the category of *animantia*. Why Pliny should make such a particular point of associating plants with life is a matter I will postpone for later discussion; for the present I only wish to note that in

---

[29] Early on in his list he includes *cortices*, typically used of tree-bark, but applicable to animal covering as well, such as shells: *OLD*² s.v. *cortex* 3b. The usage here is ambiguous, but in view of the fact that Pliny concludes by naming trees explicitly, perhaps it is better to interpret *cortices* as a general animal-covering reference, which would make it consistent with the others in the list.

associating plants more closely with animals than with minerals, Pliny is expressing a view similar to the younger Seneca's,[30] and is in fact consistent with Aristotelian theory.[31]

Murphy, then, is right that a polarity ultimately structures the categories of animals, plants, and minerals in the *Natural History*, but his line of division should be shifted to the right so that it divides animals and plants from minerals, rather than dividing animals from plants and minerals. Moreover, I would contest that Pliny conceives of these divisions in terms of stark antithesis. Pliny's use of *animantia* in Book 7, as largely synonymous with *animalia* except for one instance, when he includes trees as if as an afterthought, suggests that he views the category of *animantia* as most typically or perfectly exemplified by animals. The trouble he takes in Book 12 to describe plants as also possessing *anima* is another sign that he thinks of plants as less perfect examples of *animantia* — much in the way we might name bears as mammals before we do anteaters. Rather than viewing animals, plants, and minerals in terms of black and white, Pliny seems to approach them as placed along a continuum, with the quality of vitality in nature existing more in shades of gray.[32]

The above discussion forms just one example of how I see it possible for the act of translation itself to exaggerate immanent differences between ancient and modern conceptualizations of analogous natural categories, and for those differences to impact our analysis of the text's structural relationships.[33] The work that Conte did to defamiliarize the modern scholar's stance toward the natural world has a role to play in the practical criticism of Pliny, both with regard to our immediate concern of describing textual organization, but also beyond. As fraught as the act of translation can be, however, when dealing with the cognitive implications of naming natural categories, I do not mean to suggest that we should avoid using modern terms to refer to relevant portions of the text. Particularly in the case of concepts lexicalized in our language but expressed in the form of descriptive phrases in the *Natural History* (as

---

[30] Sen. 58.10: "But certain things have soul and are not animals. For it is generally accepted that the soul exists within trees too" (*sed quaedam animam habent nec sunt animalia. placet enim satis et arbustis animam inesse*).

[31] For discussion of plants as possessing the quality of life also cf. *HA* 8.1 588b6–11; *PA* 2.10 655b33–4, 4.10 687a4–5; *GA* 2.3 732a13.

[32] In this respect too he is consistent with Aristotle's view of the *scala naturae* as a continuum: cf. *HA* 8.1 588b4–6; *PA* 4.5 681a10–15.

[33] Related to this issue is the scholarly tendency to anachronistically translate or reframe the work's major subjects in terms of the modern scientific disciplines, e.g. by labelling Book 7 on man as Pliny's 'anthropology', Books 8–11 as the books of 'zoology', and so on. Cf. e.g. the Italian translation edited by Conte, Barchiesi and Ranucci (1982–1988); Isager (1991) 48; Naas (2002) 196.

we have just seen with 'plants' and 'minerals'), there is a matter of convenience to consider. My point, rather, is merely that the endeavor of representing the character of ancient thought obliges us to be vigilant about misalignments between ancient and modern methods of framing the natural world, and to try to foreground in such instances the attributes implied in the Latin.

Methods of Segmentation

Now that we have sorted out the different constructions that have been placed on the task of studying organization in Pliny, let us confine our survey to the method, by far the more common, that concerns itself with the arrangement of material in the text. Here we find yet another divergence, for the scholarship has so far applied two methods of segmenting the text. One method involves putting parts of the text into different discursive categories, as by distinguishing passages of anecdotes from passages that impart factual information, or digressive passages from the main exposition. An analogy is the kind of narrative analysis applied to epic that has furnished our critical vocabulary with terms such as ekphrasis, type scene, simile, and so on. The other method simply follows the sequence of topics presented in the text — let us call this the 'topical' approach. Because this latter method blocks the text off in an array of segments that correspond to the units successively articulated by Pliny in his partitioning statements, it yields a better description of the mental picture that would have been imagined by Pliny and readers who read the text linearly.

For obvious reasons the second method has been the predominant approach; the discursive method has formed the centerpiece of only one analysis thus far, by A. Locher.[34] Locher argues that it is possible to break the exposition down into discrete sections distinguished by "type of information", namely straight facts, historical anecdotes, and eyewitness accounts, and also into distinct "philosophical and moral considerations".[35] The types of information, Locher claims, correspond to the *res* (or *medicinae*), *historiae*, and *observationes* that Pliny himself identifies and scrupulously tallies up in his summarium, and provide

---

[34] For full citation cf. n.5. One may also put in this category Sconocchia (1987), an article which observes that the *Natural History* has a tripartite structure composed of prefatory epistle, index, and main text. However, despite his title, Sconocchia is in fact not interested in analyzing the *Natural History*'s structure *per se*, but rather in using this format to argue for the existence of a distinctive category of Latin technical and encyclopedic writing from antiquity to the Middle Ages: hence his work cannot truly be counted a study of organization. Murphy (2004) 30–2, 37–8 on digressive passages incorporates elements of the discursive method.

[35] Locher (1986) 24.

indirect testimony for Pliny's system of working from notecards.[36]

I mention Locher and his minority approach not to evaluate his results, but rather to point out the potential of his method to emphasize structural aspects of the *Natural History* that have been less explored by the topical approach. In this area, too, a synthesis in methodologies can benefit our understanding of Plinian organization. Because it is the purpose of the topical approach to trace, from beginning to end, the exposition's progress from one subject to the next, the method tends to stress a linear perspective, especially when the text is considered macroscopically. But when one's purpose is to search for occurrences of a limited number of pre-defined discursive categories (in Locher's case, four), one's attention is naturally drawn to the fact of recurrences, and with it, to recurrent patterns in positioning.

The most obvious pattern formed by the recurrent appearance of topics in the work is a chiastic or circular pattern formed at the macroscopic level by its central books.[37] It is usual, when describing the work's overall structure, to list the topics in a linear sequence. Below are three typical descriptions which are largely in agreement with one another; I reproduce book numbers where originally given:[38]

NAAS[39]

II:	cosmologie
III–VI:	géographie
VII:	anthropologie
VIII–XI:	zoologie
XII–XIX:	botanique
XX–XXVII:	médicine végétale
XXVIII–XXXII:	médicine animale
XXXIII–XXXVII:	minéralogie

---

[36] Locher (1986) 23–8. I follow Doody (2001) 2 in preferring the term 'summarium' over alternatives such as 'index' or 'table of contents'.

[37] Incidentally mentioned by Della Corte (1982) 25; Naas (2002) 197; but for Henderson (2011) 144, 151–71 and Laehn (2013) 6–31 this structure forms the basis for interpretation.

[38] A diagram provided by Della Corte is another major structural model, but because his analysis is more complicated, I postpone it for later discussion (pp.228–31 below).

[39] Naas (2002) 209–10.

	MURPHY[40]	**DOODY**[41]
2	heavens	heavens
3–6	earth/geography	lands and seas of Earth
7–11	humans and animals	man and other animals
12–19	plants	plants
20–32	medicines from plants	uses of animals and plants
	and animals	in medicine
33–7	metals and minerals	rocks and minerals

We can see from these summaries that the recurrent treatment of plants and animals, in reverse order, in the form of medicines made from them, is universally recognized as occurring in Books 20–27 and 28–32 (or 20–32, if all medicines are taken together as a single group).[42] However, the recurrence has not until recently been made much of.[43] Here is an alternative format that maintains emphasis on the linear experience of following the exposition from beginning to end while at the same time bringing the work's circularity (and symmetry) more to the foreground:

Books 2–6	**7–11**	**12–19**	**20–7**	**28–32**	**33–7**
graphically-based	animals	plants	plants	animals	minerals
discussion of two-			(medicines	from)	
sphere universe					
5 books	**5 books**	**8 books**	**8 books**	**5 books**	**5 books**[44]

I have, purely for illustrative purposes and the sake of brevity, only listed the recurrence of topics here at the very largest level, but as one can imagine, Pliny retreads subject matter in the central books at smaller levels as well — sometimes in sequences that recapitulate, in intriguingly imperfect ways, the original order.[45]

In addition to the chiastic or circular patterning of topics that attention to recurrences can bring out, a better sense of the recurrent *posi-*

---

[40] Murphy (2004) 30.

[41] Doody (2010) 27.

[42] Notable is the different structuration given by the Italian translation edited by Conte, Barchiesi and Ranucci (1982-1988). Instead of dividing the middle books between 12–19 and 20–32, this edition groups 12–19 and 20–27 together under the single header "botanica"; and labels only 28–32 "medicina e farmacologia".

[43] Henderson (2011) 154–65; Laehn (2013) 10.

[44] Cf. Henderson (2011) 153–4. Laehn (2013) 10 counts the books as I do, but additionally sees a perfect symmetry of content, analyzing Books 2–6 and 33–7 as both about "inanimate matter"; I do not agree with him on this point. Naas (2002) 197 notes only the thematic symmetry of the plant and animal books, and the numerical symmetry of the plant books.

[45] In Books 28–32 for example, the topics of man, land animals, aquatic animals, birds, and insects are recapitulated in the original sequence except for aquatic animals, which is postponed to the end. A more detailed study of sequence recapitulation in the central mirroring books of the *Natural History*, especially in Books 19 and 20, is in progress.

tioning of repeated textual phenomena can also bring some balance to current descriptions of the *Natural History*'s organization. Valérie Naas has already explored the question to good effect: finding that there is a higher concentration of lengthy book introductions and conclusions in the second half of the work, she argues that the increased density reflects Pliny's increasing concern with stressing the essentials of his thought and approach.[46] Along these lines there remains much to be explored on the question of Pliny's ordering schemes, applied at subordinate levels in the text and widely regarded as remarkably multifarious. As a natural by-product of its pursuit of other interests, the scholarship has seldom done more than identify an illustrative selection, naming for example schemes based on magnitude, merit, utility, price, number, degree of foreignness, time and chronology, and the alphabet.[47] There is evidence, however, that Pliny has a habit of reprising certain schemes at certain junctures — the tendency of alphabetical lists to be relegated to final or quasi-final position comes to mind as one example.[48] A more intensive examination of when and how often Pliny repeats his small-scale methods of organization may well turn up patterns that complement or corroborate the sense of orderly design intimated by the symmetrical ring-pattern evident at the large scale.

Balance, I wish to stress, is ultimately the goal best served by greater attention to recurrences and the patterns formed by them, not an attempt to turn the critical tide so that we replace the prevailing rhetoric of unpredictability with one that asserts the opposite extreme. Cultural context, as it has been pointed out, gave Pliny incentive to incorporate erratic elements into his text: not only the general aesthetic of variety cultivated in the early imperial era,[49] but also the practices of intellectual life, which featured as a central component a type of learned convivial conversation in which participants juxtaposed capsule knowledge in playful and unexpected ways.[50] But too much stress on the text's mutability can be heuristically limiting, because it makes it harder to imagine and explain the cognitive processes involved, on the author's side, in managing information with the discipline that is manifestly on

---

[46] Naas (2002) 224.

[47] Della Corte (1982) 27 and *passim*; Naas (2002) 199; Doody (2010) 27.

[48] Cf. e.g. *NH* 27 (the last book devoted to botanic medicine); 32.145–52 (the end of the last book devoted to animal medicine and the whole section on medicines); 37.138 (near the end of gemstones and the entire work).

[49] On the aesthetics of intricacy in the *Natural History* cf. Murphy (2004) 38–40; Doody (2010) 25–30 for the entertainment value of *variatio*.

[50] On the use of textual forms of "morselized" knowledge such as the anecdote for oral reperformance cf. Goldhill (2009); in sympotic contexts 109–110.

display, and on the reader's, in retaining and retrieving from memory information found in the text. Although the inclusion of a so-called index may seem to have obviated the need to rely on memory, doubt has been plausibly cast on its functionality as a search tool,[51] and memory was still unquestionably the predominant mode of retrieval in that era. Thus by looking more deeply into the matter of recurrences, we may form a better picture of how the text was structurally predictable, and thereby gain some insight into Plinian organizational thinking, as well as how the work internally facilitated its self-proclaimed ambition of utility.

Part II: Taxonomic Structure and its Cognitive Implications

I have structured the first part of this article to take us in two steps from a wider to a narrower understanding of what it has meant to study organization in the *Natural History*, using minority approaches along the way to suggest methods by which the dominant approach could bolster and develop its findings. To be clear, my main interest in Plinian organization lies in the work's arrangement of its topics of discussion, what we commonly (but not inevitably, it appears) mean when we refer to the structure of a work.

Focusing now just on the work's arrangement of topics, let me begin by making note of one matter on which it is vital to achieve clarity, as it can have — and indeed already has had, as I will detail — profound impact on different levels of analysis, from the way we describe and assess the work's structure to the conclusions we draw about Pliny's thinking processes and systems of thought. This matter has to do with the fact that Pliny's topics of discussion represent concepts (largely concrete phenomena or objects of nature) that organize themselves into a tiered hierarchy: the sharing of attributes causes certain concepts to fall under the umbrella of a larger category; a set of those larger categories may share further attributes that group them into still larger ones; and so on. An example of such a tiered hierarchy in the *Natural History* is peacock → plumage-bird → bird → animal.[52] All of Pliny's topics of discussion must therefore be imagined as positioned within a two-dimensional matrix, each with both vertical and horizontal axes of relations; one may visualize the matrix as a collection of tree diagrams.

---

[51] Doody (2001); Riggsby (2007) 95–8.
[52] On the peacock as a plumage-bird cf. *NH* 10.43.

This type of vertical hierarchy is known as a taxonomy, and, especially because I have just described it in the context of a work commonly viewed as a forerunner of modern natural history, it has undoubtedly brought to the reader's mind the artificial classification system of Linnaeus. It is important to recognize, however, that artificial systems represent a special application of a fundamental cognitive process that we perform reflexively in our daily lives. The cognitive psychologist Eleanor Rosch, who has performed a series of influential experiments on category perception in culture, has articulated a particularly clear definition that may serve as a useful reference:

> By *category* is meant a number of objects that are considered equivalent. Categories are generally designated by names (e.g. *dog, animal*). A *taxonomy* is a system by which categories are related to one another by means of class inclusion. The greater the inclusiveness of a category within a taxonomy, the higher the level of abstraction. Each category within a taxonomy is entirely included within one other category (unless it is the highest level category) but is not exhaustive of that more inclusive category. Thus the term *level of abstraction* within a taxonomy refers to a particular level of inclusiveness.[53]

In what follows I shall continue to use the word 'concepts' to refer to Pliny's topics of discussion or objects of thought, but interchange it with 'categories' on occasions when I wish to emphasize the perceived existence of boundaries that enable vertical and horizontal sorting to occur. I shall also use the terms 'taxonomy' and 'level of abstraction' (or 'inclusiveness') in the manner defined above.[54]

Because in the topical approach, it is the categories of nature that serve as the basis for segmenting the discourse, a maximally thorough description of textual structure would map onto the conceptual taxonomy formed from analyzing the semantic relations among all the categories either named or discussed in the *Natural History*. In fact, paratextual divisions of various sizes are often employed to visually reflect and aid in this segmentation — the modern reader has access to paragraphs, chapter, and section numbers introduced by editors, in addition to the book units that are attested by the text as original.[55] To take the book unit as an example, parallel categories at a higher level of abstraction would be described as occupying certain groups of books

---

[53] Rosch (1999) 191–2.
[54] These terms are not unique to Rosch; I have merely chosen to reproduce a definition I found to be especially elegant and economical.
[55] Similar issues concerning editorial intervention are discussed by Riggsby (2007) 94–6 in relation to the summarium. Cf. Naas (2002) 197–8 on internal cross-references to other books (*volumine* in Pliny).

(say, plants from 12–19 and minerals from 33–7), while those at a lower level of abstraction would correspond to smaller groups of books or individual ones (say, metals from 33–4, clays in 35, stones in 36, gems in 37).

It is not necessary for paratextual divisions to map consistently onto the conceptual segments formed by these categories, however, and we sometimes find this to be the case with book units. A category at the same level of abstraction as others that occupy whole books might turn out to take up only part of a book. For instance, insects in Book 11 is parallel to humans, land animals, aquatic animals, and birds (Books 8, 9, and 10 respectively), but unlike its counterparts the subject does not cover the whole book but only extends up to chapter 120.[56] Conversely, categories at that same level of abstraction might run over the space of an individual book, such as metals, which as we saw extends from 33 to 34, while its counterparts, clays, stones, and gems, each take up only one book. The presence of these variations means that in order to preserve methodological consistency throughout one's analysis of textual structure, one must choose either to prioritize paratextual principles (the division offered by the book unit) in identifying significant segments in the work, or to prioritize the conceptual segmentation offered by the categories themselves.

In the synoptic descriptions of textual structure produced in recent scholarship it appears that the book unit has sometimes interfered with a general intent to follow a conceptual method of segmentation. This inconsistency is notably exemplified in the way the heavens and earth are listed as separate subjects occupying Books 2 and 3–6 respectively.[57] A more precise description would take account of the fact that earth is introduced at the end of Book 2, not at the beginning of 3, with a formulaic transitional phrase that Pliny uses often to indicate expository progress: "earth is next" (*sequitur terra*, 2.154). Here, Pliny additionally marks the significance of the topical shift by prefacing the discussion with a rhetorical proem of some length (154–9). The rest of the book gives an overview of earth as sphere, with a natural scientific orientation that includes total geographic measurements. What changes between the end of Book 2 and the beginning of 3 is not the subject matter, then, but rather the perspective from which a continued subject is considered. Pliny's purpose in discussing earth in Book 2 is to look at it as a whole and in the context of the rest of the universe; in 3–6 his purpose is to work through the parts of the earth one piece at a time.

---

[56] Similarly garden plants in 19 begins only at chapter 49.
[57] Cf. my reproduction of three structural breakdowns on pp.221–2.

This change in perspective is the kind of transition that Pliny's introduction to Book 3 conveys: "up to now we have discussed the situation and marvels of earth, water, and stars, and the workings and measurement of the totality. Now on to the parts" (*hactenus de situ et miraculis terrae aquarumque et siderum ac ratione universitatis atque mensura. nunc de partibus*, 3.1). The use of earth to bridge over Books 2 and 3 creates a rhetorical momentum that binds these books closer together, and complements the use of a shared graphical method of exposition to set off, as I have argued, the first five books as a single integrated unit. Whether we take Books 2–6 as one block or as divided between 2 and 3–6 may seem a minor matter, but in this case the difference in perception is great: on it turns the question of whether or not there is numerical symmetry in the work, with the first and last portions each occupying equal blocks of five books. The aesthetic question, in turn, will affect qualitative assessments of Plinian organization, which condition the kind of textual features we look for or notice.

There is another way in which the segmentation offered by the book unit may have had a subtle effect on the way we have approached organization in the *Natural History*. When the work is being considered synoptically, the book unit presents itself as a major divider of convenience. Using the book unit as reference point promotes a bipartite view of structure: on the one hand, we speak of the large-scale structure of the work as a whole (the pattern formed from taking the books in sequence), and on the other, the small-scale structures to be found in each individual book. However, if we approach structural analysis purely from a conceptual point of view, the taxonomies produced would all exceed two levels — in the peacock's case we saw a total of four (possibly five). In theory the scholarship does appear to recognize that the concepts organize themselves into multiple levels of abstraction, but in practice there is a tendency for analysis to be cast in bipartite terms. So, for example, we find discussions that contrast the "internal organization of books" with the "organization of the work",[58] or the work's "overall organization" (referring to book units) with "information within the individual books",[59] or the text's "partitions, its larger structural divisions" with "what we find within those partitions",[60] or its "macro level" with the "smaller scale".[61]

These dichotomous formulations have several consequences for thinking about organization. First, in promoting a foreshortened view

---

[58] Naas (2002) 199, 209.
[59] Carey (2003) 27.
[60] Murphy (2004) 37.
[61] Doody (2010) 27.

of Pliny's taxonomies, they may inaccurately assimilate to each other the organizational logic of certain proximate levels of abstraction. Second and related to the first point, the inevitable consequence of stressing two levels rather than more is that we artificially constrain our knowledge of vertical relationships. Finally, the terminology does not make clear which level of abstraction is being referred to — even if the book unit is used as a benchmark for distinguishing between larger and smaller scales, we still can find two levels of abstraction at or above the book unit (for example, "animals" and "birds"), and at least two below ("plumage-birds" and "peacocks").[62]

It must be noted, however, that while the more recent scholarship has emphasized a bipartite approach to Plinian organization, one earlier analysis does exist that attempts to represent schematically the taxonomic relationships of several higher-order categories. This is the diagram that accompanies Della Corte's article on the *Natural History*'s structure. Figure 1 (opposite) reproduces this diagram, which was printed both originally in the collected proceedings of the 1979 Como conference, and reproduced as part of the same piece reprinted as the introductory essay in the companion Italian translation of the *Natural History*.[63] This article is important in modern studies of Plinian organization because it has enjoyed a citation history of unqualified success: not only is it the most frequently cited of such studies, but its conclusions have also never been contested.[64]

Close examination of the diagram, however, shows that revision is necessary. To begin with, the diagram's tree structure does indeed appear, as we would instinctively conclude, to be an attempt to represent the nesting of smaller categories within larger, more inclusive ones. One area of the diagram that represents this relation well is at "Animalia" and its subdivisions, on the third and fourth levels: under the general topic of animals encompassing Books 8–11 we find books individually devoted to "Terrestria", "Aquatilia", "Volucres", and "Insecta". From this part of the diagram we may conclude that by reading from top to bottom we follow categories as they proceed from more to less inclusive. In addition, this part of the diagram, like most other parts, labels the book numbers in which each of the topics is treated.

---

[62] So, for example, Doody's assertion, (2010) 27, that the "named object is the building block of the narrative" does not clearly distinguish among lexicalized concepts at different levels of abstraction.

[63] Boscherini *et al.* (1984).

[64] Cf. Sconocchia (1987) 624 n.3; Conte (1994) 100 n.35; Naas (2002) 196 n.97. Isager (1991) 49 reproduces Della Corte's diagram; Murphy (2004) 6 n.11 cites the Isager reproduction. Henderson (2011) 142 n.3 lists it as one of the "standard accounts", which he intends to reaffirm but tweak.

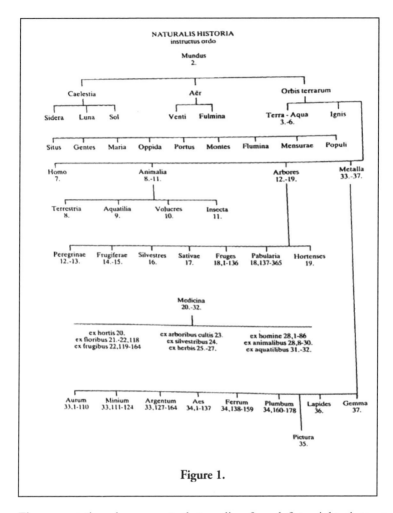

Figure 1.

The presentation also suggests that reading from left to right gives us the sequence of Pliny's discussion.

The cues given by this section thus make it confusing to read certain other parts of the diagram. The top, where Della Corte indicates discussion of the heavens and earth, does not faithfully represent the order and character of Pliny's exposition. For example, in Pliny's text the sun is named before the moon, contrary to what the diagram suggests, where "Luna" is placed to the left of "Sol";[65] and there is no

---

[65] Following the spatial organization of the exposition: 2.35–6 (sun), 41 (moon). Possibly

special section in the early part of the work expressly devoted to fire (a fact which may account for the diagram's illogicality, as the positioning of "Ignis" suggests that the topic occupies a space somewhere between the end of Book 6 and the beginning of Book 7). That the parallel topics of "Aër", "Terra", "Aqua", and "Ignis" should be divided, counterintuitively, between two levels may be a deliberate attempt to represent the way Pliny conflates two strands of philosophical thought: one that describes the *caelestia, aër,* and *orbis terrarum* as contained within the *mundus,* and the other that describes the distribution of those elements within the universe. But the location of "Ignis" would be inaccurate even so, since the text asserts that fire is the element from which stars are made (2.10).

As we continue to the right from "Ignis", we see represented on the same level "Homo", "Animalia", "Arbores", and "Metalla". These four categories reflect Della Corte's view that Pliny uses the Aristotelian *scala naturae* to structure his work from Book 7 on. Note that Della Corte lists "Homo" separately from "Animalia" and places them on the same level, perhaps to underscore the ancient view of man's exceptionalism. In the context of a tree diagram, however, this leaves the impression that Pliny classifies man as a species entirely separate from the animal kingdom. That is an impression directly contradicted by Pliny's text. In the proem to Book 7, Pliny is intent on reminding us of man's inclusion among animals. Man is indeed exceptional in Pliny's account, but in a sly reversal of the Aristotelian hierarchy,[66] portrayed as exceptionally inferior to them:

> hominem tantum nudum et in nuda humo natali die abicit ad vagitus statim et ploratum, nullumque tot animalium aliud ad lacrimas …. ab hoc lucis rudimento quae ne feras quidem inter nos genitas vincula excipiunt …. itaque feliciter natus iacet manibus pedibusque devinctis, flens animal ceteris imperaturum ….

> quam diu palpitans vertex, summae inter cuncta animalia inbecillitatis indicium!

> Only man naked on bare earth on the day of his birth does [nature] immediately give up to wailing and crying, and no other animal out of so many [nature gives up] to tears …. Bonds whisk him away from this meager light, bonds which [fetter] not even the beasts born

---

Della Corte is basing his reading on Pliny's discussion of lunar eclipses (41–8) before the size of the sun (49–52), but I consider the entire section to be a subsidiary discussion in Book 2.

[66] Cf. *PA* 2.10 656a5–9, 4.10 686a26–687a26 (esp. 687a24–6 where Aristotle asserts that those who say that humans are inferior to animals are deeply mistaken); *GA* 2.4 737b25–7.

among us, …. so lies the healthy baby, with its hands and feet bound
up, weeping, the animal meant to command the rest ….

For how long does its head quiver, an indication of its utmost weakness among all animals.   *NH* 7.2–4

The language repeatedly stresses our membership in the animal kingdom: from the partitive genitive in the phrase *nullum tot animalium*, to
two uses of the preposition *inter* relating man to animals, to the outright
labelling of humans as animals in conjunction with characterizing other
animals as "the rest" (*animal ceteris imperaturum*). It should be noted
that the error in the diagram is probably no more than a representational
oversight, as in the text of his article Della Corte indicates that he has
interpreted Pliny as I have.[67] However, because the same taxonomic
slip has appeared elsewhere in the work of other scholars, it seems
important to underscore the point at this juncture.[68]

Other parts of the diagram label categories erroneously. The label
"Arbores" for Books 12–19 cannot stand, as the term encompasses a
semantic field too narrow to include the types of vegetation discussed
in those books (other scholars usually characterize this section as
'plants'). The use of this label is the source for the logical error we find
on the next level, where "Fruges", "Pabularia", and "Hortenses" are
presented as types of trees.

Della Corte's choice of "Metalla" for the subject covered in Books
33–37 raises similar questions about semantic field. Does he intend
metalla as equivalent to 'mineral', or 'mineral kingdom'? Latin usage
does provide some textual support for construing *metalla* in this
broader fashion, but Plinian usage more strongly suggests that we
should take the word restrictively, as equivalent to our concept
'metals'.[69] That being the case, the subjects of Books 35–7, identified
in the diagram as "Pictura", "Lapides", and "Gemmae", should be
shown on the same level as "Metalla", not subordinate to it.

The absence of criticism of Della Corte's diagram, particularly its

---

[67] Della Corte (1982) 25, summarizing this passage writes, "gli altri animali".

[68] Cf. Naas (2002) , who represents "VII: anthropologie" separately from "VIII–XI: zo-
ologie"; also Locher (1986) 21; Isager (1991) 48. Beagon (2005) 40–50 is the only one
to my knowledge to explicitly argue in favor of treating Book 7 separately from 8–11,
but this is done on thematic grounds; it is clear that she implicitly accepts the classificatory point. For criticism of Beagon cf. Laehn (2013) 20–1.

[69] For the wider usage cf. the citations in *OLD*[2] s.v. *metallum* 2. On Plinian usage, I draw
this conclusion especially from the way he mentions *metalla* separately from *lapides*
and *gemmae* in passages meant to survey the mineral kingdom (e.g. 2.158, 207; 33.1),
from his use of the word to separate the topics of Book 33–4 from 35–7 (cf. the
headers for Books 33 and 34 in the summarium; the proem at 33.1 together with the
retrospective comments at 35.1 and 35.29, 30), and from numerous instances where
gold, silver, bronze, or iron is used as a qualifier for *metallum*.

misrepresentation of taxonomic relationships, combined with subsequent scholarship's tendency to stress a bipartite way of approaching the text, are two major indications that it would be beneficial at this point to devote more explicit attention to the matter of the work's vertical organization. The ultimate goal of this analysis would not simply be to obtain greater clarity on an important way to describe textual structure, but to understand more precisely the nature of Pliny's organizational thinking. By 'thinking' I mean both cognitive process and sum of ideas — taking the evidence of the text to understand, on the one hand, thought in the traditional sense, by asking what sources (such as cultural and intellectual modes of thought) underlie or motivate the way in which his categories of nature are perceived and framed as they are. And on the other, using the text as a basis for exploring the very process of recognizing and sorting categories, for better understanding the mechanics, as it were, of Plinian organization by situating any potential patterns in the text within cultural practice (such as those that may have been aimed at developing mental skills of organization) and within scientific theories of cognition.

In what follows I shall offer a first foundation for these avenues of research. I begin by presenting a revised version of Della Corte's taxonomic analysis, which is based on close readings I have done of the partitioning statements that Pliny makes at major transitions (a sample of which was given above, on the relation of *homo* to *animalia*). For the sake of clarity and simplicity I leave out the medical books, the topically recursive part of the text. This diagram shows levels of abstraction only down to the whole book, what we may call the work's higher order categories. The taxonomy of lower order categories, the categories found within an individual book, will be incorporated only in discussion.

Following Della Corte's practice, I use Latin terms to designate categories, but I differ from him in that I use terminology drawn only from Pliny's partitioning statements. As I discussed earlier, using modern labels to render ancient categories can sometimes introduce or magnify implications about certain attributes, or relationships with other categories, that do not well represent their original conceptualization. Here, I retain Latin terms drawn from these passages deliberately to bring attention to the way in which Pliny presents categories at crucial points in his text. Because transitions often serve as a platform for Pliny's rhetorical passages, they are good places for measuring how his conception of natural categories fit with the general moral or natural philosophical attitudes he articulates. Further, the introductory transitions show us how Pliny chooses to orient his reader (at least, those reading linearly) toward the categories he treats. These initial descriptions each establish a baseline that functions subsequently as a cognitive guide, and thus are useful for tracing to what extent Pliny sustains or deviates from that baseline in the rest of his discussion of the category in question.

The final part of this article will show how my analysis can yield new questions about Pliny's methods of categorization and organization, especially as they relate to taxonomic structure. I will use my results to highlight a number of notable features, including what appears to be instability in the attributes used to define certain categories, the recycling of organizational patterns across levels, and imbalance in the taxonomic inflection of different categories. My approach is informed by an interest in thinking about the thinking process — that is, in what the sequential unfolding of the text may suggest about Pliny's acts and habits of mental retrieval. Separately, I will demonstrate, for one of the issues I discuss, how it may be methodologically expedient to draw from modern scientific work in seeking to illuminate questions that arise from the text.

Taxonomic Analysis of Select Categories in the Natural History

These are the higher order categories in Books 2–6:

Level 1	Level 2	Level 3
mundus/caelum (2.1–153)[70]	aër[71]/caelum (2.12–153)	
	terra/terrarum orbis[72] (2.154–BK 6)	Europa (3–4) Africa (5.1–46) Asia (5.47–6.205)

Table 1.

---

[70] Numbering is a difficult issue here: technically the *mundus* encompasses all reality, so could be conceived of as a subject covering 2–37; however, in discussion Pliny seems to restrict the discussion to the contents of the heavens, so for this reason I have elected to have the numbering extend only up to the treatment of earth.

[71] Later on, in a difficult passage, Pliny seems to further subdivide the *aër* into two sections, the upper air and the sublunary region, 2.102.

[72] *terra* (in the sense of the sphere as a whole) at 2.154; *terrarum orbis* at 3.3.

And in Books 7–37 (exclusive of 20–32):

Level 1	Level 2	Level 3	Level 4
animantia (7-32)	animalia (7-11)	homo (7) terrestria (8) [animalia] aequorum, amnium, stagnorumque[73] (9) volucres/aves[74] (10.1-170) insecta[75] (11.1-120)	
	terra edita (12-19)	arbores (12-17)[76]	externae (12-13) communes[77] (14-15) silvestres/ glandiferae[78] (16) quae arte et humanis ingeniis fiunt[79] (17)
		fruges (18.48-end) [quae] neque inter fruges neque inter hortensia (19.1-48) hortorum cura/ hortensia[80] (19.49-end)	
[carentia anima][81]	[terra] eruta (33-7)	metalla (33-4) terrae (35) lapides (36) gemmae (37)	

Table 2.

Note that I have made two separate diagrams for the contents of Books 2–6 and for 7–37 (exclusive of 20–32), in contrast to Della Corte, who

---

[73] Della Corte uses *aquatilia*, which has justification as the term is used in the summarium to describe the topic of the book, as well as in Book 9 and 31–32 (medicines from aquatic creatures).

[74] *volucres* at 9.1 and 186, *aves* at 10.1.

[75] Insects appear to be a fuzzy category in relation to the preceding modes of classification; for Pliny they have features of both *terrestria* and *volucres* (11.1).

[76] The category of *frutices* is retrospectively mentioned at 18.1 but never formally introduced.

[77] The beginning and end of this category is ambiguous. At 15.35 Pliny transitions to fruit-trees, which he had foreshadowed with *frugiferae* earlier, and which he seems to follow up with the retrospective reference *pomiferae* at 16.1.

[78] Called *silvestres* at 15.138; *glandiferae* at 16.1; summed up as *sponte sua provenientia* at 17.1. On these referential changes see below.

[79] Della Corte labels this category *sativae*, also drawn from the summarium describing Book 17.

[80] *ad hortorum curam* at 19.49; *hortensia* at the summation at 19.189 and the recap at 20.2

[81] A category so framed has to be inferred from the proem in Book 12.

represents them in a continuous sequence (see Figure 1). My preference for keeping them separated is not based on active disagreement with Della Corte's interpretation of the categories' ontological relations with each other — that is, I do not dispute the idea implied by Della Corte's diagram, that the earth, as physical host to "Terra-Aqua", "Ignis", "Homo", "Animalia", "Arbores", and "Metalla", may be viewed as including or encapsulating all these categories.[82] However, as I have mentioned before, fundamentally different modes of logic rationalize the ordering of subjects in Books 2–6 and 7–37 — a predominantly physical or spatial relationship in the case of the former, a complex mix of relations in the latter case, and my object is to present the taxonomies so that logical sequences may be easy to follow.

Another major difference between my presentation and not only Della Corte's, but other structural models as well, is that in adhering to the language found at partitioning statements my model brings attention to a noteworthy feature in Pliny's method of identifying categories. Whereas other structural models have presented the categories as if they were all representable by a single name, my analysis shows that for Pliny, some concepts are more distinctly lexicalized than others. These referential differences suggest a varying degree of native comfort with the concepts he is attempting to organize, as phrases, by their circuitous and descriptive nature, imply less clarity about a concept than single words. Keeping track of the differences between names and phrases may thus serve as a useful tool in global analyses of Plinian thought on nature, such as in assessing how well he has fused Greek and other foreign knowledge with Roman folk ideas. There is evidence, at lower levels of abstraction, of a difference between superficial and deep methods of organization, as Pliny can be found at times to introduce partitions that he subsequently fails to sustain clearly.[83] Taxonomizing is not a neat process in the *Natural History*, but that messiness provides valuable clues to the sources of his thinking and the extent to which he has absorbed particular ideas. To render all his categories homogeneously by single-word names, against his actual practice,

---

[82] So also Beagon (1992) 13. At the beginning of Book 7, when Pliny introduces the subject of *animantia*, he mentions that they are located within the *mundus*: *animantium in eodem* [sc. *mundo*] *natura nullius prope partis contemplatione minore, etsi ne hic quidem omnia exsequi humanus animus queat* ("the nature of living beings that dwell in this same [universe] is worthy of no less contemplation than practically any other part, even if here too the human mind is incapable of pursuing the subject in its entirety."). This reminds us that the *mundus* is a physical container.

[83] One example is the way in which Pliny initially establishes a clear distinction between *oscines* and *alites* at 10.43, but in his subsequent list of subtypes does not bother to identify to which of the two categories a bird species belongs.

would efface this important fact.

Consider for example the categories of *terra edita* and [*terra*] *eruta* at level 2, described circuitously by Pliny but to us readily referrable by names: 'plants' and 'minerals'. In the first place, we should keep in mind that this relatively innocuous translation does involve bridging over a considerable intellectual divide, in which (scientifically-informed) oppositions reflexively brought to our minds, such as the difference between organic and inorganic matter, or between living and non-living, may not have occurred to the Roman one with the same promptitude. In fact the very act of lexicalizing the concepts in question implies that they were entrenched in the natural language of Latin in a manner that presumes a degree of cultural familiarity with thinking at that level of abstraction. Keeping focus on the phrases *terra edita* and *terra eruta* — "things produced by earth" and "things dug up from the earth" — reminds us that, on the contrary, Pliny was acting as early exponent and interpreter of ideas developed in Aristotelian philosophy.

Indeed, Pliny's phrasing shows how very Roman his interpretation was. The two concepts are defined by a polarized relationship to the earth, the one involving a cooperative, the other a coercive, means of obtainment. By characterizing plants as earth's yields, Pliny suggests a measure of autonomous will that contrasts with his characterization of minerals as things that are by nature extracted. The polarity limned in these phrases, drawn from the proem to Book 12, is echoed and more fully developed in other key transitional passages at the beginning and end of the work. In the proem to Book 33, the first book of five devoted to the subject of minerals, Pliny reveals, with anthropomorphizing vividness, the full implication of his earlier mode of description:

> persequimur omnes eius fibras .... imus in viscera et in sede manium opes quaerimus, tamquam parum benigna fertilique qua calcatur. et inter haec minimum remediorum gratia scrutamur, quoto enim cuique fodiendi causa medicina est? quamquam et hoc summa sui parte tribuit ut fruges, larga facilisque in omnibus, quaecumque prosunt. illa nos peremunt, illa nos ad inferos agunt, quae occultavit atque demersit, illa, quae non nascuntur repente ....

> We search out all her nerves .... We enter into her vitals and we look for wealth in the seat of the shades, as if too little generous and fertile is the part on which we tread. And in the midst of this, we look least of all on account of remedies, for how much is medicine the reason for digging for each of us? Although she has given even this on her topmost part, as she has given us crops, generous and easy in everything, whatever profits us. The things that destroy us, that drive us to

the shades, are what she has hidden and submerged, the things that
are not spontaneously given birth to ....   *NH* 33.1–3[84]

To consider minerals things "dug up" from earth, and plants things
"produced" is, evidently, to view the two categories in starkly moral
terms. Plants are the healthful things that earth is both quick to give and
generous in her giving; their life-sustaining function and the peaceable
manner in which we come by them seem to make goodness a condition
of their existence, as if morality were an attribute of plants as much as
biological qualities like the possession of root and leaf. Conversely,
minerals are by definition bad, death-dealing objects that are nothing
but illicitly and violently obtained. There is no neutrality in viewing
them as things that are gotten from the act of digging, for digging signifies the evisceration of a body that is all but described as maternal.

Similarly, a mirror image of these tropes appears early in the work,
at the transition to earth in Book 2. Here earth is configured by plants
and minerals just as plants and minerals are later configured by earth.
She initially appears as a function of the vegetable products she bears:

> at haec benigna, mitis, indulgens ususque mortalium semper ancilla,
> quae coacta generat, quae sponte fundit, quos odores saporesque,
> quos sucos, quos tactus, quos colores! ... quae nostra causa alit! ...
> illa medicas fundit herbas et semper homini parturit ....

> But this (earth) is kindly, gentle, indulgent and always handmaid to
> the needs of mortals, one who is both compelled to produce and bears
> of her own accord, what fragrances and tastes, what juices, what tex-
> tures, what colors! ... What does she foster for our sake! ... She
> brings forth healing herbs, and always gives birth for man! *NH* 2.155

By passage's end she is recast as the source of minerals: "we penetrate
into her entrails, digging up veins of gold and silver, the metals of
bronze and iron. We even seek gems and certain little stones by driving

---

[84] Strictly speaking, Pliny here announces only the local subject of metals (treated in
Books 33–4), but at the same time seems to have a global mentality, since he briefly
ranges over most of the other subcategories of *terra eruta* (only stones are excepted) in
the part of the introduction that precedes the quoted passage (33.1): *metalla nunc
ipsaeque opes et rerum pretia dicentur, tellurem intus exquirente cura multiplici
modo, quippe alibi divitiis foditur quaerente vita aurum, argentum, electrum, aes, alibi
deliciis gemmas et parietum lignorumque pigmenta, alibi temeritati ferrum, auro
etiam gratius inter bella caedesque* ("Metals now, and wealth itself, and the prices of
objects, will be discussed, care being taken to seek them out inside the earth in manifold ways. Indeed in some places, for wealth, they dig up (since life demands it) gold,
silver, electrum, copper; in other places, for luxury, [they dig up] gems and pigments
for walls and wood; in yet other places, for bravura, iron, more pleasing even than
gold in times of war and massacre"). Note that Pliny does not use the term *terra eruta*
or any equivalent phrase, an avoidance that reinforces the impression that the superordinate category of mineral does not easily come to mind.

shafts deep into her. We drag out her entrails, so that a gem could be displayed on the finger by which it is sought". (*penetramus in viscera, auri argentique venas et aeris ac plumbi metalla fodientes, gemmas etiam et quosdam parvulos quaerimus lapides scrobibus in profundum actis. viscera eius extrahimus, ut digito gestetur gemma, quo petitur,* 2.158). The contrast between earth's two roles could not be more visceral. Although in the first section the harsh word *coacta*, an allusion to agriculture, introduces a slight note of discord, the overall picture is one of a harmonious relationship between earth and mankind. This harmony is utterly negated at the passage's end, as earth the bountiful, compliant mother is transformed into a victim of rape and torture.

The consistency of thought in evidence across the work suggests that for Pliny, thinking at that level of abstraction is strongly identified with moral questions. The idea that plants and minerals have a moral essence proceeds, in turn, from regarding them as intrinsically possessing a use value — plants and minerals are respectively good and evil because of their employment in human health, subsistence, and luxury. The prominence of utility and morality in Pliny's basic conceptualization of plants and minerals marks the effects of cultural conditioning on his thinking — utility and morality have frequently been cited as elements that contribute to the distinctively Roman flavor of his presentation of nature.[85] In the very sentence where Pliny sums plants and minerals up as *terra edita* and *terra eruta* (12.1.1), we witness his effort to take account of the Aristotelian definition: plants are entities that "also do not lack the soul" (*neque ipsa anima carentia*). But in the cryptic gloss that follows it, "seeing that nothing lives without [the soul]" (*quandoquidem nihil sine ea vivit*), he seems to pivot away from the Aristotelian idea of immanence towards a view that defines an entity by its external effects. For because this gloss leads directly into the framing of plants as "products of earth", and because, as other passages reveal, "products of earth" are to be construed as exclusively life-giving entities, the comment that nothing lives without the soul reads, in retrospect, as a synecdochic prolepsis: the life-giving quality of soul is taken over and absorbed by plants *qua* "products of earth", the entities that in Pliny's eyes truly confer life. To put it another way, the utterance of the phrase *terra edita* triggers associations that end up eclipsing the original characterization of plants as things that also do not lack soul.[86] In this subtle change of frame we

---

[85] Cf. Beagon (2005) 12 on the "utilitarian ethos" in the context of Flavian revival of the old Roman virtues.

[86] Pliny could have chosen, as Seneca did in *Ep.* 58.10, to translate Greek φυτόν with the

perhaps see exemplified what happens when a Roman mind processes a Greek concept.

Analyzing Organization Across Levels

The preceding discussion has been intended to clarify some general aspects of the diagram, in particular the sometimes cumbersome language (drawn from Pliny's own text) used to render major categories. Now we turn to questions raised by the taxonomic analysis itself. Referring back to Table 2, observe that there is one anomalous part of the diagram: trees. Pliny has so much to say about trees that it takes an additional level of subordination to reach the same paratextual unit — about one or two books — allotted to all the other subjects. This means that at the level of the whole book, Pliny is thinking about trees with greater specificity than about any other subject. The telescoping of trees observable at these higher levels of analysis exemplifies a general phenomenon about taxonomic length in the *Natural History,* and that is its lack of uniformity. Different families of concepts, pursued from most to least inclusive, are longer or shorter than other families. For animals and plants, for example, we can find anything between one and three further levels of inflection within books. [87]

This variability in taxonomic length is potentially cognitively significant. A series of psychological experiments developed and led by Eleanor Rosch has shown that there is a correlation between knowledge and taxonomic ability. [88] The main object of these experiments was to test the theory of the "basic level object". This theory proposed that humans tend to conceptualize concrete objects by obtaining the most information about them with the least amount of mental work (maximum cognitive economy), and that these concepts exist at one level of abstraction, which Rosch designates as basic. The basic level is situated in the middle of three-level taxonomy, as can be seen below: [89]

---

more neutral *satum.*

[87] The one to three further levels of inflection apply to trees as well, so at least in a general way you can say that trees are in fact as a whole one level more inflected than other categories.

[88] The experiments are documented in Rosch (1976).

[89] These categories were tested in her experiments; the table is reproduced from Rosch (1999) 193.

Superordinate	Basic level	Subordinate
Furniture	Chair	Kitchen chair
		Living-room chair
	Table	Kitchen table
		Dining-room table
	Lamp	Floor lamp
		Desk lamp
Tree	Oak	White oak
		Red oak
	Maple	Silver maple
		Sugar maple
	Birch	River birch
		White birch

Table 3.

As Rosch explains, basic objects correspond to "natural discontinuities"; that is, the categories we form of the concrete world are not
arbitrary but respond to the objective reality wherein surface attributes
in objects in the environment are unevenly distributed. A chair is
objectively structured to have more "sit-on-able-ness" than a cat, she
writes by way of illustration.[90]

The most relevant part of Rosch's research for us, however, is the
following point. While basic objects have a real world correspondence,
the way an object is perceived depends on the perceiver's degree of
familiarity with it. Thus two factors influence the level of abstraction
that counts as basic: aspects of the external environment ranging from
variations in climate and ecology to culture, and an individual's
personal knowledge.[91]

Two examples from Rosch's experiments will help clarify this point.
One experiment tested the status of 'airplane' as a basic level object.
Results showed that one subject was able to list considerably more
attributes relevant to planes than other subjects, and consequently
taxonomized airplanes at far greater depth. This aberrant subject happened to be a former airplane mechanic, while the rest were college
students. The answers he gave led experimenters to conclude that expertise telescopes a person's classificatory ability such that more than
one level of abstraction is considered basic — perceived with the kind

[90] Rosch (1999) 190.
[91] Rosch (1976) 430, 434–5.

of reflexive ease accorded to just one level by the general population.[92]

Conversely, in another experiment Rosch and her collaborators hypothesized that species of trees such as oak, maple, and birch were basic level objects, and that 'tree' was a superordinate category (see Table 3). Unexpectedly they found that their city-dwelling subjects could not differentiate among tree species at a high enough level to fulfill their criteria for basic level objects, so after the experiment they had to modify their scheme to show 'tree' as a basic level and 'oak', 'maple', 'birch' as subordinate.[93] Here, lack of expertise corroborated through opposite means the implications of the airplane experiment, proving that the less you know, the more broadly you have to think.

For our purposes, the utility of Rosch's experiments lies in the way she was able to show empirically how taxonomic length can be an index of firsthand knowledge. Put another way, her experiments demonstrate well the insight that increased familiarity brings a closeness in perception that enhances our ability to differentiate and to categorize. Taxonomic variability in the *Natural History* thus has the potential to serve as a tool for exploring the contours of Plinian, Roman, or ancient knowledge, acting as a kind of plumb line for taking a preliminary measure of areas of expertise and ignorance. If, for instance, it were to be found that there is an average or typical number of inflections in the work, deviations can turn into interesting problems. We have already seen that from a global perspective at least, trees in the *Natural History* are pursued in more detail than other subjects, which helps to present them as a speciality. How might the status of trees as a speciality contribute to Pliny's authorial self-positioning as a source of authority? Or how might it help us refine our understanding of his intended audience of elites' relationship to arboriculture, described by Columella as the "greatest part of rural affairs" (*sequitur arborum cura, quae pars rei rusticae vel maxima est, DRR* 3.1.1) and, judging from the evidence of other agricultural treatises as well as from Pliny's own anecdotes about gentleman farmers, a matter of passionate interest among them?[94] My point, in short, is that in taxonomic analysis

---

[92] Rosch (1976) 430.

[93] Rosch (1976) 390–3, 432.

[94] Cf. also the separate treatise by Columella devoted to trees, *De Arboribus*; Var. *RR* 1.2.6–10 (esp. the argument that all Italy is an orchard, and the fame of G. Tremelius Scrofa's collections of fruit); Cato *Agri.* 1.7 (note the prominence of trees in his catalogue of the best kind of farm). Pliny reports stories of farmers' competitive zeal in importing new species of trees and developing new hybrids: cf. e.g. *NH* 12.12 (an imperial freedman's endeavors), 15.47 (the consular Sextus Papinius), 15.83 (Vitellius) and 91 (Vitellius and the equestrian Pompeius Flaccus), 17.122 (the equestrian Corellius and his freedman Tereius).

the number of levels of inflection becomes a relevant datum, and modern psychological research gives us a reason to think that it is not an empty datum, but rather a significant item in considerations of knowledge.

To conclude my exploration of the critical uses of taxonomic analysis, consider trees in Table 2 a final time. At the fourth level of abstraction, we see that its typology appears to be unstable. Pliny starts out by using geography as a criterion for organization — so the first pair of subcategories, occupying Books 12–13 and 14–15 respectively, is presented as a transition from discussing exotics (*externae*) to discussing regionally "common" trees, or trees that are found to thrive both domestically and on foreign soil (*communes*). At the beginning of 16, however, Pliny points to type of fruit as the main criterion, retrospectively describing previous books (14–15) as about "fruit-bearing" (*pomiferae*) trees while announcing "acorn-bearing" (*glandiferae*) trees as his next subject (the contents of Book 16). But at Book 17's proem Pliny changes again, summing up Book 16 as about trees that grow wild (Pliny writes *sua sponte provenientium*) in order to contrast them with the upcoming subject of cultivated trees (*arte et humanis ingeniis fiunt*). The additional characterization of trees in Book 16 as *silvestres* comes from the final sentence in Book 15, announcing the upcoming subject.

Shifts like these can leave the impression that Pliny is disorganized, lacks method, or is just employing variety for variety's sake. Taxonomic analysis tells a different story. If we look within Books 8, 9, and 10 for the fourth level of abstraction, we will see that Pliny adopts fairly conservative methods of organizing categories. In the middle of discussing land animals, Pliny abruptly introduces organization into what had been a disconnected list when he announces his intention to treat domesticated animals (8.142): "out of those animals too *that live with us* many are worth knowing about" (*ex his quoque animalibus, quae nobiscum degunt, multa sunt cognitu digna*). This comment suggests that the preceding animals, a list that began with creatures such as elephants, lions, and panthers and concluded with the lizards of Arabia and India, were characterized by their wildness or nondomesticity. I construe the phrase "animals that live with us" as "domesticated" (giving us a wild/tame axis) and not as "native to these parts" (which would give us a foreign/domestic axis) because foreign examples of animals are treated in the section on "animals that live with us" — Pliny's discussion of dogs for example, his first topic in this section, includes mention of African and Indian dogs. Moreover, Pliny follows the section on domesticated animals with a section that looks at species possessing both tame and wild varieties, as if he were attempting to bridge a pre-established polarity.

In Book 9 on aquatic animals the default mode of organization is by morphology. Several times Pliny attempts to classify animals by parts of the body. The first time he chooses the animal's outer covering to serve as the distinguishing attribute, noting:

> alia corio et pilo integuntur ut vituli et hippopotami, alia corio tantum ut delphini, cortice ut testudines, silicum duritia ut ostreae et conchae, crustis ut locustae, crustis et spinis ut echini, squamis ut pisces, aspera cute ut squatina ..., molli ut murenae, alia nulla ut polypi.

> Some have hide and hair like seals and hippopotamuses, others only hide like dolphins, others shell like turtles, others a flinty hard substance like oysters and mussels, others rind like lobsters, others rind and spines like sea-urchins, others scales like fishes, others a rough skin like the angel-fish ..., others soft skin like morays, and others none at all like octopuses.   *NH* 9.40

He follows up this method of distinction by speaking briefly of the difference between animals with hair and those without (9.41–3). After a diversion in which he abandons this mode of organization, Pliny returns to morphology, this time choosing the number of gills as the distinguishing attribute (9.69). Soon afterwards he changes to body shape, then number of fins (9.72–3). Then, apparently turning from fishes to crustaceans, which he calls "bloodless fishes", he returns to type of outer covering to subdivide them (9.83): "we will speak of those fishes that lack blood. Here there are three types: first those which are called 'soft', then those covered with thin rinds, finally those enclosed in hard shells" (*piscium sanguine carent de quibus dicemus. sunt autem tria genera: primum quae mollia appellantur, dein contecta crustis tenuibus, postremo testis conclusa duris*). What follows is perhaps the most organized stretch in the book, as the creatures he lists in order (barring digressions) follow his pre-established classificatory system.

Book 10 on birds is interesting. By taking note of his transitional statements we can see that two methods of organization are distinct in his mind. The first is to classify birds according to whether they are known or unknown, or domestic vs. foreign, as is made evident when Pliny transitions from treating ostriches and phoenixes, which he identifies as native to Africa, Ethiopia, and Arabia, to treating eagles, vultures, hawks, and kites, birds he introduces with the phrase (Book 10.6), "out of those we know about" (*ex his quas novimus*). The second method of organization is also clearly articulated. After kites Pliny writes that birds are best distinguished by their feet, and have either hooked talons, toes, or webbed feet (10.29).

Books 8, 9, and 10, then, respectively offer us three ways to classify: by the wild/tame axis, the foreign/domestic axis, and by morphology. All are employed at the fourth level of abstraction. These methods line up with those Pliny employs to classify trees, also at the fourth level. If we return to Table 2, we see that Pliny begins with the foreign/domestic axis (*externae* vs. *communes* at Books 12–13 and 14–15); from 14–15 to 16, he changes to classifying by morphology, using the class of fruit (*pomum* vs. *glans*) as the dividing attribute; and finally, at 16 to 17, changes again to wild/tame, with 'cultivated' being the vegetable equivalent of 'tame'. The parallelism suggests that Pliny had a persistent or characteristic style of thinking, an ingrained habit of reaching for one of several predetermined organizational modes after he moved beyond the third level of abstraction.

I hope to have shown through this analysis that the constant mutability of Pliny's modes of organization is more apparent than real. There is method in the madness. Our awareness that Pliny, in his section on trees, is recycling organizational modes used in previous books encourages a new perspective on his unstable framing of tree categories. Rather than view Pliny as serially changing his mind, we should see him as progressively unveiling, through successive proems, the bundle of attributes through which he had formed and systematized the relevant concepts. Our model for Pliny's methods should be one of layering, not replacing: the vine and olive-trees that make up the principal subjects of Books 14 and 15 are typified both by their universality of growth and their fruit; the oak, fir, ash, and others discussed in Book 16 are typified both by the acorns they bear and their uncultivated nature. What we are witnessing from proem to proem is a process of selection. Putting the focus on selection rather than change, by helping us keep in mind that concepts are formed through the perception of multiple attributes, serves the useful heuristic purpose of encouraging a more enriched model of the way thinking works.

Works Cited

Bakker, E. (1997). *Poetry in Speech*. Ithaca and London

Beagon, M. (1992). *Roman Nature*. Oxford

Beagon, M. (2005). *The Elder Pliny on the Human Animal*. Oxford

Bonifazi, A., Drummen, A. and de Kreij, M. (forthcoming). *Particles in Ancient Greek Discourse*. Washington D.C. and Cambridge, Mass.

Borst, A. (1994). *Das Buch der Naturgeschichte*. Heidelberg

Boscherini, S. *et al.* (1984). (trans.) *Plinii Naturalis historia. Plinio Storia naturale*. Pisa. 5 vols.

Carey, S. (2003). *Pliny's Catalogue of Culture*. Oxford

Citroni Marchetti, S. (1991). *Plinio il Vecchio e la tradizione del moralismo romano*. Pisa

Conte, G.B., Barchiesi, A. and Ranucci, C. (1982–8). (edd.) *Naturalis historia. Storia naturale*. Turin. 5 vols.

Conte, G.B. (1994). 'The inventory of the world: form of nature and encyclopedic project in the work of Pliny the Elder' in G.B. Conte (ed.) (trans. G. Most, originally published 1982 in Italian) *Genres and Readers*. Baltimore and London. 67–104

Della Corte, F. (1982). 'Tecnica espositiva e struttura della *Naturalis Historia*' in Spallino, Alfonsi, and Ronconi (1982) 19–30

Doody, A. (2001). 'Finding facts in Pliny's encyclopaedia: the summarium of the *Natural History*' *Ramus* 30.1–22

Doody, A. (2010). *Pliny's Encyclopedia*. Cambridge

French, R. and Greenaway, F. (1986). (edd.) *Science in the Early Roman Empire*. London and Sydney

Glare, P.G.W. (2012). (ed.) *Oxford Latin Dictionary*. Oxford[2]. 2 vols [= *OLD*[2]]

Goldhill, S. (2009). 'The anecdote: exploring the boundaries between oral and literate performance in the Second Sophistic' in Johnson and Parker (2009) 96–113

Henderson, J. (2011). 'The nature of man: Pliny, *Historia Naturalis* as cosmogram' *MD* 66.139–71

Isager, J. (1991). *Pliny on Art and Society*. Odense

Johnson, W.A. and Parker, H.N. (2009). (edd.) *Ancient Literacies*. Oxford

Klotz, F. and Oikonomopoulou, K. (2011). (edd.) *The Philosopher's Banquet*. Oxford

König, J. and Whitmarsh, T. (2007). (edd.) *Ordering Knowledge in the Roman Empire*. Cambridge

Laehn, T. (2013). *Pliny's Defense of Empire*. New York and London

Locher, A. (1986). 'The structure of Pliny the Elder's *Natural History*' in French and Greenaway (1986) 20–9

Maraglino, V. (2012). (ed.) *La Naturalis Historia di Plinio nella tradizione medievale e umanistica*. Bari

Margolis, E. and Laurence, S. (1999). (edd.) *Concepts*. Cambridge, Mass. and London

Mayhoff, C. (1892–1909). (ed.) *C. Plini Secundi Naturalis historiae libri XXXVII*. Leipzig

McHam, S.B. (2013). *Pliny and the Artistic Culture of the Italian Renaissance*. New Haven and London

Minchin, E. (2001). *Homer and the Resources of Memory*. Oxford

Morgan, T. (2011). 'The Miscellany and Plutarch' in Klotz and Oikonomopoulou (2011) 49–73

Murphy, T. (2004). *Pliny the Elder's* Natural History. Oxford

Naas, V. (2002). *Le projet encyclopédique de Pline l'Ancien*. Paris and Rome

Pigeaud, J. and Oroz, J. (1987). (edd.) *Pline l'Ancien: témoin de son temps*. Salamanca and Nantes

Riggsby, A. (2007). 'Guides to the wor(l)d' in König and Whitmarsh (2007) 88–107

Rosch, E. (1976). 'Basic objects in natural categories' *Cognitive Psychology* 8.382–439

Rosch, E. (1999). 'Principles of categorization' in Margolis and Laurence (1999) 189–206

Sconocchia, S. (1987). 'La structure de la *NH* dans la tradition scientifique et encyclopédique romaine' in Pigeaud and Oroz (1987) 623–32

Simpson, J. (2014). (ed.) *Oxford English Dictionary*. Oxford. Online edition

Small, J.P. (1997). *Wax Tablets of the Mind*. London and New York

Spallino, A., Alfonsi, L., and Ronconi, A. (1982). (edd.) *Plinio il Vecchio sotto il profilo storico e letterario*. Como

The Authority of Greek Poetry
in Pliny's *Natural History* 18.63–65

Aude Doody
University College Dublin

Pliny the Elder is a quirky writer. His range of knowledge is vast, his curiosity perhaps unparalleled, and his mind apparently worked in some very strange ways. This is an encyclopedist who begins his account of animals with elephants, 'because they are the biggest, and most like humans in intellect', who begins his section on humanity by talking about Scythian cannibals, and whose fact-filled *Natural History* contained wonders and marvels that were to haunt the European imagination for centuries to come.[1] Gian Biagio Conte writes that Pliny's *Natural History* finds a sort of unity in the author's will to astonish and the reader's willingness to be astonished.[2] This article explores a passage from the *Natural History* that, if not exactly astonishing, is perhaps puzzling. It is from Book 18, where Pliny is focusing on cereal crops and Roman farming:

> [63] Tritici genera plura, quae fecere gentes. Italico nullum equidem comparaverim candore ac pondere, quo maxime decernitur. montanis modo comparetur Italiae agris externum, in quo principatum tenuit Boeotia, dein Sicilia, mox Africa. tertium pondus erat Thracio, Syrio, deinde et Aegyptio, athletarum [cum] decreto, quorum capacitas iumentis similis quem diximus ordinem fecerat. Graecia et Ponticum laudavit, quod in Italiam non pervenit. [64] ex omni autem genere grani praetulit dracontian et strangian et Selinusium argumento crassissimi calami. itaque pingui solo haec genera adsignabat. levissimum et maxime inane speudian, tenuissimi calami, in umidis seri iubebat, quoniam multo egeret alimento. [65] haec fuere sententiae Alexandro Magno regnante, cum clarissima fuit Graecia atque in toto orbe terrarum potentissima, ita tamen ut ante mortem eius annis fere CXLV Sophocles poeta in fabula Triptolemo frumentum Italicum ante cuncta laudaverit, ad verbum tralata sententia: et fortunatam Italiam frumento serere candido. quae laus peculiaris hodieque Italico

---

[1] Elephants, *HN* 8.1, cannibals, *HN* 7.9; on marvels in Pliny's *Natural History*, see Beagon (2005), (2007), (2011), Doody (2010) 31–7, Mudry (2004), Naas (2001), (2004), (2008), (2011), Wallace-Hadrill (1990).
[2] Conte (1994) 102.

est; quo magis admiror posteros Graecorum nullam mentionem huius fecisse frumenti.

There are several kinds of wheat, that have been produced by various races. For my own part I should not rank any of them with Italian wheat for whiteness and for weight, for which it is particularly distinguished. Foreign wheat can only be compared with that of the mountainous regions of Italy; among foreign kinds Boeotia has obtained first rank, then Sicily, and after that Africa. The third place for weight used to belong to Thracian and Syrian wheat and later also to Egyptian, by the vote of athletes in those days, whose capacity for cereals, resembling that of cattle, had established the order of merit that we have stated. Greece also gave praise to wheat from Pontus, which did not get through to Italy; but of all the varieties of grain Greece gave preference to dracontias, strangias and the wheat of Selinunte, recognised by the thickness of the straw, because of which it used to count these kinds as appropriate for a rich soil. For sowing in damp soils Greece prescribed speudias, a very light and extremely scanty-growing grain with a very thin stalk, because it required a great deal of nourishment.

These were the opinions held in the reign of Alexander the Great, when Greece was most famous and the most powerful state in the whole world, although nevertheless about 145 years before his death the poet Sophocles in his play *Triptolemus* praised Italian corn before all other kinds, in the phrase of which a literal translation is: 'And Italy shines blessed with bright white wheat'; and also today the Italian wheat is especially distinguished for whiteness, which makes it more surprising to me that the later Greeks have made no mention of this corn.   (Pliny *HN* 18.63–5; trans. H. Rackham, adapted)

This is the patriotic opening to Pliny's treatment of wheat ('triticum'). Pliny offers his own view that Italy's wheat is best, and then characteristically proceeds to list other types in a hierarchical list, beginning with the best. The opinions of Greek writers from the time of Alexander the Great are identified with 'Greece', and Pliny draws a contrast between the state of knowledge of Greeks at this time with that of Sophocles some 145 years earlier. He then expresses amazement that no Greek since Sophocles has acknowledged the surpassing excellence of Italian wheat. This seems an odd coming together of disparate sources, subjects, and wounded *amour propre*. What has Sophocles got to do with Roman farming, and why might Pliny believe that a Greek writer of tragedies is a valuable authority on agriculture? Why is Pliny so concerned with dating here?

Although Romans saw farming as central to their cultural heritage, here, as in other areas of knowledge, the Greeks had been there before them. Pliny is conspicuous among ancient scholars for the way in which he attempts to give credit to the authorities (*auctores*) whose work he has read and used. Book 1 of the *Natural History* consists of a prefatory letter to Titus, followed by lists of the contents of each of the following 36 books, together with lists of authorities, and the number of facts that the books contain. These lists of authorities, or sources, provide us with intriguing clues as to the wealth of ancient scholarship we have lost, as well as to what an educated polymath like Pliny might have been able to read in the first century. The question of how Pliny uses his sources is an important one for the history of Classical scholarship. Pliny's lists of authorities in Book 1 and Pliny the Younger's description of his uncle's working methods provide some of our best information on how scholars could work and what they might read.[3] In the late nineteenth and early twentieth centuries, detailed close readings of Pliny's text were used to try to recover information on the many lost works alluded to in the lists of authorities. Quellenforschung, as this methodology was called, is now usually considered to have been too optimistic about what is recoverable of these missing works, but it is possible to trace how Pliny uses and adapts material when sources are still extant.[4] In the case of this passage on wheat, the unnamed source for much of its information is Theophrastus, whose work here represents 'the opinions held in the time of Alexander the Great'.[5] I want to revisit the question of Pliny's relationship to his sources, by examining how Sophocles, Theophrastus and Alexander the Great are used — and what they can represent — in this passage. I will begin with Alexander and the problematic lack of attention to the superiority of Roman wheat in the writings of Theophrastus; in the second half of the article, I will explore Pliny's use of Sophocles here in the broader context of Pliny's approach to poetry and poets as authorities. As we will see, unpicking the logic behind Pliny's amazement here can cast light on his model of scholarship in the *Natural History* as a whole.

Greece, Theophrastus and Alexander the Great

When Pliny says writers on plants from the time of Alexander the Great, he is referring to Theophrastus, from whom most of the information in this passage comes. Theophrastus is a very important source

---

[3] Plin. *Ep.* 3.5. On Pliny's working methods, Dorandi (1991), Naas (1996), (2002) 108–36. On how Pliny the Elder is represented in the letter, see Citroni Marchetti (2011) 56–8, 100–102, Henderson (2002).

[4] On how Pliny uses his sources, see especially Murphy (2003), (2004) 47–73, Naas (2002) 137–70. For a recent nuanced attempt to determine the sources for Pliny's geography, see Sallmann (2003).

[5] On Pliny and Theophrastus, see André (1955), (1959), Doody (2011), Lloyd (1983) 140–46, Stannard (1965).

for Pliny's books on plants, but we know this mainly because
Theophrastus' works, *De Causis Plantarum* and *Historia Plantarum*,
are both extant. If we were going by Pliny's direct references to Theophrastus, this debt would not be at all obvious, as Theophrastus is very
rarely mentioned by name in these books, although he duly shows up in
the list of sources that Pliny gives for them in Book 1. As we will see,
there are significant differences in the ways Theophrastus is used when
he is an unnamed source, and how he is used when he is cited by name
in the *Natural History*. In the absence of Theophrastus as a named
source here, the emphasis of the passage falls on Alexander the Great
and on the authority of Greek cultural knowledge at a time when, Pliny
says, Greek power was at its height. Alexander is something of a hero
for Pliny in the *Natural History*. He is mentioned frequently in the text,
as a great general, as an art lover, but also, crucially, as a leader who
combined his military expeditions with the pursuit of knowledge in a
way that might serve as an example for the Romans of Pliny's day.[6] As
I will discuss, the gap between the knowledge of Sophocles and the
knowledge of Theophrastus that Pliny detects here resonates within a
broader discourse on the acquisition of knowledge in the *Natural
History*, the ways in which it can be gained, and the ways in which can
be lost.

Most, but not all, of Pliny's information on wheat in this passage
comes from two passages in Theophrastus, one from the *Historia
Plantarum*, the other from the *De Causis Plantarum*:

κουφότατος μὲν οὖν ὡς ἁπλῶς εἰπεῖν πυρὸς ὁ Ποντικός· βαρύτερος
δὲ τῶν εἰς τὴν Ἑλλάδα παραγιγομένων ὁ Σικελός· τούτου δ' ἔτι
βαρύτερος ὁ Βοιωτός· σημεῖον δὲ λέγουσιν ὅτι οἱ μὲν ἀθληταὶ ἐν τῇ
Βοιωτίᾳ τρί' ἡμιχοίνικα μόλις ἀναλίσκουσιν, Ἀθήναζε δὲ ὅταν
ἔλθωσι πένθ' ἡμιχοίνικα ῥᾳδίως. κοῦφος δὲ καὶ ὁ ἐν τῇ Λακωνικῇ.
τούτων μὲν οὖν ἕν τε ταῖς χώραις καὶ τῷ ἀέρι τὸ αἴτιον.

Lightest of all we may say is the Pontic wheat; the Sicilian is heavier
than most of those imported into Hellas, but heavier still than this is
the Boeotian; in proof of which it is said that the athletes in Boeotia
consume scarcely three pints, while, when they come to Athens, they
easily manage five. The Laconian kind is also light. The reason for
these differences is to be found in the respective soils and in the
climate.   (Theophrastus *HP* 8.4.5; trans. A. Hort)

τῶν δὲ πυρῶν ὁ μὲν τρίμηνος ἐν ταῖς λεπτογείοις καλλίων, σύμ-
μετρος γὰρ ἡ τροφὴ κούφη κούφοις· ὁ δὲ Λιβυκὸς και ὁ Δρακοντίας
καὶ ὁ στλεγγίας καὶ ὁ Σελινούσιος ἐν ἀγαθῇ, πολύτροφοι γάρ

---

[6]   On Pliny and Alexander, see Ash (2011) 8–9, Naas (2011) 58–9. For the link between
       imperial conquest and the accumulation of knowledge in Pliny's work, see Murphy
       (2004) 49–73, Naas (2002) 416–37, Naas (2011).

(σημεῖον δ᾿, ὅτι κάλαμον ἔχουσι παχύν· ἁπλῶς δὲ καὶ εἴ τις ἄλλος τοιοῦτος).

Of the varieties of wheat, the three-months kind is finer in country with lean soil, for light food is just right for light wheat. But the Libyan, Dracontias, stlengias and Selinuntine varieties are finest in good soil, since they need plenty of food (proof of this is their thick haulm, and this is true of all thick-haulmed varieties).
(Theophrastus *CP* 3.21.2; trans. B. Einarson & G.K.K. Link)

Pliny constructs a narrative of competition and nationalism in his organisation of this material on wheat. Pliny's preferred structure, the hierarchical list, provides some of the impetus here for his desire to identify the best, second best and so on, and the motif of competition between people, animals, and inanimate objects emerges partly from this dominant ordering system.[7] Pliny's statement that Boeotian wheat, followed by Sicilian, is best for weight is derived from Theophrastus, though the contenders for third place are not mentioned in this section of Theophrastus. The reference to Pontic wheat as the lightest is probably behind Pliny's reference to Greek praise for this variety. The information on Dracontis and Selinuntine wheat comes from *De Causis Plantarum*, a quite different context. Speudias is not mentioned in Theophrastus, and Pliny's information here presumably comes from a lost source. It is possible that the point about athletes in Pliny's text also comes from some other source, but it looks like Pliny has expanded on Theophrastus' simpler anecdote. In Theophrastus's version, proof that Boeotian wheat is heavier than Athenian is provided by the fact that Boeotian athletes require a much larger quantity when they arrive in Athens. In Pliny's account, this point is expanded to produce a longer hierarchy of wheat types that includes wheat from Thrace, Syria and Egypt. National types compete with each other, a little like the athletes who establish Pliny's 'order of merit', and can be judged by writers like Pliny, Sophocles, and Theophrastus (under the aegis of Alexander).

Spotting omissions and mistakes in Pliny's reading of Theophrastus has a long and distinguished history in scholarship on the text. In the late fifteenth century, the humanist Niccolo Leonicenò's discovery of factual errors in Pliny on the basis of reading Theophrastus sparked one of the most bitter and most famous controversies in humanist scholarship, one that has often been discussed as a clash between scholastic culture, that looked to the text for its authority, and a new, medical, proto-scientific approach that championed experience over book-

---

[7]   On hierarchical lists in Pliny, see Doody (2010) 23–30, 162–9.

learning, Greek knowledge over Roman.[8] More recently, scholars have documented several different types of error in Pliny's use of Theophrastus.[9] Sometimes Pliny seems to have misheard or confused similar Greek names — as in the case of ivy, *kissos*, and rock-rose, *kisthos* (*HN* 12.74, *HN* 16.145) — sometimes he seems to have mis-understood Theophrastus' Greek or been reliant on a bad copy of Theophrastus' text, as when he offers a confused account of mistletoe in Book 16. Even when Pliny accurately represents Theophrastus' text, information that is true for Greece can be wrong for Italy: so, for instance, the times of year that Pliny gives for the budding of cornel and laurel trees are more accurate for Greece than for Italy (*HN* 16.97). Ironically, Pliny is aware of the potential for this type of error, and criticises Virgil and others in Book 17 for being too prescriptive about the correct situation of vineyards, explaining that local conditions are key (*HN* 17.19–24).

Pliny's reading of Theophrastus silently underpins a great deal of the information on plants in the *Natural History*, including the section on wheat, but Pliny rarely cites Theophrastus by name when he is drawing on him for this sort of information. When Theophrastus is mentioned by name to support a fact, it is often something miraculous or a digressive point of interest: so, for instance, at *HN* 28.54, Theo-phrastus is given as the authority for the information that lying on the right side aids digestion, and a little later at *HN* 28.57, Pliny remarks that Theophrastus tells us that old people find it harder to sneeze; at *HN* 31.13, Theophrastus is the source for the dubious fact that a particular river in Crathis can turn cattle and sheep white, while another in Sybaris turns them black; and at *HN* 26.99, Pliny criticises Theophrastus for exaggerating the effects of an aphrodisiac plant, as well as being vague about its name and its type (*HP* IX.18.9). This is not unusual for Pliny: sources are often invoked to support an apparently miraculous fact, or as part of a display of erudition, when Pliny weighs the opinions of different sources to indicate his own scholarship.[10]

But one of the key reasons that Pliny cites other writers is to mark time: to demonstrate the state of knowledge in a particular period and to comment on the distance between then and now. In Pliny's treatment of plants and agriculture, Cato the Elder is by far the most commonly cited source. This is partly because Cato is a key model for Pliny: a great conservative statesman who found time to produce practical

[8] See Davies (1995), Doody (2011), Fera (1996), French (1986), Godman (1998) 80–134, Nauert (1979).
[9] André (1956).
[10] Naas (2002) 347–52.

scholarship, one of the first Romans to do so.[11] Cato is also useful, however, because he allows Pliny to show how Roman agriculture has advanced in the intervening centuries, while implicitly drawing attention to the fullness of his own account in comparison to that of his illustrious predecessor.[12] So, at *HN* 14.44–6, Pliny praises Cato for his military and political career, which, he says, is second in importance to his achievement as a scholar. Cato's actual information on vines is interesting to Pliny and his readers more for its historical significance than for its practical value:

> Catonum ille primus, triumpho et censura super cetera insignis, magis tamen etiamnum claritate litterarum praeceptisque omnium rerum expetendarum datis generi Romano, inter prima vero agrum colendi, ille aevi confessione optimus ac sine aemulo agricola, pauca attigit vitium genera, quarundum ex his iam etiam nominibus abolitis. [45] separatim toto tractatu sententia eius indicanda est, ut in omni genere noscamus quae fuerint celeberrima anno DC urbis, circa captas Carthaginem ac Corinthum, cum supremum is diem obiit, et quantum postea CCXXX annis vita profecerit.

> The elder Cato, who was exceedingly celebrated for his triumph and his censorship, though yet more for his literary distinction and for the precepts that he has given to the Roman nation upon every matter of utility, and in particular as to agriculture — a man who by the admission of his contemporaries was a supremely competent and unrivalled agriculturalist — has dealt with only a few varieties of the vine, including some even the names of which are now extinct. His opinion deserves to be set out separately and handled at full length, to make us acquainted with the varieties which were the most famous in the whole of this class in the year 154 B.C., about the time of the taking of Carthage and Corinth, the period of Cato's demise — and to show us how great an advance civilization has made in the subsequent 230 years.   (Pliny *HN* 14.44–5; trans. H. Rackham)

As in the passage on wheat, Pliny contextualises the state of knowledge about agriculture in terms of the political situation at the time, though here it is Roman expansion, rather than Alexander's conquests that provides the backdrop, and knowledge has been gained rather than lost over time. Pliny is interested in charting changes in practice and changes in the state of knowledge, where he has the sources to do so.

Theophrastus is used in this way repeatedly in the *Natural History*. In the account of ancient Latium in Book 3, Pliny praises Theophrastus

---

[11] Hine (2009) 28.
[12] For advances since Cato's time, see *HN* 14.44–6 on vines, *HN* 15.24 on artificial oil, *HN* 15.44 and 15.46 on plums, *HN* 15.72 on figs, *HN* 15.84 on the medlar, *HN* 15.90 on almonds, *HN* 15.122 on myrtle, *HN* 15.127 on laurel, *HN* 17.111–12 17.115–16 and 17.119 on methods of grafting, *HN* 19.147–51 on asparagus.

as one of the first Greeks to have real knowledge of Italy:

> mirum est quod hac de re tradere hominum notitiae possumus.
> Theophrastus, qui primus externorum aliqua de Romanis diligentius
> scripsit — nam Theopompus, ante quem nemo mentionem habuit,
> urbem dumtaxat a Gallis captam dixit, Clitarchus, ab eo proximus,
> legationem tantum ad Alexandrum missam — hic iam plus quam ex
> fama Cerceiorum insulae et mensuram posuit stadia LXXX in eo
> volumine, quod scripsit Nicodoro Atheniensium magistratu, qui fuit
> urbis nostrae CCCCXL anno. quicquid ergo terrarum est praeter X p.
> ambitus adnexum insulae, post eum annum accessit Italiae.

> The facts we are able to publish for the information of the world on
> this subject [ancient Latium] are remarkable. Theophrastus, the first
> foreigner to write with special care about the Romans — for Theo-
> pompus, before whom nobody mentioned them, merely states that
> Rome was taken by the Gauls, and Clitarchus, the next after him,
> only that an embassy was sent to Alexander — Theophrastus, I say,
> relying on more than rumour, has actually given the measurement of
> the island of Circello as 80 furlongs in the volume that he wrote in
> the archonship of Nicodorus at Athens, which was the 440th year of
> our city. Whatever land therefore has been joined to the island be-
> yond the circumference of 10 miles was added to Italy after that year.
> (Pliny *HN* 3.57–8; trans. H. Rackham)

Theophrastus's statement about the size of Circello is taken as so
reliable that any difference between Theophrastus' figures and the
current measurements are taken to represent a change in its size over
time. In another example, Theophrastus is given a position of honour at
the very start of Book 15 and his dates are again carefully noted:

> Oleam Theophrastus e celeberrimis Graecorum auctoribus urbis
> Romae anno circiter CCCCXL negavit nisi intra XXXX passuum ab
> mari nasci, Fenestella vero omnino non fuisse in Italia Hispaniaque
> aut Africa Tarquinio Prisco regnante, ab annis populi Romani
> CLXXIII, quae nunc pervenit trans Alpis quoque et in Gallias
> Hispaniasque medias.

> One of the most celebrated Greek authors, Theophrastus, who
> flourished about 314 B.C., stated that the olive only grows at places
> within forty miles of the sea, while Fenestella says that in 581 B.C.,
> during the reign of Tarquinius Priscus, it was not found at all in Italy
> and Spain or in Africa; whereas at the present day it has penetrated
> even across the Alps and into the middle of the Gallic and Spanish
> provinces.   (Pliny *HN* 15.1; trans. H. Rackham)

Pliny uses Theophrastus' information on olives as a starting point for
discussing the development of their cultivation in the intervening
centuries. It is this ability of a source to reflect the knowledge of its era
that is at stake in Pliny's amazement at the change in knowledge of

Italy's pre-eminence in wheat production that we began with.

Already in Theophrastus' time, varieties of wheat from far-flung regions are imported from across the Hellenistic world, and can be compared and contrasted with each other by the scholar at the centre. But in Pliny's discussion of Italian wheat, it is Alexander the Great, not Theophrastus, who is named and given prominence. Pliny makes frequent mention of the historians who followed Alexander the Great, and holds him up as something of a pioneering hero in the pursuit of knowledge about the natural world:

> Aristoteles diversa tradit, vir quem in his magna secuturus ex parte praefandum reor. Alexandro Magno rege inflammato cupidine animalium naturas noscendi delegataque hac commentatione Aristoteli, summo in omni doctrina viro, aliquot milia hominum in totius Asiae Graeciaeque tractu parere iussa, omnium quos venatus, aucupia piscatusque alebant quibusque vivaria, armenta, alvaria, pisciniae, aviaria in cura erant, ne quid usque genitum ignoraretur ab eo. quos percunctando quinquaginta ferme volumina illa praeclara de animalibus condidit. quae a me collecta in artum cum iis, quae ignoraverat, quaeso ut legentes boni consulant, in universis rerum naturae operibus medioque clarissimi regum omnium desiderio cura nostra breviter peregrinantes.

> King Alexander the Great being fired with a desire to know the natures of animals and having delegated the pursuit of this study to Aristotle as a man of supreme eminence in every branch of science, orders were given to some thousands of people throughout the whole of Asia and Greece, all those who made their living by hunting, fowling and fishing and those who were in charge of warrens, herds, apiaries, fishponds and aviaries, to obey his instructions, so that he might not fail to be informed about any creature born anywhere. His enquiries addressed to those persons resulted in the composition of his famous works on zoology, in nearly 50 volumes. To my compendium of these, with the addition of facts unknown to him, I request my readers to give a favourable reception while making a brief excursion under our direction among the whole of the works of Nature, the central interest of the most glorious of all sovereigns.
>
> (Pliny *HN* 8.44; trans. H. Rackham)

Alexander's conquests open up the natural world to the scrutiny of the natural philosopher, as we see in Pliny's discussion of exotic trees in Book 12:

> Nunc eas exponemus, quas mirata est Alexandri Magni victoria orbe eo patefacto.

> We will now describe the trees that aroused the wonder of the victorious expedition of Alexander the Great when that part of the world was first revealed.   (Pliny *HN* 12.21; trans. H. Rackham)

As recent scholarship on the *Natural History* has emphasised, it is this alliance between the pursuit of knowledge and the pursuit of empire that Pliny would like to see the Romans emulate.[13]

At the start of Book 14, Pliny laments that Romans have not made the most of the opportunities provided by empire to expand their knowledge of the world:

> illud satis mirari non queo, interisse quarundam memoriam atque etiam nominum quae auctores prodidere notitiam. quis enim non communicato orbe terrarum maiestate Romani imperii profecisse vitam putet commercio rerum ac societate festae pacis omniaque, etiam quae ante occulta fuerant, in promiscuo usu facta? [3] at Hercules non reperiuntur qui norint multa ab antiquis prodita. tanto priscorum cura fertilior aut industria felicior fuit, ante milia annorum inter principia litterarum Hesiodo praecepta agricolis pandere orso subsecutisque non paucis hanc curam eius, unde nobis crevit labor, quippe cum requirenda sint non solum postea inventa, verum etiam ea quae invenerant prisci, desidia rerum internecione memoriae indicta.

> There is one thing at which I cannot sufficiently wonder — that of some trees the very memory has perished, and even the names recorded by authors have passed out of knowledge. For who would not admit that now that intercommunication has been established throughout the world by the majesty of the Roman Empire, life has been advanced by the interchange of commodities and by partnership in the blessings of peace, and that even things that had previously lain concealed have all now been established in general use? Still, it must be asserted, we do not find people acquainted with much that has been handed down by the writers of former days: so much more productive was the research of the men of old, or else so much more successful was their industry, when a thousand years ago, at the dawn of literature Hesiod began putting forth rules for agriculture, and not a few writers followed him in these researches — which has been a source of more toil to us, inasmuch as nowadays it is necessary to investigate not only subsequent discoveries but also those that had already been made by the men of old, because general slackness has decreed an utter destruction of records.

> (Pliny *HN* 14.2–3; trans. H. Rackham)

As he goes on to indicate, luxurious and extravagant living have impeded the progress of scholarship at Rome. Elsewhere, Pliny points to the foreign kings and generals who have written on agriculture as an example to Romans who have abandoned knowledge of agriculture to their slaves:

---

[13] See, especially, Carey (2003) 17–40, Murphy (2004) 49–73, Naas (2002) 416–37, (2011).

Igitur de cultura agri praecipere principale fuit etiam apud exteros, siquidem et reges fecere, Hiero, Philometor, Attalus, Archelaus, et duces, Xenophon et Poenus etiam Mago, cui quidem tantum honorem senatus noster habuit Carthagine capta, ut, cum regulis Africae bibliothecas donaret, unius eius duodetriginta volumina censeret in Latinam linguam transferenda, cum iam M. Cato praecepta condidisset, [23] peritisque Punicae dandum negotium, in quo praecessit omnes vir clarissimae familiae D. Silanus. sapientiae vero auctores et carminibus excellentes quique alii illustres viri conposuissent, quos sequeremur, praetexuimus hoc in volumine, non in grege nominando M. Varrone, qui LXXXI vitae annum agens de ea re prodendum putavit.

Consequently to give instructions for agriculture was an occupation of the highest dignity even with foreign nations, inasmuch as it was actually performed by kings such as Hiero, Attalus Philometor and Archelaus, and by generals such as Xenophon and also the Carthaginian Mago, on whom indeed our senate bestowed such a great honour, after the taking of Carthage, that when it gave away the city's libraries to the petty kings of Africa it passed a resolution that in his case alone his twenty-eight volumes should be translated into Latin, in spite of the fact that Marcus Cato had already compiled his book of precepts, and that the task should be given to persons acquainted with the Carthaginian language, an accomplishment in which Decimus Silanus, a man of most distinguished family, surpassed everybody. But we have given at the beginning a list of the philosophers of originality and the eminent poets and other distinguished authors whom we shall follow in this volume, although special mention must be made of Marcus Varro, who felt moved to publish a treatise on this subject in the eighty-first year of his life.

(Pliny HN 18.22–3; trans. H. Rackham)

Foreign sources include not just Greek texts but the voluminous writings of Mago the Carthaginian, which were translated into Latin on the orders of the Roman Senate, despite the fact, Pliny notes, that Cato's work had already been published (*HN* 18.23).[14] Pliny praises foreign scholarship here, though his emphasis on the scholarship of Silanus and Varro may indicate a certain patriotic unease, but in practice, external sources could present practical problems. In agriculture, local conditions matter and these conditions change over time. As Pliny indicates, what is true of Italian wheat generally does not extend to the wheat produced in its mountainous regions; the region that holds third place for wheat has also changed over time.[15]

---

[14] On Mago and the politics of Roman translations of his work, see Devillers and Krings (1996), Heurgon (1976).

[15] Pliny highlights the importance of local differences at, for example, *HN* 17.19–24 on the best aspect for vineyards, *HN* 18.27 on buying land, *HN* 18.190 on the importance of knowing the nature of local soil and water. On changes over time, see the examples

In Pliny's view, knowledge can be lost as well as gained with the passing of time.[16] In the preface, he famously says that many subjects have fallen into obscurity, while others are over done, and that is not books but storehouses that are needed to keep up with the proliferation of information (*HN* pr.14, 17). The failure of Theophrastus and the other scholars of Alexander's Greece to remember their Sophocles is part of this pattern: knowledge from an earlier era is forgotten with the vexatious result that Greece at its height does not recognise Italy's superior wheat. In other circumstances, Pliny tends to accept Theophrastus' information as an accurate reflection of the situation at the time in which he wrote. Here, because Sophocles had written of Italian wheat earlier, and because Pliny patriotically believes in its continued excellence, he can spot the surprising lacuna in scholarship. This was perhaps especially disappointing to Pliny, given his celebration of Theophrastus as the first to write knowledgeably about Italy, and his admiration of Alexander's promotion of the pursuit of knowledge alongside empire. Even in the best of circumstances, Greek scholarship has its blind spots. New research is not enough: scholars must, like Pliny, read the old writers if knowledge is not to be lost.

Poetry and Authority in the *Natural History*

For Pliny, these old writers include poets as much as philosophers. As he says at the start of Book 18, 'But we have given at the beginning a list of the philosophers of originality and the eminent poets and other distinguished authors whom we shall follow in this volume' (*HN* 18.23). Still, using Sophocles to correct Theophrastus on agriculture seems like an odd thing to do on the face of it. Sophocles is not, in fact, listed as one of the sources for Book 18 in Pliny's list in Book 1; part of the point of the quotation is perhaps to show off Pliny's translation. But as we will see, Sophocles is cited purely for his information without any decorative quotations at a number of points in the *Natural History*. I am going to put this in context by looking first at Pliny's approach to poetic source material in the *Natural History*, and in particular in the agricultural books. Poets could be particularly authoritative sources in the field of agriculture. Pliny looks back to Hesiod's didactic poem, *Works and Days*, as the Ur-text for writing on agriculture (*HN* 18.201);

---

in note 12 above.

[16] On scholarship and time in Pliny, see especially Murphy (2004) 66–73, Naas (2002) 399–415.

more recently, Virgil had produced the *Georgics*, and Columella had pretended to finish Virgil's work by writing about gardens in verse in Book 10 of his work on agriculture.[17] Does the style in which a text is written matter to Pliny's assessment of its substance? How far does the genre in which Sophocles writes affect the authority of his information?

The simple answer to both these questions is 'surprising little, from our perspective'. In Pliny's discussion of failures in Roman scholarship at the start of Book 14, not only do people not read all the books they should, they also only want to work on prestigious subjects. And here Pliny contrasts his own scholarship with that of Virgil:

> sed nos oblitterata quoque scrutabimur, nec deterrebit quarundam rerum humilitas, sicuti nec in animalibus fecit, quamquam videmus Vergilium praecellentissimum vatem ea de causa hortorum dotes fugisse et in his quae rettulit flores modo rerum decerpsisse, beatum felicemque gratiae quindecim omnino generibus uvarum nominatis, tribus oleae, totidem pirorum, malo vero tantum Assyrio, ceteris omnibus neglectis.

> We, however, will carry our researches even into matters that have passed out of notice, and will not be daunted by the lowliness of certain objects, any more than we were when dealing with animals, although we see that Virgil, the prince of poets, was lead by this consideration to make omissions among the resources of the garden and in those which he as recorded has only culled the flower of his subject, happy and gracious as he is: he has only named fifteen kinds of grapes in all and three of olives and as many pears, and of apples only the Assyrian citron, neglecting all the rest.

> (Pliny *HN* 14.7; trans. H. Rackham)

The fact that Virgil is writing poetry does not seem to be a good excuse for his lack of thoroughness in the *Georgics*. For Pliny, poetry and elevated style more generally can be problematic in so far as they mitigate against the detailed engagement with humble subject matter that Pliny thinks is important.[18] But poetry or prose makes no difference to Pliny's expectations that the information should be correct. As Bruère has shown, Pliny is quite critical of Virgil in the *Natural History*: lines of poetry are rarely quoted, but mistaken information is often highlighted.[19]

Didactic poetry could function as an important vehicle for transmitting information on the natural world in antiquity, with a long

---

[17] On Columella's poetry, see Gowers (2000), Henderson (2002). On genre and technical literature, see especially Asper (2007), Kullmann, Althoff and Asper (1998), Taub (2008).

[18] Doody (2007).

[19] Bruère (1956). On Virgil as a source on agriculture, see Doody (2007), Spurr (1999).

tradition stretching back to Hesiod, that could include Aratus, Lucretius, the Aetna poet.[20] The expectation that Virgil be right, in this context, is perhaps not surprising. Columella is considerably more alive to the aesthetics of the *Georgics* than Pliny, and quotes it extensively, but he too occasionally flags up factual errors.[21] We might expect statements from a tragedian or an epic poet to be used differently than information from writers who, whatever other ambitions they might have had, wrote to inform. Recent work on quotations of poetry in ancient technical writing has highlighted the ways in which authors can use poetry in the construction of their authorial personae, or to make claims for the literary nature of their own work.[22] In the preface to the *Natural History*, Pliny shows off his literary skills by 'fixing' Catullus 1, offering a small change in the word order that, he says, smoothes the scansion.[23] Here too, Pliny's Latin translation of the line from Sophocles' *Triptolemus* is offered with a self-deprecating disclaimer, but he has obviously taken some trouble with his choice of words: *et fortunatam Italiam frumento serere candido* ('And Italy shines blessed with bright white wheat'). On one level, Pliny is displaying his discernment and sophisticated engagement with Greek literature, but it also matters to his argument that Sophocles be correct.

Sophocles is cited for his information more often than he is quoted for his poetry in the *Natural History*. So in Book 21, when Pliny is discussing the medical uses of trefoil, he brings in Sophocles as an authority:

> Trifolium scio credi praevalere contra serpentium et scorpionum ictus, seminis granis XX potis vel foliis et tota herba decocta, serpentesque numquam in trifolio aspici; praeterea a celebratis auctoribus contra omnia venena pro antidoto sufficere XXV grana eius, quod minyanthes ex eo appellavimus, tradi, multa alia praeterea in remediis eius adscribi. [153] sed me contra sententias eorum gravissimi viri auctoritas movet, Sophocles enim poeta venenatum id dicit, Simos quoque ex medicis, decocti aut contriti sucum infusum corpori easdem uredines facere, quas si percussis a serpente inponatur. ergo non aliter utendum eo quam contra venena censuerim. fortassis enim et his venenis inter se contraria sit natura, sicut multis aliis.

> I know it is believed that trefoil is an antidote for the bites of snakes and scorpions, twenty grains of the seed being taken in a drink of wine or of vinegar and water, or leaves of the whole plant are boiled

---

[20] For an introduction to the relationships between technical literature and poetry, see the essays collected in Horster and Reitz (2005).

[21] Saint-Denis (1971).

[22] Totelin (2012), Coxhead (2012).

[23] On Pliny and Catullus, see Gibson (2011), Howe (1985), Morello (2011).

down to make a decoction; that snakes too are never seen in trefoil; I know too that it is reported by famous authorities that twenty-five grains of the trefoil I have called minyanthes serve as an antidote to all poisons, and that many other virtues besides are attributed to it as a remedy.

But I am led to oppose their views by the authority of a very reliable man; for the poet Sophocles asserts that it is poisonous, as does Simos also among the physicians, saying that the juice of the decocted or pounded plant, when poured upon the body, produces the same sensation of burning as those felt by persons bitten by a serpent, when this plant is applied to the wound. Wherefore I should be of the opinion that it should not be used otherwise than as a counter-poison. For perhaps these poisons have a mutually counteracting quality, as many other things have.   (Pliny *HN* 21.152–3; trans. W.H.S. Jones)

Here Pliny cites Sophocles among other sources in a show of erudition on the uses of trefoil. Sophocles' views on trefoil are out of step with Pliny's other evidence for its use, but Pliny takes it seriously because of Sophocles' *gravitas* and *auctoritas*, and finds a way for everyone to be (more or less) right.

Only twenty-one fragments of Sophocles' *Triptolemus* survive, and of these, only ten are more than a single word.[24] We do not know what the plot was, but both the surviving fragments and the wider mythological tradition around Triptolemus provide some clues as to the context for Pliny's quotation. Triptolemus is a hero god associated with the Eleusinian mysteries who welcomes Demeter to Eleusis when she is wandering in grief for her daughter, Persephone. Demeter rewards Triptolemus with the gift of knowledge about how to sow wheat, and gives him a chariot pulled by snakes in order to spread this knowledge around the world. In his list of inventors and discoverers in Book 7, Pliny tells us that it was Triptolemus (or alternatively Byzges the Athenian) who introduced the ox and plough (*HN* 7.199). Strabo tells us that Sophocles' *Triptolemus* included a description of the many lands that Triptolemus visited when he was sowing the land with seed (Strabo 1.2.20). Several of the longer fragments of the play seem to refer to this journey: one line refers to two dragons curled around the axle of a chariot (*FrGT* 596), and the longest fragment, three lines quoted by Dionysius of Halicarnassus, is a speech of Demeter, apparently addressed to Triptolemus, in which she points out the land beneath him, Oenotria, the Tyrrhenian Gulf and Liguria, which will receive him (*FrGT* 598).[25] It is likely that Italy and its white wheat was

---

[24] Radt (1999) = *FrGT* 596–617
[25] There is also a line in which Triptolemus greets the borders of Carthage (*FrGT* 602), and a reference to Charnabon, who rules the Getae (*FrGT* 604).

a picturesquely far-flung example in a longer list of regions over which Triptolemus passed.

Pliny uses the quotation as authoritative evidence of Italian wheat's superiority over the wheat produced in the rest of the world, and Sophocles testifies to the state of Greek knowledge in his period. It is interesting, then, to find Strabo using the description of Triptolemus' wanderings in his critique of Sophocles as an unreliable authority on geography. This critique comes in the context of Strabo's defence of Homeric geography against Eratosthenes' charge that, like all poets, Homer wrote to entertain, not to teach, and sometimes invented 'facts' in the service of this aim (Strabo 1.1.10, 1.2.3).[26] Strabo's defence of Homer is important for what it tells us about the ways in which Homer in particular and poets in general could be thought of as authorities in ancient scholarly discourse.[27] In the course of his discussion, Strabo suggests that Homer sometimes writes to entertain and sometimes to instruct, and grants that while the poet may not have the same knowledge of the various skills he writes about — geography, generalship, agriculture, rhetoric — as that of a specialist, Homer is still someone of vast learning. Strabo presents poetry as a form of moral philosophy, and myth is a method used to instruct listeners, particularly when those listeners are not well educated. The excellent poet, he tells us, is also an excellent person. Strabo refers to specific instances of Homer's success in accurately describing the geography of the world, and contrasts his care in cataloguing places based on their relative locations with the higgledy-piggledy ordering employed by Euripides in the *Bacchae* and Sophocles in his *Triptolemus*:

> Τὸ δ' ὅλον οὐκ εὖ τὸ τὴν Ὁμήρου ποίησιν εἰς ἓν συνάγειν τῇ τῶν ἄλλων ποιητῶν εἴς τε τἆλλα καὶ εἰς αὐτὰ τὰ νῦν προκείμενα τὰ τῆς γεωγραφίας καὶ μηδὲν αὐτῷ πρεσβεῖον ἀπονέμειν. καὶ γὰρ εἰ μηδὲν ἄλλο, τόν γε Τριπτόλεμον τὸν Σοφοκλέους ἢ τὸν ἐν ταῖς Βάκχαις ταῖς Εὐριπίδου πρόλογον ἐπελθόντα καὶ παραβαλόντα τὴν Ὁμήρου περὶ τὰ τοιαῦτα ἐπιμέλειαν, ῥᾷον ἦν αἰσθέσθαι τὴν ὑπερβολὴν ἢ τὴν διαφοράν ... οἱ δ' ἐφ' ὧν τάξεως χρεία, ὁ μὲν τὸν Διόνυσον ἐπιόντα τὰ ἔθνη φράζων, ὁ δὲ τὸν Τριπτόλεμον τὴν κατασπειρομένην γῆν, τὰ μὲν πολὺ διεστῶτα συνάπτουσιν ἐγγύς, τὰ δὲ συνεχῆ διασπῶσι· "λιπὼν δὲ Λυδῶν τὰς πολυχρύσους γύας Φρυγῶν τε Περσῶν θ' ἡλιοβλήτους πλάκας Βάκτριά τε τείχη, τήν τε δύσχειμον χθόνα Μήδων ἐπελθὼν Ἀραβίαν τ' εὐδαίμονα." τοιαῦτα δὲ καὶ ὁ Τριπτόλεμος ποιεῖ.

---

[26] Seneca makes a similar claim about Virgil's aims in the *Georgics* (*Ep.* 86.15). See Spurr (1999).

[27] On Strabo and Homer, see Biraschi (2005), Dueck (2002) 31–39, Kim (2007), Kim (2010) 47–84, Schenkeveld (1976).

> Generally speaking, it is wrong to place the poetry of Homer on the same level with that of other poets, and to decline to rank him above them in any respect, and particularly in the subject that now occupies our attention, namely, geography. For if you did no more than go over the *Triptolemus* of Sophocles or the prologue to the *Bacchae* of Euripides, and then compare Homer's care with respect to geographical matters, it would be easy for you to perceive this difference, which lies on the surface. ... But Sophocles and Euripides, even where there is need of orderly sequence — the latter when he describes the visits of Dionysus to the various peoples, and the former when he tells Triptolemus visiting the earth that is being sown with seed — both poets, I say, bring near together regions that are very widely separated, and separate those that are contiguous: "I have left behind me," says Dionysus, "the gold-bearing glades of Lydia and of Phrygia, and I have visited the sun-stricken plains of Persia, the walled towns of Bactria, the wintry lands of the Medes, and Arabia the Blest." And *Triptolemus* does the same sort of thing.
>
> (Strabo 1.2.20; trans. H.L. Jones)

Euripides and Sophocles fall short of Homer's success, but there is an expectation that they should have done better in their descriptions of the world, an expectation of accuracy from poets and their writing, even though it is acknowledged that they also have other aims.

In Pliny's work, we find this same expectation that poetry should be accurate, and that poets should be moral people. Ironically, Pliny only gives us his reasons for finding Sophocles so compelling an authority at the point at which he is most critical of him. This is in Book 37 of the *Natural History*, when Pliny sets out to expose the appalling errors about amber he has found in the work of Greek writers. This is a key passage in any discussion of Pliny's attitude to the Greeks, and important, as we shall see, for his approach to poetry as a source of information. It is quite a long diatribe, but it begins:

> Occasio est vanitatis Graecorum detegendae: legentes modo aequo perpetiantur animo, cum hoc quoque intersit vitae scire, non quidquid illi prodidere mirandum.

> Here is an opportunity for exposing the falsehoods of the Greeks. I only ask my readers to endure these with patience since it is important for mankind just to know that not all that the Greeks have recounted deserves to be admired.
>
> (Pliny *HN* 37.31; trans. D.E. Eichholz)

Pliny's resentful but enormous admiration for Greek learning is at the root of both his chagrin and his glee in recounting the 'mistakes' he has found in references to amber across the whole spectrum of Greek literature. From our perspective, many of these 'mistakes' look like myths, or poetic license, employed by writers who had no intention of

informing later Romans on the subject of amber. He begins with
Aeschylus and Euripides among other poets, commenting that their
ignorance on amber is only matched by their ignorance of geography,
and proceeds to list the opinions of a large number of Greeks, including
Theophrastus (who mistakenly states amber is found in Liguria at *De
Lap.* 29), Ctesias and Mithridates VI.

In his conclusion, Pliny makes Sophocles the culmination of all this
Greek wrongness:

> super omnes est Sophocles poeta tragicus, quod equidem miror, cum
> tanta gravitas ei cothurni sit, praeterea vitae fama alias principi loco
> genito Athenis et rebus gestis et exercitu ducto. hic ultra Indiam fieri
> dixit e lacrimis meleagridum avium Meleagrum deflentium. [41]
> quod credidisse eum aut sperasse aliis persuaderi posse quis non
> miretur? quamve pueritiam tam inperitam posse reperiri, quae avium
> ploratus annuos credat lacrimasve tam grandes avesve, quae a
> Graecia, ubi Meleager periit, ploratum adierint Indos? quid ergo? non
> multa aeque fabulosa produnt poetae? sed hoc in ea re, quae cotidie
> invehatur atque abundet ac mendacium coarguat, serio quemquam
> dixisse summa hominum contemptio est et intoleranda mendaciorum
> inpunitas.

> But all these authors are surpassed by the tragic poet Sophocles, and
> this greatly surprises me seeing that his tragedy is so serious and,
> moreover, his personal reputation in general stands so high, thanks to
> his noble Athenian lineage, his public achievements and his leader-
> ship of an army. Sophocles tells us how amber is formed in the lands
> beyond India from the tears shed for Meleager by the birds known as
> Meleager's Daughters. Is it not amazing that he should have held this
> belief or have hoped to persuade others to accept it? Can one ima-
> gine, one wonders, a mind so childish and naïve as to believe in birds
> that weep every year or that shed such large tears or that once
> migrated from Greece, where Meleager died, to the Indies to mourn
> for him? Well then, are there not many other equally fabulous stories
> told by the poets? Yes; but that anyone should seriously tell such a
> story regarding such a substance as this, a substance that every day of
> our lives is imported and floods the market and so confutes the liar, is
> a gross insult to man's intelligence and an insufferable abuse of our
> freedom to utter falsehoods.   (Pliny *HN* 40–41; trans. D.E. Eichholz)

This is scathing. It is a stupid story, Pliny says, and while poets tell
many unbelievable stories, what Pliny finds offensive about this is that
it is a mythical story about an ordinary substance: mythical bird tears
do not get sold in Roman markets.

But there is a moral issue here too. Pliny assumes that Sophocles
believed in the literal truth of the mythic origins of amber that appears
in his play, and wished to persuade others of it. And this amazes him
because of the high regard he has for Sophocles. His respect for

Sophocles is founded on a number of factors: his writing is part of it —
and here it is the gravitas of his tragedy that is highlighted — but Pliny
goes on to list his noble birth, his success as a general and in public
life, his reputation in Athens. Pliny is not simply using Sophocles'
tragedy as a source; it is Sophocles the man that Pliny is citing as an
authority. And this is something that Trevor Murphy has illuminated in
his work on Pliny's sources: Pliny's *auctores* always remain people
rather than books in Pliny's mind, people with whom he is engaged in
an exchange of ideas governed by the rules of elite social behaviour.[28]
In his discussion of Sophocles' writing on amber, Pliny's reading of
poetry appears naïve to us. But his apparently naïve use of the information he finds in Sophoclean tragedy (or Virgilian didactic) makes
more sense if we see him appealing to the authority of the poet rather
than to the poem as a source. The fact that it is poetry matters less
because it is the poet himself who is at issue.

When Pliny praises Italy in Book 3 and again in his valedictory praise
that concludes the *Natural History*, the fertility of the land and the
abundance of its crops is one of the *topoi* that Pliny invokes; Italian
wheat is praised by Varro and by Columella. So when Pliny champions
Italian wheat as the best in the world in Book 18, he is speaking from
patriotism but also voicing what he believes is a standard view. He
finds confirmation of a sort in Sophocles, but the Greece of Alexander
the Great unexpectedly fails to acknowledge Roman superiority in
wheat production. This article had its roots in my own surprise at
Pliny's amazement at the failure of the Greeks. What I hope to have
shown is that Pliny's expectations of his Greek sources are consistent
with a particular model of scholarship that he promotes throughout the
Natural History. Sophocles' reputation as a general and statesman, no
less than the weight of his tragedy, underpins his authority to speak on
agriculture. What people of this sort say is expected to be accurate,
regardless of the style they adopt in saying it. The scholars of
Alexander's time, and this includes Theophrastus, produced a partial
account of wheat because they failed to cull information from all the
sources at their disposal, despite the advantageous conditions in which
they worked. For Pliny, a good authority is a serious man with a
reputation in the public sphere, and the good scholar reads everything
to makes new knowledge out of old facts. If this seems to be a
somewhat reflexive model of authoritative scholarship, that is perhaps
not at all surprising.

---

[28] Murphy (2003), (2004) 52–66; see also Sinclair (2003), Lao (2011).

Works Cited

André, J. (1955). 'Pline l'Ancien botaniste' *REL* 33.297–318

— (1959). 'Erreurs de traduction chez Pline l'Ancien' *REL* 37.203–15

Asper, M. (2007). *Griechische Wissenschaftstexte: Formen, Funktionen, Differenzierungsgeschichten.* Stuttgart

Beagon, M. (2005). *The Elder Pliny on the Human Animal: Natural History v.7.* Oxford

— (2007). 'Situating Nature's Wonders in Pliny's *Natural History*' in E. Bispham, G. Rowe and E. Matthews (edd.) *Vita Vigilia Est. Essays in Honour of Barbara Levick.* London. 19–40

— (2011). 'The Curious Eye of the Elder Pliny' in Gibson and Morello (2011) 71–88

Biraschi, A.M. (2005). 'Strabo and Homer: a chapter in cultural history' in D. Dueck, H. Lindsay and S. Pothecary (edd.) *Strabo's Cultural Geography: The Making of a Kolossourgia.* Cambridge. 73–85

Boyle, A.J. and Dominic, W.J. (2003). (edd.) *Flavian Rome: Culture, Image, Text.* Leiden and Boston

Bruère, R.T. (1956). 'Pliny the Elder and Virgil' *Classical Philology* 51.228–46

Carey, S. (2003). *Pliny's Catalogue of Culture. Art and Empire in the Natural History.* Oxford

Citroni Marchetti, S. (2011). *La scienza della natura per un intellettuale romano: studi su Plinio il Vecchio.* Pisa

Coxhead, M.A. (2012). 'A close examination of the pseudo-Aristotelian Mechanical Problems: The homology between mechanics and poetry as techne' *Studies in History and Philosophy of Science* Part A, 43(2).300–306

Davies, M. (1995). 'Making Sense of Pliny in the Quattrocento' *Renaissance Studies* 9.240–57

Devillers, O. and Krings, V. (1996). 'Autour de l'agronome Magon' in M. Khanoussi, P. Ruggeri and C. Vismara (edd.) *L'Africa romana: Atti dell' XI convegno di studio, Cartagine, 15–18 dicembre 1994.* Ozieri. 489–516

Doody, A. (2007). 'Virgil the Farmer? Critiques of the Georgics in Columella and Pliny' *Classical Philology* 102(2).180–97

— (2010). *Pliny's Encyclopedia: the Reception of the Natural History.* Cambridge

Dueck, D. (2002). *Strabo of Amasia: a Greek Man of Letters in Augustan Rome.* London and New York

Einarson, B. and Link, G.K.K. (1976–1990). (edd.) *Theophrastus: De causis plantarum.* Cambridge MA

Fera, V. (1995). 'Un laboratorio filologico di fine quattrocento: la *Naturalis historia*' in O. Pecere and M. Reeve (edd.) *Formative Stages of Classical Traditions: Latin Texts from Antiquity to the Renaissance.* Spoleto. 435–66

French, R. (1986). 'Pliny and Renaissance Medicine' in R. French and F.

Greenaway (edd.) *Science in the Early Roman Empire: Pliny the Elder, his Sources and Influence*. London and Sydney. 252–81

Gibson, R. (2011). 'Elder and Better: The *Naturalis Historia* and the *Letters* of the Younger Pliny', in Gibson and Morello (2011) 187–205

Gibson, R.K. and Morello, R. (2011). (edd.) *Pliny the Elder: Themes and Contexts*. Leiden and Boston

Godman, P. (1998). *From Poliziano to Machiavelli. Florentine Humanism in the High Renaissance*. Princeton

Gowers, E. (2000). 'Vegetable love: Virgil, Columella, and Garden Poetry' *Ramus* 29(2).127–48

Henderson, J. (2002). 'Knowing Someone through their Books: Pliny on Uncle Pliny' *Classical Philology* 97(3).256–84

— (2002). 'Columella's Living Hedge: The Roman Gardening Book' *JRS* 92.110–33

Heurgon, J. (1976). 'L'agronome carthaginois Magon et ses traducteurs en latin et en grec' *Comptes rendus de l'Académie des Inscriptions et Belles-Lettres*, 441–56

Hine, H. (2009). 'Subjectivity and Objectivity in Latin Scientific and Technical Literature' in L.C. Taub & A. Doody (edd.) *Authorial Voices in Greco-Roman Technical Writing*. Trier. 13–30

Horster, M. and Reitz, C. (2005). (edd.) *Wissensvermittlung in dichterischer Gestalt*. Stuttgart

Hort, A. (1916). (ed.) *Theophrastus: Enquiry into Plants, and Other Minor Works on Odours and Weather Signs*. Cambridge, MA

Howe, N.P. (1985). 'In Defence of the Encyclopedic Mode: on Pliny's *Preface* to the *Natural History*' *Latomus* 44.561–76

Jones, H.L. (1917–1932). (ed.) *Strabo: Geography*. Cambridge MA

Kim, L. (2007). 'The Portrait of Homer in Strabo's Geography' *Classical Philology* 102(4).363–88

— (2010). *Homer between History and Fiction in Imperial Greek Literature*. Cambridge

Kullmann, W., Althoff, J. and Asper, M. (1998). *Gattungen wissenschaftlicher Literatur in der Antike*. Tübingen

Lao, E. (2011). 'Luxury and the Creation of a Good Consumer' in Gibson and Morello (2011) 35–56

Lloyd, G.E.R. (1983). *Science, Folklore and Ideology*. Cambridge

Lloyd-Jones, H. (1996). (ed.) *Sophocles: The Fragments*. Cambridge MA

Morello, R. (2011). 'Pliny and the Encyclopaedic Addressee' in Gibson and Morello (2011) 147–66

Mudry, P. (2004). '«Mirabilia» et «magica»: essai de définition dans l'«Histoire naturelle» de Pline l'Ancien' in O. Bianchi, O. Thévenaz and P. Mudry (edd.) *Conceptions et représentations de l'extraordinaire dans le monde antique: actes du colloque international, Lausanne, 20–22 mars 2003*. Bern and Frankfurt am Main. 239–52

Murphy, T. (2003). 'Pliny's Natural History: the Prodigal Text' in Boyle and Dominic (2003) 301–22

— (2004). *Pliny the Elder's Natural History. The Empire in the Encyclopedia.* Oxford

Naas, V. (2001). '«Est in his quidem, tametsi mirabilis, aliqua ratio» (NH, IX, 178): modes de construction du savoir et imaginaires de Pline l'Ancien' in M. Courrént & J. Thomas (edd.) *Imaginaire et modes de construction du savoir antique dans les textes scientifiques et techniques: actes du colloque de Perpignan, 12–13 mai 2000.* Perpignan. 15–34

— (2002). *Le projet encyclopédique de Pline l'Ancien.* Rome

— (2004). '«Ratio… multis inuoluta miraculis» (Pline l'Ancien, Naturalis historia, II, 62): autour de la «ratio» plinienne' in V. Naas (ed.) *En deçà et au-delà de la «ratio»: actes de la journée d'étude, université de Lille 3, 28 et 29 septembre 2001.* Villeneuve-d'Asq. 29–37

— (2008). 'Pline l'Ancien a-t-il cru à ses mythes?' *Pallas* 78.133–51

— (2011). 'Imperialism, *Mirabilia*, and Knowledge: Some Paradoxes in the *Naturalis Historia*' in Gibson and Morello (2011) 57–70

Nauert, C. (1979). 'Humanists, Scientists and Pliny: Changing Approaches to a Classical Author' *American Historical Review* 84.72–85

Rackham, H., Jones, W.H.S. and Eichholz, D.E. (1938–1962). (edd.) *Pliny: Natural history / with an English translation.* Cambridge MA

Sallmann, K. (2003). 'Quellenangaben und Namenszitate in der plinianischen Geographie' *Hyperboreus* 9(2).330–54

Schenkeveld, D.M. (1976). 'Strabo on Homer' *Mnemosyne* 29.52–64

Sinclair, P. (2003). 'Rhetoric of Writing and Reading in the Preface to Pliny's *Natural History*' in Boyle and Dominic (2003) 277–99

Spurr, M.S. (1999). 'Agriculture and the *Georgics*' in P. Hardie (ed.) *Virgil. Critical Assessments of Classical Authors* Vol. 2. London and New York. 1–24

Stannard, J. (1965). 'Pliny and Roman Botany' *Isis* 56.420–25

Taub, L.C. (2008). *Aetna and the Moon: Explaining Nature in Ancient Greece and Rome.* Corvallis OR

Totelin, L.M.V. (2012). 'And to End on a Poetic Note: Galen's Authorial Strategies in the Pharmacological Books' *Studies in History and Philosophy of Science* Part A, 43(2).307–15

Wallace-Hadrill, A. (1990). 'Pliny the Elder and Man's Unnatural History' *Greece and Rome* 1.80–96

Notes from Underground: the Curious Katabasis of Dionysodorus

Trevor Murphy
University of California, Berkeley

Book 2 of Pliny's *Natural History* closes on a strange note. The subject of Book 2 is the universe as a whole, embracing the fields known today as astronomy, geology, and meteorology, and it ends by dealing with the question of the world's size. Pliny quickly surveys different estimates of the Earth's size advanced by three Greek scholars, Eratosthenes, Hipparchus, and Dionysodorus. This last man, an otherwise unknown geometer, gives Pliny occasion for the bizarre anecdote that closes Book 2, in which Eratosthenes' estimate of Earth's circumference is confirmed by evidence provided from beyond the grave by a mathematician for whom death posed no barrier to publication. Previous interpretations of this story have tended to avoid dealing with its grotesque framing in order to focus on the accuracy of Dionysodorus' measurement; as I will show, this approach fundamentally misses Pliny's point.

Some of the most brilliant thinkers of antiquity attempted to answer the question of how big the Earth was by applying the principles of geometry to astronomical and geographical observations. Aristotle estimated Earth's circumference to be 400,000 stades; Dicaearchus of Messene reckoned it at 300,000 stades. The most famous of these ancient estimates, one recognized today as a milestone in the history of science, was advanced by Eratosthenes of Cyrene (c. 285–194 BCE) in his treatise *On the Measurement of the Earth*.[1] This treatise is known only from the testimonies of later writers, who give differing accounts of Eratosthenes' procedure and conclusion; the most common version is as follows: it was accepted that Syene on Egypt's southern frontier lay on the solar tropic, because at noon on the summer solstice the sun cast no shadow down a deep well (Strabo 17.1.48). On the summer solstice the noonday shadow of the pointer on a sundial in Alexandria, which was understood to lie due north of Syene, was read as one-

---

[1] Geus (2004) 1–26; Roller (2010) 12–13, 157–8; Thomson (1947) 159–60.

fiftieth of the sundial's bowl (that is, 7°12′: Eratosthenes antedates the system of measuring in degrees). From this difference Eratosthenes deduced the Earth's circumference to be fifty times the distance from Syene to Alexandria, reported to be 5000 stades. Accordingly he estimated the circumference as either 250,000 stades, as transmitted by one source,[2] or (more commonly reported) 252,000 stades. (It has been surmised Eratosthenes may have added 2000 stades to yield a number divisible by 60.)[3] By either number Eratosthenes' estimate comes reasonably close to the Earth's actual circumference (polar: 40,008 km; equatorial: 40,007.5 km) though because of the variable length of the stade in antiquity it is impossible to gauge exactly how close.[4]

Eratosthenes' reckoning of Earth's size was, Pliny states, an exceptionally brilliant achievement: "a wickedly conceited venture, but established with such refined calculation that it seems embarrassing to disbelieve it". The phrasing reveals no little ambivalence. It is all very wonderful, to be sure, but faced with such rarified cleverness, how is a lay person to frame an intelligent objection? "I see everyone agrees with Eratosthenes," says Pliny (*quem cunctis probari video*), but adds in almost the same breath "Hipparchus, employing that remarkable energy typical of all his projects to pick Eratosthenes apart, corrects him by adding a little less than 26,000 stades to the circumference".[5] So are we to take it that Pliny preferred Hipparchus' figure of 278,000 stades over Eratosthenes' 252,000? On what grounds is the non-geometer to choose between them? No further hint is offered. The circumference of the Earth, it would seem, does not lend itself to commonsense discussion.

It is on this note that Pliny narrates the anecdote that concludes *Natural History* 2, which puts the question on a more pragmatic plane. Eratosthenes and Hipparchus were celebrated geometers, but neither

----

[2] Cleomedes *Elementary Theory* 1.7, available in Bulmer-Thomas (1941) II 266–273; published as Eratosthenes fragment M6 in Roller (2010) 265–6.

[3] Roller (2010) 13 n.73.

[4] Roller (2010) 271 gives a range of 177.7 meters to 197.3 meters to the stadion, adding "There is no reason to believe Eratosthenes always used the same length of stadion." Thomson (1947) 161–2 (with useful diagrams) describes several variant stades proposed by scholars for use with Eratosthenes' estimate: the 'ordinary' stade of 185 meters; the Attic stade of 177.6 meters; and a posited (but not attested) Ptolemaic stade used by royal surveyors of 157.5 meters, which would yield a total very near the modern measurement.

[5] *universum autem circuitum Eratosthenes, in omnium quidem litterarum subtilitate, set in hac utique praeter ceteros solers, quem cunctis probari video, CCLII milium stadiorum prodidit, quae mensura Romana conputatione efficit trentiens quindeciens centena milia passuum: inprobum ausum, verum ita subtili argumentatione conprehensum, ut pudeat non credere. Hipparchus, et in coarguendo eo et in reliqua omni diligentia mirus, adicit stadiorum paulo minus XXVI.*

had measured the Earth in person. Enter a third Greek mathematician, Dionysodorus of Melos, less famous but (perhaps) better placed to speak with authority. Despite all their cleverness, neither Eratosthenes nor Hipparchus ever gave firsthand testimony about the distance from Earth's outside to its center:

> alia Dionysodoro fides. neque enim subtraham exemplum vanitatis Graecae maximum. Melius hic fuit, geometricae scientia nobilis; senecta diem obiit in patria. funus duxere ei propinquae, ad quas pertinebat hereditas. hae cum secutis diebus iusta peragerent, invenisse dicuntur in sepulchro epistulam Dionysodori nomine ad superos scriptam: pervenisse eum a sepulchro ad infimam terram; esse eo stadiorum $\overline{XLII}$. nec defuere geometrae qui interpretarentur, significare epistulam a medio terrarum orbe missam, quod deorsum ab summo longissimum esset spatium et idem pilae medium. ex quo consecuta conputatio est, ut circuitum esse $\overline{CCLII}$ stadiorum pronuntiarent.

> To Dionysodorus, on the other hand, I attach quite another sort of credence. I will not supress this gigantic example of Greek nonsense. He was a Melian, renowned for his command of geometry, and died in his old age in his homeland. His funeral was managed by female relatives who inherited his property. The story goes that when they were completing the funeral rites some days later they found in the tomb a letter in Dionysodorus' name addressed TO THOSE ABOVE. He had passed, it said, from his tomb to the lowest level of the Earth, a distance of 42,000 stades. There were found geometers to explain what the letter meant: it had been sent from the center of the Earth, that is, the maximum distance from its surface, identical with the center of the sphere. From which the estimate followed that the circumference of the world is 252,000 stades.

> *(Natural History 2.248)*

Needless to say, this story contains striking elements of the fantastic: in a stunning instance of posthumous scholarly achievement, Dionysodorus not only measured Earth's radius as he descended to Hades, but also found some way of conveying a letter from Hades to his tomb to secure publication of his findings. Note also the heavy sarcasm with which Pliny frames the tale: it is *exemplum vanitatis Graecae maximum*, "a gigantic example of Greek nonsense." Nevertheless, despite its fantastic content and ironic presentation, commentators have been willing to detect behind this anecdote a serious attempt at reckoning the Earth's size, because of its possible relevance to Eratosthenes. Assuming a value of 3 for π, Dionysodorus' 42,000–stade radius confirms Eratosthenes' 252,000–stade circumference. Little enough is known about Eratosthenes himself, the context of his work in Alexandria, or how his ideas were received by his contemporaries, and in Pliny's tale possibly we have evidence bearing on all those questions. That there was such a person called Dionysodorus is not in itself implausible, as Dionysodorus was a rather common name in antiquity. No fewer than 24 individuals of that name are known to the *RE*, and a few of them are known to have been intellectuals.[6] One is tantalized by the idea of a mathematician who, independent of Eratosthenes, proposed a figure for Earth's radius that confirmed his reckoning.

So Alexander Jones[7] and Ivor Bulmer-Thomas[8] identify Pliny's Dionysodorus of Melos with a mathematician mentioned by Strabo (12.3.16). Jones would bypass the supernatural element of the tale ("a foolish anecdote") by interpreting the letter (*epistula*) as Pliny's misreading of a "funeral inscription." The story's supernatural element — the improbability of the letter from the dead — can be explained as due to Pliny's garbling or misunderstanding his source. Of course we are familiar with the figure of Pliny the bungler, mistranslating and misunderstanding his sources with his rapid and indiscriminating consumption of books. The "funeral inscription" could have been designed by Dionysodorus during his lifetime as a way of using his monument to assert ownership of a mathematical proof. A famous contemporary parallel (not adduced by Jones) can be found in the case of Archimedes in Syracuse, whose tomb displayed the figures of a sphere and a cylinder to demonstrate Archimedes' formula for calculating their relative sizes (Cicero *Tusculans* 5.64–6).[9] But this hypothesis runs into problems in accounting for the shape and emphasis of the narrative as Pliny transmits it. Short as it is, the anecdote works as a story with a beginning, middle, and end, and contains a surprising amount of circumstantial detail. At what point in the garbling were Dionysodorus's female heirs introduced, for instance, or the resumption of the funeral rites after a pause of some days, or the address "To Those Above"? This looks less like a case of details accidentally misunderstood than the marks of a creative fictional narrative.

---

[6] Pliny's is the only secure attestation of Dionysodorus of Melos. Not including Pliny's Dionysodorus we know of at least two Greek mathematicians with the name, Dionysodorus of Kaunos and Dionysodorus of Amisene. Strabo (12.3.16; C 548) distinguishes Dionysodorus of Amisene from another Dionysodorus, τῷ ἴκενι γεωμέτρῃ, where ἴκενι seems to be the corruption of a demonym. Tyrwhitt conjectured Μηλίῳ, which was accepted by Meineke (1877), and appears in Jones' Loeb (1917–1932), but has been rejected on paleographical grounds by Radt, the latest editor of Strabo (2002–2011).

[7] Jones (2008) 266 .

[8] Bulmer-Thomas (1971) IV 108–10.

[9] For other examples of monuments publicizing mathematical proofs see Fraser (1972) I 411–13, including a poem by Eratosthenes himself on doubling the cube.

Another hypothesis relieves Pliny of responsibility for the fantasy and puts it on the shoulders of Dionysodorus' survivors: Roller has proposed that the finding of Dionysodorus' letter was a spurious miracle performed to inspire awe and command belief. "The story has the character of a staged event to give folkloric wisdom to arcane mathematical calculations, and thus to provide popular support, perhaps even to supersede Eratosthenes."[10] Certainly it is a vivid and memorable episode, but this explanation runs into improbabilities of its own. The question of what motivated the staging of the supposed miracle is a serious obstacle. If the plan was to influence Eratosthenes' reputation by producing a forged letter from a dead geometer, by what means did the discoverers imagine the letter would effect such change? It is hard to imagine a mechanism by which the miraculous letter would be reasonably expected to win popular support; it is even harder to imagine the link between popular support and acceptance by intellectuals. No matter how dramatically it was brandished in public, this was not a letter to electrify bystanders or persuade the masses; its contents could not be comprehended by non-specialists. Given modern norms of how geometry is taught, the use of a given radius to calculate a circle's circumference may not seem especially arcane, but it was not so transparent in antiquity, and, on Pliny's showing, the significance of the 42,000–stade figure was not understood till the letter had been interpreted by experts in geometry. Even supposing that after explication the letter had somehow generated popular support, I cannot recall a case in antiquity where popular support — created by a miracle or any other means — counted toward acceptance of a mathematical proof by the educated elite.

A third possibility is to see Dionysodorus himself as the deceiver. In his *RE* article on Dionysodorus (#20) Friedrich Hultsch[11] proposed that the geometer had calculated the Earth's radius following Eratosthenes' estimate of its circumference. As Hultsch conjectured, thinking his female next-of-kin gullible enough to swallow anything Dionysodorus decided to play a practical joke on them in the last days of his life. Composing a letter about his descent from the tomb, he entrusted it to a confidant (*Vertrauensmann*), with instructions that he should claim to have found it at the grave some days after the burial. Of the different interpretations of the episode, Hultsch's suggestion is the simplest and the most persuasive. He was certainly right to emphasize the story's black and misogynistic humor. What else could motivate the careful re-

---

[10] Roller (2010) 43.
[11] *RE* s.v. 'Dionysodorus' (20) (Hultsch) V:1 cols. 1005–1006.

mark that Dionysodorus' funeral was conducted by the "female relatives who inherited his property" (*propinquae ad quas pertinebat hereditas*)? On the other hand, once the finding of the letter is understood to be a prank, it is not quite logical to treat the letter's content, the 42,000 stade measurement, as a sincere attempt by Dionysodorus to calculate the Earth's radius, exempt from the general black humor. Making such an exception would seem to be motivated by a predisposition in favor of what seems at first sight to agree with Eratosthenes. It is also problematic that to make the prank feasible, Hultsch has had to posit the action of a third party — Dionysodorus' unnamed male confidant. Nothing in the text supports the agency of such a man, and as I will show, the existence of such a co-conspirator is contrary to the internal logic of the anecdote.

The tendency to see the anecdote as originating in an account of a historical Dionysodorus, partisan of Eratosthenes, has worked powerfully against the proper appreciation of its fantasy and grotesque humor. But we have seen that the grounds for a historical reading are slender. There is no evidence outside Pliny for a Dionysodorus with the demonym *Melius* ("of Melos"). The identification of Pliny's geometer with the Dionysodorus of Strabo 12, accepted by Jones and Bulmer-Thomas, rests on an obsolete textual conjecture. Absent this, the only point at which the story impinges on history is the compatibility of Dionysodorus' radius with Eratosthenes' circumference. There is no reason to assume the composer of the story meant his audience to connect it with any particular Dionysodorus; similarly, there is no reason to see it as directed toward Eratosthenes with friendly intent.

It is the anecdote's circumstantial details that suggest we are dealing with an imaginative narrative meant to entertain, and that, as Hultsch understood, there is a grim joke somewhere behind it. When we read the story as fantasy, taking its black humor as our starting-point, what had looked like apparently pointless details are seen to make sense. For example, the address of Dionysodorus' letter, "To Those Above," *ad superos,* is a pun, a trap laid for the unwary reader. "To the ones above" is a literal rendering. "Above what?" one asks oneself. The natural way of taking it is "to those above us" on the assumption that the writer of the letter and the recipient have the same sense of direction and orientation. On this assumption, the referent of *superi* are the gods, an easy inference in Greco-Roman antiquity when "those above" was a traditional way of designating the (non-infernal) deities.[12]

---

[12] Oxford Latin Dictionary, v.l. '*superus*'; Liddell and Scott ἄνω.

So it was taken by Hultsch.[13] But "above" is of course potentially ambiguous, and when Dionysodorus' message is understood it emerges
that the writer of the letter orients himself according to points of
reference quite different from his readers. The trap is sprung and the
reader winces, as we tend to when victims of a pun: Dionysodorus
directed the letter not to the gods above but to us, to the people on the
surface.

Similarly, the anecdote is careful to specify the gender of Dionysodorus' heirs because ancient sexual stereotypes are in play here.
Dionysodorus' property was inherited by his female relatives, who
conducted his funeral, managed his tomb, and discovered his letter. A
standard part of Greek funerary culture was the offering of ritual meals
at the deceased's grave on the ninth and thirtieth day after death.[14]
Since his female heirs are said to have been completing the rites, they
were presumably carrying out the *triakostia*, the thirtieth day ceremony, but *iusta peragerent,* translated as "completing the rites" might
only mean "fulfilling the rites," in which case the ninth-day ceremony,
the *ennata* cannot be excluded.[15] But it is clear enough in either case
that it was Dionysodorus' female heirs who found his letter, and in
antiquity this was certainly not a point in the letter's favor. The pre-
supposition was that women were credulous; they made poor witnesses.
To the second century CE Platonist Celsus, for instance, marshalling
arguments against the Christians, it seemed a vulnerability of the
Gospels that evidence of Jesus' resurrection should depend on paltry
female witnesses: what god, Celsus asked, intending to announce to the
universe his triumph over death, would start by revealing himself to a
hysterical woman (γυνὴ πάροιστρος) and similar hole-and-corner
rabble?[16]

---

[13] Hultsch (n.11) 1006.

[14] Garland (2001) 39–40.

[15] This prompts one to wonder how long a soul needs to get to Hades, and poses the
contingent question of how quickly mail travels underground. If Pliny's source used
specific names for the ceremonies, the *triakostia* would indicate a putative journey of
half a month, *ennata,* just four and a half days, assuming, of course, that it takes as
long to go up as to go down. Perhaps Dionysodorus could have shed light for us on the
meaning of Heraclitus fragment B60, ὁδὸς ἄνω κάτω μία καὶ ὡυτή.

[16] Origen *Contra Celsum* 2.55: τίς τοῦτο εἶδε; Γυνὴ πάροιστρος, ὥς φατε, καὶ εἴ τις
ἄλλος τῶν ἐκ τῆς αὐτῆς γοητείας, ἤτοι κατά τινα διάθεσιν ὀνειρώξας καὶ κατὰ τὴν
αὐτοῦ βούλησιν δόξῃ πεπλανημένη φαντασιωθείς, ὅπερ ἤδη μυρίοις συμβέβηκεν, ἤ,
ὅπερ μᾶλλον, ἐκπλῆξαι τοὺς λοιποὺς τῇ τερατετείᾳ θελήσας καὶ διὰ τοῦ τοιούτου
ψεύσματος ἀφορμὴν ἄλλοις ἀγύρταις παρασχεῖν.: "But who really saw this? A hysterical woman, as you admit and perhaps one other person — both deluded by his
sorcery, or else so wrenched with grief at this failure that they hallucinated him risen
from the dead by a sort of wishful thinking. This mistaking a fantasy for reality is not
at all uncommon; indeed, it has happened to thousands. Just as possible, these deluded

But the joke here has another, more bitter target than Dionysodorus' female heirs — Pliny calls it proof of Greek silliness, not female silliness. Rather, the target of the joke is Dionysodorus himself, as a man without male connections. Though Pliny says he was famous as a geometer (*geometricae scientia nobilis*), his life considered from an ancient Greek or Roman perspective must be judged to have been a social and sexual failure. For all his fame, he died without leaving a son or student to be his successor and carry on his work. He was, it seems, a social oddball whose death was the kind that laws of inheritance were intended to prevent.[17] If all his heirs were women, he must have lacked even a male cousin or a nephew in the female line to whom to leave his property. Viewed in this light, Dionysodorus was a feckless, ineffectual man to be pitied, perhaps even to be despised. His life had borne no fruit. Only in dying did he forge a significant connection with another male, taking on the role of ancillary supporter to Eratosthenes. All this considered, it cannot have been a good thing for Eratosthenes' estimate to be confirmed by a figure so evidently weak and ridiculous.

Pliny's skepticism toward Dionysodorus' letter is consistent with the generally skeptical attitude toward the souls of the dead (called variously *manes, umbrae*, or *inferi*) voiced throughout the *Natural History*. The eschatology implied by Dionysodorus' letter — the dead traveling through physical and measurable space down from their graves to the bottom of the earth (*ad infimam terram*) where they enjoy an existence corporeal enough to write and send letters home — is obviously absurd. To pose just the most obvious of the many questions that it begs, who carries the letters? The conceptual absurdity is made visible in the awkwardness of Pliny's language, which juxtaposes two incommensurate descriptive modes, the technical language of geometry (e.g. "the maximum distance extending downward from its surface, identical with the center of the sphere, *quod deorsum ab summo longissimum esset spatium et idem pilae medium*) combining uneasily with the homely idea of a physical subterranean region where the dead dwell. Elsewhere, in the discussion of death and the soul in *Natural History* 7, Pliny's book on the human condition, the logical contradictions and

---

women wanted to impress the others." (trans. Hoffman (1987) 68).

[17] Harrison (1968) I 132–3: "If a man died leaving behind no sons but only a daughter or daughters and if he had not married off the daughters to men whom he adopted, the daughters became ἐπίκληροι ... The distinguishing mark of an ἐπίκληρος was that she was also ἐπίδικος; that is to say, her hand could be claimed in marriage by her father's nearest male kin." MacDowell (1978) 95: "A woman or girl left in this position was called *epikleros* ... she did not really own the property herself in the sense of being able to dispose of it as she wished; it just remained with her until her son was ready to inherit."

absurdities of this eschatology give an occasion for an outpouring of joyous scorn as he rails against its *vanitas* — the word he used in *NH* 2.248 to condemn "Greek nonsense":

> Post sepulturam vanae manium ambages, omnibus a supremo die eadem quae ante primum, nec magis a morte sensus ullus aut corpori aut animae quam ante natalem. eadem enim vanitas in futurum etiam se propagat et in mortis quoque tempora ipsa sibi vitam mentitur, alias inmortalitatem animae, alias transfigurationem, alias sensum inferis dando et manes colendo deumque faciendo qui iam etiam homo esse desierit, ceu vero ullo modo spirandi ratio ceteris animalibus distet aut non diuturniora in vita multa reperiantur, quibus nemo similem divinat inmortalitatem.

> The mazy wanderings of the *manes* beyond the grave are nonsensical (*vanae*): everyone who reaches their last day has the same condition as before their first, and neither body nor spirit has any more consciousness after death than before birth. The same nonsense (*vanitas*) extends itself into the future and imagines for itself life continuing even into epochs of death, in some cases as immortality of the soul, or as a change of shape, or by endowing the shades below with consciousness and worshipping the *Manes* and making into a god that which has ceased to be human. As if the mechanism of our breathing differed from that of the other animals, or as if there were no animals with life-spans longer than ours! No one prophesies immortality for them. (*NH* 7.188)

This is just the beginning of a long and vigorous attack on the notion of life after death. At its peak Pliny takes aim at the idea that the *manes* reside in the depths of the earth as a particular improbability:

> quae deinde sedes quantave multitudo tot saeculis animarum vel umbrarum? puerilium ista delenimentorum avidaeque numquam desinere mortalitatis commenta sunt ... quaeve genitis quies umquam, si in sublimi sensus animae manet, inter inferos umbrae? perdit profecto ista dulcedo credulitasque praecipuum naturae bonum, mortem.

> What housing do they have, and how big is the population of the souls or the ghosts, over the course of so many centuries? These are childish fantasies, productions of a mortal life eager never to reach an end ... What rest will there ever be for us poor creatures, if consciousness persists for the soul on the surface-world and the ghost retains it in the underworld? Gullible acceptance of this sweet fantasy does away with nature's greatest benefit: death. (*NH* 7.189–190)

The skepticism towards life after death voiced here is as sharp as that of Lucretius in *De Rerum Natura* 3, and Pliny, though no Epicurean, helps himself to many of the same images and arguments.[18] In short, he argues that the primitive notion of the *Manes* surviving under the

---

[18] Lucretius *De Rerum Natura* 3.978–1023; compare Seneca *Epistulae Morales* 24.18.

ground cheapens the dignity of human life and produces needless anxiety; the concept is not compatible with the relative values of life and death as illustrated in *NH* 7.

Pliny does not consistently demonstrate such thorough skepticism as this to ghosts and the *Manes* everywhere in the *Natural History,* but his tone toward the topic is always dismissive and sardonic. For example, Pliny cites them in his many attacks on the exponents of magic (*magi,* sorcerers). Among their many other false claims, they promised customers evocations and colloquies with the dead; these promises were found to be a complete fraud by the experiments of the *princeps* Nero, their illustrious dupe (*NH* 30.14; compare with 37.192). In a similar manner, Pliny uses the *manes* to give point to tirades against mining as a violent abuse of the Earth: *si ulli essent inferi, iam profecto illos avaritiae atque luxuriae cuniculi refodissent* (If residents of the underworld *(inferi)* did exist, the excavations undertaken in our avarice and luxury would certainly have dug them up by now, 2.158). When Pliny returns to the theme of mining in the preface to Book 33, about metals, his skepticism is less overt:

> persequimur omnes eius fibras vivimusque super excavatam, mirantes dehiscere aliquando aut intremescere illam, ceu vero non hoc indignatione sacrae parentis exprimi possit. imus in viscera et in sede manium opes quaerimus, tamquam parum benigna fertilique qua calcatur.

> We hunt through all Earth's innards, we build our homes above the excavated void, and then feel shock when she quakes or splits open, as if we could not recognize when our sacred parent vents her anger. In the home of the *manes* we scrounge for wealth, as if Earth were not already generous and fertile enough where we tread on her.
>
> (*NH* 33.2)

Though Pliny mentions the *manes* here as if he believed in them, the tone here is every bit as sarcastic as in Book 2. 158; clearly the *manes* appear only in the service of hyperbole.

Collectively the stock of images and motifs describing the underworld like Minos' judgment, the punishments of Tantalus, or asphodel fields, stemming from epic *katabasis* narratives[19] were combined with daemonic terrors like Cerberus and personalities from popular eschatology like Charon to make up a stereotyped discourse of great flexibility in Greek and Roman literature. The imagery of the dead and their infernal realm was employed not only to suggest pathos, bereavement, horror, or dread, but also for frivolous jokes and satire. In some

---

[19] The heroic journey to the underworld: above all the Nekyia of *Odyssey* 11, but see also *Odyssey* 24.1–204 and *Iliad* 23.69–79)

literary fantasies the horror was combined with paradox and ridicule, as in this example from Juvenal, an outrageous piece of special pleading on the topic of cannibalism during siege: *uentribus abnueret dira atque inmania passis, / et quibus illorum poterant gnoscere manes / quorum corporibus uescebantur?* (Who would refuse to forgive stomachs that suffered terrible, monstrous pangs? They [the Vascones] would have been forgiven even by the *manes* of the corpses they were eating! – Juvenal 15.104–6). But considered as a dramatic location, Hades gave writers a place where gods and porters could be depicted interacting on the same level (as Dionysus and Xanthias in Aristophanes' *Frogs*), where philosophers could be juxtaposed with buffoons, revered ancestors with their descendants. The use of the tropes of Hades did not commit the author to believing in any aspect of the afterlife; sometimes belief was specifically disavowed:

> esse aliquos manes et subterranea regna,
> Cocytum et Stygio ranas in gurgite nigras,
> atque una transire uadum tot milia cumba
> nec pueri credunt, nisi qui nondum aere lauantur.
> sed tu vera puta: Curius quid sentit et ambo
> Scipiadae, quid Fabricius manesque Camilli,
> quid Cremerae legio et Cannis consumpta iuuentus,
> tot bellorum animae, quotiens hinc talis ad illos
> umbra uenit? cuperent lustrari, si qua darentur
> sulpura cum taedis et si foret umida laurus.

Not even kids — no one old enough to have to pay for entrance to the baths — believe in the *manes* and their underground kingdom, Cocytus and the black frogs of the Stygian stream, and so many thousands crossing the water in one little boat. But just suppose: what does Curius think, and the two Scipios, what does Fabricius think, and the soul of Camillus, the ghosts of the legion lost at Cremera and the army killed at Cannae, the souls perished in so many wars, what do they think when the shade of one of our contemporaries joins them in Hades? They'd want to be cleansed, if they could get hold of some sulfur and torches and a wet laurel sprig.

(Juvenal *Satires* 2.149–54)

Though Juvenal is of course after Pliny's time, the use of underworld tropes for comic effect was already old, going back at least as far as Aristophanes in the fifth century BCE. His brilliant exploitation of the underworld's comic potential in *Frogs*, pitting Aeschylus against Euripides in a fantasy *agon* that makes recondite issues of literary criticism into broad comedy, is too well-known to need comment here. In Eratosthenes' own lifetime (the first half of the third century BCE) this literary mode was given new impetus and an extended range of targets

by the Cynic Menippus of Gadara.[20] This Cynic philosopher demonstrated how the clichés of Hades could serve to juxtapose incongruous
elements and puncture lofty reputations. Though Menippus' writings
— a series of *spoudogeloios* (serio-comic) prose-and-verse satires —
elude reconstruction in detail, it seems in his *Nekyia* that he portrayed
himself as a ghost-cum-social critic. Having died in the regular way, as
he framed his account, he was sent back from Hades in the costume of
a junior Fury, deputized to monitor the follies of the living.[21] The targets of Menippus' satires remain shadowy, but his influence was wide
and lasting. It was felt in Rome in the last century BCE by Varro, who
composed scores of Menippean satires, as well as in the early Principate, in Seneca's *Apocolocyntosis* where the climactic descent to
Hades of Emperor Claudius completes his humiliation. Menippus' influence is evident above all in Lucian, many of whose works feature
trips to Hades in which self-satisfied intellectuals are disconcerted or
their reputations punctured (*Menippus; Icaromenippus, Kataplous;
Charon; Lover of Lies; Dialogues of the Dead*); in some of these
Menippus himself appears as a character.

The grotesque humor that makes the Dionysodorus anecdote sit
awkwardly in the history of science makes much more sense when seen
in the tradition of satiric infernal fantasy. Its fantastic premise and its
strong element of mockery (the female heirs and the letter's address *ad
superos*) bear an unmistakable resemblance to *Frogs*, Lucian, and other
use of underworld tropes for ridicule and parody. Pliny introduces the
anecdote as an example of nonsense; our interpretation cannot begin by
minimizing the mockery and teasing. A reading that sees it as praising
either Dionysodorus or Eratosthenes is hardly plausible. If the Dionysodorus of the anecdote is to be identified with an actual geometer, we
must conclude the author's object was not to promote him but to make
fun of him. If, as is more likely, this Dionysodorus is fictional, whoever
made him up and connected him with Eratosthenes' *Measurement of
the Earth* was not motivated by friendly intentions. As little as Eratosthenes seems to us to deserve it, Pliny's story originated in ridicule.

Who would want to mock Eratosthenes? When did the ridicule
originate? Who circulated it? It is impossible to give definite answers
to these questions, but even from the scanty records of his life it is clear

---

[20] See the reconstruction of Menippus' philosophy and works outlined by Relihan (1993)
39–48. Menippus' dates are approximately 299–250 BCE. Diogenes Laertius gives a
list of thirteen titles for Menippus' writings, among which the following seem the most
relevant to the Dionysodorus anecdote: *Nekyia*; *Treatises Against Physikoi*; *Against
Mathematikoi*; *Testaments* (sc. of Philosophers). The epithet '*spoudogeloios*' was
applied to Menippus by Strabo, 16.29 C759.
[21] Relihan (1993) 45–7.

that Eratosthenes had competitors and critics. We have already seen from Pliny that in the second century BCE the astronomer Hipparchus corrected Eratosthenes' *Measurement of the Earth*; from Strabo we know that Hipparchus subjected his *Geographica* to extensive criticism.[22] Other critics of the *Geographica* included Polybius, Artemidorus of Ephesus, and Polemon of Ilium.[23] Besides criticism directed at his work, Eratosthenes attracted a certain amount of personal teasing. He was famous for having spread himself too thin among many different fields (besides mathematics and geography, he published on chronology, grammar, and literary criticism) which perhaps explains why he founded no school and left no direct intellectual successors.[24] Certainly it is recorded that his failure to achieve first rank in any one of his many fields gave rise to two nicknames: *Beta*, "Second place," and *Pentathlos*, "All-round-athlete," in the dismissive sense of our "Jack-of-all-trades."[25] These nicknames point to the agonistic culture of scholarship in his time. In a competitive world few if any scholars made their reputation without experiencing the opposition of rivals — certainly no scholar eminent enough to be appointed Librarian at Alexandria. In this environment, where scholars enjoyed coining spiteful nicknames for Eratosthenes, it is not hard to imagine how someone might make up a character like the hapless Dionysodorus, whose fruitlessness could have been a glance at Eratosthenes' lack of a direct intellectual heir, and to circulate such a story about him. It is probable that in its original form the story was no longer or more ambitious than the narrative Pliny transmits. Nothing inclines us to posit that the original story was a literary production on the scale of Lucian's or the *Apocolocyntosis*. Say rather a bilious joke intended to be shared behind the famous man's back. "Eratosthenes may say he's got the measure of the world's circumference, but he's never said he laid eyes on its radius, has he? Have you heard the one about the little friend of his who *did* …?"

If the circumstances of the anecdote's creation must necessarily remain speculative, it is easier to speak in positive terms about Pliny's reasons for relating it at the end of *Natural History* 2. As we saw at the outset of this article, Pliny described Eratosthenes' feat of reasoning in

---

[22] See Strabo 2.1.5, 2.1.10–11, 2.1.29, and 2.1.36 (= Roller (2010) 71–3; 77–9) as well as 2.1.34 (= Roller (2010) 89) for methodological criticisms levelled by Hipparchus against Eratosthenes.

[23] Roller (2010) 9

[24] Fraser (1972) I 458: "It is significant that we hear of no Ἐρατοσθένειοι; this versatile man started no formal tradition of scholarship, though he is said to have numbered Aristophanes of Byzantium among his pupils." See further Fraser II 662 n.94.

[25] Fraser (1972) I 777, II 1084 n.425.

ambivalent terms, as brilliant, commanding agreement, but not entirely
safe. It is a "wickedly conceited venture" (*improbum ausum*) in *NH*
2.247. As Beagon notes, Pliny uses *improbus* for things it is good to
keep at a respectful distance; what is immense, dangerous, or in-
human.[26] She draws a parallel with Pliny's reaction to Hipparchus, who
"dared a thing wicked even for a god" (*ausus rem etiam deo inprobam*)
in publishing a comprehensive catalogue of stars organized by magnitude, position, and time of rising (*NH* 2.95). Though one may be
embarrassed to disagree with Eratosthenes because of the elegance and
power of his calculation, all the same it is not canny. Contrast this with
the self-assurance evident in the preceding paragraph of the *Natural
History,* on the dimensions of the world's climatic zones (2.246). Here,
noting the uncertainty of his sources, Pliny intervenes with a
straightforward observation of his own:

> Artemidorus ulteriora inconperta existimavit, cum circa Tanain
> Sarmatarum gentes degere fateretur ad septentriones versus; Isidorus
> adiecit |XII| L usque ad Thylen, quae coniectura divinationis est. ego
> non minore quam proxime dicto spatio Sarmatarum fines nosci
> intellego. et alioqui quantum esse debet quod innumerabiles gentes
> subinde sedem mutantes capiat?

> The regions north of the mouth of the river Don have been judged by
> Artemidorus to be uncertain, though he admitted the Sarmatian tribes
> at the Don do extend toward the north. Isidorus added 1,250 miles
> from the Don to Thule, which is based on a guess. I myself under-
> stand that the territory of the Sarmatians is known to be at least as
> large as that last quoted figure. And looking at it from another angle,
> how large must the region be to accommodate those teeming, ever-
> migrating tribes?

Here Pliny shows no hesitation about using his own judgment (resting
not just on his reading but also on his experiences as a veteran of the
German wars, provincial procurator, and *principis amicus*) to fine-tune
earlier geographers' ideas of the northern limit of the temperate zone.[27]
The vital difference is that Pliny was comfortable with the underlying

---

[26] Beagon (1992) 44–5.

[27] In reference to Earth's climatic zones Eratosthenes seems to have conflated the
habitable or inhabited world (*oikoumene*) with the temperate zone of the northern
hemisphere, bracketed on either side by zones of uninhabitable cold or heat
(Eratosthenes F30 Roller; see also Geus (2004) 16). Pliny's purpose in this passage is
to find the north-south measure of the temperate zone / known world (called by Pliny
latitudo, 'breadth') beginning from the Aethiopic Ocean in the south up through the
familiar lands of the Mediterranean and into the hazily known north. For the Greek
geographers of Hellenistic times the northern limit of habitation was associated either
with the mouth of the Tanais / river Don, on the continent or, after Pytheas (c. 330
BCE) the obscure land of Thule (in the Ocean). Pliny was in a position to be more
specific.

procedures of conventional geography, which relied on hodological data on the one hand, that is, distances inferred from the durations of journeys and voyages, and on the other, comparative measurements of the longest period of daylight at the solstice in different cities. Given the constraints of ancient technology for measuring time, both of these methods were necessarily imprecise, and an informed layperson might justly feel entitled to disagree with conclusions reached by either method. Compared to conventional geography, the mathematical geo-graphy practiced by Eratosthenes in *Measurement of the Earth* was a horse of a different color, capable of much greater precision, supported by ratiocination both inspiring and intimidating in its power. It would seem that were this method developed further, it might render conventional geography obsolete, putting the field entirely outside non-specialists' power to intervene.[28] Though he seems to have felt that in the boldness of his intellectual ambition Eratosthenes was overreaching human propriety, this was not a method Pliny felt capable of criticizing.

Pliny's ambivalence explains why he juxtaposes the discussion of Eratosthenes with the Dionysodorus anecdote and makes this the book-end to *Natural History* 2. He has found in it a narrative counter for Eratosthenes. He does not attack Eratosthenes' ideas by offering a more persuasive alternative; he deflates mathematical geography as a whole by associating it with the ridiculous. The Dionysodorus anecdote brings together two wildly incommensurate ways of imagining the world, the abstract reasoning of the geometer and the fantastic subterranean realm of the literary *katabasis*, and in this combination Pliny found an apt means of parodying the methods of mathematical geographers. Despite the logical force of the one and the absurdity of the other, they have in common a reliance on the mind's eye. The anecdote reminds us that, while Minos or Tantalus are not perceptible to the physical eye, neither are the cones and planes manipulated in a typical geometrical calcu-lation. Geometers have persuaded us that the Earth has a central point, as all spheres do; no one tries to proves its existence by digging with a shovel, just as no one in the ancient world attempted to tunnel a way

---

[28] Hipparchus, who criticized Eratosthenes' later work *Geographica* for its dependence on conventional hodological measurements as opposed to the more strictly mathe-matical approach of *Measurement of the Earth*, did in fact attempt to develop the field in this direction. His criticisms of Eratosthenes are known from Strabo's attempts to rebut them; see n.22 above. Perceiving the need for a system of longitude grounded in astronomy, Hipparchus tried to erect such a framework on the basis of recorded lunar eclipses, correlating the various times at which a given eclipse had been observed in different cities of the *oikoumene* with the east-west distances between them. The idea was brilliant, but thwarted by the scantiness of the records and the imprecision of ancient means of time-keeping. See Stückelberger (2004) 35–7.

down to Hades. They were content, insofar as they believed in it, to let Hades remain an object of their mind's eye. The Dionysodorus anecdote is deployed at the end of *NH* 2 as a rhetorical strategy: it gives us a concrete memorable image to hold in mind as a counter to the abstract image of the world as conjured by Eratosthenes. While acknowledging mathematical geography's descriptive power, Pliny retells the story of Dionysodorus' *katabasis* to deny Eratosthenes the last word, keeping the cosmos in play as a space for Roman moral discourse.

List of Works Cited

Beagon, M. (1992). *Roman Nature: the Thought of Pliny The Elder.* Oxford

— (2005). *The Elder Pliny on the Human Animal.* Oxford

Bulmer-Thomas, I. (1971). s.v. 'Dionysodorus' *Dictionary of Scientific Biography* (Detroit: Charles Scribner's Sons) IV 108–10

Hoffman R.J. (1987). (trans.) *Celsus. On the True Doctrine.* Oxford

Fraser, P.M. (1972). *Ptolemaic Alexandria.* 2 vols, Oxford

Garland, R. (2001). *The Greek Way of Death.* 2nd edn, Ithaca NY

Geus, K. (2004). 'Measuring the earth and the oikoumene: zones, meridians, sphragides and some other geographical terms used by Eratosthenes of Kyrene' in R.J.A. Talbert and K. Brodersen (edd.) *Space in the Roman World: its Perception and Presentation.* Antike Kultur und Geschichte 5. Münster. 11–26.

Harrison, A.R.W. (1968). *The Law of Athens.* Oxford

Hultsch, F. 'Dionysodorus' (20). *Paulys Real-encyclopädie der classischen Altertumswissenschaft.* München and Stuttgart, 1893–1963. V:1 columns 1005–1006

Jones, A. (2008). s.v. 'Dionusodoros (of Kaunos?)' *Biographical Encyclopedia of Ancient Natural Scientists.* London

MacDowell, D.M. (1978). *The Law in Classical Athens.* London

Relihan, J.C. (1993). *Ancient Menippean Satire.* Baltimore

Roller, D.W. (2010). *Eratosthenes' Geography: Fragments Collected and Translated, with Commentary and Additional Material.* Princeton

Bulmer-Thomas, I. (1941). (ed. and trans.) *Selections Illustrating the History of Greek Mathematics.* Cambridge MA

Stückelberger, A. (2004). 'Ptolemy and the problem of scientific perception of space' in R.J.A Talbert, and K. Brodersen (edd.) *Space in the Roman World: its Perception and Presentation.* Antike Kultur und Geschichte 5. Münster. 28–41

Thomson, J.O. (1947). *History of Ancient Geography.* Cambridge

Pliny the Elder on Pythagoras

Trevor S. Luke
The Florida State University

Roman thinkers were captivated by the figure of Pythagoras, and it is not difficult to understand why.[1] To many he embodied Hellenic wisdom planted in Italian soil. Some even believed that Rome's second king, Numa, was Pythagoras' student.[2] During the Samnite wars, when the Romans were instructed by the Delphic oracle to erect statues to the bravest and wisest of the Greeks, they chose Alcibiades and Pythagoras respectively.[3] Ennius' proem to the *Annales* prominently features the poet's vision of Homer teaching the Pythagorean doctrine of the transmigration of souls to explain how Homer was reborn within Ennius.[4] When the works of Numa came to light in 181 BC, it was found that he had written, at least according to some historians of the time, books of Pythagorean philosophy.[5] Interest in Pythagoras and the Pythagoreans continued in the first century BC (even though by then Roman intellectuals realized that the link with Numa was unhistorical).[6] Varro was buried in Pythagorean style and Cicero went out of his way to visit Pythagoras' chair in Metapontum.[7] Roman fascination with Pythagoras lasted for centuries thereafter, inspiring new comment in succeeding generations.

This article explores how Pliny the Elder dealt with the legacy of Pythagoras in his *Naturalis Historia*. Although he treated Pythagoras in accordance with the philosopher's fame and demonstrated his own respect for him, he also distanced himself from Pythagoras in various ways and critiqued his work. Close examination will reveal the complexity of Piny's engagement with Pythagoras as an icon of Greek wisdom in contrast with the younger Roman intellectual tradition. One

---

[1] Kahn (2001) 86–93; Riedweg (2005) 123–4; Joost-Gaugier (2007) 25–43.
[2] Forsythe (2006) 362.
[3] Plin. *NH* 34.26.
[4] Aicher (1989).
[5] See Plin. *NH* 13.86–7 for citations of Cassius Hemina and Piso Frugi identifying some of Numa's books as Pythagorean.
[6] Cic. *Rep.* 2.28–29; *Tusc.* 4.3; D. H. 2.59; Liv. 1.18.2–3.
[7] Varro's burial: Plin. *NH* 17.6. Cicero's visit to Metapontum: *De finibus* 5.2.

goal of this exploration is to test the idea that Pliny was a mere assembler of information with fairly limited intellectual tools, even for his day[8] — an assessment inspired partly by factual contradictions in Pliny's *Naturalis Historia* and partly by his nephew's account of watching his uncle at work with a reader on one side and a scribe on the other.[9] Today, accustomed as we are to powerful electronic resources, we might be tempted to see in Pliny a kind of proto-search engine, scouring books as quickly as possible for facts and then recording and arranging them without analysis, for the convenience of others. Pythagoras makes a good test case for such a theory, since Pliny mentions the philosopher numerous times and cites his pseudepigrapha (accepted as authentic by Pliny) extensively. If there is no discernible consistency in Pliny's view of Pythagoras, then one may conclude that there was no real method at work in his reportage on Pythagoras.[10] If, on the other hand, a coherent interpretation emerges from his treatment of Pythagoras, then the notion of Pliny's critical absence from his own work will be shown to be problematic.[11]

1. Culture, science, and theology

In the preface to the *Naturalis Historia* Pliny establishes a cultural hierarchy for his work that bears on the question of his treatment of Pythagoras.[12] Situating himself firmly in the Roman tradition of scholarship, Pliny, while recognizing the accomplishments of the Greeks, consistently privileges and emphasizes 'Roman' authors.[13] Not only does he primarily engage with these Romans,[14] but he also opens

---

[8] Murphy (2004) 3, 9–11.

[9] Plin. *Ep.* 3.5.

[10] Murphy (2004) 10: "[R]eaders who want to find a unitary Pliny at the bottom of the *Natural History* will be driven to making an arbitrary division between the surface of the text, to be dismissed as merely rhetoric or tradition, and the real thoughts of the author. This means privileging whatever passages can be found that may contain authorial reflection ... mining for a voice, a consistency, an individual perspective that is not elsewhere in evidence." For a contrasting view, see Howe (1985) 561–76.

[11] Paparazzo (2011) has already demonstrated Pliny's coherent application of Stoic thought in the *Naturalis Historia*. He states (110): "Besides accomplishing the unprecedented gigantic task of addressing the articles of *Natura* in a single work ... Pliny should also be granted the distinction of having taken up the challenge of treating this subject matter using an extended Stoic approach which has no equal among writings ever put down in Rome, apart from Seneca's *Natural Questions*."

[12] On Pliny's preface, see Howe (1985); Sinclair (2003) 277–300; Baldwin (2005) 91–5.

[13] Here "Roman" means, not authors of the city of Rome, but authors writing in Latin.

[14] Sinclair (2003) 279–80 notes: "[H]is preface contains quotations from earlier authors whom he invokes for support (like Cicero [7, 22], Cato [9, 30] and Varro [18, 24], or

and closes the preface with them. First comes Catullus, Pliny's 'fellow countryman' (*conterraneus*), whose work Pliny creatively adapts at the beginning[15] and with whom he compares himself favorably in terms of humility; and the preface ends with the antiquarian Valerius Soranus,[16] renowned for learning but not for eloquence,[17] who was killed during the Sullan civil war, allegedly for revealing the secret name of Rome.[18] Mention of individual Greek authors does not begin until chapter 22. Pliny's treatment of them is comparatively sparing, and it heavily favors philosophers and historians: these are (in order of appearance) Plato (22), Crantor (22), Panaetius (22), Diodorus (25), Apion (25), Homer (28), and Theophrastus (29). The first three occur only in the context of a discussion of Cicero's candor about his reliance on certain sources: here the subject is Cicero, not Plato, Crantor, or Panaetius. Pliny praises Diodorus for departing from the misleading titles of earlier Greek writers by entitling his work simply and usefully *Library*, but he says nothing else about either the author or his work. Apion is the single Greek writer whom Pliny quotes in his preface, but only to ridicule him for his self-promoting vanity:[19] *immortalitate donari a se scripsit ad quos aliqua componebat* (he wrote that he endowed with immortality those to whom he dedicated a work).[20] Homer is referred to only indirectly in the word *Homeromastigae*,[21] i.e. merely as the target for hosts of nameless critics. As for Theophrastus, Pliny reports that his work was not only criticized, but criticized by a woman (an indignity that deserved the backlash she received, in Pliny's view); moreover, Theophrastus' divine name (*nomen divinum*) merely refers to its etymology, from *theos* (god) and *phrazein* (to talk), not to any divine attribute the author might possess.[22] In general, Pliny says (*NH praef.* 24), Greek writers are worthy of criticism because, although their works have superb titles (*inscriptionis ... mira felicitas*), there is nothing inside them (*nihil in medio*); Roman writers by contrast give

---

others (like Livy [16]) with whose views of literature and politics he disagrees."
[15] Plin. *NH praef.* 1. On Pliny's adaptation of Catullus, see Howe (1985) 567–8; Sinclair (2003) 285–6, 291–2; Baldwin (2005) 93–4. See Baldwin (2005) 94 on the reading *conterraneum*.
[16] Plin. *NH praef.* 33; Sinclair (2003) 290–91.
[17] The most learned of Romans: Cic. *Or.* 3.43; lack of eloquence: Cic. *Brut.* 169.
[18] Plin. *NH* 3.65; Murphy (2004) 127–37; Cairns (2010) 245–66.
[19] For Pliny's overall depiction of Apion, see Damon (2011) 131–45.
[20] Damon (2011) 136–45.
[21] The fact that Pliny refers to Homer indirectly through his critics sets his preface apart from the proem of Ennius' *Annales*, where the author's personal identification with Homer is to the fore (*Ann.* 1 fr.3: *visus Homerus adesse poeta*). See also below p.289.
[22] According to Strabo (13.2) and Diogenes Laertius (5.38), Aristotle gave his student Tyrtamus the name Theophrastus because of his eloquence.

their works titles that are fitting and accurate. Pliny's introduction aligns the author strongly with the Roman literary and intellectual tradition, which is treated as superior to that of the Greeks.

As noted above, Pliny's arrangement of authors' names in the preface is quite deliberate. Theophrastus and Soranus are the two final named authors in the preface, one Greek, one Roman, both of whose works are comparable to Pliny's own project. Although Theophrastus' reputation is clearly problematized along with that of other Greek authors, his importance to Pliny, as an Aristotelian who wrote works on nature (*Meteorologia*, *Causae Plantarum*, etc.), cannot be gainsaid. While Theophrastus' works on nature may be closer to Pliny's *Naturalis Historia* than anything Soranus wrote, it is Soranus with whom Pliny identifies culturally and socially; so he highlights Soranus' *Epoptides*[23] but does not name any title by Theophrastus. Nevertheless it is probable that Theophrastus is placed in the honorific last position of named Greek authors precisely because Pliny views his work as a forerunner to the *Naturalis Historia*.

Before leaving the preface, something should be said about certain absences. Pythagoras makes no appearance, and Homer is introduced only indirectly: Pliny (*praef.* 28) implicitly compares himself to Homer when he makes the admission that his works are incomplete (*adici posse multa*, 'much can be added'), to safeguard himself against the carpings of *Homeromastigae*. This follows hard on the heels of praise for Apelles and Polyclitus (*praef.* 26–7) for saying that their sculptures were 'works in progress' (*faciebat*), not finalized (*fecit*). (One cannot help but note that in expressing his humility, Pliny has compared himself to two of the greatest artists and the greatest poet of all Greece.) The indirect reference to Homer in the term *Homeromastigae* draws attention to his absence and the absence of other Greek poets from the preface, especially striking given the prominence of Catullus at the beginning.

Conspicuously absent from the list of named Latin poets are both Ennius and Lucretius. Ennius was the first extant Latin poet to offer a *de rerum natura*: as a pioneer in the description of nature in Latin literature, he would have been an obvious candidate for Pliny to mention at the opening of his *Naturalis Historia*. Ennius' absence is even odder when one considers that Lucretius (*DRN* 1.117) had accorded him special praise in recognition of his role as a predecessor: *Ennius ut noster cecinit, qui primus amoeno/ detulit ex Helicone*

---

[23] Pliny's immediate reason for naming Soranus last, immediately before the table of contents, is Soranus' own inclusion of a table of contents.

perenni fronde coronam,/ per gentis Italas hominum quae clara clueret.[24] Lucretius nevertheless goes on to criticize Ennius' description of the afterlife and his vision of Homer (*DRN* 1.120–26). Pliny might have offered Ennius similarly qualified praise, but he excludes both Ennius and Lucretius.

Pliny does, however, engage with their works. His quasi-invocation of the Camenae (*praef.* 1) evokes Ennius (*Ann.* sed. inc. fr.487), who was the first Latin epic poet to equate the Camenae explicitly with the Muses: *Musas quas memorant nosces nos esse Camenas*. Others of the period had referred only to Camena or the Camenae.[25] By mentioning the Camenae and not the Muses, Pliny departs from Ennius, and also from Lucretius, who first addresses Venus Genetrix (*DRN* 1.1–2) and later the Muses (1.925–47). In this way, Pliny implicitly reduces his Greek inspiration. In fact, his emphasis on shunning the Greek love of praise (24–5) appears to be a pointed swipe at Lucretius, who links his love of the Muses with his hope for praise (1.922–5: *sed acri/ percussit thyrso laudis spes magna meum cor/ et simul incussit suavem mi in pectus amorem/ Musarum*. Pliny, who hoped to avoid undue criticism and who criticized the love of praise, chooses the Camenae and leaves the Muses out.

Pliny nevertheless arguably alludes to Homer's greeting to Ennius (*Ann.* 1, fr.5) in his own epistolary introduction written to Titus. After appearing to Ennius, Homer greets the poet: *O pietas animi!* Likewise, in the midst of Pliny's greetings to Titus and praise of him, Pliny (*praef.* 5) writes: *quantus in poetica es! O magna fecunditas animi!* It hardly seems coincidental, much less an expression of genuine humility, that Pliny assumes the role of Homer in addressing Titus as his Ennius. If this is correct, then this gesture is yet one more way in which Pliny makes a point of not identifying with his natural literary predecessor Ennius. In light of the current discussion, this distinction may also underline the difference between the two writers' views of nature. Ennius' *de rerum natura* is decidedly Pythagorean in character,[26] in that Homer explains his presence by means of the Pythagorean doctrine

---

[24] See Harrison (2002) on Lucretius' depiction of Ennius.

[25] See Dominik (2003) 39. On the priority of the Camenae in Ovid, see Hardie (2010); Tissol (2014) 210–14.

[26] Aicher (1989) 227–32. Skutsch (1968) 8 viewed the Pythagorean elements of Ennius' proem as ancillary. Aicher (230) sees the gesture as more central to the poet's navigation of a dual, Greek and Roman, literary and intellectual tradition: "The Pythagorean theory helps to create a linguistic environment in which the liberties that Ennius takes in modeling Latin on Greek will appear not so much to violate a Latin tradition as to continue an older one." Pliny's preface does not reveal an author who would be sympathetic to such a conception of the relationship between the two traditions.

of the transmigration of souls.[27] As will be emphasised below, Pliny did not believe in the immortality of the soul; he therefore could not accept Ennius' Pythagorean poetics as literal.[28] Indeed, in omitting any explicit mention of Ennius and Pythagoras from his preface, Pliny may have sought to distance himself from both the Ennian tradition of writing about nature and the Pythagorean school that inspired it. Instead Pliny would leave the summoning of a dead Homer to the likes of the discredited Apion.

2. Hipparchus as hero astronomer

Pliny's preface sets down what appear to be relatively simple and intelligible, albeit dubious, criteria for understanding his predictably patriotic cultural hierarchy. In the rest of the work, however, this simple schema is both enriched and problematized when the relative merits of individual Greek writers and thinkers are at issue. Apion is a case in point. Cynthia Damon has argued that the title of Apion's work, which Pliny includes in his preface, was Ἱστορία ἀληθὴς τῶν Αἰγυπτια-κῶν (True History of the Egyptians), and that Pliny spoofed it by twisting Apion's boasts about this work to imply that his 'truth' was as reliable as his promise of immortality.[29] After making Apion the butt of his humor, Pliny congratulates himself for not emulating Apion in choosing an interesting title. In the history of magic (Book 30), Pliny builds on this line of abuse by adding another disparaging anecdote of a similar kind. Apion is said to have raised Homer from the dead (perhaps with the aid of an herb (*osiritis*) named after the Egyptian god of resurrection, Osiris), in order to ask the poet questions (*NH* 30.18). Apion's procedure differs so strikingly from Pliny's own opinions on modesty and magic that one cannot help but wonder whether Pliny is setting him up as a kind of anti-type.

Pliny's assessment of certain Greek philosophers, however, is quite

[27] Enn. *Ann.* 1, fr.9: *memini me fiere pavom*; Aicher (1989) 227.

[28] In his *Tusculanae Quaestiones* (1.38), Cicero credits Pherecydes with the invention of the doctrine of the immortality of the soul and singles out Pythagoras as the conduit through which Plato acquired it. Interestingly, Pliny, who did not believe in the immortality of the soul (*NH* 7.188), mentions neither Pherecydes nor Pythagoras in connection with the soul's immortality. Aside from his reference to Pherecydes' prediction of the earthquake, Pliny only refers to Pherecydes to discuss the sage's bizarre death (7.172), sixteen chapters before taking up the subject of the immortality of the soul. In other words, Pliny killed off Pherecydes before discussing his most famous teaching, and, perhaps deliberately, did not credit Pherecydes with inventing the doctrine.

[29] Damon (2011) 141–4.

positive. Hipparchus is a case in point. He is named in Book 2 (along with Thales) in the context of a paean of praise for astronomers (2.54), whom Pliny apostrophizes as *viri ingentes supraque mortalium naturam* (giants surpassing the nature of mere mortals). By deciphering the divine bodies (*tantorum numinum lege deprehensa*), these 'giants' have liberated the pitiable minds of human beings from fear. The praise reaches a devotional climax with *macti ingenio este, caeli interpretes rerumque naturae capaces, argumenti repertores quo deos hominesque vicistis!* (*NH* 2.53–5). This recalls Lucretius' portrait of Epicurus, who, surpassing humankind in genius (*DRN* 3.1044: *qui genus humanorum ingenio superavit*), is both praised for liberating men from fear born of superstition (1.62–71; 3.1043–5) and called a god (5.8: *dicendum est, deus ille fuit, deus, inclute Memmi*).[30] It also responds to Vergil *Aeneid* 9.641–2: *macte nova virtute, puer, sic itur ad astra,/ dis genite et geniture deos*.[31] The context in Vergil is martial: Apollo is congratulating the boy Ascanius on his first kill in battle, a victory which leads to the stars, the realm of the gods. For Pliny, it is the astronomers who, by freeing mortals from the fear of celestial signs, conquer not only men but the gods too. In Lucretian fashion, Pliny's science thus outdoes martial achievement as the true route to the stars, and Hipparchus stands tall in the company of the heavenly scientists.[32]

Pliny's Apion and Hipparchus are therefore contrasting types. Both are renowned intellectuals, but one (Apion) is criticized as engaging in vain self-promotion and charlatanry, while the other (Hipparchus) is given the highest possible praise for substantive discoveries that freed humankind from superstitious fear. In the context of Pliny's depiction of Pythagoras it is important to note that Pliny's characterizations of both Apion and Hipparchus are implicated in the author's theological stance. For Pliny, there is no such thing as immortality, and Nature is god.[33] Pliny's Apion fails the intellectual test implied by these views: he boasts of giving immortality to others, and, even if Apion had intended this immortality to be understood metaphorically, in relating this claim Pliny likely alludes to Apion's literal belief in an afterlife, since Pliny also mentions Apion's claim to have summoned the ghost

---

[30] See Tatum (2007) 142.
[31] See also Hor. *S.* 1.2.31; Liv. 10.40; Sen. *Ep.* 66.
[32] Buchheit (1971) 303–23.
[33] Disbelief in immortality: *NH* 7.188. Nature as god: *NH* 2.27 ... *declaratur haut dubie naturae potentia, idque esse quod deum vocemus*; cf. Beagon (1992) 92–5, esp. 92: "The only form of deity acceptable to Pliny is *divina Natura*, the spirit of the universe, an all-embracing unity". Pliny's predecessor Seneca took the same view of Nature as god: *quid deus est? quod vides totum et quod non vides totum* (Sen. *Nat.* 1 *praef.* 13); and see Williams (2012) 3–4.

of Homer. In contrast, Hipparchus, Pliny reports at *NH* 2.53, 'prophesied' (*praececinit*) the course of the sun and the moon for a 600-year period, according to his contemporaries, 'by no other means than partaking in the councils of nature' (*haut alio modo quam consiliorum naturae particeps*) — high praise indeed from a man who considered Nature to be the only god. In his idealized depiction of Hipparchus, Pliny is following Seneca, who, in his *Quaestiones Naturales*, identified the duty of the philosopher as self-purification undertaken so as to commune fully with Nature and see the workings of the heavens.[34]

If it is accepted that Pliny regards Hipparchus as an ideal scientist/ astronomer, then the religious language he uses to describe Hipparchus' scientific activities cannot be critical or dismissively humorous. Pliny has, rather, appropriated and repurposed the language of divination and divinities in his praise of astronomers in a manner that is consistent with his theological views about nature and apotheosis. In fact, Pliny's treatment of the philanthropic scientists is similar to his treatment of the emperor Vespasian, whom Pliny eulogizes as an example of the adage *deus est mortali iuvare mortalem* for his rescue of a fatigued world (*NH* 2.18). Pliny will adhere to this linguistic-theological framework as he proceeds in Book 2 to discuss the science of prediction, whether it involves reading fires in the sky or foretelling earthquakes.

3. Scientific prediction: Pythagoras and Pherecydes

Pythagoras first appears in the *Naturalis Historia* in Book 2, as one of the astronomers whom Pliny classed as *viri ingentes*. At 2.37 Pythagoras is credited with discovering Venus' relationship to the rising and setting of the sun. Next, at 2.83–4, he is the person who discovered the distances between the planets in a series of mathematical proportions and attempted to relate these to musical proportions. Finally at 2.191, a passage dealing primarily with Anaximander of Miletus and Pherecydes of Samos, he is referred to as

---

[34] A partnership with nature/god is the purpose behind the quest for virtue at Sen. *Nat.* 1 *praef.* 6–7. The acquisition of virtue enables one to acquire celestial knowledge: *praeparat ad cognitionem caelestium.* Pliny's Hipparchus seems to have attained Seneca's ideal celestial perspective; see Williams (2012) 3–4. Beagon (2011) 71–88 argues that Pliny's cosmos is essentially the same as Seneca's, but Pliny's focus is on the terrestrial, Seneca's on the celestial. Pliny takes as his subject Seneca's *totum* (*Nat.* 1 *praef.* 13, cited in n.33 above).

the pupil of the latter.

In the second of these references, Pliny's Pythagoras uses his *sagax animus* when measuring the distance between the planets to 'deduce' (*colligere*) the right answer.[35] The phrase *vir sagacis animi*, deserves closer examination; it further clarifies Pliny's view of Pythagoras and his methods. In *De Rerum Natura*, Lucretius employed *sagax animus* several times when he discussed the power of 'reasoned observation' or the 'reasoning faculty of keen sense.'[36] According to the poet, reason could help one to discern the mysteries of nature beyond the limits achievable by the senses alone. Pliny's depiction in *Naturalis Historia* Book 2 of Anaximander, Pherecydes, and Pythagoras fits the Lucretian model of the person possessing a *sagax animus*, despite the fact that the broader tradition about these men included miraculous feats that likened them to magicians. Pliny did not, of course, need to be a doctrinaire Epicurean, or self-identify as an Epicurean at all, to appropriate Lucretian ideas.[37] The concept of the *sagax animus* allowed Pliny to account for Pythagoras' amazing insights without attributing to him supernatural abilities.[38] In other words, Pythagoras belongs among those giants (*viri ingentes*) of the field of astronomy, such as Hipparchus, whose scientific interpretations of the heavens allowed them to attain heroic status and conquer gods and men. As such a scientist, Pythagoras is, in Pliny's view, worthy of reverence but not for the superstitious reasons popularly cultivated.

The third reference to Pythagoras in Book 2, as the pupil of Pherecydes, further helps to show how Pliny skirted round the problems created by the fantastical portraits of early Greek philosopher-scientists, among whom Pythagoras was perhaps the most famous, in order to establish a more rational depiction of the philosopher. There was a rich but dubiously factual tradition regarding the relationship between Pherecydes and Pythagoras rooted in the two men's similar intellectual concerns, teachings, and abilities.[39] Like Pythagoras, Pherecydes, in addition to being a philosopher, was sometimes characterized as a kind of prophet and wonderworker.[40] This may help explain why Pythagoras

---

[35] *OLD* s.v. *colligo*, 11.

[36] Lucr. 1.150, 2.840, 4.912; Lehoux (2013) 134–6. To say that Pliny appropriated a Lucretian concept is not to equate the philosophical and epistemological views of the two authors. On the epistemological differences between Pliny and Lucretius, see Kennedy (2013) 61–3.

[37] Pliny's rejection of the immortality of the soul is reminiscent of Lucretius. See Plin. *NH* 7.188. Even Pliny's dedication resembles Lucretius' dedication. On the latter, Plin. *NH* pr. 1; Luc. *DRN* 1.947; Healey (1999), 40 n.11.

[38] Note also *Hipparchi sagacitate conpertum est et lunae defectum* (*NH* 2.57).

[39] Riedweg and Rendall (2008) 9. Apollonius *Historiae Mirabiles* 6.

[40] D.L. 1.116–18.

was thought to have studied under him. Indeed, the paradoxographer Apollonius (ca. second century BC) reports that Pythagoras learned thaumaturgy from Pherecydes, and, like his teacher, predicted the sinking of a ship as he watched it sail.[41] Interestingly, Pliny does not dwell on the alleged thaumaturgy of either man, although he might have mentioned any one of a plethora of such stories.[42] In the case of Pherecydes, he chooses to relate how the philosopher predicted an earthquake in his hometown while drawing water from a well.[43]

Pherecydes' prediction of the earthquake is the second account of a pair of such feats. It will be useful to examine the first in order to understand the Plinian context of Pherecydes' prediction and the relationship between Pliny's version of these paired accounts and his source, Cicero's *De Divinatione*. Anaximander of Miletus also foretold a catastrophic earthquake, this time at Sparta (*NH* 2.191):

> Praeclara quaedam et inmortalis in eo, si credimus, <u>divinitas</u> perhibetur Anaximandro physico, quem ferunt Lacedaemoniis praedixisse ut urbem ac tecta custodirent, instare enim motum terrae, et tum urbs tota eorum corruit et Taygeti montis magna pars ad formam puppis eminens abrupta cladem eam insuper ruina oppressit.

> The natural philosopher Anaximander was held to possess, if we believe it, a certain remarkable and immortal *divinitas*. They say that he warned the Spartans in advance that they should watch over their city and homes, for an earthquake was imminent. Then their entire city collapsed and a big piece of Mt. Taygetus, projecting like the prow of a ship, having broken off, brought devastation down on top of the ruins.

Pliny does not say whether he himself believes that Anaximander's powers of prediction were due to his *praeclara et inmortalis divinitas*, but he does not necessarily dismiss it. The question is Pliny's definition of *divinitas*. It is clear, because he rejects the traditional forms of the gods, that Pliny would not interpret this *divinitas* to be 'a deity'.[44]

---

[41] *Historiae Mirabiles* 6. Apollonius also reports such things as Pythagoras biting and killing a poisonous snake in Etruria, being greeted by a river god's divine voice in Samos, and revealing his golden thigh in a theater.

[42] This is consistent with Pliny's distaste for magicians who claim to manipulate Nature; see Beagon (1992) 102–13. For examples of the wonders, see the citations at nn40, 41.

[43] Pliny mentions Pherecydes three times, of which this is the first. He also reports that Pherecydes invented the prose oration in the reign of Cyrus (7.205); and that he died of phthiriasis (7.172; this is rendered as a host of serpents bursting out of his body).

[44] For Pliny's criticism of traditional polytheism, see *NH* 2.14–21. *Divin-* in *NH* Book 2 (82, 87, 149, 191, 246) always comes in divinatory contexts. This is so even at 2.82, where the presence of Jupiter might suggest that *divinus* has its usual meaning: having rationalized the thunder-bolts of Jupiter (*Iovem fulmina iaculari*) as fires from three of the planets, Pliny explains that, whether attached to the planets or flung from it, these fires are the objects of divinatory speculations (*divina ... opera*). At *NH* 7.119,

Pliny's understanding of the scientist's *divinitas* was established in his account of the predictive powers of Hipparchus at *NH* 2.53, where Hipparchus as observer of the heavenly bodies is a kind of prophet. The language of divination is likewise used here of Anaximander's ability to predict earthly phenomena. This is consistent with the idea that Pliny, while accepting Seneca's vision of the cosmos, rejected his exclusive privileging of celestial observation (see n.34 above). Pliny's Anaximander can predict things on the earth in the same way that Hipparchus is able to predict things in the heavens.

The same gesture can be seen in the parallel anecdote of Pherecydes that immediately follows: *perhibetur et Pherecydi, Pythagorae doctori, alia coniectatio, sed et illa divina, haustu aquae e puteo praesensisse ac praedixisse civibus terrae motum* (another conjecture, and a divine one also,[45] is credited to Pherecydes, the teacher of Pythagoras: that from a draught of water from a well he realized an earthquake was imminent, and predicted it to the citizens,). Pliny might have chosen another of Pherecydes' predictions, in some of which the method employed to foretell an event is not at all clear. In this instance, however, there is an implicit connection between Pherecydes' observation of the water and his subsequent prediction of the earthquake. Pliny's choice of this story is thus consistent with his avowed belief in the epistemological importance of observation.[46]

By conjoining the two anecdotes, Pliny implicitly equates Pherecydes' *coniectatio ... divina* with Anaximander's *divinitas*. In the case of Pherecydes, it is much clearer that Pliny sees the *coniectatio* as a surmise based on evidence, not a divine miracle. Pherecydes observes one part of nature (well water) to predict what is about to happen in another. In short, Pliny saw the predictions of Anaximander and Pherecydes as the same sort of educated guesswork that Pythagoras exercised in determining the distance between the planets — which may be why Pherecydes is here described as *Pythagorae doctor*.

4. Pliny engages with Cicero

An examination of Pliny's source for *NH* 2.191, Cicero *De Divinatione* 1.112, tells us more about Pliny's unique construction of the *sagax*

---

divinitas et quaedam caelitum societas nobilissima ex feminis in Sibylla fuit, ex viris in Melampode apud Graecos, apud Romanos in Marcio, the Sibyls, Melampus, and Marcius are again all oracular or prophetic figures.

[45] See *OLD* s.v. *sed* for *sed et* as 'and also'. I thank Professor Francis Cairns for bringing this reading to my attention.

[46] On the importance of observation in Pliny's epistemology, see Lloyd (1999) 135–49.

animus. The two passages are very close, but there are telling differences that reflect the contrast in philosophical approach between the two men. Cicero (in the mouth of his brother Quintus) wrote:

> Multa medici multa gubernatores, agricolae etiam multa praesentiunt, sed nullam eorum divinationem voco, ne illam quidem, qua ab Anaximandro physico moniti Lacedaemonii sunt, ut urbem et tecta linquerent armatique in agro excubarent, quod terrae motus instaret, tum cum et urbs tota corruit et e monte Taygeto extrema [montis] quasi puppis avolsa est. Ne Pherecydes quidem, ille Pythagorae magister, potius divinus habebitur quam physicus, quod, cum vidisset haustam aquam de iugi puteo, terrae motus dixit instare.

> Doctors and helmsmen predict many things, farmers do too, but I do not call their predictions divination; not even that prediction whereby the Spartans were warned by Anaximander the natural philosopher to leave their homes and city and keep armed watch in the fields, because an earthquake was imminent; this was when the whole city collapsed and a peak, similar to the prow of a ship, was torn off from Mt. Taygetus. Not even Pherecydes, the teacher of Pythagoras, will be held a prophet rather than a natural philosopher for saying, when he had observed a draught of water from a fresh well, that an earthquake was imminent.

Here Cicero has Quintus say that the predictions of experienced professionals (such as doctors, navigators, or farmers) have nothing to do with divination. Similarly both Anaximander and Pherecydes may have appeared to be diviners when they predicted earthquakes, but this was not the case. Both men were *physici* (natural philosophers).[47]

When Pliny paraphrases Cicero on Anaximander and Pherecydes, he is less emphatic than Cicero's Quintus. Unlike Cicero, Pliny has no need to contrast the *divinus* and the *physicus*, since he has already contextualized the significance of Anaximander's *divinitas* and Pherecydes' *coniectatio divina* through his account of Hipparchus. In Pliny's view, Anaximander and Pherecydes were prophetic figures inasmuch as they, like Hipparchus, were *consiliorum naturae participes*. Pliny's shift of the sense of *divinus* from its association with the traditional gods to this idea of scientific observation made it possible for Pliny to overcome the apparent conundrum Cicero wrestled with: namely, the problematic distinction between the *ars divinationis* and other forms of expertise. For Pliny, such a problem simply did not exist.

Pliny differs even more strikingly from Cicero in the credit he gives to these scientific predictions. Cicero's dialogical persona, responding to his fictional interlocutor Quintus, later casts doubt on the historicity

---

[47] Wardle (2013) 374–5 states that the discussion of divination is here informed by the teachings of Cratippus. See also Gregory (2013) 53–4.

of such predictions, taking the Pherecydean anecdote as an example
(*De Div.* 2.31):

> parum, credo, inpudenter, quod, cum factus est motus, dicere audent,
> quae vis id effecerit; etiamne futurum esse aquae iugis colore prae-
> sentiunt? Multa istius modi dicuntur in scholis, sed credere omnia
> vide ne non sit necesse.

> It would not, doubtless, be too presumptuous for <natural
> philosophers> to venture an explanation of the cause of an
> earthquake after the event; but do they foresee, from the appearance
> of moving water, that an earthquake is going to occur? Many things
> like this are heard in the schools, but one does not have to believe
> them all!

Pliny, on the other hand, apparently believed that it was possible to
predict an earthquake by such means, since he does not question
Anaximander's and Pherecydes' feats. Indeed, he responds to Cicero's
second passage about Pherecydes directly after his paraphrase of the
first. Whereas the Cicero of the dialogue ironically casts doubt on the
ability of physical philosophers to explain the physical causes of
earthquake, let alone predict one, Pliny unapologetically goes on to
assert that winds cause earthquakes (*ventos in causa esse non dubium
reor NH* 2.192).

Pliny is thus also engaging with Cicero's discussion of what
constitutes divination. At *De Divinatione* 2.13 Cicero quotes Quintus'
definition: *divinationem esse earum rerum praedictionem et praesensionem quae essent fortuitae* (divination is the foretelling and
foreseeing of those things that happen by chance), and then points out
that the element of chance was stipulated to exclude those experts who
would be able to predict what was going to happen by experience,
knowledge, and interpretation of physical signs. The combination
praedictionem et praesensionem is echoed in Pliny's account of
Pherecydes, who sensed in advance and foretold (*praesensisse ac
praedixisse*) the earthquake at Syros. If these stories are true, Pliny
asks, how far were these men from divinity, even in their own lifetimes
(*quae si vera sint, quantum a deo tandem videri possunt tales distare,
dum vivant?*, 2.192)? His definition of divinity in this passage,
however, must be interpreted in the context of his heroization of
Hipparchus and also of his formula: *deus est mortali iuvari mortalem.*
By predicting earthquakes, Anaximander and Pherecydes gave others
the opportunity to avoid calamity and thus merited their uniquely
Plinian superhuman status.

Pliny's treatment of Pherecydes' *coniectatio divina* shows that he is
more deeply engaged with his sources than Murphy (see n.10 above)

might lead us to suppose. Pliny both engages with Cicero's discussion of prediction, and distinguishes his own view from it. Unlike the Cicero of the dialogue, Pliny believes philosopher scientists could use their knowledge to predict the future. In effect, he sees himself as being in pursuit of 'divine' aims through the transmission of knowledge, the possession of which might enable his reader to accomplish deeds like those of Anaximander and Pherecydes. These two are set apart from others not by their supernatural abilities (in this he agrees with Cicero), but by the knowledge they possess and use to help others. Pythagoras, too, fits this model. Pliny follows Cicero in mentioning the teacher-student relationship between Pherecydes and Pythagoras, but one must interpret his revision of Cicero within the theoretical arc beginning in his preface which I have attempted to delineate in §§1–3 of this paper. Pliny's characterization of Pherecydes thus reflects on his presentation of Pythagoras.

5. Pythagoras, magic, and Greek shamanism

Despite the fact that Pliny establishes Pythagoras' reliability in this way (he must lest he undercut his own work), he is obliged to deal with a Pythagorean tradition in which the sage often appears as much a holy man or wizard as a philosopher.[48] A first indication of Pliny's gentle criticism comes in his report of Pythagoras' discovery of the harmony of the spheres (*NH* 2.84). After summing up the essentials of Pythagoras' teaching on the tones, ending with Saturn moving in the Dorian mode, Jupiter in the Phrygian, and so on with the other planets, Pliny comments that Pythagoras' assignment of particular musical modes to these planets was done *iucunda magis quam necessaria subtilitate* (with a refinement that is pleasant rather than necessary). In other words, this degree of Pythagorean theorizing, while entertaining, adds nothing important to our understanding of the cosmos. An intriguing possibility lies in *magis*: could Pliny be intending his readers to see a double entendre in which it is the dative of *magus*? Could he be hinting that such rarified ideas about the spheres are 'pleasing to magicians' but otherwise pointless?[49] He did, after all, accept the tradition that Pythagoras studied with the magi of the East, as he reports in Books 24 and 25, and in his somewhat derogatory history of

---

[48] Burkert (1972) 112–65; Riedweg and Stendall (2005) 2–5.
[49] I am not, however, suggesting that the pun is a *lectio melior*.

magic in Book 30.[50] These magi were also renowned astrologers (Plin. *Nat.* 30.2).

It is in his account of Pythagoras' eastern education in the virtues of various plants that Pliny tries to thread a more difficult needle. On the one hand, his own extensive reliance on the botanical works of Pythagoras and Democritus obliged him to legitimize them. On the other, he cannot appear unconscious or gullible with respect to these philosophers' sources or the exaggerated claims therein.

He begins his discussion of the two men's botanical works with an apologetic representation of Pythagoras: *ab eo Pythagoras clarus sapientia primus volumen de effectu earum composuit, Apollini, Aesculapio et in totum dis immortalibus inventione et origine adsignata* (*NH* 25.13). Pythagoras, famous for wisdom, (*clarus sapientia*) was the first to write a volume on the properties of plants; the gods, Apollo and Asclepius chief among them, are assigned the credit for their discovery and creation. Pythagoras himself is grammatically distanced from the attribution: while he commands the verb as the nominative subject (*Pythagoras ... composuit*), the gods are credited in an ablative absolute construction (*dis immortalibus inventione et origine adsignata*). In this way Pythagoras is made out to be a collector of knowledge, not, in this instance at least, the originator of it — an important distinction since some of the botanical knowledge he transmits is of questionable value.

The account continues with the tradition of the two philosophers' travels to learn from the magi: *ambo peregratis Persidis, Arabiae, Aethiopiae, Aegypti magis, adeoque ad haec attonita antiquitas fuit, ut adfirmaverit etiam incredibilia dictu.* (Both men visited the magi of Persia, Arabia, Ethiopia and Egypt, and antiquity was so astonished at these teachings that it maintained even things unbelievable to relate, *ibid.*) Pliny necessarily exercises great care in his handling of this topic. With the travels of Pythagoras and Democritus, the issue of the classification of sources as native or *externi*, which is an important organizational feature of his indices of sources, is raised, albeit implicitly. Pliny qualifies the value of Pythagoras' and Democritus' botanical works not simply because they are Greeks, but more importantly because they derived some of their knowledge from

---

[50] *NH* 24.156: *quae enim mirabiliores primi eas in nostro orbe celebravere Pythagoras atque Democritus, consectati magos*; 25.13: *ambo* [Pythagoras and Democritus] *peragratis Persidis, Arabiae, Aethiopiae, Aegypti magis, adeoque ad haec attonita antiquitas fuit, ut adfirmaverit etiam incredibilia dictu*; 30.9: *certe Pythagoras, Empedocles, Democritus, Plato ad hanc discendam navigavere exiliis verius quam peregrinationibus susceptis, hanc reversi praedicavere, hanc in arcanis habuere.*

sources further east (from an *aliena terra*, in other words). At the same
time, Pliny does not discredit his sources entirely; this would be
counterproductive. He does not question the fact that Pythagoras and
Democritus visited the Eastern magi, but he blames unnamed people
from the past (*antiquitas*) for embellishing the tradition of the two
men's teachings with marvels that resulted from their shock at seeing
things they did not understand. The latter point can be related back to
Pliny's discussion of folk theologies in Book 2: such theologies exist,
but they arise from ignorance. Thus it is at the very point where Pliny
needs his reader to trust the words of Pythagoras and Democritus — his
introduction to the discussion of the properties of plants — that Pliny is
obliged to distance them from thaumaturgy by attributing such reports
to ignorant people of the past.

A similar gesture is made in Pliny's history of magic in *NH* 30.1–
12.[51] After describing how people had long sought literary fame and
glory by exhibiting knowledge of magic (a category to which Apion
must implicitly belong), Pliny lists men about whom this was believed
to be true, including Pythagoras, Empedocles, Democritus, and Plato.
He adds the odd comment, however, that they studied magic as exiles
rather than as willing travelers (*exiliis verius quam peregrinationibus
susceptis*). Pliny thus seems to excuse the magical education of
philosophers as something undertaken in circumstances where better
options were unavailable. Ultimately, however, he cannot either deny
or wrap his mind around the idea that renowned philosophers not only
studied magic but even praised it and transmitted its secrets to others:
*quae recepta ab ullis hominum atque transisse per memoriam aeque ac
nihil in vita mirandum est; in tantum fides istis fasque omne deest, adeo
ut qui cetera in viro probant, haec opera eius esse infitientur* (Nothing
in life is more remarkable than the fact that these things were received
by anyone and passed down in memory; it is all so lacking in credi-
bility and propriety that those who approve of everything else about
[Democritus] deny that these works are his, *NH* 30.10). This magical
knowledge, which Pythagoras and other philosophers obtained from
eastern magi, is, according to Pliny, entirely lacking in *fides* and *fas* —
in other words, incompatible with good Roman values.[52]

While the absurdities of magic are especially associated with the
work of Democritus, it is notable that Pythagoras' interest in magic also

---

[51] For scholarly discussion of Pliny's history of magic, see Crippa (2010) 115–25;
Stannard (1986) 95–106. Dickie (2001) contains much useful discussion of Pliny's
history of magic but offers no separate discussion of the history itself.

[52] Recall that shortly after listing the great Greek scientists in Book 7 (123–25), Pliny
offers his boast regarding the surpassing virtue of the Romans (7.130).

diminished his legacy in Pliny's mind. Pliny consequently ranked the
vir sagacis animi below Socrates. Indeed, he expresses astonishment
over the Romans selecting Pythagoras in preference to Socrates (and
Alcibiades over Themistocles) when, during the Samnite War, Pythian
Apollo had commanded them to erect statues in the Comitium to the
wisest and to the bravest of the Greeks (*NH* 34.26). The Romans chose
Pythagoras despite the fact that Apollo had earlier identified Socrates
as the wisest of men.[53]

Pliny had a vision of the traditions of Greek philosophy and science
as being tainted by a *vanitas* that owed much to eastern influences, and,
even more fundamentally, was rooted in the human inability to observe
moderation.[54] While he acknowledges and appreciates the scientific
and philosophical contributions of the Greeks, he does not refrain from
criticizing what he understands to be an admixture of foolishness in
their contributions. One can see his strategy for separating the valuable
from the foolish in the references to Pythagoras discussed above.
Pythagoras' system of the harmony of the spheres was important but
included a superfluous refinement regarding Greek musical modes.
Pythagoras' teachings on herbs were mysticized by ignorant observers
who did not understand them. Pythagoras studied magic, but only
because he had nothing better to do during his exile. In each case, Pliny
establishes Pythagoras' superior wisdom, subtly undercuts the
Pythagorean legacy, and yet maintains a sufficiently favorable posture
toward the philosopher to preserve the usefulness of Pythagorean
knowledge for his own work.

The story of Dionysodorus the geometrician from Melos at *NH*
2.248 also aligns closely with the author's treatment of Pythagoras.[55]
The deceased Dionysodorus' female relatives, who performed the
customary funeral rites, produced from his tomb a letter, which they
maintained was written by him. In it he, as though dead and writing
from below the surface of the earth, addressed the people above and
told them he had descended from his tomb to the lowest part of the
earth. The distance he had traveled confirmed, for certain other
geometricians who had interpreted his account and performed their
own calculations, Eratosthenes' measurement of the earth's circumference. Pliny holds Dionysodorus in lower regard than the other geometricians he discusses for reasons similar to his reservations regarding
Pythagoras. He characterizes this tale of underworld revelation as an

---

[53] At *NH* 7.118 and 120 Socrates is again said to be the wisest of the Greeks on authority
of the Delphic oracle
[54] On the impact of a lack of moderation on medicine, see *NH* 26.20.
[55] On Dionysiodorus see now the paper by Trevor Murphy in this volume.

exemplum vanitatis Graecae maximum worthy of less credit (*alia fides*) than the other scientific discoveries of geometry he has discussed up to that point. Here Pliny uses the terms *vanitas* and *fides*, which also appear in his discussion of the history of magic, probably because he sees Dionysodorus' hoax as belonging to the same category of useless or deceptive embellishment of practical knowledge as magic.

One cannot help but see a further parallel between the underworld letter of Dionysodorus and Democritus' discovery of the grimoire of Dardanus the Phoenician in the latter's tomb: *Democritus ... Dardanum e Phoenice inlustravit voluminibus Dardani in sepulchrum eius petitis, suis vero ex disciplina eorum editis* (Democritus brought to light ... Dardanus the Phoenician; he sought Dardanus' books in the latter's tomb, and Democritus' own books were published from their teachings, *NH* 30.9).[56] Indeed, Pliny's portrayal of Dionysodorus' mummery suggests he attributed the geometrician's hoax to the same desire for fame that motivated many authors to demonstrate a familiarity with magic in their works (Plin. *Nat.* 30.2).

Such stories of messages from the underworld and buried books also abound in the Pythagorean tradition.[57] Hermippus transmitted a story of Pythagoras receiving tablets from his mother while he lived in an underground chamber he had dug for himself.[58] Using the information from the tablets, he was able, upon his return to the world above, to bamboozle the people with his pretended supernatural knowledge of their doings. Much earlier Herodotus relates the story of Zalmoxis, the putative slave of Pythagoras, who used a similar technique to impress the Getae.[59] Burkert contextualizes such tales in the ritual tradition of mysteries of the Great Mother, who represents the earth in these subterranean journeys.[60] Dionysodorus' hoax fits this model perfectly. He has transmitted his statement on the circumference of the earth (the Great Mother) in a manner that was easily recognizable to initiates in the mysteries of the Great Mother. Pliny, in any case, will have none of it. Whereas Lucretius highlighted the allegorical value of Cybele's exotic cult trappings in Rome, Pliny emphasizes the foolishness of tarting up scientific knowledge with the costume of the shaman.[61]

---

[56] *NH* 30.9.
[57] Burkert (1972) 155–65; Heilen (2009) 49–50.
[58] D.L. 8.41; *FGrH* 1026 F24.
[59] Herod. 4.94–6.
[60] Burkert, 160.
[61] Lucr. 2.598–643. On Lucretius' allegorical reading of Cybele's Roman cult, see also Jope (1985) 250–62; Clayton (1999) 69–84; Markovic (2008) 112–15; Fratantuono (2015) 121–7.

6. Pythagoras and Numa

Given the extent of Pliny's engagement with the Pythagorean tradition, one might have expected him to weigh in on the question of Pythagoras' reputed relationship with Rome's second king, Numa Pompilius. Surprisingly, Pliny has nothing explicit to add to the controversy. His silence does not indicate, however, that interest in the subject had declined. Soon Plutarch would revisit the topic, even though Cicero in the middle of the first century BC had already sensibly concluded it was a chronological impossibility.[62] The one place where Pliny does bring the two figures together is in his discussion of papyrus in Book 13, in which he offers detailed coverage of the discovery of the Books of Numa in 181 BC.[63] In his account of the books, Pliny quotes a whole cadre of Roman writers from the second and first centuries B.C., a fact that suggests he was much exercised about the topic.

This unusual investment is perhaps due to Pliny's ostensible purpose in discussing Numa's books: to present counter-evidence for Varro's claim that the invention of paper post-dated Alexander the Great's conquest of Egypt (Plin. *NH* 13.69). Indeed, Pliny uses his discussion of the books as an opportunity to cite Varro against himself. Thus, whatever else one might say of Pliny's historical acumen, his belief in the authenticity of Numa's books does him no credit. Pliny, in fact, regularly cites other obvious literary forgeries in an apparently uncritical manner. His account of Numa's books is arguably the prime example of this critical laxness. He cites Cassius Hemina for the fact that the books were discovered by a scribe, which on the face of it makes the entire episode highly dubious, and for the inclusion of Pythagorean philosophy in the books, which is a chronological impossibility.[64] Pliny appears to be more impressed with the early date of his source (mid-second century BC) — *Cassius Hemina, vetustissimus auctor annalium* (*NH* 13.84) — than he is concerned about the telltale signs of forgery. Indeed, drawing an inference from this passage, one might conclude that Pliny *contra* Cicero accepts Pythagoras' influence on Numa. Yet Pliny never explicitly connects

---

[62] Plu. *Numa* 1, 8; Cic. *Tusc.* 4.1.2–3.

[63] Plin. *NH* 13.84–7. On Numa's books, see Prowse (1964) 36–42; Forsythe (1994) 207–16; Willi (1998) 139–72.

[64] Scribe: *Cn. Terentium scribam agrum suum in Ianiculo repastinantem effodisse arcam in qua Numa, qui Romae regnavit, situs fuisset* (*NH* 13.84). Pythagorean books: *in iis libris scripta erant philosophiae Pythagoricae — eoque combustos a Q. Petilio praetore, quia philosophiae scripta essent* (*NH* 13.86).

Numa to Pythagoras. In fact, throughout the *Natural History* Pliny endeavors to keep the two men as separate as possible, the discussion of Numa's books being the single exception. This separation may be partly attributed to the nature of the sources on Numa Pliny consulted. Still, while Pliny quotes Pythagorean works, some of which were spuriously attributed to the philosopher himself, he does not quote any purported writings of Numa.

The idea that no forged writings of Numa existed in Pliny's day beggars belief. If a desire to read Numa's writings was felt, as it surely was, then someone will have written Books of Numa to satisfy the demand. The amazing thing is that we never read of such post-second-century-BC Numan pseudepigrapha. This may be a consequence, intended or not, of Petilius' brilliant stroke of having the first such books ceremonially burned in the Comitium (before the statue of Pythagoras?): the well-publicized, official destruction of Numa's supposed authentic works forever cast the pall of illegitimacy on every other forgery.[65] Doubtless the plan was not foolproof and other forgeries were made, but learned society could always point to the events of 181 as the basis for dismissing such works out of hand. This process of weeding out forgeries began in the first half of the second century BC, and may have involved dismissing writings on Pythagorean magic in the guise of teachings of Numa. The desire to rescue Numa from any association with Greek magic may be the reason why Cassius Hemina stressed the philosophical nature of the Pythagorean material in Numa's books. What one does not see in Pliny's discussion of the Books of Numa is any reference to thaumaturgical material therein, whether directly derived from Pythagorean sources or bearing the stamp of Pythagorean influence.

Pliny's account of Numa's books may serve as one more means through which the author is able to compare Roman judgment favorably with the inferior judgment of the Greeks. He does not question the authenticity of the pseudepigraphic Pythagorean work on plants that he frequently quotes because it does not strain credulity either in its provenance or its contents. There are limits to the value of Pliny's

---

[65] See *NH* 34.26 for the statue of Pythagoras in the Comitium. Pliny, however, says only that the books were burned, not where it happened. In the first instance, he is quoting Hemina (13.86): *eosque combustos a Q. Petilio praetore.* At 13.87 he cites Antias for the detail that the books were burned in accordance with a decree of the senate: *idem tertio et SC. ponit quo comburi eos placuerit.* It is Plutarch (*Num.* 22.5), citing Antias, who mentions the location of their destruction in the Comitium. Coincidental or not, the fact that Pliny does not mention this but does mention the placement of Pythagoras' statue in the Comitium may be yet another instance of Pliny avoiding Numa-Pythagoras connections.

method. What is interesting, however, is the way the story of Numa's books contrasts with Pliny's treatment of other forgeries in the Pythagorean mode. Pliny ridicules the letter of Dionysodorus as the supreme example of Greek foolishness (*vanitas*), and he dismisses Democritus' writings on magic as filled with sacrilegious nonsense. All of these works, including the books of Numa, share a connection with death and the underworld, a common theme in Pythagorean shamanic tales.

Pliny's representation of Numa's books and their discovery, however, differs from his depiction of other forgeries in ways that conform to Roman mores regarding the dead. Pliny reports that Cn. Terentius, while digging up his own field on the Janiculum, excavated a box (*arca*) containing the books of Numa. Assuming that the discovery of the books was, in fact, a hoax, one supposes that Terentius was concerned about the community's sensibilities when he and others contrived to bury and then uncover these fake relics. Implicit in Pliny's quotation of Hemina, the oldest annalistic source, is the fact that the books were preserved whereas Numa's missing body was presumably consumed by worms.[66] Found on Terentius' own property and empty of human remains, the discovery would have seemed, from Pliny's point of view, free of the taint of a religious violation or problems of uncertain ownership.[67] Thus the books are legitimized in a way that contrasts with Democritus' recovered grimoire of Dardanus, and Terentius is absolved of any possible guilt. Not only does Pliny present the discovery of Numa's books in a manner consistent with Roman values, he effectively diminishes the association of the books with the Pythagorean tradition. According to Hemina, the books contained Pythagorean philosophy, and, for that reason, the praetor Q. Petilius burned them. Pliny then cites other sources specifically for their coverage of the books' contents, such that his reader is left with a more diffuse impression of the books, which, based on this survey of sources, might have included everything from decrees of Numa alone to pontifical books and books of Greek philosophy (not specifically Pythagorean).[68]

---

[66] Plin. *NH* 13.86: *In eo lapide insuper libros III sitos fuisse; propterea arbitrarier computuisse. et libros citratos fuisse; propterea arbitrarier tineas non tetigisse.* The terms for decay and consumption by worms also apply to a human body and suggest that Hemina compared the preservation of the books to the decay and disappearance of Numa's remains.

[67] Rives (2012) 165–80 discusses the status of graves, including those missing the body. For the law on the discovery of treasure, see Lee (2007) 139.

[68] 13.87. Piso Censorius: *libros septem iuris pontificii, totidem Pythagoricos fuisse*; Tuditanus: *Numae decretorum fuisse.* Varro: *humanarum antiquitatum VII.* Antias: *XII pontificales Latinos, totidem Graecos praecepta philosophiae continentes.*

Beyond the subject of the Books of Numa, Pliny's depiction of Numa offers vanishingly little of uniquely Pythagorean interest, as his citations of Numa's contributions to Roman culture and politics will bear out. Toward the organization of society, Numa contributed the guilds of braziers and potters.[69] In the area of religion, he initiated the practices of offering wheat to the gods and propitiating them with salted cakes,[70] established the agrarian festivals of Robigalia, Fornicalia, Terminalia, and others,[71] and erected one of the very first religious images in Rome, a statue of Janus.[72] Furthermore, Numa proscribed the offering of fish without scales to the gods at festivals in order, as Pliny opines, to limit the cost of such religious observances.[73] Pliny also reports Numa's law against sprinkling wine on funeral pyres on the grounds that wine was in short supply; and his law against libations of wine from unpruned vines to prevent accidents that would result from climbing to reach grapes on unpruned vines.[74] Pliny's interest in Numa's frugality in religious practices is consistent with the his own condemnation of the burning of costly incense as a form of *superstitio*.[75]

Overall, Pliny's portrait of Numa idealizes the king in a way that is consistent with the author's own values of simplicity, practicality, and frugality.[76] None of this material about Numa resembles the tradition of Pythagoras as shaman or wizard. This is not to say, however, that Pliny's Numa has no conceivable association with Pythagorean sensibilities. Numa's institution of non-meat sacrifices would have met with the approval of those Pythagoreans who practiced vegetarianism.[77] It is also interesting that Pliny refers to Varro's burial in Pythagorean style directly after he mentions Numa's institution of the guild of potters

---

[69] *NH* 34.1, 35.159.

[70] *NH* 18.7.

[71] *NH* 18.8, 285.

[72] Plin. *NH* 34.33. Pliny's mention of Numa's erection of a statue of Janus is interesting in view of Terentius' discovery of the Books of Numa on Janus' hill, the Janiculum.

[73] Plin. *NH* 32.20, citing Cassius Hemina. The second-century BCE author Agatharcides of Cnidus wrote of the Boeotian eel sacrifice; see *FGrH* 3.192. Pliny was aware of Agatharcides and consulted his work or quotations of it.

[74] Plin. *NH* 14.88.

[75] Plin. *NH* 22.118. See also Martin (2009) 129.

[76] Beagon (1992) 99 notes the way Pliny describes Numa's law on wine offerings in terms of its practical benefits.

[77] Riedweg (2005) 68–9. R. (68) contends that Pythagorean vegetarianism is early: "The strict renunciation of eating meat follows almost inevitably from the doctrine of the transmigration of souls as it can be derived from the oldest reports about Pythagoras." In *On Abstinence* (1.3, 13–26), Porphyry mentions one philologist named Clodius of Neapolis (Italy), who criticized vegetarianism and traced its origins to Pythagoras. Clodius may have written in the late first century BCE. See O'Meara (1990) 27–8, 28 n.70.

(Varro was buried in an earthenware sarcophagus).[78] It is difficult to avoid the conclusion that Pliny had either consulted a work in which the two facts were placed next to each other, or that he made the connection himself. In any case, one can hardly suppose that Pliny was unaware of Numa's long association with Pythagoras. On the other hand, it is remarkable that, for the most part, Pliny's Numa lacks those elements of wonderworking and charlatanry that elsewhere make him resemble Pythagoras. Pliny's Numa does not capture Picus and Faunus as does Ovid's and Plutarch's.[79] He does not converse with Jupiter. He does not sleep with Egeria or claim to do so as a mechanism for cultivating respect for his laws. As with Pythagoras, but even more aggressively, Pliny sanitizes the Numan tradition of those things he likely considered to be utter rubbish.

The one datum in Pliny regarding Numa that is arguably thaumaturgical in nature is his reputed ability to summon lightning, which, according to Pliny, he practiced rather often (*saepius factitatum*).[80] Once again, Pliny seems to part ways with Varro in his decision to feature Numa's ceraunomancy instead of his hydromancy;[81] Varro's history of hydromancy traced its use from the Persians to Numa and, later, Pythagoras. Pliny's divergence from Varro is particularly interesting in light of his willingness to discuss the hydromancy of Anaximander and Pherecydes in terms identical to the astronomy of his scientific hero Hipparchus. In other words, Pliny does not connect Numa and Pythagoras through hydromancy, even though he had earlier valorized the hydromancy Pythagoras had learned from Pherecydes, and though he might have used Varro to claim that Numa had used hydromancy before either man.

Although it is true that Pliny provided an explanation of the scientific foundations of ceraunomancy in Book 2, the ability to *summon* lightning is still exactly the kind of wonder one would expect of magicians, witches, and Pythagorean heroes.[82] Pliny does not refer

---

[78] *NH* 35.160. Kahn (2001) 88–89 discusses the possibility that Varro was a Pythagorean. See also Joost-Gaugier (2007) 28–9, 98, 251. Blank (2012) 251, 266–7, 286 argues that Varro got much of his Pythagorean doctrine from Antiochus of Ascalon.

[79] Pliny does mention Faunus in connection with his mythical son, King Stercutus, who is credited with introducing the use of manure. See *NH* 17.50.

[80] *NH* 2.140. Healy (1999) 110 attributes Pliny's discussion of lightning summoning to his uncritical reliance on historians and scholars like Piso Frugi. On the death of Hostilius, see also *NH* 28.14. For discussion of Pliny's use of Frugi, see Cornell (2013) 200–202.

[81] Augustine (*De civ.* 7.35) cites Varro's *Curio* on Numa's use of hydromancy to receive instruction from the gods — a method later employed by Pythagoras. See Blank (2012) 266.

[82] Seneca's Medea claims to have received power over lightning from Phaethon: Sen.

to the lightning-summoning of any such figures, however. At *NH* 2.140, aside from Numa, Pliny cites only Lars Porsenna's use of lightning against the monster Olta that attacked Volsinium and Tullus Hostilius' death resulting from his ritual error in trying to imitate Numa in the conjuring of lightning. One may suppose that the choice of examples is not the result of selection so much as the sources he relied upon in his coverage of the topic. One of these sources was the historian Piso Frugi, who related the information about Numa and Tullius Hostilius. Less certain is Pliny's source for the story of Porsenna.

So, it may be the case that none of Pliny's sources on lightning dealt with the use of magic or shamanic abilities to summon it. Pliny's knowledge of hydromancy and his handling of the topic of lightning conjuration, however, does suggest that he was aware of Greek stories of weather manipulation and strove to avoid associating Italian lightning lore with Greek magical and philosophical traditions. Pliny precedes his listing of Italians who summoned lightning by saying that the method involved certain rites and prayers (*sacris quibusdam et precationibus vel cogi fulmina vel impetrari*, *NH* 2.140). He chooses his words carefully, lest he appear to be saying that Porsenna, Numa, and Hostilius were engaging in magic. His intention to defend Numa again emerges in the statement that follows (*NH* 2.141):

> imperare naturae sacra audacis est credere, nec minus hebetis beneficiis abrogare vires, quando in fulgurum quoque interpretatione eo profecit scientia ut ventura alia finito die praecinat ... innumerabilibus ... publicis privatisque experimentis

> It is rash to believe that ceremonies control nature, and no less stupid to deny power to their services, since in the interpretation of lightning-bolts too knowledge has made such progress that it predicts others will come at a fixed time ... through numberless experiments both public and private.[83]

On the one hand, it is surely hubris, in Pliny's view, to imagine that a man can use rites to command (*imperare*) nature; such a person we might characterize as a wizard or a witch. On the other, it would be foolish to deny the power of these benefits (*beneficiis ... vires*) when the science of ceraunoscopy has been confirmed by countless experiments. It is in the reference to such experiments that we see the clearest contrast between Pliny's depictions of Numa and of Pythagoras. His

---

Med. 826–7. Lucan's Erichtho is said to chase after lightning at night: Luc. *BC* 6.520. Control over lightning is implicit in Empedocles' control of the weather: Diels fr.111; see Gregory (2013) 183.

[83] Plin. *NH* 2.141.

tentative approval of Numa's involvement with lightning is consistent with his earlier discussion of the scientific basis of ceraunoscopy: Jove's lightning-bolts are fires from three planets.[84] Pliny thus assimilates, however unconvincingly, Numa's involvement in the summoning of lightning to scientific astrology and other similar forms of scientific prediction, which rely upon knowledge, not magic and false belief. In contrast, Pliny depicted a Pythagoras who had departed from his usual wisdom in seeking from foreign magi the vanities of a magic lacking in *fides* and *fas*. Such vanities probably include the control of weather that Pythagoras and other Pythagorean heroes were believed to possess. It is difficult not to see a certain degree of tendentiousness in Pliny's attempt to distinguish Numa from Pythagoras. Nevertheless, Pliny is consistent in attempting to distinguish them.

According to Pliny, Numa's ritual skills in the summoning of lightning are legitimized through their association with the science of ceraunoscopy, which has been proven by many trials. What seemed miraculous in the past is now, after repeated exposure, *scientia*. This epistemological position is alluded to again, albeit briefly, near the beginning of Book 6, There, dealing with the customs and rites of people living on the margins of the world, Pliny says: *prodigiosa aliqua et incredibilia multis visum iri haud dubito. quis enim Aethiopas ante quam cerneret credidit? aut quid non miraculo est, cum primum in notitiam venit?* (I have no doubt to many some things will seem portentous and unbelievable. Who, for example, would believe in the existence of Ethiopians before seeing them? Or, what is not taken for a miracle, the first time it comes to notice? *NH* 7.6)[85] The importance to Pliny of careful observation and testing appearances is also illustrated well in the contest between Zeuxis and Parrhasius (*NH* 35.65), in which Zeuxis was able to fool Parrhasius into mistaking his painting of a curtain for the real thing.[86]

Pliny made use of the writings of the Pythagorean tradition and wrote of those figures, such as Dionysodorus, whose scientific persona included wonderworking. The encyclopedist found in these figures a relatively easy way to distinguish himself as superior in judgment to some of the greatest figures of the Hellenic philosophical tradition. Armed with the values of a member of the educated Roman imperial elite, he chastised Greek scientists for failing to observe *moderatio* in

---

[84] See n.44 above.
[85] On this passage as an abbreviated statement of Pliny's epistemology, see Cummings (2004) 178.
[86] Pliny does not often live up to his own avowed ideals regarding observation. For a critical view of Pliny's methods, see Lloyd (1999) 135–49.

their search for knowledge and embracing practices lacking in *fides* and *fas*. Against the unfortunate extravagances of men like Pythagoras, Democritus, and Dionysodorus, Pliny offers us a whitewashed version of Numa, whose most apparently thaumaturgical activity — the summoning of lightning — is legitimized by its association with the science of ceraunoscopy. In doing so, he gives wide berth to a long tradition in which Pythagoras and Numa were quite closely related. Pliny was aware of this tradition, and acknowledges it in a limited way in his account of the discovery of the Books of Numa. His Numa, however, bears little resemblance to the Numa of Ovid or Plutarch, whose use of miracle and deception accord well with the Pythagorean tradition. Judging solely through the lens of Pliny's construction of Numa, one would expect that Numa's books of Pythagorean philosophy, had they survived, would have been free of the magical extravagances Pliny inveighed against regularly.

Summary

This paper has sought to show how Pliny's depiction of Pythagoras fits within Pliny's complex framework for understanding scientific investigation in the context of his Stoic theology. Pliny, following Seneca the Younger, adapted the language of divination to scientific investigation, but, unlike Seneca, Pliny applied this language to the investigation of earthly as well as celestial phenomena. At either end of the spectrum of scientific legitimacy, Pliny located Hipparchus, a scientist whose methods Pliny valorized, on the one extreme, and Apion, a vain charlatan, on the other.

Pliny's Pythagoras falls somewhere between these two figures. Although Pythagoras is praised for his contributions to science, and indeed is placed among Pliny's scientific 'giants' (*viri ingentes*), it is clear that in Pliny's mind Pythagoras came too close to the figure of Apion to avoid criticism altogether. In Pliny's view, Pythagoras both needlessly embellished his discovery of the harmony of spheres and also contributed to the study of the disreputable art of magic. Pythagoras is also downplayed in Pliny's depiction of Numa, when Rome's second king is carefully separated from a tainted Pythagorean legacy with which he was not infrequently associated. Only in Pliny's discussion of Numa's lost books is Pythagoras explicitly connected to Numa, but that connection is subsequently undercut through other, contradicting sources. Likewise, it is in the discussion of lightning alone that Pliny's Numa comes close to appearing like a Pythagorean wizard, but Pliny's treatment seeks to counteract such potential conclusions by rationalizing, however clumsily, Numa's manipulation of lightning.

In the course of the investigation, our understanding of Pliny's engagement with his sources has expanded. Past scholarship on the preface of the *Naturalis Historia* demonstrated Pliny's playful engagement with Catullus; this article points out further ways in which Pliny interacted with the work of his predecessors in writing *de rerum natura*, Ennius and Lucretius. In addition, it has explored how Pliny adapted Cicero's accounts of Anaximander and Pherecydes in the *De Divinatione* while simultaneously responding to Cicero's ideas. Pliny's response to Cicero was well integrated with his own scientific thought. Indeed, the degree of complexity and consistency in Pliny's framework for understanding and evaluating human science and its heroes suggests that there is an identifiable Pliny in the *Naturalis Historia*, whose views are, by his design, imprinted in his text. If that is the case, then the seductive portrait of Pliny the mechanistic collector and arranger of contradictory facts must be tempered to include the natural philosopher who critically engaged with works in the philosophical and scientific traditions and presented his own views, at least on certain topics, consistently.

Bibliography

Aicher, P. (1989). 'Ennius' Dream of Homer' *AJP* 110(2).227–32

Baldwin, B. (2005). 'Stylistic Notes on the Elder Pliny's Preface' *Latomus* 64(1).91–95

Barton, T. (2002). *Ancient Astrology*. London and New York

Beagon, M. (1992). *Roman Nature. The Thought of Pliny the Elder.* Oxford

— (2011). 'The curious eye of the Elder Pliny' in Gibson and Morello (2011) 71–88

Blank, D. (2012). 'Varro and Antiochus' in D. Sedley (ed) *The Philosophy of Antiochus*. Cambridge and New York. 250–89.

Buchheit, V. (1971). 'Epikurs Triumph des Geistes' *Hermes* 99.303–23

Burkert, W. (1972). *Lore and Science in Ancient Pythagoreanism*. Cambridge, Mass.

Cairns, F. (2010). '*Roma* and Her Tutelary Deity: Names and Ancient Evidence' in C. Shuttleworth Kraus, J. Marincola, and C.B.R. Pelling (edd.) *Ancient Historiography and its Contexts: Studies in Honour of A.J. Woodman.* Oxford and New York. 245–66

Clayton, B. (1999). 'Lucretius' Erotic Mother: Maternity as a Poetic Construct in *De Rerum Natura*' *Helios* 26(1).69–84

Cornell, T.J. (2013). *The Fragments of the Roman Historians, vol. 3, Commentary.* Oxford

Crippa, S. (2010). 'Magic and Rationality in Pliny: Transmission of Knowledge: the Medical-Magical Pharmacopoiea' *Palamedes* 5.115–25

Cummings, B. (2004). 'Animal Language in Renaissance Thought' in E. Fudge (ed.) *Renaissance Beasts: Of Animals, Humans, and Other Wonderful Creatures.* Urbana-Champagne. 164–85

Damon, C. (2011). 'Pliny on Apion' in Gibson and Morello (2011) 111–46

Dickie, M. (2001). *Magic and Magicians in the Greco-Roman World.* London

Dominik, W.J. 'From Greece to Rome: Ennius' *Annales*' in A.J. Boyle (ed.) *Roman Epic.* London and New York. 37–58

Forsythe, G. (1994). *The Historian L. Calpurnius Piso Frugi and the Roman Annalistic Tradition.* Lanham, MD

Forsythe, G. (2006). *A Critical History of Early Rome: From Prehistory to the First Punic War.* Berkeley

Fratantuono, L. (2015). *A Reading of Lucretius' De Rerum Natura.* London and New York

Gibson, R.K. and R. Morello (2011). (edd.) *Pliny the Elder: Themes and Contexts.* Leiden

Goldstein, B.R. and A.C. Bowen (1995). 'Pliny and Hipparchus' 600–Year Cycle' *JHA* 26(2).155–58

Gregory, A. (2013). *The Presocratice and the Supernatural: Magic, Philosophy, and Science in Early Greece.* London and New York

Hardie, A. (2010). '*Canens*: (Ovid *Metamorphoses* 14.320–434)' *SIFC* ser. 8(1).11–67

Harrison, S.J. (2002). 'Ennius and the prologue to Lucretius *DRN* 1 (1.1–148)' *LICS* 1.4.13p, online at http://lics.leeds.ac.uk/

Healey, J.F. (1999). *Pliny the Elder on Science and Technology.* Oxford

Heilen, S. (2009). 'Ptolemy's Doctrine of the Terms and Its Reception' in A. Jones (ed.) *Ptolemy in Perspective: Use and Criticism of his Work from Antiquity to the Nineteenth Century.* Dordrecht and New York. 45–94

Howe, N.P. (1985). 'In Defense of the Encyclopedic Mode: On Pliny's "Preface" to the "Natural History"' *Latomus* 44(3).561–76

Joost-Gaugier, C.L. (2007). *Measuring Heaven: Pythagoras and His Influence on Thought and Art in Antiquity and the Middle Ages.* Ithaca, NY

Jope, J. (1985). 'Lucretius, Cybele, and Religion' *Phoenix* 39.250–62

Kahn, C.H. (2001). *Pythagoras and the Pythagoreans: A Brief History.* Indianapolis

Kennedy, D.F. (2013). 'The Political Epistemology of Infinity' in D. Lehoux, A.D. Morrison, and A. Sharrock (edd.) *Lucretius: Poetry, Philosophy, Science.* Oxford. 51–67

Lee, R.W. (2007). *The Elements of Roman Law: With a Translation of the*

Institutes of Justinian. London

Lehoux, D. (2013). 'Seeing and Unseeing, Seen and Unseen' in D. Lehoux, A. D. Morrison, and A. Sharrock (edd.) *Lucretius: Poetry, Philosophy, Science.* Oxford. 131–51

Lloyd, G.E.R. (1999). *Science, Folklore, and Ideology: Studies in the Life Sciences in Ancient Greece.* London and Indianapolis

Luke, T. (2010). 'A Healing Touch for Empire: Vespasian's Healings in Domitianic Rome' *G&R* 57(1).77–106

Markovic, D. (2008). *The Rhetoric of Explanation in Lucretius' De Rerum Natura.* Leiden and Boston

Martin, D.B. (2009). *Inventing Superstition: From the Hippocratics to the Christians.* Cambridge, Mass.

Murphey, T. (2004). *Pliny the Elder's Natural History: The Empire in the Encyclopedia.* Oxford and New York

Murphy, T.M. (2004). 'Privileged Knowledge: Valerius Soranus and the Secret Name of Rome' in A. Barchiesi, J. Rüpke, and S.A. Stephens (edd.) *Rituals in Ink: A Conference on Religion and Literary Production in Ancient Rome Held at Stanford University in February 2002.* Stuttgart. 127–37

O'Meara, D.J. (1990). *Pythagoreanism Revived: Mathematics and Philosophy in Late Antiquity.* Oxford

Paparazzo, E. (2011). 'Philosophy and Science in the *Naturalis Historia*' in Gibson and Morello (2011) 89–111

Prowse, K.R. (1964). 'Numa and the Pythagoreans: A Curious Incident' *G&R* 11(1).36–42

Riedweg, C. (2005). *Pythagoras: His Life, Teaching, and Influence* (tr. S. Rendall). Ithaca, NY

Rives, J. (2012). 'Control of the Sacred in Roman Law' in O. Tellegen-Couperus (ed.) *Law and Religion in the Roman Republic.* Leiden and Boston. 165–80

Sinclair, P. (2003). 'Rhetoric of Writing and Reading in the Preface to Pliny's *Naturalis Historia*' in A.J. Boyle and W.J. Dominik (edd.) *Flavian Rome: Culture, Image, Text.* Leiden and Boston. 277–300

Skutsch, O. (1968). *Studia Enniana.* London

Stannard, J. (1986). 'Herbal Medicine and Magic in Pliny's Time' *Helmantica* 37.95–106

Tatum, W.J. (2007). 'The Presocratics in Book 1' in M.R. Gale (ed.) *Oxford Readings in Lucretius.* Oxford and New York. 132–45

Tissol, G. (2014). *The Face of Nature: Wit, Narrative, and Cosmic Origins in Ovid's Metamorphoses.* Princeton, NJ

Wardle, D. (2013). *Cicero: On Divination Book 1.* Oxford

Willi, A. (1998). 'Numa's Dangerous Books: The Exegetic History of a Roman Forgery' *MH* 55(3).139–72

Williams, G. (2012). *The Cosmic Viewpoint: A Study of Seneca's Natural Questions.* Oxford and New York

Cicero as Role-Model in the Self-Definition of Pliny the Elder

Sandra Citroni Marchetti
Università di Firenze

-I-

On the nineteenth of September, 44 BC, Marcus Antonius delivered a major invective against Cicero in the Roman senate. This was Antonius' retaliation for an earlier senate speech by Cicero, in which he had listed the illegal actions of Antonius as consul. In his invective against Cicero, Antonius accused Cicero of responsibility for almost everything that had gone wrong in Rome in the previous years. Among other things he blamed him for the murder of Clodius, for the Civil War, and for Caesar's assassination — and he mocked Cicero's poetry. Cicero was unable to reply because he was not present at that senate meeting. But he wrote a response, framing it as the speech he would have delivered if he had been in the senate that day. This is the work we now know as the *Second Philippic*, one of the most famous and memorable of all Cicero's compositions. In it Cicero responds (among other things) to Antonius' mockery of his poetry: he starts with a brief witticism, and then continues with a passage which has great significance for the subject of this paper, and which might have implanted itself in the mind of Pliny the Elder:

> nec vero tibi de versibus plura respondebo: tantum dicam breviter, te neque illos neque ullas omnino litteras nosse; me nec rei publicae nec amicis umquam defuisse, et tamen omni genere monumentorum meorum perfecisse operis subsicivis ut meae vigiliae meaeque litterae et iuventuti utilitatis et nomini Romano laudis aliquid adferrent.
>
> Cic. *Phil.* 2.20

First of all, this passage documents the political conflict between Cicero and Antonius at that particular point in time. Secondly, it sets out Cicero's attitude to culture in a way which is basically consistent with declarations made elsewhere by Cicero on this subject. And thirdly, the declaration comes from a work which is itself the product of Cicero's highest cultural efforts: not only was the *Philippic* never delivered, but in essence it is a literary composition with political aims which keeps its 'occasional' character very much in the background.[1]

There are several major points of contact between Cicero's self-presentation in the *Second Philippic* and sections sixteen and eighteen of Pliny the Elder's preface to his *Naturalis Historia*:

> equidem ita sentio, peculiarem in studiis causam eorum esse, qui difficultatibus victis utilitatem iuvandi praetulerint gratiae placendi, idque iam et in aliis operibus ipse feci et profiteor mirari me T. Livium, auctorem celeberrimum, in historiarum suarum, quas repetit ab origine urbis, quodam volumine sic orsum: "iam sibi satis gloriae quaesitum, et potuisse se desidere, ni animus inquies pasceretur opere." profecto enim populi gentium victoris et Romani nominis gloriae, non suae, composuisse illa decuit. maius meritum esset operis amore, non animi causa, perseverasse et hoc populo Romano praestitisse, non sibi. [...] nec dubitamus multa esse quae et nos praeterierint; homines enim sumus et occupati officiis subsicivisque temporibus ista curamus, id est nocturnis, ne quis vestrum putet his cessatum horis. dies vobis inpendimus, cum somno valetudinem computamus, vel hoc solo praemio contenti, quod, dum ista, ut ait M. Varro, musinamur, pluribus horis vivimus. profecto enim vita vigilia est.   *NH pr.*16–18

Cicero refers to his 'nocturnal vigils', and Pliny confines his studies to the night hours. Cicero speaks of the utility of his works for the young (*iuventuti utilitatis ... aliquid adferrent*), while Pliny writes of the *utilitas iuvandi* of his *studia*. Pliny, incidentally, sees *utilitas* as being in opposition to providing entertainment. Furthermore, both Cicero and Pliny speak of the enhancement which their works will bring to the reputation of Rome. I am not arguing that the Pliny passage necessarily derives from the *Second Philippic*. It is enough that the *Philippic* passage is characteristic of Cicero's thought, and that it contains a number of elements which reappear in Pliny the Elder, concentrated in a section of his preface which specifically refers to his current work, but which also provides a more general cultural agenda, and defines the attitude that Pliny considers appropriate to a man of culture.

There is moreover a fourth element in common between the two texts which I have kept to this point because of the uncertainty surrounding it. This is the striking coincidence of *operis subsicivis*

---

[1] The *Second Philippic* can thus be placed firmly within that body of Cicero's work whose cultural worth is acknowledged by Pliny in these words: *quae volumina ediscenda, non modo in manibus cotidie habenda nosti* (*pr.* 22). Pliny mentions *De Republica*, the *Consolatio* and *De Officiis*, but his judgement cannot be regarded as being limited to these three works, nor just to Cicero's philosophical writings. By saying *nosti* (you know), Pliny associates the emperor Titus, to whom his work is dedicated, with this judgment, connoting him as a cultured man.

(spare-time activities) in Cicero and *subsicivisque temporibus* in Pliny (bits of spare time). The uncertainty lies in the fact that the words *operis subsicivis* are found in only one branch of the manuscript tradition of Cicero.[2] But even if these words were inserted subsequently into Cicero's text, the reason must have been that the phrase was recognized as characteristic of the way in which both Cicero himself and the characters in his dialogues speak of their cultural activities. Thus in *De Legibus* we find *subsiciva tempora* (*subsiciva quaedam tempora incurrunt, quae ego perire non patior*, 1.9; *his subsicivis, ut ais, temporibus*, 1.13), and in *De Oratore* we find the same phrase, *subsicivis operis*, as is found in some manuscripts of the *Second Philippic* (*quae ego sero, quae cursim arripui, quae subsicivis operis, ut aiunt*, 2.364). Hence, whether or not Cicero wrote *operis subsicivis* in the *Second Philippic*, when Pliny in his preface speaks of himself as a man who is *occupatus* and who devotes only *subsiciva tempora* to his studies, he is thinking in Ciceronian terms.

The closeness of Pliny's adherence to a Ciceronian mindset in his preface can be perceived more clearly if we examine the evolution after Cicero of the term *subsicivus*, when used of study and scholarship.[3] Already in the Neronian age the Ciceronian relationship between other occupations and study had been overturned radically by Seneca. Seneca advised that one should free oneself from other occupations in order to dedicate all one's time to study. He refused to qualify study as *subsicivus* because for Seneca study was the study of philosophy: *philosophia non est res subsiciva* (philosophy is not a thing to be followed at odd times).[4] In subsequent authors, however, the term *subsicivus* was no longer used to signal an opposition between time given to other occupations and time given to study. Rather it was connected with the notion of dividing up the time allocated for study between different subjects. *Subsicivum tempus* is time taken away from studies con-

---

[2] Among modern editors, *operis subsicivis* is omitted by W.C.A. Ker (Cambridge Mass. and London 1963 [1926]), P. Fedeli (Leipzig 1982), W.K. Lacey (Warminster 1986). It is retained by A. Boulanger and P. Wuilleumier (Paris 1959); D.R. Shackleton Bailey (Chapel Hill and London 1986); J.T. Ramsey (Cambridge 2003).

[3] Prior to Cicero there is an attestation of *subsicivus* in reference to studies in Lucilius 762 M. *haec subsiciva si quando voles oper<a>*.

[4] Sen. *Epist.* 53.9: *omnia inpedimenta dimitte et vaca bonae menti: nemo ad illam pervenit occupatus. exercet philosophia regnum suum; dat tempus, non accipit; non est res subsiciva*. Seneca's affirmation that philosophy is not *res subsiciva* seems to be a polemical response to Cicero's comments about the period of his public career, when he was able to devote to philosophy only the time left over from his activities on behalf 'of friends and the state': *posteaquam honoribus inservire coepi meque totum rei publicae tradidi, tantum erat philosophiae loci, quantum superfuerat amicorum et rei publicae tempori* (*Off.* 2.4). But Cicero himself, late on in his life, denied that the study of philosophy could be moderated or limited (*Fin.* 1.2).

sidered more conventional and more legitimate and given to less worthy subjects. Quintilian, for example, describes as *subsicivum* the time that pupils dedicate to arts such as music and mathematics, something that should be permitted only so they will not become bored by simply following the lessons of the *grammaticus*: *ergo cum grammaticus totum diem occupare non possit, nec debeat ne discentis animum taedio avertat, quibus potius studiis haec temporum uelut subsiciva donabimus?* (*Inst.* 1.12.13–14).

In the *Noctes Atticae* of Gellius, the last author in whom *subsicivus* is attested in connection with studies, the characters make use of this term to indicate that, within their entire cultural activity, they set aside a certain time for subjects which are not their main interest:

> "etiamsi" inquit Favorinus "opera mihi princeps et prope omnis in litteris disciplinisque Graecis sumpta est, non usque eo tamen infrequens sum vocum Latinarum, quas subsicivo aut tumultuario studio colo, ut hanc ignorem … interpretationem.   13.25.4

> quantum habui temporis subsicivi, medicinae quoque disciplinae libros attigi.   18.10.8

Thus in Gellius not only does *subsicivus* not mark an opposition between time spent on fulfilling duties and time spent on study, but on the contrary it serves to underline the status of his characters as men of learning, men for whom a predominant commitment to one cultural field is no obstacle to other areas of study. But Gellius also used the term *subsicivus* in his preface with reference to the work that he was introducing, his own *Noctes Atticae*, and he created the same opposition between the time for other occupations and the time for study as Pliny had done:

> volumina commentariorum ad hunc diem viginti iam facta sunt. quantum autem vitae mihi deinceps deum voluntate erit quantumque a tuenda re familiari procurandoque cultu liberorum meorum dabitur otium, ea omnia subsiciva et subsecundaria tempora ad colligendas huiuscemodi memoriarum delectatiunculas conferam.   *pr.* 22–3

The difference however was that for Gellius the occupations from which the *subsiciva tempora* had to be subtracted for studies were exclusively of a private nature. Pliny is therefore the only author of the Imperial age who uses the term *subsicivus* in the Ciceronian sense, to indicate a personal choice between public duty and cultural activity.

One author of this same intervening period who also uses *subsicivus* has not yet been mentioned. This is Pliny the Younger, who employs the term in a passage specifically about Cicero and about his behavior as a man of letters. Pliny the Younger had been invited to take part of his time away from his studies and to dedicate it as *subsicivum* time to the reading of the poetic collections of a friend. The friend had backed up his request by recalling the kindness and accessibility of Cicero to poets:

> petis ut libellos tuos in secessu legam examinem, an editione sint digni; adhibes preces, adlegas exemplum: rogas enim, ut aliquid sub-sicivi temporis studiis meis subtraham, impertiam tuis, adicis M. Tullium mira benignitate poetarum ingenia fovisse. *Epist.* 3.15.1

Although the figure of Cicero is involved here, the term *subsicivus* does not refer to the Ciceronian opposition between studies and more meritorious activities. Rather it indicates, as in Quintilian and in Gellius, the process of taking some time away from one's usual studies and dedicating it to other literary activities. But Pliny the Younger is not making a casual reference to the link between Cicero and poetry. Pliny the Younger says that he has decided to write poetry, and to write lascivious poems in particular, in imitation of Cicero, an orator who had also dedicated himself to this kind of study:

> incidit epigramma Ciceronis ... coepi reputare maximos oratores hoc studii genus et in oblectationibus habuisse et in laude posuisse.[5]
> *Epist.* 7.4.3–4

-II-

Pliny the Younger was rounding out his own imitation of Cicero, different from that of his uncle, an imitation which he had pursued in all aspects of his public life, as a senator, as a political and judicial orator, and as a man involved in *officia*, by adopting also the partial persona of the uncommitted man of letters, something which had been quite marginal in the case of Cicero. The sort of analogy that Pliny the Younger was trying to construct between himself and Cicero, both of them senators and both of them consuls, was one from which his uncle Pliny the Elder was inevitably at least partly excluded, since Pliny the Elder was equestrian in rank and an imperial functionary. In one letter, in fact, the nephew himself underlines that his uncle's political and social involvement is different from that of Cicero and different from his own involvement. Cicero's reflection on his own status as a man of letters in the *Second Philippic* was preceded by a claim of commitment to the State and to his friends which placed those commitments above his commitment to his studies: *me nec rei publicae nec amicis umquam*

---

[5] The same language is used by Pliny in reference to the pleasure and glory he himself seeks in light verse: *incipio enim ex hoc genere studiorum non solum oblectationem verum etiam gloriam petere* (9.25.2).

defuisse (I never failed in my duty either to the state or to my friends, *Phil.* 2.20). Pliny the Younger, in a letter recalling the works and personality of his uncle, and comparing his uncle and himself, says that his own devotion to studies is hindered by his public duties and his duties to his friends: *me ... quem partim publica partim amicorum officia distringunt* (*Epist.* 3.5.19). In this statement Pliny the Younger recognizes himself as the heir of Cicero. He also seemingly intends to establish continuity with the lifestyle of his uncle, since he had already defined his uncle's commitments by referring both to public duties and to friendship. But the references are not in exactly the same terms. With regard to his uncle, Pliny the Younger spoke of *officia* (or *maxima officia*) and of friendship with the *principes* or friendship with the *princeps*:

> miraberis si scieris illum aliquamdiu causas actitasse, decessisse anno sexto et quinquagensimo, medium tempus distentum impeditumque qua officiis maximis qua amicitia principum egisse.   *Epist.* 3.5.7

> Nonne videtur tibi recordanti, quantum legerit quantum scripserit, nec in officiis ullis nec in amicitia principis fuisse...?   *Epist.* 3.5.18

The Ciceronian terminology which he used of his own activities and which mentioned both his state duties and his duties of friendship — while keeping them distinct — has a narrower compass when his nephew speaks of Pliny the Elder. He specifies that the *amicitia*, the friendship, of Pliny the Elder, was directed towards those same *principes* who are the recipients of Pliny the Elder's *officia*, the public tasks making up his assignments as an imperial functionary. In this way Pliny the Younger describes his uncle's position in flattering terms, but excludes his uncle from the natural and direct continuity which he wishes to establish between himself and Cicero.

Expressions of commitment to the state and to one's friends were standard among the Roman elite, and before them, among the elite of the Greek polis.[6] Pliny the Younger feels that he is heir to the status claimed by Cicero, that of an eminent citizen who acts autonomously both in his political and his social life. Pliny the Elder could have no such illusions, and the re-use of the terms *officia* and *amicitia* in connection with his uncle by Pliny the Younger does not, as we have seen, bridge the gap. However in reality the condition of Pliny the

---

[6]   Such commitment is affirmed in a particular marked way in the works of Xenophon. In *De Oratore,* the usefulness of oratory for friends and the state is precisely the goal proposed by Cicero in exhorting the young to study it: *in id studium ... incumbite, ut et vobis honori et amicis utilitati et rei publicae emolumento esse possitis* (1.34). For the use of the formula in Cicero, see also *De Or.* 1.3; 1.78; *Off.* 1.92 (in reference to the financial aspect); 1.123 (and see *Sen.* 38); 2.4; *Fam.* 4.6.2.

Younger was very different from that of Cicero. For a Roman citizen of Cicero's day, services to the state and to friends implied *libertas*, but for Pliny the Younger, living under the domination of an Emperor, any such notion was illusory.[7] As for Pliny the Elder, he never imagined organizing his life in a way that was free and independent of the *princeps*, and Pliny the Younger, in writing of his uncle, never thought in those terms either.[8] Indeed, if we take the words of Pliny the Elder literally, he devotes all his time to the *princeps* and to his family. This situation is close to the one described by Seneca for the imperial freedman Polybius. In attempting to comfort this imperial freedman, Seneca tells him that suffering must not distract him *ab occupationibus tuis, id est a studio et a Caesare* (from your occupations, which are study and Caesar, *ad Polyb.* 5.2; cf. also 8.1–2 *omnia in te Caesar tenebit ... non est quod ullum tempus vacare patiaris a studiis*).

The life program set out by Pliny the Elder was identical: service to the *princeps* and study. Pliny the Elder was of course not an imperial freedman, but such freedmen were powerful figures in the imperial age, and from the viewpoint of Roman ethical and cultural values the program prescribed by Seneca for Polybius is the same as that traditionally upheld by members of the upper classes in Rome.[9] In one further

---

[7] As indicated by the paradoxical words Pliny the Younger addresses to Trajan, in which he makes the liberty of citizens dependent on the direct will of the Emperor: *iubes esse liberos: erimus* (*Paneg.* 66.4). When, under the rule of Caesar, Sulpicius Rufus wrote to Cicero consoling him for the death of Tullia, one source of comfort he mentions is that she would not at any rate have had children who could "use their liberty" in dealing with the state and friends: *liberos ... qui ... essent in re publica, in amicorum negotiis libertate sua <us>uri* (*Fam.* 4.5.3). For more about the relation between Pliny the Younger and Cicero from the point of view of both their political and their literary careers, see Riggsby (1995); Gibson and Steel (2010); Gibson (2012).

[8] What Pliny the Elder affirms before the *princeps* in the preface is not liberty, but license, petulance and impudence (*pr.* 1 *licentiore epist<u>la*; 2 *hac mea petulantia ... in alia procaci epist<u>la nostra*), that is to say, a kind of relationship in which an inferior 'takes liberties' with respect to a superior. The distance between himself and the *princeps* is, on the other hand, greatly dilated by Pliny, who transposes the dedication of his work onto the plane of a religious offering.

[9] Two cases can be cited in which the same traits found in Cicero and Pliny serve for the ennobling depiction of the imperial freedman. Seneca invites Polybius to adopt an appearance dissimilar to his inner state in order to hide his pain: *indue dissimilem animo tuo vultum et, si potes, proice omnem ex toto dolorem, si minus, introrsus abde et contine, ne appareat* (*ad Polyb.* 5.5). After the death of Tullia, Cicero strove to maintain an outer composure, even though his soul was oppressed by pain: *omnia ... nitor non ad animum sed ad vultum ipsum, si queam, reficiendum* (*Att.* 12.14.3). Seneca says that Polybius, though grief-stricken, should simulate *hilaritas*, as commanders do to prevent their soldiers losing heart: *Quod duces magni faciunt rebus adfectis, ut hilaritatem de industria simulent et adversas res adumbrata laetitia abscondant ne militum animi, si fractam ducis sui mentem viderint, et ipsi conlabantur, id nunc tibi quoque faciendum est* (*ad Polyb.* 5.4). Pliny the Younger, in the letter in which he describes his uncle's final hours, says that he dined *aut hilaris aut (quod aeque*

respect Pliny the Elder's position was perhaps closer to that of Polybius than to that of Cicero. Cicero devoted himself to his studies when he was unable to take part in the direct management of the state. Intellectual activities thus became completely absorbing for Cicero when a single figure took over command of the Roman state. But the Elder Pliny could represent these activities as having not only their intrinsic attractions, but as being a sort of collaboration with the power of the *princeps*.

This raises another question: Pliny the Elder expresses fervent praise of Cicero in Book 7 of the *Naturalis Historia*. There Pliny exemplifies the greatness of Cicero's intellect by referring exclusively to his activities in his consulate, and specifically to the speeches made by Cicero in his consulate which influenced the citizen body directly and determined its behaviour:[10]

> sed quo te, M. Tulli, piaculo taceam, quove maxime excellentem insigni praedicem? quo potius quam universi populi illius genti<um> amplissimi testimonio, e tota vita tua consulatus tantum operibus electis? te dicente legem agrariam, hoc est alimenta sua, abdicarunt tribus; te suadente Roscio theatralis auctori legis ignoverunt notatasque se discrimine sedis aequo animo tulerunt; te orante proscriptorum liberos honores petere puduit; tuum Catilina fugit ingenium; tu M. Antonium proscripsisti. salve primus omnium parens patriae appellate, primus in toga triumphum linguaeque lauream merite et facundiae Latiarumque litterarum parens aeque (ut dictator Caesar, hostis quondam tuus, de te scripsit) omnium triumphorum laurea maiorem, quanto plus est ingenii Romani terminos in tantum promovisse quam imperii.   *NH* 7.116–17

What Pliny underlines several times is the direct link between Cicero the politician-orator and the citizens of Rome. Compared with Pliny's own concrete experience as a collaborator of the *princeps*, a role which he consciously accepts and makes his own, the Cicero of *Naturalis Historia* Book 7 is a very distant model, almost a myth.

But it is a myth with positive implications. Pliny is assimilating the

---

magnum) similis hilari ('*hilaris*' or, something equally grand, similar to him who is '*hilaris*', *Epist.* 6.16.12). This expression, which remains ambiguous in Pliny the Younger, is fully explained in the Senecan passage just quoted, together with reference to its specific field of application (the behavior of military leaders).

[10] See the analysis of the passage in Wolverton (1964); see also Grüninger (1976); de Oliveira (1992) 172, 191ff. As regards the presence in the passage of the figure of Caesar, who pays homage to Cicero's intellect, Wolverton rightly points out the difference from cases where Pliny represents the tribute of a man of power to a man of culture; de Oliveira also acknowledges that Caesar is presented not as being of superior power, but as "a political rival". For more about the rhetorical and political strategies through which Cicero himself had tried to shape his 'public persona' and pass it on to posterity, in particular that of the 'orator-statesman', see Van der Blom (2010).

Republican past, as represented both politically and culturally by Cicero, into his own present. Pliny's purpose is to suggest continuity, and what lends authenticity to that continuity is Pliny's strong sense of Romanness. That is the essential difference between the Roman *eques* Pliny and the freedman Polybius. Pliny sees his link with the *princeps* as the same link that he has with Rome. Behind the *princeps* Pliny sees a *respublica.* This emerges in the way that Pliny in the preface to the *Naturalis Historia* concludes the list of the roles played by Vespasian's son Titus: "You are all these things for the *Respublica*" (*omnia ... haec rei publicae es*):[11]

> triumphalis et censorious tu sexiesque consul ac tribuniciae potestatis particeps et, quod his nobilius fecisti, dum illud patri partiter et equestri ordini praestas, praefectus praetorii eius omniaque haec rei publicae es.   *pr.* 3

It is because Pliny is able to recognize in the *princeps* the heir of the great political tradition of Rome that he can proudly foreground his collaboration with the *princeps* both as a functionary and as a man of letters. So Pliny's exaltation of Cicero from both a cultural and a political viewpoint is not as ingenuous as it might appear. On the contrary it is totally consistent with Pliny's own self-representation as a man involved both in public life and in letters, an heir of the Ciceronian tradition but within a new contemporary context.

-III-

If this is the significance that Cicero had for the Elder Pliny as a man of politics and culture, how did Pliny in his capacity as author see Cicero as a model, and in particular how did he see Cicero as a model for the *Naturalis Historia*? It must be significant that, when Cicero crops up for the first time in the preface of the *Naturalis Historia,* it is in a passage in which Pliny sees himself as writing for a public that is not over-learned, but average. Pliny presents this choice of audience as following a similar choice made by Cicero, who himself had quoted Lucilius as a precedent:

> praeterea est quaedam publica etiam eruditorum reiectio. utitur illa et M. Tullius extra omnem ingeni<i> al<e>am positus et, quod miremur, per advocatum defendítur: "nec doctissimis. Manium Persium haec legere nolo, Iunium Congium volo". quod si hoc Lucilius, qui primus condidit stili nasum, dicendum sibi putavit,

---

[11] Listed together with the offices of the Republican tradition (the censorship, the consulate, the tribunate of the plebs) is the post of the pretorian prefect, established in the imperial age. Pliny significantly stresses that this pertains to the equestrian order.

Cicero mutuandum, praesertim cum de re publica scriberet, quanto
nos causatius ab aliquo iudice defendimur?   *pr.* 7

A middle-of-the-road public was probably Pliny's personal
preference, but in practical terms he expands his horizons to include a
wide of range of potential readers. They peak with the Emperor, but
they start with the massed ranks of farmers and craftsmen: *humili vulgo
scripta sunt, agricolarum, opificum turbae* (*pr.* 6). We may of course
speculate about whether farmers and craftsmen really read the
Naturalis Historia. Book 18 offers a clue: it provides the astronomical
information needed for agriculture, and on one level it might seem that
Pliny is discussing the subject in terms suitable for this uneducated
element of the public. But Nature herself then comes to the farmer and
asks "Why should you look at the sky, farmer? Why should you search
for the stars, countryman?" (*cur caelum intuearis, agricola? cur sidera
quaeras, rustice?*, 18.251). This is a hint, not just that farmers should
not trouble to look at the sky, but that they should not trouble to read
Pliny's text explaining the constellations. The affectionately ironic
reference to the *agricola* and the *rusticus* is a sly nod to his real public,
the averagely learned and the truly learned. But at the same time it does
not detract from the status of the *agricola*, in whom Pliny sees the heir
of the archaic *rusticus*, the free Roman with his Roman cultural and
ethical values. It is this figure who is the nominal reader of the
Naturalis Historia, although the practicalities of that reading are not
entered into.[12]

Pliny's references to farmers and to their supposed status as his
readers are primarily ideological. But his relations with the *opifices*, the
craftsmen, who are mentioned in the preface along with the *agricolae*
as readers, are different. The *Naturalis Historia* interests itself in the
activities of craftsmen, partly because crafts are a contemporary reality,
and partly because natural objects are the raw material employed by

---

[12] The image of the *rusticus* as a person of modest level is in line with the treatment of
agriculture in the *Naturalis Historia*. Columella had searched for the perfect farmer,
just as Cicero had searched for the perfect orator. Pliny was far removed from such a
cultural project: the desire to transpose onto agriculture the ideal of perfection that
Cicero had sought for oratory is extraneous to him. When Pliny depicted Cincinnatus
and the other peasant-warriors, he was familiar with Cato's speech in the *De Senec-
tute*, and also the beginning of Columella's work, but he did not limit himself to
extolling the pleasantness of rural labor, as Cicero did, nor to deploring the decline of
agriculture, like Columella. Contributing to his evocation of the peasant-warriors was
a state of mind probably shared by many readers, which stemmed from a rejection of
the organization of labor on the *latifundia*, and also (irrespective of the economic
motivations) of the human type to which such work was entrusted: the men he saw
chained and branded (*NH* 18.21) were, for Pliny, the negation of the free Roman
peasant (free 'man').

craftsmen in the craft process. From the moment that an object offers itself as a product of Nature until it ends up as a product to be consumed, that object is subject to human intervention, which modifies it in accordance with its desired use. The term *opifices* (craftsmen) appears only rarely in the *Naturalis Historia*, but *officina* (workshop) is more frequent. The *Naturalis Historia* does not teach craftsmen their trades; rather it informs its readers about the contributions of craftsmen. A craftsman might of course learn something from the *Naturalis Historia*, and he might even read it in the same way as any generic reader, or because he was interested in reading about his own trade. But however the *opifex* might read the work, what matters is that it talks his own language and speaks about his specific area of interest. In this respect, the *Naturalis Historia* resembles technical works like Vitruvius's *De Architectura*. The difference is that the *Naturalis Historia* does not start as a technical work, but instead acquires technical characteristics as the raw materials of crafts leave their natural state and are transformed and made usable by man.[13] Thus the *Naturalis Historia* was conceived by a man of letters, as were the works of Cicero in different areas, but it was conceived and brought to fruition by a man of letters who consciously broadened the areas of interest of a man of letters, and who opened up his work to embrace farmers and craftsmen, whom he ostensibly welcomes as readers and includes as essential members of his world.

-IV-

Pliny the Elder's decision to write a work about nature which also becomes a technical work and excludes no sort of reader involved a modification of existing visions of society and of the relationship between society and culture.[14] In this respect we may contrast Cicero with Pliny. In his *De Officiis* Cicero gives a list of the professions that he considers *liberales* and those he considers *sordidae*. In this list the

---

[13] Vitruvius claimed a 'humanistic' culture for himself: on Vitruvius's attempt to "elevate himself from technician to intellectual", see Romano (1987) 84. Romano points out the importance Vitruvius attributed to the Ciceronian cultural model: 68ff. and *passim*.

[14] Among the various negative views of manual craft activities passed down to us from classical antiquity, I would like to cite two, because of their particular pertinence for the topic of our discussion. Xenophon contrasted the manual arts to the way of life of those who, thanks to the free time they enjoyed, could 'attend to friends and the city', in line with the pattern we have already seen: *Oec.* 4.3. On the basis of this, Xenophon separates craft activities from farming. He regards farming as pertaining to ἀνὴρ καλός τε κἀγαθός, and places the formative activity of this human type in opposition to the manual arts: he defines it in fact as the art which leaves the most time free to 'attend to friends and the city': *Oec* 6.9.

opifices appear to be representatives of an *ars sordida* in a working environment, the *officina*, which excludes what is free. Then Cicero contrasts craftwork with agriculture, which he considers to be the most noble activity of a free man:

> iam de artificiis et quaestibus, qui liberales habendi, qui sordidi sint, haec fere accepimus. primum improbantur ii quaestus, qui in odia hominum incurrunt, ut portitorum, ut feneratorum. inliberales autem et sordidi quaestus mercennariorum omnium, quorum operae, non quorum artes emuntur; est enim in illis ipsa merces auctoramentum servitutis. sordidi etiam putandi, qui mercantur a mercatoribus, quod statim vendant; nihil enim proficiant, nisi admodum mentiantur; nec vero est quicquam turpius vanitate. opificesque omnes in sordida arte versantur; nec enim quicquam ingenuum habere potest officina. minimeque artes eae probandae, quae ministrae sunt voluptatum ... quibus autem artibus aut prudentia maior inest aut non mediocris utilitas quaeritur ut medicina, ut architectura, ut doctrina rerum honestarum, eae sunt iis, quorum ordini conveniunt, honestae. mercatura autem, si tenuis est, sordida putanda est ... omnium autem rerum, ex quibus aliquid adquiritur, nihil est agri cultura melius, nihil uberius, nihil dulcius, nihil homine libero dignius. Cic. *Off.* 1.150–51

Pliny is not only well aware of the concept of liberal arts, but he is the Latin writer who places most emphasis on their connection with *libertas* (*a maximo bono liberales dictae artes, NH* 14.5). He shows consciousness of the category of the liberal arts in Book 23 too (*NH* 23.32), where he distances himself from professional doctors and does so in the name of Roman *gravitas* and *artium liberalium adpetentia* (the pursuit of the liberal arts).[15] But in actual fact craftsmen and craft workshops are everywhere in the *Naturalis Historia*, and Pliny, unlike Cicero, never explicitly contrasts agriculture as the most noble art with the vulgar activities of craftsmen.

We do not know exactly what Latin authors meant when they used the term *encyclios paedeia*. But the equivalence between arts which are *encyclioi* and liberal arts, which is first attested in Seneca, encourages us to believe that when Pliny uses the term *encyclios paedeia* in his preface, he too is referring to the liberal arts.[16] Pliny does not however include the *Naturalis Historia* in this category, but he does include the sources upon which he drew for the *Naturalis Historia*. Some of these

---

[15] In one case Pliny states that he has excluded the description of a technical procedure because it is not part of the liberal arts: *nec tinguendi tamen rationem omisissemus, si umquam ea liberalium artium fuisset* (22.4). For more about Pliny's criticism of Greek physicians, see Nutton (1986). For the relation between professional medicine and the treatment of medicinal herbs in Pliny, see Scarborough (1986) (in particular p.61, on the need for a more comprehensive medicine practiced not only by physicians).

[16] See Naas (2002) 23.

sources, he opined, had fallen into obscurity; others, he thought, had been given so much public exposure that people were bored with them. Just before making these statements Pliny had talked about scholars of his own day dedicating themselves to enjoyable topics and leaving difficult questions untouched. Immediately after these statements he stressed that he wanted to bring to light obscure matters and to return to favor things that had become tedious:

> an<te> omnia attingenda quae Graeci τῆς ἐγκυκλίου παιδείας vocant, et tamen ignota aut incerta ingeniis facta; alia vero ita multis prodita, ut in fastidium sint adducta. res ardua vetustis novitatem dare, novis auctoritatem, obsoletis nitorem, obscuris lucem, fastiditis gratiam, dubiis fidem.   *pr.* 14–15

A similar aspiration can be found in Cicero *Partitiones Oratoriae* 12: *parva magnis, simplicia coniunctis, obscura dilucidis, laeta tristibus, incredibilia probabilibus inteximus.* Pliny is employing the language of rhetoric at this point. But more specifically he is claiming a Ciceronian heritage when he stresses the need to bring to light obscure matters. The ability to overcome the obscurity of a subject by means of a lucid presentation was considered very important in the rhetorical works of Cicero: *'atqui vides' inquit Antonius 'quam alias res agamus, qui adduci possimus ... relictis ut rebus omnibus te sectemur; ita de horridis rebus nitida, de ieiunis plena, de pervulgatis nova quaedam est oratio tua'* (*De Or.* 3.51–2). We can specify more clearly the kind of culture that Pliny the Elder was bringing to his public if we keep in mind this particular Ciceronian concept.

If we can place Pliny in the tradition of Cato and Varro, it is not because they were writing encyclopedias and Pliny himself wrote an encyclopedia, but because Cato and Varro were, like Pliny, polymaths.[17] It is this quality that links Cato, Varro and Celsus in the

---

[17] The terms of the question are correctly posed by Doody (2010) 55: "The common link between Cato, Varro, Cicero and Celsus is something that they hold in common with Homer: they all stand as figures of the polymath ... and it is this archetype that Quintilian is using to guarantee the ideal of education that he has been advocating in the course of the *Institutio Oratoria.*" I believe it is also possible to share what Doody says about the need to reconsider the customary view of the *Naturalis Historia* as an 'encyclopedia' to be situated within an 'encyclopedic' genre: see 1ff., 40ff., esp. 43f.: "There was no ancient genre of encyclopedia that ancient writers and readers understood as such; it was never Pliny's intention to write 'an encyclopedia', and genre is probably not a helpful model for understanding the relationship between Pliny and Varro's work ... If Pliny's *Natural History* is an encyclopedia it is not because of authorial intention, and its first audience could not have recognised it as part of an encyclopedic genre of texts that included the *Ad Filium,* the *Disciplinae* and the *Artes.* If any of these texts are encyclopedias, it is because of their reception history, rather than because they belong to a shared ancient category of writing." Some limitations on the characterization of the *Naturalis Historia* as an 'encyclopedia' had already been

twelfth book of Quintilian's *Institutio Oratoria*, and Quintilian added Cicero to the ranks of the encyclopedists, because Cicero too was an expert on many subjects:

> M. igitur Cato, idem summus imperator, idem sapiens, idem orator, idem historiae conditor, idem iuris, idem rerum rusticarum peritis- simus fuit ... quam multa, paene omnia tradidit Varro! Quod instru- mentum dicendi M. Tullio defuit? quid plura? cum etiam Cornelius Celsus, mediocri vir ingenio, non solum de his omnibus conscripserit artibus, sed amplius rei militaris et rusticae et medicinae praecepta reliquerit, dignus uel ipso proposito ut eum scisse omnia illa credamus.   Quintil. *Inst.* 12.11.23–4

Quintilian specifies that the reason for Cicero's widespread know- ledge was his activity as an orator, and he describes the areas of Cicero's expertise as his *instrumenta dicendi*. Quintilian was of course writing about rhetoric, and this was the basis for his judgment and his approval of Cicero. Just before, in the same passage, he mentioned Plato and Aristotle as polymaths, Plato because he covered all the literary arts, and Aristotle because he went beyond philosophy and rhetoric to study animals and plants:

> ceterum, ut de Homero taceam, in quo nullius non artis aut opera perfecta aut certe non dubia vestigia reperiuntur, ut Elium Hippian transeam, <qui non> liberalium modo disciplinarum prae se scientiam tulit, sed vestem et anulum crepidasque quae omnia manu sua fecerat in usu habuit, atque ita se praeparavit ne cuius alterius ope egeret ... quae tandem ars digna litteris Platoni defuit? quot saeculis Aristoteles didicit ut non solum quae ad philosophos atque oratores pertinent scientia complecteretur, sed animalium satorumque naturas omnis perquireret?   *Inst.* 12.11.21–2

Pliny seems to have adopted the same attitude as Quintilian's poly- maths. He had already dealt with rhetoric, grammar and historiography in his other works, and in the *Naturalis Historia* he enlarges his field of knowledge to include arts that are by definition vulgar, treating them not in a systematic way but whenever treatment was required at speci- fic points in his work. But Pliny's announcement in his Preface that they would be discussed is in itself significant.

The polymathic vision which Quintilian presents in his account of Cato, Varro, Celsus and their Greek predecessors is not, however, as

---

set in place by Beagon (1992), who noted (13) how its unitary nature differentiated it from the tradition represented by Varro and Celsus. On the relationship of the *Natu- ralis Historia* with the liberal arts and the encyclopedic tradition, see also Naas (2002) 15ff., who highlights the innovative nature of Pliny's work, especially as it was inspired, besides the ideology of *paideia*, by that of *humanitas*, for which Pliny in turn found a model in Cicero (see p.32 in particular).

open and all-embracing as it might at first seem. This can be seen in the attitude of Quintilian, and of some other Latin authors, to the sophist Hippias, who extended his practice of the arts beyond those generally considered liberal, and who therefore even ran the risk of being seen as a figure of ridicule, as a man who made all his own clothes and other objects of daily use.[18] The passage in Quintilian opens with a mention of Homer and then of Hippias, about whom no explicit comment is actually made. A comment can be found, instead, in Cicero, who wrote of Hippias in the *De Oratore* as someone not only acquainted with all the liberal arts but also with a knowledge and practice of the vulgar arts. Cicero made it clear that he regarded Hippias as excessive, but not as a negative *exemplum*:[19] in fact, it was precisely through the excessive enthusiasm with which he embraced the *artes sordidae* that Hippias demonstrated how much the ancient orators loved the higher arts:

> illos veteres doctores auctoresque dicendi nullum genus disputationis a se alienum putasse accepimus semperque esse in omni orationis ratione versatos; ex quibus Elius Hippias, cum Olympiam venisset … gloriatus est … nihil esse ulla in arte rerum omnium quod ipse nesciret; nec solum has artis, quibus liberales doctrinae atque ingenuae continerentur, geometriam, musicam, litterarum cognitionem et poetarum atque illa, quae de naturis rerum, quae de hominum moribus, quae de rebus publicis dicerentur, <se tenere> sed anulum, quem haberet, pallium … soccos … sua manu confecisse. scilicet nimis hic quidem est progressus, sed ex eo ipso est coniectura facilis, quantum sibi illi oratores de praeclarissimis artibus appetierint, qui ne sordidiores quidem repudiarint.   Cic. *De Orat*. 3.126–8

Cicero, though baulking at the idea of making objects personally, is broadly receptive to forms of knowledge that are not *liberales* and

---

[18] In Quintilian the mention of Hippias is followed by a reference to Gorgias as an expert in rhetoric alone, whose illusionistic aspect he developed: *inlusisse tot <malis> quot summa senectus habet universae Graeciae credimus Gorgian, qui quaerere auditores de quo quisque vellet iubebat* (12.11.21). In Pliny's list of the capacities of rhetoric (*pr*. 15 *res ardua* …), the lesson of Gorgias can still be detected. But Pliny never applies the resources of rhetoric in the illusionistic sense of denying the objective data of reality (for example, in the specific case of the ailments of old age, for Pliny they are inevitably ailments: 7.168).

[19] Cicero always refers to Hippias in contexts regarding rhetoric. See Cic. *Brut*. 30 *ut intellectum est quantam vim haberet accurata et facta quodam modo oratio, tum etiam magistri dicendi multi subito exstiterunt. Tum Leontinus Gorgias, Thrasymachus Calchedonius, Protagoras Abderites, Prodicus Ceius, Hippias Eleius in honore magno fuit*. Naas (2002) 24 attributes value to the passage from *De Oratore* containing the reference to Hippias, regarding it as testimony to a kind of education that Cicero inherited from the Greeks (see 15ff. for the whole treatment of Pliny's position in ancient literature). Beagon (1992) 13 argued that the link between the *Naturalis Historia* and the encyclopedic tradition should be limited, considering it preferable to relate the work to the "arts of living" of which Hippias was an exponent.

ingenuae, and recognizes that everything giving rise to the liberal arts and the *sordidae* arts is part and parcel of the same unique impulse towards knowledge. It is this space, extended, due to the desire for knowledge, from the liberal arts to include the vulgar ones, that Pliny uses; and the lesson of Cicero, who theorized such an extension, probably influenced him. This willingness to look beyond a central core of rhetoric and literature towards the vulgar arts was not, however, a given. Reference to Hippias can be found in the *Florida* of Apuleius, where there is no widening of vision on the part of an intellectual, but rather a narrowing. Apuleius is directly at odds with Hippias, and in the face of the latter's technical constructions, affirms the entirely literary nature of his own output: poetry of all kinds, historic works, orations, philosophical dialogues. It is a corpus of literary works that he wants to offer to the proconsul to whom his work is dedicated:[20]

> plura ... mea extant in Camenis quam Hippiae in opificiis opera ... et Hippias e numero sophistarum est, artium multitudine prior omnibus, eloquentia nulli secundus ... venit Hippias iste quondam certamine Olympio Pisam ... quis autem non laudabit hominem tam numerosa arte multiscium, totiugi scientia magnificum, tot utensilium peritia daedalum? quin et ipse Hippian laudo, sed ingenii eius fecunditatem malo doctrinae quam supellectilis multiformi instrumento aemulari ... pro his praeoptare me fateor uno chartario calamo me reficere poemata omnigenus apta virgae, lyrae, socco, coturno, item satiras ac <g>riphos, item <h>istorias varias rerum nec non <o>rationes laudatas disertis nec non dialogos laudatos philosophis atque haec <et> alia [et] eiusdem modi tam Graece quam Latine, gemino voto, pari studio, simili stilo. quae utinam possem equidem non singillatim ac discretim, sed cunctim et coacervatim tibi, proconsul [ut] optime, offerre ac praedicabili testimonio tuo ad omnem nostram Camenam frui!   Apul. *Flor.* 9.41–92

The preface of the *Naturalis Historia* takes a different stance: the work that Pliny is offering to Titus is a work of low literary level closely related to the world of manual arts.

But there is also a striking point of similarity between Apuleius' preface and that of Pliny. The passage which Apuleius devotes to the contrast/comparison between himself and Hippias opens and closes with the term *Camena*, a term which refers above all to poetry and which is chosen to mark Apuleius' preference for strictly literary arts and for poetry in particular. But a reference to the *Camenae* is also found in Pliny's preface. At the very beginning of the *Naturalis*

---

[20] Lee (2005) 97 rightly points out that Apuleius, who depends on Plato *Hipp. Min.* 368be, does not talk about Hippias' literary works, which are listed in Plato, but uses that type of list to his own advantage.

Historia, when he dedicates his work to the *princeps*, he describes it as *novicium Camenis Quiritium tuorum opus* (a novel task for the native Muses of your Roman citizens):

> PLINIVS SECVNDVS VESPASIANO CAESARI SVO S. Libros Naturalis Historiae, novicium Camenis Quiritium tuorum opus ... licentiore epist<u>la narrare constitui tibi, iucundissime Imperator; sit enim haec tui praefatio, verissima ... "namque tu solebas nugas esse aliquid meas putare", ut obiter emolliam Catullum conterraneum meum (agnoscis et hoc castrense verbum).   *pr.* 1

Thus Pliny places his *Naturalis Historia* under the protection of the *Camenae*, but — in the very same part of his dedication — he characterizes it as a work involved with the lowest aspects of life and with the workers who are engaged in them (*pr.* 6 *ista ... humili vulgo scripta sunt, agricolarum, opificum turbae*; 13 *rerum natura, hoc est vita, narratur, et haec sordidissima sui parte*). The references to the *Camenae* thus function in opposite ways in the two authors. For Apuleius the reference excludes anything not appropriate to a strictly literary environment. For Pliny the reference serves to blend low-life material with a high literary tradition. Pliny's inclusive attitude thus continues and further develops Cicero's appreciation of those who extend their commitment to the liberal arts and take an interest in the vulgar arts. Pliny and Apuleius thus represent two extremes, with Quintilian and Cicero occupying an intermediate position. For all these authors it was of course the knowledge of artisan techniques that was under discussion, not the manufacture of objects. In this respect Hippias remained a colorful outsider.

-V-

I want to end by looking further at the presence of the *Camenae* at the beginning of the *Naturalis Historia*, and by considering first how Pliny relates the Camenae to their main area of responsibility, poetry, and second, how the *Camenae* are linked to Pliny's image of Cicero.[21]

---

[21] Pliny's affirmation that no one, from amongst the Greek and Latin authors, had dealt with all the subjects of his work (*pr.* 14: *iter est non trita auctoribus via nec qua peregrinari animus expet<a>t. Nemo apud nos qu<i> idem temptaverit, nemo apud Graecos qui unus omnia ea tractaverit*) has a sole parallel, I believe, in the poet Manilius (the usual aspiration was to enrich Latin literature with works capable of replacing Greek models). Pliny and Manilius share certain common prefatory elements. Both employ the method, derived from Lucretius, of referring to the subject matter with the image of a path that has to be trod: Lucr. 1.926–7 *avia Pieridum peragro loca nullius ante / trita solo*; Manil. 2.50–53 *omnis ad accessus Heliconos semita trita est /... integra quaeramus rorantis prata per herbas*; Plin. *pr.* 14 *iter est non trita auctoribus via nec qua peregrinari animus expet<a>t*. Both affirm that they

Pliny the Elder was not himself a poet, and for him poets were primarily sources of information, so he quotes verses of Cicero for didactic purposes.[22] But Cicero also becomes an object of poetry in the *Naturalis Historia* when Pliny quotes some eulogistic verses by one of Cicero's freedmen which were inscribed on one of his villas. They speak of Cicero being 'read all over the world', and Pliny repeats this concept when he says that he is including the verses because he wants them to be known everywhere.[23] By implication the *Naturalis Historia* is a work which, like the writings of Cicero, is destined to be read all over the world:[24]

---

are not committing a literary theft: Manil. 2.58 *nec furtum sed opus veniet*; Plin. *pr.* 23 *infelicis ingenii est deprehendi in furto malle.* This motif (used by Terence in the prologue of *Eunuchus*: *peccatum inprudentiast / poetae, non quo furtum facere studuerit,* 27–8) also crops up in the prologue of Book VII of Vitruvius: *oportere ... non furta sed scripta probare* (7 *pr.* 7). Such elements were readily accessible. But their concentration in Manilius and Pliny shows that they both began their discourse with a 'literary' attitude: in Manilius this was typically poetic, while in Pliny the tendency towards poetry was programmatically blocked by the declaration of the humble prosaicness of the work.

[22] *NH* 18.228: *Ciceronis sententiam ipsius verbis subsignabimus: "Iam vero semper viridis semperque gravata / lentiscus triplici solita est grandescere fetu / ter fruges fundens tria tempora monstrat arandi".* The value attributed to Cicero by Pliny is confirmed by the fact that he places him in the same company as Homer. The superlative Greek poet is judged to be the first of the great human intellects, while alongside him, in second place, Pliny puts Cicero: *fons ingeniorum Homerus ... Cicero, lux doctrinarum altera* (*NH* 17.37–8). One area of Cicero's output to which Pliny appears to refer concerns the *mirabilia*: *NH* 31.12 would seem to suggest the existence of a work by Cicero entitled *Admiranda*, to which other passages in Pliny might also refer (see Garbarino (1984) 30ff.; 96ff.).

[23] A penetrating analysis of the passage from Pliny can be found in Morgan (2007) 113ff., who pinpoints the reasons why Pliny was able to see in Laurea's verses "a sympathetic text." As the verses extolling the villa called Academia and the salubrious waters discovered nearby were written by one of Cicero's freedmen, Pliny traces the poetic skills of the freedman back to Cicero himself, regarding them as an extension of the "splendor" of his genius. In these verses, Cicero is addressed as *vindex clarissime Romanae linguae*; the waters, insofar as they are good for the eyes, are considered to be an honorary gift of the place to an author who "is read endlessly all around the world" (*totum legitur sine fine per orbem*). This reference to Cicero's popularity is picked up by Pliny, who informs us that in the villa Cicero composed the volumes of the same name, and that in the same villa he also established a monument to himself that is only one of those he has erected for himself all over the world: *in qua et monumenta sibi instauraverat, ceu vero non et in toto terrarum orbe fecisset.* In Book 13, using the term *monumentum*, Pliny applies to Cicero's intellectual production the same terminology with which, as we have seen, Cicero referred to himself in *Phil* 2.20: *me ... omni genere monumentorum meorum perfecisse ... ut meae ... litterae ... nomini Romano laudis aliquid adferrent* (see above p.315): see *NH* 13.21: *in M. Ciceronis monumentis invenitur unguenta gratiora quae terram quam quae crocum sapiant* (as for Cicero's sentence, this can be found in 17.38, with small variations which suggest that Pliny cited them from memory: *meliora, inquit, unguenta sunt quae terram, quam quae crocum sapiunt*).

[24] The ideological importance of this passage can be appreciated even better by recalling

... villa est ab Averno lacu Puteolos tendentibus inposita litori, celebrata porticu ac nemore, quam vocabat M. Cicero Academiam ab exemplo Athenarum, ibi compositis voluminibus eiusdem nominis, in qua et monumenta sibi instauraverat, ceu vero non et in toto terrarum orbe fecisset. huius in parte prima exiguo post obitum ipsius Antistio Vetere possidente eruperunt fontes calidi perquam salubres oculis, celebrati carmine Laureae Tulli, qui fuit e libertis eius, ut protinus noscatur etiam ministeriorum haustus ex illa maiestate ingenii. ponam enim ipsum carmen, <ut> ubique et non ibi tantum legi <queat>.

> quo tua, Romanae vindex clarissime linguae,
>   silva loco melius surgere iussa viret
> atque Academiae celebratam nomine villam
>   nunc reparat cultu sub potiore Vetus,
> hoc etiam apparent lymphae non ante repertae,
>   languida quae infuso lumina rore levant.
> nimirum locus ipse sui Ciceronis honori
>   hoc dedit, hac fontes cum patefecit ope,
> ut, quoniam totum legitur sine fine per orbem,
>   sint plures oculis quae medeantur aquae.   *NH* 31.6–8

But let us concentrate again on the beginning of the preface to the *Naturalis Historia*, where the name of the *Camenae* denotes culture in a broad sense. Here we will perhaps find something that refers us to Cicero as a persona, to his way of practicing culture, and also to his way of fostering social relationships in the city. We are at the beginning of the dialogue with Titus, addressed by Pliny as *Caesar* and *imperator.* The solemnity of the word *imperator* is tempered by being placed alongside the informal adjective *iucundissime*, which probably already anticipates the reference to Catullus that follows immediately afterwards:[25] as a learned joke Pliny proposes improving a line of Catullus' *nugae*.[26] In part this is Pliny's way of presenting himself to

---

how much value Pliny attributed to inscriptions and monuments (2.154: the greatest merit of Mother Earth is to sustain them on herself, thus enabling human memory to survive). But the book is something more: it permits the written word to detach itself from the immobility of a support and to spread without limit. Pliny's praise of the custom of inserting pictures of illustrious men into books (35.11) is also part of this ideology, which values the spread of knowledge and memory. Some important ways in which the concrete presence of monuments and inscriptions seen by Pliny is reflected in his text have been clearly outlined by Carey (2003) *passim*.

[25] The form — *iucundissime* — used by Pliny to address the *princeps* can be found in Catullus (*iucundissime Calve*, 14.2). It is otherwise rare and informal: it is used by Dolabella for Cicero, *Fam* 9.9.3, Martial for his friend Julius Martialis, 10.47.2. In the other attested cases, the particularity of the form is that it is used in letters written by a 'Caesar': Caes. Aug. Oct. *Epist* 12.1 *vale, iucundissime Tiberi, et feliciter rem gere*; 22.2 *Ave, mi Gai, meus asellus iucundissimus*; Aur. Caes. 1.2.2 *Vale mihi Fronto iucundissime* (in other letters, Marcus Aurelius commonly addresses Fronto as *iucundissime magister*); Script. Hist. Aug. *Aurelian.* 11.1.3; 47.4.

[26] Improving other people's poems was a common practice in rhetorical exercises: see

Titus as a cultured person who can involve himself with nugatory poetry. But Catullus serves another purpose too. Pliny describes him by using the term *conterraneum*, and he then asks the emperor if he recognizes this term as belonging to military slang. By referring to military life Pliny is able to allude to his longstanding link with Titus as his comrade-in-arms. But for us the allusion is also evocative of another military situation involving Cicero, where the subject of conversation was similarly culture. When Quintus Cicero was Caesar's lieutenant in Gaul, Cicero asked his brother what Caesar thought of his verses:

> sed heus tu! celari videor a te. quo modo nam, mi frater, de nostris
> versibus Caesar? nam primum librum se legisse scripsit ad me ante,
> et prima sic ut neget se ne Graeca quidem meliora legisse.
>
> *Q. Fr.* 2.16.5

The two brothers encouraged each other to write poetry, either epic or laudatory. Cicero was writing a poem on the glory of Caesar, and he invited Quintus to write a poem on the expedition to Britain in the following words:

> te vero ὑπόθεσιν scribendi egregiam habere video. quos tu situs, quas
> naturas rerum et locorum, quos mores, quas gentis, quas pugnas,
> quem vero ipsum imperatorem habes!   *Q. fr.* 2.16.4

This invitation can be compared with the subjects of Books 3–6 of the *Naturalis Historia* as they appear in Pliny's Index:

> Libro III (IV, V, VI) continentur situs, gentes, maria, oppida, portus,
> montes, flumina ...   *NH* 1

Thus the geographical contents of Pliny's prose work largely coincide with those of the planned poetic celebration of Caesar's conquest, and of course we may recollect that Cicero himself, a few years earlier, had planned to write a work on geography.

These overlaps again foreground the similarities between Pliny and Cicero: both started out from a rhetorical and literary education; both

---

Sen. *Contr.* 7.1.27. Offering the *Naturalis Historia* to the *princeps* by making reference to Catullus' presentation of the *nugae*, while coherent with its qualification as *levioris operae libelli*, is incongruous with respect to the size of the work and its declared prosaicness. The interest stirred by the reference to Catullus in recent studies of Pliny is testified by Gibson (2011), who compares it with the more eulogistic reference to Catullus by Pliny the Younger in *Epist.* 1.16; Morello (2011), esp. 164: "Stylistically ... the decision to open with an incongruous reference to a writer whose persona could hardly be more different from his own makes a powerful statement of a literary ambition to attempt the impossible and to make the lion lie down with the lamb, as it were." A particular interest in aspects of literary elaboration in *Naturalis Historia* can be found in Lao (2008).

are men of action with a larger commitment to the state; in both their cultural formation and their political life are closely connected; and in both their culture supports and celebrates the greatness of Rome and her conquests. There is, however, one new element in Cicero's outline of his poetic project: the leader. This element does not appear in Pliny's list of geographical data. But its absence is only apparent. The leader, who is *Caesar* and *imperator*, as was the individual with whom Cicero and Quintus were glad to be linked (*coniuncti*), is already present in the title of the *Naturalis Historia* and in the beginning of its dedication: *Vespasiano Caesari suo ... Imperator* (To his dear Vespasian Caesar ... Emperor"). The figure of the *princeps*, who gave the work its initial stamp of approval, is an essential presence throughout the *Naturalis Historia* in the sense that he is, in his own person, the Roman Empire, and is thus to a certain extent consubstantial with the work.[27] Cicero was tempted by his closeness to Julius Caesar, but the passage of the *Second Philippic* with which we started, which presents him as the defender of the free *respublica*, is more true to Cicero's personality as a citizen and as a man of literature. But the letter to Quintus contains its own truth because it predicts the future relationships which will exist within the Roman elite, and the future culture which they will share.

-VI-

I started at the heart of Roman politics with an oration, the *Second Philippic*, which is, however, preeminently a literary product. I would like to end with a document which is highly stylistic poetry but which also perceives and reveals important elements of reality. This is Ovid *Ex Ponto* 1.5.43–54, in which the poet offers us a portrait of himself which is very different from Pliny's self-depiction.

> quid potius faciam? non sum qui segnia ducam   43
>   otia: mors nobis tempus habetur iners.
>   ...
> cum dedimus somno quas corpus postulat horas,   47
>   quo ponam vigilans tempora longa modo?
>   ...
> cum bene quaesieris quid agam, magis utile nil est   53
>   artibus his quae nil utilitatis habent.

Pliny writes of himself as someone who devotes very little time to

---

[27] On the relationship of Pliny's work with power (not just Roman power in general, but power as represented by the figure of the *princeps*), see Murphy (2004), in particular 24: "A triangle existed between Pliny's book, the world that it describes, and the ruling powers to whom the book was dedicated."; 164: "The eye that reads the *orbis terrarum* is the eye of its ruler."

sleep, fills his days with useful activity, and equates life with wakefulness. Ovid, up to a point, expresses a concept similar to Pliny's *vita
vigilia est* (life is staying awake) when, writing from exile, he states
that he considers the time that passes in idleness as death. And like
Pliny, Ovid does not prolong his sleep beyond what is strictly necessary. But, and this is the difference, Ovid does not know how to spend
the long hours of his wakefulness, a predicament absolutely opposite to
that of Pliny. Then again, Ovid writes poetry, and he proclaims this as
his choice among the liberal arts. But his statement as regards the
utility of his poetry is paradoxical. He says that he does the most useful
thing because nothing is more useful than the arts that have no utility.
And then there is the final element, the most fundamental difference
between the two characters: the presence of a city in Pliny's case, and
the absence of a city in Ovid's. Because he is far away from Rome, the
place of participation, Ovid can take no action on behalf of the city or
his friends, and his friends can take no action on his behalf — because
he has lost the *amicitia principis* (the favor of the Emperor).

A set of elements recurs in the texts of the authors we have been
considering: an awareness of their legitimate choices within a series of
arts; a reflection on the utility of their choices; a declared ability to act
on behalf of the city and to foster social relationships within the city
(an ability which is lost when a person is in exile). This recurring set of
elements is adaptable to political circumstances, so that new elements,
such as the *amicitia principis*, can be absorbed into it in such a way that
it remains clearly recognizable as part of the culture of the Roman elite
citizen. We might even say that this set of elements characterizes the
Roman citizen in his status as an intellectual.

Works Cited

Beagon, M. (1992). *Roman Nature. The Thought of Pliny the Elder.* Oxford
Carey, S. (2003). *Pliny's Catalogue of Culture. Art and Empire in the Natural
    History.* Oxford
de Oliveira, F. (1992). *Les Idées Politiques et Morales de Pline l'Ancien.*
    Coimbra
Doody, A. (2010). *Pliny's Encyclopedia. The Reception of the Natural History.*
    Cambridge
Garbarino, G. (1984). (ed.) *M. Tulli Ciceronis Fragmenta ex Libris Philoso-
    phicis, ex aliis Libris Deperditis, ex Scriptis Incertis.* Torino.
Gibson, R.K. (2011). 'Elder and Better: the Naturalis Historia and the Letters
    of the Younger Pliny' in Gibson and Morello (2011) 187–205

Gibson, R.K. (2012). 'Epistolary Models. Cicero and Seneca' in R.K. Gibson and R. Morello *Reading the Letters of Pliny the Younger: an Introduction.* Cambridge. 74–103

Gibson, R.K. and Steel C., 2010, 'The Indistinct Literary Careers of Cicero and Pliny the Younger' in P. Hardie and H. Moore (edd.) *Classical Literary Careers and their Reception.* Cambridge. 118–37

Gibson, R.K. and Morello, R. (2011). (edd.) *Pliny the Elder: Themes and Contexts.* Leiden and Boston

Grüninger, G. (1976). *Untersuchungen zur Persönlichkeit des älteren Plinius: die Bedeutung wissenschaftlicher Arbeit in seinem Denken.* Freiburg

Healy, J.F. (1999). *Pliny the Elder on Science and Technology.* Oxford

Lao, E. (2008). *Restoring the Treasury of Mind: the Practical Knowledge of the Natural History.* Ann Arbor

Lee, B.T. (2005). *Apuleius' Florida. A Commentary.* Berlin and New York

Morgan, L. (2007). '*Natura narratur*: Tullius Laurea's Elegy for Cicero (Pliny, *Nat.* 31, 8)' in S.J. Heyworth (ed.) *Classical Constructions. Papers in Memory of Don Fowler, Classicist and Epicurean.* Oxford. 113–40

Morello, R. (2011). 'Pliny and the Encyclopaedic Addressee' in Gibson and Morello (2011) 147–65

Murphy, T. (2004). *Pliny the Elder's Natural History. The Empire in the Encyclopedia.* Oxford

Naas, V. (2002). *Le Projet Encyclopédique de Pline l'Ancien.* Rome

Nutton, V. (1986). 'The Perils of Patriotism: Pliny and Roman Medicine' in R. French and F. Greenaway (edd.) *Science in the Early Roman Empire: Pliny the Elder, his Sources and Influence.* London and Sidney. 30–58

Riggsby, A.M. (1995). 'Pliny on Cicero and Oratory: Self-Fashioning in the Public Eye' *AJPh.* 116.123–35

Romano, E. (1987). *La Capanna e il Tempio: Vitruvio o dell'Architettura.* Palermo

Scarborough, J. (1986). 'Pharmacy in Pliny's *Natural History*: Some Observations on Substances and Sources' in R. French and F. Greenaway (edd.) *Science in the Early Roman Empire: Pliny the Elder, his Sources and Influence.* London and Sydney. 53–85

Schultze, C. (2011). 'Encyclopaedic Exemplarity in Pliny the Elder' in Gibson and Morello (2011) 167–86

Van der Blom, H. (2010). *Cicero's Role Models. The Political Strategy of a Newcomer.* Oxford

Wolverton, R.E. (1964). 'The Encomium of Cicero in Pliny the Elder' in C. Henderson (ed.) *Classical, Medieval and Renaissance Studies in Honour of B. L. Ullman.* Rome. I. 159–64

ARCA
Classical and Medieval Texts, Papers and Monographs

ISSN 0309-5541
General Editors: Neil Adkin, Francis Cairns, Robin Seager, Frederick Williams.

The Bishops' Synod ("The First Synod of St. Patrick"). A Symposium with Text, Translation and Commentary
Edited by M.J. FARIS
ARCA 1. 978-0-905205-01-4. vi+63pp. 11 illustrs. Paper. 1976.

Papers of the Liverpool Latin Seminar 1976.
Classical Latin Poetry; Medieval Latin Poetry; Greek Poetry
Edited by FRANCIS CAIRNS
ARCA 2 (=PLLS 1). 978-0-905205-00-7. vi+310pp. Paper. 1977.

Papers of the Liverpool Latin Seminar, Second Volume, 1979.
Vergil and Roman Elegy; Medieval Latin Poetry and Prose; Greek Lyric and Drama
Edited by FRANCIS CAIRNS
ARCA 3 (=PLLS 2). 978-0-905205-03-8. viii+360pp. Paper. 1979.

Form and Universal in Aristotle
A.C. LLOYD
ARCA 4. 978-0-905205-05-2. vi+89pp. Paper. 1981, repr. 2006

Court and Poet. Selected Proceedings of the Third Congress of the International Courtly Literature Society (Liverpool 1980)
Edited by GLYN S. BURGESS
ARCA 5. 978-0-905205-06-9. xiv+364pp. 1981.

The Fragmentary Classicising Historians of the Later Roman Empire
I. Eunapius, Olympiodorus, Priscus and Malchus
R.C. BLOCKLEY
ARCA 6. 978-0-905205-07-6. xii+196pp. 1981. Pb repr. 978-0-905205-51-9. 2009

Papers of the Liverpool Latin Seminar, Third Volume, 1981
Edited by FRANCIS CAIRNS
ARCA 7 (=PLLS 3). 978-0-905205-08-3. vi+423pp. 1981.

Late Latin and Early Romance in Spain and Carolingian France
ROGER WRIGHT
ARCA 8. 978-0-905205-12-0. xii+322pp. 1982.

Statius and the Silvae.
Poets, Patrons and Epideixis in the Graeco-Roman World
ALEX HARDIE
ARCA 9. 978-0-905205-13-7. viii+261pp. 1983.

The Fragmentary Classicising Historians of the Later Roman Empire.
II. Text, Translation and Historiographical Notes
R.C. BLOCKLEY
ARCA 10. 978-0-905205-15-1. x+515pp. 1983. Pb repr. 978-0-905205-49-6. 2007

Papers of the Liverpool Latin Seminar, Fourth Volume, 1983
Edited by FRANCIS CAIRNS
ARCA 11 (=PLLS 4). 978-0-905205-17-5. viii+369pp. 1984.

Fracastoro's Syphilis. Introduction, Text, Translation and Notes
GEOFFREY EATOUGH
ARCA 12. 978-0-905205-20-5. viii+295pp. 1984.

A Historical Commentary on Sallust's Bellum Jugurthinum
G.M. PAUL
ARCA 13. 978-0-905205-16-8. xxvi+276pp. 1984.

Sextus Aurelius Victor: a Historiographical Study
H.W. BIRD
ARCA 14. 978-0-905205-21-2. x+175pp. 1984.

Sheep-Rearing and the Wool Trade in Italy during the Roman Period
JOAN M. FRAYN
ARCA 15. 978-0-905205-22-9. x+208pp. 13 ills., 8 plates. 1984.

Biblical Epic and Rhetorical Paraphrase in Late Antiquity
MICHAEL ROBERTS
ARCA 16. 978-0-905205-24-3. x+253pp. 1985.

The History of Menander the Guardsman. Introductory Essay, Text, Translation and Historiographical Notes
R.C. BLOCKLEY
ARCA 17. 978-0-905205-25-0. xiii+307pp. 1985. Pb. repr. 978-0-905205-45-8. 2006

Bionis Smyrnaei Adonidis Epitaphium. Testo critico e commento
MARCO FANTUZZI
ARCA 18. 978-0-905205-27-4. 165pp. 1985.

Papers of the Liverpool Latin Seminar, Fifth Volume, 1985
Edited by FRANCIS CAIRNS
ARCA 19 (=PLLS 5). 978-0-905205-28-1. viii+502pp. 1986.

Ovid: Amores. Text, Prolegomena and Commentary, in four volumes
Volume I: Text and Prolegomena
J.C. McKEOWN
ARCA 20. 978-0-905205-69-4 (four-volume set 978-0-905205-68-7). x+220pp. 1987.

Herodotus and his 'Sources'. Citation, Invention and Narrative Art
DETLEV FEHLING.
Translated by J.G. Howie, from *Die Quellenangaben bei Herodot* (de
Gruyter: Berlin/New York, 1971)
ARCA 21. 978-0-905205-70-0. x+276pp. 1989.

Ovid: Amores. Text, Prolegomena and Commentary, in four volumes
Volume II: A Commentary on Book One
J.C. McKEOWN
ARCA 22. 978-0-905205-71-7 (four-volume set 978-0-905205-68-7). xxvi+421pp. 1989.

Masters of Roman Prose. From Cato to Apuleius. Interpretative
Studies
MICHAEL VON ALBRECHT. Translated by Neil Adkin
ARCA 23. 978-0-905205-72-4. xii+192pp. 1989.

Intellectual Culture in Elizabethan and Jacobean England. The
Latin Writings of the Age
J.W. BINNS
ARCA 24. 978-0-905205-73-1. xxvi+762pp. 1990.

A Lexicon of Ancient Latin Etymologies
ROBERT MALTBY
ARCA 25. 978-0-905205-74-8. xvii+669pp 1991. Pb. repr. 978-0-905205-47-2. 2006

Arae: The Curse Poetry of Antiquity
LINDSAY WATSON
ARCA 26. 978-0-905205-75-5. viii+263pp.1991.

The Fifth-Century Chroniclers. Prosper, Hydatius, and the Gallic
Chronicler of 452
STEVEN MUHLBERGER
ARCA 27. 978-0-905205-76-2. xii+329pp. 1990. Pb. repr. 978-0-905205-46-5. 2006

Greek Philosophers and Sophists in the Fourth Century A.D.
Studies in Eunapius of Sardis
ROBERT J. PENELLA
ARCA 28. 978-0-905205-79-3. x+165pp. 1990.

Papers of the Leeds International Latin Seminar, Sixth Volume.
Roman poetry and drama; Greek epic, comedy, rhetoric
Edited by FRANCIS CAIRNS & MALCOLM HEATH
ARCA 29 (=PLLS 6). 978-0-905205-81-6. viii+375pp.1990.

East Roman Foreign Policy. Formation and Conduct from Diocletian to Anastasius
R.C. BLOCKLEY
ARCA 30. 978-0-905205-83-0. xiv+283pp. 1992.

Doctrine and Exegesis in Biblical Latin Poetry
DANIEL J. NODES
ARCA 31. 978-0-905205-86-1. x+147pp. 1993.

Papers of the Leeds International Latin Seminar, Seventh Volume. Roman poetry and prose; Greek rhetoric and poetry
Edited by FRANCIS CAIRNS & MALCOLM HEATH
ARCA 32 (=PLLS 7). 978-0-905205-87-8. viii+219pp.1993.

Papers of the Leeds International Latin Seminar, Eighth Volume. Roman comedy, Augustan poetry, historiography
Edited by R. BROCK & A.J. WOODMAN
ARCA 33 (=PLLS 8). 978-0-905205-89-2. x+307pp. 1995.

Papers of the Leeds International Latin Seminar, Ninth Volume. Roman Poetry and Prose, Greek Poetry, Etymology, Historiography
Edited by FRANCIS CAIRNS & MALCOLM HEATH
ARCA 34 (=PLLS 9). 978-0-905205-90-8. viii+350pp.1996.

Augustus and the Principate. The Evolution of the System
W.K. LACEY
ARCA 35. 978-0-905205-91-5. x+245pp. 1996.

Ovid: *Amores.* Text, Prolegomena and Commentary, in four volumes Vol. III. A Commentary on Book Two
J.C. McKEOWN
ARCA 36. 978-0-905205-92-2 (four-volume set 978-0-905205-68-7). xxxii+433 pp. 1998.

Rome and Persia at War, 502–532
GEOFFREY GREATREX
ARCA 37. 978-0-905205-93-9. xvi+301pp., 14 maps and plans. 1998.
Pb. repr. 978-0-905205-48-9, 2006

Papers of the Leeds International Latin Seminar, Tenth Volume, 1998. Greek Poetry, Drama, Prose; Roman Poetry
Edited by FRANCIS CAIRNS & MALCOLM HEATH
ARCA 38 (=PLLS 10). 978-0-905205-95-3. vi + 409pp. 1998.

Vergil's *Aeneid* and the *Argonautica* of Apollonius Rhodius
DAMIEN NELIS
ARCA 39. 978-0-905205-97-7. xii+519 pp. 2001.

Ancient Etymologies in Ovid's *Metamorphoses*: a Commented Lexicon
ANDREAS MICHALOPOULOS
ARCA 40. 978-0-905205-98-4. viii+204 pp. 2001.

Tibullus: Elegies. Text, Introduction and Commentary
ROBERT MALTBY
ARCA 41. 978-0-905205-99-1. xii+529 pp. 2002

Jerome on Virginity. A Commentary on the *Libellus de virginitate observanda* (Letter 22)
NEIL ADKIN
ARCA 42. 978-0-905205-38-0. xxxv+458 pp. 2003.

Papers of the Langford Latin Seminar. Eleventh Volume (2003). Caesar against Liberty? Perspectives on his Autocracy
Edd. FRANCIS CAIRNS and ELAINE FANTHAM
ARCA 43 (= PLLS 11). 978-0-905205-39-7. xxii+234 pp. 2003.

Papers of the Langford Latin Seminar. Twelfth Volume (2005). Greek and Roman Poetry, Greek and Roman Historiography
Edited by FRANCIS CAIRNS
ARCA 44 (=PLLS 12). 978-0-905205-41-0. viii+343 pp. 2005.

Properzio. Elegie Libro II. Introduzione, testo e commento
PAOLO FEDELI
ARCA 45. 978-0-905205-42-7. x+1072 pp. 2005.

Anastasius I. Politics and Empire in the Late Roman World
F.K. HAARER
ARCA 46. 978-0-905205-43-4. xiv+351 pp. 2006

Ovid *Heroides* 16 and 17. Introduction, Text and Commentary
ANDREAS N. MICHALOPOULOS
ARCA 47. 978-0-905205-44-1. x+420 pp. 2006

Papers of the Langford Latin Seminar 13 (2008)
Hellenistic Greek and Augustan Latin Poetry, Flavian and post-Flavian Latin Poetry, Greek and Roman Prose
Edited by FRANCIS CAIRNS
ARCA 48. 978-0-905205-50-2. viii+390 pp. 2008

Bacchylides. Five Epinician Odes (3, 5, 9, 11, 13)
Text, Introductory Essays, and Interpretative Commentary
D.L. CAIRNS. Translations by D.L. Cairns and J.G. Howie
ARCA 49. 978-0-905205-52-6. xiv + 380 pp. 2010

Papers of the Langford Latin Seminar, 14 (2010)
Health and Sickness in Ancient Rome; Greek and Roman Poetry and Historiography
Edited by FRANCIS CAIRNS and MIRIAM GRIFFIN
ARCA 50 (=PLLS 14). ISBN 978-0905205-53-3. vi + 393pp. 2010.

Papers of the Langford Latin Seminar, 15 (2012)
Edited by FRANCIS CAIRNS
ARCA 51 (=PLLS 15). ISBN 978-0905205-55-7. vi + 376pp. 2012.

Cult, Myth, and Occasion in Pindar's Victory Odes
A Study of *Isthmian* 4, *Pythian* 5, *Olympian* 1, and *Olympian* 3
EVELINE KRUMMEN
Translated by J.G. Howie from *Pyrsos Hymnon. Festliche Gegenwart und mythisch-rituelle Tradition als Voraussetzung einer Pindarinterpretation (Isthmie 4, Pythie 5, Olympie 1 und 3)* (de Gruyter: Berlin/New York, 1990)
ARCA 52. 978-0-905205-56-4. xii+346pp. 2014.

Justinian's Balkan Wars
Campaigns, Diplomacy and Development in Illyricum, Thrace and the Northern World A.D. 527-65
ALEXANDER SARANTIS
ARCA 53. 978-0-905205-58-8. xxviii+550pp. 13 maps, 20 plates. 2016

Papers of the Langford Latin Seminar, 16 (2016)
Greek and Roman Poetry; The Elder Pliny
Edited by FRANCIS CAIRNS and ROY GIBSON
ARCA 54 (=PLLS 16). ISBN 978-0905205-59-5. vi + 337pp. 2016.

All ARCA titles are in print. Further volumes are in preparation

COLLECTED CLASSICAL PAPERS

ISSN 0951-7405

Roman Studies, Literary and Historical
T.P. WISEMAN
CCP 1. ISBN 978-0-905205-62-5. xii+418pp. 1987. (Out of print)

Future Currents in Aqueduct Studies
Edited by A. TREVOR HODGE
CCP 2. ISBN 978-0-905205-80-9. x+181pp., 8 b&w plates. 1991.

Exemplum and Myth, Creation and Criticism
J.G. HOWIE
CCP 3. ISBN 978-0-905205-54-0. xvii+443pp., 38 b&w illustrs. 2012.

Greek Music, Drama, Sport, and Fauna
The Collected Classical Papers of E. K. Borthwick
E.K. BORTHWICK
Edited by Calum Maciver
CCP 4. ISBN 978-0-905205-57-1. xvi+446 pp. 2015

Further titles are in preparation.